The William Stallings Books on Computer and Data Communications Technology

OPERATING SYSTEMS

A state-of-the art survey of operating system principles. Covers fundamental technology as well as contemporary design issues, such as threads, real-time systems, multiprocessor scheduling, distributed systems, and security.

HANDBOOKS OF COMPUTER-COMMUNICATIONS STANDARDS

VOLUME I
THE OPEN SYSTEMS INTERCONNECTION (OSI) MODEL AND OSI-RELATED STANDARDS, SECOND EDITION

A description of the master plan for all computer-communications standards: the OSI model. The book also provides a detailed presentation of OSI-related standards at all 7 layers, including HDLC, X.25, ISO internet, ISO transport, ISO session, ISO presentation, Abstract Syntax ONE (ASN.1), and common application service elements (CASE).

VOLUME 2
LOCAL AREA NETWORK STANDARDS, SECOND EDITION

A detailed examination of all current local network standards, including logical link control (LLC, IEEE 802.2), CSMA/CD (IEEE 802.3), token bus (IEEE 802.4), token ring (IEEE 802.5), and fiber distributed data interface (FDDI, ANS X3T9.5).

VOLUME 3
THE TCP/IP PROTOCOL SUITE, SECOND EDITION

A description of the protocol standards that are mandated on all DOD computer procurements and are becoming increasingly popular on commercial local network products, including TCP, IP, FTP, SMTP, and TELNET. The network management standards, SNMP and CMOT, are also presented.

William Stallings, Ph.D.

COMPUTER ORGANIZATION AND ARCHITECTURE

Principles of Structure and Function

THIRD EDITION

MACMILLAN PUBLISHING COMPANY
New York

MAXWELL MACMILLAN CANADA
Toronto

MAXWELL MACMILLAN INTERNATIONAL
New York   Oxford   Singapore   Sydney

To my loving wife, Tricia

Editor: John Griffin
Production Supervisor: John Travis
Production Manager: Sandra E. Moore
Cover Designer: Robert Freese

This book was set in 10/12 Palatino by York Graphic Services, Inc. printed by R.R. Donnelley, Inc., and bound by R.R. Donnelley. The cover was printed by Lehigh Press, Inc.

(Acknowledgments are listed on page viii.)

Macmillan Publishing Company is part of the Maxwell Communication Group of Companies.

Macmillan Publishing Company
866 Third Avenue, New York, New York 10022

Maxwell Macmillan Canada, Inc.
1200 Eglinton Avenue East
Suite 200
Don Mills, Ontario M3C 3N1

Library of Congress Cataloging in Publication Data
Stallings, William.
    Computer organization and architecture : principles of structure and function / William Stallings. — 3rd ed.
        p.   cm.
    Includes bibliographical references and index.
    ISBN 0-02-415495-4
    1. Computer organization.   2. Computer architecture.   I. Title.
QA76.9.C643S73   1993
004.2'2—dc20   92-6986
                                                                        CIP

PREFACE

Objectives

This book is about the structure and function of computers. Its purpose is to present, as clearly and completely as possible, the nature and characteristics of modern-day computer systems.

This task is a challenging one for several reasons.

First, there is a tremendous variety of products that can rightly claim the name computer, from single-chip microcomputers costing a few dollars to supercomputers costing tens of millions of dollars. Variety is exhibited not only in cost, but in size, performance, and application. Second, the rapid pace of change that has always characterized computer technology continues with no letup. These changes cover all aspects of computer technology, from the underlying integrated circuit technology used to construct computer components, to the increasing use of parallel organization concepts in combining those components.

In spite of the variety and pace of change in the computer field, certain fundamental concepts apply consistently throughout. To be sure, the application of these concepts depends on the current state of technology and the price/performance objectives of the designer. The intent of this book is to provide a thorough discussion of the fundamentals of computer organization and architecture, and to relate these to contemporary computer design issues.

The subtitle suggests the theme and the approach taken in this book. A computer system, like any system, consists of an interrelated set of components. The system is best characterized in terms of structure—the way in which components are interconnected, and function—the operation of each individual component. A computer's organization is hierarchic. Each major component can be further described by decomposing it into its major subcomponents and describing their structure and function. For clarity and ease of understanding, this hierarchical organization is described from the top down:

- *Computer System:* Major components are CPU, memory, and I/O
- *CPU:* Major components are control unit, registers, and ALU
- *Control Unit:* Major components are control memory, microinstruction sequencing logic, and registers.

The objective is to present the material in a fashion that keeps new material in a clear context. This should minimize the chance that the reader will get lost and should provide better motivation than a bottom-up approach.

Throughout the discussion, aspects of the system are viewed from points of view of both architecture (those attributes of a system visible to a machine-language programmer) and organization (the operational units and their interconnections that realize the architecture.)

Example Systems

Throughout this book, many examples from dozens of different machines are used to clarify and reinforce the concepts being presented. Many, but by no means all, of the examples are drawn from three computer families: the mainframe IBM 370, the minicomputer VAX, and the microprocessor Intel 80X86.

Intended Audience

This book is intended for both an academic and a professional audience. It can be used as a textbook in a computer science curriculum and covers topics specified in courses CS.3 and CS.4 of ACM Curriculum '78 and Subject Area 8 of the 1983 IEEE Computer Society Model Program in Computer Science and Engineering.

The book also serves as a basic reference volume and is suitable for self-study.

Plan of the Text

The book is divided into five parts:

  I. *Prologue:* This part provides an overview and context for the remainder of the book.
 II. *The Computer System:* A computer system consists of CPU, memory, and I/O modules, plus the interconnections among these major components. With the exception of the CPU, which is sufficiently complex to be explored in Part III, this part examines each of these aspects in detail.
III. *The Central Processing Unit:* The CPU consists of a control unit, registers, the arithmetic and logic unit, and the interconnections among these components. This part examines these components primarily from an architectural point of view. That is, the functionality of the CPU is determined by the machine instruction set and data types is examined. Organizational issues, such as pipelining, are also explored.
 IV. *The Control Unit:* The control unit is that part of the CPU that activates the various components of the CPU. This part looks at the functioning of the control unit and its implementation using microprogramming.
  V. *Epilogue:* The final part of the book looks at several advanced topics: parallel organization and RISC architecture.

A more detailed, chapter-by-chapter, summary appears at the end of Chapter 1.

Related Materials

A videotape course specifically designed for use with *Computer Organization and Architecture* is available from the Association for Media-Based Continuing Education for Engineers, Inc.; 430 Tenth Street, NW; Suite 8-208; Atlanta, GA 30318; telephone (404) 894-3362.

The Third Edition

In the three years since the last edition of Computer Organization and Architecture was published, the field has seen continued innovations and improvements. Thirty-two bit, high-performance microprocessors now dominate the marketplace, and such systems come equipped with sophisticated memory management, pipelining, and I/O facilities to enhance performance. RISC systems are now commercially widespread and RISC-based superscalar computers are finding growing use. There is increased use of parallel organizations and multiprocessor computers. Optical storage has become increasingly widespread and is having a dramatic effect on the way in which computers are used.

The increasing pervasiveness of computers and the increasing sophistication of personal computers confirms the need for a book that covers the fundamentals of computer organization and architecture and presents the most important recent innovations. The author is gratified by the positive response to the first two editions of this book and has tried to respond to constructive suggestions for improvements in this third edition.

Virtually the same chapter organization has been retained, but much of the material has been revised and new material has been added. As an indication of this, about one-quarter of the tables and one-fifth of the figures are new, 89 new references have been added, and 23 new homework problems have been included. A general theme of this revision is an increasing emphasis on microprocessor technology. Some of the most noteworthy changes are the following:

- In Chapter 3, two bus interfacing specifications have been added: VMEbus, which is the most popular microprocessor bus scheme, and Futurebus+, which looks to become the most important bus standard in the next few years.
- In Chapter 4, the material on multilevel memories is handled in a more systematic and, hopefully, a clearer fashion. The Intel 80486 on-chip cache is introduced as an example.
- In Chapter 5, the material on interrupt handling has been expanded.
- The material in Chapters 8 and 9 has been augmented with examples from the 80386/80486 architecture.
- The material on branch prediction in Chapter 10 has been expanded, and the 80486 instruction pipeline is presented as an example.
- In Chapter 12, the material on bit-slice architecture, which is becoming less important in the era of VLSI, has been dropped. A major new example of microprogrammed implementation has been introduced: the Texas Instruments ACT8800. This example should help clarify the somewhat confusing concepts of microprogrammed processor control.

- The example systems used to illustrate RISC architecture have been updated. The two systems now used are the Motorola 88000 and the MIPS R4000.
- An entirely new chapter has been added on superscalar systems. The chapter covers design fundamentals and uses the IBM RS/6000 and the Intel 80960 as examples.

The revision of this text has been an interesting and rewarding experience for the author, and it is hoped that its readers find it a useful guide to this fascinating field.

W.S.

ACKNOWLEDGMENTS

Permission is gratefully acknowledged for use of the following figures and tables:

Fig. 2-3 from J. Vallee, *The Network Revolution*, 1982, by permission of And/Or Press, Berkeley, California.

Figures 2-2, 2-6, 2-7, and Table 8-2 from J. Hayes, *Computer Architecture and Organization*, 1978, by permission of McGraw-Hill Book Company, New York.

Figure 2-14 reprinted with permission from *Computer Engineering: A DEC View of Hardware Systems Design* by Bell, Mudge and McNamara. Copyright © Digital Press/Digital Equipment Corporation (Bedford, MA), 1978.

Figure 3-6 from D. Siewiorek et al., *Computer Structures: Principles and Examples*, 1982, by permission of McGraw-Hill Book Company, New York.

Figures 4-10 and 4-11 from *Introduction to Computer Architecture* by Harold S. Stone (ed.), et al. Copyright © Science Research Associates, Inc. 1980, 1975. Reprinted by permission of the publisher.

Figures 6-8, 6-12, 6-15 and 6-16 from J. Peterson et al., *Operating System Concepts*, 2nd ed., 1985, by permission of Addison-Wesley Publishing Company, Reading, MA.

Figures 7-17(b) and 9-5 from Andrew S. Tanenbaum, *Structured Computer Organization*, 2nd ed. © 1984, p. 452. Adapted by permission of Prentice-Hall, Inc., Englewood Cliffs, New Jersey.

Figure 11-6 from V. Hamacher, *Computer Organization*, 2nd ed., 1984, by permission of McGraw-Hill Book Company, New York.

Figures 12-6, 12-7, and 12-8 from B. Cline, *Microprogramming Concepts and Techniques*, 1981, by permission of Petrocelli Books, Princeton, NJ.

Table 13-3 from Burt H. Liebowitz/John H. Carson, *Multiple Processor Systems for Real-Time Applications*, © 1985, p. 161. Adapted by permission of Prentice-Hall, Inc., Englewood Cliffs, New Jersey.

Figure 13-2 from M. Katevenis, *Reduced Instruction Set Computer Architectures for VSLI*, 1985, by permission of MIT Press, Cambridge, MA.

Figures A-15 (a), A-15 (b), and A-16 from T. Bartee, *Digital Computer Fundamentals*, 6th ed., 1985, by permission of McGraw-Hill Book Company, New York.

CONTENTS

PART I

OVERVIEW

T he purpose of Part I is to provide an overview and a context for the remainder of the book. It does this in two ways.

First, Chapter 1 introduces the concept of the computer as a hierarchical system. A computer can be viewed as a structure of components and its function described in terms of the collective function of its cooperating components. Each component can, in turn, be described in terms of its internal structure and function. The major levels of this hierarchical view are introduced. The remainder of the book is organized, top down, in terms of these levels.

Second, Chapter 2 is a brief history of the development of computers from their mechanical ancestors to present-day systems. This history serves to highlight some important computer design features and to provide a top-level view of computer structure.

CHAPTER 1

Introduction

This book is about the structure and function of computers. Its purpose is to present, as clearly and completely as possible, the nature and characteristics of modern-day computer systems. This task is a challenging one for two reasons.

First, there is a tremendous variety of products, from single-chip microcomputers costing a few dollars to supercomputers costing tens of millions of dollars, that can rightly claim the name computer. Variety is exhibited not only in cost, but in size, performance, and application. Second, the rapid pace of change that has always characterized computer technology continues with no letup. These changes cover all aspects of computer technology, from the underlying integrated circuit technology used to construct computer components to the increasing use of parallel organization concepts in combining those components.

In spite of the variety and pace of change in the computer field, certain fundamental concepts apply consistently throughout. To be sure, the application of these concepts depends on the current state of technology and the price/performance objectives of the designer. The intent of this book is to provide a thorough discussion of the fundamentals of computer organization and architecture and to relate these to contemporary computer design issues. This introductory chapter discusses briefly the descriptive approach to be taken and provides an overview of the remainder of the book.

1.1

ORGANIZATION AND ARCHITECTURE

In describing computer systems, a distinction is often made between *computer architecture* and *computer organization*. Although it is difficult to give precise definitions for these terms, a consensus exists about the general areas covered by each (e.g., see [VRAN80], [LANG82], [SIEW82a], and [BELL78a]).

Computer architecture refers to those attributes of a system visible to a programmer, or put another way, those attributes that have a direct impact on the logical execution of a program. Computer organization refers to the operational

3

units and their interconnections that realize the architectural specifications. Examples of architectural attributes include the instruction set, the number of bits used to represent various data types (e.g., numbers, characters), I/O mechanisms, and techniques for addressing memory. Organizational attributes include those hardware details transparent to the programmer, such as control signals, interfaces between the computer and peripherals, and the memory technology used.

An example from [LORI82] illustrates this distinction. It is an architectural design issue whether a computer will have a multiply instruction. It is an organizational issue whether that instruction will be implemented by a special multiply unit or by a mechanism that makes repeated use of the add unit of the system. The organizational decision may be based on the anticipated frequency of use of the multiply instruction, the relative speed of the two approaches, and the cost and physical size of a special multiply unit.

Historically, and still today, the distinction between architecture and organization has been an important one. Many computer manufacturers offer a family of computer models, all with the same architecture but with differences in organization. Consequently, the different models in the family have different price and performance characteristics. Furthermore, an architecture may survive many years but its organization changes with changing technology. A prominent example of both these phenomena is the IBM System/370 architecture. This architecture was first introduced in 1970 and included a number of models. The customer with modest requirements could buy a cheaper, slower model and, if demand increased, later upgrade to a more expensive, faster model without having to abandon software that had already been developed. Over the years, IBM has introduced many new models with improved technology to replace older models, offering the customer greater speed, lower cost, or both. These newer models retained the same architecture so that the customer's software investment was protected. Remarkably, the System/370 architecture, with a few enhancements, has survived to this day and continues as the flagship of IBM's product line.

In a class of systems called microcomputers, the relationship between architecture and organization is very close. Changes in technology not only influence organization but also result in the introduction of more powerful and richer architectures. Generally, there is less of a requirement for generation-to-generation compatibility for these smaller machines. Thus, there is more of an interplay between organizational and architectural design decisions. An intriguing example of this is the reduced instruction set computer (RISC), which we examine at the end of the book.

This book examines both computer organization and computer architecture. The emphasis is perhaps more on the side of organization. However, because a computer organization must be designed to implement a particular architectural specification, a thorough treatment of organization requires a detailed examination of architecture as well.

1.2

STRUCTURE AND FUNCTION

A computer is a complex system; contemporary computers contain millions of elementary electronic components. How, then, can one clearly describe them? The key is to recognize the hierarchic nature of most complex systems, including the computer [SIMO69]. A hierarchic system is a set of interrelated subsystems, each of the latter, in turn, hierarchic in structure until we reach some lowest level of elementary subsystem.

The hierarchic nature of complex systems is essential to both their design and their description. The designer need only deal with a particular level of the system at a time. At each level, the system consists of a set of components and their interrelationships. The behavior at each level depends only on a simplified, abstracted characterization of the system at the next lower level. At each level, the designer is concerned with structure and function [KOES78]:

- *Structure:* The way in which the components are interrelated.
- *Function:* The operation of each individual component as part of the structure.

In terms of description, we have two choices: starting at the bottom and building up to a complete description, or beginning with a top-view and decomposing the system into its sub-parts. Evidence from a number of fields suggests that the top-down approach is the clearest and most effective [WEIN75].

The approach that is taken in this book follows from this viewpoint. The computer system will be described from the top down. We begin with the major components of the system, describing their structure and function, and proceed to successively lower layers of the hierarchy. The remainder of this section provides a very brief overview of this plan of attack.

Function

Both the structure and functioning of a computer are, in essence, simple. Figure 1-1 depicts the basic functions that a computer can perform. In general terms, there are only four:

- Data Processing
- Data Storage
- Data Movement
- Control

The computer, of course, must be able to *process data.* The data may take a wide variety of forms and the range of processing requirements is broad. However, we shall see that there are only a few fundamental methods or types of data processing.

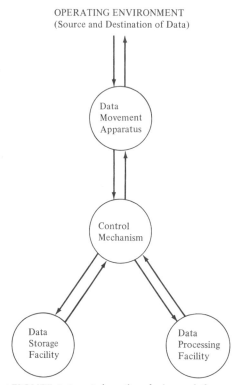

FIGURE 1-1. A functional view of the computer

It is also essential that a computer *store data*. Even if the computer is processing data on the fly (i.e., data come in and get processed, and the results go right out), the computer must temporarily store at least those pieces of data that are being worked on at any given moment. Thus there is at least a short-term data storage function. Equally important, the computer performs a long-term data storage function. Files of data are stored on the computer for subsequent retrieval and update.

The computer must be able to *move data* between itself and the outside world. The computer's operating environment consists of devices that serve as either sources or destinations of data. When data are received from or delivered to a device that is directly connected to the computer, the process is known as *input–output* (I/O), and the device is referred to as a *peripheral*. When data are moved over longer distances, to or from a remote device, the process is known as *data communications*.

Finally, there must be *control* of these three functions. Ultimately, this control is exercised by the individual(s) who provides the computer with instructions. Within the computer system, a control unit manages the computer's resources and orchestrates the performance of its functional parts in response to those instructions.

At this general level of discussion, the number of possible operations that can be performed is few. Figure 1-2 depicts the four possible types of operations. The computer can function as a data movement device (Figure 1-2a), simply transferring data from one peripheral or communications line to another. It can also function as a data storage device (Figure 1-2b), with data transferred from the external environment to computer storage (read) and vice versa (write). The final two diagrams show operations involving data processing, on data either in storage (Figure 1-2c) or en route between storage and the external environment.

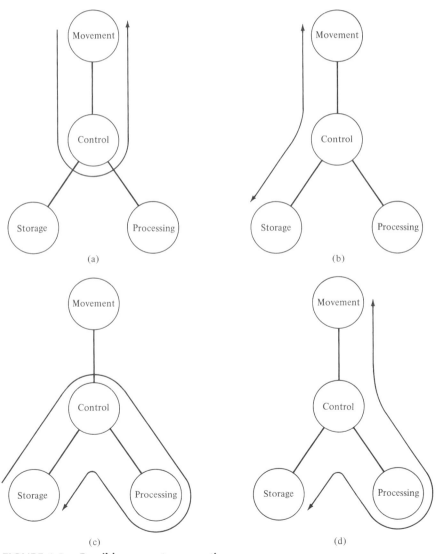

FIGURE 1-2. Possible computer operations

The preceding discussion may seem absurdly generalized. It is certainly possible, even at a top level of computer structure, to differentiate a variety of functions, but, to quote [SIEW82a]:

> There is remarkably little shaping of computer structure to fit the function to be performed. At the root of this lies the general-purpose nature of computers, in which all the functional specialization occurs at the time of programming and not at the time of design.

Structure

Figure 1-3 is the simplest possible depiction of a computer. The computer is an entity that interacts in some fashion with its external environment. In general, all of its linkages to the external environment can be classified as peripheral devices or communication lines. We will have something to say about both types of linkages.

But of greater concern in this book is the internal structure of the computer itself which is shown at a top level in Figure 1-4. There are four main structural components:

- *Central Processing Unit (CPU):* Controls the operation of the computer and performs its data processing functions. Often simply referred to as *processor.*
- *Main Memory:* Stores data.
- *I/O:* Moves data between the computer and its external environment.
- *System Interconnection:* Some mechanism that provides for communication among CPU, main memory, and I/O.

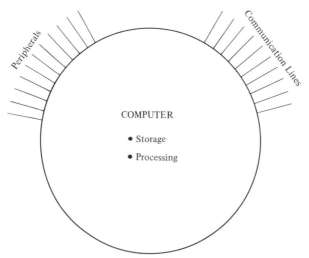

FIGURE 1-3.   The computer

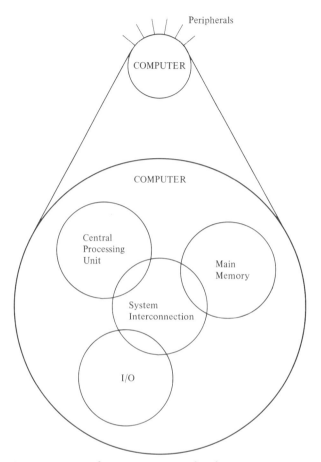

FIGURE 1-4. The computer: top-level structure

There may be one or more of each of the above components. Traditionally, there has been just a single CPU. In recent years, there has been increasing use of multiple processors in a single system. Some design issues relating to multiple processors crop up and are discussed as the text proceeds; Chapter 15 focuses on such systems.

Each of these components will be examined in some detail in Part II. However, for our purposes, the most interesting and in some ways the most complex component is the CPU, and its structure is depicted in Figure 1-5. Its major structural components are

Control Unit: Controls the operation of the CPU and hence the computer.
Arithmetic and Logic Unit (ALU): Performs the computer's data processing functions.
Registers: Provides storage internal to the CPU.

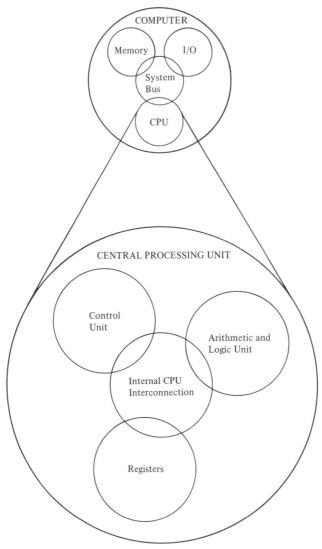

FIGURE 1-5. The CPU

- *CPU Interconnection:* Some mechanism that provides for communication among the control unit, ALU, and registers.

Each of these components will be examined in some detail in Part III. Again, for our purposes, the most interesting component is the control unit. Now, there are several approaches to the implementation of the control unit, but the most common by far is a *microprogrammed* implementation. With this approach, the structure of the control unit can be depicted as in Figure 1-6. This structure will be examined in Part IV.

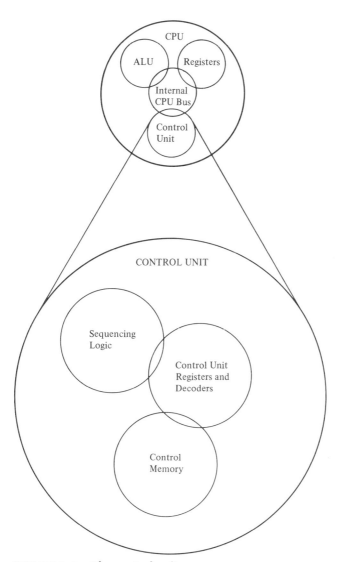

FIGURE 1-6.   The control unit

1.3
OUTLINE OF THE BOOK

This chapter, of course, serves as an introduction to the entire book. A brief synopsis of the remaining chapters follows.

A Brief History

Chapter 2 serves two purposes. First, a discussion of the history of computers is an easy and interesting way of being introduced to the subject. Second, this discussion of necessity describes the basic structure and function of computers and hence serves as an overview of the remainder of the book.

Computer Interconnection Structures

At a top level, a computer consists of processor, memory, and I/O components. The functional behavior of the system consists of the exchange of data and control signals among these components. To support this exchange, these components must be interconnected in some fashion. Chapter 3 begins with a brief examination of the computer's components and their input–output requirements. The chapter then examines the major structural approaches to interconnection, including considerations of timing and arbitration. The bulk of the chapter is devoted to the most common approach, the bus structure. The central-switched structure, used on IBM and other mainframes, is also examined.

Internal and External Memory

Memory is that portion of a computer system used for the storage, and subsequent retrieval, of data and instructions. Computer memory exhibits a wide range of type, technology, organization, performance, and cost. The typical computer system is equipped with a hierarchy of memory subsystems, some internal (directly accessible by the processor) and some external (accessible by the processor via an I/O module). Chapter 4 discusses key characteristics of memory subsystems and surveys the memory hierarchy, including an examination of

• Cache
• Semiconducter Main Memory
• Bubble Memory
• Magnetic Disk
• Magnetic Tape

Input/Output

In addition to processor and memory components, the third key element of a computer system is a set of I/O modules. Each module is interconnected with the processor and memory, and controls one or more external devices. Chapter 5 examines the mechanisms by which an I/O module interacts with the rest of the computer system, using the techniques of programmed I/O, interrupt I/O, and direct memory access (DMA). The interface between an I/O module and external devices is also described.

Operating Systems

At this point, it is appropriate to look at the operating system, to explain how the basic computer components are managed to perform useful work. Chapter 6 begins with a brief history, which serves to identify the major types of operating systems and to motivate their use. Next, multiprogramming is explained by examining the long-term and short-term scheduling functions. Finally, an examination of memory management includes a discussion of swapping, partitioning, paging, and virtual memory.

Computer Arithmetic

Chapter 7 begins a detailed examination of the CPU. One of the essential functions of the CPU is computer arithmetic, performed by the arithmetic and logic unit (ALU). Computer arithmetic is commonly performed on two types of numbers: fixed point and floating point. In both cases, the representation chosen is a crucial design issue and is treated first, followed by a discussion of arithmetic operations.

Machine Instructions

From a programmer's perspective, the best way to understand the operation of a processor is to learn the machine instructions that it executes. Chapter 8 examines the key characteristics of machine instruction sets. It covers the various data types and operation types commonly found in a machine instruction set. Then the relationship of machine instructions to assembly language is briefly explained. In Chapter 9, the various addressing modes possible are examined. Finally, the issue of instruction format is explored, including a discussion of tradeoffs.

CPU Structure and Function

Chapter 10 is devoted to a discussion of the internal structure and function of the CPU. The overall CPU organization (ALU, control unit, register file) is reviewed. Then, the organization of the register file is discussed. The remainder of the chapter describes the functioning of the CPU in executing machine instructions. The instruction cycle is examined to show the function and interrelationship of fetch, indirect, execute, and interrupt cycles. Finally, the use of pipelining to improve performance is examined.

Control Unit Operation

Chapter 11 turns to a discussion of how CPU functions are performed or, more specifically, how the various elements of the CPU are controlled to provide these functions. Thus the chapter describes the control unit, which is that component of the CPU that controls its operation. It is shown that each instruction cycle is made up of a set of micro-operations that generate control signals. Execution is accomplished by the effect of these control signals, emanating from the control unit to the ALU, registers, and system interconnection structure. Finally, an approach to the implementation of the control unit, referred to as hardwired, is presented.

Microprogrammed Control

Chapter 12 shows how the control unit can be implemented using the technique of microprogramming. First, micro-operations are mapped into microinstructions. Then the layout of a control memory containing a microprogram for each machine instruction is described. The structure and function of the microprogrammed control unit can then be explained. The chapter closes with a discussion of bit-slice architecture.

Reduced Instruction Set Computers

One of the most interesting and, potentially, one of the most significant innovations in computer organization and architecture in recent years is the reduced instruction set computer (RISC). RISC architecture is a dramatic departure from the historical trend in CPU architecture. An analysis of this new approach brings into focus many of the important issues in computer organization and architecture. Chapter 13 presents the RISC approach and compares it to more conventional approaches.

Superscalar Processors

Chapter 14 examines an even more recent and equally important design innovation: the superscalar processor. Although superscalar technology can be used in any processor, it is especially well suited to a RISC architecture.

Parallel Organization

Traditionally, the computer has been viewed as a sequential machine. As computer technology has evolved, and the cost of computer hardware has dropped, computer designers have increasingly sought opportunities for parallelism, usually to improve performance and, in some cases, to improve reliability. Chapter 15 looks at two of the most prominent and successful applications of parallel organization: multiprocessing and vector organization.

Digital Logic

The body of the text treats binary storage elements and digital functions as the fundamental building blocks of computer systems. The appendix to the text describes how these storage elements and functions can be implemented in digital logic. The appendix begins with a brief review of Boolean algebra. Next, the concept of a gate is introduced. Finally, combinational and sequential circuits, which can be constructed from gates, are discussed.

CHAPTER 2

A Brief History

We begin our study of computers with a brief history of computers. This history is interesting in itself and also serves the purpose of providing an overview of computer structure and function. This chapter, of course, is by no means complete; only selected highlights are surveyed.

2.1

MECHANICAL AND ELECTROMECHANICAL ANCESTORS

The history of the computer properly begins with the first electronic digital computer, built shortly after the end of World War II. But this history is predated by influential and significant work whose highlights are summarized in Table 2-1. Much of the technical strategy for the modern computer was worked out in these mechanical ancestors.

Early Developments

The ancestry of the modern computer can be traced as far back as the seventeenth century, when machines capable of automatically performing the four basic arithmetic operations (addition, subtraction, multiplication, and division) first appeared.

   The first machine to attract widespread attention was built by the French philosopher and scientist Blaise Pascal in 1642. This was a mechanical counter for performing addition and subtraction. It consisted of two sets of six gears with teeth, or *counter wheels* for representing decimal numbers. Each gear had the ten decimal digits engraved on it, with the position of the dial indicating the decimal value. Each set of dials was used as a *register* to temporarily hold a number. One register acted as an *accumulator* in which a running total was kept. The other register was used to enter a number to be added to or subtracted from the accumulator. When the machine was set in motion, the numbers in the two sets of dials were added, with the result appearing in the accumulator. The two main

TABLE 2-1   Milestones in the Development of Mechanical Computers

Date	Inventor: Machine	Capability	Technical Innovation
1642	Pascal	Addition, subtraction	Automatic carry transfer, complement number representation
1671	Leibniz	Addition, subtraction, multiplication, division	"Stepped reckoner" mechanism
1801	Jacquard: Loom	Automatic control of weaving process	Operation under program control
1822	Babbage: Difference Engine	Polynomial evaluation by finite differences	Automatic multistep operation
1834	Babbage: Analytical Engine (never completed)	General-purpose computation	Automatic sequence control mechanism, print-out of results
1941	Zuse: Z3	General-purpose computation	The first operational general-purpose computers
1944	Aiken: Mark I		

Source: [HAYE88].

technical innovations were (1) a ratchet device to transfer a carry automatically from one place to the next, and (2) a means of storing negative numbers, known as "complements representation," so that subtraction as well as addition could be accomplished.

A little later, around 1671, the German philosopher and mathematician Gottfried Leibniz constructed a calculator that could perform multiplication and division as well as addition and subtraction. Leibniz's machine contained a duplicate of the Pascal calculator, plus two additional sets of wheels that could perform multiplication and division in a repetitive step-by-step fashion, using chains and pulleys. Leibniz's machine was the forerunner of many machines that are now called *four-function calculators*.

In an entirely unrelated area, developments in the technology of weaving were ultimately to serve as one of the roots of modern computers. The manual weaving of multiple copies of patterned materials is a time-consuming, error-prone process. By 1750, the practice of using punched cards to specify the pattern had been developed. Thus the first use of symbols stored on punched cards was to represent instructions, rather than numbers or text. At first, these instructions were simply interpreted by a man or, more likely, a boy. The process was slow and mistakes were made. A series of modifications to the loom incorporated the punch card more mechanically into the process. The last step was made by Joseph Jacquard in 1801 when he produced a very successful loom in which all the power was supplied mechanically and all the control via the punched card. In essence, cards were moved through the loom apparatus. The presence or absence of a hole dictated the movement of parts of the loom to create the desired pattern. Thus the Jacquard loom was a programmable process-control machine, with the "program" supplied on a deck of cards. One of the most famous such programs wove a portrait of Jacquard himself, on a five-foot-square tapestry; 24,000 cards were used.

Charles Babbage

The next important steps in the development of calculating machines did not occur until the nineteenth century, and they were taken by an Englishman, Charles Babbage, who might be considered the grandfather of the modern computer. He designed two computers: the Difference Engine and the Analytical Engine.

The Difference Engine

In the late eighteenth and early nineteenth centuries, it was the practice to employ large groups of clerks, under the direction of a mathematician, to calculate extensive tables of figures, which were used for navigation. Following explicit directions, the clerks carried out a repetitive series of additions and multiplications. Interestingly, it was found that the number of mistakes could be reduced if the clerks had very little mathematical training because then they followed their directions more readily and did not take shortcuts. However, even with elaborate checking procedures, it was impossible to eliminate errors. Many of the mistakes were made in the final step of preparing the printed tables. This need for simple, accurate, and repetitive arithmetic operations and for reliable output stimulated Babbage to develop the Difference Engine. Furthermore, Babbage expected the machine to be less expensive than large groups of clerks.

The Difference Engine was designed to calculate the entries of a table automatically and transfer them via steel punches to an engraver's plate, from which the tables could be printed. Like Pascal's machine, the Difference Engine could perform only addition and subtraction. However, using a mathematical technique known as *finite differences*, a large number of useful formulas could be computed, either exactly or approximately, using just additions (see Problem 2.1). These included polynomials and trigonometric functions (e.g., the sine function).

The Difference Engine consisted of a number of *mechanical registers*. Each register consisted of a set of counter wheels and could store a decimal number. Pairs of adjacent registers were connected by an adding mechanism similar in principle to Pascal's. To compute a result, initial values were loaded into the registers. The Difference Engine, when driven by a suitable motor (such as a steam engine), would then perform a series of steps to "crank out" an answer.

Several difference engines were constructed and operated, including one that could handle third-degree polynomials and 15-digit numbers. Babbage proposed to build one that would accommodate sixth-degree polynomials and 20-digit numbers. The project was begun in 1823 with funding from the British government but was abandoned before completion almost 20 years later. Babbage found that despite tight design specifications and exhortations to workers, the smallest imperfections were enough to throw the tons of brass, pewter rods, and gears of the machine out of whack. After spending £17,000 to no avail, the British government withdrew its support. (A British prime minister later stated that the only use he could see for the Difference Engine was for calculating the large amount of money spent on it.)

In the meantime, Babbage was already losing interest in the project because he had conceived a much more powerful and ambitious machine he called the Analytical Engine.

The Analytical Engine

Babbage designed the Analytical Engine to be a general-purpose device, capable of performing any mathematical operation automatically. Figure 2-1 shows the structure of Babbage's final design. The key components are

- *The Store:* A memory unit consisting of sets of counter wheels.
- *The Mill:* An arithmetic unit capable of performing the four basic arithmetic operations. It operated on pairs of mechanical registers and produced a result stored in another mechanical register, all of which were located in the store.
- *Operation Cards:* These cards, of the type developed for the Jacquard loom, selected one of four arithmetic operations by activating the mill to perform the selected function.
- *Variable Cards:* These cards selected the memory locations to be used by the mill for a particular operation (i.e., the source of the operands and the destination of the results).
- *Output:* Was to a printer or a card punch device.

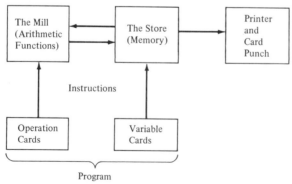

FIGURE 2-1.   Structure of Babbage's analytical engine

The Equations:

$$a_{11}x_1 + a_{12}x_2 = b_1$$

$$a_{21}x_1 + a_{22}x_2 = b_2$$

Have the solutions:

$$x_1 = \frac{a_{22}b_1 - a_{12}b_2}{a_{11}a_{22} - a_{12}a_{21}}$$

$$x_2 = \frac{a_{11}b_2 - a_{21}b_1}{a_{11}a_{22} - a_{12}a_{21}}$$

To compute the values of x_1 and x_2: Let w_0, w_1, ... denote the number locations in the store. Assign $w_0 = a_{11}$, $w_1 = a_{12}$, $w_2 = b_1$, $w_3 = a_{21}$, $w_4 = a_{22}$, $w_5 = b_2$.

Program for x_1.

Operation Cards	Variable Cards		Comments
	Source	Destination	
X	w_2, w_4	w_8	$w_8 \leftarrow a_{22}b_1$
X	w_1, w_5	w_9	$w_9 \leftarrow a_{12}b_2$
X	w_0, w_4	w_{10}	$w_{10} \leftarrow a_{11}a_{22}$
X	w_1, w_3	w_{11}	$w_{11} \leftarrow a_{12}a_{21}$
−	w_8, w_9	w_{12}	$w_{12} \leftarrow a_{22}b_1 - a_{12}b_2$
−	w_{10}, w_{11}	w_{13}	$w_{13} \leftarrow a_{11}a_{22} - a_{12}a_{21}$
÷	w_{12}, w_{13}	w_{14}	$w_{14} \leftarrow w_{12} \div w_{13}$

FIGURE 2-2. A program for the analytical engine

Figure 2-2 is an example of a program for the Analytical Engine. It was devised by L. F. Menebrea, a contemporary of Babbage's. In each operation, two numbers from the required locations are brought into the mill and stored in registers in the mill. A calculation is carried out and the result returned to the store at the specified address. All of these operations are controlled by a version of the Jacquard loom.

A major advantage of this design over earlier efforts by Babbage, Leibniz, and Pascal is that it is general-purpose and programmable. Another technical innovation is the provision of automatic sequence control, which enabled a program to alter the sequences of its operations. The engine could test the sign of a number and take a different course of action for a positive or negative result. There was also a mechanism for both advancing and reversing the control cards to permit continuing execution of any desired instruction. In modern terms, Babbage had devised conditional and branching instructions.

This design of Babbage's is truly remarkable. It is fundamentally the same design used in modern computers. The Analytical Engine includes memory, a central processing unit, input/output, and the use of a programming language— all of the key elements in today's computers.

Typically, Babbage proposed to build his engine on a grand scale. The store was to have a capacity of 1,000 50-digit decimal numbers. He estimated that the addition of two numbers would take a second and multiplication, a minute.

Only a small part of this machine was ever built. Babbage succeeded only in showing that his design was ahead of the required technology. Further developments had to await the development of electrical technology.

Electromechanical Devices

After Babbage, no significant attempts to build a general-purpose digital computer were made until the 1930s. Two names stand out: Zuse and Aiken.

Zuse

Zuse was a German engineering student obsessed with the idea of building a computer (and had, in fact, designed mechanical computing models out of an Erector set as a child). He was apparently not aware of Babbage's work, but had he been so, he would have rejected the basic operating principle of its computation unit. Zuse's idea was to use mechanical relays or switches that could be either opened or closed automatically. This necessitated the use of a binary rather than a decimal system.

In 1936, Zuse gave up his regular job and his studies to devote himself to his brainchild. His first machine, the Z1, had a primitive processing machine and a primitive memory based on mechanical relays. It was driven from a keyboard and displayed its binary results by light bulb. His third model, the Z3, was finished in 1941. This machine differed in a number of respects from the Z1. It made use of electromechanical relays and is believed to have been the first fully operational general-purpose program-controlled computer. For input, the Z3 used a punched tape mechanism. The medium was discarded photographic film, in which Zuse punched holes to give instructions to his computer.

By 1943, Zuse was working on his Z4 model, which still used electromagnetic relays and inspired a line of machines that were applied to aircraft and missile design. The Allied bombing raids of Berlin destroyed most of Zuse's machines and the work ended. After the war, Zuse managed to get backing first from IBM and then from Remington Rand, and he installed a number of relay computers throughout Europe. Nevertheless, Zuse's accomplishment was not recognized for many years after the war and had very little influence on the subsequent development of computers.

Aiken

At the time of Zuse's work in Germany, the same technology was being pursued in the United States by Howard Aiken, a physicist and mathematics professor at Harvard University. Unlike Zuse, Aiken was aware of Babbage's work and designed a machine along the same lines. Aiken managed to convince IBM to invest a million dollars in the development of an American computer, and work began in 1939. The first model, the Mark I, became operational in 1944. Like Babbage's machines, the Mark I employed decimal-digit counter wheels for its memory, but it used electromechanical relays for its computational structure. It had a storage capacity of 72 23-digit decimal numbers. Instructions were provided by means of a punched paper tape, which combined the functions of Babbage's operation cards and variable cards. Each instruction had the format

A_1 A_2 OP

where OP was an operation to be performed (e.g., $+$, $-$, $\times$, $\div$) and A_1 and A_2 were registers storing the operands.

The Mark I became operational in 1944. It could do a single addition in 6 seconds and a division in 12 seconds. Aiken soon began work on a Mark II machine. This effort marks the end of the mechanical era, for the Mark II was obsolete before it could be turned on. The electronic era and the first "real" computers were under way.

2.2

THE FIRST GENERATION: VACUUM TUBES

The computers of the mechanical era suffered from two serious drawbacks:

- The inertia of moving parts limited computing speed.
- The movement of data by mechanical means (gears, levers, etc.) was cumbersome and unreliable.

What was needed was a switching and storing mechanism with no moving parts. The triode vacuum tube, invented in 1906, provided the basic building block. As these devices became less expensive and more reliable, the way was open for the development of the electronic computer.

False Starts

Turing

The British mathematician Alan Turing is best known for the theory of the Turing machine, which he described in 1937. This machine, when supplied with the necessary instructions via punched paper tape, could imitate the behavior of any other machine used for computation. In this way, Turing defined the essence of the computing function and the theoretical groundwork for the modern digital computer.

Less well known is Turing's contribution to the design and development of the computer. In the 1930s, the Germans developed a machine named Enigma, which was used for encryption of messages. It was, among its other tasks, the key to U-boat deployment. The British obtained one of these machines and set about to build a decryption device, with Turing responsible for the design. The result was Colossus, which was a machine capable of emulating encryption devices. It was constructed with vacuum tubes and used punched-paper-tape input. The first Colossus machine became operational in 1943.

After the war, Turing turned to the design of a general-purpose digital computer. This design would ultimately be implemented as the Automatic Computing Engine (ACE) in 1950. By that time however, discouraged by the slow pace dictated by British bureaucracy, Turing had left the project and gone on to other efforts. Many of his ideas would be realized first in American computers, and it is only recently that Turing's importance to the historical development of computers has been recognized.

Atanasoff

John Vincent Atanasoff was an associate professor of physics and mathematics at Iowa State College in the 1930s. He designed a special-purpose machine for solving simultaneous linear equations of the type found in physics. Aided by a student named Clifford Berry, he constructed a working machine using vacuum tubes in 1939. The machine became known as the Atanasoff-Berry Computer, or the ABC. Atanasoff and Iowa State never filed a patent for the device, which was dismantled after the inventor had gone to work at the Naval Ordnance Laboratory.

Atanasoff's desire to build a general-purpose version of the ABC was never realized. However another physicist, John Mauchly, was greatly inspired by what he saw during his visits to Iowa State, and he incorporated these concepts into a later machine called the ENIAC. This relationship came to light only when Sperry Rand, which had acquired the patent rights to ENIAC, sued Honeywell, charging that Honeywell had infringed upon the ENIAC patent. In his 1974 decision, Judge Larson stated,

> Eckert and Mauchly did not themselves invent the automatic electronic digital computer, but instead derived that subject matter from a Dr. John Vincent Atanasoff.

The significance of all this is that while the ENIAC was the first electronic general-purpose digital computer, had Atanasoff been able to pursue his work, he might have gotten there first.

ENIAC

The ENIAC (Electronic Numerical Integrator And Computer), designed by and constructed under the supervision of John Mauchly and John Presper Eckert at the University of Pennsylvania, was the world's first general-purpose electronic digital computer.

The project was a response to U.S. wartime needs. The Army's Ballistics Research Laboratory (BRL), an agency responsible for developing range and trajectory tables for new weapons, was having difficulty supplying these tables accurately and within a reasonable time frame. Without these firing tables, the new weapons and artillery were useless to gunners. The BRL employed more than

200 people, mostly women, who, using desktop calculators, solved the necessary ballistics equations. Preparation of the tables for a single weapon would take one person many hours, even days.

Mauchly, a professor of electrical engineering at the University of Pennsylvania, and Eckert, one of his graduate students, proposed to build a general-purpose computer using vacuum tubes to be used for the BRL's application. In 1943, this proposal was accepted by the Army and work began on the ENIAC. The resulting machine was enormous, weighing 30 tons, occupying 15,000 square feet of floor space, and containing over 18,000 vacuum tubes. When operating, it consumed 140 kilowatts of power. It was also substantially faster than any electromechanical computer, being capable of 5,000 additions per second.

The ENIAC was a decimal rather than a binary machine. That is, numbers were represented in decimal form and arithmetic was performed in the decimal system. Its memory consisted of 20 "accumulators," each capable of holding a 10-digit decimal number. Each digit was represented by a ring of 10 vacuum tubes. At any time, only one vacuum tube was in the ON state, representing one of the ten digits. The major drawback of the ENIAC was that it had to be programmed manually by setting switches and plugging and unplugging cables.

The ENIAC was completed in 1946, too late to be used in the war effort. Instead, its first task was to perform a series of complex calculations that were used to help determine the feasibility of the H-bomb. The use of the ENIAC for a purpose other than that for which it was built demonstrated its general-purpose nature. Thus, 1946 ushered in the new era of the electronic computer, culminating years of effort (Figure 2-3). The ENIAC continued to operate under BRL management until 1955, when it was disassembled.

The von Neumann Machine

As was mentioned, the task of entering and altering programs for the ENIAC was extremely tedious. The programming process could be facilitated if the program could be represented in a form suitable for storing in memory alongside the data. Then, a computer could get its instructions by reading them from memory, and a program could be set or altered by setting the values of a portion of memory.

This idea, known as the *stored-program concept*, is usually attributed to the ENIAC designers, most notably the mathematician John von Neumann, who was a consultant on the ENIAC project. The idea was also developed at about the same time by Turing. The first publication of the idea was in a 1945 proposal by von Neumann for a new computer, the EDVAC (Electronic Discrete Variable Computer).

In 1946, von Neumann and his colleagues began the design of a new stored-program computer, referred to as the IAS computer, at the Princeton Institute for Advanced Studies. The IAS computer, although not completed until 1952, is the prototype of all subsequent general-purpose computers.

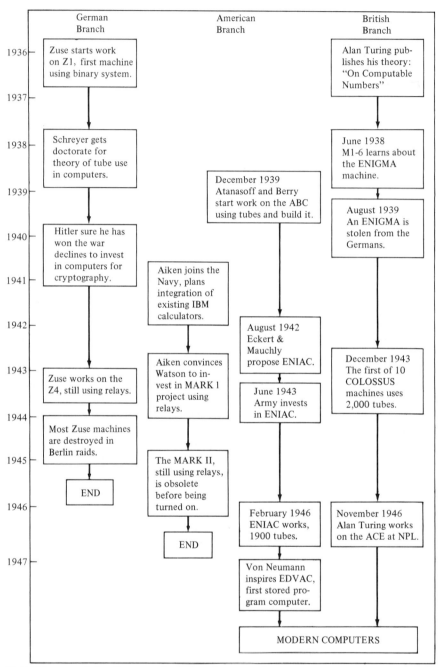

FIGURE 2-3. A family tree of electronic computers

Figure 2-4 shows the general structure of the IAS computer. It consists of

- A main memory which stores both data and instructions.
- An arithmetic-logical unit (ALU) capable of operating on binary data.
- A control unit which interprets the instructions in memory and causes them to be executed.
- Input and output (I/O) equipment operated by the control unit.

This structure was outlined in von Neumann's earlier proposal, which is worth quoting at this point [VONM45]:

2.2 First: Since the device is primarily a computer, it will have to perform the elementary operations of arithmetics most frequently. These are addition, subtraction, multiplication and division: $+$, $-$, $\times$, $\div$. It is therefore reasonable that it should contain specialized organs for just these operations.

It must be observed, however, that while this principle as such is probably sound, the specific way in which it is realized requires close scrutiny. . . At any rate a *central arithmetical* part of the device will probably have to exist and this constitutes *the first specific part: CA.*

2.3 Second: The logical control of the device, that is, the proper sequencing of its operations, can be most efficiently carried out by a central control organ. If the device is to be *elastic,* that is, as nearly as possible *all purpose,* then a distinction must be made between the specific instructions given for and defining a particular problem, and the general control organs which see to it that these instructions—no matter what they are—are carried out. The former must be stored in some way; the latter are represented by definite operating parts of the device. By the *central control* we mean this latter function only, and the organs which perform it form *the second specific part: CC.*

2.4 Third: Any device which is to carry out long and complicated sequences of operations (specifically of calculations) must have a considerable memory. . .

(b) The instructions which govern a complicated problem may constitute considerable material, particularly so, if the code is circumstantial (which it is in most arrangements). This material must be remembered. . .

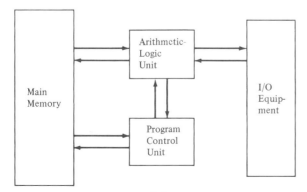

FIGURE 2-4.   Structure of the IAS computer

At any rate, the total *memory* constitutes *the third specific part of the device: M.*

2.6 The three specific parts CA, CC (together C), and M correspond to the *associative* neurons in the human nervous system. It remains to discuss the equivalents of the *sensory* or *afferent* and the *motor* or *efferent* neurons. These are the *input* and *output* organs of the device. . .

The device must be endowed with the ability to maintain input and output (sensory and motor) contact with some specific medium of this type (cf. 1.2): The medium will be called the *outside recording medium of the device: R.* . .

2.7 Fourth: The device must have organs to transfer . . . information from R into its specific parts C and M. These organs form its *input, the fourth specific part: I.* It will be seen that it is best to make all transfers from R (by I) into M and never directly into C. . .

2.8 Fifth: The device must have organs to transfer . . . from its specific parts C and M into R. These organs form its *output, the fifth specific part: O.* It will be seen that it is again best to make all transfers from M (by O) into R, and never directly from C. . .

With rare exceptions, all of today's computers have this same general structure and function and are thus referred to as von Neumann machines. Thus, it is worthwhile at this point to briefly describe the operation of the IAS computer [BURK46]. Following [HAYE88], the terminology and notation of von Neumann are changed in the following to conform more closely to modern usage; the examples and illustrations accompanying this discussion are based on that latter text.

The memory of the IAS consists of 1000 storage locations, called *words,* of 40 binary digits (bits) each. Both data and instructions are stored there. Hence, numbers must be represented in binary form, and each instruction also has to be a binary code. Figure 2-5 illustrates these formats. Each number is represented by a sign bit and a 39-bit value. A word may also contain two 20-bit instructions,

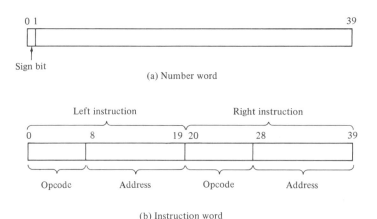

(a) Number word

(b) Instruction word

FIGURE 2-5.   IAS memory formats

with each instruction consisting of an 8-bit operation code (opcode) specifying the operation to be performed and a 12-bit address designating one of the words in memory (numbered from 0 to 999).

The control unit operates the IAS by fetching instructions from memory and executing them one at a time. To explain this, a more detailed structure diagram is needed, as indicated in Figure 2-6. This figure reveals that both the control unit and the ALU contain storage locations, called *registers*, defined as follows:

- *Memory Buffer Register (MBR):* Contains a word to be stored in memory, or is used to receive a word from memory.
- *Memory Address Register (MAR):* Specifies the address in memory of the word to be written from or read into MBR.
- *Instruction Register (IR):* Contains the 8-bit opcode instruction being executed.
- *Instruction Buffer Register (IBR):* Employed to temporarily hold the right-hand instruction from a word in memory.
- *Program Counter (PC):* Contains the address of the next instruction-pair to be fetched from memory.

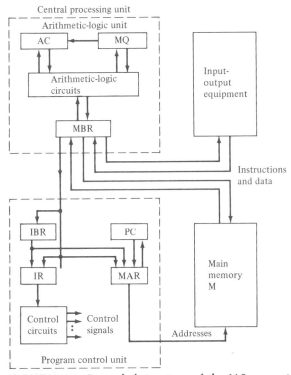

FIGURE 2-6.   **Expanded structure of the IAS computer**

• *Accumulator (AC) and Multiplier-Quotient (MQ):* Employed to temporarily hold operands and results of ALU operations. For example, the result of multiplying two 40-bit numbers is an 80-bit number; the most significant 40 bits are stored in the AC and the least significant in the MQ.

The IAS operates by repetitively performing an *instruction cycle,* as shown in Figure 2-7. Each instruction cycle consists of two subcycles. During the *fetch cycle,* the opcode of the next instruction is loaded into the IR and the address portion is loaded into the MAR. This instruction may be taken from the IBR, or it can be obtained from memory by loading a word into the MBR, and then down to the IBR, IR, and MAR.

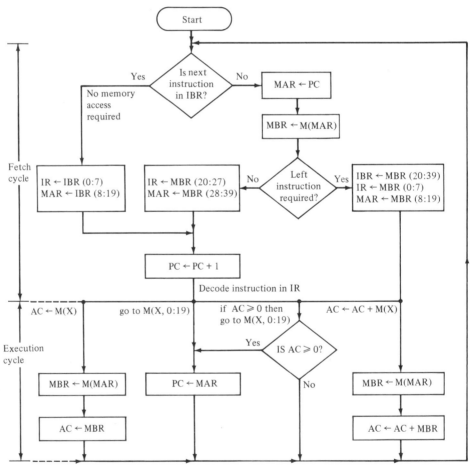

(MX) = contents of memory location whose address is X
(X : Y) = bits X through Y

FIGURE 2-7. Partial flowchart of IAS operation

Why the indirection? Well, all of these operations are controlled by electronic circuitry and result in the use of data paths. To simplify the electronics, there is only one register that is used to specify the address in memory for a read or write, and only one register to be used for the source or destination.

Once the opcode is in the IR, the *execute cycle* is performed. Control circuitry interprets the opcode and executes the instruction by sending out the appropriate control signals to cause data to be moved or an operation to be performed by the ALU.

The IAS computer had a total of 21 instructions, which are listed in Table 2-2. These can be grouped as follows:

- *Data Transfer:* Move data between memory and ALU registers or between two ALU registers.
- *Unconditional Branch:* Normally, the control unit executes instructions in sequence from memory. This sequence can be changed by a branch instruction. This facilitates repetitive operations.
- *Conditional Branch:* The branch can be made dependent on a condition, thus allowing decision points.
- *Arithmetic:* Operations performed by the ALU.
- *Address Modify:* Permit addresses to be computed in the ALU and then inserted into instructions stored in memory. This allows a program considerable addressing flexibility.

Table 2-2 presents instructions in a symbolic, easy-to-read form. Actually, each instruction must conform to the format of Figure 2-5b. The opcode portion (first 8 bits) specifies which of the 21 instructions is to be executed. The address portion (remaining 12 bits) specifies which of the 1000 memory locations is to be involved in the execution of the instruction.

Figure 2-7 shows several examples of instruction execution by the control unit. Note that each operation requires several steps. Some of these are quite elaborate. The multiplication operation requires 39 suboperations, one for each bit position except that of the sign bit!

So, the IAS is used by writing a program using the instruction set of Table 2-2. As an example, Menebrea's program for the Analytical Engine (Figure 2-2) is rewritten for the IAS computer in Figure 2-8. Memory locations M(0) through M(5) correspond to number locations W_0 through W_5. Note that the IAS version is longer. This is so because it is a *one-address* machine, permitting only one memory address per instruction, whereas the Analytical Engine permits three addresses per instruction.

Commercial Computers

The 1950s saw the birth of the computer industry with two companies, Sperry and IBM, dominating the marketplace.

TABLE 2-2   The IAS Instruction Set

Instruction Type	Opcode	Symbolic Representation	Description
Data transfer	00001010	LOAD MQ	Transfer contents of register MQ to the accumulator AC
	00001001	LOAD MQ,M(X)	Transfer contents of memory location X to MQ
	00100001	STOR M(X)	Transfer contents of accumulator to memory location X
	00000001	LOAD M(X)	Transfer M(X) to the accumulator
	00000010	LOAD −M(X)	Transfer −M(X) to the accumulator
	00000011	LOAD |M(X)|	Transfer absolute value of M(X) to the accumulator
	00000100	LOAD −|M(X)|	Transfer −|M(X)| to the accumulator
Unconditional branch	00001101	JUMP M(X,0:19)	Take next instruction from left half of M(X)
	00001110	JUMP M(X,20:39)	Take next instruction from right half of M(X)
Conditional branch	00001111	JUMP+ M(X,0:19)	If number in the accumulator is nonnegative, take next instruction from left half of M(X)
	00010000	JUMP+ M(X,20:39)	If number in the accumulator is nonnegative, take next instruction from right half of M(X)

TABLE 2-2   (continued)

Instruction Type	Opcode	Symbolic Representation	Description
Arithmetic	00000101	ADD M(X)	Add M(X) to AC; put the result in AC
	00000111	ADD |M(X)|	Add |M(X)| to AC; put the result in AC
	00000110	SUB M(X)	Subtract M(X) from AC; put the result in AC
	00001000	SUB |M(X)|	Subtract |M(X)| from AC; put the remainder in AC
	00001011	MUL M(X)	Multiply M(X) by MQ; put most significant bits of result in AC, put least significant bits in MQ
	00001100	DIV M(X)	Divide AC by M(X); put the quotient in MQ and the remainder in AC
	00010100	LSH	Multiply accumulator by 2, i.e., shift left one bit position
	00010101	RSH	Divide accumulator by 2, i.e., shift right one bit position
Address modify	00010010	STOR M(X,8:19)	Replace left address field at M(X) by 12 rightmost bits of AC
	00010011	STOR M(X,28:39)	Replace right address field at M(X) by 12 rightmost bits of AC

Instruction	Comments
$MQ \leftarrow M(1)$	Transfer a_{12} to MQ
$AC, MQ \leftarrow MQ \times M(3)$	Compute $a_{12}a_{21}$
$M(11) \leftarrow AC$	Transfer $a_{12}a_{21}$ to M(11)
$MQ \leftarrow M(0)$	Transfer a_{11} to MQ
$AC, MQ \leftarrow MQ \times M(4)$	Compute $a_{11}a_{22}$
$AC \leftarrow AC - M(11)$	Compute $a_{11}a_{22} - a_{12}a_{21}$
$M(13) \leftarrow AC$	Transfer $a_{11}a_{22} - a_{12}a_{21}$ to M(13)
$MQ \leftarrow M(1)$	Transfer a_{12} to MQ
$AC, MQ \leftarrow MQ \times M(5)$	Compute $a_{12}b_2$
$M(9) \leftarrow AC$	Transfer $a_{12}b_2$ to M(9)
$MQ \leftarrow M(4)$	Transfer a_{22} to MQ
$AC, MQ \leftarrow MQ \times M(2)$	Compute $a_{22}b_1$
$AC \leftarrow AC - M(9)$	Compute $a_{22}b_1 - a_{12}b_2$
$MQ, AC \leftarrow AC \div M(13)$	Compute x_1
$M(14) \leftarrow AC$	Transfer remainder of x_1 to M(14)
$AC \leftarrow MQ$	Transfer quotient of x_1 to AC
$M(15) \leftarrow AC$	Transfer quotient of x_1 to M(15)

FIGURE 2-8. An IAS version of Menebrea's program

In 1947, Eckert and Mauchly formed the Eckert-Mauchly Computer Corporation to manufacture computers commercially. Their first successful machine was the UNIVAC I (Universal Automatic Computer), which was commissioned by the Bureau of the Census for the 1950 calculations. The Eckert-Mauchly Computer Corporation became part of the UNIVAC division of Sperry-Rand Corporation, which went on to build a series of successor machines.

The UNIVAC I was the first successful commercial computer. It was intended, as the name implies, for both scientific and commercial applications. The first paper describing the system listed matrix algebraic computations, statistical problems, premium billings for a life insurance company, and logistical problems as a sample of the tasks it could perform.

The UNIVAC II, which had greater memory capacity and higher performance than the UNIVAC I, was delivered in the late 1950s and illustrates several trends that have remained characteristic of the computer industry. First, advances in technology allow companies to continue to build larger, more powerful computers. Second, each company tries to make its new machines *upward compatible* with the older machines. This means that the programs written for the older machines can be executed on the new machine. This strategy is adopted in the hopes of retaining the customer base; that is, when a customer decides to buy a newer machine, he is likely to get it from the same company to avoid losing the investment in programs.

The UNIVAC division also began development of the 1100 series of computers, which was to be its bread and butter. This series illustrates a distinction that existed at one time. The first model, the UNIVAC 1103, and its successors for many years were primarily intended for scientific applications, involving long and complex calculations. Other companies concentrated on business applications, which involved processing large amounts of text data. This split has largely disappeared, but it was evident for a number of years.

IBM, which had helped build the Mark I and was then the major manufacturer of punched-card processing equipment, delivered its first electronic stored-program computer, the 701, in 1953. The 701 was intended primarily for scientific applications [BASH81]. In 1955, IBM introduced the companion 702 product, which had a number of hardware features that suited it to business applications. These were the first of a long series of 700/7000 computers that established IBM as the overwhelmingly dominant computer manufacturer.

2.3

THE SECOND GENERATION: TRANSISTORS

The first major change in the electronic computer came with the replacement of the vacuum tube by the transistor. The transistor is smaller, cheaper, and dissipates less heat than a vacuum tube but can be used in the same way as a vacuum tube to construct computers. Unlike the vacuum tube, which requires wires, metal plates, a glass capsule, and a vacuum, the transistor is a *solid-state device,* made from silicon.

The transistor was invented at Bell Labs in 1947 and by the 1950s had launched an electronic revolution. It was not until the late 1950s, however, that fully transistorized computers were commercially available. IBM again was not the first company to deliver the new technology. NCR, and more successfully RCA, were the front-runners with some small transistor machines. IBM followed shortly with the 7000 series.

The use of the transistor defines the *second generation* of computers. It has become widely accepted to classify computers into generations based on the fundamental hardware technology employed (Table 2-3). Each new generation is characterized by greater speed, larger memory capacity, and smaller size than the previous one.

But there are other changes as well. The second generation saw the introduction of more complex arithmetic and logic units and control units, the use of

TABLE 2-3   COMPUTER GENERATIONS

Generation	Approximate Dates	Technology	Typical Speed (operations per second)
1	1946-1957	Vacuum tube	40,000
2	1958-1964	Transistor	200,000
3	1965-1971	Small and medium scale integration	1,000,000
4	1972-1977	Large scale integration	10,000,000
5	1978-	Very large scale integration	100,000,000

high-level programming languages, and the provision of *system software* with the computer.

The second generation is noteworthy also for the appearance of the Digital Equipment Corporation (DEC). DEC was founded in 1957 and, in that year, delivered its first computer, the PDP-1. This computer and this company began the minicomputer phenomenon that would become so prominent in the third generation.

The IBM 7094

From the introduction of the 700 series in 1952 to the introduction of the last member of the 7000 series in 1964, this IBM product line underwent an evolution that is typical of computer products. Successive members of the product line show increased performance, increased capacity, and/or lower cost.

Table 2-4 illustrates this trend. The size of main memory, in multiples of 2^{10} 36-bit words, grew from 2K ($1K = 2^{10}$) to 32K words, while the time to access one word of memory, the *memory cycle time*, fell from 30 μs to 1.4 μs. The number of opcodes grew from a modest 24 to 185.

The final column indicates the relative execution speed of the CPU. Speed improvements are achieved by improved electronics (e.g., a transistor implementation is faster than a vaccum tube implementation) and more complex circuitry. For example, the IBM 7094 includes an Instruction Backup Register (IBR), which is used to buffer the next instruction. The control unit fetches two adjacent words from memory for an instruction fetch. Except for the occurrence of a branching instruction, which is typically infrequent, this means that the control unit has to access memory for an instruction on only half the instruction cycles. This prefetching significantly reduces the average instruction cycle time.

The remainder of the columns of Table 2-4 will become clear as the text proceeds.

Figure 2-9 shows a large (many peripherals) configuration for an IBM 7094, which is representative of second-generation computers [BELL71a]. Several differences from the IAS computer are worth noting. The most important of these is the use of *data channels*. A data channel is an independent I/O module with its own processor and its own instruction set. In a computer system with such devices, the CPU does not execute detailed I/O instructions. Such instructions are stored in a main memory to be executed by a special-purpose processor in the data channel itself. The CPU initiates an I/O transfer by sending a control signal to the data channel, instructing it to execute a sequence of instructions in memory. The data channel performs its task independently of the CPU and signals the CPU when the operation is complete. This arrangement relieves the CPU of a considerable processing burden.

Another new feature is the *multiplexor*, which is the central termination point for data channels, the CPU, and memory. The multiplexor schedules access to the memory from the CPU and data channels, allowing these devices to act independently.

TABLE 2-4   Example Members of the IBM 700/7000 Series

Model Number	First Delivery	CPU Technology	Memory Technology	Memory Cycle Time (μs)	Memory Size (K)	Number of Opcodes	Number of Index Registers	Hardwired Floating-point	I/O Overlap (Channels)	Instruction Fetch Overlap	Speed Ratio (Approximate)
701	1952	Vacuum tubes	Electrostatic tubes	30	2-4	24	0	no	no	no	1
704	1955	Vacuum tubes	Core	12	4-32	80	3	yes	no	no	2.5
709	1958	Vacuum tubes	Core	12	32	140	3	yes	yes	no	4
7090	1960	Transistor	Core	2.18	32	169	3	yes	yes	no	25
7094 I	1962	Transistor	Core	2	32	185	7	yes (double precision)	yes	yes	30
7094 II	1964	Transistor	Core	1.4	32	185	7	yes (double precision)	yes	yes	50

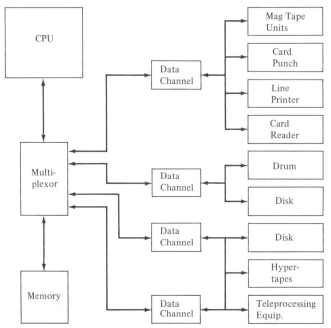

FIGURE 2-9. An IBM 7094 configuration

THE THIRD GENERATION: INTEGRATED CIRCUITS

A single, self-contained transistor is called a *discrete component*. Throughout the 1950s and early 1960s, electronic equipment was composed largely of discrete components—transistors, resistors, capacitors, and so on. Discrete components were manufactured separately, packaged in their own containers, and soldered or wired together onto masonite-like circuit boards, which were then installed in computers, oscilloscopes, and other electronic equipment. Whenever an electronic device called for a transistor, a little tube of metal containing a pinhead-sized piece of silicon had to be soldered to a circuit board. The entire manufacturing process, from transistor to circuit board, was expensive and cumbersome.

These facts of life were beginning to create problems in the computer industry. Early second-generation computers contained about 10,000 transistors. This figure grew to the hundreds of thousands, making the manufacture of newer, more powerful machines increasingly difficult.

In 1958 came the achievement that revolutionized electronics and started the era of microelectronics: the invention of the integrated circuit. It is the integrated circuit that defines the third generation of computers. In this section we provide a brief introduction to the technology of integrated circuits. Then, we look at perhaps the two most important members of the third generation, both of which were introduced at the beginning of that era: the IBM System/360 and the DEC PDP-8.

Microelectronics

Microelectronics means, literally, "small electronics." Since the beginnings of digital electronics and the computer industry there has been a persistent and consistent trend toward the reduction in size of digital electronic circuits. Before examining the implications and benefits of this trend, we need to say something about the nature of digital electronics. A more detailed discussion is found in Appendix A.

The basic elements of a digital computer, as we know, must perform storage, movement, processing, and control functions. Only two fundamental types of components are required (Figure 2-10): gates and memory cells. A gate is a device that implements a simple Boolean or logical function, such as IF *A* AND *B* ARE TRUE THEN *C* IS TRUE (AND gate). Such devices are called gates because they control data flow in much the same way that canal gates do. The memory cell is a device that can store one bit of data; that is, the device can be in one of two stable states at any time. By interconnecting large numbers of these fundamental devices, we can construct a computer. We can relate this to our four basic functions as follows:

- *Data Storage:* Provided by memory cells.
- *Data Processing:* Provided by gates.

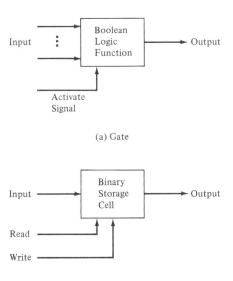

FIGURE 2-10.   Fundamental computer elements

- *Data Movement:* The paths between components are used to move data from memory to memory and from memory through gates to memory.
- *Control:* The paths between components can carry control signals. For example, a gate will have one or two data inputs plus a control signal input that activates the gate. When the control signal is ON, the gate performs its function on the data inputs and produces a data output. Similarly, the memory cell will store the bit on its input lead when the WRITE control signal is ON and will place that bit on its output lead when the READ control signal is ON.

Thus, a computer consists of gates, memory cells, and interconnections among these elements. The gates and memory cells are, in turn, constructed of simple digital electronic components.

Although the transistor technology introduced in the second computer generation was a major improvement over vacuum tubes, problems remained. The transistors were individually mounted in separate packages and interconnected on printed circuit boards by separate wires. This was a complex, time-consuming, and error-prone process.

The integrated circuit exploits the fact that such components as transistors, resistors, and conductors can be fabricated from a semiconductor such as silicon. It is merely an extension of the solid-state art to fabricate an entire circuit in a tiny piece of silicon rather than assemble discrete components made from separate pieces of silicon into the same circuit. Hundreds and even thousands of transistors can be produced at the same time on a single wafer of silicon. Equally important, these transistors can be connected with a process of metallization to form circuits.

Figure 2-11 depicts the key concepts in an integrated circuit. A thin *wafer* of silicon is divided into a matrix of small areas, each a few millimeters square. The identical circuit pattern is fabricated in each area, and the wafer is broken up into *chips*. Each chip consists of many gates plus a number of input and output attachment points. This chip is then packaged in housing that protects it and provides pins for attachment to devices beyond the chip. A number of these packages can then be interconnected on a printed-circuit board to produce larger and more complex circuits.

Initially, only a few gates or memory cells could be reliably manufactured and packaged together. These early integrated circuits are referred to as *small-scale integration* (SSI). As time went on, it became possible to pack more and more components on the same chip. This growth in density is illustrated in Figure 2-12; it is one of the most remarkable technological trends ever recorded. Beginning at unity in 1959, the number of devices per chip doubled annually in the 1960s. In the 1970s, the rate declined, but only to the still remarkable level of quadrupling every three years. That level should persist through the early 1990s, when the effects of physical limits will probably slow the rate of growth again. Nevertheless, according to the more optimistic prediction, gigascale integration (GSI)—a one-billion-component chip—will be achieved by the end of the century. (The projections differ in assumptions about limits imposed by chip-fabrication processes.)

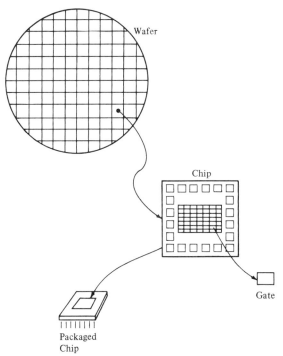

FIGURE 2-11.   Relationship between wafer, chip, and gate

For the computer manufacturer, the use of ever-more densely packed ICs provides many benefits:

1. The cost of a chip has remained virtually unchanged during this period of rapid growth in density. This means that the cost of computer logic and memory circuitry has fallen at a dramatic rate.
2. Because logic and memory elements are placed closer together on more densely packed chips, the electrical path length is shortened, increasing operating speed.
3. The computer becomes smaller, making it more convenient to place in a variety of environments.
4. There is a reduction in power and cooling requirements.
5. The interconnections on the integrated circuit are much more reliable than solder connections. With more circuitry on each chip, there are fewer interchip connections.

IBM System/360

By 1964, IBM had a firm grip on the computer market with its 7000 series of machines. In that year, IBM announced the System/360, a new family of computer products. Although the announcement itself was no surprise, it contained

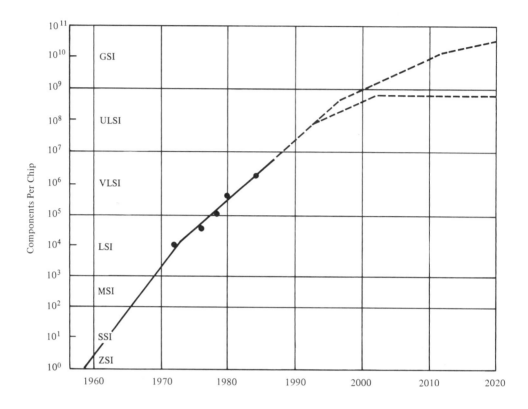

ZSI = Zero-scale Integration (Descrete Components)
SSI = Small-Scale Integration
MSI = Medium-scale Integration
LSI = Large-scale Integration
VLSI = Very-large-scale Integration
ULSI = Ultra-large-scale Integration
GSI = Giga-scale Integration

FIGURE 2-12. Growth in chip density [MEIN87]

some unpleasant news for current IBM customers: the 360 product line was incompatible with older IBM machines. Thus the transition to the 360 would be difficult for the current customer base. This was a bold step by IBM but one they felt was necessary to break out of some of the constraints of the 7000 architecture and to produce a system capable of evolving with the new integrated circuit technology [PADE81, GIFF87]. The strategy paid off both financially and technically. The 360 was the success of the decade and cemented IBM as the overwhelmingly dominant computer vendor with a market share above 70%. And, with some modifications and extensions, the architecture of the 360 remains to this day the architecture of IBM's large computers. Examples using this architecture can be found throughout this text.

The System/360 was the industry's first planned family of computers. The family covered a wide range of performance and cost. Table 2-5 indicates some of the key characteristics of the various models in 1965 (each member of the family

TABLE 2-5   Key Characteristics of the System/360 Family

Characteristic	Model 30	Model 40	Model 50	Model 65	Model 75
Maximum memory size (bytes)	64K	256K	256K	512K	512K
Data rate from memory (M bytes/sec)	0.5	0.8	2.0	8.0	16.0
Processor cycle time (μsec)	1.0	0.625	0.5	0.25	0.2
Relative speed	1	3.5	10	21	50
Maximum number of data channels	3	3	4	6	6
Maximum data rate on one channel (K bytes/sec)	250	400	800	1250	1250

is distinguished by a model number). The various models were compatible in that a program written for one model should be capable of being executed by another model in the series, with only a difference in the time it takes to execute.

The concept of a family of compatible computers was both novel and extremely successful. A customer with modest requirements and a budget to match could start with the relatively inexpensive Model 30. Later, if the customer's needs grew, it was possible to upgrade to a faster machine with more memory without sacrificing the investment in already-developed software. The characteristics of a family are

- *Similar or Identical Instruction Set:* In many cases, the exact same set of machine instructions obtains on all members of the family. Thus, a program that executes on one machine will also execute on any other. In some cases, the lower end of the family has an instruction set that is a subset of that of the top end of the family. This means that programs can move up but not down.
- *Similar or Identical Operating System:* The same basic operating system is available for all family members. In some cases, additional features are added to the higher-end members.
- *Increasing Speed:* The rate of instruction execution increases in going from lower to higher family members.
- *Increasing Number of I/O Ports:* In going from lower to higher family members.
- *Increasing Memory Size:* In going from lower to higher family members.
- *Increasing Cost:* In going from lower to higher family members.

How could such a family concept be implemented? Differences were achieved based on three factors: basic speed, size, and degree of simultaneity [STEV64]. For example, greater speed in the execution of a given instruction could be gained by the use of more complex circuitry in the ALU, allowing suboperations to be carried out in parallel. Another way of increasing speed was to increase the width of the data path between main memory and the CPU. On the Model 30, only 1 byte (8 bits) could be fetched from main memory at a time, whereas 8 bytes could be fetched at a time on the Model 70.

The System/360 not only dictated the future course of IBM but also had a profound impact on the entire industry. Many of its features have become standard on other large computers.

DEC PDP-8

In the same year that IBM shipped its first System/360, another momentous first shipment occurred: DEC's PDP-8. At a time when the average computer required an air-conditioned room, the PDP-8 (dubbed a minicomputer by the industry, after the miniskirt of the day) was small enough that it could be placed on top of a lab bench or be built into other equipment. It could not do everything the mainframe could, but at $16,000, it was cheap enough for each lab technician to have one. It contrast, the System/360 series of mainframe computers introduced just a few months before cost hundreds of thousands of dollars.

The low cost and small size of the PDP-8 enabled another manufacturer to purchase a PDP-8 and integrate it into a total system for resale. These other manufacturers came to be known as original equipment manufacturers (OEMs), and the OEM market became and remains a major segment of the computer marketplace.

The PDP-8 was an immediate hit and made DEC's fortune. This machine and other members of the PDP-8 family that followed it (see Table 2-6) achieved a production status formerly reserved for IBM computers, with about 50,000 machines sold over the next dozen years. As DEC's official history puts it, the PDP-8 "established the concept of minicomputers, leading the way to a multibillion dollar industry." It also established DEC as the number one minicomputer vendor, and, by the time the PDP-8 had reached the end of its useful life, DEC was the number two computer manufacturer, behind IBM.

In contrast to the central-switched architecture (Figure 2-9) used by IBM on its 700/7000 and 360 systems, later models of the PDP-8 used a structure that is now virtually universal for minicomputers and microcomputers: the bus structure. This is illustrated in Figure 2-13. The PDP-8 bus, called the Omnibus, consists of 96 separate signal paths, used to carry control, address, and data signals. Since all system components share a common set of signal paths, their use must be controlled by the CPU. This architecture is highly flexible, allowing modules to

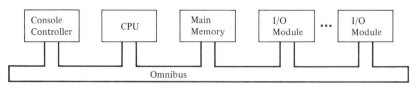

FIGURE 2-13.   PDP-8 bus structure

TABLE 2-6 Evolution of the PDP-8 [VOEL88]

Model	First Shipped	Cost of Processor + 4K 12-bit Words of Memory ($1,000s)	Data Rate from Memory (words/μsec)	Volume (cubic feet)	Innovations and Improvements
PDP-8	4/65	16.2	1.26	8.0	Automatic wire-wrapping production
PDP-8/S	9/66	8.79	0.08	3.2	Serial instruction implementation
PDP-8/I	4/68	11.6	1.34	8.0	Medium-scale integrated circuits
PDP-8/L	11/68	7.0	1.26	2.0	Smaller cabinet
PDP-8/E	3/71	4.99	1.52	2.2	Omnibus
PDP-8/M	6/72	3.69	1.52	1.8	Half-size cabinet with fewer slots than 8/E
PDP-8/A	1/75	2.6	1.34	1.2	Semiconductor memory; floating-point processor

be plugged into the bus to create various configurations. Figure 2-14 shows a large PDP-8/E configuration.

2.5

LATER GENERATIONS

Beyond the third generation there is less general agreement on defining generations of computers. Table 2-3 suggests that there have been a fourth and a fifth generation, based on advances in integrated-circuit technology. With the introduction of large-scale integration (LSI), over 1,000 components can be placed on a single integrated-circuit chip. Very-large-scale integration (VLSI) achieved over 10,000 components per chip, and current VLSI chips can contain over 100,000 components.

With the rapid pace of technology, the high rate of introduction of new products, and the importance of software and communications as well as hardware, the classification by generation becomes less clear and less meaningful. It could be said that the commercial application of new developments resulted in a major change in the early 1970s and that the results of these changes are still being worked out. In this section, we mention two of the most important of these results.

Semiconductor Memory

The first application of integrated-circuit technology to computers was construction of the processor (the control unit and the arithmetic and logic unit) out of integrated circuit chips. But it was also found that this same technology could be used to construct memories.

In the 1950s and 1960s, most computer memory was constructed from tiny rings of ferromagnetic material, each about a sixteenth of an inch in diameter. These rings were strung up on grids of fine wires suspended on small screens inside the computer. Magnetized one way, a ring (called a *core*) represented a one: magnetized the other way, it stood for a zero. Magnetic-core memory was rather fast; it took as little as a millionth of a second to read a bit stored in memory. But it was expensive, bulky, and used destructive readout: the simple act of reading a core erased the data stored in it. It was therefore necessary to install circuits to restore the data as soon as it had been extracted.

Then, in 1970, Fairchild produced the first relatively capacious semiconductor memory. This chip, about the size of a single core, could hold 256 bits of memory. It was nondestructive and much faster than core. It took only 70 billionths of a second to read a bit. However, the cost per bit was higher than for that of core.

In 1974, a seminal event occurred: the price per bit of semiconductor memory dropped below the price per bit of core memory. Following this, there has been a continuing and rapid decline in memory cost accompanied by a corresponding

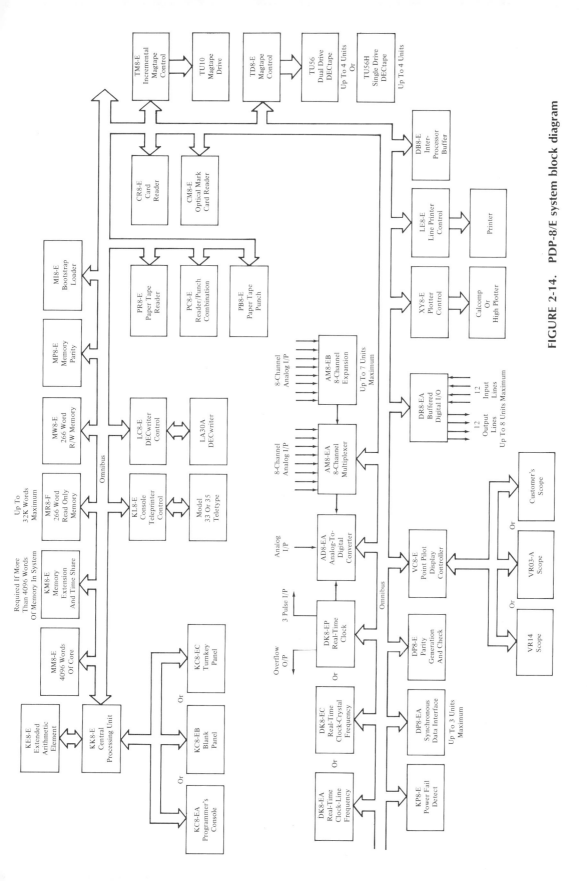

FIGURE 2-14. PDP-8/E system block diagram

increase in physical memory density. This has led the way to smaller, faster machines with memory sizes of larger and more expensive machines with a time lag of just a few years. Developments in memory technology, together with developments in processor technology to be discussed next, changed the nature of computers in less than a decade. Although bulky, expensive computers remain a part of the landscape, the computer has also been brought out to the "end user," with office machines and personal computers.

Since 1970, semiconductor memory has been through six generations: 1K, 4K, 16K, 64K, 256K, and now 1M bits on a single chip ($1K = 2^{10}$, $1M = 2^{20}$). Each generation has provided four times the storage density of the previous generation, accompanied by declining cost per bit and declining access time.

Microprocessors

Just as the density of elements on memory chips has continued to rise, so has the density of elements on processor chips. As time went on, more and more elements were placed on each chip so that fewer and fewer chips were needed to construct a single computer processor.

A breakthrough was achieved in 1971, when Intel developed its 4004. The 4004 was the first chip to contain *all* of the components of a CPU on a single chip: the microprocessor was born.

The 4004 can add two 4-bit numbers and can multiply only by repeated addition. By today's standards, the 4004 is hopelessly primitive, but it marked the beginning of an ongoing evolution of microprocessor capability and power.

This evolution can be seen most easily in the number of bits that the processor deals with at a time. There is no clear-cut measure of this, but perhaps the best measure is the data bus width: the number of bits of data that can be brought into or sent out of the processor at a time. Another measure is the number of bits in the accumulator or in the set of general-purpose registers. Often, these measures coincide, but not always. For example, there are a number of microprocessors that operate on 16-bit numbers in registers but can only read and write 8 bits at a time.

The next major step in the evolution of the microprocessor was the introduction in 1972 of the Intel 8008. This was the first 8-bit microprocessor and was almost twice as complex as the 4004.

Neither of these steps was to have the impact of the next major event: the introduction in 1974 of the Intel 8080. This was the first general-purpose microprocessor. Whereas the 4004 and the 8008 had been designed for specific applications, the 8080 was designed to be the CPU of a general-purpose microcomputer. Like the 8008, the 8080 is an 8-bit microprocessor. The 8080, however, is faster, has a richer instruction set, and has a large addressing capability.

About the same time, 16-bit microprocessors began to be developed. However, it wasn't until the end of the 1970s that powerful, general-purpose 16-bit microprocessors appeared. One of these was the 8086. The culmination of this trend occurred in 1981, when both Bell Labs and Hewlett-Packard developed

TABLE 2-7   Evolution of Intel Microprocessors

Feature	8008	8080	8086	80386	80486
Year introduced	1972	1974	1978	1985	1989
Number of instructions	66	111	133	154	235
Address bus width	8	16	20	32	32
Data bus width	8	8	16	32	32
Number of flags	4	5	9	14	14
Number of registers	8	8	16	8	8
Memory addressability	16 KB	64 KB	1 MB	4 GB	4 GB
I/O ports	24	256	64K	64K	64K
Bus bandwidth	—	0.75 MB/sec	5 MB/sec	32 MB/sec	32 MB/sec
Register-to-register add time	—	1.3 μsec	0.3 μsec	0.125 μsec	0.06 μsec

32-bit, single-chip microprocessors. Intel introduced its own 32-bit microprocessor, the 80386, in 1985 (Table 2-7). At least for the foreseeable future, the step to 32 bits is in a sense a final one [ZORP85b]. For both microcomputers and minicomputers, 32 bits represent the top of the line, and this size is becoming the standard for mainframe computers. Further development is to be found in increasing the complexity of the ALU, the variety of instructions, and the number of registers. All of this can be done with the 32-bit word length.

2.6

CONTEMPORARY COMPUTERS

There is a wide variety of computers on the marketplace today, in terms of physical size, price, capacity, and performance. The variety is so wide that it is sometimes difficult to see those elements that are shared by many computers and those elements that tend to differ among computers.

For some time now, engineers, manufacturers, and users of computers have found it convenient to group the many computers into three main classes:

• Microcomputers
• Minicomputers
• Mainframes

This classification is very useful to gaining an understanding of the key elements of computer architecture and the key differences among computers. It is important to realize, though, that these classes are not precisely defined. This is for two reasons:

• There is actually a spectrum of computer types, and the differences among computers within each of the three classes are as great as the differences between neighboring classes.

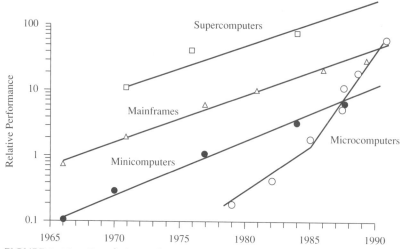

FIGURE 2-15.   Trends in performance growth by computer class [HENN91]

- Computer technology is evolving rapidly, so that the microcomputer of today is as powerful as the minicomputer of a few years ago, and the minicomputer of today is as powerful as the mainframe of a few years ago.

  This latter point is illustrated in Figure 2-15, which shows the major classes of computers over time. By almost any measure of computer power, each class has grown in power over time. Going up the chart diagonally, one sees that a class of computers becomes more powerful as time goes on. Going across the chart horizontally, one sees that, as time goes on, the same computing power can be provided by smaller, cheaper computers.[1]

  This classification (microcomputer, minicomputer, mainframe), of course, implies differences between classes in one or more characteristics. In the 1960s, before the microcomputer, there was a clear-cut distinction between minicomputers and mainframes. The most important characteristics that could be used to differentiate the two types of computers were

- Speed
- Instruction Repertoire
- Number of CPU Registers
- Word Length
- Main Memory Size
- Complexity of I/O Modules
- Operating System Complexity

[1]The plot only reflects CPU performance for general-purpose applications. Performance for classes other than microprocessor are underestimated because I/O performance is not taken into account.

- Physical Size
- Cost
- Virtual Address Space
- Secondary Memory Size
- Degree of Multiprogramming

(The last three terms have not yet been defined but are discussed later in this text.) The mainframe possessed more of each of these characteristics than the minicomputer. When the microcomputer was first introduced, this same list could be used to differentiate the microcomputer from the minicomputer. With the ongoing evolution in technology, the boundaries between the three types of machines have become blurred. Also, a new class has emerged: the supercomputer. Table 2-8 gives examples of each class.

The remainder of this section provides a brief commentary on each of these classes.

Microcomputer

The microcomputer class can be more precisely defined than the other classes. Simply, a microcomputer is a computer whose CPU is a microprocessor. As we saw in the preceding section, a microprocessor is a processor all of whose components are on a single integrated-circuit chip.

The microcomputer has become such a common part of everyday life that little need be said about it here. Home computers and personal office computers have proliferated, bringing computing power and literacy to more and more people. In terms of numbers of units, microcomputer sales dwarf those of all other types of computers combined.

Minicomputer

By the early 1960s, economic and technical factors combined to make small, inexpensive computers attractive for many applications. Many computing tasks could be accomplished with less power than was then available on contemporary mainframe computers. For example, computers could be used to control some industrial or data acquisition process, such as checkout of the electronic system of a product on an assembly line. This type of task could not be economically performed by a mainframe, but a small, relatively inexpensive computer could be used. While mainframe machines were run by staffs of operators, such costs could not be justified for the inexpensive minicomputer. Thus, direct interaction between the minicomputer and the user was required.

A key development in the minicomputer field was the introduction of the 16-bit minicomputer, of which the PDP-11 from DEC, introduced in 1970, was the most prominent and widely used. Earlier minicomputers employed a variety of shorter bit lengths, with 8-bit and 12-bit machines being common. By the late

TABLE 2-8   Characteristics of Some Contemporary Computers [GIBS88, RYAN88]

	Cray Y-MP	IBM 3090/600	VAX 8842	IBM AS/400/B60	IBM PS/2/50
Class	Supercomputer	Mainframe	Minicomputer	Minicomputer	Microcomputer
First installed	3Q/88	8/88	4Q/88	8/88	3Q87
Instruction execution rate	2.6 GFLOPS	102 MIPS	22 MIPS	N/A	2 MIPS
Machine cycle time (nsec)	6	15	45	60	100
Memory in bytes	256M	128M-512M	256M-1G	32M-96M	1M-16M
Disk transfer rate (MB/sec)	9.6	3-4.5	2.8	3	1.25
Number of I/O channels	81	64-128	N/A	N/A	8
Base price	$20M	$12.4M	$1.735	$300K	$4K

N/A = Not available.
MIPS = Millions of instructions per second.
GFLOPS = Billions of floating-point operations per second.

1970s, virtually all minicomputers were 16-bit machines. Compared to shorter word-length machines, the 16-bit computer boasted the following advantages:

- The 16-bit word length allows for a relatively rich set of machine instructions and a relatively large address field. This provides a more powerful machine that can be used in a wide variety of applications.
- The 16-bit word length is efficient for storage and handling of text. Thus, it lends itself to business applications as well as scientific applications.

As the speed, instruction repertoire, memory size, and other characteristics of minicomputers increased with advances in technology, its role changed. Many of the stand-alone or dedicated applications began to be performed by micro-computers. The minicomputer became a multi-user, or shared, system. Throughout the 1960s and 1970s, advances in technology led to the increasing functionality of the minicomputer. Instruction sets were enhanced to include operations on floating-point numbers for scientific processing and on character strings for commercial applications. The availability of low-cost memory allowed a dramatic increase in the size of main memory attached to the minicomputer. The speed of instruction execution increased.

All of these improvements occurred within a 16-bit architecture. But there are limitations imposed by that architecture:

- *Instruction repertoire:* With the use of 16-bit instructions, the number of available opcodes is limited.
- *Higher-precision arithmetic:* The "natural" form of arithmetic on a 16-bit machine operates on 16-bit numbers. Higher precision can be obtained by storing a single number in two or more words. A more efficient operation can be achieved with a larger word size to store numbers.
- *Address range:* The addressing capability is generally limited by the number of bits that can be stored in address registers. So, on a 16-bit machine, a maximum of 64K unique addresses is allowed.

Of these limitations, the last is the most important and the most fundamental. Addresses are used by computer programs to reference data locations and program locations. As the power of the minicomputer increased, a mismatch developed between the 64K address range and the multi-megabyte physical address space. For large applications, two trends developed: (1) minicomputer users wanted to process large arrays of data; this showed up particularly in FORTRAN programs; and (2) application programs were growing rapidly in size, particularly large COBOL programs. The programmer had to resort to various "tricks" to cope with this mismatch.

These considerations led to the introduction in the late 1970s of the 32-bit minicomputer, which was quickly dubbed the *supermini*. The superminicomputer continues the trend established for the 16-bit minicomputer, supporting more simultaneous users and handling more peripheral devices and larger memories than previous minicomputers. With the virtual disappearance of the

16-bit minicomputer, the term supermini has been dropped in favor of simply minicomputer or mid-range system.

Mainframe

Although there has been some blurring of the boundaries between minicomputers and mainframes, the mainframe remains a distinct class of computers.

Some of the key differences between the high end of the mainframe class and the high end of the minicomputer class are highlighted for the IBM 3090 and the VAX 8842 in Table 2-8. One of the most dramatic differences is in the speed of the two classes. A common measure of speed is *millions of instructions per second* (MIPS); this is the rate at which machine instructions are executed. It is sometimes dangerous to compare the MIPS rating of dissimilar machines, since the typical instruction on one machine might do more than the typical instruction on another. However, the instruction sets of mainframes and superminis are comparable, and so this is a fair comparison. Another dramatic area of difference is price, as is also shown in the table.

In terms of dollar volume, mainframes are the largest sector of the computer hardware market, and the marketplace continues to grow. The question might arise of why such expensive machines continue to survive in the world of microcomputers and low-cost minis. Indeed, predictions of the death of the mainframe have appeared regularly for the past 15 years or more (e.g., [HEAL83]). The answer is twofold [POWE83, VERI87]: (1) mainframes have more than kept up with the other classes of computers in terms of price and performance improvements, and (2) there is a legitimate function uniquely served by the mainframe. Let us briefly examine these two points.

The dramatic improvements in the performance of minicomputers led many observers to believe that the expensive mainframe was out of date by the mid-1970s. An event that represented a turning point for the mainframe industry was the beginning of volume shipments of *plug-compatible* systems by Amdahl Corp. in 1976 [AMDA79]. These machines were identical in function to the IBM CPU and could run all software developed for IBM machines. Amdahl offered improvements in price and performance over the current IBM mainframes and this introduced true competition to this sector of the industry. The result was a strong response from IBM. From 1970 to 1976, the top-of-the-line mainframe from IBM went from 1.8 MIPS to 2.5 MIPS; from 1976 to 1982, it went from 2.5 MIPS to 14 MIPS. During this period, prices remained steady. This price/performance improvement exceeded that experienced in the minicomputer industry over the same period of time.

Nevertheless, a full-size mainframe is a huge investment. With the development of distributed data processing technology, many observers felt that even large applications could be handled by a network of minicomputers instead of by a mainframe. This has happened in some areas. But in one area, the mainframe continues to be dominant. The primary function of mainframes today is to support large databases. Large business and government organizations need a central repository of data that can be managed and controlled centrally. Only the mainframe has the processing power to handle large database systems.

Supercomputer

Although the performance of mainframe general-purpose computers continues to improve relentlessly, there remain applications that are beyond the reach of the contemporary mainframe. There is a need for computers to solve mathematical problems of real processes, such as occur in disciplines including aerodynamics, seismology, meteorology, and atomic, nuclear, and plasma physics.

Typically, these problems are characterized by the need for high precision and a program that repetitively performs floating-point arithmetic operations on large arrays of numbers. Most of these problems fall into the category known as continuous-field simulation. In essence, a physical situation can be described by a surface or region in three dimensions (e.g., the flow of air adjacent to the surface of a rocket). This surface is approximated by a grid of points. A set of differential equations defines the physical behavior of the surface at each point. The equations are represented as an array of values and coefficients, and the solution involves repeated arithmetic operations on the arrays of data.

To handle these types of problems, the supercomputer has been developed. These machines are typically capable of hundreds of millions of floating-point operations per second and cost in the 10 to 15 million-dollar range. Although a supercomputer is capable of the general-purpose applications found on mainframes, it is optimized for the type of numerical calculation involving arrays. Its architecture is examined in Chapter 15.

The supercomputer has limited use and, because of its price tag, a limited market. Only a few dozen of these machines are operational, mostly at research centers and some government agencies with scientific or engineering functions. As with other areas of computer technology, there is a constant demand to increase the performance of the supercomputer. In some current applications in aerodynamics and nuclear physics, as many as 10^{13} arithmetic operations, absorbing more than two days of computing time on a contemporary supercomputer, are needed for a single problem. Thus the technology and performance of the supercomputer continues to evolve.

2.7

RECOMMENDED READING

There are a number of good books that cover the material in Sections 2-1 and 2-2. [WULF82], [SHUR84], [MORE84], and [EVAN81] are readable and entertaining. [GOLD72] provides an insider's view of the American developments.

A description of the IBM 7000 series can be found in [BELL71a]. There is good coverage of the IBM 360 in [SIEW82a] and of the PDP-8 in [BELL87a]. These latter three references also contain many examples of other computers from the second, third, and later generations. [GUPT83] provides an excellent history and survey of microprocessors.

2.8

PROBLEMS

2.1 (a) The method of finite differences can be explained as follows. A polynomial of order N has the form:

$$P(X) = \sum_{i=0}^{N} a_i X^i$$

The jth difference of $P(X)$, $\Delta^j P(X)$, is defined recursively as follows:

$$\Delta^0 P(X) = P(X)$$
$$\Delta^1 P(X) = P(X + 1) - P(X)$$
$$\Delta^2 P(X) = \Delta P(X + 1) - \Delta P(X)$$

$$\Delta^j P(X) = \Delta^{j-1} P(X + 1) - \Delta^{j-1} P(X)$$

Show that $\Delta^N P(X)$ equals a constant and that $\Delta^k P(X) = 0$ for $k > N$.
(b) We can rearrange the equations above to get

$$P(X) = P(X - 1) + \Delta^1 P(X - 1)$$
$$\Delta P(X) = \Delta P(X - 1) + \Delta^2 P(X - 1)$$
$$\Delta^2 P(X) = \Delta^2 P(X - 1) + \Delta^3 P(X - 1)$$

$$\Delta^N P(X) = \text{constant}$$

Thus, if $P(0)$, $\Delta P(0)$, . . . $\Delta^N P(0)$ are known, then all subsequent values of $P(X)$, $\Delta P(X)$. . .$\Delta^N P(X)$ can be easily calculated with simple additions. This is the method of finite differences used in Babbage's Difference Engine.

Consider the polynomial $X^2 + X + 1$. For this problem, a difference engine with three registers is needed. Once the registers are initialized, the procedure is as follows: the third register (D_2) is added to the second, the second to the first, and the result recorded. The procedure may be repeated until a register overflow (number too big for a register) occurs. This was one of the first polynomials computed by Babbage on his first machine. It was a particular favorite of his owing to its first 39 values all being prime numbers [DUBB78].

Construct a table showing the result of applying this technique to the first 10 values of X.

2.2 Let A = A(1), A(2). . ., A(1,000) and B = B(1), B(2). . . B(1,000) be two vectors (one-dimensional arrays) comprising 1,000 numbers each that are to be added to form an array C such that C(I) = A(I) + B(I) for I = 1, 2,. . ., 1,000. Using the IAS instruction set, write a program for this problem.

2.3 For the flowchart of Figure 2-7, add the logic for the remaining IAS instructions, except for those involving a multiply or a divide.

2.4 In the IBM 360 Models 65 and 75, addresses are staggered in two separate main memory units (e.g., all even-numbered words in one unit and all odd-numbered words in another). What might be the purpose of this technique?

2.5 Discuss the advantages and disadvantages of storing programs and data in the same memory.

2.6 List those instructions in Table 2-2 that are redundant. An instruction is redundant if the identical function can be performed by some combination of other instructions from the instruction set. In each case, demonstrate the redundancy by showing an alternative sequence of instructions.

2.7 Discuss the relative merits of the central switch and bus architectures.

PART II

THE COMPUTER SYSTEM

A computer system consists of CPU, memory, I/O, and the interconnections among these major components. With the exception of the CPU, which is sufficiently complex to be explored in Part III, Part II examines each of these aspects in detail.

At the highest level, we can understand the function of each of the major components by describing the structure of their interconnection and the type of signals exchanged among them. This is done in Chapter 3. The next two chapters (4 and 5) examine memory and I/O, respectively. Finally, Chapter 6 describes the principles of operating systems, which helps to illuminate the manner in which the CPU controls the entire computer system.

Computer Interconnection Structures

At a top level, a computer consists of CPU, memory, and I/O components, with one or more modules of each type. These components are interconnected in some fashion to achieve the basic function of the computer, which is to execute programs. Thus, at a top level, we can describe a computer system by (1) describing the external behavior of each component, that is, the data and control signals that it exchanges with other components, and (2) describing the interconnection structure and the controls required to manage the use of the interconnection structure.

This top-level view of structure and function is important because of its explanatory power in understanding the nature of a computer. Equally important is its use to understand the increasingly complex issues of performance evaluation. A grasp of the top-level structure and function offers insight into system bottlenecks, alternate pathways, the magnitude of system failures if a component fails, and the ease of adding performance enhancements. In many cases, requirements for greater system power and fail-safe capabilities are being met by changing the design rather than merely increasing the speed and reliability of individual components.

This chapter focuses on the basic structures used for computer component interconnection. As background, the chapter begins with a brief examination of the basic components and their interface requirements. Then, a functional overview is provided.

We are then prepared to survey the major structural approaches, with an emphasis on the most popular, the bus structure.

COMPUTER COMPONENTS

As discussed in Chapter 2, virtually all contemporary computer designs are based on concepts developed by John von Neumann at the Institute for Advanced Studies, Princeton. Such a design is referred to as the *von Neumann architecture* and is based on three key concepts:

- Data and instructions are stored in a single read–write memory.
- The contents of this memory are addressable by location, without regard to the type of data contained there.
- Execution occurs in a sequential fashion (unless explicitly modified) from one instruction to the next.

The reasoning behind these concepts was discussed in Chapter 1 but is worth summarizing here. There is a small set of basic logic components that can be combined in various ways to store binary data and to perform arithmetic and logical operations on that data. If there is a particular computation to be performed, a configuration of logic components designed specifically for that computation can be constructed. We can think of the process of connecting together the various components in the desired configuration as a form of programming. The resulting "program" is in the form of hardware and is termed a *hardwired program.*

If all programming were done in this fashion, very little use would be made of this type of hardware. But now consider this alternative. Suppose we construct a general-purpose configuration of arithmetic and logic functions. This set of hardware will perform various functions on data depending on control signals applied to the hardware. In the original case of customized hardware, the system accepts data and produces results (Figure 3-1a). With general-purpose hardware, the system accepts data and control signals and produces results. Thus, instead of rewiring the hardware for each new program, the programmer merely needs to supply a new set of control signals.

How shall control signals be supplied? The answer is simple but subtle. The entire program is actually a sequence of steps. At each step, some arithmetic or logical operation is performed on some data. For each step, a new set of control signals is needed. Let us provide a unique code for each possible set of control signals, and let us add to the general-purpose hardware a segment that can accept a code and generate control signals (Figure 3-1b).

Programming is now much easier. Instead of rewiring the hardware for each new program, all we need to do is provide a new sequence of codes. Each code is, in effect, an instruction, and part of the hardware interprets each instruction and generates control signals. To distinguish this new method of programming, a sequence of codes or instructions is called *software.*

Figure 3-1b indicates two major components of the system: an instruction interpreter and a module of general-purpose arithmetic and logic functions.

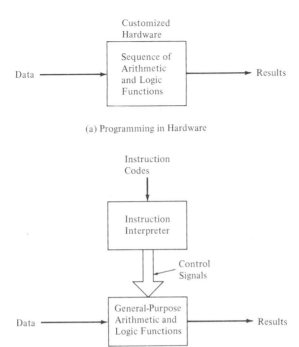

(a) Programming in Hardware

(b) Programming in Software

FIGURE 3-1.   Hardware and software approaches

These two constitute the CPU. Several other components are needed to yield a functioning computer. Data and instructions must be put into the system. For this we need some sort of input module. This module contains basic components for accepting data and instructions in some form and converting them into an internal form of signals usable by the system. A means of reporting results is needed, and this is in the form of an output module. Taken together these are referred to as *I/O components*.

One more component is needed. An input device will bring instructions and data in sequentially. But a program is not invariably executed sequentially; it may jump around (e.g., the IAS jump instruction). Similarly, operations on data may require access to more than just one element at a time in a predetermined sequence. Thus there must be a place to temporarily store both instructions and data. That module is called *memory*, or *main memory* to distinguish it from external storage or peripheral devices. Von Neumann pointed out that the same memory could be used to store both instructions and data. Data would be treated as data upon which computations were performed. Instructions would be treated as data to be interpreted as codes for generating control signals.

Figure 3-2 illustrates these top-level components and suggests the interactions among them. The CPU is typically in control. It exchanges data with memory.

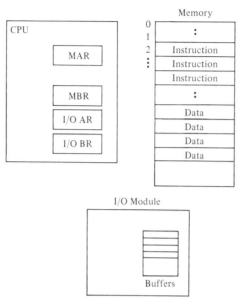

FIGURE 3-2. Computer components: top-level view

For this purpose, it typically makes use of two internal (to the CPU) registers: a memory address register (MAR), which specifies the address in memory for the next read or write, and a memory buffer register (MBR), which contains the data to be written into memory or receives the data read from memory. Similarly, an I/O address register (I/OAR) specifies a particular I/O device. An I/O buffer register is used for the exchange of data between an I/O module and the CPU.

A memory module consists of a set of locations, defined by sequentially numbered addresses. Each location contains a binary number that can be interpreted as either an instruction or data. An I/O module transfers data from external devices to CPU and memory, and vice versa. It contains internal buffers for temporarily holding this data until it can be sent on.

Having looked briefly at these major components, we now turn to an overview of how these components function together to execute programs.

3.2

COMPUTER FUNCTION

The basic function performed by a computer is program execution. The program to be executed consists of a set of instructions stored in memory. The central processing unit (CPU) does the actual work by executing instructions specified in the program.

In order to gain a greater understanding of this function and of the way in which the major components of the computer interact to execute a program, we need to look in more detail at the process of program execution. The simplest point of view is to consider instruction processing as consisting of two steps: The CPU reads *(fetches)* instructions from memory one at a time, and executes each instruction. Program execution consists of repeating the process of instruction fetch and instruction execution. Of course, the execution of an instruction may itself involve a number of steps (see, for example, the lower portion of Figure 2-7). At this stage, we can justify the breakdown of instruction processing into the two stages of fetch and execution as follows: The instruction fetch is a common operation for each instruction, and consists of reading an instruction from a location in memory. The instruction execution may involve several operations and depends on the nature of the instruction.

The processing required for a single instruction is called an *instruction cycle*. Using the simplified two-step description explained above, the instruction cycle is depicted in Figure 3-3. The two steps are referred to as the *fetch cycle* and the *execute cycle*. Program execution halts only if the machine is turned off, some sort of unrecoverable error occurs, or a program instruction that halts the computer is encountered.

The Fetch and Execute Cycles

At the beginning of each instruction cycle, the CPU fetches an instruction from memory. In a typical CPU, a register called the program counter (PC) is used to keep track of which instruction is to be fetched next. Unless told otherwise, the CPU always increments the PC after each instruction fetch so that it will fetch the next instruction in sequence (i.e., the instruction located at the next higher

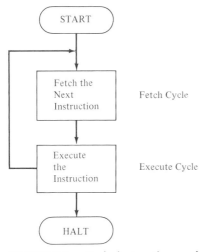

FIGURE 3-3. Basic instruction cycle

memory address). So, for example, consider a computer in which each instruction occupies one 16-bit word of memory. Assume that the program counter is set to location 300. The CPU will next fetch the instruction at location 300. On succeeding instruction cycles, it will fetch instructions from locations 301, 302, 303, and so on. This sequence may be altered, as explained presently.

The fetched instruction is loaded into a register in the CPU known as the instruction register (IR). The instruction is in the form of a binary code that specifies what action the CPU is to take. The CPU interprets the instruction and performs the required action. In general, these actions fall into four categories:

- *CPU–Memory:* Data may be transferred from the CPU to memory or from memory to CPU.
- *CPU–I/O:* Data may be transferred to or from the outside world by transferring between the CPU and an I/O module.
- *Data Processing:* The CPU may perform some arithmetic or logic operation on data.
- *Control:* An instruction may specify that the sequence of execution be altered (e.g., the IAS jump instruction, Table 2-2). For example, the CPU may fetch an instruction from location 149, which specifies that the next instruction be fetched from location 182. The CPU will remember this fact by setting the program counter to 182. Thus, on the next fetch cycle, the instruction will be fetched from location 182 rather than 150.

Of course, an instruction's execution may involve a combination of these actions.

Let us consider a simple example using a hypothetical machine that includes the characteristics listed in Figure 3-4. The CPU contains an accumulator (AC) to

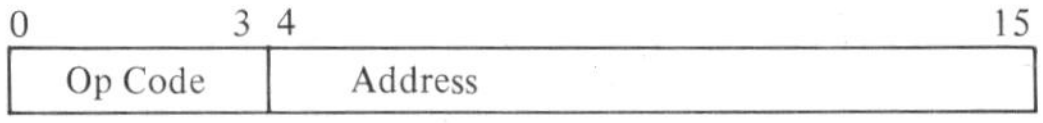

```
0        3 4                              15
┌────────┬──────────────────────────────┐
│ Op Code│  Address                     │
└────────┴──────────────────────────────┘
```
(a) Instruction Format

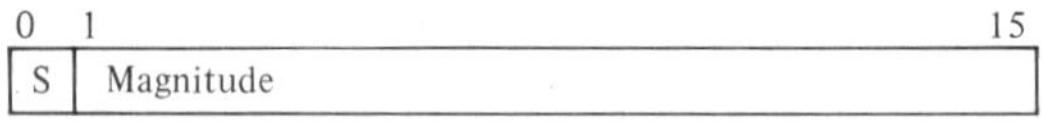

```
0  1                                     15
┌──┬─────────────────────────────────────┐
│ S│ Magnitude                          │
└──┴─────────────────────────────────────┘
```
(b) Integer Format

Program Counter (PC) = Address of Instruction
Instruction Register (IR) = Instruction Being Executed
Accumulator (AC) = Temporary Storage

(c) Internal CPU Registers

0001 = Load AC from Memory
0010 = Store AC to Memory
0101 = Add to AC from Memory

(d) Partial List of Opcodes

FIGURE 3-4. Characteristics of a hypothetical machine

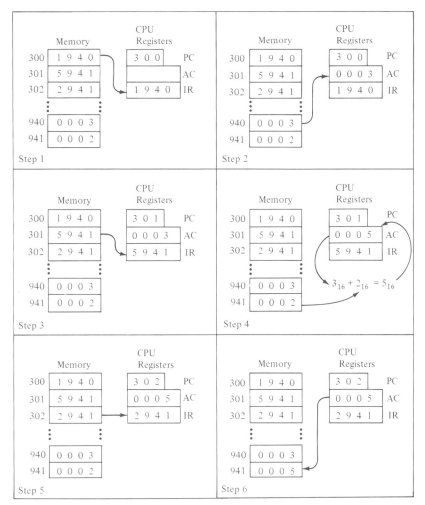

FIGURE 3-5. Example of program execution

temporarily store data. Both instructions and data are 16 bits long. Thus it is convenient to organize memory using 16-bit locations, or words. The instruction format indicates that there can be as many as $2^4 = 16$ different opcodes, and up to $2^{12} = 4,096$ (4K) words of memory can be directly addressed.

Figure 3-5 illustrates a partial program execution, showing the relevant portions of memory and CPU registers. The notation used is hexadecimal.[1] The program fragment shown adds the contents of the memory word at address

---

[1] In hexadecimal notation, each digit represents four bits. This is the most convenient notation for representing the contents of memory and registers when the word length is a multiple of 4 (e.g., 8, 16, or 32). For the reader unfamiliar with this notation, it is reviewed in the appendix to Chapter 7.

940_{16} to the contents of the memory word at address 941_{16} and stores the result in the latter location. Three instructions, which can be described as three fetch and three execute cycles, are required:

1. The program counter (PC) contains 300, the address of the first instruction. This address is loaded into the instruction register (IR). Note that this process would involve the use of a memory address register (MAR) and a memory buffer register (MBR). For simplicity, these intermediate registers are ignored.
2. The first 4 bits in the IR indicate that the accumulator (AC) is to be loaded. The remaining 12 bits specify the address, which is 940.
3. The PC is incremented and the next instruction is fetched.
4. The old contents of the AC and the contents of location 941 are added and the result is stored in the AC.
5. The PC is incremented and the next instruction is fetched.
6. The contents of the AC are stored in location 941.

In this example, three instruction cycles, each consisting of a fetch cycle and an execute cycle, are needed to add the contents of location 940 to the contents of 941. With a more complex set of instructions, fewer cycles would be needed. Most modern CPUs include instructions that contain more than one address. The PDP-11 instruction expressed symbolically as ADD B,A stores the sum of the contents of memory locations B and A into memory location A. A single instruction cycle with the following steps occurs:

1. Fetch the ADD instruction.
2. Read the contents of memory location A into the CPU.
3. Read the contents of memory location B into the CPU. In order that the contents of A are not lost, the CPU must have at least two registers for storing memory values, rather than a single accumulator.
4. Add the two values.
5. Write the result from the CPU to memory location A.

Thus the execution cycle for a particular instruction may involve more than one reference to memory. Also, instead of memory references, an instruction may specify an I/O operation. With these additional considerations in mind, Figure 3-6 provides a more detailed look at the basic instruction cycle of Figure 3-3. The figure is in the form of a state diagram. For any given instruction cycle, some states may be null and others may be visited more than once. The states can be described as follows:

- *instruction.address.calculation (iac):* Determine the address of the next instruction to be executed. Usually, this involves adding a fixed number to the address of the previous instruction. For example, if each instruction is 16 bits long and memory is organized into 16-bit words, then add 1 to the previous address. If, instead, memory is organized as individually addressable 8-bit bytes, then add 2 to the previous address.

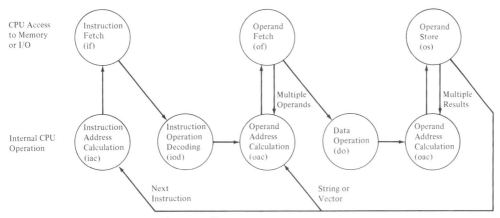

FIGURE 3-6.   Instruction cycle state diagram

- *instruction.fetch (if):* Read instruction from its memory location into the CPU.
- *instruction.operation.decoding (iod):* Analyze instruction to determine type of operation to be performed and operand(s) to be used.
- *operand.address.calculation (oac):* If the operation involves reference to an operand in memory or available via I/O, then determine the address of the operand.
- *operand.fetch (of):* Fetch the operand from memory or read it in from I/O.
- *data.operation (do):* Perform the operation indicated in the instruction.
- *operand.store (os):* Write the result into memory or out to I/O.

States in the upper part of Figure 3-6 involve an exchange between the CPU and either memory or an I/O module. States in the lower part of the diagram involve only internal CPU operations. The oac state appears twice, since an instruction may involve a read, a write, or both. However, the action performed during that state is fundamentally the same in both cases, so only a single-state identifier is needed.

Also note that the diagram allows for multiple operands and multiple results, since some instructions on some machines require this. For example, the PDP-11 instruction ADD A,B results in the following sequence of states: iac, if, iod, oac, of, oac, of, do, oac, os.

Finally, on some machines, a single instruction can specify an operation to be performed on a vector (one-dimensional array) of numbers or a string (one-dimensional array) of characters. As Figure 3-6 indicates, this would involve repetitive operand fetch and/or store operations.

Interrupts

Virtually all computers provide a mechanism by which other modules (I/O, memory) may interrupt the normal processing of the CPU. Table 3-1 lists the

TABLE 3-1   Classes of Interrupts

Program	Generated by some condition that occurs as a result of an instruction execution, such as arithmetic overflow, division by zero, attempt to execute an illegal machine instruction, and reference outside a user's allowed memory space.
Timer	Generated by a timer within the processor. This allows the operating system to perform certain functions on a regular basis.
I/O	Generated by an I/O controller, to signal normal completion of an operation or to signal a variety of error conditions.
Hardware failure	Generated by a failure such as power failure or memory parity error.

most common classes of interrupts. The specific nature of these interrupts is examined later in this book, especially in Chapters 5 and 10. However, we need to introduce the concept now in order to understand more clearly the nature of the instruction cycle and the implications of interrupts on the interconnection structure. The reader need not be concerned at this stage about the details of the generation and processing of interrupts, but only focus on the communication between modules that results from interrupts.

Interrupts are provided primarily as a way to improve processing efficiency. For example, most external devices are much slower than the processor. Suppose that the processor is transferring data to a printer using the instruction cycle scheme of Figure 3-3. After each write operation, the processor will have to pause and remain idle until the printer catches up. The length of this pause can be on the order of many hundreds or even thousands of instruction cycles that do not involve memory. Clearly, this is a very wasteful use of the processor. With interrupts, the processor can be engaged in executing other instructions while an I/O operation is in progress.

Figure 3-7a illustrates this state of affairs for the application referred to in the preceding paragraph. The user program performs a series of WRITE calls interleaved with processing. Code segments 1, 2, and 3 refer to sequences of instructions that do not involve I/O. The WRITE calls are calls to an I/O program that is a system utility and that will perform the actual I/O operation. The I/O program consists of three sections:

• A sequence of instructions, labeled 4 in the figure, to prepare for the actual I/O operation. This may include copying the data to be output into a special buffer, and preparing the parameters for a device command.
• The actual I/O command. Without the use of interrupts, once this command is issued, the program must wait for the I/O device to perform the requested function. The program might wait by simply repeatedly performing a test operation to determine if the I/O operation is done.
• A sequence of instructions, labeled 5 in the figure, to complete the operation. This may include setting a flag indicating the success or failure of the operation.

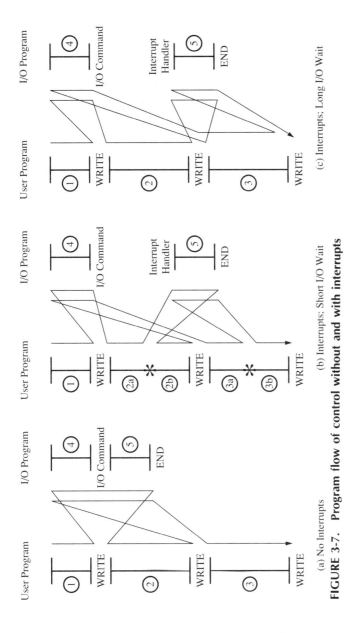

(a) No Interrupts

(b) Interrupts; Short I/O Wait

(c) Interrupts; Long I/O Wait

FIGURE 3-7. Program flow of control without and with interrupts

Because the I/O operation may take a relatively long time to complete, the I/O program is hung up waiting for the operation to complete; hence, the user program is stopped at the point of the WRITE call for some considerable period of time.

Interrupts and the Instruction Cycle

With interrupts, the processor can be engaged in executing other instructions while an I/O operation is in progress. Consider the flow of control in Figure 3-7b. As before, the user program reaches a point at which it makes a system call in the form of a WRITE call. The I/O program that is invoked in this case consists only of the preparation code and the actual I/O command. After these few instructions have been executed, control returns to the user program. Meanwhile, the external device is busy accepting data from computer memory and printing it. This I/O operation is conducted concurrently with the execution of instructions in the user program.

When the external device becomes ready to be serviced, that is, when it is ready to accept more data from the processor, the I/O module for that external device sends an *interrupt request* signal to the processor. The processor responds by suspending operation of the current program, branching off to a program to service that particular I/O device, known as an interrupt handler, and resuming the original execution after the device is serviced. The points at which such interrupts occur are indicated by an asterisk (*) in Figure 3-7b.

From the point of view of the user program, an interrupt is just that: an interruption of the normal sequence of execution. When the interrupt processing is completed, execution resumes (Figure 3-8). Thus, the user program does not have to contain any special code to accommodate interrupts; the processor and the operating system are responsible for suspending the user program and then resuming it at the same point.

To accommodate interrupts, an *interrupt cycle* is added to the instruction cycle, as shown in Figure 3-9. In the interrupt cycle, the processor checks to see if any interrupts have occurred, indicated by the presence of an interrupt signal. If no interrupts are pending, the processor proceeds to the fetch cycle and fetches the next instruction of the current program. If an interrupt is pending, the processor does the following:

1. It suspends execution of the current program being executed and saves its context. This means saving the address of the next instruction to be executed (current contents of the program counter) and any other data relevant to the processor's current activity.
2. It sets the program counter to the starting address of an *interrupt handler* routine.

The processor now proceeds to the fetch cycle and fetches the first instruction in the interrupt handler program, which will service the interrupt. The interrupt handler program is generally part of the operating system. Typically, this pro-

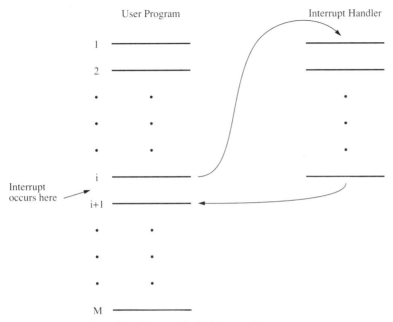

FIGURE 3-8. Transfer of control via interrupts

gram determines the nature of the interrupt and performs whatever actions are needed. For example, in the example we have been using, the handler determines which I/O module generated the interrupt, and may branch to a program

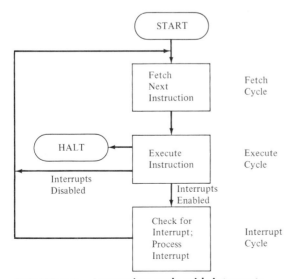

FIGURE 3-9. Instruction cycle with interrupts

that will write more data out to that I/O module. When the interrupt handler routine is completed, the processor can resume execution of the user program at the point of interruption.

It is clear that there is some overhead involved in this process. Extra instructions must be executed (in the interrupt handler) to determine the nature of the interrupt and to decide on the appropriate action. Nevertheless, because of the relatively large amount of time that would be wasted by simply waiting on an I/O operation, the processor can be employed much more efficiently with the use of interrupts.

To appreciate the gain in efficiency, consider Figure 3-10, which is a timing diagram based on the flow of control in Figure 3-7a and 3-7b.

Figures 3-7b and 3-10 assume that the time required for the I/O operation is relatively short: less than the time to complete the execution of instructions between write operations in the user program. The more typical case, especially for a slow device such as a printer, is that the I/O operation will take much more time than executing a sequence of user instructions. Figure 3-7c indicates this

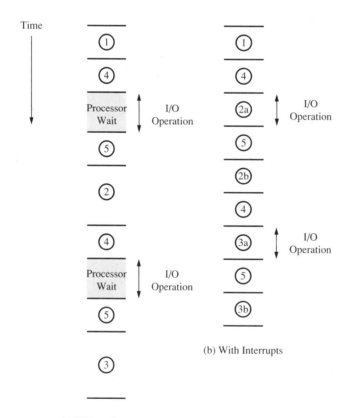

(b) With Interrupts

(a) Without Interrupts

FIGURE 3-10. Program timing; short I/O wait

state of affairs. In this case, the user program reaches the second WRITE call before the I/O operation spawned by the first call is complete. The result is that the user program is hung up at that point. When the preceding I/O operation is completed, this new WRITE call may be processed, and a new I/O operation may be started. Figure 3-11 shows the timing for this situation with and without the use of interrupts. We can see that there is still a gain in efficiency because part of the time during which the I/O operation is under way overlaps with the execution of user instructions.

Figure 3-12 shows a revised instruction cycle state diagram that includes interrupt cycle processing.

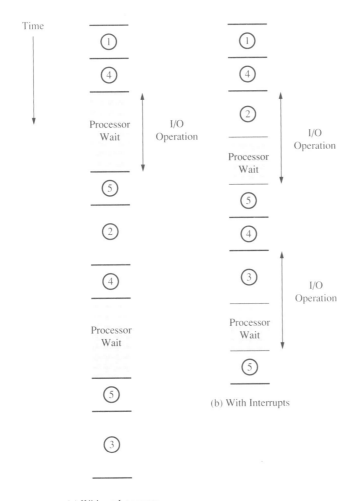

(a) Without Interrupts

FIGURE 3-11.   Program timing; long I/O wait

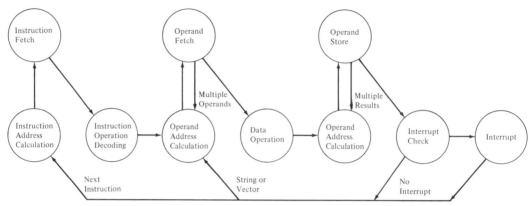

FIGURE 3-12. Instruction cycle state diagram, with interrupts

Multiple Interrupts

The discussion so far has only discussed the occurrence of a single interrupt. Suppose however that multiple interrupts can occur. For example, a program may be receiving data from a communications line and printing results. The printer will generate an interrupt every time that it completes a print operation. The communication line controller will generate an interrupt every time a unit of data arrives. The unit could either be a single character or a block, depending on the nature of the communications discipline. In any case, it is possible for a communications interrupt to occur while a printer interrupt is being processed.

Two approaches can be taken to dealing with multiple interrupts. The first is to disable interrupts while an interrupt is being processed. A *disabled interrupt* simply means that the processor can and will ignore that interrupt request signal. If an interrupt occurs during this time, it generally remains pending and will be checked by the processor after the processor has enabled interrupts. Thus, when a user program is executing and an interrupt occurs, interrupts are disabled immediately. After the interrupt handler routine completes, interrupts are enabled before resuming the user program, and the processor checks to see if additional interrupts have occurred. This approach is nice and simple, as interrupts are handled in strict sequential order (Figure 3-13a).

The drawback to the above approach is that it does not take into account relative priority or time-critical needs. For example, when input arrives from the communications line, it may need to be absorbed rapidly to make room for more input. If the first batch of input has not been processed before the second batch arrives, data may be lost.

A second approach is to define priorities for interrupts and to allow an interrupt of higher priority to cause a lower-priority interrupt handler to be itself interrupted (Figure 3-13b).

As an example of this second approach, consider a system with three I/O devices: a printer, a disk, and a communications line, with increasing priorities

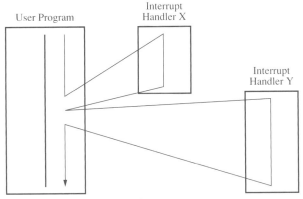

(a) Sequential Interrupt Processing

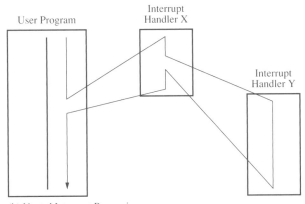

(b) Nested Interrupt Processing

FIGURE 3-13. Transfer of control with multiple interrupts

of 2, 4, and 5 respectively. Figure 3-14 illustrates a possible sequence. A user program begins at $t = 0$. At $t = 10$, a printer interrupt occurs; user information is placed on the system stack and execution continues at the printer interrupt service routine (ISR). While this routine is still executing, at $t = 15$, a communications interrupt occurs. Since the communications line has higher priority than the printer, the interrupt is honored. The printer ISR is interrupted, its state is pushed onto the stack, and execution continues at the communications ISR. While this routine is executing, a disk interrupt occurs ($t = 20$). Since this interrupt is of lower priority, it is simply held, and the communications ISR runs to completion.

When the communications ISR is complete ($t = 25$), the previous processor state is restored, which is the execution of the printer ISR. However, before even

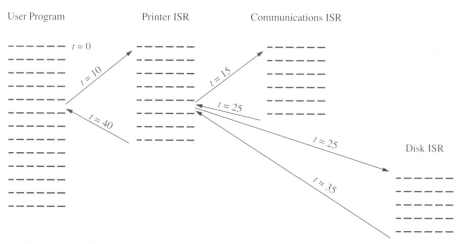

FIGURE 3-14.   Example time sequence of multiple interrupts

a single instruction in that routine can be executed, the processor honors the higher-priority disk interrupt and control transfers to the disk ISR. Only when that routine is complete ($t = 35$) is the printer ISR resumed. When that routine completes ($t = 40$), control finally returns to the user program.

I/O Function

Thus far, we have discussed the operation of the computer as controlled by the CPU, and we have looked primarily at the interaction of CPU and memory. The discussion has only alluded to the role of the I/O component. This role is discussed in detail in Chapter 5, but a brief summary is in order here.

An I/O module can exchange data directly with the CPU. Just as the CPU can initiate a read or write with memory, designating the address of a specific location, the CPU can also read data from or write data to an I/O module. In this latter case, the CPU identifies a specific device that is controlled by a particular I/O module. Thus an instruction sequence similar in form to that of Figure 3-5 could occur, with I/O instructions rather than with memory-referencing instructions.

In some cases, it is desirable to allow I/O exchanges to occur directly with memory. In such a case, the CPU grants to an I/O module the authority to read from or write to memory, so that the I/O–memory transfer can occur without tying up the CPU. During such a transfer, the I/O module issues read or write commands to memory, relieving the CPU of responsibility for the exchange. This operation is known as *direct memory access* (DMA), and will be examined in detail in Chapter 5. For now, all that we need to know is that the interconnection structure of the computer may need to allow for direct memory–I/O interaction.

3.3

INTERCONNECTION STRUCTURES

A computer consists of a set of components or modules of three basic types (CPU, memory, I/O) that communicate with each other. In effect, a computer is a network of basic modules. Thus there must be paths for connecting the modules together.

The collection of paths connecting the various modules is called the *interconnection structure*. The design of this structure will depend on the exchanges that must be made between modules.

Figure 3-15 suggests the types of exchanges that are needed by indicating the major forms of input and output for each module type:

- *Memory:* Typically, a memory module will consist of N words of equal length. Each word is assigned a unique numerical address $(0, 1, \ldots, N - 1)$. A word of data can be read from or written into the memory. The nature of the operation is indicated by Read and Write control signals. The location for the operation is specified by an address.
- *I/O Module:* From an internal (to the computer system) point of view, I/O is functionally similar to memory. There are two operations, read and write. Further, an I/O module may control more than one external device. We can refer to each of the interfaces to an external device as a *port* and give each a unique address (e.g., $0, 1, \ldots, M - 1$). In addition, there are external data paths for the input and output of data with an external device. Finally, an I/O module may be able to send interrupt signals to the CPU.
- *CPU:* The CPU reads in instructions and data, writes out data after processing, and uses control signals to control the overall operation of the system. It also receives interrupt signals.

The preceding list defines the data to be exchanged. The interconnection structure must support the following types of transfers:

- *Memory to CPU:* The CPU reads an instruction or a unit of data from memory.
- *CPU to Memory:* The CPU writes a unit of data to memory.
- *I/O to CPU:* The CPU reads data from an I/O device via an I/O module.
- *CPU to I/O:* The CPU sends data to the I/O device.
- *I/O to or from Memory:* For these two cases, an I/O module is allowed to exchange data directly with memory, without going through the CPU, using direct memory access (DMA).

Over the years a number of interconnection structures have been tried. Virtually all of these can be classified into four architectural types that are defined by the control point for the I/O modules [AUER79, MALL82]:

- I/O to CPU
- I/O to Memory

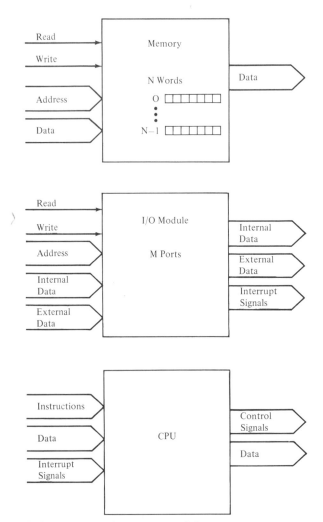

FIGURE 3-15. Computer modules

- I/O to Central Switch
- I/O to Bus

Each of these architectures is designed to exploit some virtue in terms of a given environment; at the same time, it usually introduces a drawback to another function.

The *I/O-to-CPU* architecture was common during the late 1940s and 1950s and is perhaps the simplest arrangement. It is still used today in modified form, for example, on some of IBM's minicomputer and small-to-medium-range mainframe systems. In this architecture, the CPU and I/O modules share the same data paths to memory and must share the same capacity. The CPU controls all exchanges and direct-memory access (DMA) by the I/O modules cannot occur: All exchanges between I/O and memory must pass through the CPU. Because of its simplicity, this structure involves the least amount of hardware and is generally the least expensive interconnection structure. The major drawback of this arrangement is that I/O activity significantly reduces CPU throughput. In earlier versions of this architecture, the CPU had to physically read from I/O and write to memory for every I/O-to-memory operation, and vice versa. In contemporary versions of this architecture, the CPU is augmented with hardware that performs the memory handling function. Even so, the CPU and I/O must share this hardware, affecting CPU performance. Figure 3-16, showing the IBM AS/400, is

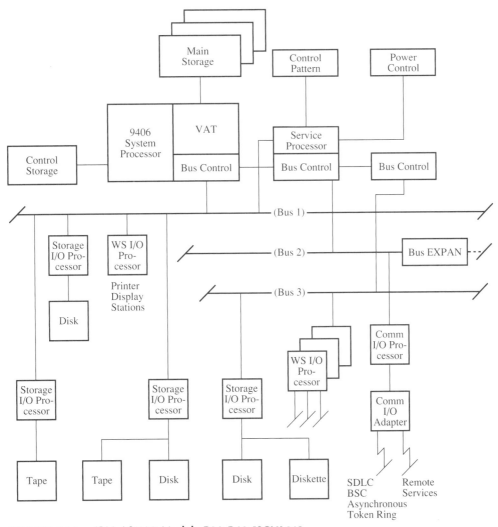

FIGURE 3-16.   IBM AS/400 Models B30-B60 [SCHL89]

an example of this architecture. The supplemental hardware consists of a bus controller and a virtual address translator, responsible for calculating physical memory addresses from logical ones.

An *I/O-to-Memory* architecture involves the direct independent access of main memory by two or more components. The memory module must contain control logic for resolving conflicts. Figure 3-17 is an example system. A strength of this system is that I/O transfers can occur directly with memory while the CPU is simultaneously performing computation. When the CPU wishes to initiate a transfer between I/O and memory, it places a request in a given location in memory. The I/O module periodically checks that memory location for the request. The main weakness is that control mechanisms are complex and relatively inflexible. That is, it is comparatively difficult to add additional modules.

With the *I/O-to-Central Switch,* there is a central switching mechanism to which all components attach. We have already seen one example of this, the IBM 7094 (Figure 2-9). The architecture has been retained by IBM in its large mainframes (e.g., Figure 3-18). The central switch controls access to memory from both the CPU and I/O modules. Because the data path between I/O and memory does not include the CPU, the CPU is freed up to do computation, as in the I/O-to-memory architecture. At the same time, it can provide constant and immediate status of activities to the CPU and provides a path between CPU and I/O that does not pass through memory. Because of the power and flexibility of this

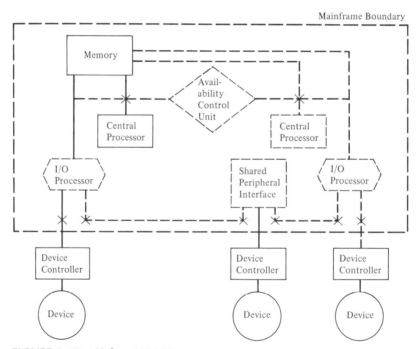

FIGURE 3-17. Unisys 1100/20

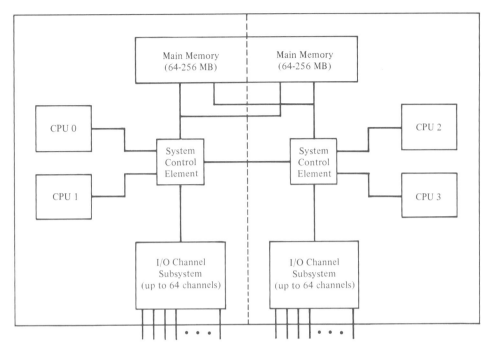

FIGURE 3-18.   IBM 3090/400

approach, it is the most popular solution for large mainframes. Its major draw-backs are the expense and complexity of the switch.

The *I/O-to-Bus* architecture shares many of the advantages of the central switch approach. In this case, there is a collection of lines that are shared by all modules. Only one module at a time can successfully transmit, and one or more of the modules must exert control over the use of the bus. We have seen one example of this architecture in the PDP-8 (Figure 2-13). Because of the simplicity and flexibility of the bus architecture, it has become near-universal for micro-computers and minicomputers. Because of its importance, we devote the re-mainder of this chapter to a study of the bus.

3.4

BUS INTERCONNECTION

A bus is a communication pathway connecting two or more devices. A key characteristic of a bus is that it is a shared transmission medium. Multiple de-vices connect to the bus, and a signal transmitted by any one device is available for reception by all other devices attached to the bus. If two devices transmit during the same time period, their signals will overlap and become garbled. Thus, only one device at a time can successfully transmit.

In many cases, a bus actually consists of multiple communication pathways, or lines. Each line is capable of transmitting signals representing binary 1 and binary 0. Over time, a sequence of binary digits can be transmitted across a single line. Taken together, several lines of a bus can be used to transmit binary digits simultaneously (in parallel). For example, an 8-bit unit of data can be transmitted over eight bus lines.

Computer systems contain a number of different buses that provide pathways between components at various levels of the computer system hierarchy. A bus that connects major computer components (CPU, memory, I/O) is called a *system bus*. The most common computer interconnection structures are based on the use of one or more system buses.

Bus Structure

A system bus consists, typically, of from 50 to 100 separate lines. Each line is assigned a particular meaning or function. Although there are many different bus designs, on any bus the lines can be classified into three functional groups (Figure 3-19): data, address, and control lines. In addition, there may be power distribution lines that supply power to the attached modules.

The *data lines* provide a path for moving data between system modules. These lines, collectively, are called the *data bus*. The data bus typically consists of 8, 16, or 32 separate lines, the number of lines being referred to as the *width* of the data bus. Since each line can carry only 1 bit at a time, the number of lines determines how many bits can be transferred at a time. The width of the data bus is a key factor in determining overall system performance. For example, if the data bus is 8 bits wide, and each instruction is 16 bits long, then the CPU must access the memory module twice during each instruction cycle.

The *address lines* are used to designate the source or destination of the data on the data bus. For example, if the CPU wishes to read a word (8, 16, 32 bits) of data from memory, it puts the address of the desired word on the address lines. Clearly, the width of the address bus determines the maximum possible memory capacity of the system. Furthermore, the address lines are generally also used to address I/O ports. Typically, the higher-order bits are used to select a particular module on the bus, and the lower-order bits select a memory location

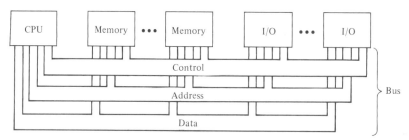

FIGURE 3-19. Bus interconnection scheme

or I/O port within the module. For example, on an 8-bit bus, address 01111111 and below might reference locations in a memory module (module 0) with 128 words of memory, and address 10000000 and above refer to devices attached to an I/O module (module 1).

The *control lines* are used to control the access to and the use of the data and address lines. Since the data and address lines are shared by all components, there must be a means of controlling their use. Control signals transmit both command and timing information between system modules. Timing signals indicate the validity of data and address information. Command signals specify operations to be performed. Typical control lines include

- *Memory Write:* Causes data on the bus to be written into the addressed location.
- *Memory Read:* Causes data from the addressed location to be placed on the bus.
- *I/O Write:* Causes data on the bus to be output to the addressed I/O port.
- *I/O Read:* Causes data from the addressed I/O port to be placed on the bus.
- *Transfer ACK:* Indicates that data have been accepted from or placed on the bus.
- *Bus Request:* Indicates that a module needs to gain control of the bus.
- *Bus Grant:* Indicates that a requesting module has been granted control of the bus.
- *Interrupt Request:* Indicates that an interrupt is pending.
- *Interrupt ACK:* Acknowledges that the pending interrupt has been recognized.
- *Clock:* Used to synchronize operations.
- *Reset:* Initializes all modules.

The operation of the bus is as follows. If one module wishes to send data to another, it must do two things: (1) obtain the use of the bus, and (2) transfer data via the bus. If one module wishes to request data from another module, it must (1) obtain the use of the bus, and (2) transfer a request to the other module over the appropriate control and address lines. It must then wait for that second module to send the data.

Physically, the system bus is actually a number of parallel electrical conductors. These conductors are metal lines etched in a card or board (printed-circuit board). The bus extends across all of the system components, each of which taps into some or all of the bus lines. A very common physical arrangement is depicted in Figure 3-20. In this example, the bus consists of two vertical columns of conductors. At regular intervals along the columns, there are attachment points in the form of slots that extend out horizontally to support a printed-circuit board. Each of the major system components occupies one or more boards and plugs into the bus at these slots. The entire arrangement is housed in a chassis.

This arrangement is most convenient. A small computer system may be acquired and then expanded later (more memory, more I/O) by adding more boards. If a component on a board fails, that board can easily be removed and replaced.

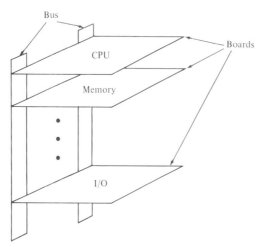

FIGURE 3-20.   Typical physical realization of a bus architecture

Elements of Bus Design

Although a variety of different bus implementations exist, there are a few basic parameters or design elements that serve to classify and differentiate buses. Table 3-2 lists key elements.

Bus Types

Bus lines can be separated into two generic types: dedicated and multiplexed. A dedicated bus line is permanently assigned either to one function or to a physical subset of computer components.

An example of functional dedication is the use of separate dedicated address and data lines, which is common to many buses. However, it is not essential. For example, address and data information may be transmitted over the same set of lines using an Address Valid control line. At the beginning of a data transfer, the address is placed on the bus and the Address Valid line is activated.

TABLE 3-2   Elements of Bus Design

Type	Bus Width
Dedicated	Address
Multiplexed	Data
Method of Arbitration	**Data Transfer Type**
Centralized	Read
Distributed	Write
Timing	Read-modify-write
Synchronous	Read-after-write
Asynchronous	Block

At this point, each module has a specified period of time to copy the address and determine if it is the addressed module. The address is then removed from the bus, and the same bus connections are used for the subsequent read or write data transfer. This method of using the same lines for multiple purposes is known as *time multiplexing*.

The advantage of time multiplexing is the use of fewer lines, which saves space and, usually, cost. The disadvantage is that more complex circuitry is needed within each module. Also, there is a potential reduction in performance since certain events that share the same lines cannot take place in parallel.

Physical dedication refers to the use of multiple buses, each of which connects only a subset of modules. A typical example is the use of an I/O bus to interconnect all I/O modules; this bus is then connected to the main bus through some type of I/O adapter module. The potential advantage of physical dedication is high throughput, because there is less bus contention. A disadvantage is the increased size and cost of the system.

Method of Arbitration

In all but the simplest systems, more than one module may need control of the bus. For example, an I/O module may need to read or write directly to memory, without sending the data to the CPU. Since only one unit at a time can successfully transmit over the bus, some method of arbitration is needed. The various methods can be roughly classified as being either centralized or distributed. In a centralized scheme, a single hardware device, referred to as a *bus controller* or *arbiter*, is responsible for allocating time on the bus. The device may be a separate module or part of the CPU. In a distributed scheme, there is no central controller. Rather, each module contains access control logic and the modules act together to share the bus. With both methods of arbitration, the purpose is to designate one device, either the CPU or an I/O module, as master. The master may then initiate a data transfer (e.g., read or write) with some other device, which acts as slave for this particular exchange. We will see examples of both methods of arbitration later in this section.

Timing

Timing refers to the way in which events are coordinated on the bus. With synchronous timing, the occurrence of events on the bus is determined by a clock. The bus includes a clock line upon which a clock transmits a regular sequence of alternating 1s and 0s of equal duration. A single 1–0 transmission is referred to as a *clock cycle* or *bus cycle* and defines a time slot. All other devices on the bus can read the clock line, and all events start at the beginning of a clock cycle. Figure 3-21a shows the timing diagram for a synchronous read operation (see Appendix 3A, page 116, for a description of timing diagrams). Other bus signals may change at the leading edge of the clock signal (with a slight reaction delay). Most events occupy a single clock cycle. In this simple example, the CPU

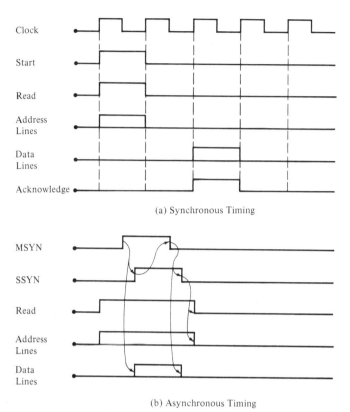

(a) Synchronous Timing

(b) Asynchronous Timing

FIGURE 3-21. Timing of a read operation

issues a read signal and places a memory address on the address bus. It also issues a start signal to mark the presence of address and control information on the bus. A memory module recognizes the address and, after a delay of 1 cycle, places the data and an acknowledgment signal on the bus.

With asynchronous timing, the occurrence of one event on a bus follows and depends on the occurrence of a previous event. In the simple example of Figure 3-20b, the CPU places address and read signals on the bus. After pausing for these signals to stabilize, it issues an MSYN (master sync) signal, indicating the presence of valid address and control signals. The memory module responds with data and an SSYN (slave sync) signal, indicating the response.

Synchronous timing is simpler to implement and test. However, it is less flexible than asynchronous timing. Because all devices on a synchronous bus are tied to a fixed clock rate, the system cannot take advantage of advances in device performance. With asynchronous timing, a mixture of slow and fast devices, using older and newer technology, can share a bus. We will see examples of both synchronous and asynchronous timing.

Bus Width

We have already addressed the concept of bus width. The width of the data bus has an impact on system performance: the wider the data bus the greater the number of bits transferred at one time. The width of the address bus has an impact on system capacity: the wider the address bus, the greater the range of locations that can be referenced.

Data Transfer Type

Finally, a bus supports various data transfer types, as illustrated in Figure 3-22. All buses support both write (master to slave) and read (slave to master) transfers. In the case of a multiplexed address/data bus, the bus is first used for specifying the address and then for transferring the data. For a read operation, there is typically a wait while the data is being fetched from the slave to be put on the bus. For either a read or a write, there may also be a delay if it is necessary

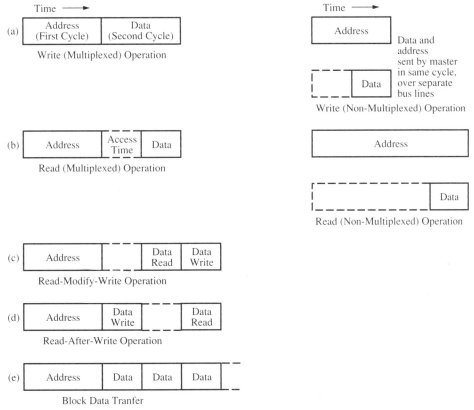

FIGURE 3-22. Bus data transfer types [GOOR89]

to go through arbitration to gain control of the bus for the remainder of the operation (i.e., seize the bus to request a read or write, then seize the bus again to perform a read or write).

In the case of dedicated address and data buses, the address is put on the address bus and remains there while the data are put on the data bus. For a write operation, the master puts the data onto the data bus as soon as the address has stabilized and the slave has had the opportunity to recognize its address. For a read operation, the slave puts the data onto the data bus as soon as it has recognized its address and has fetched the data.

There are also several combination operations that some buses allow. A read-modify-write operation is simply a read followed immediately by a write to the same address. The address is only broadcast once at the beginning of the operation. The whole operation is typically indivisible in order to prevent any access to the data element by other potential bus masters. The principal purpose of this capability is to protect shared memory resources in a multiprogramming system (see Chapter 6).

Read-after-write is an indivisible operation consisting of a write followed immediately by a read from the same address. The read operation may be performed for checking purposes.

Some bus systems also support a block data transfer. In this case, one address cycle is followed by n data cycles. The first data item is transferred to or from the specified address; the remaining data items are transferred to or from subsequent addresses.

Example Bus Structures

To illustrate the concepts of bus interconnection, let us consider the case of the VAX organization, which relies on three key buses: Unibus, SBI, and Massbus.

The Unibus was introduced by DEC in 1970 for its PDP-11 computer family. It is a single bus to which all system components are attached.

The Synchronous Backplane Interconnect (SBI) is used by DEC on many of the members of its VAX family of 32-bit minicomputers. Figure 3-23 shows its use on the VAX 11/780 (the original VAX system) and the higher-performance VAX 8600. As can be seen, no I/O modules connect directly to the SBI, which is optimized for high-speed operations. Instead, I/O modules connect to the Unibus or Massbus, which in turn are connected to the SBI via adapters. The Unibus is used primarily for low- and medium-speed connections, such as terminals, printers, and communication lines. The Massbus is a special-purpose bus intended for peripheral storage devices, such as disk and tape. Note that for the VAX 11/780, the CPU and memory communicate across the SBI. In the case of the VAX 8600, there is a central switch, called the MBOX, which connects CPU, memory, and the SBI. Thus, this architecture is a mixture of the I/O-to-bus and I/O-to-central-switch. The VAX 8600 architecture provides several benefits over the VAX 11/780:

- The MBOX supports direct CPU-to-memory operations. The MBOX provides greater throughput than the SBI and hence provides more rapid memory access.
- The MBOX is capable of supporting two SBI interfaces, greatly increasing the I/O capability of the system.

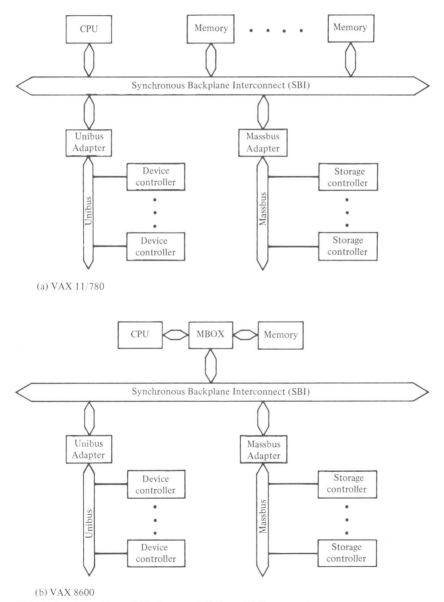

(a) VAX 11/780

(b) VAX 8600

FIGURE 3-23. Use of Unibus and SBI on VAX computers

Example Bus Specifications

In the remainder of this section, we will examine the two most widely used bus specifications: Multibus II and VMEbus.

Multibus II is a 32-bit bus specification released by Intel in 1983 as a follow-on to its highly successful 16-bit Multibus. Multibus II was standardized by the Institute of Electrical and Electronics Engineers in 1987 as ANSI/IEEE Standard 1296. Tables 3-3 and 3-4 define the 96 lines of Multibus II.

VMEbus (Versa Module European bus) is also a 32-bit bus specification. It is based on Motorola's 16-bit Versabus, and was issued jointly in 1981 by Motorola, Mostek Corp. and N. V. Philips/Signetics. VMEbus was issued as ANSI/IEEE Standard 1014 in 1987. Table 3-5 defines the VMEbus lines.

Both Multibus and VMEbus are designed to support a variety of microprocessor-based configurations, including both single- and multiple-processor systems. Accordingly, each provides a general-purpose set of functions, which support a wide range of microprocessor families. The fact that each is a standard assures that products built by different vendors will be compatible.

Table 3-6 compares the two specifications. As you can see, Multibus II uses synchronous timing and a distributed arbitration scheme; VMEbus uses asynchronous timing and a centralized arbitration scheme. Thus, an examination of the two schemes covers most of the issues in bus design. In this section, we will look at the arbitration and data transfer capabilities of the two buses; a discussion of interrupt capability is deferred until Chapter 5.

The reader may also be interested in a more recent bus standard, Futurebus+. Futurebus+ is intended as a follow-on to today's microprocessor bus systems, including Multibus II and VMEbus. Appendix 3B provides an overview of Futurebus+.

TABLE 3-3   Signal Groups for the Multibus II Parallel System Bus

Signal Group Name	Description
Arbitration Cycle Signal Group	Provides the bus requesting and bus granting signals and identifies the priority of a bus request.
Address/Data Bus Signal Group	Provides the address, data, and parity signals for read and write operations.
System Control Signal Group	Provides the control signals needed to transfer address and data on the address/data signal group.
Exception Control Signal Group	Provides the error indication signals to stop transfer cycles.
Central Control Signal Group	Provides system-wide services such as reset and initialization control.

TABLE 3-4   Multibus II Lines

Designation	No. of Lines	Description
Arbitration Cycle		
Bus request	1	Request access to bus
Arbitration	6	Agents requesting access to the bus use these lines for arbitration. The agent's ID is on ARB4-ARB0; ARB5 indicates high priority.
Address/Data		
Address/data	32	During request phase, contain address for ensuing transfer cycle; during reply phase, contain 8, 16, 24, or 32 bits of data.
Parity	4	Each parity signal generates an even parity for eight bits of the 32-bit address/data bus. Even parity causes the total number of 1s to be an even number.
System Control		
System control	8	Used by agents to define commands or report status depending on the phase of the transfer cycle (Table 3-3). The requesting agent drives all lines during request phase, and lines SC7 through SC4 during reply phase.
Parity	2	Each parity signal generates an even parity for four of the system control lines.
Exception Cycle		
Bus error	1	Indicates detection of data integrity problem during a transfer.
Time-out	1	Signaled by central services module whenever it detects a failure of a module to complete a handshake.
Central Control		
Reset	1	System-level initialization.
Reset-not-complete	1	Agents generate this signal to extend the initialization time period provided by the central services module.
DC power low	1	Provides warning of imminent power failure.
Protect	1	Informs all bus interfaces to ignore any transitions on the bus as power is lost.
Bus clock	1	Clock signal with maximum frequency of 10 MHz.
Central clock	1	Auxiliary clock at twice the frequency of the bus clock.
ID latch	1	During reset phase, signal from central services module to read ID lines.
Power		
Power	30	Voltage sources
Reserved	4	Reserved

TABLE 3-5   VME Bus Lines

Designation	Number of Lines	Description
		Data Transfer Bus
Address (A01-A31)	31	Address of the slave being selected by the current bus master initiating a data transfer cycle.
Address modifier (AM0-AM5)	6	Provide additional information about the type of transfer that is going to be performed by the current bus master, such as address size, cycle type, protection information.
Address strobe (AS)	1	High-to-low transition indicates valid address information on A01-A31.
Data (D00-D31)	32	Dynamically assigned on each transfer for byte (8), word (16), or long-word (32) transfer.
Data strobe (DS0-DS1)	2	Indicate during byte and word transfers that a data transfer will occur on data bus lines D00-D07 and D08-D15, respectively.
LWORD	1	Indicate that the current transfer is a 32-bit transfer.
Data transfer acknowledge (DTACK)	1	Asserted by slave when it has taken data from the data bus or has placed data on the data bus.
WRITE	1	Set high to indicate a write operation (transfer of data from master to slave); set low to indicate a read operation (transfer of data from slave to master).
Bus error (BERR)	1	Indicates a type of transfer that cannot be performed by the slave or some other error condition.
		Data Transfer Arbitration Bus
Bus grant in (BG0IN-BG3IN); Bus grant out (BG0OUT-BG3OUT)	8	BGOUT line in daisy-chain arrangement; connected to BGIN line of lower priority master. Four daisy chains may be constructed. For each daisy chain, the BGIN signal indicates to this board that it may become the next bus master; the BGOUT indicates it to the next board.
Bus request (BR0-BR3)	4	Request access to bus for one of the four daisy-chained groups.
Bus busy (BBSY)	1	Set by current master to indicate that it is using the bus.
Bus clear (BCLR)	1	Set by arbiter to indicate to the current master that a higher priority request of the bus is pending and that it should release the bus.

TABLE 3-5 VME Bus Lines (*continued*)

Designation	Number of Lines	Description
Priority Interrupt Bus		
Interrupt request (IRQ1-IRQ7)	7	Prioritized interrupt request lines driven by the interrupter, with IRQ7 having the highest priority.
Interrupt acknowledge (IACK)	1	Used to signal that an interrupt handler is responding to an interrupt request.
Interrupt acknowledge in (IACKIN)	1	Interrupt acknowledge input line in daisy chain.
Interrupt acknowledge out (IACKOUT)	1	Interrupt acknowledge output line in daisy chain.
Utility Bus		
System clock (SYSCLOCK)	1	Constant 16-MHz clock.
Serial clock (SERCLK)	1	Provides a periodic timing signal that synchronizes operation of the VMSbus.
Serial data (SERDAT)	1	Used for serial communication with the VMS bus.
System failure (SYSFAIL)	1	Indicates a failure in the system; it can be generated by any module on the VMEbus.
System reset (SYSRESET)	1	When low, causes system to be reset.
AC failure (ACFAIL)	1	Indicates that the main input to the power supply is no longer provided.

Arbitration

Multibus II

Multibus II provides a distributed, synchronous arbitration scheme.

Associated with the bus is a clock with a 100-ns period. Each board attached to Multibus II is assigned a 5-bit identification (ID), allowing a total of 32 boards (called *agents*). There are six arbitration lines, ARB5 through ARB0. Five of these are used to hold an agent's ID. When an agent wishes to gain control of the bus, it places its ID on the lines ARB4 through ARB0. If the agent is the only one to attempt to seize the bus, then it will gain access for the next time slot. If, however, more than one agent wishes to use the bus, then all contending agents will simultaneously attempt to drive the bus. This means that if, for example, any of the IDs has a 1 bit in the first position, then ARB5 will be driven high. If all agents have a 0 bit in the first position, then ARB5 will remain low. Thus, the bit pattern that is on the 5 lines corresponds to the logical AND of all of the IDs.

As an example, suppose that three agents simultaneously attempt to gain control of the bus. Their IDs are, respectively, 10101, 10100, and 10011. As Table 3-7a illustrates, the resulting pattern on ARB5 through ARB0 is 10111. It is this

TABLE 3-6   A Comparison of Multibus II and VMEbus

	Multibus II	VMEbus
Data Transfer Capability		
Transfer timing	Synchronous	Asynchronous
Transfer rate	40	40
Number of data lines	32	32
Multiplexed address/data	Yes	No
Address bus width	32	16/24/32
Interrupt Handling Capability		
Number of interrupt lines	N/A	8
Bus vectored interrupts	No	Yes
Bus Master Capability		
Multiple masters	Yes	Yes
Arbitration method	Distributed	Centralized
Arbitration algorithms	Fair;	Release on request;
	Priority	Release when done
Mechanical Features		
User-defined pins	Yes	Yes
Board dimensions (in)	8.7 × 9.2 or 8.7 × 14.4	3.9 × 6.3 or 6.3 × 9.2
Number of pins	96	96
Maximum number of devices	21	21
Maximum bus length (m)	0.5	0.5

TABLE 3-7   Multibus II Arbitration Example

(a) Multiple IDs on Line			
	Agent 1 ID 10101	Agent 2 ID 10100	Agent 3 ID 10011	Actual Signal on Line
ARB4	High	High	High	High
ARB3	Low	Low	Low	Low
ARB2	High	High	Low	High
ARB1	Low	Low	High	High
ARB0	High	Low	High	High

(b) ID Comparison and Arbitration			
Bit Position	Start 543210	Period 1 543210	Period 2 543210
Agent 1 ID	010101	010100P (win)	010101 (win)
Agent 2 ID	010100	010100 (win)	010100 (lose)
Agent 3 ID	010011	010000P (lose)	010000P (lose)
ID on the bus	010111	010100	010101

Notes: 1. P = pseudo-ID driven onto bus.
       2. Bit 5 is the high priority bit on the bus; ARB5 = 0 for normal priority.

logical-AND result of agent contention that is used for arbitration. The rules of the arbitration are as follows:

1. At the beginning of a time slot, all agents that wish access to the bus place their ID on bus lines ARB4 through ARB0.
2. During that time slot (period 1), each agent compares its ID with the actual state of each of the 5 bus lines, beginning with ARB4. If an agent detects a mismatch, it immediately stops driving that bit and the bits below it. This creates a "pseudo-ID," consisting of the agent's ID up to the point of mismatch, and 0s from that point on. The pseudo-IDs are driven onto the bus and, again, compared.
3. An agent "wins" in period 1 if its ID or pseudo-ID matches the pattern on the bus. An agent that wins puts its true ID on the bus for period 2. An agent that loses in period 1 continues to put its pseudo-ID on the bus for period 2.
4. During period 2, all of the winners from period 1 compare their ID with the pattern on the bus. The agent whose ID matches the bus pattern wins and is granted bus ownership.

Table 3-7b gives an example of the arbitration. Note that the higher the binary value of the ID, the higher the priority.

The above discussion describes the way in which competing requests for bus access are resolved. We are now in a position to describe the overall bus arbitration algorithm. When the bus is idle, all agents that enter a requesting state (need to gain control of the bus) during one clock cycle assert the bus request line (BREQ) and form a batch. An agent in the batch competes during one or more arbitrations until it has been granted ownership of the bus. An agent that generates a new request while a batch is in progress must wait for the batch to end before asserting BREQ and competing for access. The end of the batch is signaled by a logical "0" on BREQ, since each agent in the batch releases the request line at the start of its bus tenure. All requests that are waiting at the end of a batch assert the shared request line and form a new batch. Agents in a batch receive service in order of their assigned IDs.

Figure 3-24 illustrates the timing of Multibus II arbitration. In this example, there are three agents: A, B, and C, with the IDs shown in Table 3-7. To begin, both A and B desire use of the bus. Each agent enters arbitration by asserting BREQ and driving its ID on the ARB4-ARB0 lines during the first clock cycle. The arbitration process described above takes two cycles. By the end of the third cycle, A's ID is stable on ARB4-ARB0 indicating that it will be the next bus owner. Meanwhile, during the arbitration phase, C desires normal use of the bus. Because BREQ is asserted, it must wait. On the next clock cycle (cycle 4), A gets ownership of the bus, removes its ID, and deactivates BREQ. Agent B still desires the bus, so it continues to assert BREQ and drive its ID. Agent C is prevented from entering arbitration because BREQ remains active.

By cycle 6, B's ID is stable on ARB4-ARB0 indicating that it will be the next bus owner. However, A retains ownership until it has completed its use of the bus.

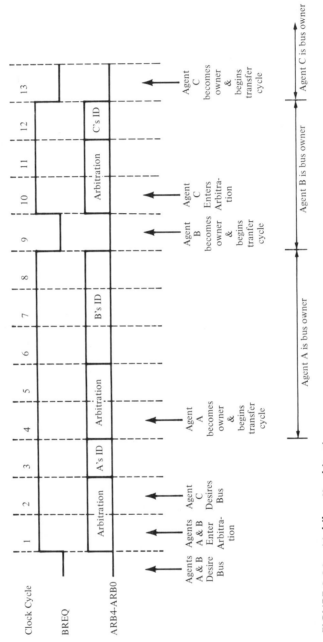

FIGURE 3-24. Multibus II arbitration

If A needs the bus for more than the time for a single read or write, it makes use of system control line SC0 to lock the bus. When the bus is unlocked, A relinquishes bus ownership and B becomes the bus owner. At this point, B removes its ID and deactivates BREQ. Since both A and B have been granted access to the bus, BREQ is inactive. C senses this, enters arbitration, and becomes the next bus owner.

All of the above is referred to as the "normal priority" process. In addition, it is possible to gain access to the bus using a high-priority request. In this case, the agent asserts ARB5 as well as putting its ID on ARB4-ARB0. Because of the nature of the arbitration algorithm depicted in Table 3-7, this has two effects:

- Any agent at normal priority will drive ARB5 at 0 and will automatically lose.
- If two or more agents request high priority access, the one with the highest priority based on ID will be serviced first.

In addition, an agent with a high-priority request need not wait for BREQ to become inactive, but may enter the next arbitration.

VMEbus

VMEbus provides a centralized, asynchronous arbitration scheme. Unlike Multibus II, which provides arbitration and control logic on each card plugged into the bus, VMEbus cards provide only bus-request logic. The VME specification assigns the arbitration logic to the card in slot 1.

The bus lines used for arbitration are illustrated in Figure 3-25. VMEbus actually supports three bus allocation policies:

- *Single-level:* The arbiter only responds to requests on BR3. Multiple cards may share the same bus request line. A bus grant line is threaded through all cards in a daisy chain, as explained below. The result is that each member of the daisy chain, in descending order of precedence, is given the opportunity to seize the bus. Because there is a single bus request line in use, a very simple bus arbiter can be used with this policy.
- *Priority-based:* The arbiter honors requests on the four bus request lines from BR3 (highest priority) to BR0 (lowest priority) on the basis of priority. The daisy-chain method is used on each of the BRn, BGnIN, BGnOUT set of lines. Thus there are two levels of arbitration involved: four levels of priority, with a daisy-chain of cards within each priority level.
- *Round-robin:* The arbiter assigns the bus on a rotating priority basis. After access has been granted on bus request line n, bus request line $n - 1$ is assigned the highest priority.

For **single-level arbitration,** a number of cards are connected to the BR3 bus request line. To resolve competing claims for bus access, all of the cards are linked together by means of the BG3IN and BG3OUT bus grant lines. The bus grant line begins as BG3OUT at the arbiter, and the line terminates (BG3IN) and restarts (BG3OUT) at each card until the last card, which only has a BG3IN line.

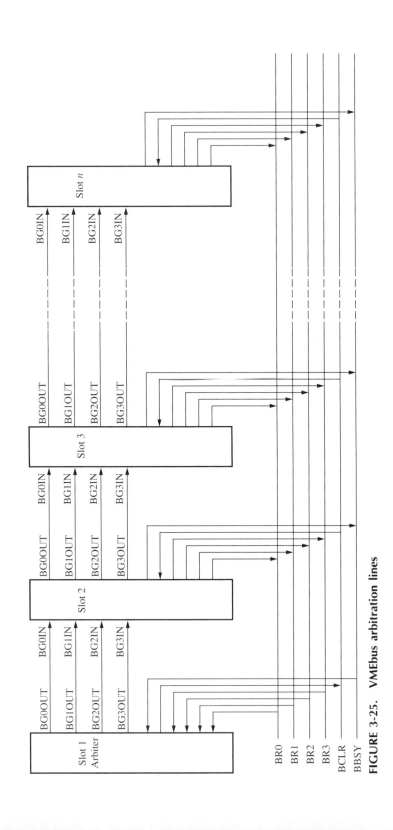

FIGURE 3-25. VMEbus arbitration lines

98

This form of interconnection is known as a daisy chain. If a card has not raised BR3, it will respond to a BG3IN signal by setting its BG3OUT line. If it has asserted BR3, it will accept a BG3IN signal as indication that it has been granted control of the bus, and will not signal on its BG3OUT line. Note that the effect of this scheme is to provide a higher priority to a card that is physically closer to the arbiter.

Figure 3-26 shows the timing sequence involved. Assume that A and B both wish to access the bus, and that A is closer to the arbiter.

1. BR3 is set by both A and B.
2. After some arbitrary amount of time, the arbiter grants control by setting BG3.
3. A receives the BG3IN signal and sets BBSY to seize the bus. It can now drop the BR3 request, but B continues to assert that line.
4. The arbiter can drop the BR3 signal when it detects the BBSY signal.
5. After an arbitrary amount of time, A completes its use of the bus and drops BBSY.
6. Now that the bus is not busy, the arbiter can grant control by setting BG3.
7. A detects the bus grant signal on BG3IN and repeats it on BG3OUT.
8–13. B's request is granted in the same fashion.

VMEbus provides for four groups of cards, each of which uses the daisy-chain scheme just described. Figure 3-27 shows the timing for **priority-based arbitration.** Assume that there are two masters requesting access to the bus, one at

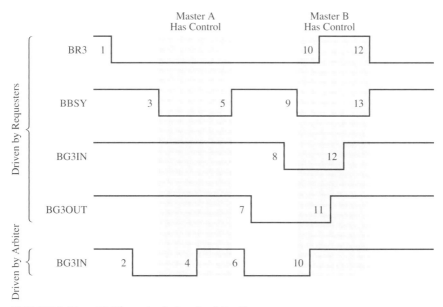

FIGURE 3-26.   VMEbus single-level arbitration

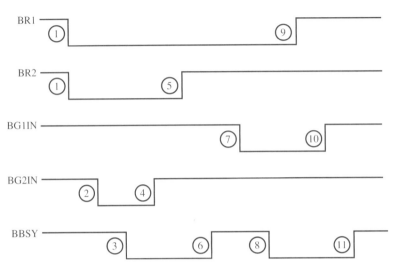

FIGURE 3-27.   VMEbus priority-based arbitration

priority level 1 (master A) and the other at priority 2 (master B). The following sequence occurs:

1. Both masters issue a request at about the same time.
2. BR2 is at higher priority, so the arbiter honors this request by issuing a signal on BG2IN.
3. B seizes the bus by signaling on BBSY.
4. The arbiter uses the BBSY signal as an acknowledgement and drops BG2IN.
5. B drops BR2.
6. B completes its use of the bus and drops BBSY.
7. A's request is still pending, so the arbiter now signals on BG1IN.
8–11. A's request is granted in the same fashion.

Round-robin arbitration operates in essentially the same fashion as priority-based arbitration. The exception is the way in which priorities are assigned to the four groups. The priority assigned to each of the BRn lines changes or rotates with each successive bus exchange operation. The system is initialized with the priority order from highest to lowest as BR3, BR2, BR1, BR0. When a bus request on bus request line n is granted, then bus request line $n - 1$ becomes the highest priority line, where priority 0 is followed by priority 3. Thus the priority order may be one of the following:

• BR3, BR2, BR1, BR0
• BR2, BR1, BR0, BR3
• BR1, BR0, BR3, BR2
• BR0, BR3, BR2, BR1

Transfer Timing

Multibus II

Figure 3-28 shows read and write operations on Multibus II, in which a single transfer takes place. For the read operation, the requesting agent, after gaining ownership of the bus, makes use of a number of the system control lines to control the operation. During the first cycle, SC0 is asserted. This indicates to all agents that the address/data bus and the SC lines contain valid request-phase information. Each agent can then read the address/data lines to determine if the request is intended for itself. The requestor sets lines SC2 and SC3 to indicate the length of data to be transferred (in this case, 16 bits), SC4 and SC5 to indicate the nature of the operation (in this case, I/O), and SC6 to indicate read or write (in this case, read). Two clock cycles are allowed to elapse to give the replier time to

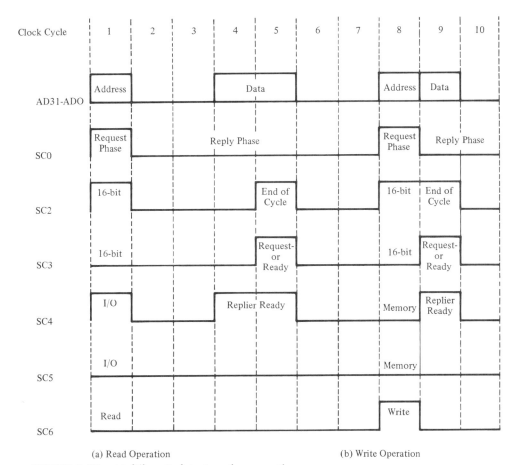

(a) Read Operation   (b) Write Operation

FIGURE 3-28. Multibus II data transfer operation

TABLE 3-8   Functions of Multibus II System Control Lines

| Signal | Request Phase | | Reply Phase | |
	Driving Agent	Functions	Driving Agent	Functions
SC0	Requesting Agent	Identify transition between request and reply phases.	Requesting Agent	Identify transition between request and reply phases.
SC1	Requesting Agent	Locks bus so that requesting agent retains control.	Requesting Agent	Locks bus so that requesting agent retains control.
SC2	Requesting Agent	Used with SC3.	Requesting Agent	Used to indicate that the current data transfer is the last, the end-of-cycle.
SC3	Requesting Agent	SC2 and SC3 identify width of data during transfer cycle (8, 16, 24, 32 bits).	Requesting Agent	Notify replying agent when ready to send or receive data. Part of reply phase handshake.
SC4	Requesting Agent	Used with SC4.	Replying Agent	Notify requesting agent when ready to send or receive data. Part of reply phase handshake.
SC5	Requesting Agent	SC4 and SC5 identify address space for transfer cycle (memory, I/O, message, interconnect).	Replying Agent	Used with SC6 and SC7.
SC6	Requesting Agent	Indicate read or write operation.	Replying Agent	Used with SC5 and SC7.
SC7	Requesting Agent	Not used.	Replying Agent	SC5, SC6, and SC7 place an error indication on the bus.

prepare the data. The replier asserts SC4 to indicate that it has placed valid data on the address/data bus. The requesting agent asserts SC3 to indicate that it is ready to accept data from the bus; it also asserts SC2 to indicate that this is the last data transfer of the current cycle and that it will relinquish control of the bus.

The first cycle of a write operation is similar to that of a read operation, with SC6 set to indicate write. The replying agent is expected to be able to accept data on the next cycle. The requesting agent places the data on the address/data bus. SC2, SC3, and SC4 are used as before.

Multibus II makes multiple uses of the same bus lines. The address/data lines carry both address and data information. The system control lines have different meanings during the request and reply phases of a data transfer (Table 3-8).

VMEbus

The VMEbus provides considerable flexibility in data transfer. The following operations may be performed:

1. Read of single byte, double byte (word), or quad byte (longword)
2. Write of single byte, double byte, or quad byte
3. Read-modify-write (RMW) of single byte, double byte, or quad byte
4. Block transfer of single bytes, double bytes, or quad bytes
5. Unaligned transfer of double bytes or quad bytes

Thus, a total of 14 different data transfer operations are defined for VMEbus.

To understand these various operations, we first need to explain the addressing conventions used in VMEbus (Table 3-9). The smallest addressable unit of memory is a byte. A byte whose address ends in 00 is denoted as BYTE(0); an address ending in 01 is denoted as BYTE(1), and so on. A set of four bytes whose addresses differ only in the two least significant bits is called a quad byte or longword, and designated BYTE(0-3). A master can access some or all of the bytes in a longword simultaneously using a single data transfer bus cycle.

To initiate a data transfer, a master must place signals on the following data transfer bus lines:

- *Address (A01-A31):* An address may be 16, 24, or 32 bits long, referred to as short, standard, and extended addresses, respectively. Actually, only the most significant 15, 23, or 31 bits are placed on the address lines, providing the address of a two-byte word. If access is desired to BYTE(1), this is indicated by the DS0 and DS1 lines.
- *Address Modifier (AM0-AM5):* These lines indicate the size of the address and whether or not this is a block transfer. For a non-block transfer, the lines indicate whether the master is operating in supervisory or nonprivileged mode and whether this is a data access or instruction fetch (Table 3-10).
- *LWORD:* A low on this line means that the master is performing a longword transfer.
- *Data Strobe (DS0, DS1):* These lines actually perform two functions. The actual value of the signals, in conjunction with LWORD and address line A01, are

TABLE 3-9   VMEbus Addressing Convention

Category	Byte Address
BYTE(0)	XXXXXX . . . XXXXXX00
BYTE(1)	XXXXXX . . . XXXXXX01
BYTE(2)	XXXXXX . . . XXXXXX10
BYTE(3)	XXXXXX . . . XXXXXX11

used to indicate the size of the data transfer and which byte of the addressed word is the first byte of the access (Table 3-11). The transition to the proper values is a signal that the remaining lines are stable and the data may now be placed on the data lines.

- *WRITE:* This line is set low to indicate a write (master to slave) and high to indicate a read (slave to master).

Now let us consider the various data transfer operations that may be performed. Figure 3-29a shows the sequence of events for a longword read (slave to master) operation:

1. Once a master has gained control of the bus (see Figures 3-26 and 3-27), it begins the operation by setting the Address, Address Modifier, and LWORD lines. It also sets the Write line to high to indicate that this is a read operation.
2. The master then pauses to account for the worst-case signal-propagation delay along the bus. It then sets the Address Strobe line to low to indicate that valid address information is on the bus.

TABLE 3-10   VMEbus Address Modifier Codes

Hexadecimal Code	Address Modifier 5	4	3	2	1	0	Function
09	0	0	1	0	0	1	Extended nonprivileged data access
0A	0	0	1	0	1	0	Extended nonprivileged program access
0B	0	0	1	0	1	1	Extended nonprivileged block transfer
0D	0	0	1	1	0	1	Extended supervisory data access
0E	0	0	1	1	1	0	Extended supervisory program access
0F	0	0	1	1	1	1	Extended supervisory block transfer
10-1F	0	1	X	X	X	X	User defined
29	1	0	1	0	0	1	Short nonprivileged I/O access
2D	1	0	1	1	0	1	Short supervisory I/O access
39	1	1	1	0	0	1	Standard nonprivileged data access
3A	1	1	1	0	1	0	Standard nonprivileged program access
3B	1	1	1	0	1	1	Standard nonprivileged block transfer
3D	1	1	1	1	0	1	Standard supervisory data access
3E	1	1	1	1	1	0	Standard supervisory program access
3F	1	1	1	1	1	1	Standard supervisory block transfer

Note: All other address modifier codes are undefined and reserved.

TABLE 3-11 Common Types of VMEbus Transfer Operations

Type of Cycle	DS1*	DS0*	A01	LWORD*
ADDRESS-ONLY	high	high	<----Note 1---->	
Single even byte transfers				
BYTE(0) READ or WRITE	low	high	low	high
BYTE(2) READ or WRITE	low	high	high	high
Single odd byte transfers				
BYTE(1) READ or WRITE	high	low	low	high
BYTE(3) READ or WRITE	high	low	high	high
Double byte transfers				
BYTE(0-1) READ or WRITE	low	low	low	high
BYTE(2-3) READ or WRITE	low	low	high	high
Quad byte transfers				
BYTE(0-3) READ or WRITE	low	low	low	low
Single byte block transfers				
SINGLE BYTE BLOCK READ or WRITE	<-------Note 2------->			high
Double byte block transfers				
DOUBLE BYTE BLOCK READ or WRITE	low	low	Note 3	high
Quad byte block transfers				
QUAD BYTE BLOCK READ or WRITE	low	low	low	low
Single byte RMW transfers				
BYTE(0) READ-MODIFY-WRITE	low	high	low	high
BYTE(1) READ-MODIFY-WRITE	high	low	low	high
BYTE(2) READ-MODIFY-WRITE	low	high	high	high
BYTE(3) READ-MODIFY-WRITE	high	low	high	high
Double byte RMW transfers				
BYTE(0-1) READ-MODIFY-WRITE	low	low	low	high
BYTE(2-3) READ-MODIFY-WRITE	low	low	high	high
Quad byte RMW transfers				
BYTE(0-3) READ-MODIFY-WRITE	low	low	low	low
Unaligned transfers				
BYTE(0-2) READ or WRITE	low	high	low	low
BYTE(1-3) READ or WRITE	high	low	low	low
BYTE(1-2) READ or WRITE	low	low	high	low

1. During ADDRESS-ONLY cycles, both data strobes are maintained, but the A01 and LWORD* lines might be either high or low.
2. During single-byte block transfers, the two data strobes are alternately driven low. Either data strobe might be driven low on the first transfer. If the first accessed byte location is BYTE(0) or BYTE(2), then DS1* is driven low first. If the first accessed byte location is BYTE(1) or BYTE(3), then DS0* is driven low first. A01 is valid only on the first data transfer (i.e., until the SLAVE drives DTACK* or BERR* low the first time) and might be either high or low, depending on which byte the single-byte block transfer begins with. If the first byte location is BYTE(0) or BYTE(1), then A01 is low. If the first byte location is BYTE(2) or BYTE(3), then A01 is high.
3. During a double-byte block transfer, the two data strobes are both driven low on each data transfer. A01 is valid only on the first data transfer (i.e., until the SLAVE drives DTACK* or BERR* low the first time) and might be either high or low, depending on what double-byte group the double-byte block transfer begins with. If the first double-byte group is BYTE(0–1), then A01 is low. If the first double-byte group is BYTE(2–3), then A01 is high.

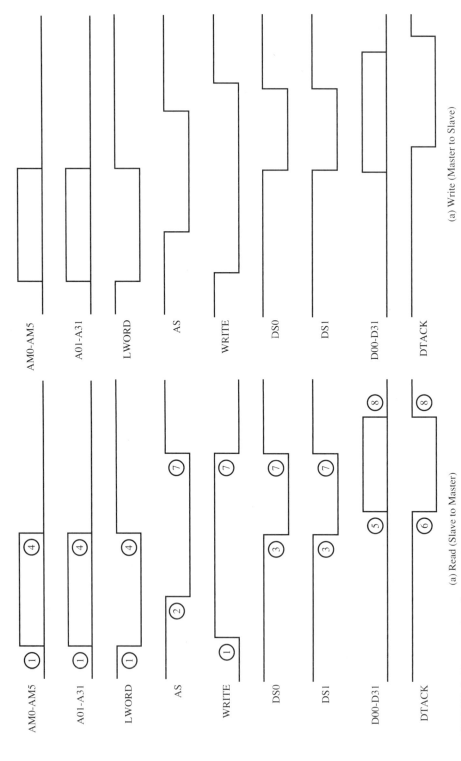

(a) Write (Master to Slave)

(a) Read (Slave to Master)

FIGURE 3-29. VMEbus longword data transfer

3. After another pause to give all slaves time to sense and compare the address lines, the master sets the DS0 and DS1 lines. These signals complete the specification of the operation to be performed (Table 3-11) and signal that the master is prepared to read the data lines.
4. The master releases the Address, AM, and LWORD lines.
5. The slave being addressed selects and accesses the four-byte group at the indicated address and loads the data onto the Data lines.
6. The slave then sets the DTACK line low, indicating that the data is stable on the data bus.
7. The master responds to DTACK by taking the data from D00-D31 and releasing the AS, WRITE, and DS lines.
8. The slave finishes the transfer cycle by releasing DTACK and the Data lines when it detects that AS, DS0, and DS1 have been released.

The timing diagram for a longword write is virtually the same as for the read (Figure 3-29b). In this case, the master sets WRITE to low to indicate a write operation, and the master loads the data onto the Data lines when it sets DS0 and DS1. The slave sets DTACK after it has read the data from the Data lines.

The timing diagrams of Figure 3-29 are also valid for read and write of a single byte and word. In the case of a single-byte transfer, only data lines D00–D07 are used, and in the case of a word transfer, data lines D00–D15 are used.

The read-modify-write operation is a combination of the read and write operations. The address is broadcast only once, at the beginning. This is followed by a read transfer and a write transfer.

Block data transfers allow for the movement of up to 256 bytes of data into consecutive memory locations. The timing diagram for a single-byte block read of 3 bytes is illustrated in Figure 3-30. The operation begins with the starting address of the transfer being placed on the address lines. As before, the AM, LWORD, and A01 lines determine the exact nature of the transfer. A series of data strobes on DS0 and DS1 are generated by the master. For write operations, data are placed on the Data lines by the master in the same fashion as for a single-byte write. For read operations, the slave places data on the Data lines following each data strobe.

Finally, VMEbus allows what are called unaligned transfers to accommodate differences in storage schemes between two modules. Typically, word transfers begin on BYTE(0) or BYTE(2) and longword transfers begin on BYTE(0). However, words may be transferred that are not stored on normal word boundaries and longwords may be transferred that are not stored on normal longword boundaries. These unaligned transfers take multiple data transfer cycles to accomplish (see Problem 3.17).

Interrupt Communication

Multibus II

Unlike most buses, Multibus II has no dedicated interrupt-control lines. Instead, an interrupting device arbitrates for the bus and passes interrupt information in a special message format.

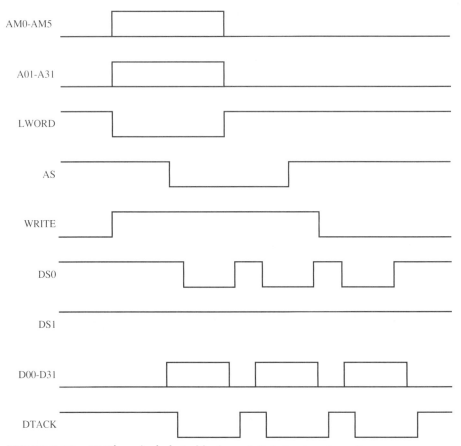

FIGURE 3-30.   VMEbus single-byte block read (3 bytes transferred)

The interrupt scheme makes use of the Multibus II message-passing facility, which provides a standardized method for one agent on the bus to send a message (command plus data) to another, using a sequence of bus cycles (Figure 3-31):

- *Request Phase:* On the first bus cycle, the source and destination of the interrupt message are identified. A special address space is defined for interrupts, using 8-bit addresses. Any module on the bus that is to be enabled to send and/or receive interrupts is assigned a message-passing address. During the request phase, the 8-bit source address identifies the bus owner, which is the agent generating the interrupt. The 8-bit destination address identifies the intended recipient of the interrupt.
- *Command Phase:* During the next bus cycle, the address/data lines are used to

	AD31 to AD24	AD23 to AD16	AD15 to AD8	AD7 to AD0
Request Phase			Source Address Byte 2	Destination Address Byte 1
Command Phase			Type Specific = Reserved	Type = 0
Data Phase (Optional)	Data Byte 3 Byte 8	Data Byte 2 Byte 7	Data Byte 1 Byte 6	Data Byte 0 Byte 5
Data Phase (Optional)	Data Byte 7 Byte 12	Data Byte 6 Byte 11	Data Byte 5 Byte 10	Data Byte 4 Byte 9
Data Phase (Optional)	Data Byte 11 Byte 16	Data Byte 10 Byte 15	Data Byte 9 Byte 14	Data Byte 8 Byte 13
Data Phase (Optional)	Data Byte 15 Byte 20	Data Byte 14 Byte 19	Data Byte 13 Byte 18	Data Byte 12 Byte 17
Data Phase (Optional)	Data Byte 19 Byte 24	Data Byte 18 Byte 23	Data Byte 17 Byte 22	Data Byte 16 Byte 21
Data Phase (Optional)	Data Byte 23 Byte 28	Data Byte 22 Byte 27	Data Byte 21 Byte 26	Data Byte 20 Byte 25
Data Phase (Optional)	Data Byte 27 Byte 32	Data Byte 26 Byte 31	Data Byte 25 Byte 30	Data Byte 24 Byte 29

FIGURE 3-31. Multibus II interrupt message

identify the type of message. For an interrupt, the Type Specific field is ignored (reserved for future use) and the Type field has a value of 0.

• *Data Phase:* Optionally, up to 28 bytes of data may be sent with the interrupt, using up to 7 additional bus cycles.

The SC2 signal (Table 3-8) is used to indicate the end of the message. When the interrupt message is sent without data (only 2 bus cycles), it functions like a standard interrupt signal line, providing an interrupt signal and a source identification. The interrupt message with data (3 to 9 bus cycles) is a more general-purpose interrupt that includes status information and other information pertaining to the interrupt. The use of the data bytes can enhance performance by eliminating the need for the interrupted agent to poll the sender for additional information.

There is no provision in Multibus II for an interrupt acknowledgment, which would let the sender know that the interrupt and its data were properly received. For particular applications, software can be added to the interrupt-handler routine to acknowledge the message.

VMEbus

VMEbus provides a markedly different approach to interrupt handling than that of Multibus II. With Multibus II, there is a potential disadvantage in real-time applications because the message-passing interrupter must arbitrate for the bus and wait its turn to issue an interrupt. In contrast, VMEbus uses the more traditional approach of dedicated interrupt lines that may be utilized without gaining possession of the bus.

Figure 3-32 illustrates the key elements of the VMEbus interrupt structure. At least one agent on the bus acts as an interrupt handler; it is also possible for there to be more than one interrupt handler. The bus provides seven interrupt-request lines. If there is one interrupt handler, then all of the IRQ lines are attached to that handler, and are treated on a priority basis, with IRQ7 having highest priority. If there are two or more interrupt handlers, then each handler controls a subset of the IRQ lines, such that each IRQ line provides input to one and only one interrupt handler. For the set of IRQ lines attached to an interrupt handler, the one with the highest number has the highest priority. Thus, in our example, the interrupt handler in slot 3 controls IRQ3 through IRQ1, in descending order of priority, and the interrupt handler in slot n controls IRQ7 through IRQ4, in descending order of priority.

Each agent that is capable of generating an interrupt request signal attaches to at least one of the IRQ lines to generate its interrupt. The IACK line provides a way for an interrupt handler to acknowledge an interrupt, as explained below.

The sequence of events in handling an interrupt are as follows:

1. An agent that wishes to signal an interrupt sets one of the IRQi lines low. Multiple agents may connect to the same IRQi line; the line is asserted if one or more agents signal on the line.
2. An interrupt handler monitors the IRQ lines that it controls. When an interrupt signal is detected, the interrupt handler must first gain control of the bus through the usual arbitration signal. It then issues an IACK. If more than one IRQ line is set, the interrupt handler responds to the request on the highest-priority line. To indicate which interrupt is being acknowledged, the interrupt handler places the request level (1 to 7) as a binary code on address lines A01–A03. The handler also sets DS0, DS1, and LWORD to indicate the size of the status information that it expects to receive.
3. Since more than one agent may share the same interrupt request priority, a daisy-chain architecture is used to prioritize the agents within a single interrupt-request priority level. The daisy chain begins at slot 1. When IACK is set, the agent in slot 1 is responsible for signaling on its IACKOUT line to start the signal down the daisy chain.
4. The IACKIN/IACKOUT signal propagates from board to board until it is blocked from going to the next board by an agent that satisfies the following conditions:
   (a) the agent has an interrupt request pending on IRQi, and
   (b) the code on address lines A01–A03 matches i.

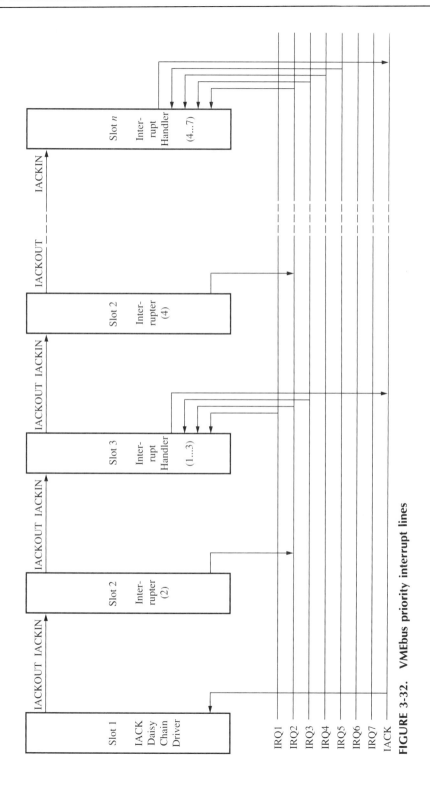

FIGURE 3-32. VMEbus priority interrupt lines

The interrupting agent places its status/id information on the data lines. The interrupter releases the IRQ line. This action is taken in one of two ways. The first method is called release on acknowledge (ROAK): After the interrupter transfers status/id information, it releases the IRQ line. The second method is called release on register access (RORA): When the interrupt handler enters the interrupt service routine, it accesses key registers within the interrupter with either a read or write operation; this register access causes the interrupter to release the IRQ line.

There are several levels of discrimination in operation to determine the order in which interrupt requests are handled. If more than one agent issues an interrupt request on the same IRQ line, the first agent on the daisy chain will have the first opportunity to deliver its interrupt. When an interrupt handler detects simultaneous requests on two IRQ lines, it first services the interrupter that has a pending request on the higher-priority request line. Finally, if there is more than one interrupt handler, and both detect an interrupt request (on separate IRQ lines), the two interrupt handlers must compete using the VMEbus arbitration mechanism for the opportunity to respond.

3.5

RECOMMENDED READING

The literature on interconnection structures is, surprisingly, not very extensive. A number of introductory texts, including [GOOR89] and [HAYE88], cover aspects of the subject. [MALL82] uses a similar classification to the one presented in this chapter.

[GIAC90] and [CRAM91] provide detailed descriptions of a number of bus specifications, including Multibus II and VMEbus. The Unibus is thoroughly described in [DEC83], and the VAX SBI in [DEC82] and [DEC86]. An excellent discussion of bus function, using the Unibus and SBI as examples, is [LEVY78]. [CONN77] and [JEND83] provide an interesting description of the Honeywell Megabus, an independent development with similarities to the Unibus and SBI. [INTE85] is a readable description of Multibus II. [KRUT88] contains a good chapter on buses and devotes a lengthy appendix to VMEbus. The following are survey articles on buses, with the emphasis on microcomputer buses and bus standards: [GUST84], [DAWS86], and [DAWS87].

3.6

PROBLEMS

3.1 For each of the IAS instructions (Table 2-2), specify the sequence of states (Figure 3-6) for the instruction cycle.

3.2 The hypothetical machine of Figure 3-4 also has two I/O instructions:

0011 = Load AC from I/O
0111 = Store AC to I/O

In these cases, the 12-bit address identifies a particular I/O device. Show the program execution (using format of Figure 3-5) for the following program:

1. Load AC from device 5.
2. Add contents of memory location 940.
3. Store AC to device 6.

3.3 Consider a computer system that contains an I/O module controlling a simple keyboard/printer teletype. The following registers are contained in the CPU and connected directly to the system bus:

INPR: Input Register—8 bits
OUTR: Output Register—8 bits
FGI: Input Flag—1 bit
FGO: Output Flag—1 bit
IEN: Interrupt Enable—1 bit

Keystroke input from the teletype and printer output to the teletype are controlled by the I/O module. The teletype is able to encode an alphanumeric symbol to an 8-bit word and decode an 8-bit word into an alphanumeric symbol.

(a) Describe how the CPU, using the first four registers listed in this problem, can achieve I/O with the teletype.
(b) Describe how the function can be performed more efficiently by also employing IEN.

3.4 On the VAX SBI bus, the lowest priority device is assigned priority 16. Why is there not a TR16 line?

3.5 In discussing SBI arbitration, it is stated that the lowest priority (16) device has the lowest average wait time. Would this always be true? If not, under what circumstances is it true?

3.6 Figure 3-33 indicates a distributed arbitration scheme that can be used with Multibus I. Agents are daisy-chained physically in priority order. The left-

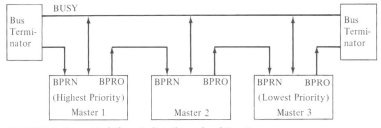

FIGURE 3-33. Multibus I distributed arbitration

most agent in the diagram receives a constant *bus priority in* (BPRN) signal indicating that no higher-priority agent desires the bus. If the agent does not wish the bus, it asserts its *bus priority out* (BPRO) line. At the beginning of a clock cycle, any agent can request control of the bus by lowering its BPRO line. This lowers the BPRN line of the next agent in the chain, which is in turn required to lower its BPRO line. Thus the signal is propagated the length of the chain. At the end of this chain reaction, there should be only one agent whose BPRN is asserted and whose BPRO is not. This agent has priority. If, at the beginning of a bus cycle, the bus is not busy (BUSY inactive), the agent that has priority may seize control of the bus by asserting the BUSY line.

It takes a certain amount of time for the BPR signal to propagate from the highest-priority agent to the lowest. Must this time be less than the clock cycle? Explain.

3.7   A memory system consists of a number of memory modules connected together on a common memory bus. When a write request is made, the bus is occupied for 100 ns by the data, address, and control signals. During the same 100 ns, and for 500 ns thereafter, the addressed memory module executes 1 cycle accepting and storing the data. The operation of the memory modules may overlap, but only one request can be on the bus at any time.

(a) Assume that there are eight such modules connected to the bus. What is the maximum possible rate (in words/second) at which data can be stored?

(b) Sketch a graph of the maximum write rate as a function of the module cycle time, assuming eight memory modules and a bus busy time of 100 ns.

3.8   To save gates, buses are often time multiplexed. Consider a machine with 48-bit words, a 10^7-bps disk, and a 600-ns main memory cycle time. Assume that each bus transmission requires 750 ns for data bits and various control "handshaking" operations. How many data bits would have to be sent in each 750-ns period to stay ahead of the disk, and what bus format would you choose? What fraction of the main memory bandwidth is consumed by a disk I/O operation?

Sketch the sequence of timing events involved in a continuous input transmission from disk to main memory; that is, show how much of the bandwidth of the disk, bus, and main memory are used.

3.9   Regarding priorities on a daisy chain—assume that devices $d_1, \ldots, d_k$ are to be put on a daisy chain and that each device, d_i, uses fraction α_i of the capacity of the bus, $0 < \alpha_i < 1$; $\sum_{i=1}^{k} \alpha_i < 1$, and the capacity of the bus has a normalized value of 1.0. How should the devices be attached to the daisy chain to obtain the maximum average remaining capacity? The remaining capacity for a device on a daisy chain is 1 minus the sum of the capacities used by all the devices with higher priorities on the daisy chain. Briefly comment on what your results mean and give an example of when they may not be applicable.

3.10 The VAX SBI bus uses a distributed, synchronous arbitration scheme. Each SBI device (i.e., processor, memory, Unibus adapter) has a unique priority and is assigned a unique transfer request (TR) line. The SBI has 16 such lines (TR0, TR1, . . . , TR15), with TR0 having the highest priority. When a device wants to use the bus, it places a reservation for a future time slot by asserting its TR line during the current time slot. At the end of the current time slot, each device with a pending reservation examines the TR lines; the highest-priority device with a reservation uses the next time slot.

A maximum of 17 devices can be attached to the bus. The device with priority 16 has no TR line. Why not?

3.11 Paradoxically, the lowest-priority device usually has the lowest average wait time. For this reason, the CPU is usually given the lowest priority on the SBI. Why does the priority 16 device usually have the lowest average wait time? Under what circumstances would this not be true?

3.12 In Multibus II, assume that the bus is not busy and that no requests are pending. At some point, a single agent wishes to make a data transfer. What is the average amount of time that it will take for the agent to seize the bus?

3.13 The largest block of data that an agent can transfer across Multibus II before relinquishing control of the bus is 32 bytes. How long will that take and what is the data transfer rate?

3.14 Multibus II uses the same lines for address and data. How many bus cycles would be required for a read and a write if there were dedicated lines for address and dedicated lines for data?

3.15 It was stated that for Multibus II, the higher the binary value of the ID, the higher the priority. Prove this.

3.16 For the Multibus II arbitration scheme, in every batch, an agent always receives service after all agents in the batch that have higher identities. For multiprocessor systems in which the processors do not continue execution while waiting for a memory request to be satisfied, this means that the lower-identity processors execute at a slower rate. Several algorithms are proposed in [VERN88] that do not exhibit this unfairness. The *round-robin algorithm* assigns priorities dynamically after each arbitration. If an agent with ID j is the winner of a given arbitration, then the round-robin algorithm assigns priorities, from high to low, to $j - 1$ through 1 and then N through j for the next arbitration. The first-come-first-served algorithm gives highest priority to the agent that has been waiting the longest for bus access. If more than one agent has been waiting the longest time, then they are serviced in priority order based on ID.

(a) Suggest a way of implementing the round-robin algorithm.

(b) Suggest a way of implementing the first-come-first-served algorithm.

3.17 A device on VMEbus might store a longword in four different ways: beginning on BYTE(0), BYTE(1), BYTE(2), or BYTE(3). If the longword is not stored beginning at BYTE(0), it is unaligned. A master could transfer the longword one byte at a time, using four single-byte data transfers. However, there are a number of sequences that can be used to improve performance. Consider a longword that straddles two 4-byte groups. We have the following two possibilities:

Cycle Sequence Used to Accomplish the Transfer	Data Bus Lines Used	Byte Location Accesses
Single-byte transfer	D00–D07	Group 1, BYTE(1)
Double-byte transfer	D00–D15	Group 1, BYTE(2-3)
Single-byte transfer	D08–D15	Group 2, BYTE(0)
Triple-byte transfer	D00–D23	Group 1, BYTE(1-3)
Single-byte transfer	D08–D15	Group 2, BYTE(0)

Note that it is possible to transmit three bytes using the 32-bit data bus. Show possible sequences for the transfer of longwords that begin on BYTE(2); for longwords that begin on BYTE(3).

APPENDIX 3A

Timing Diagrams

In this chapter, timing diagrams are used to illustrate sequences of events and dependencies among events. For the reader unfamiliar with timing diagrams, this appendix provides a brief explanation.

Communication among devices connected to a bus takes place along a set of lines capable of carrying signals. Two different signal levels (voltage levels), representing binary 0 and binary 1, may be transmitted. A timing diagram shows the signal level on a line as a function of time (Figure 3-34a). By convention, the binary 1 signal level is depicted as a higher level than that of binary 0. Usually, binary 0 is the default value. That is, if no data or other signal is being transmitted, then the level on a line is that which represents binary 0. A signal transition from 0 to 1 is frequently referred to as the signal's *leading edge*; a transition from 1 to 0 is referred to as a *trailing edge*. For clarity, signal transitions are often depicted as occurring instantaneously. In fact, a transition takes a nonzero amount of time, but this transition time is usually small compared to the duration of a signal level. On a timing diagram, it may happen that a variable or at least irrelevant amount of time elapses between events of interest. This is depicted by a gap in the time line.

Signals are sometimes represented in groups (Figure 3-34b). For example, if data are transferred a byte at a time, then eight lines are required. Generally, it is not important to know the exact value being transferred on such a group, but rather whether signals are present or not.

A signal transition on one line may trigger an attached device to make signal changes on other lines. For example, if a memory module detects a read control

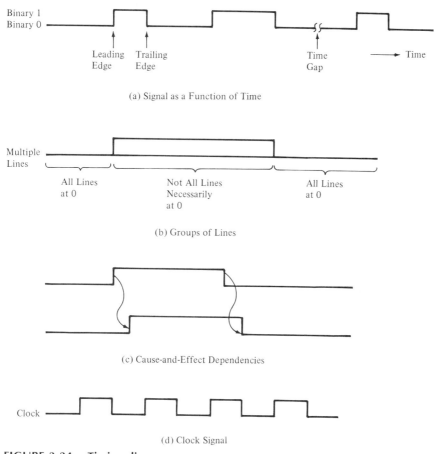

(a) Signal as a Function of Time

(b) Groups of Lines

(c) Cause-and-Effect Dependencies

(d) Clock Signal

FIGURE 3-34.   Timing diagrams

signal (0 or 1 transition), it will place data signals on the data lines. Such cause-and-effect relationships produce sequences of events. Arrows are used on timing diagrams to show these dependencies (Figure 3-34c).

A clock line is often part of a system bus. An electronic clock is connected to the clock line and provides a repetitive, regular sequence of transitions (Figure 3-34d). Other events may be synchronized to the clock signal.

APPENDIX 3B

Futurebus+

Futurebus+ is a high-performance asynchronous bus standard developed by IEEE. An initial version, called Futurebus, was issued as ANSI/IEEE Std 896 in 1987. This initial version was for a 32-bit bus that was intended to be technology-independent. Since 1987, the initial Futurebus standard has been revised and expanded. To emphasize the difference, the standard is now known as Futurebus+. The plus sign refers to the extensible nature of the specification, and the hooks provided to allow further evolution to meet unanticipated needs of specific application architectures. This appendix is based on the current (1992) version of that standard.

The Futurebus+ committee defined eight requirements upon which the design is based [ANDR90]. The bus had to

- be architecture-, processor-, and technology-independent
- have a basic asynchronous transfer protocol
- allow for optional source-synchronized protocol
- have no technology-based upper limit to performance
- be composed of fully distributed parallel arbitration protocols, supporting both circuit-switched and split-transaction protocols
- provide support for fault-tolerant and high-reliability systems
- offer direct support for cache-based shared memory
- provide a compatible message transport definition

The importance of Futurebus+ is the likelihood that it will supplant most current microprocessor bus schemes. Consider the following observation [ANDR91]:

> The Futurebus+ committee has created the ultimate in bus enhancements. When it's through, there will probably be little left for future generations of bus designers to modify. When it's called up for its mandatory review five years after final acceptance, the committee may well look at the Futurebus+ spec and say, "there's nothing to add."

The key differences between the 1987 Futurebus standard and the current Futurebus+ specification are the following:

- Futurebus supports a 32-bit data bus; Futurebus+ supports data bus widths of 32, 64, 128, and 256 bits.
- Futurebus supports a distributed arbitration protocol. Futurebus+ supports both distributed and centralized models.
- Only Futurebus+ includes a 3-bit capability field to allow a module to declare its ability to accommodate major modes of bus transactions.

Futurebus+ is a complex bus specification. It introduces some innovative concepts in bus design. As a result, the standard includes a number of new and redefined terms that will become increasingly familiar in the next few years; Table 3-12 summarizes some of the most important terms. Table 3-13 lists the bus lines defined for Futurebus+.

The intent of this appendix is to provide an overview to give the reader a feel for the nature of this important bus standard.

TABLE 3-12   Some Futurebus+ Terminology

Arbitrated Message

A number broadcast on the arbitrated message lines to all modules on the bus.

Beat

An event that begins with the transition on a synchronization line by the master followed by the release of an acknowledge line by one or more slaves. Command and data information may be transferred from the master to one or more slaves in the first half of the beat. During the second half of the beat the slaves may transfer capability, status, and data information back to the master.

Bus Tenure

The duration of a master's control of the bus; i.e., the time during which a module has the right to initiate and execute bus transactions.

Bus Transaction

An event initiated with a connection phase and terminated with a disconnection phase. Data may or may not be transferred during a bus transaction.

Compelled Data Transfer Protocol

A technology independent transfer mechanism in which the slave is compelled to provide a response before the master proceeds to the next transfer.

Locking

A facility whereby a module is requested to guarantee exclusive access to addressed data, blocking other modules from accessing that data. This allows indivisible operations to be performed on addressed resources.

Parallel Contention Arbitration

A process whereby modules assert their unique arbitration number on a parallel bus and release signals according to an algorithm such that after a period of time the winner's number appears on the bus.

Split Transaction

A system transaction in which the request is transmitted in one bus transaction and the response is transmitted in a separate subsequent bus transaction.

Starvation

A system condition which occurs when one or more modules perform no useful work for an indefinite period of time due to lack of access to the bus or other system resources.

System Transaction

A complete operation such as a memory read or write as viewed from the initiating unit. A system transaction can be translated into one or more bus transactions by the Futurebus+ interface to complete the operation.

3B-1 *Addressing*

Each module on the bus gets assigned a unique geographical address, which is hard-wired into each slot of the backplane. When a board plugs into a slot it senses the 5-bit number of lines GA(4 . . . 0) to determine which slot it resides in. This feature promotes high availability in the following way. Boards can be inserted and withdrawn without having to power down the system and without having to configure an address.

3B-2 *Arbitration*

The Futurebus+ arbitration process operates in parallel with data transfers on the bus. Futurebus+ supports both distributed and centralized arbitration

TABLE 3-13 Futurebus+ Bus Lines

Symbol	Designation	Number of Lines				Description
	Data Path Width:	32	64	128	256	Used during the execution of bus transactions.
	Information Lines					
AD(63 . . . 0)	Address/Data	32	64	64	64	Carry address during address transfer; carry data during data transfer.
D(255 . . . 64)	Data	—	—	64	192	Carry data during data transfer.
BP(31 . . . 0)	Bus Parity	4	8	16	32	One parity line for every 8 address/data lines.
TG(7 . . . 0)	Tag	8	8	8	8	Carry additional information related to the address/data lines; standard does not prescribe specific use.
TP	Tag Parity	1	1	1	1	Parity code for tag lines.
CM(7 . . . 0)	Command	8	8	8	8	Carry command information from master to one or more slaves for the current transaction.
CP	Command Parity	1	1	1	1	Parity code for command lines.
ST(7 . . . 0)	Status	8	8	8	8	Carry information about the status of a slave and its disposition in regards to the requested transfer.
CA(2 . . . 0)	Capability	3	3	3	3	Activated by a module to declare its ability to accommodate major modes of bus transactions.

TABLE 3-13   Futurebus+ Bus Lines

Symbol	Designation	Number of Lines				Description
		32	64	128	256	
	Data Path Width:					Coordinate the exchange of address, command, capability, status, and data during a transaction.
	Synchronization Lines					
AS, AK, AI	Address Handshake	3	3	3	3	Address Synchronization: asserted by master to inform slaves that the address and command information are valid. Address Acknowledge: released by by modules to indicate to master that their status information is valid. Address Acknowledge Inverse: released by modules to indicate to master that their status and capability information are valid.
DS, DK, DI	Data Handshake	3	3	3	3	Data Synchronization: asserted by master to inform slaves that the write data and command information are valid or that the master is ready to receive read data. Data Acknowledge, Data Acknowledge Inverse: released by participating slaves to indicate to master that status information and read data are valid or that write data has been received.
ET	End of Tenure	1	1	1	1	Released by current master to notify master-elect that it is the new master.

TABLE 3-13   Futurebus+ Bus Lines (continued)

Symbol	Designation	Number of Lines				Description
	Data Path Width:	32	64	128	256	
	Arbitrated Message Lines					Manage distributed arbitration mechanisms.
AB(7 . . . 0)	Arbitrated Message Bus	8	8	8	8	Carry a number that signifies the precedence of competitors during the arbitrated message process and the distributed arbitration process.
ABP	Arbitrated Message Bus Parity	1	1	1	1	Parity code for AB(7 . . . 0)
AP, AQ, AR	Arbitrated Message Synch.	3	3	3	3	Handshake lines that perform a cyclic handshake sequence that controls the sequencing of the arbitrated message process and the distributed arbitration process.
AC(1 . . . 0)	Arbitrated Message Condition	2	2	2	2	Control the arbitrated message process and the distributed arbitration process.
	Reset/Bus Initialize Line					
RE	Reset	1	1	1	1	Initializes the bus interface logic of all modules.
	Central Arbitration					Used for bus master selection in systems with central arbiter.
RQ(1 . . . 0)	Request	2	2	2	2	One or both lines are asserted to request bus mastership.
GR	Grant	1	1	1	1	Asserted by central arbiter to grant bus mastership.
PE	Preemption	1	1	1	1	Asserted by central arbiter to indicate to current master that a preemptive condition exists and the master should relinquish bus mastership.
GA(4 . . . 0)	Geographical Address	5	5	5	5	A unique identifier assigned to each physical module slot on the bus and assumed by any module connected to that slot.
Total active signals		96	132	204	348	

schemes. The most powerful one, and the one most likely to be used on a given implementation, is the distributed arbitration scheme.

Distributed Arbitration

Each module on the bus has a unique arbitration number that is used in a parallel contention algorithm during competition to become master. Before explaining the process for acquiring bus mastership, we need to look at the competition mechanism.

Parallel Contention Mechanism. During parallel contention, any number of modules may compete using the 8-bit arbitrated message bus. The module that applies the largest number to the bus wins the competition. Each competitor applies its competition number, cn(7 . . . 0), to bus lines AB(7 . . . 0). The signal on any particular line is the OR of all the signals applied to that line; thus the line has a logical 1 if any of the competing modules applies a 1. The arbitration logic in each module (Figure 3-35) senses the resulting bus values and modifies the number it is applying to the bus according to the following rule: If, for any bit of a module's arbitration number that is zero, the corresponding arbitration bus line shows a one, all lower-order bits of the number are withdrawn from the bus. Eventually, the module with the highest arbitration number will find that its number matches the number remaining on the bus and is therefore the winner.

To understand the logic diagram,[1] note that each of the module's bits is inverted prior to application to the bus, so that a logical 1 is a HIGH level in the module but a LOW level on the bus, and vice versa. The result is that the OR gate will produce a zero (forcing a lose) only if the cn bit is a logical zero and the corresponding AB bit is a logical 1.

Arbitration Process. The arbitration process requires that all competing modules (distributed arbiters) move through the same sequence of states together, at the speed of the slowest arbiter. To achieve this, a rather ingenious protocol involving three bus lines (AP, AQ, AR) has been developed. The protocol makes use of different bus lines than the data transfer protocol and can therefore take place concurrently with data transfer transactions driven by the current bus master.

The arbitration process consists of six phases (Figure 3-36). The beginning and end of each phase is defined by a transition on one of the arbitration synchronizing signals (AP, AQ, AR):

- *Phase 0—Idle:* Identified by AP and AQ released (HIGH) and AR asserted (LOW); no competition is in progress.
- *Phase 1—Decision:* Any arbiter requesting mastership asserts AP. Any arbiter that wishes to compete applies its competition number to AB(7 . . . 0). All

---

[1]See Appendix A for a discussion of digital logic.

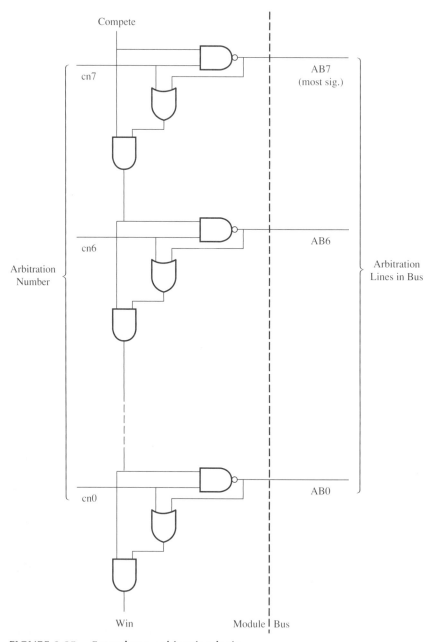

FIGURE 3-35. Futurebus+ arbitration logic

modules synchronize with the arbitration process by releasing AR; only when all of the modules have released AR is it HIGH on the bus, signaling the end of phase 1.

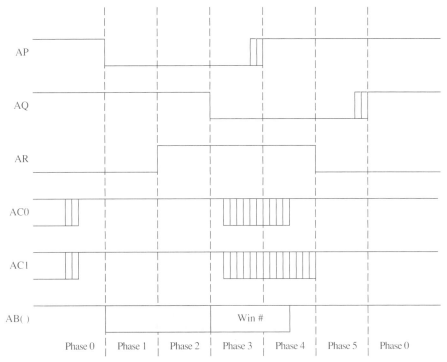

FIGURE 3-36. Futurebus+ arbitration phases

- *Phase 2—Competition:* During this phase, competitors monitor their internal "win" signal for a time that allows for the competition logic (Figure 3-35) to settle to a final state. The winner asserts AQ and becomes "master-elect."
- *Phase 3—Error Check:* During this phase, all competition losers check that the winning competition number is greater than their own. Any modules detecting an error condition assert AC0 and AC1. This phase continues as long as the current master holds the bus. The current master signals the end of a transaction by releasing AS. Each module releases AP when it detects the release of AS.
- *Phase 4—Master Release:* The winning number is removed from AB(7 . . .). If the master wishes to retain the bus, it asserts AC1; otherwise it asserts AR.
- *Phase 5—Tenure:* All modules save the state of AC0 and AC1 to determine if tenure transfer is to take place or if some other action is appropriate. Once they have captured the status, they release AQ. When all modules have released AQ, the phase is over and a new arbitration cycle may begin.

If the above sequence of steps occurs once and, at the end of phase 5, the master-elect assumes mastership, this is referred to as a single-pass arbitration. In other cases, two passes are required. In those cases, there is more than one winner at the end of the first pass, and phases zero through five are repeated.

The value of the arbitration numbers used by modules in the competition determine whether one or two passes are required. Each pass of the arbitration cycle consists of an arbitration competition using the 8-bit competition numbers supplied by each module. An arbitration number consists of three fields as shown in Figure 3-37a: priority, round-robin, and geographical address. A module's arbitration number maps onto one or two competition numbers. The bit cn7 indicates whether the module requires another arbitration pass, so that a single-pass arbitration number defeats a two-pass arbitration number.

The 8-bit priority field PR(7 . . .) selects one of 256 priority levels for the request (255 = highest, 0 = lowest). The highest two priority levels, with all but PR0 set to 1, use the single-pass competition cycle.[2]

Parking.   In a lightly loaded system, there may be a number of instances in which there are no bus requests pending. To save time, the current master retains control under such circumstances and may begin a new transaction without having to arbitrate. It is only when the master sees that an arbitration has taken place and that a master-elect exists that it may decide to release control to the master-elect. Even then, if the current master has higher priority than the master-elect, it may retain the bus.

Deposing the Master-Elect.   The master-elect must wait for some period of time for the current master to finish using the bus. During that period, a module of higher priority may have need of the bus. If so, that module may force a new arbitration cycle and a new competition to establish a new master-elect. Thus, the cycle begins again at phase 1.

Round-Robin.   The round-robin feature ensures a fair and equitable allocation of bus tenure between competing modules of the same priority. The value of a module's round-robin bit is adjusted each time a transfer of tenure to another module in its priority class occurs. The bit is set when tenure is granted to a module in the same priority class but higher geographical address, and cleared for a module in the same priority class but lower geographical address. Thus, once the round-robin bit is cleared, the module will lose in any subsequent arbitration competition with modules in its priority class for which the bit is set. The effect of this feature is to assure a round-robin type of allocation under heavy load.

Arbitration Message.   The arbitration number of the master-elect, since it is visible to all modules, can also be used to broadcast information to the entire system. This is referred to as an arbitration message. The arbitration message can be used to issue a system-wide interrupt or emergency message.

---

[2] This is possible because when PR(7. . .1) are all set to 1, the requestor would always win a first pass, so that it can be skipped in this case. For efficiency, in a system with only one or two priority levels, priorities 255 and 254 should be used.

Bit	cn7	cn6	cn6	cn4	cn3	cn2	cn1	cn0
Single Pass								
Pass 1	1	PR0	RR	GA4	GA3	GA2	GA1	GA0
Two Pass								
Pass 1	0	PR7	PR6	PR5	PR4	PR3	PR2	PR1
Pass 2	1	PR0	RR	GA4	GA3	GA2	GA1	GA0

(a) Distributed Arbitration Request Fields (Distributed Arbiter)

Bit	cn7	cn6	cn6	cn4	cn3	cn2	cn1	cn0
Pass 1	1	1	1	1	1	1	1	1
Pass 2	1	AM6	AM5	AM4	AM3	AM2	AM1	AM0

(b) Distributed Arbitration Message Fields (Distributed Arbiter)

Bit	cn7	cn6	cn6	cn4	cn3	cn2	cn1	cn0
Pass 1	1	AM6	AM5	AM4	AM3	AM2	AM1	AM0

(c) General Arbitrated Message Fields (Central Arbiter)

Bit	cn7	cn6	cn6	cn4	cn3	cn2	cn1	cn0
Pass 1	0	PR7	PR6	PR5	PR4	PR3	PR2	PR1
Pass 2	1	PR0	RQ	GA4	GA3	GA2	GA1	GA0

(d) Central Arbitrated Message Fields (Central Arbiter)

FIGURE 3-37.   Futurebus+ arbitrated messages

Arbitration messages look like any other priority request and follow the same sequence outlined above and illustrated in Figure 3-36. The arbitration message (Figure 3-37b) uses all 1s on the first pass to drive out any priority arbitration messages of priority less than 254. The actual message is conveyed on the second pass; it is up to the system to assign meanings to each message number.

The only change in the arbitration cycle is that the issuer of the arbitration message does not assume mastership after winning the arbitration.

Centralized Arbitration

A Futurebus+ system can also be organized with a central arbiter. The central arbitration scheme makes use of the RQ(1 . . . 0), GR, and PE lines. The RQ and GR lines are not actually part of the common bus; rather there are two separate request lines and one grant line from the central arbiter to each module on the bus. This configuration avoids the need for address resolution in dealing with multiple simultaneous requests.

Arbitration Process. A module may assert RQ0 or RQ1 to request the bus at one of two priority levels. The actual priority of each module is determined by the arbiter, based on the identity of the module and the priority level at which it is making its request. The arbiter indicates to a module that it is the new master-elect by asserting the GR line for that module. The module may then assume bus mastership when it detects that ET is released by the current bus master. The central arbiter may also assert PE to signal to the current bus master that it should relinquish control to the master-elect as soon as possible.

Arbitrated Messages.   When the central arbiter is used, the arbitrated message lines are still available, and are used solely for the transmission of arbitrated messages. Two types of messages are provided: general arbitrated messages and central arbitrated messages (Figure 3-37c and d). The numbering scheme used assures that general messages have precedence over central messages.

General messages are intended for broadcasting messages to other modules on the bus. As with distributed arbitration messages, they can be used to convey interrupts and other emergency messages.

Central messages are directed to the arbiter and are a means of sending priority information to the arbiter. The RQ field indicates whether RQ0 or RQ1 is the subject of this message. The priority field PR(7 . . . 0) selects the priority level to be assigned to a selected RQ line for this module.

3B-3   Data Transfer

Futurebus+ provides a wide variety of data transfer capabilities. In this subsection we present one example of a write, taken from [JONE91], as an illustration of the Futurebus+ approach.

In general, a Futurebus+ transaction consists of an address beat, followed by zero or more data beats. In this example, a block of four data words are being transferred. The sequence is as follows (Figure 3-38):

1. The sender gains control of the bus using one of the arbitration techniques described above.
2. The sender loads the address, as well as command information, onto the bus and asserts AS to indicate this.
3. All other modules read the address. Each module then asserts AK to indicate that it has read the address. Thus AK on the bus will be asserted as soon as the fastest module responds.
4. Each module also releases AI at the time that it asserts AK. Thus, AI is not released until the slowest module responds. This signals the end of the address beat. The master can now safely remove the address from the bus.

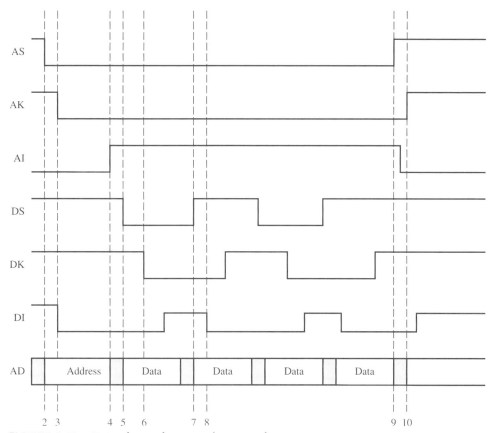

FIGURE 3-38.   Futurebus+ data transfer example

The master now loads data onto the bus, signaled by asserting DS.

The recipient captures the data from the bus and asserts DK and then releases DI to signal successful capture.

The master loads the next data word onto the bus and releases DS to signal that the data is now valid.

The recipient captures the data from the bus and asserts DI and then releases DK to signal successful capture.

Data transfer continues in this fashion, one word at a time, with each transition of DS and DK/DI, until the master has no more data to send. The master signals the end of the transaction by releasing AS.

The recipient, and all other slaves, acknowledge the release of AS by asserting AI and releasing AK. This completes the transaction.

This example illustrates the way in which Futurebus+ is independent of technology. Each event is causally related to the previous event only, with no other timing constraints.

CHAPTER 4

Internal and External Memory

Memory is that portion of a computer system that is used for the storage, and subsequent retrieval, of data and instructions. Although seemingly simple in concept, computer memory exhibits perhaps the widest range of type, technology, organization, performance, and cost of any feature of a computer system. No one technology is optimal in satisfying the memory requirements for a computer system. As a consequence, the typical computer system is equipped with a hierarchy of memory subsystems, some internal to the system (directly accessible by the CPU), and some external (accessible by the CPU via an I/O module).

This chapter explores this range of computer subsystems. In the first section, we begin by looking at key characteristics of computer memories and address the question of why such a wide range exists. Remaining sections examine specific memory subsystems.

4.1

COMPUTER MEMORY SYSTEM OVERVIEW

Characteristics of Memory Systems

The complex subject of computer memory is made more manageable if we classify memory systems according to their key characteristics. The most important of these are listed in Table 4-1.

We begin with the most visible aspect of memory: its *location*. As the title of this chapter suggests, there is memory both internal and external to the computer. Internal memory is often equated with main memory. But there are other forms of internal memory. The CPU requires its own local memory, in the form of registers (e.g., see Figure 2-6). Further, as we shall see, the control unit portion of the CPU may also require its own internal memory. We will defer discus-

TABLE 4-1   Key Characteristics of Computer Memory Systems

Location	Performance
CPU	Access time
Internal (main)	Cycle time
External (secondary)	Transfer rate
Capacity	**Physical Type**
Word size	Semiconductor
Number of words	Magnetic surface
Unit of Transfer	**Physical Characteristics**
Word	Volatile/nonvolatile
Block	Erasable/nonerasable
Access Method	**Organization**
Sequential access	
Direct access	
Random access	
Associative access	

sion of these latter two types of internal memory to later chapters. External memory consists of peripheral storage devices, such as disk and tape, that are accessible to the CPU via I/O controllers.

An obvious characteristic of memory is its *capacity*. For internal memory, this is typically expressed in terms of bytes (1 byte = 8 bits) or words. Common word lengths are 8, 16, and 32 bits. External memory capacity is typically expressed in terms of bytes.

A related concept is the *unit of transfer*. For internal memory, the unit of transfer is equal to the number of data lines into and out of the memory module. This is often equal to the word length, but may not be. To clarify this point, consider three related concepts for internal memory:

- *Word:* The "natural" unit of organization of memory. The size of the word is typically equal to the number of bits used to represent a number and to the instruction length. Unfortunately there are many exceptions. For example, the CRAY-1 has a 64-bit word length but uses a 24-bit integer representation. The VAX has a stupendous variety of instruction lengths, expressed as multiples of bytes, and a word size of 32 bits.
- *Addressable Units:* In many systems, the addressable unit is the word. However, some systems allow addressing at the byte level. In any case, the relationship between the length A of an address and the number N of addressable units is $2^A = N$.
- *Unit of Transfer:* For main memory, this is the number of bits read out of or written into memory at a time. The unit of transfer need not equal a word or an addressable unit. For external memory, data are often transferred in much larger units than a word, and these are referred to as blocks.

One of the sharpest distinctions among memory types is the *method of accessing* units of data. Four types may be distinguished:

- *Sequential Access:* Memory is organized into units of data, called records. Access must be made in a specific linear sequence. Stored addressing information is used to separate records and assist in the retrieval process. A shared read/write mechanism is used, and this must be moved from its current location to the desired location, passing and rejecting each intermediate record. Thus the time to access an arbitrary record is highly variable. Tape units, discussed in Section 4-6, are sequential access.
- *Direct Access:* As with sequential access, direct access involves a shared read–write mechanism. However, individual blocks or records have a unique address based on physical location. Access is accomplished by direct access to reach a general vicinity plus sequential searching, counting, or waiting to reach the final location. Again, access time is variable. Disk units, discussed in Section 4-5, are direct access.
- *Random Access:* Each addressable location in memory has a unique, physically wired-in addressing mechanism. The time to access a given location is independent of the sequence of prior accesses and is constant. Thus, any location can be selected at random and directly addressed and accessed. Main memory systems are random access.
- *Associative:* This is a random-access type of memory that enables one to make a comparison of desired bit locations within a word for a specified match, and to do this for all words simultaneously. Thus a word is retrieved based on a portion of its contents rather than its address. As with ordinary random-access memory, each location has its own addressing mechanism, and retrieval time is constant independent of location or prior access patterns. Cache memories, discussed in Section 4-3, may employ associative access.

From a user's point of view, the two most important characteristics of memory are capacity and *performance*. Three performance parameters are used:

- *Access Time:* For random-access memory, this is the time it takes to perform a read or write operation, that is, the time from the instant that an address is presented to the memory to the instant that data have been stored or made available for use. For nonrandom-access memory, access time is the time it takes to position the read-write mechanism at the desired location.
- *Memory Cycle Time:* This concept is primarily applied to random-access memory and consists of the access time plus any additional time required before a second access can commence. This additional time may be required for transients to die out on signal lines or to regenerate data if they are read destructively.
- *Transfer Rate:* This is the rate at which data can be transferred into or out of a memory unit. For random-access memory, it is equal to 1/(Cycle Time). For nonrandom-access memory, the following relationship holds:

$$T_N = T_A + \frac{N}{R}$$

where

T_N = Average time to read or write N bits
T_A = Average access time
 N = Number of bits
 R = Transfer rate, in bits per second (bps)

A variety of *physical types* of memory have been employed. The two most common today are semiconductor memory, using LSI or VLSI technology, and magnetic surface memory, used for disk and tape.

Several *physical characteristics* of data storage are important. In a volatile memory, information decays naturally or is lost when electrical power is switched off. In a nonvolatile memory, information once recorded remains without deterioration until deliberately changed; no electrical power is needed to retain information. Magnetic-surface memories are nonvolatile. Semiconductor memory may be either volatile or nonvolatile. Nonerasable memory cannot be altered, except by destroying the storage unit. Semiconductor memory of this type is known as *read-only memory* (ROM). Of necessity, a practical nonerasable memory must also be nonvolatile.

For random-access memory, the organization is a key design issue. By *organization* is meant the physical arrangement of bits to form words. The obvious arrangement is not always used, as will be explained presently.

The Memory Hierarchy

The design constraints on a computer's memory can be summed up by three questions: How much? How fast? How expensive?

The question of how much is somewhat open-ended. If the capacity is there, applications will likely be developed to use it. The question of how fast is, in a sense, easier to answer. To achieve greatest performance, the memory must be able to keep up with the CPU. That is, as the CPU is executing instructions, we would not want it to have to pause waiting for instructions or operands. The final question must also be considered. For a practical system, the cost of memory must be reasonable in relationship to other components.

As might be expected, there is a tradeoff among the three key characteristics of memory, namely cost, capacity, and access time. At any given time, a variety of technologies are used to implement memory systems. Across this spectrum of technologies, the following relationships hold:

- Smaller access time, greater cost per bit
- Greater capacity, smaller cost per bit
- Greater capacity, greater access time

The dilemma facing the designer is clear. The designer would like to use memory technologies that provide for large-capacity memory, both because the capacity is needed and because the cost per bit is low. However, to meet performance requirements, the designer needs to use expensive, relatively lower-capacity memories with fast access times.

The way out of this dilemma is not to rely on a single memory component or technology, but to employ a *memory hierarchy*. A typical hierarchy is illustrated in Figure 4-1a. As one goes down the hierarchy, the following occur:

(a) Decreasing cost/bit
(b) Increasing capacity
(c) Increasing access time
(d) Decreasing frequency of access of the memory by the CPU

Thus smaller, more expensive, faster memories are supplemented by larger, cheaper, slower memories. The key to the success of this organization is the last item, decreasing frequency of access. We will examine this concept in detail

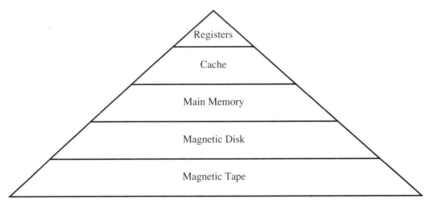

(a) Traditional Memory Hierarchy

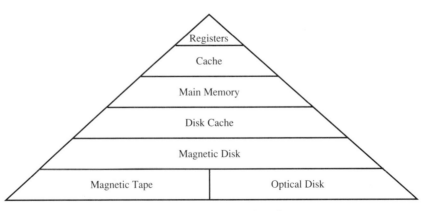

(b) Contemporary Memory Hierarchy

FIGURE 4-1. The memory hierarchy

when we discuss the cache, later in this chapter, and virtual memory, in Chapter 6, but we give a brief explanation here.

If memory can be organized according to items (a) through (c) above, and if the data and instructions can be distributed across this memory according to (d), then it should be intuitively clear that this scheme will reduce overall costs while maintaining a given level of performance. We give a simple example to illustrate this point.

Suppose that the CPU has access to two levels of memory. Level 1 contains 1,000 words and has an access time of 1 μs. Level 2 contains 100,000 words and has an access time of 10 μs. Assume that if a word to be accessed is in Level 1, then the CPU accesses it directly. If it is in Level 2, then the word is first transferred to Level 1 and then accessed by the CPU. For simplicity, we ignore the time required for the CPU to determine whether the word is in Level 1 or Level 2. Figure 4-2 shows the average total access time as a function of the percentage of time that the desired word is already in Level 1. As can be seen, for high percentages of Level 1 access, the average total access time is much closer to that of Level 1 than of Level 2.

This example illustrates that the strategy works in principle. It will work in practice if conditions (a) through (d) apply. Figures 4-3 and 4-4 show typical characteristics of contemporary alternative memory systems. Figure 4-3 shows that by employing a variety of technologies, a spectrum of memory systems

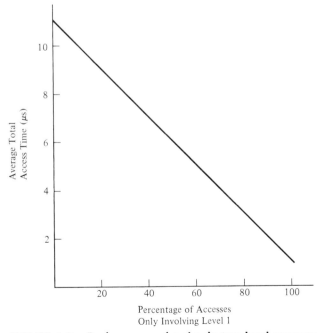

FIGURE 4-2. **Performance of a simple two-level memory**

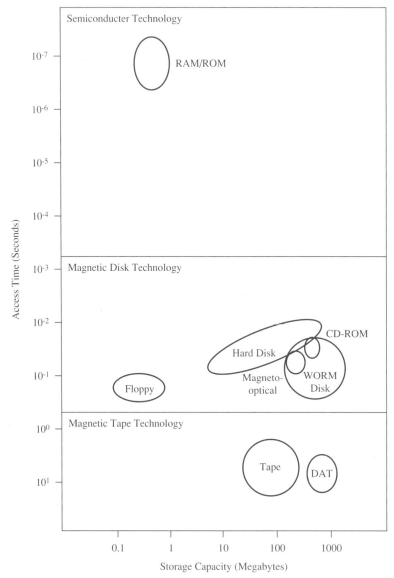

FIGURE 4-3. Storage comparison

exists that satisfy (b) and (c), and Figure 4-4 confirms that condition (a) is satisfied. Fortunately, condition (d) is also generally valid.

The basis for the validity of condition (d) is a principle known as *locality of
reference* [DENN68]. During the course of execution of a program, memory references by the processor, for both instructions and data, tend to cluster. Programs
typically contain a number of iterative loops and subroutines. Once a loop or

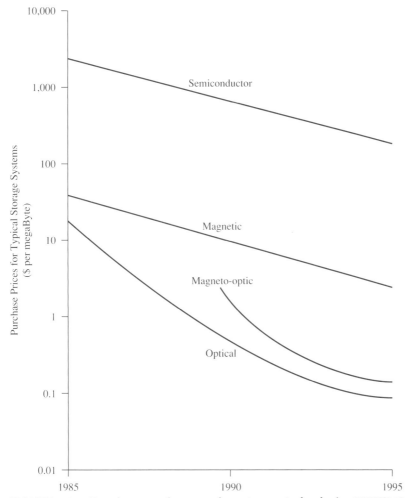

FIGURE 4-4. Cost forecasts for secondary storage technologies [WEIZ91]

subroutine is entered, there are repeated references to a small set of instructions. Similarly, operations on tables and arrays involve access to a clustered set of data words. Over a long period of time, the clusters in use change, but over a short period of time, the processor is primarily working with fixed clusters of memory references.

Accordingly, it is possible to organize data across the hierarchy such that the percentage of accesses to each succeedingly lower level is substantially less than of the level above. Consider the two-level example already presented. Let Level 2 memory contain all program instructions and data. The current clusters can be temporarily placed in Level 1. From time to time, one of the clusters in Level 1 will have to be swapped back to Level 2 to make room for a new cluster coming into Level 1. On average, however, most references will be to instructions and data contained in Level 1.

This principle can be applied across more than two levels of memory. Consider the hierarchy shown in Figure 4-1a. The fastest, smallest, and most expensive type of memory consists of the registers internal to the processor. Typically, a processor will contain a few dozen such registers, although some machines contain hundreds of registers. Skipping down two levels, main memory, also referred to as real memory, is the principal internal memory system of the computer. Each location in main memory has a unique address, and most machine instructions refer to one or more main memory addresses. Main memory is usually extended with a higher-speed, smaller cache. The cache is not usually visible to the programmer or, indeed, to the processor. It is a device for staging the movement of data between main memory and processor registers to improve performance.

The three forms of memory just described are, typically, volatile and employ semiconductor technology. The use of three levels exploits the fact that semiconductor memory comes in a variety of types, which differ in speed and cost. Data are stored more permanently on external mass storage devices, of which the most common are magnetic disk and tape. External, nonvolatile memory is also referred to as secondary or auxiliary memory. These are used to store program and data files and are usually visible to the programmer only in terms of files and records, as opposed to individual bytes or words. Disk is also used to provide an extension to main memory known as virtual storage or virtual memory, which is discussed in Chapter 6.

Other forms of memory may be included in the hierarchy. For example, large IBM mainframes include a form of internal memory known as Expanded Storage. This uses a semiconductor technology that is slower and less expensive than that of main memory. Strictly speaking, this memory does not fit into the hierarchy but is a side branch: data can be moved between main memory and expanded storage but not between expanded storage and external memory. Other forms of secondary memory include optical disks and bubble memory devices. Finally, additional levels can be effectively added to the hierarchy in software. A portion of main memory can be used as a buffer to temporarily hold data that is to be read out to disk. Such a technique, sometimes referred to as a disk cache,[1] improves performance in two ways:

- Disk writes are clustered. Instead of many small transfers of data, we have a few large transfers of data. This improves disk performance and minimizes processor involvement.
- Some data destined for write-out may be referenced by a program before the next dump to disk. In that case, the data is retrieved rapidly from the software cache rather than slowly from the disk.

---

[1] Disk cache is generally a purely software technique, and is not examined in this book. See [STAL91] for a discussion.

Figure 4-1b shows a contemporary memory hierarchy that includes a disk cache and optical disk as an additional type of secondary memory.

Appendix 4A, page 183, examines the performance implications of multilevel memory structures.

4.2

SEMICONDUCTOR MAIN MEMORY

In earlier computers, the most common form of random-access storage for computer main memory employed an array of doughnut-shaped ferromagnetic loops referred to as *cores*. Hence main memory was often referred to as *core*, a term that persists to this day. The advent of, and advantages of, microelectronics has long since vanquished the magnetic core memory. Today, the use of semiconductor chips for main memory is almost universal. Key aspects of this technology are explored in this section.

Types of Random-Access Semiconductor Memory

All of the memory types that we will explore in this section are random access. That is, individual words of memory are directly accessed through wired-in addressing logic.

Table 4-2 lists the major types of semiconductor memory. The most common is referred to as *random-access memory* (RAM). This is, of course, a misuse of the term, since all of the types listed in the table are random access. One distinguishing characteristic of RAM is that it is possible both to read data from the memory and to easily and rapidly write new data into the memory. Both the reading and writing are accomplished through the use of electrical signals.

TABLE 4-2   Semiconductor Memory Types

Memory Type	Category	Erasure	Write Mechanism	Volatility
Random-access memory (RAM)	Read-write memory	Electrically, byte-level	Electrically	Volatile
Read-only memory (ROM)	Read-only memory	Not possible	Masks	Nonvolatile
Programmable ROM (PROM)				
Erasable PROM (EPROM)	Read-mostly memory	UV light, chip-level	Electrically	
Flash memory		Electrically, block-level		
Electrically Erasable PROM (EEPROM)		Electrically, byte-level		

The other distinguishing characteristic of RAM is that it is volatile. A RAM must be provided with a constant power supply. If the power is interrupted, then the data are lost. Thus RAM can be used only as temporary storage.

RAM technology has divided into two technologies: static and dynamic. A *dynamic RAM* is made with cells that store data as charge on capacitors. The presence or absence of charge in a capacitor is interpreted as a binary 1 or 0. Because capacitors have a natural tendency to discharge, dynamic RAMs require periodic charge refreshing to maintain data storage. In a *static RAM*, binary values are stored using traditional flip-flop logic-gate configurations (see Appendix A for a description of flip-flops). A static RAM will hold its data as long as power is supplied to it.

Both static and dynamic RAMs are volatile. A dynamic memory cell is simpler and hence smaller than a static memory cell. Thus a dynamic RAM is more dense (smaller cells = more cells per unit area) and less expensive than a corresponding static RAM. On the other hand, a dynamic RAM requires the supporting refresh circuitry. For larger memories, the fixed cost of the refresh circuitry is more than compensated for by the smaller variable cost of dynamic RAM cells. Thus dynamic RAMs tend to be favored for large memory requirements. A final point is that static RAMs are generally somewhat faster than dynamic RAMs.

In sharp contrast to the RAM is the *read-only memory* (ROM). As the name suggests, a ROM contains a permanent pattern of data that cannot be changed. While it is possible to read a ROM, it is not possible to write new data into it. An important application of ROMs is microprogramming, discussed in Part IV. Other potential applications include:

* Library subroutines for frequently wanted functions
* System programs
* Function tables

For a modest-sized requirement, the advantage of ROM is that the data or program is permanently in main memory and need never be loaded from a secondary storage device.

A ROM is created like any other integrated-circuit chip, with the data actually wired-in to the chip as part of the fabrication process. This presents two problems:

* The data insertion step includes a relatively large fixed cost, whether one or thousands of copies of a particular ROM are fabricated.
* There is no room for error. If one bit is wrong, the whole batch of ROMs must be thrown out.

When only a small number of ROMs with a particular memory content is needed, a less expensive alternative is the *programmable ROM* (PROM). Like the ROM, the PROM is nonvolatile and may be written into only once. For the PROM, the writing process is performed electrically and may be performed by a supplier or customer at a time later than the original chip fabrication. Special equipment is required for the writing or "programming" process. PROMs provide flexibility and convenience. The ROM remains attractive for high-volume production runs.

Another variation on read-only memory is the read-mostly memory, which is useful for applications in which read operations are far more frequent than write operations but for which nonvolatile storage is required. There are three common forms of read-mostly memory: EPROM, EEPROM, and flash memory.

The optically *erasable programmable read-only memory* (EPROM) is read and written electrically, as with PROM. However, before a write operation, all the storage cells must be erased to the same initial state by exposure of the packaged chip to ultraviolet radiation. This erasure process can be performed repeatedly; each erasure can take as much as 20 minutes to perform. Thus, the EPROM can be altered multiple times, and like the ROM and PROM, holds its data virtually indefinitely. For comparable amounts of storage, the EPROM is more expensive than PROM, but it has the advantage of the multiple update capability.

A more attractive form of read-mostly memory is *electrically erasable programmable read-only memory* (EEPROM). This is a read-mostly memory that can be written into at any time without erasing prior contents; only the byte or bytes addressed are updated. The write operation takes considerably longer than the read operation, on the order of several hundred microseconds per byte. The EEPROM combines the advantage of nonvolatility with the flexibility of being updateable in place, using ordinary bus control, address, and data lines. EEPROM is more expensive than EPROM and also is less dense, supporting fewer bits per chip.

The newest form of semiconductor memory is *flash memory* (so named because of the speed with which it can be reprogrammed). First introduced in the mid-1980s, flash memory is intermediate between EPROM and EEPROM in both cost and functionality. Like EEPROM, flash memory uses an electrical erasing technology. An entire flash memory can be erased in one or a few seconds, which is much faster than EPROM. In addition, it is possible to erase just blocks of memory rather than an entire chip. However, flash memory does not provide byte-level erasure. Like EPROM, flash memory uses only one transistor per bit, and so achieves the high density (compared to EEPROM) of EPROM.

Organization

The basic element of a semiconductor memory is the memory cell. Although a variety of electronic technologies are used, all semiconductor memory cells share certain properties:

- They exhibit two stable (or semi-stable) states, which can be used to represent binary 1 and 0.
- They are capable of being written into (at least once), to set the state.
- They are capable of being read to sense the state.

Figure 4-5 depicts the operation of a memory cell. Most commonly, the cell has three functional terminals capable of carrying an electrical signal. The select

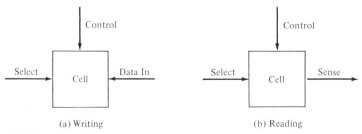

(a) Writing   (b) Reading

FIGURE 4-5. Memory cell operation

terminal, as the name suggests, selects a memory cell for a read or write operation. The control terminal indicates read or write. For writing, the other terminal
provides an electrical signal that sets the state of the cell to 1 or 0. For reading,
that terminal is used for output of the cell's state. The details of the internal
organization, functioning, and timing of the memory cell depend on the specific
integrated-circuit technology used and are beyond the scope of this book. For
our purposes, we will take it as given that individual cells can be selected for
reading and writing operations.

Chip Organization

As with other integrated-circuit products, semiconductor memory comes in
packaged chips (Figure 2-11). Each chip contains an array of memory cells. With
current technology, 64K-bit and 256K-bit chips are common. Chips with 1M-bit
capacity have become dominant in the marketplace, with 4M-bit chips starting to
be used.

In the memory hierarchy as a whole, we saw that there are tradeoffs among
speed, capacity, and cost. These tradeoffs also exist when we consider the organization of memory cells and functional logic on a chip. For semiconductor
memories, two organizational approaches have been used: 2D and 2½D.

Figure 4-6 depicts the 2D organization. In this case, the physical arrangement
of cells in the array is the same as the logical arrangement of words in memory as
perceived outside the memory. The array is organized into W words of B bits
each. For example, a 1K-bit chip might contain 64 16-bit words. The elements of
the array are connected by both horizontal (row) and vertical (column) lines.
Each horizontal line connects to the Select terminal of each cell in its row; each
vertical line connects to the Data-In/Sense terminal of each cell in its column.

The figure also depicts some of the supporting circuitry needed on the chip.
Address lines supply the address of the word to be selected. A total of $\log_2 W$
lines are needed. In our example, 6 address lines are needed to select one of 64
words. These lines are fed into a decoder. The decoder, resident on the chip, has
$\log_2 W$ inputs and W outputs. Its function is to activate a single output based on
the bit pattern of the input. For example, an input of 000101 causes the sixth
output line (numbering the lines from 0 to $W - 1$) to be activated. This output is

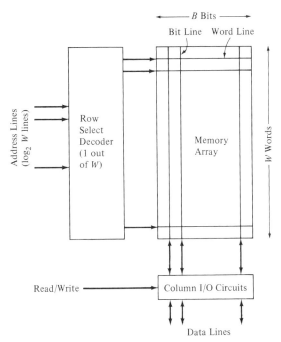

FIGURE 4-6.   2D memory organization

then used to drive one of the word lines. Data lines are used for the input and output of B bits simultaneously to and from a data buffer. On input (write), the bit driver of each bit line is activated for a 1 or 0 according to the value of the corresponding data line. On output (read), the value of each bit line is passed through a sense amplifier and presented to the data lines. The word line, of course, selects which row of cells is used for reading or writing.

Now, this organization is conceptually simple and may produce less delay than other organizations. There are, however, a number of disadvantages, which are best described after presenting the 2½D organization.

With the 2D organization, all of the bits of any given word are on the same chip. With 2½D organization, the bits of a particular word are spread across multiple chips. For example, a 16-bit word might be stored as four bits each on four different chips. The most extreme, and most common, organization is to allow only 1 bit of a given word on a chip. This organization is depicted in Figure 4-7. As before, the chip contains an array of bits. The array is typically square. The array itself functions in the same fashion as for 2D. That is, each cell is connected to a row line and a column line and, for any operation, an entire row of cells is selected. To select the bit of a particular word, the word address is split in two. Part of the address is presented to a decoder that selects one row, as before. The remainder of the address is directed to another decoder connected to the column lines. This decoder activates only one column line for write and

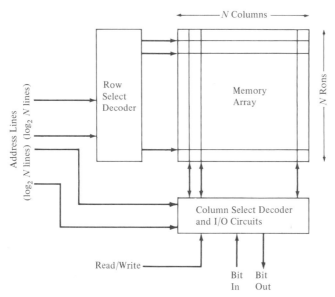

FIGURE 4-7.   2 1/2D one-bit-per-chip memory organization

passes through only one column line for read. The result is that a single bit is read or written in the array. Clearly, other memory chips must be used to supply the remaining bits of the desired word, and we will discuss that shortly. But first, we need to compare the 2D and 2½D organizations and say something about chip packaging.

It should be apparent that there are several disadvantages to the 2D organization as compared to the 2½D. First, consider that, although the 2½D array may be square, the 2D physical structure is very long and narrow, consisting of a relatively large number of words with relatively few bits per word. This leads to an increased logic or circuit requirement compared to 2½D. For a 2D array, each word line must have one signal driver, and each driver must be connected to one logic gate of the decoder. One driver and one sense amplifier are required for each bit line. These requirements are summarized in Table 4-3. The table also shows the requirements for a square, 1-bit-per-chip array. As an example, consider a 256K-bit chip. This could be used, in a 2D organization, to hold 8K words of 32 bits per word. This leads to a circuit count of over 16K, which is equivalent to a modest-sized microprocessor CPU. With a square array of A bits, we have $\sqrt{A} = 512$, and the circuit count is about 1K or 2K, a considerable savings.

Another physical drawback of the 2D organization is that it requires a large number of external data lines. In our example, 32 data lines are needed for the 2D organization, and only 1 for the 2½D. Because pins are a precious commodity on chip packages, the 2½D organization is very desirable.

A final drawback of the 2D organization is the difficulty of making effective use of error-correction circuitry. As we shall see below, it is possible to add logic

TABLE 4-3   Circuit Requirements for Alternative Random-access Memory Organizations

Function	2D	2½D (One-bit, Square Array)
Decoding gates		
Word lines	W	$\sqrt{A}$
Bit lines	O	$\sqrt{A}$
Read/write drivers		
Word lines	W	$\sqrt{A}$
Bit lines	B	1
Sense AMPS	B	1

Note:
A = Number of bits in array
W = Number of 2D words
B = Number of bits per 2D word
A = W · B

and bits to a memory to both detect and correct errors. If the bits of a word are spread across multiple chips, then an electromagnetic disturbance is likely to affect only 1 bit of any given word, and correction is possible. If all the bits of a word are on the same chip, then multiple bits in a single word may be altered, and correction is impossible.

As a final topic related to chip organization, we briefly discuss packaging. As was mentioned in Chapter 2, an integrated circuit is mounted on a package that contains pins for connection to the outside world.

Typically, read-only and read-mostly chips use a 2D organization with all the bits of each word on the chip. As an example, the package for the Intel 27010 EPROM, which is 1 Mbit organized as 128K × 8, is shown in Figure 4-8. The package includes 32 pins, which is one of the standard chip package sizes. The pins support the following signal lines:

- The address of the word being accessed. For 128K words, a total of 16 (2^{16} = 128K) pins are needed (A0-A15).
- The data to be read out, consisting of 8 lines (D0-D7).
- The power supply to the chip (V_{CC}).
- A ground pin (GND).
- A chip enable (CE) pin. Since there may be more than one memory chip, each of which is connected to the same address bus, the CE pin is used to indicate whether or not the address is valid for this chip. The CE pin is activated by logic connected to the higher-order bits of the address bus (i.e., address bits above A15). The use of this signal is illustrated presently.
- An output enable (OE) pin. This is an output control and is used to gate data from the memory array to the output, or data, pins and hence onto the data bus.
- A program (PGM) pin. Initially, and after each erasure, all bits of the EPROM

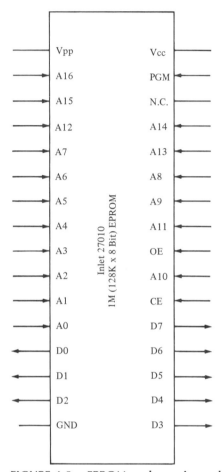

FIGURE 4-8.   EPROM package pins and signals

are in the 1 state. Data is introduced by selectively programming 0s into the desired bit locations. When the program pin and chip enable pins are active, the pattern of 1s and 0s on the data bus is used to program the chip, one byte at a time.

- A program voltage (V_{PP}) that is supplied during programming (write operation).
- An unused pin, labeled N.C. (no internal connect).

A RAM chip is often organized as 1 bit per chip, and a typical pin configuration is shown in Figure 4-9 for the Intel 51C256L 256K × 1-bit RAM. There are several differences from a ROM chip. First, since a RAM can be updated, there are pins for both data in and data out. However, only 1 of each is needed since only 1 bit at a time is accessed. The two states of the write enable (WE) pin are used to designate whether this is a read or a write.

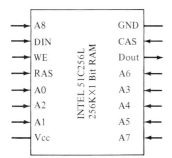

FIGURE 4-9. RAM package pins and signals

Note that there are only 9 address pins (A0-A8), half the number you would expect for a 256K array. This is done to save on the number of pins. The 18 address lines for the 256K bits are passed through select logic external to the chip and multiplexed onto the 9 address lines. First, 9 address signals are passed to the chip to define the row address of the array and then the other 9 address signals are presented for the column address. These signals are accompanied by row address select (RAS) and column address select (CAS) signals to provide timing to the chip. Thus only 11 pins (A0-A8, RAS, CAS) are needed to specify 256K addresses. The package also includes a ground and a power supply.

Incidentally, multiplexed addressing plus the use of square arrays result in a quadrupling of memory size with each new generation of memory chips. One more pin devoted to addressing doubles the number of rows and columns, so the size of the internal memory can grow by a factor of 4. So far, we have gone through the following generations, at a rate of roughly one every three years: 1K, 4K, 16K, 64K, 256K, 1M, 4M.

Module Organization

If a RAM chip contains only 1 bit per word, then clearly we will need at least a number of chips equal to the number of bits per word. As an example, Figure 4-10 shows how a memory module consisting of 256K 8-bit words could be organized. For 256K words, an 18-bit address is needed and is supplied to the module from some external source (e.g., the address lines of a bus to which the module is attached). The address is presented to 8 256K × 1-bit chips, each of which provides the input/output of 1 bit.

This organization works as long as the size of memory equals the number of bits per chip. In the case in which larger memory is required, an array of chips is needed. Figure 4-11 shows the possible organization of a memory consisting of 1 M-word by 8 bits per word. In this case, we have four columns of chips, each column containing 256K words arranged as in Figure 4-8. For 1 M-word, 20 address lines are needed. The 18 least significant bits are routed to all 32 modules. The high-order 2 bits are input to a group select logic module that sends a chip enable signal to one of the four columns of modules.

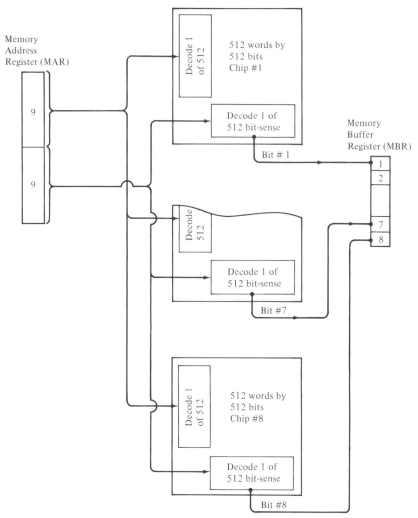

FIGURE 4-10.   256K-byte memory organization

Error Correction

A semiconductor memory system is subject to errors. These can be categorized as hard failures and soft errors. A *hard failure* is a permanent physical defect so that the memory cell or cells affected cannot reliably store data, but become stuck at 0 or 1 or switch erratically between 0 and 1. Hard errors can be caused by harsh environmental abuse, manufacturing defects, and wear. A *soft error* is a random, nondestructive event that alters the contents of one or more memory cells, without damaging the memory. Soft errors can be caused by power supply problems or alpha particles. These particles result from radioactive decay and

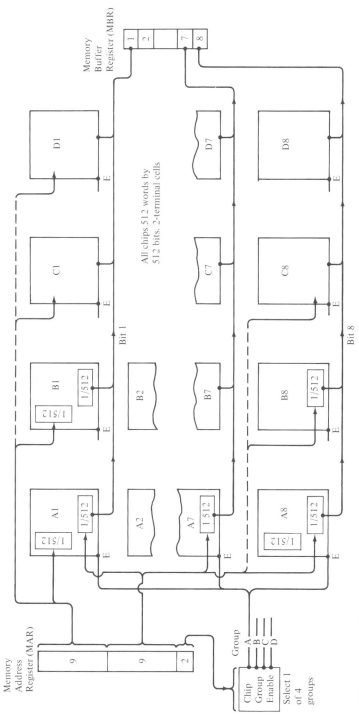

FIGURE 4-11.   1M-byte memory organization

are distressingly common because radioactive nuclei are found in small quantities in nearly all materials. Both hard and soft errors are clearly undesirable, and most modern main memory systems include logic for both detecting and correcting errors.

Figure 4-12 illustrates in general terms how the process is carried out. When data are to be read into memory, a calculation, depicted as a function f, is performed on the data to produce a code. Both the code and the data are stored. Thus, if an M-bit word of data is to be stored, and the code is of length K bits, then the actual size of the stored word is M + K bits.

When the previously stored word is read out, the code is used to detect and possibly correct errors. A new set of K code bits is generated from the M data bits and compared to the fetched code bits. The comparison yields one of three results:

- No errors are detected. The fetched data bits are sent out.
- An error is detected and it is possible to correct the error. The data bits plus error-correction bits are fed into a corrector, which produces a corrected set of M bits to be sent out.
- An error is detected, but it is not possible to correct it. This condition is reported.

Codes that operate in this fashion are referred to as *error-correcting codes*. A code is characterized by the number of bit errors in a word that it can correct and detect.

The simplest of the error-correcting codes is the *Hamming code* devised by Richard Hamming at Bell Laboratories. Figure 4-13 uses Venn diagrams to illustrate the use of this code on 4-bit words (M = 4). With three intersecting circles, there are seven compartments. We assign the 4 data bits to the inner compartments (Figure 4-13a). The remaining compartments are filled with what are called *parity bits*. Each parity bit is chosen so that the total number of 1s in its circle is even (Figure 4-13b). Thus, since circle A includes three data 1s, the

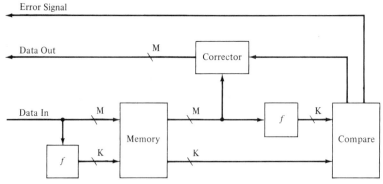

FIGURE 4-12. Error-correcting code function

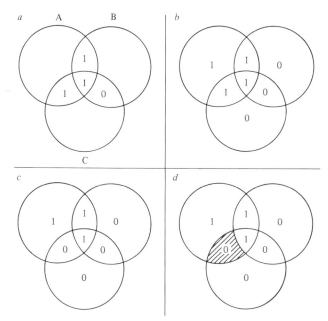

FIGURE 4-13. Hamming error-correcting code

parity bit in that circle is set to 1. Now, if an error changes one of the data bits (Figure 4-13c), it is easily found. By checking the parity bits, discrepancies are found in circle A and circle C but not in circle B. Only one of the seven compartments is in A and C but not B. The error can therefore be corrected by changing that bit.

To clarify the concepts involved, we will develop a code that can detect and correct single-bit errors in 8-bit words (example based on [ALTN79]).

To start, let us determine how long the code must be. Referring to Figure 4-12, the comparison logic receives as input two K-bit values. A bit-by-bit comparison is done by taking the exclusive-or of the two inputs. The result is called the *syndrome word*. Thus, each bit of the syndrome is 0 or 1 according as there is or is not a match in that bit position for the two inputs.

The syndrome word is therefore K bits wide and has a range of 2^K values between 0 and $2^K - 1$. The value 0 indicates that no error was detected, leaving $2^K - 1$ values to indicate, if there is an error, which bit was in error. Now, since an error could occur on any of the M data bits or K check bits, we must have

$$2^K - 1 \geq M + K$$

This equation gives the number of bits needed to correct a single bit error in a word containing M data bits. Table 4-4 lists the number of check bits required for various data word-lengths.

TABLE 4-4 Increase in Word Length With Error Correction

Data Bits	Single-Error Correction		Single-Error Correction/ Double-Error Detection	
	Check Bits	% Increase	Check Bits	% Increase
8	4	50	5	62.5
16	5	31.25	6	37.5
32	6	18.75	7	21.875
64	7	10.94	8	12.5
128	8	6.25	9	7.03
256	9	3.52	10	3.91

From this table, we see that a word of 8 data bits requires 4 check bits. For convenience, we would like to generate a 4-bit syndrome with the following characteristics:

- If the syndrome contains all 0's, no error has been detected.
- If the syndrome contains one and only one bit set to 1, then an error has occurred in one of the 4 check bits. No correction is needed.
- If the syndrome contains more than one bit set to 1, then the numerical value of the syndrome indicates the position of the data bit in error. This data bit is inverted for correction.

To achieve these characteristics, the data and check bits are arranged into a 12-bit word as depicted in Figure 4-14. The bit positions are numbered from 1 to 12. Those bit positions whose position numbers are powers of 2 are designated as check bits. The check bits are calculated as follows, where the symbol $\oplus$ designates the exclusive-or operation:

$$C1 = M1 \oplus M2 \oplus \quad\quad M4 \oplus M5 \quad\quad \oplus M7$$
$$C2 = M1 \oplus \quad\quad M3 \oplus M4 \quad\quad \oplus M6 \oplus M7$$

```
Bit Position
    Position
    Number  Check Bit
            Data Bit
12  1 1 0 0    M8
11  1 0 1 1    M7
10  1 0 1 0    M6
 9  1 0 0 1    M5
 8  1 0 0 0 C8
 7  0 1 1 1    M4
 6  0 1 1 0    M3
 5  0 1 0 1    M2
 4  0 1 0 0 C4
 3  0 0 1 1    M1
 2  0 0 1 0 C2
 1  0 0 0 1 C1
```

FIGURE 4-14. Layout of data bits and check bits

$$C4 = \quad M2 \oplus M3 \oplus M4 \qquad\qquad\qquad \oplus M8$$
$$C8 = \qquad\qquad\qquad\qquad M5 \oplus M6 \oplus M7 \oplus M8$$

Each check bit operates on every data bit position whose position number contains a 1 in the corresponding column position. Thus data bit positions 3, 5, 7, 9, and 11 all contain the term 2^0; bit positions 3, 6, 7, 10, and 11 all contain the term 2^1; bit positions 5, 6, 7, and 12 all contain the term 2^2; and bit positions 9, 10, 11, and 12 all contain the term 2^3. Looked at another way, bit position n is checked by those bits C_i such that $\Sigma i = n$. For example, position 7 is checked by bits in position 4, 2, and 1; and $7 = 4 + 2 + 1$.

Let us verify that this scheme works with an example. Assume that the 8-bit input word is 00111001, with data bit M1 in the rightmost position. The calculations are as follows:

$$C1 = 1 \oplus 0 \oplus 1 \oplus 1 \oplus 0 = 1$$
$$C2 = 1 \oplus 0 \oplus 1 \oplus 1 \oplus 0 = 1$$
$$C4 = 0 \oplus 0 \oplus 1 \oplus 0 = 1$$
$$C8 = 1 \oplus 1 \oplus 0 \oplus 0 = 0$$

Suppose now that data bit 3 sustains an error and is changed from 0 to 1. When the check bits are recalculated, we have

$$C1 = 1 \oplus 0 \oplus 1 \oplus 1 \oplus 0 = 1$$
$$C2 = 1 \oplus 1 \oplus 1 \oplus 1 \oplus 0 = 0$$
$$C4 = 0 \oplus 1 \oplus 1 \oplus 0 = 0$$
$$C8 = 1 \oplus 1 \oplus 0 \oplus 0 = 0$$

When the new check bits are compared with the old check bits, the syndrome word is formed.

	C8	C4	C2	C1
	0	1	1	1
$\oplus$	0	0	0	1
	0	1	1	0

The result is 0110, indicating that bit position 6, which contains data bit 3, is in error.

Figure 4-15 illustrates the above calculation. The data and check bits are positioned properly in the 12-bit word. By laying out the position number of each data bit in columns, the 1s in each row indicate the data bits checked by the check bit for that row. Since the result is affected only by 1s, only the columns containing 1s are circled for identification. The check bits can then be calculated along the rows. The results are shown for the original data bits and for the data bits including the error.

The code just described is known as a *single-error-correcting* (SEC) code. More commonly, semiconductor memory is equipped with a single-error-correcting, double-error-detecting (SEC-DED) code. As Table 4-4 shows, such codes require 1 additional bit compared to SEC codes.

Bit Position	12	11	10	9	8	7	6	5	4	3	2	1	
Data Bit	M8	M7	M6	M5		M4	M3	M2		M1			
Check Bit					C8				C4		C2	C1	
	1	1	1	1	0	0	0		0				C8 0
	1	0	0	0		1	1	1	0				C4 1
	0	1	1	0		1	1	0			1		C2 1
	0	1	0	1		1	0	1			1		C1 1
Word Stored As:	0	0	1	1	0	1	0	0	1	1	1	1	
Word Fetched As:	0	0	1	1	0	1	1	0	1	1	1	1	
	1	1	1	1	0	0	0		0				C8 0
	1	0	0	0		1	1	1	0				C4 0
	0	1	1	0		1	1	0			1		C2 0
	0	1	0	1		1	0	1			1		C1 1

FIGURE 4-15. Check bit generation

Figure 4-16 illustrates how such a code works, again with a 4-bit data word. The sequence shows that if two errors occur (Figure 4-16c), the checking procedure goes astray (d), and worsens the problem by creating a third error (e). To overcome the problem, an eighth bit is added that is set so that the total number of 1s in the diagram is even. The extra parity bit catches the error (f).

An error-correcting code enhances the reliability of the memory at the cost of added complexity. With a one-bit-per-chip organization, a SEC-DED code is generally considered adequate. For example, the IBM 30XX implementations use an 8-bit SEC-DED code for each 64 bits of data in main memory. Thus, the size of main memory is actually about 12% larger than is apparent to the user. The VAX computers use a 7-bit SEC-DEC for each 32 bits of memory, for a 22% overhead.

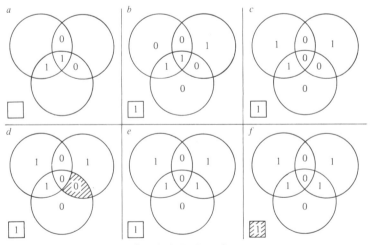

FIGURE 4-16. Hamming SEC-DEC code

4.3

CACHE MEMORY

Motivation

On all instruction cycles, the CPU accesses memory at least once, to fetch the instruction, and often one or more additional times to fetch operands or store results. The rate at which the CPU can execute instructions is clearly limited by the memory cycle time. This limitation has in fact been a significant problem because of the persistent mismatch between processor and main memory speeds. Figure 4-17, which may be considered representative, illustrates this by comparing, over time, the memory cycle time and the processor cycle time. The latter is the time required for the CPU to perform the shortest "primitive" operation, such as memory reading or writing, opcode execution, or checking for interrupts.

The figure shows that memory speed has not kept up with processor speed. What we are faced with here is a tradeoff among speed, cost, and size. Ideally, the main memory should be built with the same technology as that of the CPU registers, giving memory cycle times comparable to processor cycle times. This has always been too expensive a strategy. The solution is to exploit the principle

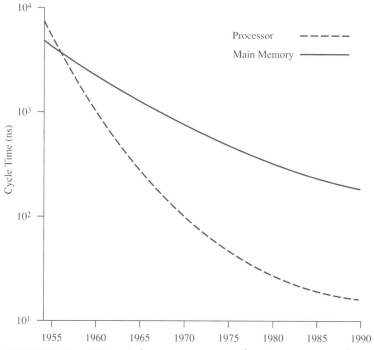

FIGURE 4-17.   IBM mainframe processor and main memory performance

of locality by providing a small, fast memory between the CPU and main memory. This memory is known as *cache memory*.

Principles

Cache memory is intended to give memory speed approaching that of the fastest memories available, and at the same time provide a large memory size at the price of less expensive types of semiconductor memories. The concept is illustrated in Figure 4-18. There is a relatively large and slower main memory together with a smaller, faster cache memory. The cache contains a copy of portions of main memory. When the CPU attempts to read a word of memory, a check is made to determine if the word is in the cache. If so, the word is delivered to the CPU. If not, a block of main memory, consisting of some fixed number of words, is read into the cache and then the word is delivered to the CPU. Because of the phenomenon of locality of reference, when a block of data is fetched into the cache to satisfy a single memory reference, it is likely that future references will be to other words in the block.

Figure 4-19 depicts the structure of a cache/main-memory system. Main memory consists of up to 2^n addressable words, with each word having a unique n-bit address. For mapping purposes, this memory is considered to consist of a number of fixed-length blocks of K words each. That is, there are $M = 2^n/K$ blocks. Cache consists of C slots of K words each, and the number of slots is considerably less than the number of main memory blocks ($C \ll M$). At any time, some subset of the blocks of memory resides in slots in the cache. If a word in a block of memory is read, that block is transferred to one of the slots of the cache. Since there are more blocks than slots, an individual slot cannot be uniquely and permanently dedicated to a particular block. Thus, each slot includes a tag that

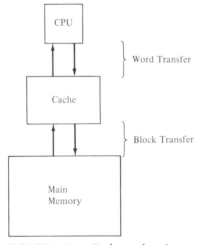

FIGURE 4-18.   Cache and main memory

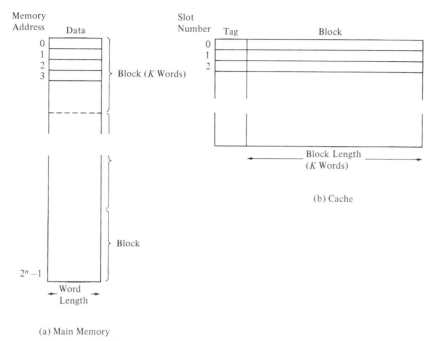

(a) Main Memory

FIGURE 4-19.   Cache/main memory structure

identifies which particular block is currently being stored. The tag is usually a portion of the main memory address, as described later in this section.

Figure 4-20 illustrates the read operation. The CPU generates the address, RA, of a word to be read. If the word is contained in the cache, it is delivered to the CPU. Otherwise, the block containing that word is loaded into the cache and the word is delivered to the CPU.

A discussion of the performance parameters related to cache use is contained in Appendix 4A.

Elements of Cache Design

Although there are a large number of cache implementations, there are a few basic design elements that serve to classify and differentiate cache architectures. Table 4-5 lists key elements.

Cache Size

The first element, cache size, has already been discussed. We would like the size of the cache to be small enough so that the overall average cost per bit is close to that of main memory alone and large enough so that the overall average access time is close to that of the cache alone. There are several other motivations for

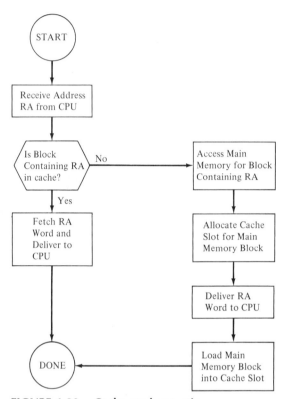

FIGURE 4-20. Cache read operation

minimizing cache size. The larger the cache, the larger the number of gates involved in addressing the cache. The result is that large caches tend to be slightly slower than small ones—even when built with the same integrated-circuit technology and put in the same place on chip and circuit board. Cache

TABLE 4-5   Elements of Cache Design

Cache Size	Write Policy
	Write through
Mapping Function	Write back
Direct	Write once
Associative	
Set-associative	**Block Size**
Replacement Algorithm	
Least-recently used (LRU)	
First-in-first-out (FIFO)	
Least-frequently used (LFU)	
Random	

size is also limited by the available chip and board area. In Appendix 4A, we point out that a number of studies have suggested that cache sizes of between 1K and 128K words would be optimum. Because the performance of the cache is very sensitive to the nature of the workload, it is impossible to arrive at an "optimum" cache size.

Mapping Function

Another key element of cache design is the mapping function, which maps blocks of memory into cache locations. Three techniques can be used: direct, associative, and set associative. We will examine these three alternatives with an example, based on an example in [INTE87]. Consider a cache that can hold 64 Kbytes. Data is transferred between main memory and the cache in blocks of 4 bytes each. This means that the cache is organized as 16K slots of 4 bytes each. The main memory consists of 16 Mbytes, with each byte directly addressable by a 24-bit address (2^{24} = 16M). For mapping purposes, we can consider the main memory to consist of 4M blocks of 4 bytes each.

Since there are fewer cache slots than main memory blocks, an algorithm is needed for mapping main memory blocks into cache slots. Further, a means is needed for determining which main memory block currently occupies a cache slot. The simplest technique, known as **direct mapping,** allows each block of main memory only one possible cache slot. This is illustrated in Figure 4-21a.[1] The mapping is:

S = A modulo C

where

S = cache slot number
A = main memory block number
C = number of slots in the cache

In the example, C = 16K = 2^{14} and S = A modulo 2^{14}. The mapping function is easily implemented using the 24-bit address. The least significant (rightmost) two bits serve to identify a unique byte within a block of main memory. The remaining 22 bits specify one of the 2^{22} = 4M blocks of main memory. The cache logic interprets these 22 bits as an 8-bit tag (most significant portion) and a 14-bit slot (least significant portion). The slot identifies a unique slot within the cache. It also gives the number of the block in main memory, modulo 2^{14}. This determines the mapping of blocks into slots. Thus, blocks 000000, 010000, . . ., FF0000 of main memory map into cache slot 0; blocks 000001, 010001, . . ., FF0001 map into cache slot 1; and so on, down to blocks 00FFF8, 01FFF8, . . ., FFFFF8, which map into slot 3FFE. Thus, the use of a portion of the address as a slot number provides a unique mapping of each block of main memory into the

---

[1] In the figure, addresses and memory values are represented in hexadecimal notation for convenience. For the reader unfamiliar with this notation, see the appendix to Chapter 7.

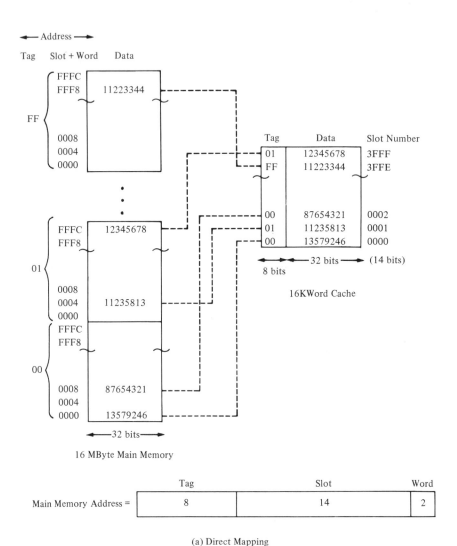

(a) Direct Mapping

FIGURE 4-21. Cache/main memory mapping

cache. When a block is actually read into its assigned slot, it is necessary to tag it to distinguish it from other blocks that can fit into that slot. The final 8 bits of the address serve this purpose. Note that no two blocks that map into the same slot have the same tag number. Thus, blocks 000000, 010000, . . ., FF0000 have tag numbers 00, 01, . . ., FF respectively.

Thus, referring back to Figure 4-20, a read operation works as follows. The cache system is presented with a 24-bit address. The 14-bit slot number is used as an index into the cache to access a particular slot. If the 8-bit tag number matches the tag number for that slot, then the 2-bit word number is used to

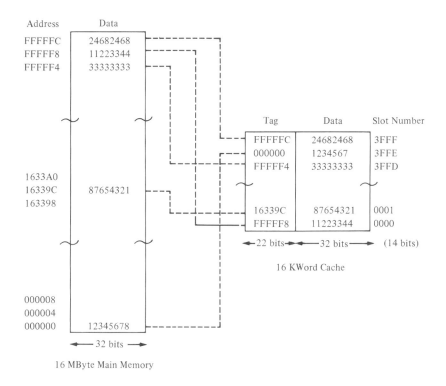

Address   Data

FFFFFC   24682468
FFFFF8   11223344
FFFFF4   33333333

1633A0
16339C   87654321
163398

000008
000004
000000   12345678

← 32 bits →

16 MByte Main Memory

Tag   Data   Slot Number

FFFFFC   24682468   3FFF
000000   1234567   3FFE
FFFFF4   33333333   3FFD

16339C   87654321   0001
FFFFF8   11223344   0000

←22 bits→ ←32 bits→   (14 bits)

16 KWord Cache

	Tag	Word
Main Memory Address =	22	2

(b) Associative Mapping

FIGURE 4-21.   (continued)

select one of the 4 bytes in that slot. Otherwise, the 22-bit tag-plus-slot field is used to fetch a block from main memory. The actual address that is used for the fetch is the 22-bit tag concatenated with two zero bits. Thus, four bytes are fetched that start on a block boundary.

The direct mapping technique is simple and inexpensive to implement. Its main disadvantage is that there is a fixed cache location for any given block. Thus, if a program happens to repeatedly reference words from two different blocks that map into the same slot, then the blocks will be continually swapped in the cache and the hit ratio will be low.

A technique that overcomes the disadvantage of the direct mapping approach is **associative mapping,** which permits a main memory block to be loaded into any slot of the cache. In our example (Figure 4-21b), the main memory address

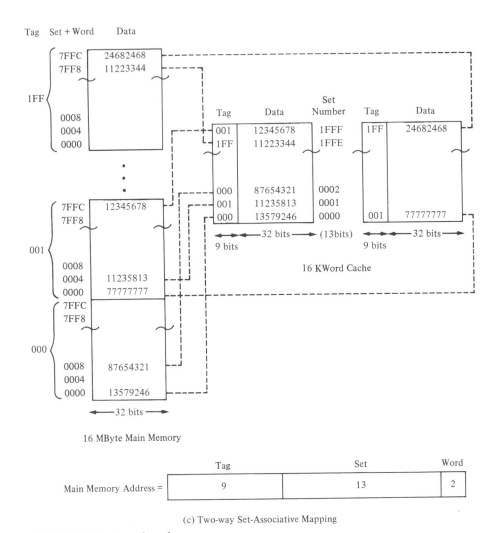

(c) Two-way Set-Associative Mapping

FIGURE 4-21. (continued)

consists of a 22-bit tag and a 2-bit byte number. A main memory block can be stored in any slot, and its 22-bit tag is stored with it. To determine whether a block is in the cache, logic is needed to simultaneously examine every slot's tag for a match.

With associative mapping, there is flexibility as to which block to replace when a new block is read into the cache. Replacement algorithms, discussed later in this section, are designed to maximize the hit ratio. The main disadvantage of the associative approach is the complex circuitry required to examine the tags of all cache slots in parallel.

Set-associative mapping is a compromise that captures the advantages of both the direct and associative approaches. In this case, the cache is divided into I sets, each of which consists of J slots. We have:

$C = I \times J$
$K = A \text{ modulo } I$

where K = cache set number. With this algorithm, the block containing address A can be mapped into any of the slots in set I. Our example (Figure 4-21c) is a two-way set associative mapping; that is, two blocks per slot. Again, as with direct mapping, the main memory address is interpreted as three fields. In this case, the 13-bit set number identifies a unique set of two slots within the cache. It also gives the number of the block in main memory, modulo 2^{13}. This determines the mapping of blocks into slots. Thus, blocks 000000, 00A000, . . ., FF1000 of main memory map into cache set 0. Since cache set 0 consists of two slots, any block can be loaded into either of the two slots in the set. Note that no two blocks that map into the same set of two slots have the same tag number. For a read operation, the 13-bit set number is used to determine which set of two slots is to be examined. Both slots in the set are examined for a match with the tag number of the address to be accessed.

Notice that in the extreme case of I = C, J = 1, the set-associative technique reduces to direct mapping, and for I = 1, J = C, it reduces to associative mapping. The use of two slots per set (I = C/2, J = 2) is the most common set-associative organization. It significantly improves the hit ratio over direct mapping. Four-way set-associative (I = C/4, J = 4) makes a small additional improvement for a relatively small additional cost [MAYB84, SMIT88, HILL89]. Further increases in set size have little effect.

Replacement Algorithms

When a new block is brought into the cache, one of the existing blocks must be replaced. For direct mapping, there is only one possible slot for any particular block, and no choice is possible. For the associative and set-associative techniques, a replacement algorithm is needed. To achieve high speed, such an algorithm must be implemented in hardware. A number of algorithms have been tried: we mention four of the most common. Probably the most effective is **least-recently used (LRU):** Replace that block in the set which has been in the cache longest with no reference to it. For two-way set-associative, this is easily implemented. Each slot includes a USE bit. When a slot is referenced, its USE bit is set to 1 and the USE bit of the other slot in that set is set to 0. When a block is to be read into the set, the slot whose USE bit is 0 is used. Since we are assuming that more-recently used memory locations are more likely to be referenced, LRU should give the best hit ratio. Another possibility is **first-in-first-out (FIFO):** Replace that block in the set which has been in the cache longest. FIFO is easily implemented as a round-robin or circular buffer technique. Still another possibility is **least-frequently used (LFU)**: replace that block in the set which has experienced the fewest references. LFU could be implemented by associating a counter with each slot. A technique not based on usage is to just pick a slot from among the candidate slots at **random.** Simulation studies have shown that random replacement provides only slightly inferior performance to an algorithm based on usage [SMIT82].

Write Policy

Before a block that is resident in the cache can be replaced, it is necessary to consider whether it has been altered in the cache but not in main memory. If it has not, then the old block in the cache may be overwritten. If it has, that means that at least one write operation has been performed on a word in that slot of the cache, and main memory must be updated accordingly. A variety of write policies, with performance and economic tradeoffs, are possible. There are two problems to contend with. First, more than one device may have access to main memory. For example, an I/O module may be able to read/write directly to memory. If a word has been altered only in the cache, then the corresponding memory word is invalid. Further, if the I/O device has altered main memory, then the cache word is invalid. A more complex problem occurs when multiple CPUs are attached to the same bus and each CPU has its own local cache. Then, if a word is altered in one cache, it could conceivably invalidate a word in other caches.

The simplest technique is called **write through.** Using this technique, all write operations are made to main memory as well as to the cache, ensuring that main memory is always valid. Any other CPU-cache module can monitor traffic to main memory to maintain consistency within its own cache. The main disadvantage of this technique is that it generates substantial memory traffic and may create a bottleneck. An alternative technique, known as **write back,** minimizes memory writes. With write back, updates are made only in the cache. When an update occurs, an UPDATE bit associated with the slot is set. Then, when a block is replaced, it is written back to main memory if and only if the UPDATE bit is set. The problem with write back is that portions of main memory are invalid, and hence accesses by I/O modules can be allowed only through the cache. This makes for complex circuitry and a potential bottleneck. Experience has shown that the percentage of memory references that are writes is on the order of 15 percent [SMIT82]. Consequently, the simple write-through policy is more commonly used than write back.

In a bus organization in which more than one device (typically a processor) has a cache and main memory is shared, a new problem is introduced. If data in one cache is altered, this invalidates not only the corresponding word in main memory, but also that same word in other caches (if any other cache happens to have that same word). Even if a write-through policy is used, the other caches may contain invalid data. A system that prevents this problem is said to maintain cache coherency. Possible approaches to cache coherency include:

- *Bus Watching with Write Through:* Each cache controller monitors the address lines to detect write operations to memory by other bus masters. If another master writes to a location in shared memory which also resides in the cache memory, the cache controller invalidates that cache entry. This strategy depends on the use of a write-through policy by all cache controllers.
- *Hardware Transparency:* Additional hardware is used to ensure that all updates to main memory via cache are reflected in all caches. Thus, if one processor modifies a word in its cache, this update is written to main memory. In addition, any matching words in other caches are similarly updated.
- *Non-cacheable Memory:* Only a portion of main memory is shared by more than one processor, and is designated as non-cacheable. In such a system, all accesses to shared memory are cache misses, because the shared memory is never copied into the cache. The non-cacheable memory can be identified using chip-select logic or high-address bits.

Cache coherency is an active field of research, and it is likely that simpler and more effective ways of ensuring consistency will be developed in the next several years.

Block Size

A final design element is the block, or line, size. When a block of data is retrieved and placed in the cache, not only the desired word but some number of adjacent words are retrieved. As the block size increases from very small to larger sizes, the hit ratio will at first increase because of the principle of locality: the high probability that data in the vicinity of a referenced word is likely to be referenced in the near future. As the block size increases, more useful data is brought into the cache. The hit ratio will begin to decrease, however, as the block becomes even bigger and the probability of using the newly fetched information becomes less than the probability of reusing the information that has to be replaced. Two specific effects come into play:

1. Larger blocks reduce the number of blocks that fit into a cache. Because each block fetch overwrites older cache contents, a small number of blocks results in data being overwritten shortly after it is fetched.
2. As a block becomes larger, each additional word is farther from the requested word, therefore less likely to be needed in the near future.

The relationship between block size and hit ratio is complex, depending on the locality characteristics of a particular program, and no definitive optimum value has been found. A size of from 4 to 8 addressable units (words or bytes) seems reasonably close to optimum [SMIT87a, PRZY88, PRZY90].

Examples

Intel 80486

One of the key differences[2] between the Intel 80386 and the 80486 is that the latter includes an on-chip cache. Figure 4-22 illustrates the architecture.

The 80486 cache size is 8K bytes, using a block size (called *line size* in the Intel literature) of 16 bytes and a four-way set associative organization. A write-through policy is used: each write to the cache also causes a contemporaneous write to external memory. Performance studies based on simulation have yielded a hit rate of 96% for DOS applications and 92% for Unix and OS/2 applications. If greater hit ratios are needed, the internal cache can be supplemented by a second external cache that is larger and slower. Thus, there are two levels of cacheing between the processor and main memory.

The replacement algorithm is referred to as pseudo-least-recently-used. It requires the use of three bits per set, compared to a true LRU policy, which would require six bits. Associated with each of the 128 sets of four lines (labeled L1, L2, L3, L4) are three bits, B0, B1, and B2. These are set according to the following rules with each access to the set:

1. If the access is to L0 or L1, $B0 \leftarrow 1$.
2. If the access is to L0, $B1 \leftarrow 1$.
3. If the access is to L1, $B1 \leftarrow 0$.
4. If the access is to L2 or L3, $B0 \leftarrow 0$.
5. If the access is to L2, $B2 \leftarrow 1$.
6. If the access is to L3, $B2 \leftarrow 0$.

The replacement algorithm works as follows (Figure 4-23): When a line must be replaced, the cache will first determine whether the most recent use was from L0 and L1 or L2 and L3. Then the cache will determine which of the pair of blocks was least recently used and mark it for replacement. When the cache is initialized or flushed, all 128 sets of three LRU bits are set to zero.

The 80486 deals with the issue of cache coherency in the following way: A separate external address monitor is attached to the 80486 and to the bus. Whenever a device other than the 80486 writes to a memory location that may be in the 80486's cache, the external logic drives the address onto the 80486 address pins and signals the 80486 over a control line. The 80486 compares the supplied address to the cache tags and, if there is a match, invalidates the cache block. This access to the cache can interfere with the normal cache access of the processor. However, the processor reads from the cache a block at a time. If the read is for program instructions, these are placed in a prefetch queue (Figure 4-22). In the absence of a branch, this minimizes the number of times that the cache must be accessed for instructions.

---

[2] The other differences: several instructions to support multiprocessing, and the inclusion of floating-point instructions.

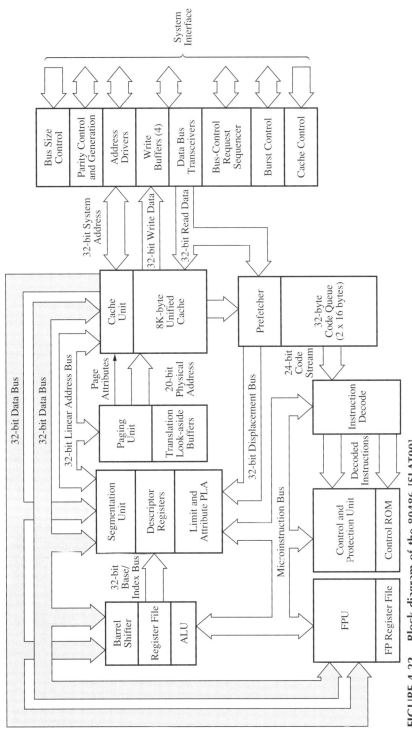

FIGURE 4-22.   Block diagram of the 80486 [SLAT90]

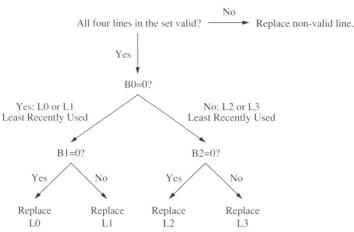

FIGURE 4-23. 80486 on-chip cache replacement strategy [INTE90]

The inclusion of an on-board cache in a microprocessor significantly affects the character of the bus traffic to and from the microprocessor. For a processor without a cache, it is typically the case that the largest fraction of bus traffic consists of program fetches, and most of the remaining data transfers are data reads. A cached system such as the 80486 satisfies most fetch and read cycles internally. All 80486 writes, however, pass through to the external bus, with the result that the majority of bus traffic is data writes. To decouple write operations from the performance of external bus and memory systems, the 80486 contains four internal write buffers. A write operation results in placing the written quantity and its address into the buffer. It is subsequently written out across the bus at the earliest opportunity. Only if all four buffers are full awaiting bus access is the processor stalled on a write operation.

The cache is controlled by two bits in one of the control registers, labeled the CD and NW bits (Table 4-6). CD enables and disables the cache; NW controls memory write-throughs and invalidate operations. There are also two 80460 instructions that can be used to control the cache: INVD flushes the cache memory and signals the external cache (if any) to flush. WBINVD performs the same function and also signals an external write-back cache to write back modified blocks before flushing.

TABLE 4-6   80486 Cache Operating Modes

Control Bits		Operating Mode		
CD	NW	Cache Fills	Write-Throughs	Invalidates
0	0	Enabled	Enabled	Enabled
1	0	Disabled	Enabled	Enabled
1	1	Disabled	Disabled	Disabled

Note: CD = 0; NW = 1 is an invalid combination.

VAX Computers

A variety of cache structures have been tried on the VAX family of computers, perhaps reflecting the fact that cache design remains an art rather than a science. The VAX architecture employs a 30-bit address that allows for a total of 1 Gbyte (billion bytes) of addressable main memory. The VAX 11/780, 11/785, and 8600 use a two-way set-associative organization, with random replacement and write-through policies. The cache size for these three models is 8 Kbytes, 32 Kbytes, and 16 Kbytes, respectively. All use a block size of 8 bytes. The VAX 8800 differs from the above in that it uses a direct mapping policy; the size of the 8800 cache is 64 Kbytes.

IBM Mainframes

The IBM 309X series of mainframe computers employs a cache size ranging from 16 to 64 Kbytes. The address size is 31 bits. A 4-way set-associative organization is used, with a block of 64 bytes. An LRU policy is used for replacing one of the four blocks in a set, and a write-through policy is used.

4.4

MAGNETIC DISK

A disk is a circular platter constructed of metal or of plastic coated with a magnetizable material. Data are recorded on and later retrieved from the disk via a conducting coil named the *head*. During a read or write operation, the head is stationary while the platter rotates beneath it.

The write mechanism is based on the fact that electricity flowing through a coil produces a magnetic field. Pulses are sent to the head, and magnetic patterns are recorded on the surface below, with different patterns for positive and negative currents. The read mechanism is based on the fact that a magnetic field moving relative to a coil produces an electrical current in the coil. When the surface of the disk passes under the head, it generates a current of the same polarity as the one already recorded.

Data Organization and Formatting

The head is a relatively small device capable of reading to or writing from a portion of the platter rotating beneath it. This gives rise to the organization of data on the platter in a concentric set of rings, called *tracks*. Each track is the same width as the head.

Figure 4-24 depicts this data layout. Adjacent tracks are separated by *gaps*. This prevents, or at least minimizes, errors due to misalignment of the head or simply interference of magnetic fields. To simplify the electronics, the same number of bits are typically stored on each track. Thus the *density*, in bits per

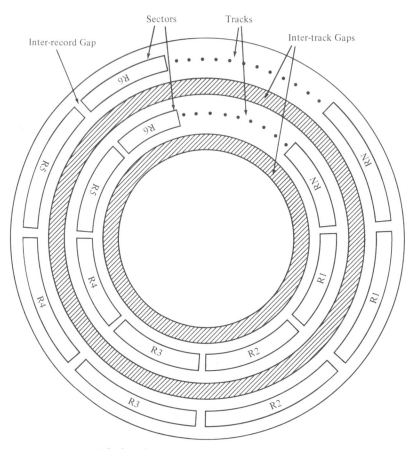

FIGURE 4-24.   Disk data layout

linear inch, increases as we move from the outermost track to the innermost track (this same phenomenon is present on a phonograph record).

As was mentioned earlier, data are transferred to and from the disk in blocks. Typically, the block is smaller than the capacity of a track. Accordingly, data are stored in block-size regions known as *sectors* (Figure 4-24). There are typically between 10 and 100 sectors per track, and these may be of either fixed or variable length. To avoid imposing unreasonable precision requirements on the system, adjacent sectors are separated by intra-track (inter-record) gaps.

How are sector positions within a track identified? Clearly, there must be some starting point on the track and a way of identifying the start and end of each sector. These requirements are handled by means of control data recorded on the disk. Thus, the disk is formatted with some extra data used only by the disk drive and not accessible to the user.

An example of disk formatting is shown in Figure 4-25. In this case, each track contains 30 fixed-length sectors of 600 bytes each. Each sector holds 512 bytes of

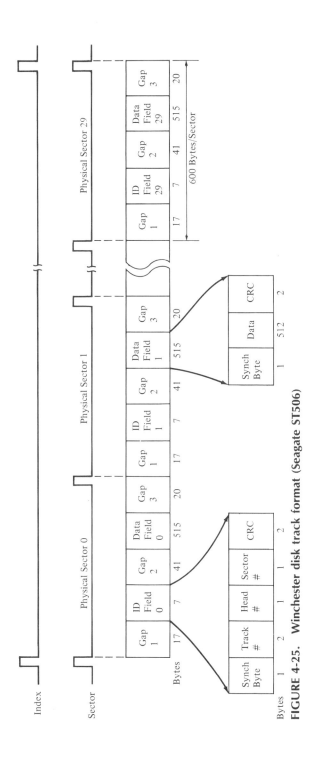

FIGURE 4-25. Winchester disk track format (Seagate ST506)

data plus control information useful to the disk controller. The ID field is a unique identifier or address used to locate a particular sector. The SYNCH byte is a special bit pattern that delimits the beginning of the field. The track number identifies a track on a surface. The head number identifies a head, since this disk has multiple surfaces (explained presently). The ID and data fields each contain an error-detecting code.

Characteristics

Table 4-7 lists the major characteristics that differentiate among the various types of disks. First, the head may either be fixed or movable with respect to the radial direction of the platter. In a *fixed-head* disk, there is one read/write head per track. All of the heads are mounted on a rigid arm that extends across all tracks (Figure 4-26a). In a movable head disk, there is only one read/write head (Figure 4-26b). As before, the head is mounted on an arm. Since the head must be able to be positioned above any track, the arm can be extended or retracted for this purpose.

The disk itself is mounted in a disk drive, which consists of the arm, a shaft that rotates the disk, and the electronics needed for input and output of binary data. A *nonremovable disk* is permanently mounted in the disk drive. The *removable disk* can be removed and replaced with another disk. The advantage of the latter type is that unlimited amounts of data are available with a limited number of disk systems. Furthermore, a disk may be moved from one computer system to another.

For most disks, the magnetizable coating is applied to both sides of the platter, which is then referred to as *double-sided*. Some less expensive disk systems use *single-sided* disks.

Some disk drives accommodate *multiple platters* stacked vertically about an inch apart (Figure 4-27). Multiple arms are provided. The platters come as a unit known as a *disk pack*.

Finally, the head mechanism provides a clear classification of disks into three types. Traditionally, the read/write head has been positioned a fixed distance

TABLE 4-7   Characteristics of Disk Systems

Head Motion	**Platters**
Fixed head (one per track)	Single-platter
Movable head (one per surface)	Multiple-platter
Disk Portability	**Head Mechanism**
Nonremovable disk	Contact (floppy)
Removable disk	Fixed gap
	Aerodynamic gap (Winchester)
Sides	
Single-sided	
Double-sided	

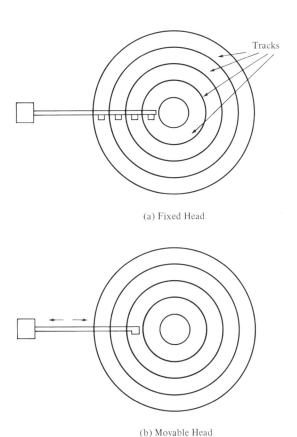

(a) Fixed Head

(b) Movable Head

FIGURE 4-26.   **Fixed and movable head disks**

above the platter, allowing an air gap. At the other extreme is a head mechanism that actually comes into physical contact with the medium during a read or write operation. This mechanism is used with the *floppy disk,* which is a small, flexible platter and the least expensive type of disk.

To understand the third type of disk, we need to comment on the relationship between data density and the size of the air gap. The head must generate or sense an electromagnetic field of sufficient magnitude to write and read properly. The narrower the head is, the closer it must be to the platter surface to function. Since a narrower head means narrower tracks and therefore greater data density, this is desirable. However, the closer the head is to the disk, the greater the risk of error from impurities or imperfections. To push the technology further, the Winchester disk was developed. Winchester heads are used in sealed drive assemblies that are almost free of contaminants. They are designed to operate closer to the disk's surface than conventional rigid disk heads, thus allowing greater data density. The head is in the shape of an aerodynamic foil which rests lightly on the platter's surface when the disk is motionless. The air

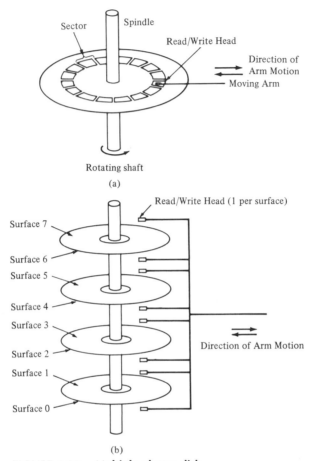

Sector   Spindle

Read/Write Head

Direction of
Arm Motion

Moving Arm

Rotating shaft

(a)

Read/Write Head (1 per surface)

Surface 7

Surface 6

Surface 5

Surface 4

Surface 3

Surface 2

Surface 1

Surface 0

Direction of Arm Motion

(b)

FIGURE 4-27. Multiple-platter disk

pressure generated by the spinning disk is enough to make the foil rise above
the surface. The resulting noncontact system can be engineered to use narrower
heads that operate closer to the platter's surface than conventional rigid disk
heads.

As a matter of historical interest, the term *Winchester* was originally used by
IBM as a code name for their 3340 disk model prior to announcement. The 3340
was a removable disk pack with the heads sealed within the pack. The term is
now applied to any sealed-unit disk drive with aerodynamic head design.

Disk Access Time

When the disk drive is operating, the disk is rotating at constant speed. To read
or write, the head must be positioned at the desired track and at the beginning of
the desired sector on that track. Track selection involves moving the head in a

movable-head system or electronically selecting one head on a fixed-head system. On a movable-head system, the time it takes to position the head at the track is known as *seek time*. In either case, once the track is selected, the system waits until the appropriate sector rotates to line up with the head. The time it takes for the sector to reach the head is known as *rotational latency*. The sum of the seek time, if any, and the rotational latency is the *access time*, the time it takes to get into position to read or write. Once the head is in position, the read or write operation is then performed as the sector moves under the head.

4.5

MAGNETIC TAPE

Tape systems use the same reading and recording techniques as disk systems. The medium is a flexible mylar tape coated with magnetic oxide. The tape and the tape drive are analogous to a home tape recorder system.

Data on tape are stored one character at a time, with either 7 or 9 bits used for each character (Figure 4-28). Normally, one of the 7 or 9 bits is a parity bit. Each bit position across the width of a head is called a *track*. As with the disk, data are read and written in contiguous blocks, called *physical records* on a tape. Blocks on the tape are separated by gaps, called *inter-record* gaps. Also as with the disk, the tape is formatted to assist in locating physical records.

A tape drive is referred to as a *sequential-access* device. If the tape head is positioned at record 1, in order to read physical record N, it is necessary to read physical records 1 through N − 1, one at a time. If the head is currently positioned beyond the desired record, it is necessary to rewind the tape a certain distance and then begin reading forward. Unlike the disk, the tape is in motion only during a read or write operation.

In contrast to the tape, a disk drive is referred to as a *direct-access* device. This reflects the fact that a disk drive need not read all the sectors on a disk sequentially to get to the desired one. It must only wait for the intervening sectors within one track and can make successive accesses to any track.

Historically, magnetic tape was the first kind of secondary memory. It is still widely used as the lowest-cost, slowest-speed member of the memory hierarchy.

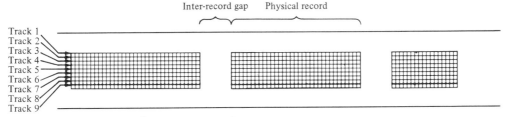

FIGURE 4-28.   Nine-track magnetic tape format

OPTICAL MEMORY

In 1983, one of the most successful consumer products of all time was introduced: the compact disk (CD) digital audio system [GUTE88]. The CD is a
nonerasable disk that can store more than 60 minutes of audio information on
one side. The huge commercial success of the CD enabled the development of
low-cost optical-disk storage technology that now promises to revolutionize
computer data storage. In the past few years, a variety of optical-disk systems
have been introduced (Table 4-8). Three of these systems are increasingly coming to be used in computer applications: CD-ROM, WORM, and the erasable
optical disk. We will briefly review each of these.

CD-ROM

Both the audio CD and the CD-ROM (compact disk read-only memory) share a
similar technology. The main difference is that CD-ROM players are more rug-
ged and have error-correction devices to ensure that data are properly transferred from disk to computer. Both types of disk are also made the same way.

TABLE 4-8   Optical Disk Products

CD

Compact Disk. A nonerasable disk that stores digitized audio information. The standard
system uses 12-cm disks and can record more than 60 minutes of uninterrupted playing
time.

CD-ROM

Compact Disk Read-Only Memory. A nonerasable disk used for storing computer data.
The standard system uses 12-cm disks and can hold more than 550 Mbytes.

CD-I

Compact Disk Interactive. A specification based on the use of CD-ROM. It describes
methods for providing audio, video, graphics, text, and machine-executable code on
CD-ROM.

DVI

Digital Video Interactive. A technology for producing digitized, compressed representation of video information. The representation can be stored on CD or other disk media.
Current systems use CDs and can store about 20 minutes of video on one disk.

WORM

Write-Once Read-Many. A disk that is more easily written than CD-ROM, making
single-copy disks commercially feasible. As with CD-ROM, after the write operation is
performed, the disk is read-only. The most popular size is 5.25-in, which can hold from
200 to 800 Mbytes of data.

Erasable Optical Disk

A disk that uses optical technology but that can be easily erased and rewritten. Both
3.25-inch and 5.25-inch disks are in use. A typical capacity is 650 Mbytes.

The disk is formed from a resin, such as polycarbonate, and coated with a highly reflective surface, usually aluminum. Digitally recorded information (either music or computer data) is imprinted as a series of microscopic pits on the reflective surface. This is done, first of all, with a finely focused, high-intensity laser to create a master disk. The master is used in turn to make a die to stamp out copies. The pitted surface of the copies is protected against dust and scratches by a top coat of clear lacquer.

Information is retrieved from a CD or CD-ROM by a low-powered laser housed in an optical-disk player or drive unit. The laser shines through the clear protective coating while a motor spins the disk past it. The intensity of the reflected light of the laser changes as it encounters a pit. This change is detected by a photosensor and converted into a digital signal.

A pit near the center of a rotating disk travels past a fixed point (such as a laser beam) slower than a pit on the outside, so some way must be found to compensate for the variation in speed so that the laser can read all the pits at the same rate. This can be done—as it is on magnetic disks—by increasing the spacing between bits of information recorded in segments of the disk. The information can then be scanned at the same rate by rotating the disk at a fixed speed, known as the **constant angular velocity (CAV).** Figure 4-29 shows the layout of a disk using CAV. The disk is divided into a number of pie-shaped sectors and into a series of concentric tracks. The advantage of using CAV is that individual blocks of data can be directly addressed by track and sector. To move the head from its current location to a specific address, it only takes a short movement of the head to a specific track and a short wait for the proper sector to spin under the head. The disadvantage of CAV is that the amount of data that can be stored on the long outer tracks is the same as what can be stored on the short inner tracks.

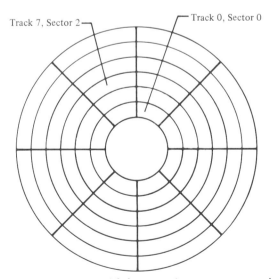

FIGURE 4-29. Disk layout using constant angular velocity

Because putting less information on the outside of a disk wastes space, the CAV method is not used on CDs and CD-ROMs. Instead, information is packed evenly across the disk in segments of the same size and these are scanned at the same rate by rotating the disk at a variable speed. The pits are then read by the laser at a **constant linear velocity (CLV).** Because the amount of data per track is not constant across the disk, addresses are expressed in the manner used in CDs, that is, in units of 0 to 59 minutes, 0 to 59 seconds, and 0 to 74 blocks. This information is carried at the beginning of each block. At 60 minutes (the usual limit), the CD-ROM can hold 270,000 blocks, each of which contains 2048 bytes of user data, for a total of 553 Mbytes. This is equivalent to more than 1300 5.25-inch floppy disks. The format of a CD-ROM block is shown in Figure 4-30. It consists of the following fields:

- *Sync:* The sync field identifies the beginning of a block. It consists of a byte of all 0s, 10 bytes of all 1s, and a byte of all 0s.
- *Header:* The header contains the block address and the mode byte. Mode 0 specifies a blank data field; mode 1 specifies the use of an error-correcting code and 2,048 bytes of data; mode 2 specifies 2,336 bytes of user data with no error-correcting code.
- *Data:* User data.
- *Auxiliary:* Additional user data in mode 2. In mode 1, this is a 288-byte error-correcting code.

Figure 4-31 indicates the layout used for CDs and CD-ROMs. Data are arranged sequentially along a spiral track. With the use of CLV, random access becomes more difficult. Locating a specific address involves moving the head to the general area, adjusting the rotation speed and reading the address, and then making minor adjustments to find and access the specific sector.

CD-ROM is appropriate for the distribution of large amounts of data to a large number of users. Because of the expense of the initial writing process, it is not appropriate for individualized applications. Compared with traditional magnetic disks, the CD-ROM has three major advantages:

- The information-storage capacity is much greater on the optical disk.
- The optical disk together with the information stored on it can be mass repli-

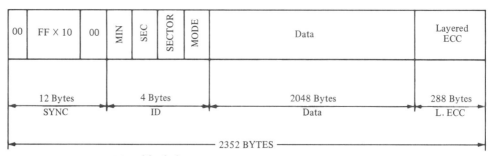

FIGURE 4-30.   CD-ROM block format

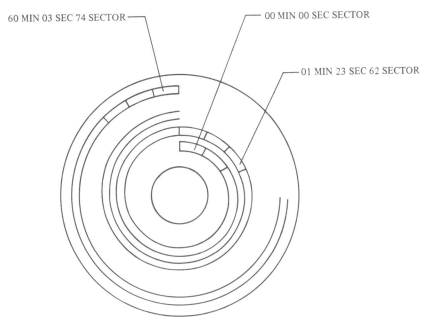

60 MIN 03 SEC 74 SECTOR

00 MIN 00 SEC SECTOR

01 MIN 23 SEC 62 SECTOR

FIGURE 4-31.   Disk layout using constant linear velocity

cated inexpensively—unlike a magnetic disk. The database on a magnetic disk has to be reproduced by copying one disk at a time using two disk drives.
- The optical disk is removable, allowing the disk itself to be used for archival storage. Most magnetic disks are nonremovable. The information on it must first be copied to tape before the disk drive/disk can be used to store new information.

The disadvantages of CD-ROM:

- It is read-only and cannot be updated.
- It has an access time much longer than that of a magnetic disk drive, as much as half a second.

WORM

To accommodate applications in which only one or a small number of copies of a set of data is needed, the write-once read-many CD has been developed. For WORM, a disk is prepared in such a way that it can be subsequently written once with a laser beam of modest intensity. Thus, with a somewhat more expensive disk controller than for CD-ROM, the customer can write once as well as read the disk. To provide for more rapid access, the WORM uses constant angular velocity, at the sacrifice of some capacity.

A typical technique for preparing the disk is to use a high-power laser to produce a series of blisters on the disk. When the preformatted medium is placed in a WORM drive, a low-powered laser can produce just enough heat to burst the prerecorded blisters. During a disk-read operation, a laser in the WORM drive illuminates the disk's surface. Since the burst blisters provide higher contrast than the surrounding area, these are easily recognized by simple electronics.

The WORM optical disk is attractive for archival storage of documents and files. It provides a permanent record of large volumes of user data.

Erasable Optical Disk

The most recent development in computer optical disks is the erasable optical disk. This disk can be repeatedly written and overwritten, as with any magnetic disk. Although a number of approaches have been tried, the only technology that has proved commercially feasible is the magneto-optical system. In this system, the energy of a laser beam is used together with a magnetic field to record and erase information by reversing the magnetic poles in a small area of a disk coated with a magnetic material. The laser beam heats a specific spot on the medium, and a magnetic field can change the orientation of that spot while its temperature is elevated. As the polarization process does not cause a physical change in the disk, the process can be repeated many times. For reading, the direction of magnetism can be detected by polarized laser light. Polarized light reflected from a particular spot will change its degree of rotation depending on the magnetic field's orientation.

The erasable optical disk has the obvious advantage over CD-ROM and WORM that it can be rewritten and thus used as a true secondary storage. As such, it competes with the magnetic disk. The principal advantages of erasable optical disks compared to magnetic disks are:

- High capacity: A 5.25-inch optical disk can hold about 650 Mbytes of data. The most advanced Winchester disks can carry less than half that amount.
- Portability: The optical disk can be removed from the drive.
- Reliability: The engineering tolerances for optical disks are much less severe than for high-capacity magnetic disks. Thus, they exhibit higher reliability and longer life.

As with WORM, the erasable optical disk uses constant angular velocity.

4.7

RECOMMENDED READING

[MAJU83] and [TRIE82], though a little dated, provide good surveys of most of the memory technologies discussed in this chapter. [STON80] contains a useful discussion of semiconductor memory organization. More recent assessments of the state of the art include [MEIN87], [POHM81], and [WILL84]. Discussions of flash, EPROM, and EEPROM can be found in [PASH89] and [LAHT90].

A good explanation of error-correcting codes is contained in [MCEL85]; extensive coverage is provided in [SIEW82c]. [CHEN84] surveys a variety of modern codes more powerful than SEC-DED. Other good papers are [SARR84] and [LEVI76].

[POHM83] contains a lengthy and worthwhile discussion of cache design and performance. [SMIT82] surveys various elements of cache design and presents the results of an extensive set of analyses. Other surveys include [ALPE88], [SMIT87], and [PRZY88]. The 80486 cache is described in [CRAW90] and [INTE90]. A description of the VAX cache system is in [LEVY89] and [DEC78]. Brief descriptions of the cache design for the VAX 8600 and VAX 8800 are contained in [TROI85] and [NATU87], respectively. Descriptions of the IBM 3033 cache system can be found in [PRAS81] and [LORI82]. A brief description of the cache design for the IBM 3090 is included in [SING86]. A detailed examination of a variety of cache design issues related to multiprogramming and multiprocessing is presented in [AGAR89a]. [HIGB90] provides a set of simple formulas that can be used to estimate cache performance as a function of various cache parameters.

A good discussion of disk and tape systems can be found in [STON80]. More recent surveys of the state of the art include [HOBB84], [KRYD86], and [KRYD87]. A worthwhile survey of disk technology is [SIER90]. CD-ROMs are well-covered in [FUJI84] and [BUDD87]. WORMs and erasable optical disks are described in [FREE88], [KRYD87], and [MEIK86]. [ZECH88] is a good analysis of the appropriate applications of the various optical disk technologies.

4.8

PROBLEMS

4.1 Draw a configuration showing a CPU, four 1K × 8-bit ROMs, and a bus containing 12 address lines and 8 data lines. Add a chip select logic block that will select one of the four ROM modules for each of the 4K addresses.

4.2 Suggest reasons why RAMs are often organized with only one bit per chip, whereas ROMs are usually organized with multiple bits per chip.

4.3 **(a)** The address lines shown in Figure 4-9 are multiplexed so that only half as many lines are needed as for dedicated address lines. Would you expect that this arrangement results in a time penalty? If not, justify the assertion that there would be no time penalty.

(b) Could address-line multiplexing be used with a 2D memory organization? Why or why not?

4.4 A dynamic RAM must be given a refresh cycle 64 times per ms. Each refresh operation requires 150 ns, and a memory cycle requires 250 ns. What percentage of the memory's total operating time must be given to memory refreshes?

4.5 Develop an SEC code for a 16-bit data word. Generate the code for the data word 0101000000111001. Show that the code will correctly identify an error in data bit 4.

4.6 Generalize Equations 4-1 and 4-2, pages 186–187, to n-level memory hierarchies.

4.7 A set-associative cache consists of 64 slots divided into 4- slot sets. Main memory contains 4K blocks of 128 words each. Show the format of main memory address.

4.8 A computer system contains a main memory of 32K 16-bit words. It also has a 4K-word cache divided into 4-slot sets with 64 words per slot. Assume that the cache is initially empty. The CPU fetches words from locations 0, 1, 2, . . ., 4,351 in that order. It then repeats this fetch sequence 9 more times. The cache is 10 times faster than main memory. Estimate the improvement resulting from the use of the cache. Assume an LRU policy for block replacement.

4.9 Describe a simple technique for implementing an LRU replacement algorithm in a four-way set-associative cache.

4.10 Consider a memory system with the following parameters:

T_c = 100 ns C_c = 0.01 ¢/bit
T_m = 1,200 ns C_m = 0.001 ¢/bit
H = 0.95

(a) What is the cost of a 1-MByte main memory?

(b) What is the cost of a 1-MByte main memory using cache technology?

(c) Design a main memory/cache system with 1 MByte of main memory whose effective cycle time is no more than 10% greater than the cache memory cycle time. What is its cost?

4.11 (a) Compare the 80486 cache replacement algorithm with a true least-recently-used algorithm. Show that the 80486 algorithm approximates LRU.

(b) In the discussion of the 80486 cache, the statement was made that a true least-recently-used replacement algorithm would require six bits per set. Demonstrate this.

4.12 Define the following for a disk system

t_s = seek time; average time to position head over track
r = rotation speed of the disk, in revolutions per second
n = number of bits per sector
N = capacity of a track, in bits
t_A = time to access a sector

Develop a formula for t_A as a function of the other parameters.

4.13 What is the transfer rate of a 9-track magnetic tape unit whose tape speed is 120 inches per second and whose tape density is 1,600 linear bits per inch?

4.14 Assume a 2,400-foot tape reel; an inter-record gap of 0.6 inch where the tape stops midway, between reads; that the rate of tape speed increase/decrease during gaps is linear; and that other characteristics of the tape are the same as in Problem 4.13. Data on the tape are organized in physical records, where each physical record contains a fixed number of user-defined units, called *logical records*.

    (a) How long will it take to read a full tape of 120-byte logical records blocked 10/physical record?

    (b) Same, blocked 30?

    (c) How many logical records will the tape hold with each of the above blocking factors?

    (d) What is the effective overall transfer rate for each of the two blocking factors above?

    (e) What is the capacity of the tape?

4.15 Calculate how much disk space (in sectors, tracks, and surfaces) will be required to store the logical records read in Problem 4.14a if the disk is fixed-sector of 512 bytes/sector, with 96 sectors/track, 110 tracks per surface, and 8 usable surfaces. Ignore any file header record(s) and track indexes, and assume that records cannot span 2 sectors.

4.16 Neglecting CPU time, how long will it take to write the records in Problem 4.15 on the disk sequentially if average track-to-track time is 8 ms and the disk rotates at 360 rpm? Assume that the head is initially above the first track to be written.

4.17 Considering the combined problems of 4.14b and 4.16, and neglecting CPU time, will the tape-to-disk copy be tape-bound (limited by tape speed) or disk-bound (limited by disk speed), assuming separate I/O modules?

4.18 For the tape unit described in Problem 4.13, what would be the effective transfer rate if the data were all numeric, packed 2 digits per byte?

4.19 In Problem 4.14a, if the tape did not slow down or stop in passing over the gaps (i.e., streaming tape), what would be the improvement in reading time for the same data?

APPENDIX 4A
_____

Performance Characteristics of Two-Level Memories

In this chapter, reference is made to a cache that acts as a buffer between main memory and processor, creating a two-level internal memory. This two-level architecture provides improved performance over a comparable one-level memory, by exploiting a property known as locality, which is explored below.

    The main memory cache mechanism is part of the computer architecture, implemented in hardware, and typically invisible to the operating system. In addition, there are two other instances of a two-level memory approach that also exploit locality and that are, at least partially, implemented in the operating system: virtual memory and the disk cache (Table 4-9). Virtual memory is explored in Chapter 6; disk cache is beyond the scope of this book but is examined in [STAL91]. In this appendix, we look at some of the performance characteristics of two-level memories that are common to all three approaches.

TABLE 4-9   Characteristics of Two-Level Memories

	Main Memory Cache	Virtual Memory (Paging)	Disk Cache
Typical access time ratios	5/1	1000/1	1000/1
Memory management system	Implemented by special hardware	Combination of hardware and system software	System software
Typical block size	4 to 128 bytes	64 to 4096 bytes	64 to 4096 bytes
Access of processor to second level	Direct access	Indirect access	Indirect access

4A-1 Locality

The basis for the performance advantage of a two-level memory is a principle known as *locality of reference* [DENN68]. This principle states that memory references tend to cluster. Over a long period of time the clusters in use change, but over a short period of time, the processor is primarily working with fixed clusters of memory references.

From an intuitive point of view, the principle of locality makes sense. Consider the following line of reasoning:

1. Except for branch and call instructions, which constitute only a small fraction of all program instructions, program execution is sequential. Hence, in most cases, the next instruction to be fetched immediately follows the last instruction fetched.
2. It is rare to have a long uninterrupted sequence of procedure calls followed by the corresponding sequence of returns. Rather, a program remains confined to a rather narrow window of procedure-invocation depth. Thus, over a short period of time references to instructions tend to be localized to a few procedures.
3. Most iterative constructs consist of a relatively small number of instructions repeated many times. For the duration of the iteration, computation is therefore confined to a small contiguous portion of a program.
4. In many programs, much of the computation involves processing data structures, such as arrays or sequences of records. In many cases, successive references to these data structures will be to closely located data items.

This line of reasoning has been confirmed in many studies. For example, let us consider point 1. A variety of studies have been made to analyze the behavior of high-level language programs. Table 4-10 includes key results, measuring the appearance of various statement types during execution, from the following studies. The earliest study of programming language behavior, performed by Knuth [KNUT71], examined a collection of FORTRAN programs used as student

TABLE 4-10   Relative Dynamic Frequency of High-Level Language Operations

Study	[HUCK83]	[KNUT71]	[PATT82a]		[TANE78]
Language	Pascal	FORTRAN	Pascal	C	SAL
Workload	Scientific	Student	System	System	System
Assign	74	67	45	38	42
Loop	4	3	5	3	4
Call	1	3	15	12	12
IF	20	11	29	43	36
GOTO	2	9	—	3	—
Other	—	7	6	1	6

exercises. Tanenbaum [TANE78] published measurements collected from over 300 procedures used in operating-system programs and written in a language that supports structured programming (SAL). Patterson and Sequein [PATT82] analyzed a set of measurements taken from compilers and programs for typesetting, CAD, sorting, and file comparison. The programming languages C and Pascal were studied. Huck [HUCK83] analyzed four programs intended to represent a mix of general-purpose scientific computing, including fast Fourier transform and the integration of systems of differential equations. There is quite good agreement in the results of this mixture of languages and applications that branching and call instructions represent only a fraction of statements executed during the lifetime of a program. Thus, these studies confirm assertion 1 above.

With respect to assertion 2, studies reported in [PATT85] provide confirmation. This is illustrated in Figure 4-32, which shows call-return behavior. Each call is represented by the line moving down and to the right, and each return by the line moving up and to the right. In the figure, a *window* with depth equal to

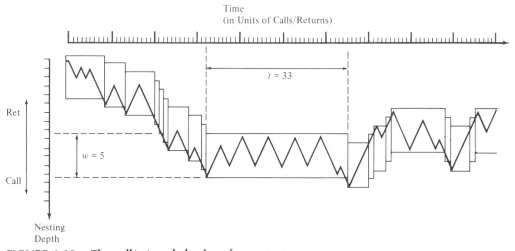

FIGURE 4-32.   The call/return behavior of programs

5 is defined. Only a sequence of calls and returns with a net movement of 6 in either direction causes the window to move. As can be seen, the executing program can remain within a stationary window for quite long periods of time. A study by the same group of C and Pascal programs showed that a window of depth 8 will need to shift only on less than one percent of the calls or returns [TAMI83].

Other studies have also demonstrated the validity of assertions 3 and 4 (e.g., [DENN80b], [CHU76]).

4A-2   Operation of Two-Level Memory

The locality property can be exploited in the formation of a two-level memory. The upper level memory (M1) is smaller, faster, and more expensive (per bit) than the lower level memory (M2). M1 is used as a temporary store for part of the contents of the larger M2. When a memory reference is made, an attempt is made to access the item in M1. If this succeeds, then a quick access is made. If not, then a block of memory locations is copied from M2 to M1 and the access then takes place via M1. Because of locality, once a block is brought into M1, there should be a number of accesses to locations in that block, resulting in fast overall service.

To express the average time to access an item, we must consider not only the speeds of the two levels of memory, but also the probability that a given reference can be found in M1. This probability is known as the hit ratio. We have

$$
\begin{aligned}
T_S &= H \times T_1 + (1 - H) \times (T_1 + T_2) \\
&= T_1 + (1 - H) \times T_2
\end{aligned} \tag{4-1}
$$

where

T_S = average (system) access time
T_1 = access time of M1 (e.g., cache, disk cache)
T_2 = access time of M2 (e.g., main memory, disk)
H = hit ratio (fraction of time reference is found in M1)

Figure 4-2 shows average access time as a function of hit ratio. As can be seen, for a high percentage of hits, the average total access time is much closer to that of M1 than M2.

4A-3   Performance

Let us look at some of the parameters relevant to an assessment of a two-level memory mechanism. First consider cost. We have

$$
C_S = \frac{C_1 S_1 + C_2 S_2}{S_1 + S_2} \tag{4-2}
$$

where

C_S = average cost per bit for the combined two-level memory
C_1 = average cost per bit of upper-level memory M1
C_2 = average cost per bit of lower-level memory M2
S_1 = size of M1
S_2 = size of M2

We would like $C_S \approx C_2$. Given that $C_1 \gg C_2$, this requires $S_1 \ll S_2$. Figure 4-33 shows the relationship.

   Next, consider access time. For a two-level memory to provide a significant performance improvement, we need to have T_S approximately equal to T_1 ($T_S \approx T_1$). Given that T_1 is much less than T_2 ($T_1 \ll T_2$), a hit ratio of close to 1 is needed.

   So, we would like M1 to be small to hold down cost, and large to improve the hit ratio and therefore the performance. Is there a size of M1 that satisfies both requirements to a reasonable extent? We can answer this question with a series of sub-questions:

• What value of hit ratio is needed to satisfy the performance requirement?
• What size of M1 will assure the needed hit ratio?
• Does this size satisfy the cost requirement?

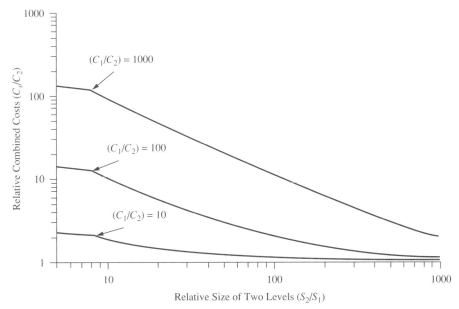

FIGURE 4-33.   Relationship of average memory cost to relative memory size for a two-level memory

To get at this, consider the quantity T_1/T_S, which is referred to as the *access efficiency*. It is a measure of how close average access time (T_S) is to M1 access time (T_1). From Equation 4-1:

$$\frac{T_1}{T_S} = \frac{1}{H + (1 - H)\dfrac{T_2}{T_1}}$$

(4-3)

In Figure 4-34, we plot T_1/T_S as a function of the hit ratio H, with the quantity T_2/T_1 as a parameter. Typically, cache access time is about five to ten times faster than main memory access time (i.e., T_2/T_1 is 5 to 10), and main memory access time is about 1000 times faster than disk access time ($T_2/T_1 = 1000$). Thus, a hit ratio in the range of 0.8 to 0.9 would seem to be needed to satisfy the performance requirement.

We can now phrase the question about relative memory size more exactly. Is a hit ratio of 0.8 or better reasonable for $S_1 \ll S_2$? This will depend on a number of factors including the nature of the software being executed and the details of the design of the two-level memory. The main determinant is, of course, the degree of locality. Figure 4-35 suggests the effect that locality has on the hit ratio. Clearly, if M1 is the same size as M2, then the hit ratio will be 1.0: all of the items in M2 are always stored also in M1. Now, suppose that there is no locality; that is, references are completely random. In that case the hit ratio should be a strictly linear function of the relative memory size. For example, if M1 is half the size of M2, then at any time, half of the items from M2 are also in M1 and the hit ratio will be 0.5. In practice, however, there is some degree of locality in

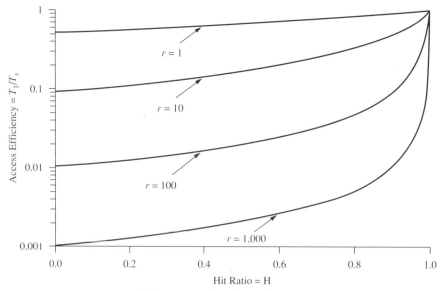

FIGURE 4-34.   Access efficiency as a function of H ($r = T_2/T_1$)

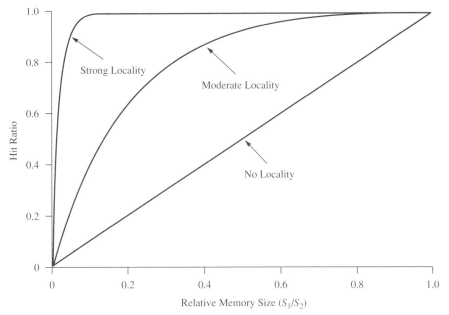

FIGURE 4-35.   Hit ratio as a function of relative memory size

the references. The effects of moderate and strong locality are indicated in the figure.

So, if there is strong locality, it is possible to achieve high values of hit ratio even with relatively small upper-level memory size. For example, numerous studies have shown that rather small cache sizes will yield a hit ratio above 0.75, *regardless of the size of main memory* (e.g., [AGAR89a], [AGAR89b], [PRZY88], [STRE83], and [SMIT82]). A cache in the range of 1K to 128K words is generally adequate, whereas main memory is now typically in the multiple-megabyte range. When we consider virtual memory and disk cache, we will cite other studies that confirm the same phenomenon, namely that a relatively small M1 yields a high value of hit ratio because of locality.

This brings us to the last question listed earlier: Does the relative size of the two memories satisfy the cost requirement? The answer is clearly yes. If we need only a relatively small upper-level memory to achieve good performance, then the average cost per bit of the two levels of memory will approach that of the cheaper lower-level memory.

CHAPTER 5

Input/Output

In addition to the CPU and a set of memory modules, the third key element of a computer system is a set of I/O modules. Each module interfaces to the system bus or central switch and controls one or more peripheral devices. An I/O module is not simply mechanical connectors that wire a device into the system bus. Rather, the I/O module contains some "intelligence," that is, it contains logic for performing a communication function between the peripheral and the bus.

The reader may wonder why one does not connect peripherals directly to the system bus. The reasons are

- There are a wide variety of peripherals with various methods of operation. It would be impractical to incorporate the necessary logic within the CPU to control a range of devices.
- The data transfer rate of peripherals is often much slower than that of the memory or CPU. Thus it is impractical to use the high-speed system bus to communicate directly with a peripheral.
- Peripherals often use different data formats and word lengths than the computer to which they are attached.

Thus, an I/O module is required. This module has two major functions (Figure 5-1).

- Interface to the CPU and memory via the system bus or central switch.
- Interface to one or more peripheral devices by tailored data links.

We begin this chapter with a brief discussion of external devices, followed by an overview of the structure and function of an I/O module. Then, we look at the various ways in which the I/O function can be performed in cooperation with the CPU and memory: the internal I/O interface. Finally, the external I/O interface, between the I/O module and the outside world, is examined.

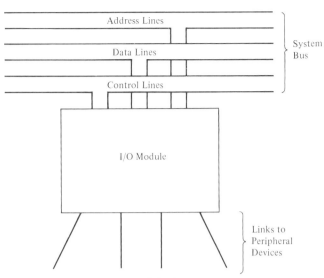

FIGURE 5-1. Generic model of an I/O module

EXTERNAL DEVICES

A computer system is of no use without some means of input and output. I/O operations are accomplished through a wide assortment of external devices that provide a means of exchanging data between the external environment and the computer. An external device attaches to the computer by a link to an I/O module (Figure 5-1). The link is used to exchange control, status, and data between the I/O module and the external device. An external device connected to an I/O module is often referred to as a *peripheral device* or, simply, a *peripheral.*

We can broadly classify external devices into three categories:

- *Human-readable:* Suitable for communicating with the computer user.
- *Machine-readable:* Suitable for communicating with equipment.
- *Communication:* Suitable for communicating with remote devices.

Examples of human-readable devices are video display terminals (VDTs) and printers. Examples of machine-readable devices are magnetic disk and tape systems, and sensors and actuators, such as are used in a robotics application. Note that we are viewing disk and tape systems as I/O devices in this chapter, whereas in Chapter 4 we viewed them as memory devices. From a functional point of view, these devices are part of the memory hierarchy, and their use is appropriately discussed in Chapter 4. From a structural point of view, these devices are controlled by I/O modules and are hence to be considered in this chapter.

Communication devices allow a computer to exchange data with a remote device, which may be a human-readable device, such as a terminal, a machine-readable device, or even another computer.

In very general terms, the nature of an external device is indicated in Figure 5-2. The interface to the I/O module is in the form of control, status, and data signals. *Data* are in the form of a set of bits to be sent to or received from the I/O module. *Control signals* determine the function that the device will perform, such as send data to the I/O module (INPUT or READ), accept data from the I/O module (OUTPUT or WRITE), report status, or perform some control function particular to the device (e.g., position a disk head). *Status signals* indicate the state of the device. Examples are READY/NOT-READY to show whether the device is ready for data transfer.

Control logic associated with the device controls the device's operation in response to direction from the I/O module. The *transducer* converts data from electrical to other forms of energy during output and from other forms to electrical during input. Typically, a buffer is associated with the transducer to temporarily hold data being transferred between the I/O module and the external environment; a buffer size of 8 to 16 bits is common.

The interface between the I/O module and the external device will be examined in Section 5.7. The interface between the external device and the environment is beyond the scope of this book, but several brief examples are given here.

Video Display Terminal

The most common means for a user to communicate with a computer is the video display terminal (VDT). A VDT consists of a keyboard and a display unit, or *screen*. The user provides input through the keyboard. This input is transmitted to the computer and may also be displayed on the screen, so that the user

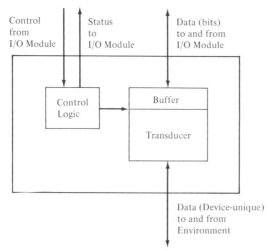

FIGURE 5-2. An external device

can see what is being transmitted. In addition, the screen displays data provided by the computer.

The basic unit of exchange is the *character*. Characters are of two types: displayable and control. Displayable characters are the alphabetic, numeric, and special characters that the user can enter at the keyboard and that can be displayed on the screen. Control characters are interpreted to cause a device-specific action, such as carriage return.

Associated with each character is a code; typical codes are from 5 to 7 bits in length. Table 5-1 shows the codes for display and control characters used in one common standard, ASCII (American Standard Code for Information Interchange). On output, this code is transmitted to the external device from the I/O module. The transducer interprets this code and sends the required electronic signals to the display unit to either display the indicated character or perform the requested control function. On input, when a key is depressed by the user, this generates an electronic signal, which is interpreted by the transducer and translated into the bit pattern of the corresponding ASCII code. At the computer, text can be stored in this same code.

Disk Drive

A disk drive contains electronics for exchanging data, control, and status signals with an I/O module plus the electronics for controlling the disk read/write mechanism. In a fixed-head disk, the transducer is capable of converting between the magnetic patterns on the moving disk surface and bits in the device's buffer (Figure 5-2). A moving-head disk must also be able to cause the disk arm to move radially in and out across the disk's surface.

5.2
I/O MODULES

Module Function

An I/O module is the entity within a computer responsible for the control of one or more external devices and for the exchange of data between those devices and main memory and/or CPU registers. Thus the I/O module must have an interface internal to the computer (to the CPU and main memory) and an interface external to the computer (to the external device).

The major functions or requirements for an I/O module fall into the following categories:

- Control and Timing
- CPU Communication
- Device Communication
- Data Buffering
- Error Detection

TABLE 5-1   The U.S. ASCII code

Bit positions 5, 6, 7:

		000	100	010	110	001	101	011	111
		0	1	2	3	4	5	6	7
0000	0	NUL	DLE	SP	0	@	P	'	p
1000	1	SOH	DC1	!	1	A	Q	a	q
0100	2	STX	DC2	"	2	B	R	b	r
1100	3	ETX	DC3	#	3	C	S	c	s
0010	4	EOT	DC4	$	4	D	T	d	t
1010	5	ENQ	NAK	%	5	E	U	e	u
0110	6	ACK	SYN	&	6	F	V	f	v
1110	7	BEL	ETB	'	7	G	W	g	w
0001	8	BS	CAN	(	8	H	X	h	x
1001	9	HT	EM	)	9	I	Y	i	y
0101	10	LF	SUB	*	:	J	Z	j	z
1101	11	VT	ESC	+	;	K	[	k	{
0011	12	FF	FS	,	<	L	\	l	|
1011	13	CR	GS	–	=	M	]	m	}
0111	14	SO	RS	.	>	N	^	n	~
1111	15	SI	US	/	?	O	–	o	DEL

Bit positions 1, 2, 3, 4:

This is the U.S. national version of CCITT alphabet number 5. The control characters are explained opposite.

TABLE 5-1 (continued)

FORMAT CONTROL

BS (Backspace): Indicates movement of the printing mechanism or display cursor backwards in one position.

HT (Horizontal Tab): Indicates movement of the printing mechanism or display cursor forward to the next preassigned "tab" or stopping position.

LF (Line Feed): Indicates movement of the printing mechanism or display cursor to the start of the next line.

VT (Vertical Tab): Indicates movement of the printing mechanism or display cursor to the next of a series of preassigned printing lines.

FF (Form Feed): Indicates movement of the printing mechanism or display cursor to the starting position of the next page, form, or screen.

CR (Carriage Return): Indicates movement of the printing mechanism or display cursor to the starting position of the same line.

TRANSMISSION CONTROL

SOH (Start of Heading): Used to indicate the start of a heading which may contain address or routing information.

STX (Start of Text): Used to indicate the start of the text and so also indicates the end of the heading.

ETX (End of Text): Used to terminate the text which was started with STX.

EOT (End of Transmission): Indicates the end of a transmission which may have included one or more "texts" with their headings.

ENQ (Enquiry): A request for a response from a remote station. It may be used as a "WHO ARE YOU?" request for a station to identify itself.

ACK (Acknowledge): A character transmitted by a receiving device as an affirmation response to a sender. It is used as a positive response to polling messages.

NAK (Negative Acknowledgment): A character transmitted by a receiving device as a negative response to a sender. It is used as a negative response to polling messages.

SYN (Synchronous/Idle): Used by a synchronous transmission system to achieve synchronization. When no data is being sent a synchronous transmission system may send SYN characters continuously.

ETB (End of Transmission Block): Indicates the end of a block of data for communication purposes. It is used for blocking data where the block structure is not necessarily related to the processing format.

INFORMATION SEPARATOR

FS (File Separator):   Information separa-
GS (Group Separator):   tors to be used in
RS (Record Separator): an optional man-
US (United Separator): ner except that
                            their hierarchy
                            shall be FS (the
                            most inclusive) to
                            US (the least inclu-
                            sive).

TABLE 5-1   (continued)

MISCELLANEOUS

NUL (Null): No character. Used for filling in time or filling space on tape when there are no data.

BEL (Bell): Used when there is need to call human attention. It may control alarm or attention devices.

SO (Shift Out): Indicates that the code combinations which follow shall be interpreted as *outside* of the standard character set until a SHIFT IN character is reached.

SI (Shift In): Indicates that the code combinations which follow shall be interpreted according to the standard character set.

DEL (Delete): Used to obliterate unwanted characters (for example, on paper tape by punching a hole in *every* bit position.

SP (Space): A nonprinting character used to separate words, or to move the printing mechanism or display cursor forward by one position.

DLE (Data Link Escape): A character which shall change the meaning of one or more contiguously following characters. It can provide supplementary controls, or permits the sending of data characters having any bit combination.

DC1, DC2, DC3 and DC4 (Device Controls): Characters for the control of ancillary devices or special terminal features.

CAN (Cancel): Indicates that the data which precedes it in a message or block should be disregarded (usually because an error has been detected).

EM (End of Medium): Indicates the physical end of a card, tape or other medium, or the end of the required or used portion of the medium.

SUB (Substitute): Substituted for a character that is found to be erroneous or invalid.

ESC (Escape): A character intended to provide code extension in that it gives a specified number of continuously following characters an alternate meaning.

During any period of time, the CPU may communicate with one or more external devices in unpredictable patterns, depending on the program's need for I/O. The internal resources, such as main memory and the system bus, must be shared among a number of activities including data I/O. Thus the I/O function includes a *control and timing* requirement, to coordinate the flow of traffic between internal resources and external devices. For example, the control of the transfer of data from an external device to the CPU might involve the following sequence of steps:

1. The CPU interrogates the I/O module to check the status of the attached device.
2. The I/O module returns the device status.
3. If the device is operational and ready to transmit, the CPU requests the transfer of data, by means of a command to the I/O module.
4. The I/O module obtains a unit of data (e.g., 8 or 16 bits) from the external device.
5. The data are transferred from the I/O module to the CPU.

If the system employs a bus, then each of the interactions between the CPU and the I/O module involves one or more bus arbitrations.

The preceding simplified scenario also illustrates that the I/O module must have the capability to engage in communication with the CPU and with the external device. *CPU communication* involves:

- *Command decoding:* The I/O module accepts commands from the CPU. These commands are generally sent as signals on the control bus. For example, an I/O module for a disk drive might accept the following commands: READ SECTOR, WRITE SECTOR, SEEK track number, and SCAN record ID. The latter two commands each include a parameter that is sent on the data bus.
- *Data:* Data are exchanged between the CPU and the I/O module over the data bus.
- *Status reporting:* Because peripherals are so slow, it is important to know the status of the I/O module. For example, if an I/O module is asked to send data to the CPU (read), it may not be ready to do so because it is still working on the previous I/O command. This fact can be reported with a status signal. Common status signals are BUSY and READY. There may also be signals to report various error conditions.
- *Address recognition:* Just as each word of memory has an address, so does each I/O device. Thus, an I/O module must recognize one unique address for each peripheral it controls.

On the other side, the I/O module must be able to perform *device communication*. This communication involves commands, status information, and data (Figure 5-2).

An essential task of an I/O module is *data buffering*. The need for this function is apparent from Table 5-2. Whereas the transfer rate into and out of main memory or the CPU is quite high, the rate is orders of magnitude lower for most

TABLE 5-2   Examples of I/O Devices Categorized by Behavior, Partner, and Data Rate [HENN90]

Device	Behavior	Partner	Data Rate (KBytes/s)
Keyboard	Input	Human	0.01
Mouse	Input	Human	0.02
Voice input	Input	Human	0.02
Scanner	Input	Human	200
Voice output	Output	Human	0.6
Line printer	Output	Human	1
Laser printer	Output	Human	100
Graphics display	Output	Human	30,000
CPU to frame buffer	Output	Human	200
Network-terminal	Input or output	Machine	0.05
Network-LAN	Input or output	Machine	200
Optical disk	Storage	Machine	500
Magnetic tape	Storage	Machine	2,000
Magnetic disk	Storage	Machine	2,000

peripheral devices. Data coming from main memory are sent to an I/O module in a rapid burst. The data are buffered in the I/O module and then sent to the peripheral device at its data rate. In the opposite direction, data are buffered so as not to tie up the memory in a slow transfer operation. Thus the I/O module must be able to operate at both device and memory speeds.

Finally, an I/O module is often responsible for *error detection* and for subsequently reporting errors to the CPU. One class of errors includes mechanical and electrical malfunctions reported by the device (e.g., paper jam, bad disk track). Another class consists of unintentional changes to the bit pattern as it is transmitted from device to I/O module. Some form of error-detecting code is often used to detect transmission errors. A common example is the use of a parity bit on each character of data. For example, the ASCII character code occupies 7 bits of a byte. The eighth bit is set so that the total number of "one"'s in the byte is even (even parity) or odd (odd parity). When a byte is received, the I/O module checks the parity to determine whether an error has occurred.

I/O Module Structure

I/O modules vary considerably in complexity and the number of external devices that they control. We will attempt only a very general description here. (One specific device, the Intel 8255A, is described in Section 5.4.) Figure 5-3 provides a general block diagram of an I/O module. The module connects to the rest of the computer through a set of signal lines (e.g., system bus lines). Data transferred to and from the module are buffered in one or more data registers. There may also be one or more status registers that provide current status information. A status register may also function as a control register, to accept detailed control information from the CPU. The logic within the module interacts with the CPU via a set of control lines. These are used by the CPU to issue commands to the

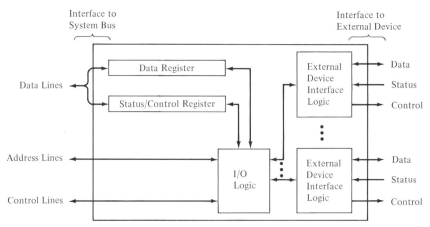

FIGURE 5-3. Block diagram of an I/O module

I/O module. Some of the control lines may be used by the I/O module (e.g., for arbitration and status signals). The module must also be able to recognize and generate addresses associated with the devices it controls. Each I/O module has a unique address or, if it controls more than one external device, a unique set of addresses. Finally, the I/O module contains logic specific to the interface with each device that it controls.

An I/O module functions to allow the CPU to view a wide range of devices in a simple-minded way. There is a spectrum of capabilities that may be provided. The I/O module may hide the details of timing, formats, and the electromechanics of an external device so that the CPU can function in terms of simple read and write commands, and possibly open and close file commands. In its simplest form, the I/O module may still leave much of the work of controlling a device (e.g., rewind a tape) visible to the CPU.

An I/O module that takes on most of the detailed processing burden, presenting a high-level interface to the CPU, is usually referred to as an *I/O channel* or *I/O processor*. An I/O module that is quite primitive and requires detailed control is usually referred to as an *I/O controller* or *device controller*. I/O controllers are commonly seen on microcomputers, whereas I/O channels are used on mainframes, with minicomputers employing a mixture.

When an I/O module is complex (I/O channel), it is usually functionally partitioned in the form of an I/O channel controlling one or more I/O controllers. An example of this is seen in Figure 2-9 (IBM 7094). The boxes labeled *Disk, Drum,* and so forth in that figure are actually I/O controllers. Figure 3-17 is another example.

In what follows, we will use the generic term *I/O module* when no confusion results and will use more specific terms where necessary.

5.3

PROGRAMMED I/O

Three techniques are possible for I/O operations. With *programmed I/O,* data are exchanged between the CPU and the I/O module. The CPU executes a program that gives it direct control of the I/O operation, including sensing device status, sending a read or write command, and transferring the data. When the CPU issues a command to the I/O module, it must wait until the I/O operation is complete. If the CPU is faster than the I/O module, this is wasteful of CPU time. With *interrupt-driven I/O,* the CPU issues an I/O command, continues to execute other instructions, and is interrupted by the I/O module when the latter has completed its work. With both programmed and interrupt I/O, the CPU is responsible for extracting data from main memory for output and storing data in main memory for input. The alternative is known as *direct memory access* (DMA). In this mode, the I/O module and main memory exchange data directly, without CPU involvement.

Table 5-3 indicates the relationship among these three techniques. In this section, we explore programmed I/O. Interrupt I/O and DMA are explored in the following two sections, respectively.

Overview

When the CPU is executing a program and encounters an instruction relating to I/O, it executes that instruction by issuing a command to the appropriate I/O module. With programmed I/O, the I/O module will perform the requested action and then set the appropriate bits in the I/O status register (Figure 5-3). The I/O module takes no further action to alert the CPU. In particular, it does not interrupt the CPU. Thus it is the responsibility of the CPU to periodically check the status of the I/O module until it finds that the operation is complete.

To explain the programmed I/O technique, we view it first from the point of view of the I/O commands issued by the CPU to the I/O module, and then from the point of view of the I/O instructions executed by the CPU.

I/O Commands

To execute an I/O-related instruction, the CPU issues an address, specifying the particular I/O module and external device, and an I/O command. There are four types of I/O commands that an I/O module may receive when it is addressed by a CPU. They are classified as control, test, read, and write.

A *control* command is used to activate a peripheral and tell it what to do. For example, a magnetic-tape unit may be instructed to rewind or to move forward one record. These commands are tailored to the particular type of peripheral device.

A *test* command is used to test various status conditions associated with an I/O module and its peripherals. The CPU will want to know that the peripheral of interest is powered on and available for use. It will also want to know if the most recent I/O operation is completed and if any errors occurred.

A *read* command causes the I/O module to obtain an item of data from the peripheral and place it in an internal buffer (depicted as a data register in Figure 5-3). The CPU can then obtain the data item by requesting that the I/O module

TABLE 5-3   I/O Techniques

	No Interrupts	Use of Interrupts
I/O-to-memory transfer through CPU	Programmed I/O	Interrupt-driven I/O
Direct I/O-to-memory transfer		Direct memory access (DMA)

place it on the data bus. Conversely, a *write* command causes the I/O module to take an item of data (byte or word) from the data bus and subsequently transmit that data item to the peripheral.

Figure 5-4a gives an example of the use of programmed I/O to read in a block of data from a peripheral device (e.g., a record from tape) into memory. Data are read in one word (e.g., 16 bits) at a time. For each word that is read in, the CPU must remain in a status-checking cycle until it determines that the word is available in the I/O module's data register. This flowchart highlights the main disadvantage of this technique: it is a time-consuming process that keeps the processor busy needlessly.

I/O Instructions

With programmed I/O, there is a close correspondence between the I/O-related instructions that the CPU fetches from memory and the I/O commands that the CPU issues to an I/O module to execute the instructions. That is, the instructions are easily mapped into I/O commands, and there is often a simple one-to-one

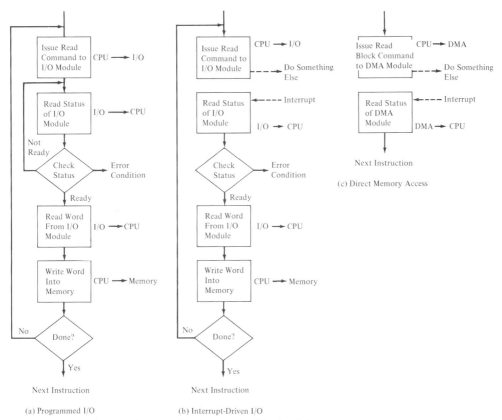

(a) Programmed I/O   (b) Interrupt-Driven I/O

FIGURE 5-4. Three techniques for input of a block of data

relationship. The form of the instruction depends on the way in which external devices are addressed.

Typically, there will be many I/O devices connected through I/O modules to the system. Each device is given a unique identifier or address. When the CPU issues an I/O command, the command contains the address of the desired device. Thus each I/O module must interpret the address lines to determine if the command is for itself.

When the CPU, main memory, and I/O share a common bus, two modes of addressing are possible: memory-mapped and isolated. With *memory-mapped I/O*, there is a single address space for memory locations and I/O devices. The CPU treats the status and data registers of I/O modules as memory locations and uses the same machine instructions to access both memory and I/O devices. So, for example, with 10 address lines, a combined total of 1,024 memory locations and I/O addresses can be supported, in any combination.

With memory-mapped I/O, a single read line and a single write line are needed on the bus. Alternatively, the bus may be equipped with memory read and write plus input and output command lines. Now, the command line specifies whether the address refers to a memory location or an I/O device. The full range of addresses may be available for both. Again, with 10 address lines, the system may now support both 1,024 memory locations and 1,024 I/O addresses. Since the address space for I/O is isolated from that for memory, this is referred to as *isolated I/O*.

Figure 5-5 contrasts these two programmed I/O techniques. Figure 5-5a shows

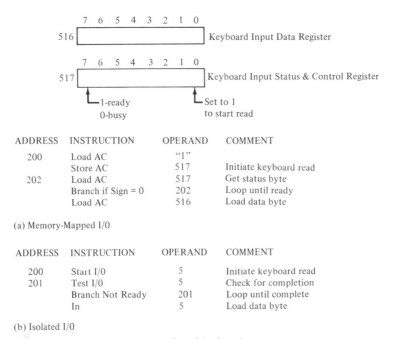

ADDRESS	INSTRUCTION	OPERAND	COMMENT
200	Load AC	"1"	
	Store AC	517	Initiate keyboard read
202	Load AC	517	Get status byte
	Branch if Sign = 0	202	Loop until ready
	Load AC	516	Load data byte

(a) Memory-Mapped I/0

ADDRESS	INSTRUCTION	OPERAND	COMMENT
200	Start I/0	5	Initiate keyboard read
201	Test I/0	5	Check for completion
	Branch Not Ready	201	Loop until complete
	In	5	Load data byte

(b) Isolated I/0

FIGURE 5-5.   Memory-mapped and isolated I/O

how the interface for a simple input device such as a terminal keyboard might appear to a programmer using memory-mapped I/O. Assume a 10-bit address, with a 512-bit memory (locations 0–511) and up to 512 I/O addresses (locations 512–1023). Two addresses are dedicated to keyboard input from a particular terminal. Address 516 refers to the data register and address 517 refers to the status register, which also functions as a control register for receiving CPU commands. The program shown will read 1 byte of data from the keyboard into an accumulator register in the CPU. Note that the CPU loops until the data byte is available.

With isolated I/O (Figure 5-5b), the I/O ports are accessible only by special I/O commands, which activate the I/O command lines on the bus.

For most types of CPUs, there is a relatively large set of different instructions for referencing memory. If isolated I/O is used, there are only a few I/O instructions. Thus, an advantage of memory-mapped I/O is that this large repertoire of instructions can be used, allowing more efficient programming. A disadvantage is that valuable memory address space is used up. Both memory-mapped and isolated I/O are in common use.

5.4

INTERRUPT-DRIVEN I/O

The problem with programmed I/O is that the CPU has to wait a long time for the I/O module of concern to be ready for either reception or transmission of data. The CPU, while waiting, must repeatedly interrogate the status of the I/O module. As a result, the level of the performance of the entire system is severely degraded.

An alternative is for the CPU to issue an I/O command to a module and then go on to do some other useful work. The I/O module will then interrupt the CPU to request service when it is ready to exchange data with the CPU. The CPU then executes the data transfer, as before, and then resumes its former processing.

Let us consider how this works, first from the point of view of the I/O module. For input, the I/O module receives a READ command from the CPU. The I/O module then proceeds to read data in from an associated peripheral. Once the data are in the module's data register, the module signals an interrupt to the CPU over a control line. The module then waits until its data are requested by the CPU. When the request is made, the module places its data on the data bus and is then ready for another I/O operation.

From the CPU's point of view, the action for input is as follows. The CPU issues a READ command. It then goes off and does something else (e.g., the CPU may be working on several different programs at the same time). At the end of each instruction cycle, the CPU checks for interrupts (Figure 3-9). When the interrupt from the I/O module occurs, the CPU saves the context (e.g., program counter and CPU registers) of the current program and processes the interrupt. In this case, the CPU reads the word of data from the I/O module and stores it in memory. It then restores the context of the program it was working on (or some other program) and resumes execution.

Figure 5-4b shows the use of interrupt I/O for reading in a block of data. Compare this to Figure 5-4a. Interrupt I/O is more efficient than programmed I/O because it eliminates needless waiting. However, interrupt I/O still consumes a lot of CPU time, since every word of data that goes from memory to I/O module or from I/O module to memory must pass through the CPU.

Interrupt Processing

Let us consider the role of the processor in I/O in more detail. The occurrence of an interrupt triggers a number of events, both in the processor hardware and in software. Figure 5-6 shows a typical sequence. When an I/O device completes an I/O operation, the following sequence of hardware events occur:

1. The device issues an interrupt signal to the processor.
2. The processor finishes execution of the current instruction before responding to the interrupt, as indicated in Figure 3-9.

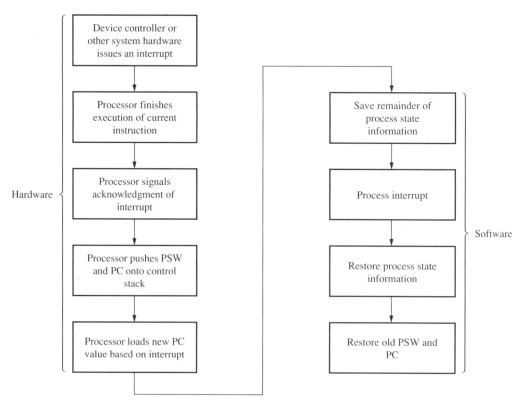

FIGURE 5-6. Simple interrupt processing

3. The processor tests for an interrupt, determines that there is one, and sends an acknowledgment signal to the device that issued the interrupt. The acknowledgment allows the device to remove its interrupt signal.
4. The processor now needs to prepare to transfer control to the interrupt routine. To begin, it needs to save information needed to resume the current program at the point of interrupt. The minimum information required is (a) the status of the processor, which is contained in a register called the program status word (PSW), and (b) the location of the next instruction to be executed, which is contained in the program counter. These can be pushed onto the system control stack[1].
5. The processor now loads the program counter with the entry location of the interrupt-handling program that will respond to this interrupt. Depending on the computer architecture and operating-system design, there may be a single program, one for each type of interrupt, or one for each device and each type of interrupt. If there is more than one interrupt-handling routine, the processor must determine which one to invoke. This information may have been included in the original interrupt signal, or the processor may have to issue a request to the device that issued the interrupt to get a response that contains the needed information.

Once the program counter has been loaded, the processor proceeds to the next instruction cycle, which begins with an instruction fetch. Since the instruction fetch is determined by the contents of the program counter, the result is that control is transferred to the interrupt-handler program. The execution of this program results in the following operations:

6. At this point, the program counter and PSW relating to the interrupted program have been saved on the system stack. However, there is other information that is considered part of the "state" of the executing program. In particular, the contents of the processor registers need to be saved, since these registers may be used by the interrupt-handler. So, all of these values, plus any other state information, need to be saved. Typically, the interrupt handler will begin by saving the contents of all registers on the stack. Figure 5-7a shows a simple example. In this case, a user program is interrupted after the instruction at location N. The contents of all of the registers plus the address of the next instruction (N + 1) are pushed onto the stack. The stack pointer is updated to point to the new top of stack, and the program counter is updated to point to the beginning of the interrupt service routine.
7. The interrupt handler may now proceed to process the interrupt. This will include an examination of status information relating to the I/O operation or other event that caused an interrupt. It may also involve sending additional commands or acknowledgments to the I/O device.
8. When interrupt processing is complete, the saved register values are retrieved from the stack and restored to the registers (e.g., see Figure 5-7b).

---

[1]See Appendix 8A for a discussion of stack operation.

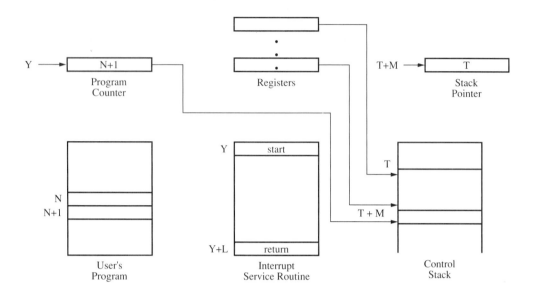

(a) Interrupt Occurs After Instruction at Location N

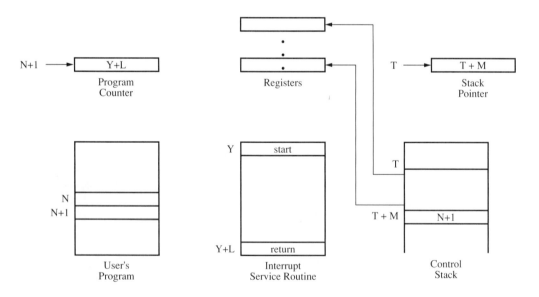

(b) Return From Interrupt

FIGURE 5-7. Changes in memory and register for an interrupt

9. The final act is to restore the PSW and program counter values from the stack. As a result, the next instruction to be executed will be from the previously-interrupted program.

Note that it is important to save all of the state information about the interrupted program for later resumption. This is because the interrupt is not a routine called from the program. Rather, the interrupt can occur at any time and therefore at any point in the execution of a user program. Its occurrence is unpredictable. Indeed, as we will see in the next chapter, the two programs may not have anything in common and may belong to two different users.

Design Issues

Two design issues arise in implementing interrupt I/O. First, since there will almost invariably be multiple I/O modules, how does the CPU determine which device issued the interrupt? And second, if multiple interrupts have occurred, how does the CPU decide which one to process?

Let us consider device identification first. Four general categories of techniques are in common use:

- Multiple Interrupt Lines
- Software Poll
- Daisy Chain (hardware poll, vectored)
- Bus Arbitration (vectored)

The most straightforward approach to the problem is to provide *multiple interrupt lines* between the CPU and the I/O modules. However, it is impractical to dedicate more than a few bus lines or CPU pins to interrupt lines. Consequently, even if multiple lines are used, it is likely that each line will have multiple I/O modules attached to it. Thus one of the other three techniques must be used on each line.

One alternative is the *software poll*. When the CPU detects an interrupt, it branches to an interrupt-service routine whose job it is to poll each I/O module to determine which module caused the interrupt. The poll could be in the form of a separate command line (e.g., TESTI/O). In this case, the CPU raises TESTI/O and places the address of a particular I/O module on the address lines. The I/O module responds positively if it set the interrupt. Alternatively, each I/O module could contain an addressable status register. The CPU then reads the status register of each I/O module to identify the interrupting module. Once the correct module is identified, the CPU branches to a device-service routine specific to that device.

The disadvantage of the software poll is that it is time-consuming. A more efficient technique is to use a *daisy chain*, which provides, in effect, a hardware poll. Examples of a daisy-chain configuration are shown in Figures 3-32 and 3-33. For interrupts, all I/O modules share a common interrupt request line. The interrupt acknowledge line is daisy-chained through the modules. When the

CPU senses an interrupt, it sends out an interrupt acknowledge. This signal propagates through a series of I/O modules until it gets to a requesting module. The requesting module typically responds by placing a word on the data lines. This word is referred to as a *vector* and is either the address of the I/O module or some other unique identifier. In either case, the CPU uses the vector as a pointer to the appropriate device-service routine. This avoids the need to execute a general interrupt-service routine first. This technique is referred to as a *vectored interrupt*.

There is another technique that makes use of vectored interrupts, and that is *bus arbitration*. With bus arbitration, an I/O module must first gain control of the bus before it can raise the interrupt request line. Thus only one module can raise the line at a time. When the CPU detects the interrupt, it responds on the interrupt acknowledge line. The requesting module then places its vector on the data lines.

The techniques listed above serve to identify the requesting I/O module. They also provide a way of assigning priorities when more than one device is requesting interrupt service. With multiple lines, the CPU just picks the interrupt line with the highest priority. With software polling, the order in which modules are polled determines their priority. Similarly, the order of modules on a daisy chain determines their priority. Finally, bus arbitration can employ a priority scheme, as discussed in Section 3.4.

We now turn to two examples of interrupt structures.

Intel 8259A Interrupt Controller

The Intel 8086 provides a single Interrupt Request (INTR) and a single Interrupt Acknowledge (INTA) line. To allow the 8086 to flexibly handle a variety of devices and priority structures, it is usually configured with an external interrupt arbiter, the 8259A [INTE88]. External devices are connected to the 8259A, which in turn connects to the 8086.

Figure 5-8 shows the use of the 8259A to connect multiple I/O modules for the 8086. A single 8259A can handle up to 8 modules. If control for more than 8 modules is required, a cascade arrangement can be used to handle up to 64 modules.

The 8259A's sole responsibility is the management of interrupts. It accepts interrupt requests from attached modules, determines which interrupt has the highest priority, and then signals the CPU by raising the INTR line. The CPU acknowledges via the INTA line. This prompts the 8259A to place the appropriate vector information on the data bus. The CPU can then proceed to process the interrupt and to communicate directly with the I/O module to read or write data.

The 8259A is programmable. The 8086 determines the priority scheme to be used by setting a control word in the 8259A. The following interrupt modes are possible.

Fully Nested: The interrupt requests are ordered in priority from 0 (IR0) through 7 (IR7).

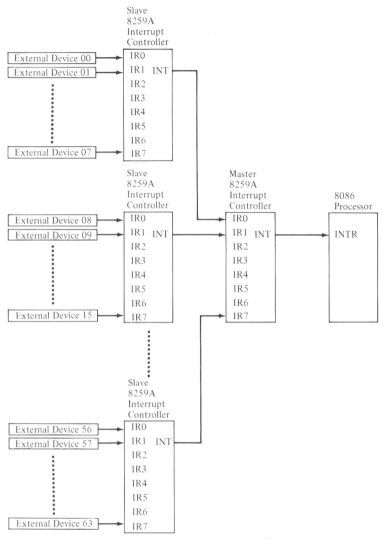

FIGURE 5-8. Use of the 8259A interrupt controller

- *Rotating:* In some applications a number of interrupting devices are of equal priority. In this mode a device, after being serviced, receives the lowest priority in the group.
- *Special Mask:* This allows the CPU to selectively inhibit interrupts from certain devices.

The Intel 8255A Programmable Peripheral Interface

As an example of an I/O module used for programmed I/O and interrupt-driven I/O, we consider the Intel 8255A Programmable Peripheral Interface [INTE88].

The 8255A is a single-chip, general-purpose I/O module designed for use with the Intel 8086 CPU. Figure 5-9 shows a general block diagram plus the pin assignment for the 40-pin package in which it is housed.

The right side of the block diagram is the external interface of the 8255A. The 24 I/O lines are programmable by the 8086 by means of the control register. The 8086 can set the value of the control register to specify a variety of operating modes and configurations. The 24 lines are divided into three 8-bit groups (A, B, C). Each group can function as an 8-bit I/O port. In addition, group C is subdivided into 4-bit groups (C_A and C_B), which may be used in conjunction with the A and B I/O ports. Configured in this manner, they carry control and status signals.

The left side of the block diagram is the internal interface to the 8086 bus. It includes an 8-bit bidirectional data bus (D0 through D7), which is used to transfer data to and from the I/O ports and to transfer control information to the control register. The two address lines specify one of the three I/O ports or the control register. A transfer takes place when the CHIP SELECT line is enabled together with either READ or WRITE line. The RESET line is used to initialize the module.

The control register is loaded by the CPU to control the mode of operation and to define signals, if any. In Mode 0 operation, the three groups of 8 external lines function as three 8-bit I/O ports. Each port can be designated as input or output. Otherwise, group A and B function as I/O ports, and the lines of group C serve as control lines for A and B. The control signals serve two principal purposes: "handshaking" and interrupt request. Handshaking is a simple timing mecha-

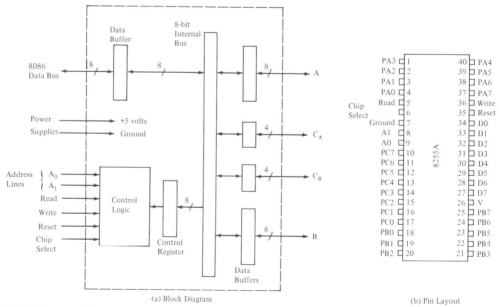

(a) Block Diagram

(b) Pin Layout

FIGURE 5-9. The Intel 8255A programmable peripheral interface

nism. One control line is used by the sender as a DATA READY line, to indicate when the data are present on the I/O data lines. Another line is used by the receiver as an ACKNOWLEDGE, indicating that the data have been read and the data lines may be cleared. Another line may be designated as an INTER-RUPT REQUEST line and tied back to the system bus.

Because the 8255A is programmable via the control register, it can be used to control a variety of simple peripheral devices. Figure 5-10 illustrates its use to control a keyboard/display terminal. The keyboard provides 8 bits of input. Two

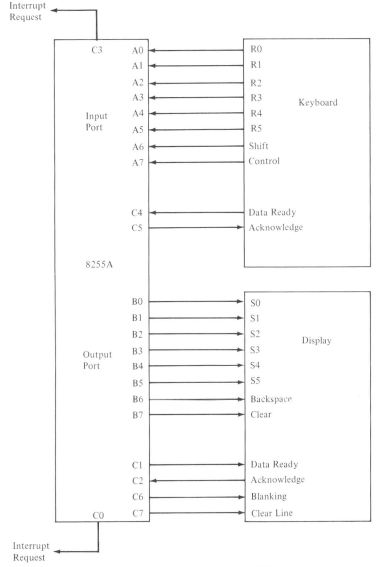

FIGURE 5-10. Keyboard/display interface to 8255A

of these bits, SHIFT and CONTROL, have special meaning to the keyboard handling program executing in the CPU. However, this interpretation is transparent to the 8255A, which simply accepts the 8 bits of data and presents them on the system data bus. Two handshaking control lines are provided for use with the keyboard.

The display is also linked by an 8-bit data port. Again, 2 of the bits have special meanings that are transparent to the 8255A. In addition to two handshaking lines, two lines provide additional control functions.

5.5

DIRECT MEMORY ACCESS

Drawbacks of Programmed and Interrupt-Driven I/O

Interrupt-driven I/O, though more efficient than simple programmed I/O, still requires the active intervention of the CPU to transfer data between memory and an I/O module, and any data transfer must traverse a path through the CPU. Thus both these forms of I/O suffer from two inherent drawbacks:

1. The I/O transfer rate is limited by the speed with which the CPU can test and service a device.
2. The CPU is tied up in managing an I/O transfer; a number of instructions must be executed for each I/O transfer (e.g., Figure 5-4).

There is somewhat of a tradeoff between these two drawbacks. Consider the transfer of a block of data. Using simple programmed I/O, the CPU is dedicated to the task of I/O and can move data at a rather high rate, at the cost of doing nothing else. Interrupt I/O frees up the CPU to some extent at the expense of I/O transfer rate. Nevertheless, both methods have an adverse impact on both CPU activity and I/O transfer rate.

When large volumes of data are to be moved, a more efficient technique is required: direct memory access (DMA).

DMA Function

DMA involves an additional module on the system bus. The DMA module (Figure 5-11) is capable of mimicking the CPU and, indeed, of taking over control of the system from the CPU. The technique works as follows. When the CPU wishes to read or write a block of data, it issues a command to the DMA module, by sending to the DMA module the following information:

- Whether a read or write is requested.
- The address of the I/O device involved.
- The starting location in memory to read from or write to.
- The number of words to be read or written.

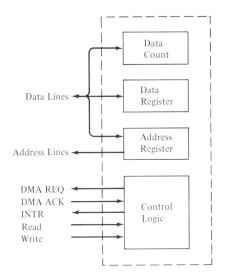

FIGURE 5-11.   Typical DMA block diagram

The CPU then continues with other work. It has delegated this I/O operation to the DMA module, and that module will take care of it. The DMA module transfers the entire block of data, one word at a time, directly to or from memory, without going through the CPU. When the transfer is complete, the DMA module sends an interrupt signal to the CPU. Thus the CPU is involved only at the beginning and end of the transfer (Figure 5-4c).

The DMA module needs to take control of the bus in order to transfer data to and from memory. For this purpose, the DMA module must use the bus only when the CPU does not need it, or it must force the CPU to temporarily suspend operation. The latter technique is more common and is referred to as *cycle-stealing* since the DMA module in effect steals a bus cycle.

Figure 5-12 shows where in the instruction cycle the CPU may be suspended. In each case, the CPU is suspended just before it needs to use the bus. The DMA module then transfers one word and returns control to the CPU. Note that this is not an interrupt; the CPU does not save a context and do something else. Rather, the CPU pauses for 1 bus cycle. The overall effect is to cause the CPU to execute more slowly. Nevertheless, for a multiple-word I/O transfer, DMA is far more efficient than interrupt-driven or programmed I/O.

The DMA mechanism can be configured in a variety of ways. Some possibilities are shown in Figure 5-13. In the first example, all modules share the same system bus. The DMA module, acting as a surrogate CPU, uses programmed I/O to exchange data between memory and an I/O module through the DMA module. This configuration, while it may be inexpensive, is clearly inefficient. As with CPU-controlled programmed I/O, each transfer of a word consumes 2 bus cycles.

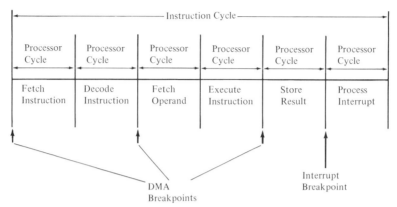

FIGURE 5-12. **DMA and interrupt breakpoints during an instruction cycle**

The number of required bus cycles can be cut substantially by integrating the DMA and I/O functions. As Figure 5-13b indicates, this means that there is a path between the DMA module and one or more I/O modules that does not include the system bus. The DMA logic may actually be a part of an I/O module,

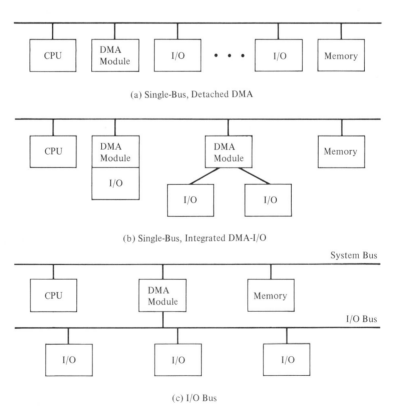

FIGURE 5-13. **Possible DMA configuration**

or it may be a separate module that controls one or more I/O modules. This concept can be taken one step further by connecting I/O modules to the DMA module using an I/O bus (Figure 5-13c). This reduces the number of I/O interfaces in the DMA module to one and provides for an easily expandable configuration. In all of these cases (Figure 5-13b and c), the system bus that the DMA module shares with the CPU and memory is used by the DMA module only to exchange data with memory. The exchange of data between the DMA and I/O modules takes place off the system bus.

5.6

I/O CHANNELS AND PROCESSORS

The Evolution of the I/O Function

As computer systems have evolved, there has been a pattern of increasing complexity and sophistication of individual components. Nowhere is this more evident than in the I/O function. We have already seen part of that evolution. The evolutionary steps can be summarized as follows:

1. The CPU directly controls a peripheral device. This is seen in simple microprocessor-controlled devices.
2. A controller or I/O module is added. The CPU uses programmed I/O without interrupts. With this step, the CPU becomes somewhat divorced from the specific details of external device interfaces.
3. The same configuration as in step 2 is used, but now interrupts are employed. The CPU need not spend time waiting for an I/O operation to be performed, increasing efficiency.
4. The I/O module is given direct access to memory via DMA. It can now move a block of data to or from memory without involving the CPU, except at the beginning and end of the transfer.
5. The I/O module is enhanced to become a processor in its own right, with a specialized set tailored for I/O. The CPU directs the I/O processor to execute an I/O program in memory. The I/O processor fetches and executes these instructions without CPU intervention. This allows the CPU to specify a sequence of I/O activities and to be interrupted only when the entire sequence has been performed.
6. The I/O module has a local memory of its own and is, in fact, a computer in its own right. With this architecture, a large set of I/O devices can be controlled, with minimal CPU involvement. A common use for such an architecture has been to control communication with interactive terminals. The I/O processor takes care of most of the tasks involved in controlling the terminals.

As one proceeds along this evolutionary path, more and more of the I/O function is performed without CPU involvement. The CPU is increasingly relieved of I/O-related tasks, improving performance. With the last two steps (5–6), a major change occurs with the introduction of the concept of an I/O module capable of executing a program. For step 5, the I/O module is often referred to as an *I/O channel*. For step 6, the term *I/O processor* is often used. However, both terms are on occasion applied to both situations. In what follows, we will use the term I/O channel.

Characteristics of I/O Channels

The I/O channel represents an extension of the DMA concept. An I/O channel has the ability to execute I/O instructions, which gives it complete control over I/O operations. In a computer system with such devices, the CPU does not execute I/O instructions. Such instructions are stored in main memory to be executed by a special-purpose processor in the I/O channel itself. Thus, the CPU initiates an I/O transfer by instructing the I/O channel to execute a program in memory. The program will specify the device or devices, the area or areas of memory for storage, priority, and actions to be taken for certain error conditions. The I/O channel follows these instructions and controls the data transfer.

Two types of I/O channels are common, as illustrated in Figure 5-14. A *selector channel* controls multiple high-speed devices and, at any one time, is dedicated to the transfer of data with one of those devices. Thus, the I/O channel selects one device and effects the data transfer. Each device, or a small set of devices, is handled by a *controller*, or I/O module, that is much like the I/O modules we have been discussing. Thus, the I/O channel serves in place of the CPU in controlling these I/O controllers. A *multiplexor channel* can handle I/O with multiple devices at the same time. For low-speed devices, a *byte multiplexor* accepts or transmits characters as fast as possible to multiple devices. For example, the resultant character stream from three devices with different rates and individual streams $A_1A_2A_3A_4 \ldots$, $B_1B_2B_3B_4 \ldots$, and $C_1C_2C_3C_4 \ldots$ might be $A_1B_1C_1A_2C_2A_3B_2C_3A_4$, and so on. For high-speed devices, a *block multiplexor* interleaves blocks of data from several devices.

IBM System/370 I/O Channel Architecture

Traditionally, the use of I/O channels has been associated with mainframe or large-scale computers. This has been so because (1) mainframes generally have a very large amount of disk and tape secondary storage and (2) many mainframes are used intensively for time sharing and transaction processing, supporting well over 100 users at a time. With the development of cheap microprocessors, the use of I/O channels is now extending to minicomputers and even microcomputers. Nevertheless, the fully developed I/O channel is best studied on the mainframe, and the best-known example is that used in IBM's large-scale systems. Although IBM now boasts a wide variety of mainframe models, all are based on the IBM System/370 architecture. Indeed, the "bible" or defining document for IBM mainframes still refers to the architecture as the IBM System/370 [IBM83]. It is to this architecture that we turn for our example.

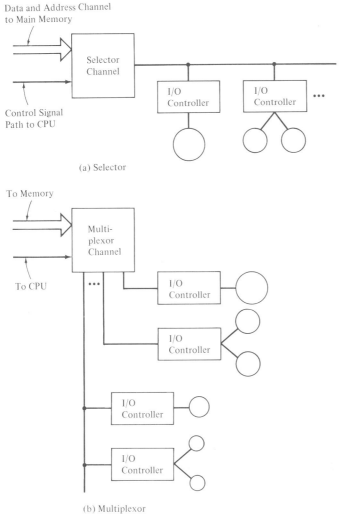

Data and Address Channel
to Main Memory

Control Signal
Path to CPU

(a) Selector

To Memory

To CPU

(b) Multiplexor

FIGURE 5-14. I/O channel architecture

Structure

The general description given so far of the system structure using I/O channels applies to the IBM 370 architecture. Figure 5-15 depicts, in general terms, the structure of the I/O subsystem for the IBM 370 family. The CPU controls one or more channels. A channel may be a byte multiplexor or block multiplexor. Each channel controls one or more I/O controllers, called *control units*. A control unit is typically concerned with a set of similar or identical devices. An example is a disk controller which controls several disk drives.

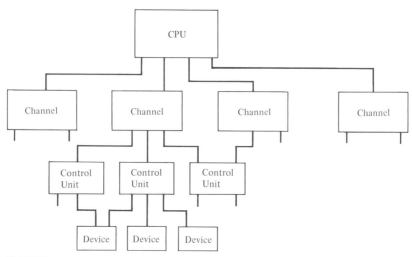

FIGURE 5-15. IBM 370 I/O structure

As the figure indicates, it is possible for one control unit to be connected to several channels and for one device to be connected to several control units. This provides for more than one physical path between the CPU and a device. Thus if one path is busy or disabled, an alternate path may be found.

The IBM 370 architecture uses, in effect, an isolated I/O addressing scheme to reference devices. Addresses on the 370 are 24 bits in length, and Figure 5-16a shows the format of a device address. Device addresses are actually only 16 bits in length; the leftmost 8 bits are set to 0. Eight bits are used to designate the channel; thus up to 256 channels are allowed. Four bits designate the control unit within the channel, and the remaining 4 bits designate the device within the control unit. When alternate paths are available, then a device will have a different address for each path.

Function

The IBM large-scale architecture defines three types of I/O directives:

- CPU I/O instructions
- Channel commands
- Control unit orders

Each type is used to control I/O processing at a different hardware level and provides a different level of detail concerning an I/O operation. This is best explained with reference to Figure 5-17, which indicates the following steps:

1. The processor controls I/O operations with a small, general set of I/O instructions issued to an I/O channel.

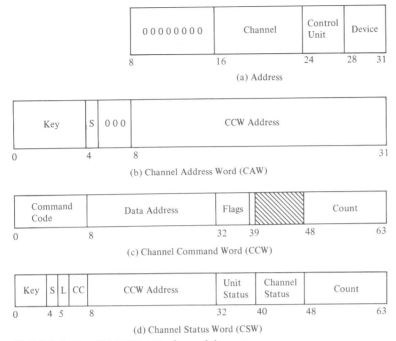

FIGURE 5-16.   IBM 370 I/O channel formats

2. More detailed instructions to the I/O channel are contained in Channel Command Words (CCWs) contained in memory. The CCWs are instructions or commands that are fetched and executed by the I/O processor.

3. Based on channel commands contained in CCWs, the channel issues control unit orders to one of its control units. During the progress of an I/O operation, control information may be exchanged back and forth between the channel and the control unit.

4. Based on the control unit orders that it receives from the channel, the control unit issues control signals to one of its devices. Again, signals may be exchanged back and forth during the course of a data transfer. These control signals represent a fourth level of I/O directives. However, these take place outside the boundary of the IBM 370 system, which is considered to be at the channel/control-unit interface, and are thus not part of the 370 architecture.

5, 6, 7. For a read, data are transferred from the device to the channel, and then from the channel directly to main memory. A write operation follows the opposite sequence.

8. Following successful or unsuccessful completion of an I/O operation, the channel issues an interrupt to the CPU.

   Let us now examine some of the details of this sequence. Table 5-4 lists the I/O instructions available on 370-class machines. These are machine instructions

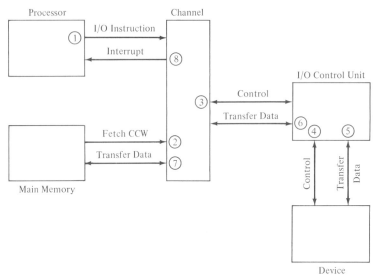

FIGURE 5-17. IBM I/O channel operation

executable by the CPU. The execution of an I/O instruction results in a CPU command being issued to an addressed channel, together with a control unit and device address. As can be seen, the I/O instructions are few in number.

An I/O operation is started when the CPU executes a START I/O (SIO) or START I/O FAST RELEASE (SIOF) instruction. The channel responds by reading the Channel Address Word (CAW) stored in location 72 of main memory. It is the responsibility of the program that issued the SIO or SIOF to load location 72 with the desired CAW. The CAW contains the following fields (Figure 5-16b):

- *Key:* A 4-bit access key is associated with every 2K- or 4K-byte block of memory. The key in the CAW is used by the channel whenever reference is made to a main memory location during the I/O operation.
- *S bit:* When set, indicates that it is possible for the CPU to suspend and later resume the I/O operation.
- *CCW address:* The location of the first CCW to be used for this operation.

The channel decodes this information and proceeds to fetch the referenced CCW. The channel will now execute an I/O program consisting of one or more CCWs. Again, these must be already stored in memory. The CCW contains the following fields (Figure 5-16c):

- *Command code:* Tells the channel what type of operation to perform. The set of commands is listed in Table 5-5. Again, the command types are few and rather general. The command codes include modifier bits that are device-specific. For example, disk commands include seek instructions and instructions to read/write control information as well as data.

TABLE 5-4 IBM 370 I/O Instructions

Start I/O (SIO)

Used for initiating an input/output operation that involves sensing the status of a device, controlling the device, and data transfer between the device and main storage. This instruction causes an I/O channel to fetch a Channel Address Word to begin an I/O operation. The start I/O instruction is initiated if (a) both subchannel and device are available, and (b) the channel is available or in the interruption-pending state and errors have not been detected. The CPU is not released until the above conditions are checked and the device selected.

Start I/O fast release (SIOF)

Similar to START I/O and used on block multiplexor channels. The main difference is that, with SIOF, the CPU is released as soon as the Channel Address Word is fetched by the I/O processor, before the status of the selected device is determined.

Test channel (TCH)

Tests whether the channel (1) is operational or not, (2) is operating in burst mode, and (3) has a pending interrupt request. Primarily used to monitor performance.

Test I/O (TIO)

Tests the status of not only the channel, but also the subchannel and the device. This instruction is used to monitor status or to respond to an interrupt.

Store channel ID (STID)

Used to obtain information about an addressed channel, such as channel type (selector, byte multiplexor, block multiplexor), and model number.

Halt I/O (HIO)

Causes the current I/O operation to be halted. A channel, subchannel, or device may be specified. This instruction provides the CPU with a means of terminating an I/O operation before all data have been transferred. This could be done to free a selector channel for a higher-priority operation or to provide real-time control on a multiplexor channel.

Halt device (HDV)

Similar to HIO. Used primarily on block multiplexor channels to halt a specific device without interfering with the other channel operations in progress.

Clear I/O (CLRIO)

Serves the same purpose as TEST I/O, and is used instead of TEST I/O for block multiplexor channels. The CLEAR I/O instruction may also cause an I/O operation to be suspended pending interrupt processing.

Clear channel (CLRCH)

Causes the channel to conclude operations on all subchannels. Status information and interruption conditions are reset on all subchannels, and a reset signal is issued to all assigned I/O devices.

Resume I/O (RIO)

Causes a currently suspended channel-program execution to be resumed with the device.

TABLE 5-5   Channel Command Word Command Codes

Write (MMMMMM01)
   Typically involves the transfer of data from main memory. For some devices, the "write" command is used for additional functions, for example, search commands in the case of the disk.

Read (MMMMMM10)
   Used to transfer data from a device to main memory.

Read backward (MMMM1100)
   Used to perform reading on a magnetic tape unit when the tape is moving backward. Data is stored in descending locations of memory.

Control (MMMMMM11)
   The modifier bits indicate a device-specific control function. In some cases, the modifier bits completely specify the function and the appropriate code is sent to the I/O device controller. In other cases, additional control information is stored in memory. This is read by the channel and sent to the device.

Sense (MMMM0100)
   Used to detect the status of the device. Status information is obtained from the device and transferred to memory.

Transfer in channel (XXXX1000)
   Used to provide chaining between CCWs that are not in contiguous locations. No I/O operation is performed. The Data Address field specifies the location of the next CCW to be fetched.

- *Data address:* Specifies the starting location in memory for a data transfer (read or write).
- *Flags:* Specify additional information about the operation to be performed. These are defined in Table 5-6.
- *Count:* Specifies the number of bytes to be transferred in this operation.

   An I/O program consists of one or more CCWs. Multiple CCWs are employed using chaining and branching. As Table 5-6 describes, CCWs can be chained together using either data chaining or command chaining. In either case, the channel will, on completion of a command, fetch the next CCW in sequence.

   The TRANSFER IN CHANNEL command is used to allow CCWs to be executed out of sequence. For example, a program to read a record with a specific ID from a disk could take the following form:

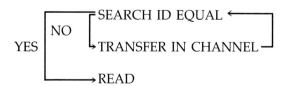

TABLE 5-6   Channel Command Word Flags

Chain data (CD)
  Used to transfer data to or from noncontiguous areas of main memory. When CD is set, and after the data transfer specified is complete, the channel fetches the next CCW and performs the same I/O operation using the new Data Address and Count fields.

Chain command (CC)
  Used to execute several CCWs using a single SIO or SIOF instruction. When CC is set, and after completion of the I/O operation specified in the command code, the channel fetches the next CCW from main memory and executes that command. Command chaining is used to set up a channel program.

Suppress length indication (SLI)
  Indicates whether an incorrect length condition is to be indicated to the program when it occurs. Incorrect length occurs when the size of the memory area assigned for the I/O operation is not equal to the number of bytes requested or offered by the I/O device.

Skip
  Instructs the channel not to transfer data to memory during a read, read backward, or sense operation. The data is absorbed by the channel as usual, but is not sent on to main memory. When combined with data chaining, skipping permits the program to store selected portions of a block of data from a device.

Program controlled interruption (PCI)
  Instructs the channel to issue an interrupt. The progress of the I/O operation is unaffected. Normally, for a chained (data or command) sequence of CCWs, the channel signals an interrupt after completion of the last CCW. The PCI provides a means of alerting the CPU to the progress of a channel I/O operation.

Indirect data address (IDA)
  Indicates that the data address field is not used to directly address the data area for the I/O operation. Rather the data address specifies the location of the first of a contiguous sequence of 32-bit Indirect Data Address Words (IDAWs). The first IDAW contains the address of a memory location until a 2K byte integral boundary is reached. The next IDAW specifies another 2K-byte block of memory, and so on until all of the data specified by the byte count field is transferred.

The first two commands are device-specific modifications of general CCW commands. First, the seek operation positions the read/write head over the required track. Then, records are read until an ID match occurs. This causes the program to skip to the READ command, which transfers in the data.

Upon completion of an operation, the channel stores the status of the operation in the Channel Status Word (CSW), in location 64 of memory, and issues an interrupt to the CPU. The CPU can determine the results of its instruction by reading the CSW, which contains the following fields (Figure 5-16d):

- *Key:* The key originally specified in the CAW for this operation.
- *S bit:* Indicates whether the operation is suspended or terminated.
- *L bit:* Indicates that a logout is pending. This means that some device-specific status information is available for the CPU. The requested I/O instruction cannot be executed until the logout is cleared.

- *Deferred Condition Code (CC):* May specify a condition that arises during an SIOF and that was not reported immediately because the CPU was released when the CAW was fetched (see definition of SIOF in Table 5-4).
- *CCW Address:* The main memory address of the byte following the last CCW that was executed.
- *Unit status:* Reports the status of the device involved in the I/O operation that caused the storing of the CSW (see Table 5-7).
- *Channel status:* Reports the status of the channel involved in the I/O operation that caused the storing of the CSW (see Table 5-7).
- *Count:* The residual count, if any, related to execution of the last CCW. The CCW count minus the CSW count equals the number of bytes actually transferred.

System/370 Extended Architecture

In 1981, IBM introduced the System/370 Extended Architecture (XA) for its large-scale systems. The XA is designed to take advantage of the changes in technology and available system resources since the introduction of the 370 architecture [BOND83]. The most visible change from System/370 to System/370-XA is the change from 24-bit to 31-bit addresses. However, virtually every aspect of the architecture is affected, including the I/O subsystem.

Several trends in large-scale systems are relevant:

- Higher execution speeds.
- The use of microprocessor rather than hard-wired logic in I/O control units.
- The use of multiple CPUs.

The first two trends are in conflict. With the use of microprocessors, the time required for a device to respond to a CPU interrogation has actually increased. Thus CPU delays are increased. In addition, the use of multiple CPUs requires coordination in the sharing of I/O control units and devices. One of the major objectives of XA is to improve overall system performance by minimizing CPU involvement in the I/O process.

The key to performance improvement is the introduction of the channel subsystem, as depicted in Figure 5-18. The channel subsystem controls all I/O devices through *subchannels*. From the processor's point of view, each device has a unique *logical subchannel* number. The channel subsystem may employ one of a number of physical paths to connect to the device. The existence of different paths and of control units is transparent to the CPU. The details of handling the status and interrupts of these lower architectural levels is hidden from the CPU.

The improvement to system performance comes about because of the increased processing power in the I/O subsystem. This allows a shift of function from the CPU to the I/O subsystem, reducing CPU program complexity and overhead. For example, testing for the availability of channels and control units and the monitoring of their status are left to the I/O channel subsystem.

TABLE 5-7   CSW Status Bits

32 Attention
   Set by the device when any significant condition occurs.

33 Status modifier
   Indicates that the device is unable to perform the requested function and cannot provide its current status.

34 Control-unit end
   The control unit has successfully completed the I/O operation and is available.

35 Busy
   The I/O device or control unit cannot execute the command because it or a required data path is busy.

36 Channel end
   The device does not need the channel any more.

37 Device end
   The device has successfully completed the I/O operation and is available.

38 Unit check
   Indicates that the I/O device or control unit has detected an unusual condition which is available in detail in response to a SENSE command.

39 Unit exception
   The I/O device detects a situation that does not usually occur, such as recognition of a tape mark.

40 Program-controlled interruption
   The CSW was created to accompany a program-controlled interruption. See definition in Table 5-6.

41 Incorrect length
   The size of the memory area assigned for the I/O operation, as specified in the CCW, is not equal to the number of bytes requested or offered by the I/O device.

42 Program check
   A programming error in a CAW or CCW was detected.

43 Protection check
   The key in the CAW did not match the key storage.

44 Channel-data check
   An error occurred during the data transfer.

45 Channel-control check
   A machine malfunction affecting channel controls has occurred.

46 Interface-control check
   An invalid signal has been received from a control unit.

47 Chaining check
   The I/O data rate for an input operation is too high to be handled by the channel and memory under current conditions.

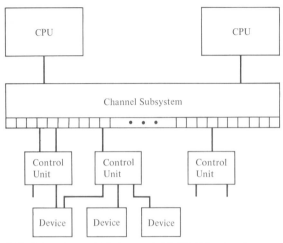

FIGURE 5-18. IBM System/370-XA I/O structure

As an example, consider a case in the 370 architecture as illustrated in Figure 5-19. With System/370, if a system has multiple CPUs, each CPU has its own set of channels. It is possible for a program in CPU 1 to request a START I/O using Channel 1-1. If a control unit busy condition is encountered, it could attempt the request on Channel 1-2. If this attempt encounters a channel-busy condition, an interrupt can be issued to CPU 2 to initiate the request from that processor. CPU 2 might require two START I/O attempts to find an available physical path. In the System/370-XA, one instruction would be issued to the channel subsystem, which would handle the details.

As the X implies, 370-XA is a compatible extension of the 370 architecture. The same or similar formats to those depicted in Figure 5-16 are used.

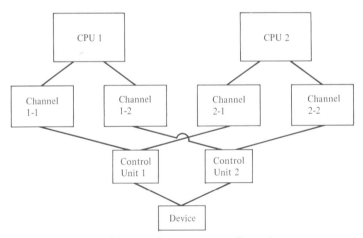

FIGURE 5-19. Multiprocessing system configuration

THE EXTERNAL INTERFACE

Types of Interfaces

The interface to a peripheral from an I/O module must be tailored to the nature and operation of the peripheral. One major characteristic of the interface is whether it is serial or parallel (Figure 5-20). In a *parallel interface*, there are multiple lines connecting the I/O module and the peripheral, and multiple bits are transferred simultaneously, just as all of the bits of a word are transferred simultaneously over the data bus. In a *serial interface*, there is only one line used to transmit data, and bits must be transmitted one at a time. A parallel interface is commonly used for higher-speed peripherals, such as tape and disk. The serial interface is more common for printers and terminals.

In either case, the I/O module must engage in a dialogue with the peripheral. In general terms the dialogue for a write operation is as follows:

1. The I/O module sends a control signal requesting permission to send data.
2. The peripheral acknowledges the request.
3. The I/O module transfers data (one word or a block depending on the peripheral).
4. The peripheral acknowledges receipt of the data.

A read operation proceeds similarly.

Key to the operation of an I/O module is an internal buffer that can store data being passed between the peripheral and the rest of the system. This buffer

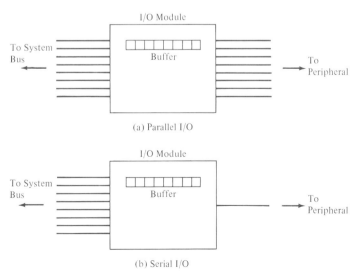

FIGURE 5-20.   **Parallel and series I/O**

allows the I/O module to compensate for the differences in speed between the system bus and its external lines.

Parallel Data Transfer

The dialogue that takes place across the interface includes the exchange of both control information and data. Two fundamental requirements occur:

• It must be possible to determine when a signal starts and ends.
• It must be possible to distinguish control information from data.

For parallel data transfer, we have already examined solutions to these requirements in Chapter 3. The timing may be either asynchronous or synchronous. In asynchronous timing, events occur in sequence, and one event depends on the occurrence of a previous event. The various operations on the Unibus exhibit this behavior. In synchronous timing, events occur during specified time slots, controlled by a clock. The VAX-11 SBI exhibits this behavior.

The differentiation between control information and data is simple with parallel transfer. Different lines are dedicated to different functions. Again the Unibus and SBI are examples.

The examples we have used are not external interfaces but internal system buses. However, the same principles apply to the external interface, as the following example shows.

Interface Between Channel and Control Unit
on the IBM System/370

One of the most widely used parallel I/O interfaces is the System/370 interface between channels and control units. As is typical of large-scale computers, the 370 architecture dictates that virtually all devices attach through control units that attach to an I/O channel. The System/370 I/O channel is used not only by IBM for its products but also by a variety of "plug compatible" vendors who sell peripheral controllers, such as disk and tape drives. Furthermore, this interface has been promulgated as a federal government standard by the National Bureau of Standards [NBS79]. Thus, many computer vendors provide this channel interface.

The System/370 I/O interface is general-purpose. It provides for a set of 34 (extendable to 48) bus lines. The channel and one or more control units attach to this bus. Table 5-8 provides a definition of each line.

Data are transferred between the channel and a control unit one byte at a time over the BUS IN and BUS OUT lines. The channel controls the use of the bus by selecting the device to be involved in the next operation and by issuing commands. The commands that are issued are those listed in Table 5-5; the modifier bits are used to tailor them to a specific type of control unit. A control unit can select a specific device by address. Alternatively, if activity is desired or expected with more than one control unit, the channel can issue an unaddressed select

TABLE 5-8   SYSTEM/370 I/O Interface Control Lines

But out (9)
   Used to transmit addresses, commands, control orders, and data to the control units. Consists of eight information lines and one parity line.

Bus in (9)
   Used to transmit addresses, status, sense information, and data to the channel. Consists of eight information lines and one parity line.

Outbound tags (3)
   Identify the type of information present on BUS OUT. The correspondence is ADDRESS OUT: a control unit; COMMAND OUT: a command; SERVICE OUT: data requested by the control unit.

Inbound tags (3)
   Identify the type of information present on BUS IN. The correspondence is ADDRESS IN: address of responding control unit; STATUS IN: status information; SERVICE IN: data associated with the current I/O operation.

Scan controls (4)
   Used for polling and selection of control units. SELECT OUT and SELECT IN form a loop from the channel through each control unit and back. HOLD OUT provides synchronization. REQUEST IN indicates that the control unit is ready to present status information or data and is a selection sequence.

Interlocks (2)
   Used to ensure that only one control unit is communicating with the channel at any given time. OPERATIONAL OUT must be up for other lines to have significance; when it is down, all lines must drop any operation currently in progress and must be reset. OPERATIONAL IN signals the channel that the control unit is selected and communicating.

Special controls (4)
   Used for metering time, suppressing other lines, and other specialized control purposes.

Note:
   OUT = signal from channel to control units
   IN = signal from control units to channel

signal. Any control unit can respond, and a daisy-chain priority scheme is employed, using the SELECT OUT and SELECT IN lines. These lines loop through all of the control units so that the unit physically closest to the channel has the highest priority, and so on. Figure 5-21 illustrates, in simplified form, the operation of the interface. The example shows the selection of a device followed by a read of 1 byte. The selection of a device proceeds with the following steps. The channel places the address of the device to be selected on the BUS OUT lines and raises ADDRESS OUT to alert the control units. The channel then raises SELECT OUT to ask for a response. If the selected unit is available, it signals this by raising OPERATIONAL IN. The channel acknowledges by dropping ADDRESS OUT. The control unit then places its address on the bus. With this coordination completed, the channel issues the read command and the control unit responds with its current status. The channel acknowledges with a SERVICE OUT signal.

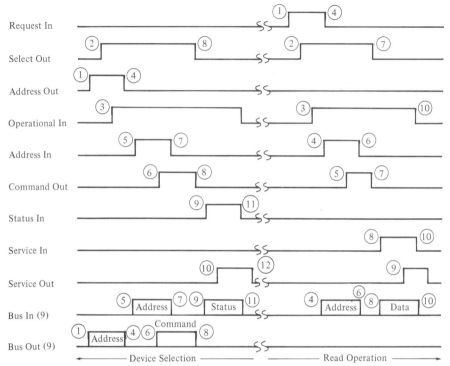

FIGURE 5-21. Channel sequence of operations

After initial selection, the control unit decodes the command it has received and sends it to the device for execution. Meanwhile, the channel may do other things. When the device operation is complete, it requests use of the bus via REQUEST IN. When it receives permission, via SELECT OUT, the control unit places the device address on the bus. The channel acknowledges with COMMAND OUT, requesting that the previous command be performed. Data transfer at last takes place.

More complex sequences are possible. A control unit may send or receive a block at a time rather than a byte at a time, and both byte and block multiplexing are permitted.

Serial Data Transfer

With serial transmission, a single path is used to handle the transfer of all control information and data between the I/O module and the device. Serial transmission is commonly used for terminal connection and for data communication lines. With just a single line available for data transfer, it is more difficult with serial transmission to provide timing. Since a sequence of bits will be transferred on the line, a fundamental requirement is that the receiver knows the starting time and duration of each bit that it receives.

The earliest and simplest scheme for meeting this requirement is *asynchronous transmission*. In this scheme, data are transmitted one character (of 5 to 8 bits) at a time. Each character is preceded by a start code and followed by a stop code (Figure 5-22a). The *start code* has the encoding for 0 and a duration of 1 bit time; in other words, the start code is 1 with a value of 0. The *stop code* has a value of 1 and a minimum duration, depending on the system, of from 1 to 2 bit times. When there are no data to send, the transmitter sends a continuous stop code. The receiver identifies the beginning of a new character by the transition from 1 to 0. The receiver must have a fairly accurate idea of the duration of each bit in order to recover all the bits of the character. However, a small amount of drift (e.g., 1% per bit) will not matter since the receiver resynchronizes with each stop code. This means of communication is simple and cheap, but it requires an overhead of 2 to 3 bits per character. This technique is referred to as *asynchronous* because characters are sent independently of each other, and the sender and receiver are not synchronized to a shared clock. Thus characters may be sent at a nonuniform rate.

A more efficient means of communication is *synchronous transmission*. In this mode, blocks of characters or bits are transmitted without start and stop codes, and the exact departure or arrival time of each bit is predictable. To prevent timing drift between transmitter and receiver, their clocks must somehow be synchronized. One possibility is to provide a separate clock line between transmitter and receiver. Otherwise, the clocking information must be embedded in the signal itself, by some form of encoding.

With synchronous transmission, there is another level of synchronization required, to allow the receiver to determine the beginning and end of a block of data. To achieve this, each block begins with a *preamble* bit pattern and ends with a *postamble* bit pattern. The data plus preamble and postamble is called a *frame*. The nature of the preamble and postamble depends on whether the block of data is character-oriented or bit-oriented.

With *character-oriented* schemes, each block is preceded by one or more "synchronization characters" (Figure 5-22b). The synchronization character, usually called *SYNC*, is chosen such that its bit pattern is significantly different from any

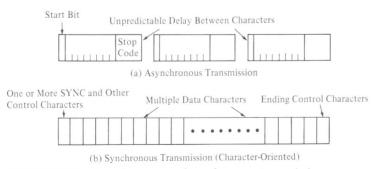

(a) Asynchronous Transmission

(b) Synchronous Transmission (Character-Oriented)

FIGURE 5-22.   **Asynchronous and synchronous transmission**

of the regular characters being transmitted. The postamble is another unique character and accepts data until the postamble character is seen. The receiver can then look for the next SYNC pattern.

Character-oriented schemes, such as IBM's BSC, are gradually being replaced by more efficient and flexible *bit-oriented schemes,* which treat the block of data as a bit stream rather than a character stream. We present an example of a bit-oriented scheme in what follows.

For serial transmission, control and data cannot be physically separated on different lines. Instead, formatting conventions are used. The example that follows illustrates this.

High-Level Data Link Control (HDLC)

One of the most common synchronous serial transmission techniques is HDLC. Developed by the International Organization for Standardization (ISO), HDLC is available from most computer vendors for both computer-to-computer and terminal-to-computer data exchange.

Three modes of operation are defined: the *normal response mode* (NRM), *asynchronous response mode* (ARM), and *asynchronous balanced mode* (ABM). Both NRM and ARM can be used in point-to-point or multipoint configurations. For each there are one *primary station* and one or more *secondary stations.* The primary station is responsible for initializing the link, controlling the flow of data to and from secondary stations, recovering from errors, and logically disconnecting secondary stations. In NRM, a secondary station may transmit only in response to a poll from the primary; in ARM, the secondary may initiate a transmission without a poll. NRM is ideally suited for a multidrop line consisting of a host computer and a number of terminals. ARM may be needed for certain kinds of loop configurations.

ABM is used only on point-to-point links, and each station assumes the role of both primary and secondary. ABM is more efficient for point-to-point lines since there is no polling overhead and both stations may initiate transmissions.

Data are transmitted in frames that consist of 6 fields (Figure 5-23).

Frame Structure

8 bits	8	8	$\geqslant 0$	16	8
Flag	Address	Control	Data	CRC	Flag

Control Field Structure

	1	2	3	4	5	6	7	8
Information	0		Seq		P/F		Next	
Supervisory	1	0	Type		P/F		Next	
Unnumbered	1	1	Type		P/F		Modifier	

FIGURE 5-23. The HDLC frame structure

- *FLAG:* Used for synchronization, these fields indicate the start and end of a frame.
- *ADDRESS:* This field identifies the secondary station of this transmission.
- *CONTROL:* This field identifies the function and purpose of the frame. It is described presently.
- *DATA:* This field contains the data to be transmitted.
- *CRC:* This is a frame check sequence field. It uses a 16-bit *cycle redundancy check* (CRC). The CRC field is a function of the contents of the address, control, and data fields. It is generated by the sender and again by the receiver. If the receiver's result differs from the CRC field, a transmission error has occurred.

Three types of frames are used, each with a different control-field format. Information frames carry the data. Supervisory frames provide basic link control functions, and unnumbered frames provide supplemental link control functions.

The P/F (poll/final) bit is used by a primary station to solicit a response. More than 1 frame may be sent in response, with the P/F bit set to indicate the last frame. The P/F may be used with supervisory and unnumbered frames to force a response.

The SEQ and NEXT fields in the information frame provide an efficient technique for both flow control and error control. A station numbers the frames that it sends sequentially modulo 8, using the SEQ field. When a station receives a valid information frame, it acknowledges that frame with its own information frame by setting the NEXT field to the number of the next frame it expects to receive. This is known as a *piggybacked acknowledgment*, since the acknowledgment rides back on an information frame. Acknowledgments can also be sent on a supervisory frame. This scheme accomplishes three important functions.

- *Flow control:* Once a station has sent seven frames, it can send no more until the first frame is acknowledged.
- *Error control:* If a frame is received in error, a station can send a NAK (negative acknowledgment) via a supervisory frame to specify which frame was received in error. This is done in one of two ways. In the *go back n protocol*, the sending station retransmits the NAK'ed frame and all subsequent frames that had already been sent. In the *selective repeat technique*, the sending station retransmits only the frame in error.
- *Pipelining:* More than 1 frame may be in transit at a time; this allows more efficient use of links with high propagation delay, such as satellite links.

The SEQ/NEXT technique is known as a *sliding-window protocol* because the sending station maintains a window of messages to be sent that gradually moves forward with transmission and acknowledgment. The process is depicted in Figure 5-24.

There are four types of supervisory frames:

- *Receive Ready (RR):* Used to acknowledge correct receipt of frames up through NEXT-1. In addition, RR is used as a poll command instructing the secondary to begin transmission with sequence number NEXT.

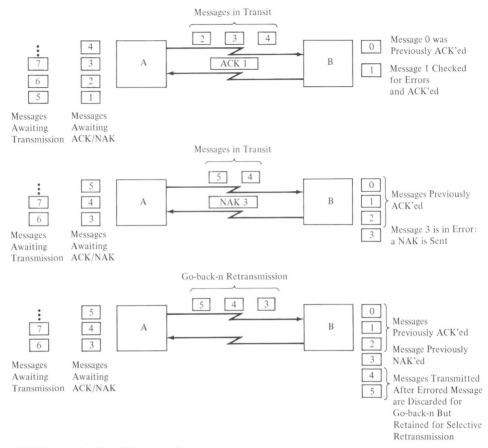

FIGURE 5-24. The sliding-window technique

- *Receive Not Ready (RNR):* Used to indicate a temporary busy condition. NEXT is used for a possibly redundant acknowledgment.
- *Reject (REJ):* Used to indicate an error in frame NEXT and to request retransmission of that and all subsequent frames.
- *Selective Reject (SREJ):* Used to request retransmission of a single frame.

The unnumbered frames have no sequence numbers and are used for a variety of special purposes, such as to initialize a station, set the mode, disconnect a station, and reject a command.

5.8

RECOMMENDED READING

[BUZE75] is a thorough survey of I/O architecture. Another survey, focusing on microcomputers, is [WAKE77]. Worthwhile accounts can be found in

[KHAM82], [SLOA83], [HAMA84], [STON80], and [MANO82]. A detailed discussion of the Intel 8255A and 8259A can be found in [BREY91].

Good descriptions of IBM 370 I/O architecture, in increasing order of completeness and complexity, are [LEBA84a], [PRAS81], and [IBM83a,b]. [CORM83] is an excellent description of the 370-XA I/O architecture. The Intel 8089, an I/O processor designed for a microcomputer, is described by [STAM79] and [ELAY79]; [INTEL83] also contains a description.

A detailed discussion of serial transmission, including asynchronous and synchronous techniques, plus an examination of HDLC can be found in [STAL91].

5.9

PROBLEMS

5.1 In Section 5.3, one advantage and one disadvantage of memory-mapped I/O, compared to isolated I/O, were listed. List two more advantages and two more disadvantages.

5.2 For vectored interrupts, why does the I/O module place the vector on the data lines rather than the address lines?

5.3 In virtually all systems that include DMA modules, DMA access to main memory is given higher priority than CPU access to main memory. Why?

5.4 Consider the disk system described in Problems 4.16 and 4.17. A CPU reads one sector from the disk using interrupt-driven I/O, with one interrupt per byte. If it takes 2.5 μs to process each interrupt, what percentage of the time will the CPU spend handling I/O (disregard seek time)?

5.5 Repeat Problem 5.4 using DMA, and assume one interrupt per sector.

5.6 A DMA module is transferring characters to memory using cycle-stealing, from a device transmitting at 9,600 bps. The CPU is fetching instructions at the rate of 1 million instructions per second (1 MIPS). By how much will the processor be slowed down due to the DMA module?

5.7 A 32-bit computer has two selector channels and one multiplexor channel. Each selector channel supports two magnetic disk and two magnetic tape units. The multiplexor channel has two line printers, two card readers, and ten VDT terminals connected to it. Assume the following transfer rates:

Disk drive	800 KBytes/s
Magnetic tape drive	200 KBytes/s
Line printer	6.6 KBytes/s
Card reader	1.2 KBytes/s
VDT	1 KBytes/s

Estimate the maximum aggregate I/O transfer rate in this system.

5.8 A computer consists of a CPU and an I/O device D connected to main memory M via a 1-word shared bus. The CPU can execute a maximum of 10^5 instructions per second. An average instruction requires five machine cycles, three of which use the memory bus. A memory read or write operation uses one machine cycle. Suppose that the CPU is continuously executing "background" programs that require 95% of its instruction execution rate but not any I/O instructions. Now the I/O device is to be used to transfer very large blocks of data to and from main memory M.

(a) If programmed I/O is used and each 1-word I/O transfer requires the CPU to execute two instructions, estimate the maximum I/O data-transfer rate r_{MAX} possible through D.

(b) Estimate r_{MAX} if DMA is used.

5.9 A number of Multibus-compatible I/O modules are to be connected to a PDP-11. A bus adapter that links Unibus to Multibus is needed. Describe the mapping needed to enable read and write operations initiated by the CPU.

5.10 Repeat Problem 5.9 for the interrupt control signals.

5.11 What is the main advantage of the IBM/370 SIOF instruction over the SIO instruction? The main disadvantage?

5.12 Can the Indirect Data Address (IDA) function (Table 5-6) for the IBM I/O function be achieved in another fashion? If so, what is the advantage or disadvantage of the IDA method?

5.13 A data source produces 7-bit ASCII characters, to each of which is appended a parity bit. Derive an expression for the maximum effective data rate (rate of ASCII data bits) over an R-bps line for the following:

(a) Asynchronous transmission, with a 1.5-unit stop bit.

(b) Bit-synchronous transmission, with a frame consisting of 48 control bits and 128 information bits.

(c) Same as (b), with a 1,024-bit information field.

(d) Character-synchronous, with 9 control characters per frame and 16 information characters.

(e) Same as (d), with 128 information characters.

5.14 The following problem is based on a suggested illustration of I/O mechanisms in [ECKE90]:

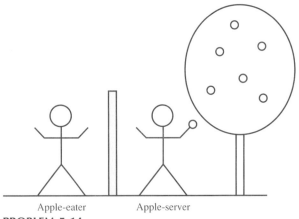

Apple-eater   Apple-server

PROBLEM 5-14.

Two boys are playing on either side of a high fence. One of the boys, named Apple-server, has a beautiful apple tree loaded with delicious apples growing on his side of the fence; he is happy to supply apples to the other boy whenever needed. The other boy, named Apple-eater, loves to eat apples but has none. In fact, he must eat his apples at a fixed rate (an apple a day keeps the doctor away). If he eats them faster than that rate, he will get sick. If he eats them slower he'll suffer malnutrition. Neither boy can talk, so the problem is to get apples from Apple-server to Apple-eater at the correct rate.

(a) Assume that there is an alarm clock sitting on top of the fence, and that the clock can have multiple alarm settings. How can the clock be used to solve the problem? Draw a timing diagram to illustrate the solution.

(b) Now assume that there is no alarm clock. Instead Apple-eater has a flag that he can wave whenever he needs an apple. Suggest a new solution. Would it be helpful for Apple-server to also have a flag? If so, incorporate this into the solution. Discuss the drawbacks of this approach.

(c) Now take away the flag and assume the existence of a long piece of string. Suggest a solution that is superior to that of (b) using the string.

CHAPTER 6

Operating Systems

Although the focus of this text is computer hardware, there is one area of software that needs to be addressed: the computer's operating system. The operating system is a program that manages the computer's resources, provides services for programmers, and schedules the execution of other programs. A limited understanding of operating systems is essential in understanding the mechanisms by which the CPU controls the computer system. In particular, explanations of the effect of interrupts and of the management of the memory hierarchy are best explained in this context.

The chapter begins with an overview, a brief history of operating systems, and a survey of the types of services provided to a programmer. The bulk of the chapter looks at the two operating-system functions that are most relevant to the study of computer organization and architecture: scheduling and memory management.

6.1

OPERATING SYSTEM OVERVIEW

Operating System Objectives and Functions

An operating system is a program that controls the execution of application programs and acts as an interface between the user of a computer and the computer hardware. An operating system can be thought of as having two objectives or performing two functions:

- *Convenience:* An operating system makes a computer system more convenient to use.
- *Efficiency:* An operating system allows the computer system resources to be used in an efficient manner.

Let us examine these two aspects of an operating system in turn.

The Operating System as a User/Computer Interface

In Chapter 1, we discussed the hierarchical nature of a computer system, referring to hardware. That view can be extended to the software that is executed on the computer, as depicted in Figure 6-1. In most cases, the ultimate use of the computer is to provide one or a set of applications. The user of those applications is called the *end user* and generally is not concerned with the computer's architecture. Thus the end user views a computer system in terms of an application. That application can be expressed in a programming language and is developed by an *application programmer*. Now, it should soon become clear that if one were to develop an *application program* as a set of machine instructions that is completely responsible for controlling the computer hardware, one would be faced with an overwhelmingly complex task. To ease this task, a set of *system programs* is provided. Some of these programs are referred to as *utilities*. These implement frequently used functions that assist in program creation, the management of files, and the control of I/O devices. A programmer will make use of these facilities in developing an application, and the application, while it is running, will invoke the utilities to perform certain functions. The most important system program is the *operating system*. The operating system masks the details of the hardware from the programmer and provides the programmer with a convenient interface for using the system. It acts as a mediator, making it easier for the programmer and for application programs to access and use those facilities and services.

Briefly, the operating system typically provides services in the following areas:

- *Program creation:* The operating system provides a variety of facilities and services to assist the programmer in creating programs. These are lumped under the generic name *utilities*.

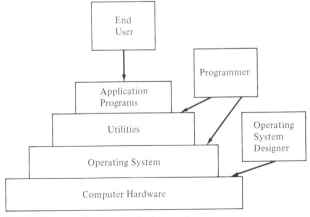

FIGURE 6-1. Layers and views of a computer system

- *Program execution:* A number of tasks need to be performed to execute a program. Instructions and data must be loaded into main memory, I/O devices and files must be initialized, and other resources must be prepared. The operating system handles all of this for the user.
- *Access to I/O devices:* Each I/O device requires its own peculiar set of instructions or control signals for operation. The operating system takes care of the details so that the programmer can think in terms of simple reads and writes.
- *Controlled access to files:* In the case of files, control must include an understanding of not only the nature of the I/O device (disk drive, tape drive) but also the file format on the storage medium. Again, the operating system worries about the details. Further, in the case of a system with multiple simultaneous users, the operating system can provide protection mechanisms to control access to shared resources, such as files.
- *System access:* In the case of a shared or public system, the operating system controls access to the system as a whole and to specific system resources.

We will not further pursue the subject of operating-system services. Our concern in this chapter is the resource-management function of the operating system, and its implications for computer organization and architecture.

The Operating System as a Resource Manager

A computer is a set of resources for the movement, storage, and processing of data and for the control of these functions. The operating system is responsible for managing these resources.

Can we say that it is the operating system that controls the movement, storage, and processing of data? From one point of view, the answer is yes; by managing the computer's resources, the operating system is in control of the computer's basic functions. But this control is exercised in a curious way. Normally, we think of a control mechanism as something external to that which is controlled or, at least, as something that is a distinct and separate part of that which is controlled. (For example, a residential heating system is controlled by a thermostat, which is completely distinct from the heat-generation and heat-distribution apparatus.) This is not the case with the operating system, which as a control mechanism is unusual in two respects:

- The operating system functions in the same way as ordinary computer software; that is, it is a program executed by the CPU.
- The operating system frequently relinquishes control and must depend on the CPU to allow it to regain control.

The operating system is, in fact, nothing more than a computer program. Like other computer programs, it provides instructions for the CPU. The only difference is in the intent of the program. The operating system directs the CPU in the use of the other system resources and in the timing of its execution of other programs. But in order for the CPU to do any of these things, it must cease executing the operating system program and execute other programs. Thus, the

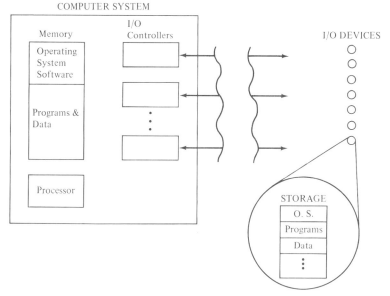

FIGURE 6-2. The operating system as resource manager

operating system relinquishes control for the processor to do some "useful" work and then resumes control long enough to prepare the CPU to do the next piece of work. The mechanisms involved in all this should become clear as the chapter proceeds.

Figure 6-2 suggests the main resources that are managed by the operating system. A portion of the operating system is in main memory. This includes the *nucleus,* which contains the most-frequently-used functions in the operating system and, at a given time, other portions of the operating system currently in use. The remainder of main memory contains other programs and data. The allocation of this resource (main memory) is controlled jointly by the operating system and memory-management hardware in the CPU, as we shall see. The operating system decides when an I/O device can be used by a program in execution and controls access to and use of files.

Types of Operating Systems

Certain key characteristics serve to differentiate various types of operating systems. The characteristics fall along two independent dimensions. The first dimension specifies whether the system is batch or interactive. In an *interactive* system, the user/programmer interacts directly with the computer, usually through a keyboard/display terminal, to request the execution of a job or to perform a transaction. Furthermore, the user may, depending on the nature of the application, communicate with the computer during the execution of the job. A *batch* system is the opposite of interactive. The user's program is batched together with programs from other users and submitted by a computer operator. After the program is completed, results are printed out for the user. Pure batch systems are rare today. However, it will be useful to the description of contemporary operating systems to briefly examine batch systems.

An independent dimension specifies whether the system employs *multiprogramming* or not. With multiprogramming, the attempt is made to keep the processor as busy as possible by having it work on more than one program at a time. Several programs are loaded into memory, and the processor switches rapidly among them. The alternative is a *uniprogramming* system that works only one program at a time.

Based on these two dimensions, we can describe four general types of operating systems, as shown in Table 6-1. The best way to describe these various types is to take a brief excursion into the history of operating systems.

Early Systems

With the earliest computers, the programmer interacted directly with the computer hardware. These machines were run from a console, consisting of display lights, toggle switches, some form of input device, and a printer. Programs in machine code were loaded via the input device (e.g., card reader). If an error halted the program, the error condition was indicated by the lights.

As time went on, additional hardware and software were developed. The hardware additions included magnetic tape and high-speed line printers. The software additions included compilers, assemblers, and libraries of common functions. Common functions could be linked together with application programs without having to be written again.

These early systems presented two main problems:

- *Scheduling:* Most installations used a sign-up sheet to reserve machine time. A user could typically sign up for a block of time in multiples of a half hour or so. A user might sign up for an hour and finish in 45 minutes; this would result in wasted computer idle time. Alternatively, the user might run into problems, not finish in the alloted time, and be forced to stop before resolving the problem.
- *Setup time:* A single program, called a *job,* could involve loading the compiler plus the high-level language program (source program) into memory, saving the compiled program (object program), and then loading and linking together

TABLE 6-1 Dimensions of an Operating System

	Batch	Interactive
One task at a time	Simple batch	Dedicated system
Multiprogrammed	Sophisticated batch	Time sharing

the object program and common functions. Each of these steps could involve mounting or dismounting tapes or setting up card decks. Thus a considerable amount of time was spent just in setting up the program to run.

Simple Batch Systems

Early machines were very expensive, and therefore it was important to maximize machine utilization. The wasted time due to scheduling and setup time was unacceptable.

To improve utilization, simple batch operating systems were developed. With such a system, also called a *monitor*, the user no longer has direct access to the machine. Rather, the user submits the job on cards or tape to a computer operator, who *batches* the jobs together sequentially and places the entire batch on an input device, for use by the monitor.

To understand how the scheme works, let us look at it from two points of view: that of the monitor and that of the CPU. From the point of view of the monitor, it is the monitor that controls the sequence of events. For this to be so, the monitor is always in main memory (hence is often called the *resident monitor*) and available for execution (Figure 6-3). The monitor reads in the jobs one at a time. As it is read in, the current job is placed in the user program area, and control is passed to this job. When the job is completed, an interrupt (internal to the CPU) occurs that returns control to the monitor, which immediately reads in the next job. The results of each job are printed out for delivery to the user.

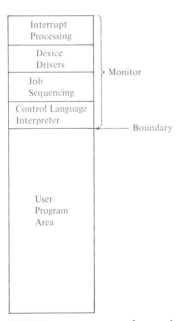

FIGURE 6-3. Memory layout for a resident monitor

Now let us consider this sequence from the point of view of the CPU. At a certain point in time, the CPU is executing instructions from the portion of main memory containing the monitor. These instructions cause the next job to be read in to another portion of main memory. Once a job has been read in, the CPU will encounter in the monitor a branch instruction that instructs the CPU to continue execution at another location in memory (the start of the user program). The CPU will then execute the instructions in the user's program until it encounters an ending or error condition. Either event causes the CPU to fetch its next instruction from the monitor program. Thus the phrase, "control is passed to a job," simply means that the CPU is now fetching and executing instructions in a user program, and "control is returned to the monitor" means that the CPU is now fetching and executing instructions from the monitor program.

It should be clear that the monitor handles the scheduling problem. A batch of jobs is queued up, and jobs are executed as rapidly as possible, with no intervening idle time.

How about the job setup problem? The monitor handles this as well. With each job, instructions are included in a *job control language.* This is just a special type of programming language used to provide instructions to the monitor. Figure 6-4 shows a simple example, with job input via cards. In this example, the user is submitting a program written in FORTRAN plus some data to be used by the program. In addition to FORTRAN and data cards, the deck includes job control instructions, which are denoted by the beginning "$."

We see that the monitor, or batch operating system, is simply a computer program. It relies on the ability of the CPU to fetch instructions from various portions of main memory in order to alternately seize and relinquish control. Certain other hardware features are also required:

• *Memory protection:* While the user program is executing, it must not alter the

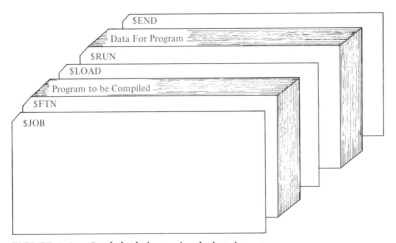

FIGURE 6-4. Card deck for a simple batch system

memory area containing the monitor. If such an attempt is made, the CPU hardware detects an error and transfers control to the monitor. The monitor aborts the job, prints out an error message, and loads in the next job.

- *Timer:* A timer is used to prevent a single job from monopolizing the system. The timer is set at the beginning of each job. If the timer expires, an interrupt occurs, and control returns to the monitor.
- *Privileged instructions:* Certain instructions are designated privileged and can be executed only by the monitor. These include I/O instructions, so that the monitor retains control of all I/O devices. This prevents, for example, a user program from accidentally reading job control instructions from the next job. If a user program wishes to perform I/O, it must request that the monitor perform the operation for it. If a privileged instruction is encountered by the CPU while it is executing a user program, the CPU hardware considers this an error and transfers control to the monitor.

Machine time thus alternates between execution of user programs and execution of the monitor. There have been two sacrifices: some main memory is now given over to the monitor and some machine time is consumed by the monitor. Both of these are forms of overhead. Even with this overhead, the simple batch system improves the utilization of the computer.

Sophisticated Batch Systems

Even with the automatic job sequencing provided by a simple batch operating system, the processor is often idle. The problem is that I/O devices are slow compared to the processor. Figure 6-5 details a representative calculation. The calculation concerns a program that processes a file of records and performs, on average, 100 machine instructions per record. In this example the computer spends over 96% of its time waiting for I/O devices to finish transferring data! Figure 6-6a illustrates this situation. The processor spends a certain amount of time executing, until it reaches an I/O instruction. It must then wait until that I/O instruction concludes before proceeding.

This inefficiency is not necessary. We know that there must be enough memory to hold the operating system (resident monitor) and one user program. Suppose that there is room for the operating system and two user programs. Now, when one job needs to wait for I/O, the processor can switch to the other job, which likely is not waiting for I/O (Figure 6-6b). Furthermore, we might expand memory to hold three, four, or more programs and switch among all of

Read one record	0.0015 seconds
Execute 100 instructions	0.0001 seconds
Write one record	0.0015 seconds
TOTAL	0.0031 seconds

Percent CPU Utilization $= \dfrac{0.0001}{0.0031} = 0.032 = 3.2\%$

FIGURE 6-5.   System utilization example

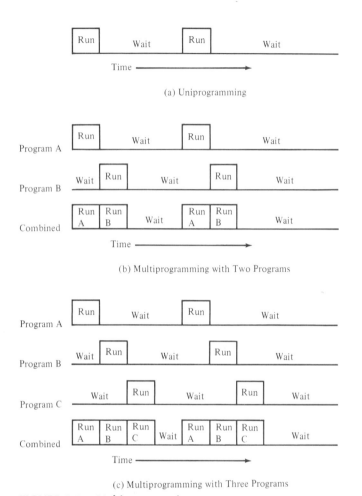

(a) Uniprogramming

(b) Multiprogramming with Two Programs

(c) Multiprogramming with Three Programs

FIGURE 6-6.   **Multiprogramming**

them (Figure 6-6c). This process is known as *multiprogramming*. It is the central theme of modern operating systems.

To illustrate the benefit of multiprogramming, let us consider an example, based on one in [TURN86]. Consider a computer with 256K words of available memory (not used by the operating system), a disk, a terminal, and a printer. Three programs, JOB1, JOB2, and JOB3, are submitted for execution at the same time, with the attributes listed in Table 6-2. We assume minimal processor requirements for JOB2 and JOB3 and continuous disk and printer use by JOB3. For a uniprogramming environment, these jobs will be executed in sequence. Thus JOB1 completes in 5 minutes. JOB2 must wait until the 5 minutes is over, and then completes 15 minutes after that. JOB3 begins after 20 minutes and completes at 30 minutes from the time it was initially submitted. The average resource utilization, throughput, and response times are shown in the

TABLE 6-2 Sample Program Execution Attributes

	JOB1	JOB2	JOB3
Type of job:	Heavy compute	Heavy I/O	Heavy I/O
Duration:	5 min	15 min	10 min
Memory required:	50K	100K	80K
Need disk?	No	No	Yes
Need terminal?	No	Yes	No
Need printer?	No	No	Yes

uniprogramming column of Table 6-3. Device-by-device utilization is illustrated in Figure 6-7. It is evident that there is gross under-utilization of all resources when averaged over the required 30-minute time period.

Now suppose that the jobs are run concurrently under a multiprogramming operating system. Since there is little resource contention between the jobs, all three can run in nearly minimum time while coexisting with the others in the computer (assuming that JOB2 and JOB3 are allotted enough processor time to keep their input and output operations active). JOB1 will still require 5 minutes to complete but at the end of that time, JOB2 will be one-third finished and JOB3 half finished. All three jobs will have finished within 15 minutes. The improvement is evident when examining the multiprogramming column of Table 6-3, obtained from the histogram shown in Figure 6-8.

As with a simple batch system, a multiprogramming batch system is a program that must rely on certain computer hardware features. The most notable additional feature that is useful for multiprogramming is the hardware that supports I/O interrupts and DMA. With interrupt-driven I/O or DMA, the CPU can issue an I/O command for one job and proceed with the execution of another job. When the I/O operation is complete, the CPU is interrupted and control is passed to an interrupt-handling program in the operating system. The operating system will then pass control to another job.

Multiprogrammed operating systems are fairly sophisticated compared to single-program or *uniprogramming* systems. In order to have several jobs ready to run, they must be kept in memory, requiring some form of *memory management*. In addition, if several jobs are ready to run, the processor must decide

TABLE 6-3 Effects of Multiprogramming on Resource Utilization

	Uniprogramming	Multiprogramming
Processor utilization:	17%	33%
Memory utilization:	30%	67%
Disk utilization:	33%	67%
Printer utilization:	33%	67%
Elasped time:	30 min	15 min
Throughput rate:	6 jobs/hour	12 jobs/hour
Mean response time:	18 min	10 min

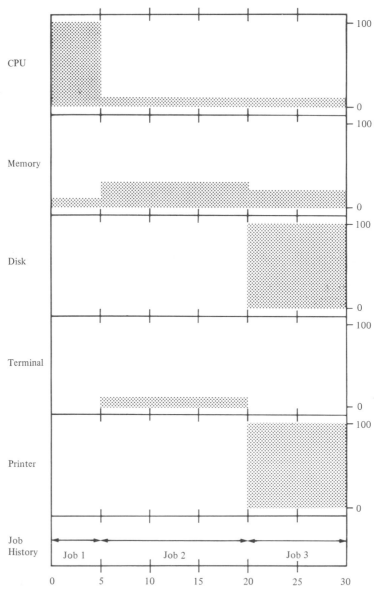

FIGURE 6-7. Uniprogramming utilization histogram

which one to run, which requires some algorithm for *scheduling*. These concepts are discussed later in this chapter.

Time Sharing

With the use of multiprogramming, batch processing can be quite efficient. However, for many jobs, it is desirable to provide a mode in which the user

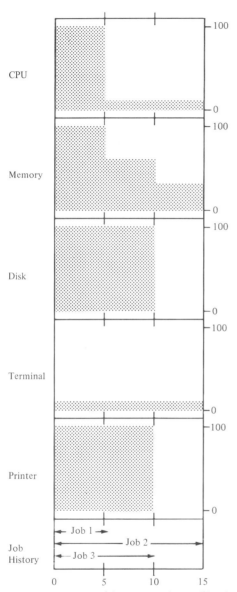

FIGURE 6-8. Multiprogramming utilization histogram

interacts directly with the computer. Indeed, for some jobs, such as transaction processing, an interactive mode is essential.

Today, the requirement for an interactive computing facility can be, and often is, met by the use of a dedicated microcomputer. That option was not available in the 1960s, when most computers were big and costly. Instead, time sharing was developed.

Just as mutliprogramming allows the processor to handle multiple batch jobs

TABLE 6-4 Batch Multiprogramming Versus Time Sharing

	Batch Multiprogramming	Time Sharing
Principle objective	Maximize processor utilization	Minimize response time
Source of instructions to operating system	Job control language instructions provided with the job	Commands entered at the terminal

at a time, multiprogramming can be used to handle multiple interactive jobs. In this latter case, the technique is referred to as *time sharing*, reflecting the fact that the processor's time is shared among multiple users. Both batch multiprogramming and time sharing use multiprogramming. The key differences are listed in Table 6-4.

Classes of Computers

Most operating system research and development has been done for mainframe computers. As first minicomputers and then microcomputers were developed, and as these systems developed increasing hardware capability, the technology developed for mainframes has been transferred to these different classes of computers.

Figure 6-9 illustrates this phenomenon. A good example of the migration of concepts and features can be seen by considering the evolution of Unix from Multics. Multics is a mainframe operating system developed jointly by M.I.T.,

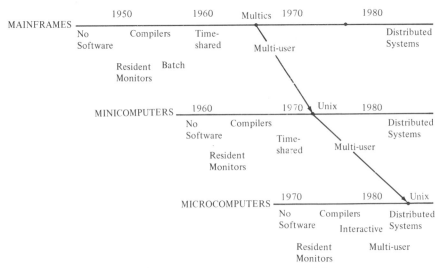

FIGURE 6-9. Migration of operating system concepts and features

Bell Laboratories, and a division of General Electric that subsequently became part of Honeywell. This operating system is still marketed by Honeywell and is still considered an advanced system, particularly in the area of security. Many of the ideas developed for Multics were subsequently used at Bell Labs in the design of Unix, which has become one of the most popular minicomputer operating systems and is now offered on many microcomputers.

6.2

SCHEDULING

The central task of modern operating systems is multiprogramming (with the exception of single-user microcomputers). With multiprogramming, multiple jobs or user programs are maintained in memory. Each job alternates between using the central processor and waiting for I/O to be performed. The processor keeps busy by executing one job while the others wait.

The key to multiprogramming is scheduling. In fact, three types of scheduling are typically involved (Table 6-5). We will explore these presently. But first, we introduce the concept of *process*. This term was first used by the designers of Multics in the 1960s. It is a somewhat more general term than *job*. Many definitions have been given for the term *process,* including

- A program in execution.
- The "animated spirit" of a program.
- That entity to which a processor is assigned.

This concept should become clearer as we proceed.

High-Level Scheduling

The high-level scheduler determines which programs are admitted to the system for processing. Thus the high-level scheduler controls the *degree of multiprogramming* (number of processes in memory). Once admitted, a job or program becomes a process and is added to a queue for the short-term scheduler. The more processes that are created, the smaller is the percentage of time that each process can be executed. The long-term scheduler may limit the degree of multiprogramming to provide satisfactory service to its current set of processes.

TABLE 6-5   Scheduling For Multiprogramming

High-level scheduling	The decision to add to the pool of programs to be executed.
Short-term scheduling	The decision as to which available process shall be executed by the processor.
I/O scheduling	The decision as to which process's pending I/O request shall be handled by an available I/O device.

In a batch system, newly submitted jobs are routed to disk and held in a queue or waiting line. The high-level scheduler adds jobs from that queue when it can. There are two decisions involved here. First, the scheduler must decide that it can take on one or more additional processes. This decision is generally made each time an existing process is completed. Second, the scheduler must decide which job or jobs to accept and turn into processes. The criteria used may include priority, expected execution time, and I/O requirements.

For time sharing, a process request is generated by the act of a user attempting to connect to the system. Time-sharing users are not simply queued up and kept waiting until the system can accept them. Rather, the operating system will accept all authorized comers until the system is saturated. At that point, a connection request is met with a message indicating that the system is full and the user should try again later.

Short-Term Scheduling

The high-level scheduler executes relatively infrequently and makes the coarse-grained decision of whether or not to take on a new process, and which one to take. The short-term scheduler, also known as the *dispatcher*, executes frequently and makes the fine-grained decision of which job to execute next.

Process States

To understand the operation of the short-term scheduler, we need to consider the concept of a process state. During the lifetime of a process, its status will change a number of times. Its status at any point in time is referred to as a *state*. The term *state* is used because it connotes that certain information exists that defines the status at that point. Typically, there are five defined states for a process (Figure 6-10):

- *New:* A program is admitted by the high-level scheduler but is not yet ready to execute. The operating system will initialize the process, moving it to the ready state.
- *Ready:* The process is ready to execute and is awaiting access to the processor.

FIGURE 6-10. Process states

- *Running:* The process is being executed by the processor.
- *Waiting:* The process is suspended from execution waiting for some system resource, such as I/O.
- *Halted:* The process has terminated and will be destroyed by the operating system.

For each process in the system, the operating system must maintain state information indicating the status of the process and other information necessary for process execution. For this purpose, each process is represented in the operating system by a *process control block* (Figure 6-11), which typically contains

- *Identifier:* Each current process has a unique identifier.
- *State:* The current state of the process (new, ready, and so on).
- *Priority:* Relative priority level.
- *Program counter:* The address of the next instruction in the program to be executed.
- *Memory pointers:* The starting and ending locations of the process in memory.
- *Context data:* These are data that are present in registers in the processor while the process is executing, and they will be discussed in Part III. For now, it is enough to say that these data represent the "context" of the process. The context data plus the program counter are saved when the process leaves the ready state. They are retrieved by the processor when it resumes execution of the process.
- *I/O status information:* Includes outstanding I/O requests, I/O devices (e.g., tape drives) assigned to this process, a list of files assigned to the process, and so on.
- *Accounting information:* May include the amount of processor time and clock time used, time limits, account numbers, and so on.

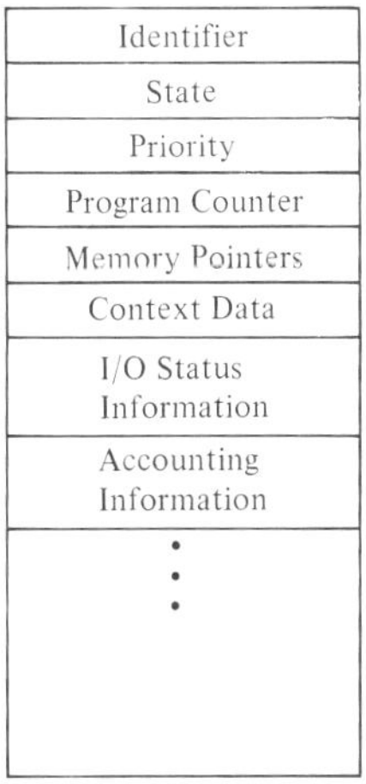

| Identifier |
| State |
| Priority |
| Program Counter |
| Memory Pointers |
| Context Data |
| I/O Status Information |
| Accounting Information |
| ⋮ |

FIGURE 6-11. Process control block

When the processor accepts a new job or user request for execution, it creates a blank process control block and places the associated process in the new state. After the system has properly filled in the process control block, the process is transferred to the ready state.

Scheduling Techniques

To understand how the operating system manages the scheduling of the various jobs in memory, let us begin by considering the simple example in Figure 6-10. The figure shows how main memory is partitioned at a given point in time. The nucleus of the operating system is, of course, always resident. In addition, there are a number of active processes, including A and B, each of which is allocated a portion of memory.

We begin at a point in time (Figure 6-12a) when process A is running. The processor is executing instructions from the program contained in A's memory partition. At some later point in time (Figure 6-12b), the processor ceases to execute instructions in A and begins executing instructions in the operating system area. This will happen for one of three reasons:

1. Process A issues a service call (e.g., an I/O request) to the operating system. Execution of A is suspended until this call is satisfied by the operating system.

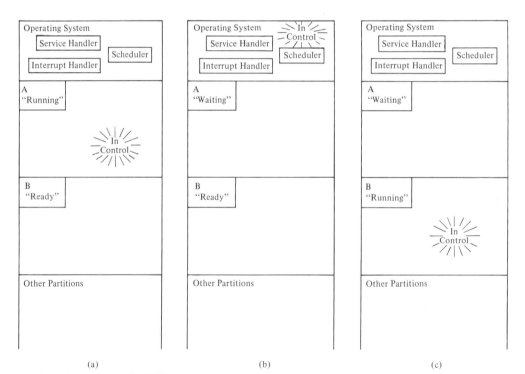

(a)   (b)   (c)

FIGURE 6-12. Scheduling example

2. Process A causes an *interrupt.* An interrupt is a hardware-generated signal to the processor. When this signal is detected, the processor ceases to execute A and transfers to the interrupt handler in the operating system. A variety of events related to A will cause an interrupt. One example is an error, such as attempting to execute a privileged instruction. Another example is a timeout; to prevent any one process from monopolizing the processor, each process is only granted the processor for a short period at a time.

3. Some event unrelated to process A that requires attention causes an interrupt. An example is the completion of an I/O operation.

In any case, the result is the following. The processor saves the current context data and the program counter for A in A's process control block and then begins executing in the operating system. The operating system may perform some work, such as initiating an I/O operation. Then the short-term-scheduler portion of the operating system decides which process should be executed next. In this example, B is chosen. The operating system instructs the processor to restore B's context data and proceed with the execution of B where it left off (Figure 6-12c).

This simple example highlights the basic functioning of the short-term scheduler. Figure 6-13 shows the major elements of the operating system involved in the multiprogramming and scheduling of processes. The operating system receives control of the processor at the interrupt handler if an interrupt occurs and at the service-call handler if a service call occurs. Once the interrupt or service call is handled, the short-term scheduler is invoked to pick a process for execution.

To do its job, the operating system maintains a number of queues. Each queue is simply a waiting list of processes waiting for some resource. The *long-term*

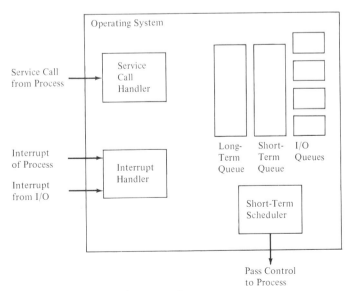

FIGURE 6-13. Key elements of an operating system for multiprogramming

queue is a list of jobs waiting to use the system. As conditions permit, the high-level scheduler will allocate memory and create a process for one of the waiting items. The *short-term queue* consists of all processes in the ready state. Any one of these processes could use the processor next. It is up to the short-term scheduler to pick one. Generally this is done with a round-robin algorithm, giving each process some time in turn. Priority levels may also be used. Finally, there is an *I/O queue* for each I/O device. More than one process may request the use of the same I/O device. All processes waiting to use each device are lined up in that device's queue.

Figure 6-14 suggests how processes progress through the computer under the control of the operating system. Each process request (batch job, user-defined interactive job) is placed in the long-term queue. As resources become available, a process request becomes a process and is then placed in the ready state and put in the short-term queue. The processor alternates between executing operating system instructions and executing user processes. While the operating system is in control, it decides which process in the short-term queue should be executed next. When the operating system has finished its immediate tasks, it turns the processor over to the chosen process.

As was mentioned earlier, a process being executed may be suspended for a variety of reasons. If it is suspended because the process requests I/O, then it is placed in the appropriate I/O queue. If it is suspended because of a timeout or because the operating system must attend to pressing business, then it is placed in the ready state and put right back into the short-term queue.

Finally, we mention that the operating system also manages the I/O queues. When an I/O operation is completed, the operating system removes the satisfied process from that I/O queue and places it in the short-term queue. It then selects another waiting process (if any) and signals for the I/O device to satisfy that process's request.

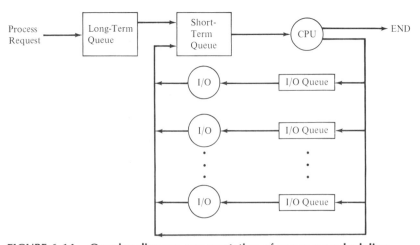

FIGURE 6-14.   Queuing diagram representation of processor scheduling

We have said that the major task of the operating system is to manage the system's resources. The queueing technique depicted in Figure 6-14 illustrates how the operating system manages processor time and I/O devices. There is one remaining major resource to manage, namely memory, and we now turn to this topic.

6.3

MEMORY MANAGEMENT

In a uniprogramming system, main memory is divided into two parts: one part for the operating system (resident monitor) and one part for the program currently being executed. In a multiprogramming system, the "user" part of memory must be further subdivided to accommodate multiple processes. The task of subdivision is carried out dynamically by the operating system and is known as *memory management.*

Effective memory management is vital in a multiprogramming system. If only a few processes are in memory, then for much of the time all of the processes will be waiting for I/O and the processor will be idle. Thus memory needs to be allocated efficiently to pack as many processes into memory as possible.

Swapping

Referring back to Figure 6-14, we have discussed three types of queues: the long-term queue of requests for new processes, the short-term queue of processes ready to use the processor, and the various I/O queues of processes that are not ready to use the processor. Recall that the reason for this elaborate machinery is that I/O activities are much slower than computation and therefore the processor in a uniprogramming system is idle most of the time.

But the arrangement in Figure 6-14 does not entirely solve the problem. It is true that, in this case, memory holds multiple processes and that the processor can move to another process when one process is waiting. But the processor is so much faster than I/O that it will be common for *all* of the processes in memory to be waiting on I/O. Thus, even with multiprogramming, a processor could be idle most of the time.

What to do? Main memory could be expanded, and so be able to accommodate more processes. But there are two flaws in this approach. First, main memory is expensive, even today. Second, the appetite of programs for memory has grown as fast as the cost of memory has dropped. So larger memory results in larger processes, not more processes.

Another solution is *swapping,* depicted in Figure 6-15. We have a long-term queue of process requests, typically stored on disk. These are brought in, one at a time, as space becomes available. As processes are completed, they are moved out of main memory. Now, the situation will arise that none of the processes in

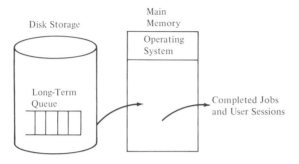

(a) Simple Job Scheduling

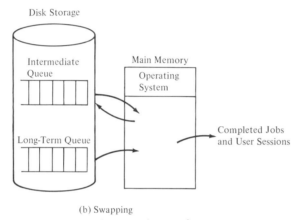

(b) Swapping

FIGURE 6-15. The use of swapping

memory are in the ready state. Rather than remain idle, the processor *swaps* one of these processes back out to disk into an *intermediate queue.* This is a queue of existing processes that have been temporarily kicked out of memory. The operating system then brings in another process from the intermediate queue, or it honors a new process request from the long-term queue. Execution then continues with the newly arrived process.

Swapping, however, is an I/O operation, and therefore there is the potential for making the problem worse, not better. But, since disk I/O is generally the fastest I/O on a system (e.g., compared to tape or printer I/O), swapping will usually enhance performance. A more sophisticated scheme, involving virtual memory, improves performance over simple swapping. This will be discussed shortly. But first, we must prepare the ground by explaining partitioning and paging.

Partitioning

The operating system occupies a fixed portion of main memory. The rest of memory is partitioned for use by multiple processes. The simplest scheme for partitioning available memory is to use *fixed-size partitions,* as shown in Figure 6-16. Note that, although the partitions are of fixed size, they are not of equal size. When a process is brought into memory, it is placed in the smallest available partition that will hold it.

Even with the use of unequal fixed-size partitions, there will be wasted memory. In most cases, a process will not require exactly as much memory as provided by the partition. For example, a process that requires 128K bytes of memory would be placed in the 192K partition of Figure 6-16, wasting 64K that could be used by another process.

A more efficient approach is to use *variable-size partitions.* When a process is brought into memory, it is allocated exactly as much memory as it requires and no more. An example is shown in Figure 6-17. Initially main memory is empty, except for the operating system. The first three processes are loaded in, starting where the operating system ends (a). This leaves a "hole" at the end of memory that is too small for a fourth process. When process 2 is swapped out (b), there is room for process 4. Since process 4 is smaller than process 2, another small hole is created. As this example shows, this method starts out well, but eventually it leads to a situation in which there are a lot of small holes in memory. As time goes on, memory becomes more and more fragmented, and memory utilization declines. One technique for overcoming this problem is *compaction:* From time to time, the operating system shifts the processes in memory to place all of the free memory together in one block. This is a time-consuming procedure, wasteful of processor time.

FIGURE 6-16.   Example of fixed partitioning

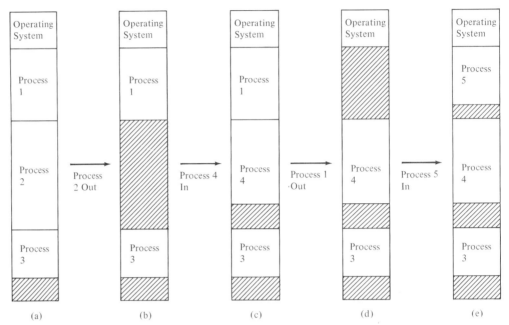

FIGURE 6-17.   **The effect of partitioning**

Before we consider ways of dealing with the shortcomings of partitioning, we must clear up one loose end. If the reader will ponder Figure 6-17 for a moment, it should become obvious that a process is not likely to be loaded into the same place in main memory each time it is swapped in. Furthermore, if compaction is used, a process may be shifted while in main memory. Now, the process in memory consists of instructions plus data. The instructions will contain addresses for memory locations of two types:

- Addresses of data items.
- Addresses of instructions, used for branching instructions.

But now we see that these addresses are not fixed! They will change each time a process is swapped in. To solve this problem, a distinction is made between logical addresses and physical addresses. A *logical address* is expressed as a location relative to the beginning of the program. Instructions in the program contain only logical addresses. A *physical address* is, of course, an actual location in main memory. When the processor executes a process, it automatically converts from logical to physical address by adding the current starting location of the process, called its *base address,* to each logical address. This is another example of a CPU hardware feature designed to meet an operating system requirement. The exact nature of this hardware feature depends on the memory management strategy in use. We will see several examples later in this section.

Paging

Both unequal fixed-size and variable-size partitions are inefficient in the use of memory. Suppose, however, that memory is partitioned into equal fixed-size chunks that are relatively small, and that each process is also divided into small fixed-size chunks of some size. Then the chunks of a program, known as *pages*, could be assigned to available chunks of memory, known as *frames*, or page frames. At most, then, the wasted space in memory for that process is a fraction of the last page.

Figure 6-18 shows an example of the use of pages and frames. At a given point in time, some of the frames in memory are in use and some are free. The list of free frames is maintained by the operating system. Process A, stored on disk, consists of four pages. When it comes time to load this process, the operating system finds four free frames and loads the four pages of the process A into the four frames.

Now suppose, as in this example, that there are not sufficient unused contiguous frames to hold the process. Does this prevent the operating system from loading A? The answer is no, because we can once again use the concept of logical address. A simple base address will no longer suffice. Rather, the operating system maintains a *page table* for each process. The page table shows the frame location for each page of the process. Within the program, each logical address consists of a page number and a relative address within the page. Recall

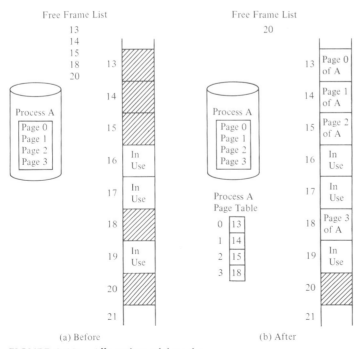

(a) Before   (b) After

FIGURE 6-18. Allocation of free frames

that in the case of simple partitioning, a logical address is the location of a word relative to the beginning of the program; the CPU translates that into a physical address. With paging, the logical-to-physical address translation is still done by CPU hardware. Now, the CPU must know how to access the page table of the current process. Presented with a logical address (page number, relative address), the CPU uses the page table to produce a physical address (frame number, relative address). An example is shown in Figure 6-19.

This approach solves the problems raised earlier. Main memory is divided into many small equal-size frames. Each process is divided into frame-size pages: smaller processes require fewer pages, larger processes require more. When a process is brought in, its pages are loaded into available frames, and a page table is set up.

Virtual Memory

Demand Paging

With the use of paging, truly effective multiprogramming systems came into being. Equally important, the simple tactic of breaking a process up into pages led to the development of another important concept: virtual memory.

To understand virtual memory, we must add a refinement to the paging scheme just discussed. That refinement is *demand paging*, which simply means that each page of a process is brought in only when it is needed, that is, on demand.

Consider a large process, consisting of a long program plus a number of arrays of data. Over any short period of time, execution may be confined to a small section of the program (e.g., a subroutine), and perhaps only one or two arrays

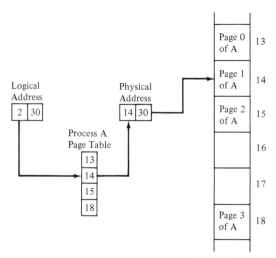

FIGURE 6-19. Logical and physical addresses

of data are being used. This is the principle of locality, which we introduced in Appendix 4A to Chapter 4. It would clearly be wasteful to load in dozens of pages for that process when only a few pages will be used before the program is suspended. We can make better use of memory by loading in just a few pages. Then, if the program branches to an instruction on a page not in main memory, or if the program references data on a page not in memory, a *page fault* is triggered. This tells the operating system to bring in the desired page.

Thus, at any one time, only a few pages of any given process are in memory, and therefore more processes can be maintained in memory. Furthermore, time is saved because unused pages are not swapped in and out of memory. However, the operating system must be clever about how it manages this scheme. When it brings one page in, it must throw another page out. If it throws out a page just before it is about to be used, then it will just have to go get that page again almost immediately. Too much of this leads to a condition known as *thrashing:* the processor spends most of its time swapping pages rather than executing instructions. The avoidance of thrashing was a major research area in the 1970s and led to a variety of complex but effective algorithms. In essence, the operating system tries to guess, based on recent history, which pages are least likely to be used in the near future.

With demand paging, it is not necessary to load an entire process into main memory. This fact has a remarkable consequence: *It is possible for a process to be larger than all of main memory.* One of the most fundamental restrictions in programming has been lifted. Without demand paging, a programmer must be acutely aware of how much memory is available. If the program being written is too large, the programmer must devise ways to structure the program into pieces that can be loaded one at a time. With demand paging, that job is left to the operating system and the hardware. As far as the programmer is concerned, he or she is dealing with a huge memory, the size associated with disk storage. The operating system uses demand paging to load portions of that process into main memory.

Because a process executes only in main memory, that memory is referred to as *real memory.* But a programmer or user perceives a much larger memory—that which is allocated on the disk. This latter is therefore referred to as *virtual memory* (Figure 6-20). Virtual memory allows for very effective multiprogramming and relieves the user of the unnecessarily tight contraints of main memory.

Paging Mechanisms

In the discussion of simple paging, we used Figure 6-19 to indicate that each process has its own page table, and when all of the pages are loaded into main memory, the page table for that process is created and loaded into main memory. Each page table entry contains the frame number of the corresponding page in main memory. The same device, a page table, is needed when we move to demand paging and virtual memory. Again, it is typical to associate a unique page table with each process. In this case, however, the page table entries be-

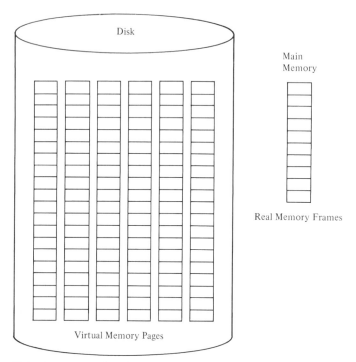

FIGURE 6-20.   Virtual memory

come more complex. Because only some of the pages of a process may be in main memory, a bit is needed in each page table entry to indicate whether the corresponding page is in main memory or not. If the bit indicates that the page is in memory, then the entry also includes the frame number for that page.

In principle then, every virtual memory reference can cause two physical memory accesses: one to fetch the appropriate page table entry, and one to fetch the desired data. Thus, a straightforward virtual memory scheme would have the effect of doubling the memory access time. To overcome this problem, most virtual memory schemes make use of a special cache for page table entries, usually called a translation lookaside buffer (TLB). This cache functions in the same way as a memory cache and contains those page table entries that have been most recently used. Figure 6-21 is a flowchart that shows the use of the TLB. By the principle of locality, most virtual memory references will be to locations in recently used pages. Therefore, most references will involve page table entries in the cache. Studies of the VAX TLB have shown that this scheme can significantly improve performance [CLAR85, SATY81].

There are several other complexities involved in the typical virtual memory scheme. First, consider the number of page table entries required. In most systems, there is one page table per process. But each process can occupy huge amounts of virtual memory. For example, in the VAX architecture, each process

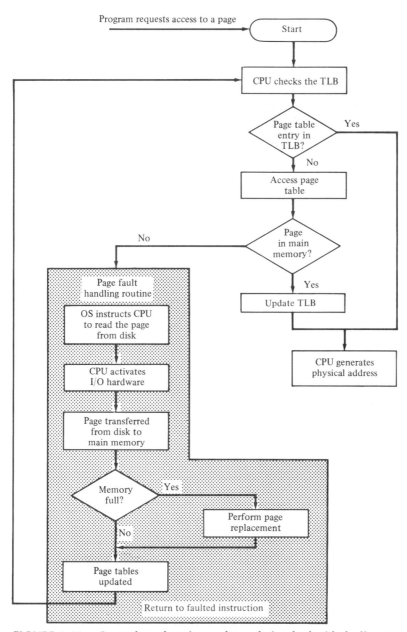

FIGURE 6-21.   Operation of paging and translation lookaside buffer (TLB) [FURH87]

can have up to 2^{31} = 2 GBytes of virtual memory. Using 2^9 = 512-byte pages, that means that as many as 2^{22} page table entries are required *per process*. Clearly, the amount of memory devoted to page tables alone could be unacceptably high. To overcome this problem, most virtual memory schemes store page tables in virtual memory rather than real memory. This means that page tables are subject to paging just as other pages are.

Finally, the virtual memory mechanism must interact with the cache system (not the TLB cache, but the main memory cache). This is illustrated in Figure 6-22. A virtual address will generally be in the form of a page number, offset. First, the memory system consults the TLB to see if the matching page table entry is present. If it is, the real (physical) address is generated by combining the frame number with the offset. If not, the entry is accessed from a page table. Once the real address is generated, which is in the form of a tag and a remainder (see Figure 4-20), the cache is consulted to see if the block containing that word is present. If so, it is returned to the CPU. If not, the word is retrieved from main memory.

The reader should be able to appreciate the complexity of the CPU hardware involved in a single memory reference. The virtual address is translated into a real address. This involves reference to a page table, which may be in the TLB, in main memory, or on disk. The referenced word may be in cache, main memory, or on disk. In the latter case, the page containing the word must be loaded into

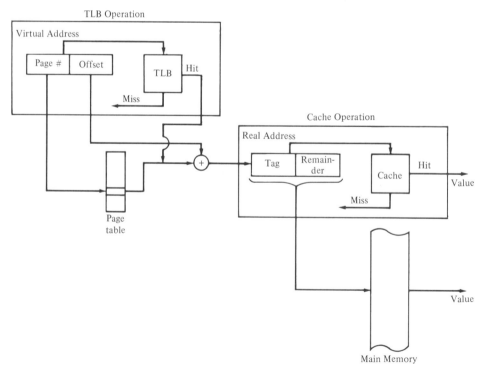

FIGURE 6-22. Translation lookaside buffer and cache operation

main memory and its block loaded into the cache. In addition, the page table entry for that page must be updated.

Segmentation

There is another way in which addressable memory can be subdivided, known as *segmentation*. Whereas paging is invisible to the programmer and serves the purpose of providing the programmer with a larger address space, segmentation is usually visible to the programmer and is provided as a convenience for organizing programs and data, and as a means for associating privilege and protection attributes with instructions and data.

Segmentation allows the programmer to view memory as consisting of multiple address spaces or segments. Segments are of variable, indeed dynamic, size. Typically, the programmer or the operating system will assign programs and data to different segments. There may be a number of program segments for various types of programs as well as a number of data segments. Each segment may be assigned access and usage rights. Memory references consist of a (segment number, offset) form of address.

This organization has a number of advantages to the programmer over a non-segmented address space:

1. It simplifies the handling of growing data structures. If the programmer does not know ahead of time how large a particular data structure will become, it is not necessary to guess. The data structure can be assigned its own segment, and the operating system will expand or shrink the segment as needed.
2. It allows programs to be altered and recompiled independently, without requiring that an entire set of programs be relinked and reloaded. Again, this is accomplished using multiple segments.
3. It lends itself to sharing among processes. A programmer can place a utility program or a useful table of data in a segment that can be addressed by other processes.
4. It lends itself to protection. Since a segment can be constructed to contain a well-defined set of programs or data, the programmer or a system administrator can assign access privileges in a convenient fashion.

These advantages are not available with paging, which is invisible to the programmer. On the other hand, we have seen that paging provides for an efficient form of memory management. To combine the advantages of both, some systems are equipped with the hardware and operating-system software to provide both.

VAX Memory Management

Address Spaces

Memory management for the VAX consists of the three mechanisms common to practically all virtual memory implementations:

1. Map virtual addresses to physical addresses.
2. Control access to memory.
3. Allow a process to execute even if all of its virtual address space is not simultaneously mapped to physical memory.

This subsection provides a brief overview of these mechanisms.

The VAX architecture employs 32-bit addresses, with addressing at the byte level (i.e., each byte is individually addressed). Thus a total *virtual address space* of 4 gigabytes (GBytes), or 2^{32} bytes, is possible. Virtual address space is divided into pages, each page containing $2^9 = 512$ bytes. This corresponds to the size of the page frame in physical memory and the size of a disk sector, and it yields a virtual address space of 2^{23} 512-byte pages. Actual main memory addresses are limited to 30 bits, resulting in a maximum *physical address space* of $2^{30} = 1$ GByte, or 2^{21} page frames.

The amount of virtual memory can actually be larger than the 32-bit virtual address indicates. This is because the CPU's interpretation of a virtual address depends upon which process is currently active. Virtual address space is divided into two halves. The first half is the per-process virtual address space, extending from address 0 to address $7FFFFFFF_{16}$. This space is distinct for each active process, giving each process its own 2-GByte virtual memory. A user process cannot reference virtual addresses in any process space but its own. Thus, instructions and data belonging to a process are automatically protected from other processes in the system.

Whereas there is one process space for each executable process, there is only a single system space, with virtual addresses from 80000000_{16} to $FFFFFFFF_{16}$. The *system space* contains the operating-system programs and data plus utility programs (e.g., an I/O handler) that are addressable by all processes, subject to access controls.

Access Control

Access to virtual memory is controlled on a page basis. Two concepts are involved here. First is the *access level*, which has three values: no access, read-only access, and read/write access. Second is *access mode*. At a given point in time, a process executes in one of four access modes. These modes, in decreasing order of privilege, are Kernel, Executive, Supervisor, and User. The VAX/VMS operating system defines these modes as follows:

- *Kernel:* Executes the kernel (most important part) of the operating system for memory management, scheduling, interrupt handling, and I/O operations.
- *Executive:* Executes many of the operating system service calls, including file and record (disk and tape) management routines.
- *Supervisor:* Executes operating-system services, such as responses to user commands.
- *User:* Executes user programs plus utilities such as compilers and debuggers.

Each page in virtual memory is defined to have a particular access level for each access mode.

As an aside, we should mention that the access mode determines not only memory access privileges but also instruction execution privileges. For example, only the kernel mode can execute a processor halt instruction. The combination of memory access and instruction execution control allows for a high degree of protection. In general, routines that execute at a particular mode can protect their programs and data from any less-privileged mode. Thus the operating system can provide a number of shared services and yet be protected from intentional or unintentional harm.

Virtual-to-Physical Address Translation

We have seen that there are two address spaces in a virtual memory system: virtual addresses and physical addresses. In the VAX architecture, a virtual address is 32 bits in length and refers to a byte in virtual memory. Such virtual addresses occur while the CPU is executing a program. The way in which these addresses appear in a program will be discussed in Chapter 8. For now, our immediate interest is the way in which such an address is handled by the CPU. If the referenced byte is in main memory, then the CPU must translate from the virtual address to a physical address. If it is not, then the CPU will be interrupted, and the operating system will be involved in replacing an existing page in main memory with the page that contains the referenced byte.

To understand these mechanisms, we begin by looking at the address formats. Figure 6-23a shows the VAX virtual address format. Bit 31 designates which of the two spaces is being referenced. The next 22 bits designate which page within

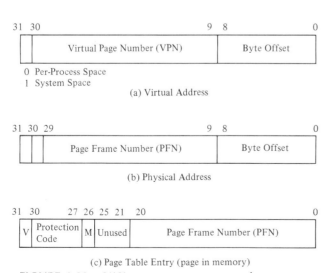

FIGURE 6-23.   VAX memory management formats

that region is being referenced. The final 9 bits designate which of the 512 bytes within the page is being referenced.

Assuming that the referenced page is in physical memory, then this virtual address must be translated into a physical address, whose format is indicated in Figure 6-23b. The actual physical size of main memory is limited to $2^{29} = 512$ MBytes. Thus the leftmost 3 bits of a 32-bit memory address are always 0. In addition, the VAX uses memory-mapped I/O, and addresses from 2^{29} to $2^{30} - 1$, indicated by bit 29 being 1, refer to I/O devices. As was mentioned, physical memory is divided into 512-byte page frames. Bits 0 through 8 of the physical address designate a byte within the frame. Bits 9 through 28 are sufficient to designate a page frame within physical memory. However, the VAX treats bits 9 through 29 as a page frame number. This allows I/O addresses to also be treated as if they were organized into pages. The reason for this is so that access control can be applied to I/O addresses as well as memory addresses. The result is an efficient scheme that allows both memory and I/O to be referenced by virtual addresses and that provides a single unified access control mechanism.

The translation from virtual to physical addresses requires the use of a *page table*. This function is performed by CPU hardware. There is one page table for the system region. The system region page table is in a fixed, known physical location in main memory. In addition, there is a page table for each process. Process page tables are accessed by virtual addresses so that the process page tables themselves may be paged. The virtual addresses of a process's page tables are part of the set of parameters associated with that process. Thus, when the process is executing, its page table addresses are known to the CPU.

Figure 6-24 illustrates the translation from virtual to physical address. Bit 31 of

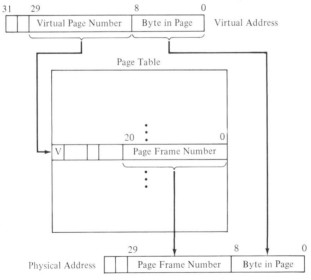

FIGURE 6-24. VAX virtual address translation

the virtual address indicates which page table is needed. The table consists of a set of 32-bit *page-table entries* (PTEs). The Virtual Page Number serves as an index into the page table to select the appropriate PTE. The leftmost bit of the PTE is the valid (V) bit. If V is set, then the referenced page exists in physical memory. In that case, bits 20 through 0 of the PTE are the Page Frame Number of the physical address. The relative location of a byte within a page is the same for both virtual and physical addresses, so those 9 bits are just carried over unchanged, completing the physical address.

The remaining bits of the PTE are shown in Figure 6-23c. The modify (M) bit is set if the page in physical memory has been altered. In that case, the page must be written back to disk before being replaced. Bits 30 through 27 contain encoded information concerning the access level for each access mode. Note that this information is associated with the virtual page, not the page frame. If the page is not in memory, then V is 0, and bits 26 through 0 are available to designate where the page may be found on the disk.

Figure 6-25 shows a sample allocation of virtual pages to physical memory. Note that there is one page table for the system space and one for each per-process space. The system page table is always in main memory. Each per-process page table is in the system space portion of virtual memory and, at any time, may or may not be in main memory.

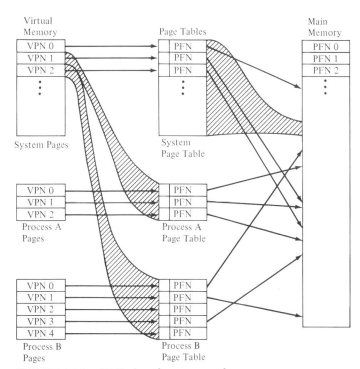

FIGURE 6-25. VAX virtual memory scheme

The VAX makes use of a translation lookaside buffer (TLB), which is organized in the same fashion as the VAX memory cache, namely, in a two-way set-associative structure (Figure 4-21c). It is divided into a system cache and a process cache each with 64 entries. This is done so that the process cache entries can be invalidated each time that a new process is activated. Access to the cache uses the following algorithm. When a virtual address is presented for translation, bit 31 is used to determine whether to check the process cache or the system cache. Bits 30 through 14 are used as the tag, and bits 13 through 9 are used as the entry number. The entry number selects the two candidate entries, and their tags are checked for a match. If there is a match, then the matching entry contains a valid PTE. Otherwise, the page table itself must be referenced to fetch the PTE.

Page Replacement

The final detail to explain is the replacement algorithm used when a desired page is not in memory. The VAX solution, performed by the operating system, is ingenious and efficient.

Each active process is allowed to keep up to a certain number of pages in memory. The set of pages in memory for a process is known as its *resident set*. Clearly, the sum of all these pages must be less than or equal to the number of page frames that constitute the memory. When paging is required, a process is paged only against itself. That is, when a new page is brought in, it replaces another page of the same process. This ensures that only those processes that need paging are affected by paging.

The page replacement algorithm, which operates on a per-process basis, is round-robin or first-in-first-out. Now, recall from our discussion of cache memory that the most-recently-referenced addresses are the ones most likely to be needed next. Thus, some sort of least-recently-used or least-frequently-used replacement algorithm would be superior to round-robin. To improve the performance of the round-robin algorithm, a replaced page is not lost but rather is transferred to one or two lists: the free page list if the page has not been modified, or the modified page list if it has.

The free page list is a list of page frames available for reading in pages. The system tries to keep some small number of frames free at all times. When a page is to be read in, the page frame at the head of the list is used. When an unmodified page is to be replaced, it remains in memory and its page frame is added to the tail of the free page list. Similarly, when a modified page is to be written out and replaced, its page frame is added to the tail of the modified page list.

The important aspect of these maneuvers is that the page in question remains in memory. Thus if the process references that page, it is returned to its resident set at little cost. In effect, the free and modified page lists act as a cache of pages. The modified page list serves another useful function: Modified pages are written out in clusters rather than one at a time. This significantly reduces the number of I/O operations and therefore the demand for disk access time.

System/370 Memory Management

The IBM System/370 architecture uses a two-level memory structure and refers to the two levels as segments and pages, although the segmentation approach lacks many of the features described earlier. For the basic 370 architecture, the page size may be either 2 KBytes or 4 KBytes, and the segment size is fixed at either 64 KBytes or 1 MByte. In the discussion that follows, we assume the 4-KByte page and 64-KByte segment. For the 370/XA architecture, the page size is 4 KBytes and the segment size is 1 MByte.

Figure 6-26a depicts the format for a virtual address, which is quite straightforward. For 370 mode, the rightmost 24 bits of a 32-bit word are used. The byte index specifies one of 4K bytes within a page; the page index specifies one of 16 pages within a segment; and the segment index indentifies one of 256 user-visible segments. Thus the user sees a virtual address space of 2^{24} = 16 MBytes. For the 370-XA, a 31-bit virtual address is used, allowing 2^{31} bytes of virtual storage.

To manage storage, segment and page tables are used. There is one *segment table* for each virtual address space. Depending on the operating system, there will be one or more virtual address spaces. For MVS, one of the most widely used 370 operating systems, there are multiple virtual address spaces, one per process, as in the VAX system. Each virtual address space is made up of a

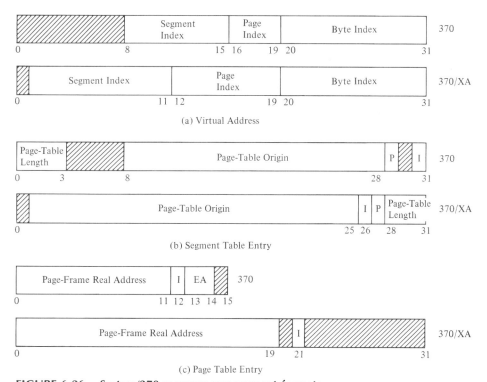

(a) Virtual Address

(b) Segment Table Entry

(c) Page Table Entry

FIGURE 6-26. **System/370 memory management formats**

number of segments, and there is one entry in the segment table per segment. Each segment has associated with it a *page table*, with one entry for each page in the segment.

The format for a segment-table entry is shown in Figure 6-26b. The Page Table Origin points to the page table for that segment. In 370 mode, 3 zero bits are appended to the right of the 21-bit field to form a 24-bit address. In 370-XA mode, 6 zero bits are appended to the 25-bit field to form a 31-bit address. The Page Table Length is 1 less than the number of entries in the page table. The bit labeled I is the segment-invalid bit. The bit is set to 1 when some malfunction or unrecoverable error occurs, indicating that the segment is unavailable. The P bit is a protection bit; when set, it prevents writes but allows reads.

The format for a page-table entry is shown in Figure 6-26c. The page-invalid (I) bit indicates whether the page is in real storage or not. If it is, the Page Frame Real Address (PFRA) indicates the location of the page. For normal 370 and 370-XA, 12 zero bits are appended to the right of this field to form the physical address. There is also an extended address (EA) feature that is employed on certain later models of the 370 architecture. In that case, the two EA bits are added to the PFRA field to form a 14-bit reference. This plus 12 zero bits yields a 26-bit address.

Figure 6-27 illustrates the address translation mechanism on the System/370. The CPU maintains in a control register the address of the segment table for the current process. The segment index of the virtual address is an index into the segment table. Since each segment-table entry is 4 bytes long, the segment index is multiplied by 4 and added to the segment table address to locate the segment table entry. This entry contains the address of the appropriate page table, which

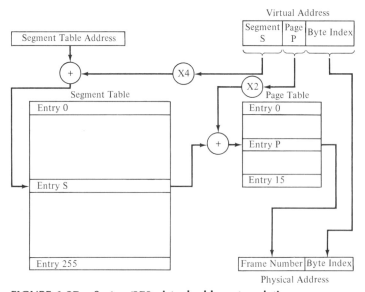

FIGURE 6-27. System/370 virtual address translation

in this case has 2-byte entries. The page index is multiplied by 2 and added to the address of the page table to find the correct entry. This entry contains the address of the page frame. Combining this with the byte index yields the physical address of the referenced byte.

Two additional aspects of System/370 memory management are worth describing: the translation lookaside buffers and the page replacement algorithms. The exact details of these depend on the system model and operating system in use. In what follows, a general description is offered.

Each memory reference involves a translation from a virtual address to a real address. The translation process, as we have seen, itself involves two memory read operations, to get the segment table and page table entries. To reduce the overhead involved in this process, a set of recently used entries is maintained in a cache called the *translation lookaside buffer* (TLB). A typical TLB will have 128 entries. Each TLB entry contains sufficient information to translate one virtual page reference to a real page frame address. The following information is needed: segment index, page index, and page table origin (see Figure 6-22). In addition, a reference bit is needed.

The process works as follows. When a virtual address is presented, the TLB is checked to determine if the (segment index, page index) reference is present. If it is, then the page origin is obtained and translation is not required. Also, the reference bit is set to 1. If the entry is not found, then translation proceeds as in Figure 6-27. In addition, a new TLB entry is created to save the page table origin of the newly referenced frame.

This new entry must replace an existing entry. The system chooses the first entry in the TLB with a reference bit equal to 0. This is a form of least-recently-used algorithm. To make this scheme work, when all entries in the TLB have a reference bit equal to 1, all are reset to 0.

Before describing the replacement algorithm, we need to know that each page frame has associated with it a 7-bit *storage key*, which may be set by the operating system. The storage key consists of

- *Access-control bits:* Contain a 4-bit access-control key. CPU memory references and DMA I/O references to storage must use a matching key to gain permission to access that block of data.
- *Fetch-protection bit:* Indicates whether the access-control key applies to writes only or to both reads and writes.
- *Reference bit:* Set to 1 when any address within the frame is referred to for a read or write. Reset when a new page is loaded into the frame.
- *Change bit:* Set to 1 when a write operation is performed to any address within the frame.

The replacement of pages in main memory is managed by the operating system. Several page frame tables are maintained. One such table maintains a list of available page frames. When a new page must be brought in, a page frame from this list is used. The reference bit associated with that frame is set to 0.

When the number of available frames drops below a certain threshold, the operating system performs a *page-stealing* operation by converting a number of active pages to available pages. The operating system chooses active pages whose reference bit has been set to 0 for the longest period of time. Various approaches are used by different operating systems for determining this. This, again, is a least-recently-used algorithm.

INTEL 80386 Memory Management

With the introduction of the 32-bit architecture, microprocessors have evolved sophisticated memory management schemes that build on the lessons learned with medium- and large-scale systems. In many cases, the microprocessor versions are superior to their larger-system antecedents. Since the schemes were developed by the microprocessor hardware vendor and may be employed with a variety of operating systems, they tend to be quite general-purpose. A representative example is the scheme used on the Intel 30836.

Address Spaces

The 80386 includes hardware for both segmentation and paging. Both mechanisms can be disabled, allowing the user to choose from four distinct views of memory:

* *Unsegmented unpaged memory:* In this case, the virtual address is the same as the physical address. This is useful, for example, in low-complexity, high-performance controller applications.
* *Unsegmented paged memory:* Here memory is viewed as a paged linear address space. Protection and management of memory is done via paging. This is favored by some operating systems—e.g., Berkeley UNIX.
* *Segmented unpaged memory:* Here memory is viewed as a collection of logical address spaces. The advantages of this view over a paged approach is that it affords protection down to the level of a single byte, if necessary. Furthermore, unlike paging, it guarantees that the translation table needed (the segment table) is on-chip when the segment is in memory. Hence, segmented unpaged memory results in predictable access times.
* *Segmented paged memory:* Segmentation is used to define logical memory partitions subject to access control and paging is used to manage the allocation of memory within the partitions. Operating systems such as UNIX System V favor this view.

Segmentation

When segmentation is used, each virtual address (called a logical address in the 80386 documentation) consists of a 16-bit segment reference and a 32-bit offset. Two bits of the segment reference deal with the protection mechanism, leaving 14 bits for specifying a particular segment. Thus, with unsegmented memory, the user's virtual memory is 2^{32} = 4 GBytes. With segmented memory, the total virtual memory space as seen by a user is 2^{46} = 64 terabytes (TBytes). The physical address space employs a 32-bit address for a maximum of 4 GBytes.

The amount of virtual memory can actually be larger than the 64 TBytes. As with the VAX, the 80386's interpretation of a virtual address depends upon which process is currently active. One-half of the virtual address space (8K segments × 4 GBytes) is global, shared by all processes; the remainder is local and is distinct for each process.

Associated with each segment are two forms of protection: privilege level and access attribute. There are four **privilege levels** from most protected (level 0) to least protected (level 3). The privilege level associated with a data segment is its "classification;" the privilege level associated with a program segment is its "clearance." An executing program may only access data segments for which its clearance level is lower than (more privileged) or equal to (same privilege) the privilege level of the data segment.

The hardware does not dictate how these privilege levels are to be used; this depends on the operating system design and implementation. It was intended that privilege level 1 would be used for most of the operating system, and level 0 would be used for that small portion of the operating system devoted to memory management, protection, and access control. This leaves two levels for applications. In many systems, applications will reside at level 3, with level 2 being unused. Specialized application subsystems that must be protected because they implement their own security mechanisms are good candidates for level 2. Some examples are: database management systems, office automation systems, and software engineering environments.

In addition to regulating access to data segments, the privilege mechanism limits the use of certain instructions. Some instructions, such as those that deal with memory-management registers, can only be executed in level 0. I/O instructions can only be executed up to a certain level that is designated by the operating system; typically this will be level 1.

The **access attribute** of a data segment specifies whether read/write or read-only accesses are permitted. For program segments, the access attribute specifies read/execute or read-only access.

The address translation mechanism for segmentation involves mapping a **virtual address** into what is referred to as a **linear address.** The format of the virtual address (Figure 6-28a) includes the following fields:

- *Table indicator (TI):* indicates whether the global segment table or a local segment table should be used for translation.
- *Segment number:* the number of the segment. This serves as an index into the segment table.
- *Offset:* The offset of the addressed byte within the segment.
- *Requested privilege level (RPL):* The privilege level requested for this access.

Each entry in a segment table consists of 64 bits, as shown in Figure 6-28c. The fields are defined in Table 6-6.

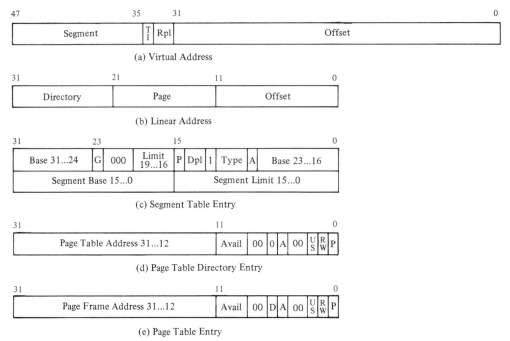

FIGURE 6-28. 80386 memory management formats

Paging

Segmentation is an optional feature and may be disabled. When segmentation is in use, addresses used in programs are virtual addresses and are converted into linear addresses, as just described. When segmentation is not in use, linear addresses are used in programs. In either case, the next subsequent step is to convert that linear address into a real 32-bit address.

To understand the structure of the linear address, you need to know that the 80386 paging mechanism is actually a two-level table lookup operation. The first level is a **page directory,** which contains up to 1024 entries. This splits the 4-GByte linear memory space into 1024 page groups, each with its own **page table** and each 4 MBytes in length. Each page table contains up to 1024 entries; each entry corresponds to a single 4-KByte page. Memory management has the option of using one page directory for all processes, one page directory for each process, or some combination of the two. The page directory for the current task is always in main memory. Page tables may be in virtual memory.

Figure 6-28 shows the formats of entries in page directories and page tables, and the fields are defined in Table 6-6. Note that access control mechanisms can be provided on a page or page group basis.

As with the VAX and System/370 memory management schemes, the 80386 makes use of a translation lookaside buffer. The buffer can hold 32 page table entries. Each time that the page directory is changed, the buffer is cleared.

TABLE 6-6   80386 Memory Management Parameters

Segment Table Entry

Limit

Defines the size of the segment. The processor interprets the limit field in one of two ways, depending on the granularity bit: in units of one byte, up to a limit of 1 MByte, or in units of 4 KBytes, up to a limit of 4 GBytes.

Base

Defines the starting address of the segment within the 4-GByte linear address space.

Accessed bit (A)

Set whenever the segment is accessed. An operating system that uses segmented nonpaged memory may use this bit to monitor frequency of segment usage for memory management purposes. In a paged system, this bit is ignored.

Type

Distinguishes between various kinds of segments and indicates the access attributes.

Descriptor privilege level (DPL)

Specifies the privilege level of the segment referred to by this segment table entry (segment descriptor).

Segment present bit (P)

Used for nonpaged systems. It indicates whether the segment is present in main memory. For paged systems, this bit is always set to 1.

Granularity bit (G)

Indicates whether the Limit field is to be interpreted in units of one byte or 4 KBytes.

Page Table Directory Entry and Page Table Entry

Page Frame Address

Provides the physical address of the page in memory if the present bit is set. Since page frames are aligned on 4K boundaries, the bottom 12 bits are zero, and only the top 20 bits are included in the entry.

Page Table Address

Provides the physical address of a page table in memory if the present bit is set.

Present bit (P)

Indicates whether the page table or page is in main memory.

Accessed bit (A)

This bit is set to one by the processor in both levels of page tables when a read or write operation to the corresponding page occurs.

Dirty bit (D)

This bit is set to one by the processor when a write operation to the corresponding page occurs.

User/Supervisor bit (US)

Indicates whether the page is available only to the operating system (supervisor level) or is available to both operating system and applications (user level).

Read/Write bit (RW)

For user-level pages, indicates whether the page is read-only access or read/write access for user-level programs.

Available bits (AVAIL)

Available for systems programmer use.

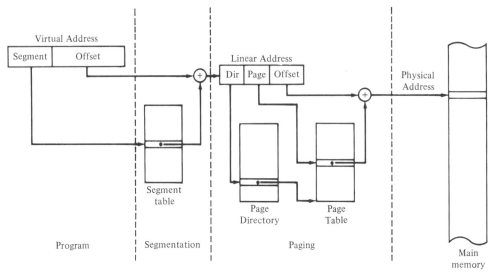

FIGURE 6-29. 80386 memory address translation mechanism

Figure 6-29 illustrates the combination of segmentation and paging mechanisms. For clarity, the translation lookaside buffer and memory cache mechanisms are not shown.

6.4

RECOMMENDED READING

[STAL92] covers the topics of this chapter in detail. In addition, as in the area of computer architecture, there is a great number of books on operating systems. [SILB91] and [DEIT90] cover the basic principles using a number of important operating systems as case studies. [TANE87] and [MILE87] take the interesting approach of providing step-by-step implementation details for small but complete UNIX-like operating systems. Other books that do a good job of covering the basic principles at a technical level are [PINK89], [FINK88], and [BIC88].

[WEIZ81] provides a brief but informative history of operating systems. [DENN84] is a good survey article.

An excellent overview on memory management is [FURH87]. Descriptions of the VAX memory management system can be found, in increasing level of detail, in [DEC82], [DEC87], [KENA84], and [DEC78a]. Descriptions of the IBM System/370 memory management system can be found in [LEBA84a], [PRAS81], and [IBM83]. That of the Intel 80386 is described in [ELAY85], [MORS87], and [INTE86].

6.5

PROBLEMS

6.1 In a certain time-sharing system, each user spends an average of 20 seconds thinking and typing between interactions. The majority of interactions require 50 ms of CPU time, but 1 in 20 requires 2 seconds. In addition, each interaction involves swap-in and swap-out times of 100 ms each.

   Describe the scheduling and swapping policies to be adopted in this system to achieve the fastest possible response time for the maximum number of users.

   Indicate how much storage your system would require (in terms of the typical job size). Derive an expression for the response time R for short interactions, in terms of the number of users N. What are the assumptions and inaccuracies of this?

6.2 Suppose we have a multiprogrammed computer in which each job has identical characteristics. In one computation period, T, for a job, half the time is spent in I/O and the other half in CPU activity. Each job runs for a total of N periods. Define the following quantities:

   • Turnaround time = actual time to complete a job.
   • Throughput = average number of jobs completed per time period, T.
   • CPU utilization = percentage of time that the CPU is active (not waiting).

   Compute these quantities for one, two, and four simultaneous jobs, assuming that the period T is distributed in each of the following ways:
   (a) I/O first half, CPU second half.
   (b) I/O first and fourth quarters, CPU second and third quarters.

6.3 Define waiting time as the amount of time that a job spends waiting in the short-term queue (Figure 6-14). Give an equation that relates turnaround time, CPU busy time, and waiting time.

6.4 An I/O-bound program is one that, if run alone, would spend more time waiting for I/O than using the CPU. A CPU-bound program is the opposite.

   Suppose a short-term scheduling algorithm favors those programs that have used little CPU time in the recent past. Explain why this algorithm favors I/O-bound programs and yet does not permanently starve CPU-bound programs.

6.5 A program computes the row sums $C_i = \sum_{j=1}^{n} a_{ij}$ of an array A that is 100 by 100. Assume that the computer uses demand paging with a page size of 1,000 words, and that the amount of main memory allotted for data is five page frames. Is there any difference in the page fault rate if A were stored in virtual memory by rows or columns? Explain.

6.6 A virtual memory system has a page size of 1,024 words, eight virtual pages, and four physical page frames. The page table is as follows:

Virtual Page Number	Page Frame Number
0	3
1	1
2	—
3	—
4	2
5	—
6	0
7	—

(a) Make a list of all virtual addresses that will cause page faults.

(b) What are the main memory addresses for the following virtual addresses: 0, 3728, 1023, 1024, 1025, 7800, 4096?

6.7 Give reasons why the page size in a virtual memory system should be neither very small nor very large.

6.8 The following sequence of virtual page numbers is encountered in the course of execution on a computer with virtual memory:

3 4 2 6 4 7 1 3 2 6 3 5 1 2 3

Assume that a least-recently-used page replacement policy is adopted. Plot a graph of page hit ratio (fraction of page references in which the page is in main memory) as a function of main-memory page capacity n for $1 \le n \le 8$. Assume that main memory is initially empty.

6.9 In the VAX, user page tables are located at virtual addresses in the system space. What is the advantage of having user page tables in virtual rather than main memory?

6.10 In the VAX translation buffer, why is it necessary to invalidate the process cache when a new process is activated?

6.11 For System/370 memory management, suggest an approach for determining which page frames are least-recently used, making use of the reference bit in the storage key.

6.12 Consider a computer system with both virtual memory and a cache. For an item that exists in main memory (and possibly in the cache), two steps are involved:

1. Translating from virtual address to main memory address.
2. Checking to see if the data in the main memory location are also in the cache.

To save time, we would like to overlap these two activities, that is, to perform them, at least partially, in parallel.

In the Amdahl 470, address translation always leaves the low-order 11 address bits (byte offset) unchanged. The cache is N-way set associative. If some of the 11 bits are used to select one of 64 cache columns, which of the following cache steps can be overlapped with the virtual-address translation of the high-order bits?

1. Column select.
2. Read N cache-address tags in selected column.
3. Compare N address tags to real address.
4. Select one of N data lines.

6.13 Consider a computer system with both segmentation and paging. When a segment is in memory, some words are wasted on the last page. In addition, for a segment size s and a page size p, there are s/p page-table entries. The smaller the page size, the less waste in the last page of the segment, but the larger the page table. What page size minimizes the total overhead?

6.14 The segmentation approach used on System/370 seems to lack many of the potential advantages of segmentation. Which advantages does it lack? What is the benefit of segmentation for the 370?

6.15 A computer has a cache, main memory, and a disk used for virtual memory. If a word is in the cache, A ns are required to access it. If it is in main memory but not in cache, B ns are first needed to load it into the cache, and then the reference is started again. If the word is not in main memory, C ns are required to fetch it from disk, followed by B ns to get it to the cache. If the cache hit ratio is $(n - 1)/n$ and the main memory hit ratio is $(m - 1)/m$, what is the average access time?

THE CENTRAL PROCESSING UNIT

So far, we have viewed the CPU essentially as a "black box" and have considered its interaction with I/O and memory. In Part III, we examine the internal structure and function of the CPU.

Recall that the major components of a CPU are the ALU, the control unit, and registers (Figure 1-5). The functionality of the ALU is addressed in Chapter 7, which focuses on the representation of numbers and techniques for implementing arithmetic operations. The functionality of the control unit is determined, in large part, by the machine instruction set. This complex topic occupies Chapters 8 and 9. With this examination, we treat the control unit as a "black box," deferring an investigation of its internal structure and function to Part IV. Finally, Chapter 10 describes the use of registers as the CPU's internal memory, and then the chapter pulls together all of the material of Part III to complete the discussion of CPU structure and function.

CHAPTER 7

Computer Arithmetic

We begin our examination of the CPU with the Arithmetic and Logic Unit (ALU). After a brief introduction to the ALU, the chapter focuses on the most complex aspect of the ALU, computer arithmetic. The logic functions that are part of the ALU are described in Chapter 8, and implementations of simple logic and arithmetic functions in digital logic are described in the appendix of this book.

Computer arithmetic is commonly performed on two very different types of numbers: integer and floating point. In both cases, the representation chosen is a crucial design issue and is treated first, followed by a discussion of arithmetic operations.

A review of number systems is provided in an appendix to this chapter.

7.1

THE ARITHMETIC AND LOGIC UNIT (ALU)

The arithmetic and logic unit (ALU) is that part of the computer that actually performs arithmetic and logical operations on data. All of the other elements of the computer system—control unit, registers, memory, I/O—are there mainly to bring data into the ALU for it to process and then to take the results back out. We have, in a sense, reached the core or essence of a computer when we consider the ALU.

An arithmetic and logic unit and, indeed, all electronic components in the computer are based on the use of simple digital logic devices that can store binary digits and perform simple Boolean logic operations. The appendix to this text explores digital logic implementation for the interested reader.

Figure 7-1 indicates, in very general terms, how the ALU is interconnected with the rest of the CPU. Data are presented to the ALU in registers, and the results of an operation are stored in registers. These registers are temporary storage locations within the CPU that are connected by signal paths to the ALU (e.g., see Figure 2-6). The ALU will also set flags as the result of an operation.

287

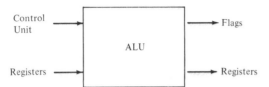

FIGURE 7-1. ALU inputs and outputs

For example, an overflow flag is set to 1 if the result of a computation exceeds the length of the register into which it is to be stored. The flag values are also stored in registers within the CPU. The control unit provides signals that control the operation of the ALU, and the movement of the data into and out of the ALU.

7.2

INTEGER REPRESENTATION

Principles

In Appendix 7A we describe the binary number system and show how numbers can be expressed using binary digits. With the aid of two symbols, the minus sign and the period, arbitrary numbers can be represented. For example,

$$-1011.0101_2 = -11.3125_{10}$$

For purposes of computer storage and processing, however, we do not have the benefit of minus signs and periods. Only binary digits (0 and 1) may be used to represent numbers. If we are limited to nonnegative integers, the representation is straightforward. An 8-bit word, for example, could be used to represent the numbers from 0 to 255:

```
00000000 = 0
00000001 = 1
00101001 = 41
10000000 = 128
11111111 = 255
```

This convention is clearly insufficient, since we will inevitably wish to represent negative as well as positive integers. There are several other conventions we could use for this. All of them involve treating the most significant (leftmost) bit in the word as a *sign bit*. If the leftmost bit is 0, the number is positive, and if the leftmost bit is 1, the number is negative.

The simplest form of representation that employs a sign bit is the *sign-magnitude* representation. In an N-bit word, the rightmost $N - 1$ bits hold the magnitude of the integer. Thus

00010010 = +18
10010010 = −18

Now, an 8-bit word can represent values in the range −127 to +127.

There are several drawbacks to this representation. One is that addition and subtraction require a consideration of both the signs of the numbers, and their relative magnitudes, in order to carry out the required operation. (We will discuss the implications of this in Section 7.3). Another drawback is that there are two representations for 0:

00000000 = 0_{10}
10000000 = -0_{10} (sign-magnitude)

This is inconvenient, since it is slightly more difficult to test for 0 (an operation performed frequently on computers) than if there were a single representation.

There are two other representations that make use of the leftmost sign bit. They differ from each other, and from sign-magnitude, in the way in which the other bits are interpreted. These representations are referred to as *1's complement* and *2's complement*. Both of them allow for more efficient addition and subtraction algorithms, as we shall see in Section 7.3. Furthermore, the 2's complement representation has only one representation for 0.

To begin, we need to distinguish between an operation and a representation. To perform the *1's-complement operation* on a set of binary digits, simply replace 0 digits with 1 digits and 1 digits with 0 digits. Thus

$$X = 01010001$$
1's complement of X = 10101110
$$Y = 10101110$$
1's complement of Y = 01010001

Now, the *1's complement representation* of binary integers is as follows. Positive integers are represented in the same way as sign-magnitude representation. A negative integer is represented by the 1's complement of the positive integer with the same magnitude. For example,

$$18 = 00010010$$
−18 = 1's complement of 18 = 11101101

Note that since all positive integers in this representation have the leftmost bit equal to 0, all negative numbers necessarily have the leftmost bit equal to 1. Thus the leftmost bit continues to function as a sign bit.

In ordinary arithmetic, the negative of the negative of a number gives you back the number (e.g., −(−18) = 18). For consistency, this should be true in 1's-complement representation, and it is. For example,

$$-18 = 11101101$$
18 = 1's complement of −18 = 00010010

As with sign-magnitude, 1's complement has two representations for 0:

$00000000 = 0_{10}$
$11111111 = -0_{10}$ (1's complement)

We turn now to 2's complement. The *2's-complement operation* consists of two steps:

1. Perform the 1's-complement operation.
2. Treating the result as an unsigned binary integer, add 1.

The *2's complement representation* of positive integers is the same as in sign-magnitude and 1's-complement representation. A negative number is represented by the 2's complement of the positive integer with the same magnitude. For example,

$$
\begin{array}{r}
18 = 00010010 \\
\text{1's complement} = 11101101 \\
+ \qquad 1 \\
\hline
-18 = \text{2's complement of } 18 = 11101110
\end{array}
$$

Again, we find that the negative of the negative of that number is itself:

$$
\begin{array}{r}
\text{2's-complement representation of } -18 = 11101110 \\
\text{1's complement} = 00010001 \\
+ \qquad 1 \\
\hline
18 = \text{2's complement of } -18 = 00010010
\end{array}
$$

The 2's complement representation has one anomaly not found with sign-magnitude or 1's complement. The bit pattern 1 followed by $N - 1$ zeros is its own 2's complement. To maintain sign-bit consistency, this bit pattern is assigned the value -2^N. For example, for 8-bit words,

$$
\begin{array}{r}
-128 = 10000000 \\
\text{1's complement} = 01111111 \\
+ \qquad 1 \\
\hline
10000000 = -128
\end{array}
$$

With this interpretation, all positive integers have a leftmost bit of 0, and all negative integers have a leftmost bit of 1. Thus the leftmost bit continues to function as a sign bit.

Some such anomaly is unavoidable. The number of different bit patterns in an N-bit word is 2^N, which is an even number. We wish to represent positive and negative integers and 0. If an equal number of positive and negative integers are represented (sign-magnitude, 1's complement), then there are two representations for 0. If there is only one representation for 0 (2's complement), then there is one more negative number than positive number represented.

Table 7-1 shows the three representations for 4-bit words. Although 2's complement is an awkward representation from the human point of view, we will see that it facilitates the most important arithmetic operations, addition and

TABLE 7-1 Comparison of Three 4-Bit Binary Number Codes

Decimal Representation	Binary Code		
	Sign-Magnitude	One's Complement	Two's Complement
+7	0111	0111	0111
+6	0110	0110	0110
+5	0101	0101	0101
+4	0100	0100	0100
+3	0011	0011	0011
+2	0010	0010	0010
+1	0001	0001	0001
+0	0000	0000	0000
−0	1000	1111	0000
−1	1001	1110	1111
−2	1010	1101	1110
−3	1011	1100	1101
−4	1100	1011	1100
−5	1101	1010	1011
−6	1110	1001	1010
−7	1111	1000	1001
−8	—	—	1000

subtraction. For this reason, it is the most commonly used computer representation for integers.

Fixed-Point Representation

Finally, we mention that all of the representations discussed in this section are sometimes referred to as *fixed point*. This is because the radix point (binary point) is fixed and assumed to be to the right of the rightmost digit. The programmer can use the same representation for binary fractions by scaling the numbers so that the binary point is implicitly positioned at some other location.

7.3

INTEGER ARITHMETIC

We have presented the 2's-complement representation for fixed-point numbers. In this section, we will examine algorithms for performing common arithmetic functions on numbers in this representation. The discussion at this point is implementation-independent. In some systems, only a few basic arithmetic functions (e.g., addition and subtraction) are performed in hardware and the rest in software. Other, more sophisticated, machines provide better performance by implementing more functions in hardware.

Addition and Subtraction

A consideration of algorithms for addition and subtraction demonstrates the motivation for the use of the 2's-complement representation.

It should be intuitively obvious that the simplest implementation is one in which the numbers involved can be treated as unsigned integers for purposes of addition. With that in mind, we can immediately reject the sign-magnitude representation. For example, these are clearly incorrect:

$$0011 = +3$$
$$+1011 = -3$$
$$\overline{1110} = -6 \text{ (sign-magnitude)}$$

$$0001 = +1$$
$$+1110 = -6$$
$$\overline{1111} = -7 \text{ (sign-magnitude)}$$

For sign-magnitude numbers, correct addition and subtraction are relatively complex, involving the comparison of signs and relative magnitudes of the two numbers.

With a complements notation, it is possible to treat the numbers as unsigned integers for purposes of addition and subtraction. First, consider 1's-complement addition:

$$0011 = +3$$
$$+1100 = -3$$
$$\overline{1111} = 0 \text{ (1's complement)}$$

$$0001 = +1$$
$$+1001 = -6$$
$$\overline{1010} = -5 \text{ (1's complement)}$$

This scheme will not always work unless an additional rule is added. If there is a carry out of the leftmost bit, add 1 to the sum. This is called an *end-around carry*. For example:

$$1101 = -2$$
$$1011 = -4$$
$$①\ \overline{1000}$$
$$\longrightarrow 1$$
$$\overline{1001} = -6 \text{ (1's complement)}$$

$$0111 = +7$$
$$1100 = -3$$
$$①\ \overline{0011}$$
$$\longrightarrow 1$$
$$\overline{0100} = 4 \text{ (1's complement)}$$

So, with 1's-complement representation, a single binary adder that operates on unsigned integers can be employed. However, this representation has the disadvantage of the need to perform an end-around carry on some additions. This problem is not found in the 2's-complement representation.

Addition in 2's complement is illustrated in Figure 7-2. The first four examples illustrate successful operation. If the result of the operation is positive, we get a positive number in ordinary binary notation. If the result of the operation is negative, we get a negative number in 2's-complement form. Note that, in some instances, there is a carry bit beyond the end of the word. This is ignored.

On any addition, the result may be larger than can be held in the word size being used. This condition is called *overflow*. When overflow occurs, the ALU must signal this fact so that no attempt is made to use the result. To detect overflow, the following rule is observed.

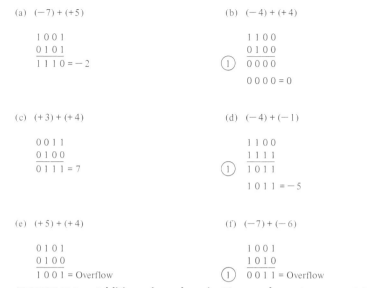

FIGURE 7-2.   Addition of numbers in 2's-complement representation

OVERFLOW RULE:

If two numbers are added, and they are both positive or both negative, then overflow occurs if and only if the result has the opposite sign.

Figures 7-2e and f show examples of overflow. Note that overflow can occur whether or not there is a carry. Subtraction is also easily handled:

SUBTRACTION RULE:

To subtract one number (subtrahend) from another (minuend), take the 2's complement of the subtrahend and add it to the minuend.

Thus subtraction is achieved using addition, as illustrated in Figure 7-3. The last two examples demonstrate that the overflow rule still applies.

Figure 7-4 suggests the data paths and hardware elements needed to accomplish addition and subtraction. The central element is a binary adder, which is presented two numbers for addition and produces a sum and an overflow indication. The binary adder treats the two numbers as unsigned integers. (A logic implementation of an adder is given in the Appendix to this book.) For addition, the two numbers are presented to the adder from two registers, designated in this case as A and B registers. The result is typically stored in one of these registers rather than a third. The overflow indication is stored in a 1-bit Overflow Flag (0 = no overflow; 1 = overflow). For subtraction, the subtrahend (B register) is passed through a complementer so that its 2's complement is presented to the adder.

(a) M = 2 = 0010
    S = 7 = 0111
    S' =   1001

       0010
    + 1001
      1011 = −5

(b) M = 5 = 0101
    S = 2 = 0010
    S' =   1110

       0101
    + 1110
  ① 0011
      0011 = 3

(c) M = −5 = 1011
    S =   2 = 0010
    S' =   1110

       1011
    + 1110
  ① 1001
      1001 = −7

(d) M = 5 = 0101
    S = −2 = 1110
    S' =   0010

       0101
    + 0010
      0111 = 7

(e) M =   7 = 0111
    S = −7 = 1001
    S' =   0111

       0111
    + 0111
      1110 = Overflow

(f) M = −6 = 1010
    S =   4 = 0100
    S' =   1100

       1010
    + 1100
  ① 0110 = Overflow

FIGURE 7-3. Subtraction of numbers in 2's-complement notation (M − S)

Multiplication

Compared to addition and subtraction, multiplication is a complex operation, whether performed in hardware or software. A wide variety of algorithms have been used in various computers. The purpose of this subsection is to give the reader some feel for the type of approach typically taken. We begin with the simpler problem of multiplying two unsigned (nonnegative) integers, and then we look at one of the most common techniques for multiplication of numbers in 2's-complement representation.

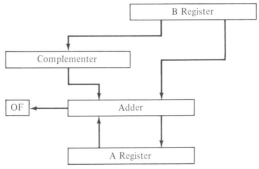

FIGURE 7-4. Block diagram of hardware for addition and subtraction

Unsigned Integers

Figure 7-5 illustrates the multiplication of unsigned binary integers, as might be carried out using paper and pencil. Several important observations can be made:

1. Multiplication involves the generation of partial products, one for each digit in the multiplier. These partial products are then summed to produce the final product.
2. The partial products are easily defined. When the multiplier bit is 0, the partial product is 0. When the multiplier is 1, the partial product is the multiplicand.
3. The total product is produced by summing the partial products. For this operation, each successive partial product is shifted one position to the left relative to the preceding partial product.
4. The multiplication of two n-bit binary integers results in a product of up to $2n$ bits in length.

Compared to the pencil-and-paper approach, there are several things we can do to make the operation more efficient. First, we can perform a running addition on the partial products rather than waiting until the end. This eliminates the need for storage of all the partial products; fewer registers are needed. Second, we can save some time on the generation of partial products. For each 1 on the multiplier, an add and a shift operation are required; but for each 0, only a shift is required.

Figure 7-6a shows a possible implementation employing these measures. The multiplier and multiplicand are loaded into two registers (Q and M). A third register, the A register, is also needed and is initially set to 0. There is also a 1-bit C register, initialized to 0, which holds a potential carry bit resulting from addition.

The operation of the multiplier is as follows. Control logic reads the bits of the multiplier one at a time. If Q_0 is 1, then the multiplicand is added to the A register and the result is stored in the A register. Then, all of the bits of the C, A, and Q registers are shifted to the right one bit, so that the C bit goes into A_{n-1}, A_0 goes into Q_{n-1}, and Q_0 is lost. If Q_0 is 0, then no addition is performed, just the shift. This process is repeated for each bit of the original multiplier. The resulting $2n$-bit product is contained in the A and Q registers. A flowchart of the

```
   1 0 1 1        Multiplicand (11)
 × 1 1 0 1        Multiplier    (13)
   1 0 1 1     ⎫
   0 0 0 0     ⎬
   1 0 1 1     ⎬  Partial Products
  1 0 1 1      ⎭
 1 0 0 0 1 1 1 1  Product (143)
```

FIGURE 7-5. Multiplication of unsigned binary integers

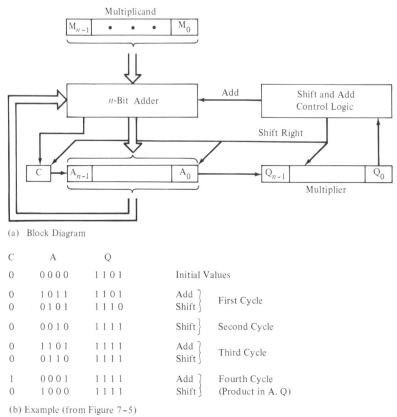

(a) Block Diagram

C	A	Q		
0	0 0 0 0	1 1 0 1	Initial Values	
0	1 0 1 1	1 1 0 1	Add	First Cycle
0	0 1 0 1	1 1 1 0	Shift	
0	0 0 1 0	1 1 1 1	Shift	Second Cycle
0	1 1 0 1	1 1 1 1	Add	Third Cycle
0	0 1 1 0	1 1 1 1	Shift	
1	0 0 0 1	1 1 1 1	Add	Fourth Cycle
0	1 0 0 0	1 1 1 1	Shift	(Product in A, Q)

(b) Example (from Figure 7–5)

FIGURE 7-6. Hardware implementation of unsigned binary multiplication (M contains 1011)

operation is shown in Figure 7-7, and an example is given in Figure 7-6b. Note that on the second cycle, when the multiplier bit is 0, there is no add operation.

Two's Complement Multiplication

We have seen that addition and subtraction can be performed on numbers in 2's-complement notation by treating them as unsigned integers. Consider:

$$\begin{array}{r} 1001 \\ +0011 \\ \hline 1100 \end{array}$$

If these numbers are considered to be unsigned integers, then we are adding 9 (1001) plus 3 (0011) to get 12 (1100). As 2's-complement integers, we are adding −7 (1001) to 3 (0011) to get −4 (1100).

Unfortunately, this simple scheme will not work for multiplication. To see

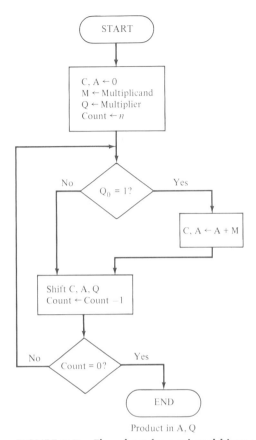

Product in A, Q

FIGURE 7-7.   Flowchart for unsigned binary multiplication

this, consider again Figure 7-5. We multiplied 11 (1011) by 13 (1101) to get 143 (10001111). If we interpret these as 2's-complement numbers, we have −5 (1011) times −3 (1101) equals −113 (10001111). This example demonstrates that straightforward multiplication will not work if both the multiplicand and multiplier are negative. In fact, it will not work if either the multiplicand or the multiplier is negative. To explain this statement, we need to go back to Figure 7-5 and explain what is being done in terms of operations with powers of 2. Recall that any unsigned binary number can be expressed as a sum of powers of 2. Thus

$$1101 = 1 * 2^3 + 1 * 2^2 + 0 * 2^1 + 1 * 2^0$$
$$= 2^3 + 2^2 + 2^0$$

Further, the multiplication of a binary number by 2^n is accomplished by shifting that number to the left n bits. With this in mind, Figure 7-8 recasts Figure 7-5 to make the generation of partial products by multiplication explicit. The only difference in Figure 7-8 is that it recognizes that the partial products should be viewed as $2n$-bit numbers generated from the n-bit multiplicand.

```
     1 0 1 1
    × 1 1 0 1
  ─────────────
  0 0 0 0 1 0 1 1        1011 × 1 × 2⁰
  0 0 0 0 0 0 0 0        1011 × 0 × 2¹
  0 0 1 0 1 1 0 0        1011 × 1 × 2²
  0 1 0 1 1 0 0 0        1011 × 1 × 2³
  ─────────────
  1 0 0 0 1 1 1 1
```

FIGURE 7-8. Multiplication of two unsigned 4-bit integers yielding an 8-bit result

Thus, as an unsigned integer, the 4-bit multiplicand 1011 is stored in an 8-bit word as 00001011. Each partial product (other than that for 2^0) consists of this number shifted to the left, with the unoccupied positions on the right filled with zeroes (e.g., a shift to the left of two places yields 00101100).

Now we can demonstrate that straightforward multiplication will not work if the multiplicand is negative. The problem is that each contribution of the negative multiplicand as a partial product must be a negative number on a $2n$-bit field; the sign bits of the partial products must line up. This is demonstrated in Figure 7-9, which shows that multiplication of 1001 by 0011. If these are treated as unsigned integers, the multiplication of $9 * 3 = 27$ proceeds simply. However, if 1001 is interpreted as the 2's complement -7, then each partial product must be a negative 2's-complement number of $2n$ (8) bits, as shown in Figure 7-9b. Note that this could be accomplished by padding out each partial product to the left with binary 1s.

It should also be clear that if the multiplier is negative, straightforward multiplication will not work. The reason is that the bits of the multiplier no longer correspond to the shifts or multiplications that must take place. For example:

$$-3 = 1101$$
$$= -(0 * 2^3 + 0 * 2^2 + 1 * 2^1 + 1 * 2^0)$$
$$= -2^1 - 2^0$$

So this multiplier cannot be used directly in the manner we have been describing.

There are a number of ways out of this dilemma. One would be to convert both multiplier and multiplicand to positive numbers, perform the multiplication, and then take the 2's complement of the result if and only if the sign of the two original numbers differed. Implementers have preferred to use techniques

```
     1 0 0 1    (9)                    1 0 0 1    (−7)
    × 0 0 1 1    (3)                   × 0 0 1 1    (3)
  ─────────────                     ─────────────
  0 0 0 0 1 0 0 1  (1001) × 2⁰      1 1 1 1 1 0 0 1  (−7) × 2⁰ = (−7)
  0 0 0 1 0 0 1 0  (1001) × 2¹      1 1 1 1 0 0 1 0  (−7) × 2¹ = (−14)
  ─────────────                     ─────────────
  0 0 0 1 1 0 1 1  (27)             1 1 1 0 1 0 1 1  (−21)
```

(a) Unsigned integers   (b) 2's complement integers

FIGURE 7-9. Comparison of multiplication of unsigned and 2's-complement integers

that do not require this final transformation step. One of the most common of these is Booth's algorithm [BOOT51]. This algorithm also has the benefit of speeding up the multiplication process, relative to a more straightforward approach.

Booth's algorithm is depicted in Figure 7-10 and can be described as follows. As before, the multiplier and multiplicand are placed in the Q and M registers, respectively. There is also a 1-bit register placed logically to the right of the least significant bit (Q_0) of the Q register and designated Q_{-1}; its use is explained shortly. The results of the multiplication will appear in the A and Q registers. A and Q_{-1} are initialized to 0. As before, control logic scans the bits of the multiplier one at a time. Now, as each bit is examined, the bit to its right is also examined. If the two bits are the same (1-1 or 0-0), then all of the bits of the A, Q, and Q_{-1} registers are shifted to the right 1 bit. If the 2 bits differ, then the multiplicand is added to or subtracted from the A register, according as the 2 bits are 0-1 or 1-0. Following the addition or subtraction, the right shift occurs. In either case, the right shift is such that the leftmost bit of A, namely A_{n-1}, not

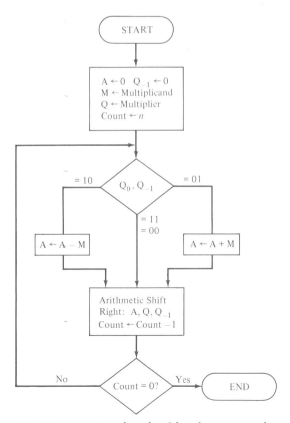

FIGURE 7-10.   Booth's algorithm for 2's-complement multiplication

only is shifted into A_{n-2}, but also remains in A_{n-1}. This is required to preserve the sign of the number in A and Q. It is known as an *arithmetic shift*, since it preserves the sign bit.

Figure 7-11 shows the sequence of events in Booth's algorithm for the multiplication of 7 by 3. More compactly, the same operation is depicted in Figure 7-12a. The rest of Figure 7-12 gives other examples of the algorithm. As can be seen, it works with any combination of positive and negative numbers. Note also the efficiency of the algorithm. Blocks of 1s or 0s are skipped over, with an average of only one addition or subtraction per block.

Why does Booth's algorithm work? Consider first the case of a positive multiplier. In particular, consider a positive multiplier consisting of one block of 1s surrounded by 0s, for example, 00011110. As we know, multiplication can be achieved by adding appropriately shifted copies of the multiplicand:

$$M * (00011110) = M * (2^4 + 2^3 + 2^2 + 2^1)$$
$$= M * (16 + 8 + 4 + 2)$$
$$= M * 30$$

The number of such operations can be reduced to two if we observe that

$$2^n + 2^{n-1} + \cdots + 2^{n-K} = 2^{n+1} - 2^{n-K} \tag{7-1}$$

Thus,

$$M * (00011110) = M * (2^5 - 2^1)$$
$$= M * (32 - 2)$$
$$= M * 30$$

So the product can be generated by one addition and one subtraction of the multiplicand. This scheme extends to any number of blocks of 1s in a multiplier, including the case in which a single 1 is treated as a block. Thus,

$$M * (01111010) = M * (2^6 + 2^5 + 2^4 + 2^3 + 2^1)$$
$$= M * (2^7 - 2^3 + 2^2 - 2^1)$$

Booth's algorithm conforms to this scheme by performing a subtraction when the first 1 of the block is encountered (1–0) and an addition when the end of the block is encountered (0–1).

A	Q	Q_{-1}		
0 0 0 0	0 0 1 1	0	Initial	
1 0 0 1	0 0 1 1	0	A ← A − M }	
1 1 0 0	1 0 0 1	1	Shift	First Cycle
1 1 1 0	0 1 0 0	1	Shift }	Second Cycle
0 1 0 1	0 1 0 0	1	A ← A + M }	
0 0 1 0	1 0 1 0	0	Shift	Third Cycle
0 0 0 1	0 1 0 1	0	Shift }	Fourth Cycle (Product in A, Q)

FIGURE 7-11. Example of Booth's algorithm (M contains 0111)

To show that the same scheme works for a negative multiplier, we need to observe the following. Let X be a negative number in 2's-complement notation:

Representation of $X = \{1 \; x_{n-2}x_{n-3} \cdots x_1x_0\}$

Then the value of X can be expressed as follows:

$$X = -2^{n-1} + x_{n-2} * 2^{n-2} + x_{n-3} * 2^{n-3} + \cdots + x_1 * 2^1 + x_0 * 2^0 \quad (7\text{-}2)$$

The reader can verify this by applying the algorithm to the numbers in Table 7-1. Also, see Problem 7.2.

Now, we know that the leftmost bit of X is 1, since X is negative. Assume that the leftmost 0 is in the Kth position. Thus X is of the form

Representation of $X = \{111 \cdots 10x_{k-1}x_{k-2} \cdots x_1x_0\}$ \quad (7\text{-}3)

Then the value of X is

$$X = -2^{n-1} + 2^{n-2} + \cdots + 2^{k+1} + x_{k-1} * 2^{k-1} + \cdots + x_0 * 2^0 \quad (7\text{-}4)$$

Now, from Equation 7-1, we can say that

$$2^{n-2} + 2^{n-3} + \cdots + 2^{k+1} = 2^{n-1} - 2^{k+1}$$

Rearranging,

$$-2^{n-1} + 2^{n-2} + 2^{n-3} + \cdots + 2^{k+1} = -2^{k+1} \quad (7\text{-}5)$$

Substituting Equation 7-5 into Equation 7-4, we have

$$X = -2^{k+1} + x_{k-1} * 2^{k-1} + \cdots + x_0 * 2^0 \quad (7\text{-}6)$$

At last we can return to Booth's algorithm. Remembering the representation of X (Equation 7-3), it is clear that all of the bits from X_0 up to the leftmost 0 are handled properly, since they produce all of the terms in Equation 7-6 but (-2^{k+1})

```
      0 1 1 1                              0 1 1 1
    × 0 0 1 1 (0)                        × 1 1 0 1 (0)
 1 1 1 1 1 0 0 1    1 − 0            1 1 1 1 1 0 0 1    1 − 0
 0 0 0 0 0 0 0     1 − 1            0 0 0 0 1 1 1     0 − 1
 0 0 0 1 1 1      0   1            1 1 1 0 0 1      1 − 0
 0 0 0 1 0 1 0 1   (21)           1 1 1 0 1 0 1 1   (−21)

(a) (7) × (3) = (21)              (b) (7) × (−3) = (−21)


      1 0 0 1                              1 0 0 1
      0 0 1 1 (0)                          1 1 0 1 (0)
 0 0 0 0 0 1 1 1   1 − 0            0 0 0 0 0 1 1 1   1 − 0
 0 0 0 0 0 0 0     1 − 1            1 1 1 1 0 0 1     0 − 1
 1 1 1 0 0 1      0 − 1            0 0 0 1 1 1      1 − 0
 1 1 1 0 1 0 1 1   (−21)           0 0 0 1 0 1 0 1   (21)

(c) (−7) × (3) = (−21)            (d) (−7) × (−3) = (−21)
```

FIGURE 7-12. Examples using Booth's algorithm

and thus are in the proper form. As the algorithm scans over the leftmost 0 and encounters the next 1 (2^{k+1}), a $1 - 0$ transition occurs and a subtraction takes place (-2^{k+1}). This is the remaining term in Equation 7-6.

As an example, consider the multiplication of some multiplicand by (-6). In 2's-complement representation, using an 8-bit word, (-6) is represented as 11111010. By Equation 7-2, we know that

$$-6 = -2^{-7} + 2^6 + 2^5 + 2^4 + 2^3 + 2^1$$

which the reader can easily verify. Thus

$$M2 * (11111010) = M * (-2^{-7} + 2^6 + 2^5 + 2^4 + 2^3 + 2^1)$$

Using Equation 7-6,

$$M * (11111010) = M * (-2^3 + 2^1)$$

which the reader can verify is still $M * (-6)$. Finally, following our earlier line of reasoning,

$$M * (11111010) = M * (-2^3 + 2^2 - 2^1)$$

But now we can see that Booth's algorithm conforms to this scheme. It performs a subtraction when the first 1 is encountered ($1 - 0$), an addition when ($0 - 1$) is encountered, and finally another subtraction when the first 1 of the next block of 1s is encountered. Thus Booth's algorithm performs fewer additions and subtractions than a more straightforward algorithm.

Division

Division is somewhat more complex than multiplication but is based on the same general principles. As before, the basis for the algorithm is the paper-and-pencil approach, and the operation involves repetitive shifting and addition or subtraction.

Figure 7-13 shows an example of the long division of unsigned binary integers. It is instructive to describe the process in detail. First, the bits of the dividend are examined from left to right, until the set of bits examined represents a number greater than or equal to the divisor; this is referred to as the divisor being able to *divide* the number. Until this event occurs, 0s are placed in the

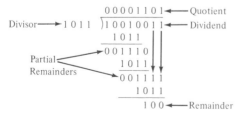

FIGURE 7-13.   Division of unsigned binary integers

quotient from left to right. When the event occurs, a 1 is placed in the quotient and the divisor is subtracted from the partial dividend. The result is referred to as a *partial remainder.* From this point on, the division follows a cyclic pattern. At each cycle, additional bits from the dividend are appended to the partial remainder until the result is greater than or equal to the divisor. As before, the divisor is subtracted from this number to produce a new partial remainder. The process continues until all of the bits of the dividend are exhausted.

Figure 7-14 shows a machine algorithm that corresponds to the long division process. The divisor is placed in the M register, the dividend in the Q register. At each step, the A and Q registers together are shifted to the left 1 bit. M is subtracted from A to determine whether A divides the partial remainder. If it

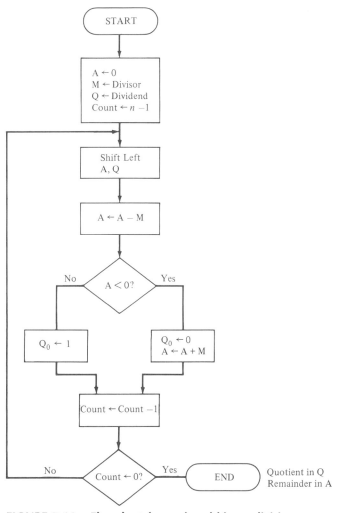

FIGURE 7-14.   Flowchart for unsigned binary division

A	Q	M = 0011
0 0 0 0	0 1 1 1	Initial Value
0 0 0 0	1 1 1 0	Shift
1 1 0 1		Subtract
0 0 0 0	1 1 1 0	Restore
0 0 0 1	1 1 0 0	Shift
1 1 1 0		Subtract
0 0 0 1	1 1 0 0	Restore
0 0 1 1	1 0 0 0	Shift
0 0 0 0		Subtract
0 0 0 0	1 0 0 1	Set Q_0 = 1
0 0 0 1	0 0 1 0	Shift
1 1 1 0		Subtract
0 0 0 1	0 0 1 0	Restore

(a) (7) ÷ (3)

A	Q	M = 1101
0 0 0 0	0 1 1 1	Initial Value
0 0 0 0	1 1 1 0	Shift
1 1 0 1		Add
0 0 0 0	1 1 1 0	Restore
0 0 0 1	1 1 0 0	Shift
1 1 1 0		Add
0 0 0 1	1 1 0 0	Restore
0 0 1 1	1 0 0 0	Shift
0 0 0 0		Add
0 0 0 0	1 0 0 1	Set Q_0 = 1
0 0 0 1	0 0 1 0	Shift
1 1 1 0		Add
0 0 0 1	0 0 1 0	Restore

(b) (7) ÷ (− 3)

A	Q	M = 0011
1 1 1 1	1 0 0 1	Initial Value
1 1 1 1	0 0 1 0	Shift
0 0 1 0		Add
1 1 1 1	0 0 1 0	Restore
1 1 1 0	0 1 0 0	Shift
0 0 0 1		Add
1 1 1 0	0 1 0 0	Restore
1 1 0 0	1 0 0 0	Shift
1 1 1 1		Add
1 1 1 1	1 0 0 1	Set Q_0 = 1
1 1 1 1	0 0 1 0	Shift
0 0 1 0		Add
1 1 1 1	0 0 1 0	Restore

(c) (−7) ÷ 3

A	Q	M = 1101
1 1 1 1	1 0 0 1	Initial Value
1 1 1 1	0 0 1 0	Shift
0 0 1 0		Subtract
1 1 1 1	0 0 1 0	Restore
1 1 1 0	0 1 0 0	Shift
0 0 0 1		Subtract
1 1 1 0	0 1 0 0	Restore
1 1 0 0	1 0 0 0	Shift
1 1 1 1		Subtract
1 1 1 1	1 0 0 1	Set Q_0 = 1
1 1 1 1	0 0 1 0	Shift
0 0 1 0		Subtract
1 1 1 1	0 0 1 0	Restore

(d) (−7) ÷ (−3)

FIGURE 7-15.   Examples of 2's-complement division

does, then Q_0 gets a 1 bit. Otherwise Q_0 gets a 0 bit and M must be added back to A to restore the previous value. The count is then decremented, and the process continues for n steps. At the end, the quotient is in the Q register and the remainder is in the A register.

This process can, with some difficulty, be extended to negative numbers. We give here one approach for 2's-complement numbers [ALEX84]. Several examples of this approach are shown in Figure 7-15. The algorithm can be summarized as follows.

1. Load the divisor into the M register and the dividend into the A, Q registers. The dividend must be expressed as a $2n$-bit 2's-complement number. Thus, for example, the 4-bit 0111 becomes 00000111, and 1001 becomes 11111001.
2. Shift A, Q left 1 bit position.
3. If M and A have the same signs, perform $A \leftarrow A - M$; otherwise, $A \leftarrow A + M$.
4. The above operation is successful if the sign of A is the same before and after the operation.
   (a) If the operation is successful or (A = 0 AND Q = 0), then set $Q_0 \leftarrow 1$.
   (b) if the operation is unsuccessful and (A $\neq$ 0 OR Q $\neq$ 0), then set $Q_0 \leftarrow 0$ and restore the previous value of A.
5. Repeat steps 2 through 4 as many times as there are bit positions in Q.
6. The remainder is in A. If the signs of the divisor and dividend were the same, then the quotient is in Q; otherwise, the correct quotient is the 2's complement of Q.

The reader will note from Figure 7-15 that $(-7) \div (3)$ and $(7) \div (-3)$ produce different remainders. This is because the remainder is defined as

$$D = Q * V + R$$

where

D = dividend
Q = quotient
V = divisor
R = remainder

The results of Figure 7-15 are consistent with this formula.

7.4

FLOATING-POINT REPRESENTATION

Principles

With a fixed-point notation (e.g., 2's complement) it is possible to represent a range of positive and negative integers centered on 0. By assuming a fixed binary or radix point, this format allows the representation of numbers with a fractional component as well.

This approach has limitations. Very large numbers cannot be represented, nor can very small fractions. Further, the fractional part of the quotient in a division of two large numbers could be lost.

For decimal numbers, one gets around this limitation by using scientific notation. Thus 976,000,000,000,000 can be represented as $9.76 * 10^{14}$, and 0.0000000000000976 can be represented as $9.76 * 10^{-14}$. What we have done, in effect, is to dynamically slide the decimal point to a convenient location and use the exponent of 10 to keep track of that decimal point. This allows a range of very large and very small numbers to be represented with only a few digits.

This same approach can be taken with binary numbers. We can represent a number in the form

$$\pm S * B^{\pm E}$$

This number can be stored in a binary word with three fields:

- Sign: plus or minus
- Significand S
- Exponent E

The base B is implicit and need not be stored since it is the same for all numbers.

The principles used in representing binary floating-point numbers are best explained with an example. Figure 7-16a shows a typical 32-bit floating-point format. The leftmost bit stores the sign of the number (0 = positive, 1 = negative). The exponent value is stored in bits 1 through 8. The representation used is known as a *biased* representation. A fixed value, called the bias, is subtracted from the field to get the true exponent value. In this case, the 8-bit field yields the numbers 0 through 255. With a bias of 128, the true exponent values are in the range −128 to +127. In this example, the base is assumed to be 2.

The final portion of the word is the *significand*, also called the *mantissa*. Now, any floating-point number can be expressed in many ways. Thus, the following are equivalent:

$$0.110 \quad * \quad 2^5$$
$$110 \quad\quad * \quad 2^2$$
$$0.0110 * \quad 2^6$$

and so on. To simplify operations on floating-point numbers, it is typically required that they be *normalized*. For our example, a normalized number is one in the form

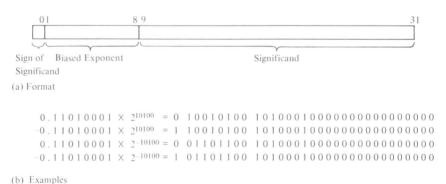

(a) Format

$$0.11010001 \times 2^{10100} = 0 \quad 10010100 \quad 10100010000000000000000$$
$$-0.11010001 \times 2^{10100} = 1 \quad 10010100 \quad 10100010000000000000000$$
$$0.11010001 \times 2^{-10100} = 0 \quad 01101100 \quad 10100010000000000000000$$
$$-0.11010001 \times 2^{-10100} = 1 \quad 01101100 \quad 10100010000000000000000$$

(b) Examples

FIGURE 7-16. Typical 32-bit floating-point format

$$\pm 0.1\ bbb \cdots b * 2^{\pm E}$$

where b is either binary digit (0 or 1). This would imply that the leftmost bit of the significand would always be 1. Since it is obviously unnecessary to store this bit, it is implicit. Thus the 23-bit field is used to store a 24-bit significand with a value between 0.5 and 1.0.

Figure 7-16b gives some examples of numbers stored in this format. Note the following features:

- The sign is stored in the first bit of the word.
- The first bit of the true significand is always 1 and need not be stored in the significand field.
- The value 128 is added to the true exponent to be stored in the exponent field.
- The base is 2.

With this representation, Figure 7-17 indicates the range of numbers that can be represented in a 32-bit word. Using 2's-complement integer representation, all of the integers from -2^{31} to $2^{31} - 1$ can be represented for a total of 2^{32} different numbers. With the example floating-point format of Figure 7-16, the following ranges of numbers are possible:

- Negative numbers between $-(1 - 2^{-24}) * 2^{127}$ and $-0.5 * 2^{-128}$
- Positive numbers between $0.5 * 2^{-128}$ and $(1 - 2^{-24}) * 2^{127}$

Five regions on the number line are not included in these ranges:

- Negative numbers less than $-(1 - 2^{-24}) * 2^{127}$, called *negative overflow*.
- Negative numbers greater than $-0.5 * 2^{-128}$, called *negative underflow*.
- Zero

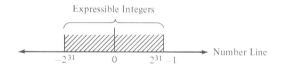

(a) 2's Complement Integers

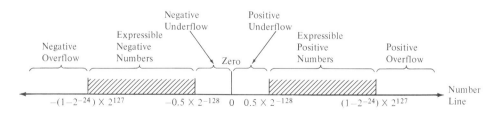

(b) Floating Point Numbers

FIGURE 7-17. **Expressible numbers in typical 32-bit formats**

- Positive numbers less than $0.5 * 2^{-128}$, called *positive underflow.*
- Positive numbers greater than $(1 - 2^{-24}) * 2^{127}$, called *positive overflow.*

The representation as presented will not accommodate a value of 0. However, as we shall see, actual floating-point representations include a special bit pattern to designate zero. Overflow occurs when an arithmetic operation results in a magnitude greater than can be expressed with an exponent of 127 (e.g., $2^{120} * 2^{100} = 2^{220}$). Underflow occurs when the fractional magnitude is too small (e.g., $2^{-120} * 2^{-100} = 2^{-220}$). Underflow is a less serious problem because the result can generally be satisfactorily approximated by 0.

It is important to note that we are not representing more individual values with floating-point notation. The maximum number of different values that can be represented with 32 bits is still 2^{32}. What we have done is to spread those numbers out in two ranges, one positive and one negative.

Also, note that the numbers represented in floating-point notation are not spaced evenly along the number line, as are fixed-point numbers. The possible values get closer together near the origin and farther apart as you move away, as shown in Figure 7-18. This is one of the tradeoffs of floating-point math: Many calculations produce results that are not exact and have to be rounded to the nearest value that the notation can represent.

In the type of format depicted in Figure 7-16, there is a tradeoff between range and precision. The example shows 8 bits devoted to the exponent and 23 to the significand. If we increase the number of bits in the exponent, we expand the range of expressible numbers. But, since only a fixed number of different values can be expressed, we have reduced the density of those numbers and therefore the precision. The only way to increase both range and precision is to use more bits. Thus, most computers offer, at least, *single-precision* numbers and *double-precision* numbers. For example, a single-precision format might be 32 bits, and a double-precision format 64 bits.

So there is a tradeoff between the number of bits in the exponent and the number of bits in the significand. But it is even more complicated than that. The implied base of the exponent need not be 2. The IBM S/370 architecture, for example, uses a base of 16. The format consists of a 7-bit exponent and a 24-bit significand. So, for example,

$$0.11010001 * 2^{10100} = 0.11010001 * 16^{101}$$

and the exponent is stored to represent 5 rather than 20.

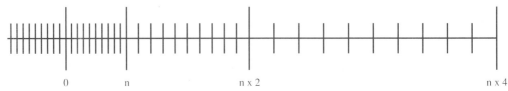

FIGURE 7-18. Density of floating-point numbers

The advantage of using a larger exponent is that a greater range can be achieved for the same number of exponent bits. But, remember, we have not increased the number of different values that can be represented. Thus, for a fixed format, a larger exponent base gives a greater range at the expense of less precision.

Examples

We now look at several example floating-point representations. Their characteristics are summarized in Table 7-2, and the formats are shown in Figure 7-19.

IBM System/370

As was mentioned, the IBM 370 family uses a 7-bit exponent with an implied base of 16. This same exponent size is used for both 32-bit and 64-bit formats. Thus, IBM opts for greater precision rather than greater range in its 64-bit format. The exponent is a biased representation, so that values from 16^{-64} to 16^{+63} are expressible.

Because the implied base is 16, a change of 1 in the exponent is equivalent to a 4-bit change in the significand. It is convenient to view the significand as consisting of 6 hexadecimal digits rather than 24 bits. A normalized floating-point number requires that the leftmost hexadecimal digit be nonzero; the implied radix point is to the left of that digit. Since there are 15 nonzero hexadecimal digits, it is not possible to use an implied bit as part of the significand.

The value of 0 in the 370 format consists of a word of all 0's.

VAX Formats

The 32-bit VAX format uses an 8-bit exponent with an implied base of 2 and a 23-bit significand. The normalized number requires a 1 bit to the right of the radix point. This bit is implied , giving an effective 24-bit significand. Within the significand, bits increase in significance from 16 through 31 and 0 through 6.

The stored exponent values from 1 to 255 are a biased representation, indicating a true binary exponent from -127 through $+127$. The stored value of 0, together with a sign bit of 0, indicates the value zero.

The VAX offers two 64-bit formats, giving the user a tradeoff between range and precision. One format provides an 8-bit exponent, the other an 11-bit exponent.

IEEE Standard 754

The IEEE Computer Society has developed a standard for floating-point representation and arithmetic [IEEE85]. The objectives of this effort are to facilitate the portability of programs from one computer to another and to encourage the development of sophisticated numerically-oriented programs. The focus is the

TABLE 7-2   Characteristics of Various Floating-Point Representations

Word Size (bits):	IBM 370		IEEE Standard		VAX		
	32	64	32	64	32	64	64
Exponent size (bits)	7	7	8	11	8	8	11
Exponent base	16	16	2	2	2	2	2
Maximum exponent	63	63	127	1023	127	127	1023
Minimum exponent	-64	-64	-126	-1022	-127	-127	-1023
Number range (base 10)	$10^{-77}, 10^{+76}$	$10^{-77}, 10^{+76}$	$10^{-38}, 10^{+38}$	$10^{-308}, 10^{+308}$	$10^{-38}, 10^{+38}$	$10^{-38}, 10^{+38}$	$10^{-308}, 10^{+308}$
Significand size (bits)	24	56	23	52	23	55	52
Number of exponents	128	128	254	2046	255	255	2047
Number of fractions	15×2^{20}	15×2^{52}	2^{23}	2^{52}	2^{23}	2^{55}	2^{52}
Number of values	1.9×2^{31}	1.9×2^{63}	1.98×2^{31}	1.99×2^{63}	1.99×2^{31}	1.99×2^{63}	1.99×2^{63}

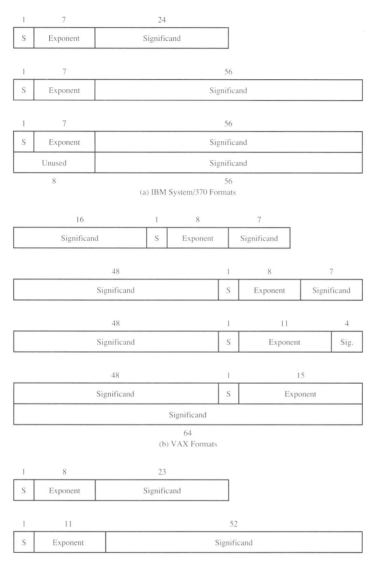

FIGURE 7-19.   Floating-point formats

microprocessor environment, where individual manufacturers may provide only limited numerical capability. As a result of this standard, vendors have developed chips that implement the standard and can be incorporated into microcomputer systems (e.g., [INTE84], [WIND85]).

The IEEE standard defines both a 32-bit and a 64-bit format, with 8-bit and 11-bit exponents, respectively. The implied base is 2. Table 7-3 indicates the values assigned to various bit patterns. We will discuss these values in the 32-bit

TABLE 7-3   Values of IEEE Floating-Point Numbers

(a) Single-Precision (32 bits)		
Exponent, e	Significand, f	Value
255	$\neq 0$	NaN
255	0	$(-1)^s\infty$
$0 < e < 255$	—	$(-1)^s 2^{e-127}(1.f)$
0	$\neq 0$	$(-1)^s 2^{-126}(0.f)$
0	0	$(-1)^s 0$
(b) Double-Precision (64 bits)		
2047	$\neq 0$	NaN
2047	0	$(-1)^s\infty$
$0 < e < 2047$	—	$(-1)^s 2^{e-1023}(1.f)$
0	$\neq 0$	$(-1)^s 2^{-1022}(0.f)$
0	0	$(-1)^s 0$

format; the same principles apply to the 64-bit format. For exponent values in the range 1 through 254, a biased representation is used, indicating a true binary exponent from -126 through $+127$. A normalized number requires a 1 bit to the left of the binary point; this bit is implied, giving an effective 24-bit significand.

The extreme exponent values of 0 and 255 are used to indicate special values, including 0 and ∞. As was mentioned, it is useful to have an exact value of 0 represented. A representation of infinity is also useful. This leaves it up to the user to decide whether to treat overflow as an error condition or to carry the value ∞ and proceed with whatever program is being executed. NaN means *not a number* and is used to signal various exception conditions.

7.5

FLOATING-POINT ARITHMETIC

Table 7-4 summarizes the basic operations for floating-point arithmetic. For addition and subtraction, it is necessary to ensure that both operands have the same exponent. This may require shifting the radix point on one of the operands to achieve alignment. Multiplication and division are more straightforward.

Problems may arise as the result of these operations. These are

- *Exponent Overflow:* A positive exponent exceeds the maximum possible exponent value. In some systems, this may be designated as $+\infty$ or $-\infty$.
- *Exponent Underflow:* A negative exponent exceeds the maximum possible exponent value. This means that the number is too small to be represented, and it may be reported as 0.
- *Significand Underflow:* In the process of aligning significands, digits may flow off the right end of the significand. As we shall discuss, some form of rounding is required.

TABLE 7-4   Floating-Point Numbers
and Arithmetic Operations

Floating-Point Numbers

$x = x_s\ B^{x_E}$

$y = y_s\ B^{y_E}$

Arithmetic Operations

$\left.\begin{array}{l} x + y = (x_s\ B^{x_E - y_E} + y_s) \times B^{y_E} \\ x - y = (x_s\ B^{x_E - y_E} - y_s) \times B^{y_E} \end{array}\right\}\ x_E \le y_E$

$x \times y = (x_s \times y_z) \times B^{x_E + y_E}$

$x \div y = (x_s \div y_s) \times B^{x_E - y_E}$

- *Significand Overflow:* The addition of two significands of the same sign may result in a carry out of the most significant bit. This can be fixed by realignment, as we shall explain.

Addition and Subtraction

In floating-point arithmetic, addition and subtraction are more complex than multiplication and division. This is because of the need for alignment. There are four basic phases of the algorithm for addition and subtraction:

1. Check for zeros.
2. Align the significands.
3. Add or subtract the significands.
4. Normalize the result.

A typical flowchart is shown in Figure 7-20. A step-by-step narrative highlights the main functions required for floating-point addition and subtraction. We assume a format similar to those of Figure 7-19. For the addition or subtraction operation, the two operands must be transferred to registers that will be used by the ALU. If the floating-point format includes an implicit significand bit, that bit must be made explicit for the operation. Typically, the exponents and significands will be stored in separate registers, to be reunited when the result is produced.

Because addition and subtraction are identical except for a sign change, the process begins by changing the sign of the subtrahend if it is a subtract operation. Next, if either operand is 0, the other is reported as the result.

The next phase is to manipulate the numbers so that the two exponents are equal. To see the need for this consider the following decimal addition:

$$123 \times 10^0 + 456 \times 10^{-2}$$

Clearly we cannot just add the significands. The digits must first be set into equivalent positions, that is, the 4 of the second number must be *aligned* with the 3 of the first. Under these conditions, the two exponents will be equal, which is

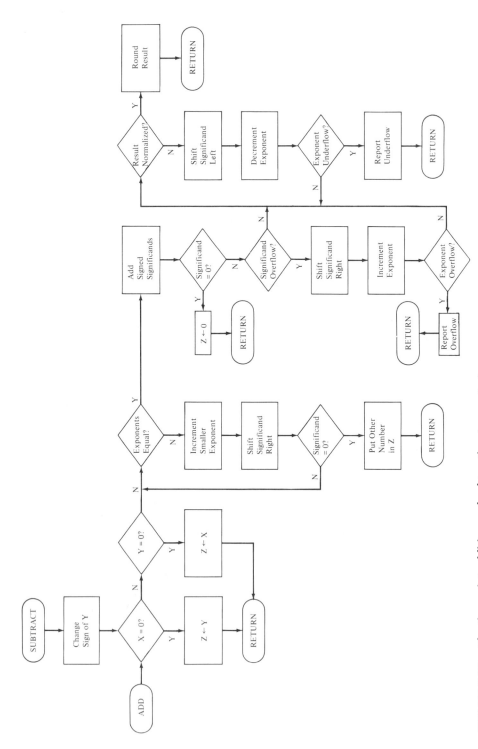

FIGURE 7-20. Floating-point addition and subtraction ($z \leftarrow x \pm y$)

the mathematical condition under which two numbers in this form can be added. Thus:

$$123 \times 10^0 + 456 \times 10^{-2} = 123 \times 10^0 + 4.56 \times 10^0 = 127.56 \times 10^0$$

Alignment is achieved by shifting either the smaller number to the right (increasing its exponent) or shifting the larger number to the left. Since either operation may result in the loss of digits, it is the smaller number that is shifted; any digits that are lost are therefore of relatively small significance. The alignment is achieved by repeatedly shifting the magnitude portion of the significand right 1 digit and incrementing the exponent until the two exponents are equal. (Note that if the implied base is 16, a shift of 1 digit is a shift of 4 bits.) If this process results in a 0 value for the significand, then the other number is reported as the result. Thus, if two numbers have exponents that differ significantly, the lesser number is lost.

Next, the two significands are added together, taking into account their signs. Since the signs may differ, the result may be 0. There is also the possibility of significand overflow by 1 digit. If so, the significand of the result is shifted right and the exponent is incremented. An exponent overflow could occur as a result; this would be reported and the operation halted.

The next phase normalizes the result. Normalization consists of shifting significand digits left until the most significant digit (bit, or 4 bits for base-16 exponent) is nonzero. Each shift causes a decrement of the exponent, and could cause an exponent underflow. Finally, the result must be rounded off and then reported. We defer a discussion of rounding until after a discussion of multiplication and division.

Multiplication and Division

Floating-point multiplication and division are much simpler processes than addition and subtraction, as the following discussion indicates.

We first consider multiplication, illustrated in Figure 7-21. First, if either operand is 0, 0 is reported as the result. The next step is to add the exponents. If the exponents are stored in biased form, the exponent sum would have doubled the bias. Thus, the bias value must be subtracted from the sum. The result could be either an exponent overflow or underflow, which would be reported, ending the algorithm.

If the exponent of the product is within the proper range, the next step is to multiply the significands, taking into account their signs. The multiplication is performed in the same way as for integers. In this case, we are dealing with a sign-magnitude representation, but the details are similar to those for 2's-complement representation. The product will be double the length of the multiplier and multiplicand. The extra bits will be lost during rounding.

After the product is calculated, the result is then normalized and rounded, as was done for addition and subtraction. Note that normalization could result in exponent underflow.

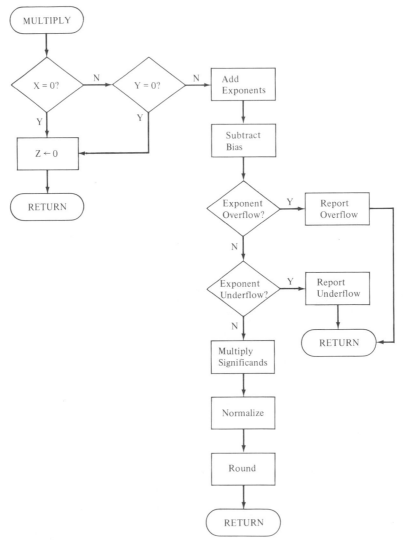

FIGURE 7-21. Floating-point multiplication ($z \leftarrow x \times y$)

Finally, let us consider the flowchart for division depicted in Figure 7-22. Again, the first step is testing for 0. If the divisor is 0, an error report is issued, or the result is set to infinity, depending on the implementation. A dividend of 0 results in 0. Next, the divisor exponent is subtracted from the dividend exponent. This removes the bias, which must be added back in. Tests are then made for exponent underflow or overflow.

The next step is to divide the significands. This is followed with the usual normalization and rounding.

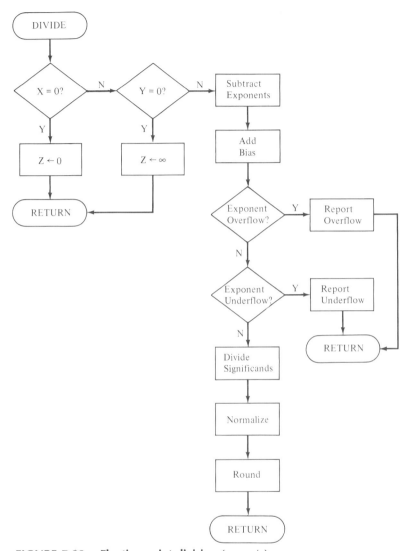

FIGURE 7-22.   Floating-point division (z ← x/y)

Precision Considerations

Guard Bits

We mentioned that, prior to a floating-point operation, the exponent and significand of each operand are loaded into ALU registers. In the case of the significand, the length of the register is almost always greater than the length of the significand plus an implied bit, if used. The register contains additional bits, called *guard bits*, that are used to pad out the right end of the significand with 0s.

The reason for the use of guard bits is illustrated in Figure 7-23. Consider numbers in the IEEE format, which has a 24-bit significand, including an implied 1 bit to the left of the binary point. Two numbers that are very close in value are $X = 1.00 \cdots 00 * 2^1$ and $Y = 1.11 \cdots 11 * 2^0$. If the smaller number is to be subtracted from the larger, it must be shifted right 1 bit to align the exponents. This is shown in Figure 7-23a. In the process, Y loses 1 bit of significance; the result is 2^{-23}. The same operation is repeated in part b with the addition of guard bits. Now, the least significant bit is not lost due to alignment, and the result is 2^{-24}, a difference of a factor of 2 from the previous answer. When the radix is 16, the loss of precision can be greater. As Figures 7-23c and d show, the difference can be a factor of 16.

Rounding

Another detail that affects the precision of the result is the rounding policy. The result of any operation on the significands is generally stored in a longer register. When the result is put back into the floating-point format, the extra bits must be disposed of.

$$
\begin{aligned}
x &= 1.000\ \ldots\ldots\ 00 \times 2^1 \\
-y &= 0.111\ \ldots\ldots\ 11 \times 2^1 \\
\hline
z &= 0.000\ \ldots\ldots\ 01 \times 2^1 \\
&= 1.000\ \ldots\ldots\ 00 \times 2^{-23}
\end{aligned}
$$

(a) Binary Example, Without Guard Bits

$$
\begin{aligned}
x &= 1.000\ \ldots\ldots\ 00 \quad 0000 \times 2^1 \\
-y &= 0.111\ \ldots\ldots\ 11 \quad 1000 \times 2^1 \\
\hline
z &= 0.000\ \ldots\ldots\ 00 \quad 1000 \times 2^1 \\
&= 1.000\ \ldots\ldots\ 00 \quad 0000 \times 2^{-24}
\end{aligned}
$$

(b) Binary Example, with Guard Bits

$$
\begin{aligned}
x &= .100000 \times 16^1 \\
-y &= .0FFFFF \times 16^1 \\
\hline
z &= .000001 \times 16^1 \\
&= .100000 \times 16^{-4}
\end{aligned}
$$

(c) Hexadecimal Example, without Guard Bits

$$
\begin{aligned}
x &= .100000 \quad 00 \times 16^1 \\
-y &= .0FFFFF \quad F0 \times 16^1 \\
\hline
z &= .000000 \quad 10 \times 16^1 \\
&= .100000 \quad 00 \times 16^{-5}
\end{aligned}
$$

(d) Hexadecimal Example, with Guard Bits

FIGURE 7-23. The use of guard bits

A number of techniques have been explored for performing rounding. In fact, the IEEE standard lists four alternative approaches:

- *Round to nearest:* The result is rounded to the nearest representable number.
- *Round toward* $+\infty$*:* The result is rounded up toward plus infinity.
- *Round toward* $-\infty$*:* The result is rounded down toward negative infinity.
- *Round toward 0:* The result is rounded toward zero.

Let us consider each of these policies in turn. **Round to nearest** is the default rounding mode listed in the standard and is defined as follows: The representable value nearest to the infinitely precise result shall be delivered; if the two nearest representable values are equally near, the one with its least significant bit zero shall be delivered.

For example, if the extra bits, beyond the 23 bits that can be stored, are 10010, then the extra bits amount to more than one-half of the last representable bit position. In this case, the correct answer is to add binary 1 to the last representable bit, rounding up to the next representable number. Now consider that the extra bits are 01111. In this case, the extra bits amount to less than one-half of the last representable bit position. The correct answer is to simply drop the extra bits (truncate), which has the effect of rounding down to the next representable number.

The standard also addresses the special case of extra bits of the form 10000 . . . . Here the result is exactly halfway between the two possible representable values. One possible technique here would be to always truncate, as this would be the simplest operation. However, the difficulty with this simple approach is that it introduces a small but cumulative bias into a sequence of computations. What is required is an unbiased method of rounding. One possible approach would be to round up or down on the basis of a random number so that, on average, the result would be unbiased. The argument against this approach is that it does not produce predictable, deterministic results. The approach taken by the IEEE standard is to force the result to be even: If the result of a computation is exactly midway between two representable numbers, the value is rounded up if the last representable bit is currently 1 and left alone if it is currently zero.

The next two options, **rounding to plus and minus infinity,** are useful in implementing a technique known as interval arithmetic. The idea behind interval arithmetic is the following: At the end of a sequence of floating-point operations, we cannot know the exact answer because of the limitations of the hardware, which introduces rounding. If we perform every calculation in the sequence twice: once rounding up and once rounding down, then the result is to maintain an upper and lower bound on the correct answer. If the range between the upper and lower bounds is sufficiently narrow, then a sufficiently accurate result has been obtained. If not, at least we know this and can perform additional analysis.

The final technique specified in the standard is **round toward zero.** This is in fact simple truncation: the extra bits are ignored. This is certainly the simplest technique. However, the result is that the magnitude of the truncated value is always less than or equal to the more precise original value, introducing a consistent downward bias in the operation. This is a more serious bias than was discussed earlier, since this bias affects *every* operation for which there are nonzero extra bits.

7.6

RECOMMENDED READING

For the serious student of computer arithmetic, a *sine qua non* is the two-volume [SWAR90a]. Volume I was originally published in 1980 and provides key papers (some very difficult to access otherwise) on computer arithmetic fundamentals. Volume II contains more recent papers, covering theoretical, design, and implementation aspects of computer arithmetic. Another valuable collection of papers is [SWAR90b]. Good textbooks on computer arithmetic include [KULI81], [SPAN81], and [GOSL80]. These are all out of print but are available in many technical libraries.

For floating-point arithmetic, [GOLD91] is well named: "What Every Computer Scientist Should Know About Floating-Point Arithmetic." The same author provides an equally good treatment, with a different emphasis, in [HENN91]. An excellent theoretical treatment of the topic is contained in [KNUT81]. Yet another approach to rounding is presented in [YOSH91].

7.7

PROBLEMS

7.1 Additional insight into 2's-complement representation can be gained by considering the following. If an N-bit sequence of binary digits, $b_{N-1}b_{N-2} \cdots b_1 b_0$, is interpreted as unsigned integer, its value is

$$X = \sum_{i=0}^{N-1} b_i 2^i$$

Define this sequence, in 2's-complement representation, to have the following interpretation:

$$X = -b_{N-1}2^{N-1} + \sum_{i=0}^{N-2} b_i 2^i$$

(a) Verify that all N-bit sequences are, in fact, in 2's-complement representation.

(b) Show that the largest negative number is -2^{N-1}.

(c) Show that the largest positive number is $2^{N-1} - 1$.

(d) Show that the only value for the b_i's that yields a value of zero is $b_i = 0$ for all i.

7.2 The 2's complement of a binary number X can be defined as follows:

$$\text{2's complement of } X = 2^N - X$$

(a) Show that the 2's complement of the 2's complement of a number is that number.

(b) Using the interpretation of Problem 7.1, show that

$$X - Y = X + (\text{2's complement of } Y)$$

7.3 Find the following differences using 2's complements:

a.	b.	c.	d.
111000	11001100	111100001111	11000011
$-$ 110011	$-$ 101110	$-$ 110011110011	$-$ 11101000

7.4 Is the following a valid alternative definition of overflow in 2's-complement arithmetic?

  If the exclusive-OR of the carry bits into and out of the leftmost column is 1, then there is an overflow condition. Otherwise, there is not.

7.5 Compare Figures 7-7 and 7-10. Why is the C bit not used in the latter?

7.6 Draw a block diagram similar to Figure 7-6 that illustrates the division process.

7.7 The division algorithm depicted in Figure 7-14 is known as the *restoral* method since the value in the A register must be restored following unsuccessful subtraction. A slightly more complex approach, known as *nonrestoral*, avoids the unnecessary subtraction and addition. Propose an algorithm for this latter approach.

7.8 Under integer arithmetic, the quotient J/K of two integers J and K is less than or equal to the usual quotient. True or false?

7.9 Prove that the multiplication of two *n*-digit numbers in base B gives a product of no more than $2n$ digits.

7.10 Compare the biased representation to sign-magnitude, 1's-complement representation, and 2's-complement representation, in terms of strengths and weaknesses.

7.11 Divide -145 by 13 in binary 2's-complement notation, using 12-bit words. Use the algorithm described in Section 7.3.

7.12 Assume that the exponent e is constrained to lie in the range $0 \le e \le X$, with a bias of q, that the base is b, and that the format is p digits in length.

(a) What are the largest and smallest positive values that can be written?

(b) What are the largest and smallest positive values that can be written as normalized floating-point numbers?

7.13 Express the following numbers in IEEE 32-bit floating-point format:

(a) -5 **(d)** 384

(b) -6 **(e)** 1/16

(c) -1.5 **(f)** $-1/32$

7.14 Express the following numbers in IBM's 32-bit floating-point format:
   (a) 1.0
   (b) 0.5
   (c) 1/64
   (d) 0.0
   (e) −15.0
   (f) $5.4 * 10^{-79}$
   (g) $7.2 * 10^{75}$

7.15 What would be the bias value for
   (a) A base-2 exponent ($B = 2$) in a 6-bit field?
   (b) A base-8 exponent ($B = 8$) in a 7-bit field?

7.16 Draw a number line similar to that in Figure 7-17b for the floating-point formats of Figure 7-19.

7.17 When people speak about inaccuracy in floating-point arithmetic, they often ascribe errors to cancellation that occurs during the subtraction of nearly equal quantities. But when X and Y are approximately equal, the difference $X - Y$ is obtained exactly, with no error. What do these people really mean?

7.18 Any floating-point representation used in a computer can represent only certain real numbers exactly; all others must be approximated. If A′ is the stored value approximating the real value A, then the relative error, r, is expressed as

$$r = \frac{A - A'}{A}$$

Represent the decimal quantity +0.4 in the following floating-point format:

• Base: 2
• Exponent: biased, 4 bits
• Significand: 7 bits

What is the relative error?

7.19 Numerical values A and B are stored in the computer as approximations A′ and B′. Neglecting any further truncation or roundoff errors, show that the relative error of the product is approximately the sum of the relative errors in the factors.

7.20 If $A = 1.427$, find the relative error if A is truncated to 1.42 and if it is rounded to 1.43.

7.21 One of the most serious errors in computer calculations occurs when two nearly equal numbers are subtracted. Consider $A = 0.22288$ and $B = 0.22211$. The computer truncates all values to four decimal digits. Thus $A' = 0.2228$ and $B' = 0.2221$.
   (a) What are the relative errors for A′ and B′?
   (b) What is the relative error for $C' = A' - B'$?

APPENDIX 7A

Number Systems

7A.1   The Decimal System

It may not have occurred to you, but in everyday life you use a system based on digits to represent numbers. In this case, we use decimal digits (0, 1, 2, 3, 4, 5, 6, 7, 8, 9) and refer to the system as the *decimal system.*

Consider what the number 83 means. It means eight tens plus three:

$$83 = 8 * 10 + 3$$

The number 4,728 means four thousands, seven hundreds, two tens, plus eight:

$$4728 = 4 * 1000 + 7 * 100 + 2 * 10 + 8$$

The decimal system is said to have a *base,* or *radix,* of ten. This means that each digit in the number is multiplied by ten raised to a power corresponding to that digit's position. Thus,

$$83 = 8 * 10^1 + 3 * 10^0$$
$$4728 = 4 * 10^3 + 7 * 10^2 + 2 * 10^1 + 8 * 10^0$$

Fractional values are represented in the same fashion. Thus,

$$472.83 = 4 * 10^2 + 7 * 10^1 + 2 * 10^0 + 8 * 10^{-1} + 3 * 10^{-2}$$

In general, for

Decimal representation of $X = \{ \cdots x_2 x_1 x_0 \cdot x_{-1} x_{-2} x_{-3} \cdots \}$

the value of X is

$$X = \sum_i x_i 10^i$$

7A.2   The Binary System

In the decimal system, ten different digits are used to represent numbers with a base of ten. In the binary system, we have only two digits, 1 and 0. Thus numbers in the binary system are represented to the base two.

To avoid confusion, we will sometimes put a subscript on a number to indicate its base. For example 83_{10} and 4728_{10} are numbers represented in decimal notation, or more briefly, decimal numbers. Now, 1 and 0 in binary notation have the same meaning as in decimal notation:

$$0_2 = 0_{10}$$
$$1_2 = 1_{10}$$

How do we represent larger numbers? As with decimal notation, each digit in a binary number has a value depending on its position:

$$10_2 = 1 * 2^1 + 0 * 2^0 = 2_{10}$$
$$11_2 = 1 * 2^1 + 1 * 2^0 = 3_{10}$$
$$100 = 1 * 2^2 + 0 * 2^1 + 0 * 2^0 = 4_{10}$$

and so on. Table 7-5 shows the first 64 8-bit binary numbers, together with their decimal equivalents (the table also shows a hexadecimal notation, explained presently).

Again, fractional values are represented with negative powers of the radix:

$$1001.101 = 2^3 + 2^0 + 2^{-1} + 2^{-3}$$

TABLE 7-5   Binary Numbers and Their Decimal and Hexadecimal Equivalents

Binary	Decimal	Hexadecimal	Binary	Decimal	Hexadecimal
00000000	0	0	00100000	32	20
00000001	1	1	00100001	33	21
00000010	2	2	00100010	34	22
00000011	3	3	00100011	35	23
00000100	4	4	00100100	36	24
00000101	5	5	00100101	37	25
00000110	6	6	00100110	38	26
00000111	7	7	00100111	39	27
00001000	8	8	00101000	40	28
00001001	9	9	00101001	41	29
00001010	10	A	00101010	42	2A
00001011	11	B	00101011	43	2B
00001100	12	C	00101100	44	2C
00001101	13	D	00101101	45	2D
00001110	14	E	00101110	46	2E
00001111	15	F	00101111	47	2F
00010000	16	10	00110000	48	30
00010001	17	11	00110001	49	31
00010010	18	12	00110010	50	32
00010011	19	13	00110011	51	33
00010100	20	14	00110100	52	34
00010101	21	15	00110101	53	35
00010110	22	16	00110110	54	36
00010111	23	17	00110111	55	37
00011000	24	18	00111000	56	38
00011001	25	19	00111001	57	39
00011010	26	1A	00111010	58	3A
00011011	27	1B	00111011	59	3B
00011100	28	1C	00111100	60	3C
00011101	29	1D	00111101	61	3D
00011110	30	1E	00111110	62	3E
00011111	31	1F	00111111	63	3F

7A.3   Converting Between Binary and Decimal

It is a simple matter to convert a number from binary notation to decimal notation. In fact, we showed several examples in the previous subsection. All that is required is to multiply each binary digit by the appropriate power of 2 and add the results.

To convert from decimal to binary, the integer and fractional parts are handled separately. Suppose it is required to convert a decimal integer N into binary form. If we divide N by 2, in the decimal system, and obtain a quotient N_1 and a remainder r_1, we may write

$$N = 2 * N_1 + r_1 \qquad r_1 = 0 \text{ or } 1$$

Next we divide the quotient N_1 by 2. Assume that the new quotient is N_2 and the new remainder r_2. Then

$$N_1 = 2 * N_2 + r_2 \qquad r_2 = 0 \text{ or } 1$$

so that

$$N = 2(2N_2 + r_2) + r_1 = 2^2 N_2 + r_2 * 2^1 + r_1 * 2^0$$

If next

$$N_2 = 2N_3 + r_3$$

we have

$$N = 2^3 N_3 + r_3 * 2^2 + r_2 * 2^1 + r_1 * 2^0$$

Continuing thus, since $N > N_1 > N_2 \cdots$, we must eventually obtain a quotient $N_k = 1$ and a remainder r_k which is 0 or 1. Then

$$N = 1 * 2^k + r_k * 2^{k-1} + \cdots + r_3 * 2^2 + r_2 * 2^1 + r_1 * 2^0$$

That is, we convert from base 10 to base 2 by repeated divisions by 2. The remainders and the final quotient, 1, give us, in order of increasing significance, the binary digits of N. Figure 7-24 shows two examples.

The fractional part involves repeated multiplication by 2, as illustrated in Figure 7-25. At each step, the fractional part of the decimal number is multiplied by 2. The digit to the left of the decimal point in the product will be 0 or 1 and contributes to the binary representation, starting with the most significant bit. The fractional part of the product is used as the multiplicand in the next step. To see that this works, let us take a positive decimal fraction $F < 1$. We can express F as

$$F = a_{-1} * \frac{1}{2} + a_{-2} * \frac{1}{2^2} + a_{-3} * \frac{1}{2^3} + \cdots$$

where each a_{-i} is 0 or 1. If we multiply this by 2, we obtain

$$2F = a_{-1} + a_{-2} * \frac{1}{2} + a_{-3} * \frac{1}{2^2} + \cdots$$

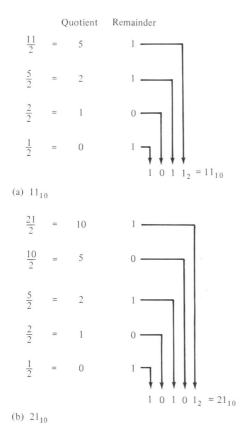

(a) 11_{10}

(b) 21_{10}

FIGURE 7-24.   Examples of converting from decimal notation to binary notation for integral numbers

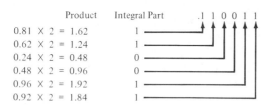

(a) $0.81_{10} = 0.110011_2$ (approximate)

(b) $0.25_{10} = 0.01_2$ (exact)

FIGURE 7-25.   Examples of converting from decimal notation to binary notation for fractional numbers

The integer parts of these two expressions must be equal. Hence the integer part of 2F, which must be either 0 or 1 since $0 < F < 1$, is simply a_{-1}. Thus $2F = a_{-1} + F_1$ where $0 < F_1 < 1$ and where

$$F_1 = a_{-2} * \frac{1}{2} + a_{-3} * \frac{1}{2^2} + \cdots$$

To find a_{-2} we now repeat the process. This process is not necessarily exact; that is, a decimal fraction with a finite number of digits may require a binary fraction with an infinite number of digits. In such cases, the conversion algorithm is usually halted after a prespecified number of steps, depending on the desired accuracy.

7A.4 Hexadecimal Notation

Because of the inherent binary nature of digital computer components, all forms of data within computers are represented by various binary codes. We have seen examples of binary codes for text and binary notation for integers. Later, we shall see examples of the use of binary codes for other types of data. However, no matter how convenient the binary system is for computers, it is exceedingly cumbersome for human beings. Consequently, most computer professionals who must spend time working with the actual raw data in the computer prefer a more compact notation.

What notation to use? One possibility is the decimal notation. We have seen, in Table 7-5, that every binary number has a decimal equivalent. This is certainly more compact than binary notation, but it is awkward because of the tediousness of converting between base 2 and base 10.

Instead, a notation known as *hexadecimal* has been adopted. Binary digits are grouped into sets of 4. Each possible combination of 4 binary digits is given a symbol, as follows:

0000 = 0	1000 = 8
0001 = 1	1001 = 9
0010 = 2	1010 = A
0011 = 3	1011 = B
0100 = 4	1100 = C
0101 = 5	1101 = D
0110 = 6	1110 = E
0111 = 7	1111 = F

Since 16 symbols are used, the notation is called *hexadecimal*, and the 16 symbols are the hexadecimal digits.

A sequence of hexadecimal digits can be thought of as representing an integer in base 16. Thus,

$$1A_{16} = 1_{16} * 16^1 + A_{16} * 16^0$$
$$= 1_{10} * 16^1 + 10_{10} * 16^0 = 26$$

But hexadecimal notation is not used just for representing integers. It is used as a concise notation for representing any sequence of binary digits, whether they represent text, numbers, or some other type of data. The reasons for using hexadecimal notation are

1. It is more compact than binary notation.
2. In most computers, binary data occupy some multiple of 4 bits, and hence some multiple of a single hexadecimal digit.
3. It is extremely easy to convert between binary and hexadecimal.

As an example of the last point, consider the binary string 110111100001. This is equivalent to

1101   1110   0001 = $DE1_{16}$
 D   E   1

This process is performed so naturally that an experienced programmer can mentally convert visual representations of binary data to their hexadecimal equivalent without written effort. It is quite possible that you will never need this particular skill. Nevertheless, since you may encounter hexadecimal notation, this discussion has been included in the text.

CHAPTER 8

Instruction Sets: Characteristics and Functions

Much of what is discussed in this book is not readily apparent to the user or programmer of a computer. If a programmer is using a high-level language, such as Pascal or Ada, very little of the architecture of the underlying machine is visible.

One boundary where the computer designer and the computer programmer can view the same machine is the machine instruction set. From the designer's point of view, the machine instruction set provides the functional requirements for the CPU: implementing the CPU is a task that in large part involves implementing the machine instruction set. From the user's side, the user who chooses to program in machine language (actually, in assembly language; see Section 8-4) becomes aware of the register and memory structure, the types of data directly supported by the machine, and the functioning of the ALU.

A description of a computer's machine instruction set goes a long way toward explaining the computer's CPU. Accordingly, we focus on machine instructions in this and the next chapter, and then we turn to an examination of the structure and function of CPUs.

8.1

MACHINE INSTRUCTION CHARACTERISTICS

The operation of the CPU is determined by the instructions it executes. These instructions are referred to as *machine instructions* or *computer instructions*. The CPU may perform a variety of functions, and these are reflected in the variety of instructions defined for the CPU. The collection of different instructions that the CPU can execute is referred to as the CPU's *instruction set*.

Elements of a Machine Instruction

Each instruction must contain the information required by the CPU for execution. Figure 8-1, which repeats Figure 3-6, shows the steps involved in instruction execution and, by implication, defines the elements of a machine instruction. These elements are

- *Operation Code:* Specifies the operation to be performed (e.g., ADD, I/O). The operation is specified by a binary code, known as the *operation code*, or *opcode*.
- *Source Operand Reference:* The operation may involve one or more source operands, that is, operands that are inputs for the operation.
- *Result Operand Reference:* The operation may produce a result.
- *Next Instruction Reference:* This tells the CPU where to fetch the next instruction after the execution of this instruction is complete.

The next instruction to be fetched is located in main memory or, in the case of a virtual memory system, in either main memory or secondary memory (disk). In most cases, the next instruction to be fetched immediately follows the current instruction. In those cases, there is no explicit reference to the next instruction. When an explicit reference is needed, then the main memory or virtual memory address must be supplied. The form in which that address is supplied is discussed in Chapter 9.

Source and result operands can be in one of three areas:

- *Main or Virtual Memory:* As with next instruction references, the main or virtual memory address must be supplied.
- *CPU Register:* With rare exceptions, a CPU contains one or more registers that may be referenced by machine instructions. If only one register exists, refer-

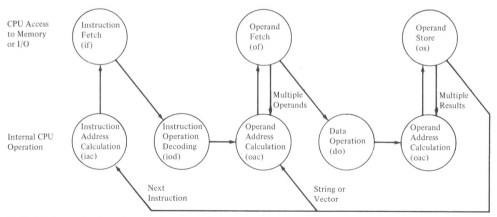

FIGURE 8-1. Instruction cycle state diagram

ence to it may be implicit. If more than one register exists, then each register is assigned a unique number, and the instruction must contain the number of the desired register.

• *I/O Device:* The instruction must specify the I/O module and device for the operation. If memory-mapped I/O is used, this is just another main or virtual memory address.

Instruction Representation

Within the computer, each instruction is represented by a sequence of bits. The instruction is divided into fields, corresponding to the constituent elements of the instruction. This layout of the instruction is known as the *instruction format.* A simple example is shown in Figure 8-2. As another example, the IAS instruction format is shown in Figure 2-5. With most instruction sets, more than one format is used. During instruction execution, an instruction is read into an instruction register (IR) in the CPU. The CPU must be able to extract the data from the various instruction fields to perform the required operation.

It is difficult for both the programmer and the reader of textbooks to deal with binary representations of machine instructions. Thus it has become common practice to use a *symbolic representation* of machine instructions. An example of this was used for the IAS instruction set, in Table 2-2.

Opcodes are represented by abbreviations, called *mnemonics,* that indicate the operation. Common examples include

ADD   Add
SUB   Subtract
MPY   Multiply
DIV   Divide
LOAD   Load data from memory
STOR   Store data to memory

Operands are also represented symbolically. For example, the instruction

ADD R, Y

may mean add the value contained in data location Y to the contents of register R. In this example, Y refers to the address of a location in memory, and R refers to a particular register. Note that the operation is performed on the contents of a location, not on its address.

Thus it is possible to write a machine-language program in symbolic form. Each symbolic op code has a fixed binary representation, and the programmer

FIGURE 8-2. A simple instruction format

specifies the location of each symbolic operand. For example, the programmer might begin with a list of definitions:

X = 513
Y = 514

and so on. A simple program would accept this symbolic input, convert op codes and operand references to binary form, and construct binary machine instructions.

Machine-language programmers are rare to the point of nonexistence. Most programs today are written in a high-level language or, failing that, assembly language, which is discussed at the end of this chapter. However, symbolic machine language remains a useful tool for describing machine instructions, and we will use it for that purpose.

Instruction Types

Consider a high-level language instruction that could be expressed in a language such as BASIC or FORTRAN. For example,

X = X + Y

This statement instructs the computer to add the value stored in Y to the value stored in X and put the result in X. How might this be accomplished with machine instructions? Let us assume that the variables X and Y correspond to locations 513 and 514. If we assume a simple set of machine instructions, this operation could be accomplished with three instructions:

1. Load a register with the contents of memory location 513.
2. Add the contents of memory location 514 to the register.
3. Store the contents of the register in memory location 513.

As can be seen, the single BASIC instruction may require three machine instructions. This is typical of the relationship between a high-level language and a machine language. A high-level language expresses operations in a concise algebraic form, using variables. A machine language expresses operations in a basic form involving the movement of data to or from registers.

With this simple example to guide us, let us consider the types of instructions that must be included in a practical computer. A computer should have a set of instructions that allows the user to formulate any data-processing task. Another way to view it is to consider the capabilities of a high-level programming language. Any program written in a high-level language must be translated into machine language in order to be executed. Thus the set of machine instructions must be sufficient to express any of the instructions from a high-level language. With this in mind we can categorize instruction types as follows:

- *Data Processing:* Arithmetic and logic instructions

- *Data Storage:* Memory instructions
- *Data Movement:* I/O instructions
- *Control:* Test and branch instructions.

Arithmetic instructions provide computational capabilities for processing numeric data. *Logic* (Boolean) instructions operate on the bits of a word as bits rather than as numbers; thus they provide capabilities for processing any other type of data the user may wish to employ. These operations are performed primarily on data in CPU registers. Therefore, there must be *memory* instructions for moving data between memory and the registers. *I/O* instructions are needed to transfer programs and data into memory and the results of computations back out to the user. *Test* instructions are used to test the value of a data word or the status of a computation. *Branch* instructions are then used to branch to a different set of instructions depending on the decision made.

We will examine the various types of instructions in greater detail later in the chapter.

Number of Addresses

One of the traditional ways of describing processor architecture is in terms of the number of addresses contained in each instruction. This dimension has become less significant with the increasing complexity of CPU design. Nevertheless, it is useful at this point to draw and analyze this distinction.

What is the maximum number of addresses one might need in an instruction? Evidently, arithmetic and logic instructions will require the most operands. Virtually all arithmetic and logic operations are either unary (one operand) or binary (two operands). Thus we would need a maximum of two addresses to reference operands. The result of an operation must be stored, suggesting a third address. Finally, after completion of an instruction, the next instruction must be fetched, and its address is needed.

The above line of reasoning suggests that an instruction could plausibly be required to contain four address references: two operands, one result, and the address of the next instruction. In practice, four-address instructions are extremely rare. Most CPUs are of the one-, two-, or three-address variety, with the address of the next instruction being implicit (obtained from the program counter).

Figure 8-3 compares typical one-, two-, and three-address instructions that could be used to compute $Y = (A - B) \div (C + D * E)$. With three addresses, each instruction specifies two operand locations and a result location. Because we would like to not alter the value of any of the operand locations, a temporary location, T, is used to store some intermediate results. Note that there are four instructions and that the original expression had five operands.

Three-address instruction formats are not common because they require a relatively long instruction format to hold the three address references. With two-address instructions, and for binary operations, one address must do dou-

Instruction	Comment
SUB Y, A, B	Y ← A − B
MPY T, D, E	T ← D × E
ADD T, T, C	T ← T + C
DIV Y, Y, T	Y ← Y ÷ T

(a) Three-Address Instructions

Instruction	Comment
MOVE Y, A	Y ← A
SUB Y, B	Y ← Y − B
MOVE T, D	T ← D
MPY T, E	T ← T * E
ADD T, C	T ← T + C
DIV Y, T	Y ← Y ÷ T

(b) Two-Address Instructions

Instruction	Comment
LOAD D	AC ← D
MPY E	AC ← AC * E
ADD C	AC ← AC + C
STOR Y	Y ← AC
LOAD A	AC ← A
SUB B	AC ← AC − B
DIV Y	AC ← AC ÷ Y
STOR Y	Y ← AC

(c) One-Address Instructions

FIGURE 8-3.   Programs to execute Y = (A − B) ÷ (C + D * E)

ble duty as both an operand and a result. Thus the instruction SUB Y, B carries out the calculation Y − B and stores the result in Y. The two-address format reduces the space requirement but also introduces some awkwardness. To avoid altering the value of an operand, a MOVE instruction is used to move one of the values to a result or temporary location before performing the operation. Our sample program expands to six instructions.

Simpler yet is the one-address instruction. For this to work, a second address must be implicit. This was common in earlier machines, with the implied address being a CPU register known as the *accumulator*, or AC. The accumulator contains one of the operands and is used to store the result. In our example, eight instructions are needed to accomplish the task.

It is, in fact, possible to make do with zero addresses for some instructions. Zero-address instructions are applicable to a special memory organization, called a *stack*. A stack is a last-in-first-out set of locations. The stack is in a known location and, often, at least the top two elements are in CPU registers. Thus zero-address instructions would reference the top two stack elements. Stacks are

TABLE 8-1   Utilization of Instruction Addresses (Nonbranching Instructions)

Number of Addresses	Symbolic Representation	Interpretation
3	OP A, B, C	A ← B OP C
2	OP A, B	A ← A OP B
1	OP A	AC ← AC OP A
0	OP	T ← T OP (T − 1)

T = Top of Stack

described in the appendix to this chapter. Their use is explored further later in this chapter and in Chapter 9.

Table 8-1 summarizes the interpretations to be placed on instructions with 0, 1, 2, or 3 addresses. In each case in the table, it is assumed that the address of the next instruction is implicit, and that one operation with two source operands and one result operand is to be performed.

The number of addresses per instruction is a basic design decision. Fewer addresses per instruction results in more-primitive instructions, which requires a less complex CPU. It also results in instructions of shorter length. On the other hand, programs contain more total instructions, which in general results in longer execution times and longer, more complex programs. Also, there is an important threshold between one-address and multiple-address instructions. With one-address instructions, the programmer generally has available only one general-purpose register, the accumulator. With multiple-address instructions, it is common to have multiple general-purpose registers. This allows some operations to be performed solely on registers. Since register references are faster than memory references, this speeds up execution. For reasons of flexibility and ability to use multiple registers, most contemporary machines employ a mixture of two- and three-address instructions.

The design tradeoffs involved in choosing the number of addresses per instruction are complicated by other factors. There is the issue of whether an address references a memory location or a register. Since there are fewer registers, fewer bits are needed for a register reference. Also, as we shall see in the next chapter, a machine may offer a variety of addressing modes, and the specification of mode takes one or more bits. The result is that most CPU designs involve a variety of instruction formats.

Instruction Set Design

One of the most interesting, and most analyzed, aspects of computer design is instruction set design. The design of an instruction set is very complex, since it affects so many aspects of the computer system. The instruction set defines many of the functions performed by the CPU and thus has a significant effect on the implementation of the CPU. The instruction set is the programmer's means of controlling the CPU. Thus, programmer requirements must be considered in designing the instruction set.

It may surprise you to know that some of the most fundamental issues relating to the design of instruction sets remain in dispute. Indeed, in recent years, the level of disagreement concerning these fundamentals has actually grown. The most important of these fundamental design issues include

- *Operation Repertoire:* How many and which operations to provide, and how complex operations should be.
- *Data Types:* The various types of data upon which operations are performed.
- *Instruction Format:* Instruction length (in bits), number of addresses, size of various fields, and so on.
- *Registers:* Number of CPU registers that can be referenced by instructions, and their use.
- *Addressing:* The mode or modes by which the address of an operand is specified.

These issues are highly interrelated and must be considered together in designing an instruction set. This book, of course, must consider them in sequence, but an attempt is made to show the interrelationships.

Because of the importance of this topic, three chapters of this book are devoted to instruction set design. Following this overview section, this chapter examines data types and the operation repertoire. Chapter 9 examines addressing modes (which includes a consideration of registers) and instruction formats. Chapter 13 examines an exciting recent development known as the *reduced instruction set computer* (RISC). RISC architecture calls into question many of the instruction set design decisions made in contemporary commercial computers.

8.2

TYPES OF OPERANDS

Machine instructions operate on data. The most important general categories of data are

- Addresses
- Numbers
- Characters
- Logical Data

We will see, in discussing modes in Chapter 9, that addresses are in fact a form of data. In many cases, some calculation must be performed on the operand reference in an instruction to determine the main or virtual memory address. In this context, addresses can be considered to be unsigned integers.

Other common data types are numbers, characters, and logical data, and each of these is briefly examined in this section. Beyond that, some machines define specialized data types or data structures. For example, there may be machine operators that operate directly on a list or a string of characters.

Numbers

All machine languages include numeric data types. Even in nonnumeric data processing, there is a need for numbers to act as counters, field widths, and so forth. An important distinction between numbers used in ordinary mathematics and numbers stored in a computer is that the latter are limited. This is true in two senses. First, there is a limit to the magnitude of numbers representable on a machine and second, in the case of floating-point numbers, a limit to their precision. Thus the programmer is faced with understanding the consequences of rounding, overflow, and underflow.

Three types of numerical data are common in computers:

- Integer or Fixed Point
- Floating Point
- Decimal

We examined the first two in some detail in Chapter 7. It remains to say a few words about decimal numbers.

Although all internal computer operations are binary in nature, the human users of the system deal with decimal numbers. Thus there is a necessity to convert from decimal to binary on input and from binary to decimal on output. For applications in which there is a great deal of I/O and comparatively little, comparatively simple computation, it is preferable to store and operate on the numbers in decimal form. The most common representation for this purpose is packed decimal.

With packed decimal, each decimal digit is represented by a 4-bit code, in the obvious way. Thus $0 = 0000$, $1 = 0001$, ..., $8 = 1000$, and $9 = 1001$. Note that this is a rather inefficient code since only 10 of a possible 16 4-bit values are used. To form numbers, 4-bit codes are strung together, usually in multiples of 8 bits. Thus the code for 246 is 0000001001000110. This code is clearly less compact than a straight binary representation, but it avoids the conversion overhead. Negative numbers can be represented by including a 4-bit sign digit at either the left or right end of a string of packed decimal digits. For example, the code 1111 might stand for the minus sign.

Many machines provide arithmetic instructions for performing operations directly on packed decimal numbers. The algorithms are quite similar to those described in Section 7-3 but must take into account the decimal carry operation.

Characters

A common form of data is text or character strings. While textual data are most convenient for human beings, they cannot, in character form, be easily stored or transmitted by data processing and communications systems. Such systems are designed for binary data. Thus a number of codes have been devised by which characters are represented by a sequence of bits. Perhaps the earliest common example of this is the Morse code. Today, the most commonly used character code in the United States is the ASCII (American Standard Code for Information

Interchange) code (Table 5-1) promulgated by the American National Standards Institute (ANSI). ASCII is also widely used outside the United States. Each character in this code is represented by a unique 7-bit pattern; thus 128 different characters can be represented. This is a larger number than is necessary to represent printable characters, and some of the patterns represent *control* characters. Some of these control characters have to do with controlling the printing of characters on a page. Others are concerned with communications procedures. ASCII-encoded characters are almost always stored and transmitted using 8 bits per character. The eighth bit may be set to 0 or used as a parity bit for error detection. In the latter case, the bit is set such that the total number of binary 1s in each octet is always odd (odd parity) or always even (even parity).

Note that for the ASCII bit pattern 011XXXX, the digits 0 through 9 are represented by their binary equivalents, 0000 through 1001, in the rightmost 4 bits. This is the same code as packed decimal. This facilitates conversion between 7-bit ASCII and 4-bit packed decimal representation.

Another code used to encode characters is the Extended Binary Coded Decimal Interchange Code (EBCDIC). EBCDIC is used on IBM S/370 machines. It is an 8-bit code. As with ASCII, EBCDIC is compatible with packed decimal. In the case of EBCDIC, the codes 11110000 through 11111001 represent the digits 0 through 9.

Logical Data

Normally, each word or other addressable unit (byte, halfword, and so on) is treated as a single unit of data. It is sometimes useful, however, to consider an *n*-bit unit as consisting of *n* 1-bit items of data, each item having the value 0 or 1. When data are viewed this way, they are considered to be *logical* data.

There are two advantages to the bit-oriented view. First, we may sometimes wish to store an array of Boolean or binary data items, in which each item can take on only the values 1 (true) and 0 (false). With logical data, memory can be used most efficiently for this storage. Second, there are occasions when we wish to manipulate the bits of a data item. For example, if floating-point operations are implemented in software, we need to be able to shift significant bits in some operations. Another example: To convert from ASCII to packed decimal, we need to extract the rightmost 4 bits of each byte.

Note that, in the preceding examples, the same data are treated sometimes as logical and other times as numerical or text. The "type" of a unit of data is determined by the operation being performed on it. While this is not normally the case in high-level languages (e.g., Pascal), it is almost always the case with machine language.

IBM 370 Data Types

The IBM S/370 architecture provides the following data types.

- *Binary Integer:* Binary integers may be either unsigned (always nonnegative) or signed. Signed binary integers are stored in 2's-complement form. Allowable lengths are 16 and 32 bits.

- *Floating Point:* Floating-point numbers of lengths 32, 64, and 128 bits are provided. We discussed the format in Chapter 7. A 7-bit exponent is used for all three formats.
- *Decimal:* Arithmetic on packed decimal integers is provided. The length is from 1 to 16 bytes. The rightmost 4 bits of the rightmost byte hold the sign. Hence signed numbers with from 1 to 31 decimal digits can be represented.
- *Binary Logical:* Operations are defined for data units of lengths 8, 32, and 64 bits, and for variable length logical data of up to 256 bytes (4K bytes on some models).
- *Character:* EBCDIC is used.

TABLE 8-2   Common Instruction Set Operations

Type	Operation Name	Description
Data Transfer	Move (transfer)	Transfer word or block from source to destination
	Store	Transfer word from processor to memory
	Load (fetch)	Transfer word from memory to processor
	Exchange	Swap contents of source and destination
	Clear (reset)	Transfer word of 0s to destination
	Set	Transfer word of 1s to destination
	Push	Transfer word from source to top of stack
	Pop	Transfer word from top of stack to destination
Arithmetic	Add	Compute sum of two operands
	Subtract	Compute difference of two operands
	Multiply	Compute product of two operands
	Divide	Compute quotient of two operands
	Absolute	Replace operand by its absolute value
	Negate	Change sign of operand
	Increment	Add 1 to operand
	Decrement	Subtract 1 from operand
Logical	AND	⎫
	OR	⎬ Perform the specified logical operation bitwise
	NOT (Complement)	
	Exclusive OR	⎭
	Test	Test specified condition; set flag(s) based on outcome
	Compare	Make logical or arithmetic comparison of two or more operands; set flag(s) based on outcome
	Set Control Variables	Class of instructions to set controls for protection purposes, interrupt handling, timer control, etc.
	Shift	Left (right) shift operand, introducing constants at end
	Rotate	Left (right) shift operand, with wraparound end
	Jump (branch)	Unconditional transfer; load PC with specified address
	Jump Conditional	Test specified condition; either load PC with specified address or do nothing, based on condition

TABLE 8-2   Common Instruction Set Operations (continued)

Type	Operation Name	Description
Transfer of Control	Jump to Subroutine	Place current program control information in known location; jump to specified address
	Return	Replace contents of PC and other registers from known location
	Execute	Fetch operand from specified location and execute as instruction; do not modify PC
	Skip	Increment PC to skip next instruction
	Skip Conditional	Test specified condition; either skip or do nothing based on condition
	Halt	Stop program execution
	Wait (hold)	Stop program execution; test specified condition repeatedly; resume execution when condition is satisfied
	No operation	No operation is performed, but program execution is continued
Input/Output	Input (read)	Transfer data from specified I/O port or device to destination, e.g., main memory or processor register
	Output (write)	Transfer data from specified source to I/O port or device
	Start I/O	Transfer instructions to I/O processor to initiate I/O operation
	Test I/O	Transfer status information from I/O system to specified destination
Conversion	Translate	Translate values in a section of memory based on a table of correspondences
	Convert	Convert the contents of a word from one form to another (e.g., packed decimal to binary)

VAX Data Types

The VAX provides an impressive array of data types. The VAX is a byte-oriented machine. All data types are in units of bytes or multiple-byte units, including the 16-bit *word*, the 32-bit *longword*, the 64-bit *quadword*, and even the 128-bit *octaword*. The data types fall into five categories:

- *Integer:* Binary integers are usually considered as signed 2's-complement numbers. However, they can be considered and operated on as unsigned integers. Allowable lengths are 8, 16, 32, 64, and 128 bits.
- *Floating Point:* The VAX provides four different floating-point representations. They are F: 32 bits with an 8-bit exponent; D: 64 bits with an 8-bit exponent; G: 64 bits with an 11-bit exponent; and H: 128 bits with a 15-bit exponent. The F type is the normal or default representation, and D is the usual double-precision representation, providing the same range as F but with greater precision.

To accommodate a variety of applications, G and H are provided to give successively increasing range and precision over F [PAYN80].

- *Decimal:* Arithmetic on decimal integers is provided. Two formats are supported. Packed decimal strings are from 1 to 16 bytes long, with 4 bits used for the sign. Unpacked numeric string data stores 1 digit, in ASCII representation, per byte with up to 31 bytes in length.
- *Character:* ASCII is used.
- *Variable Bit Field:* These are small integers packed together in a large data unit. A bit field is specified by three operands: address of byte containing the start of the field, starting bit position within the byte, and the length in bits of the field. This data type is used to increase memory efficiency.

Intel 80386/80486 Data Types

The Intel 80386/80486 can deal with data types of 8 (byte), 16 (word), and 32 (doubleword) bits in length. To allow maximum flexibility in data structures and efficient memory utilization, words need not be aligned at even-numbered addresses. Nor do doublewords need to be aligned at addresses evenly divisible by four. However, when data is accessed across Multibus II or some other 32-bit bus, data transfers take place in units of doublewords, beginning at addresses divisible by four. The processor converts the request for misaligned values into a sequence of requests for the bus transfer.

Table 8-3 summarizes the data types used in the 80386/80486 processors.

TABLE 8-3   Intel 80386/80486 Data Types

Data Type	Description
General	Byte, word (16 bits), and doubleword (32 bits) locations with arbitrary binary contents
Unpacked Binary Coded Decimal (BCD)	Unsigned byte values, with one digit in each byte
Packed BCD	Packed byte representation of two decimal digits; value in the range 0 to 99
Bit Field	A contiguous sequence of bits in which the position of each binary digit is considered as an independent unit; up to 32 bits in length
Bit String	Like a bit field, a bit string is a continuous sequence of bits. The string may be up to $2^{32} - 1$ bits long.
Near Pointer	A 32-bit logical address that represents the offset within a segment
Far Pointer	A 48-bit logical address of two components: a 16-bit segment selector and a 32-bit offset
Integer	A signed binary value contained in a byte, word, or doubleword, using 2's complement representation
Ordinal	An unsigned binary value contained in a byte, word, or doubleword
String	A contiguous sequence of bytes, words, or doublewords, containing from zero to $2^{32} - 1$ bytes

8.3

TYPES OF OPERATIONS

The number of different opcodes varies widely from machine to machine. However, the same general types of operations are found on all machines. A useful and typical categorization is the following:

- Data Transfer
- Arithmetic
- Logical
- Conversion
- I/O
- System Control
- Transfer of Control

Table 8-2 (based on [HAYE88]) lists common instruction types in each category. This section provides a brief survey of these various types of operations, together with a brief discussion of the actions taken by the CPU to execute a particular type of operation (summarized in Table 8-4). The latter topic is examined in more detail in Chapter 10.

Data Transfer

The most fundamental type of machine instruction is the data transfer instruction. The data transfer instruction must specify several things. First, the location

TABLE 8-4   CPU Actions For Various Types of Operations

Data Transfer	Transfer data from one location to another
	If memory is involved:
	Determine memory address
	Perform virtual-to-actual-memory address transformation
	Check Cache
	Initiate Memory Read/Write
Arithmetic	May involve data transfer, before and/or after
	Perform function in ALU
	Set condition codes and flags
Logical	Same as arithmetic
Conversion	Similar to arithmetic and logical. May involve special logic to perform conversion
Transfer of Control	Update program counter. For subroutine call/return, manage parameter passing and linkage
I/O	Issue command to I/O module
	If memory-mapped I/O, determine memory-mapped address

of the source and destination operands must be specified. Each location could be memory, a register, or the top of the stack. Second, the length of data to be transferred must be indicated. Third, as with all instructions with operands, the mode of addressing for each operand must be specified. This latter point is discussed in Chapter 9.

The choice of data transfer instructions to include in an instruction set exemplifies the kinds of tradeoffs the designer must make. For example, the general location (memory or register) of an operand can be indicated in either the specification of the opcode or the operand. Table 8-5 shows examples of the most common IBM S/370 data transfer instructions. Note that there are variants to indicate the amount of data to be transferred (8, 16, 32, or 64 bits). Also, there are different instructions for register to register, register to memory, and memory to register transfers. In contrast, the VAX has a move (MOV) instruction with variants for different amounts of data to be moved, but it specifies whether an operand is register or memory as part of the operand. The VAX approach is somewhat easier for the programmer, who has fewer mnemonics to deal with. However, it is also somewhat less compact than the IBM S/370 approach, since the location (register versus memory) of each operand must be specified separately in the instruction. We will return to this distinction when we discuss instruction formats, in the next chapter.

In terms of CPU action, data transfer operations are perhaps the simplest type. If both source and destination are registers, then the CPU simply causes

TABLE 8-5   Examples of IBM S/370 Data Transfer Operations

Operation Mnemonic	Name	Number of Bits Transferred	Description
L	Load	32	Transfer from memory to register
LH	Load Halfword	16	Transfer from memory to register
LR	Load	32	Transfer from register to register
LER	Load (Short)	32	Transfer from floating-point register to floating-point register
LE	Load (Short)	32	Transfer from memory to floating-point register
LDR	Load (Long)	64	Transfer from floating-point register to floating-point register
LD	Load (Long)	64	Transfer from memory to floating-point register
ST	Store	32	Transfer from register to memory
STH	Store Halfword	16	Transfer from register to memory
STC	Store Character	8	Transfer from register to memory
STE	Store (Short)	32	Transfer from floating-point register to memory
STD	Store (Long)	64	Transfer from floating-point register to memory

data to be transferred from one register to another; this is an operation internal to the CPU. If one or both operands are in memory, then the CPU must perform some or all of the following actions:

1. Calculate the memory address, based on the address mode (discussed in Chapter 9).
2. If the address refers to virtual memory, translate from virtual to actual memory address.
3. Determine whether addressed item is in cache.
4. If not, issue command to memory module.

Arithmetic

Most machines provide the basic arithmetic operations of add, subtract, multiply, and divide. These are invariably provided for signed integer (fixed-point) numbers. Often they are also provided for floating-point and packed decimal numbers.

Other possible operations include a variety of single-operand instructions; for example,

- Absolute: Take the absolute value of the operand
- Negate: Negate the operand
- Increment: Increment the operand by 1
- Decrement: Decrement the operand by 1.

The execution of an arithmetic instruction may involve data transfer operations to position operands for input to the ALU, and to deliver the output of the ALU. Figure 3-5 illustrates the movements involved in both data transfer and arithmetic operations. In addition, of course, the ALU portion of the CPU performs the desired operation.

Logical

Most machines also provide a variety of operations for manipulating individual bits of a word or other addressable unit, often referred to as "bit twiddling." They are based upon Boolean operations (see appendix to this book).

Some of the basic logical operations that can be performed on Boolean or binary data are shown in Table 8-6. The NOT operation inverts a bit. AND, OR,

TABLE 8-6   Basic Logical Operations

P	Q	NOT P	NOT Q	P AND Q	P OR Q	P XOR Q	P = Q
0	0	1	1	0	0	0	1
0	1	1	0	0	1	1	0
1	0	0	1	0	1	1	0
1	1	0	0	1	1	0	1

and Exclusive OR (XOR) are the most common logical functions with two operands. EQUAL is a useful binary test.

These logical operations can be applied bitwise to n-bit logical data units. Thus, if two registers contain the data

(R1) = 10100101
(R2) = 00001111

then

(R1) AND (R2) = 00000101

Thus the AND operation can be used as a *mask* that selects certain bits in a word and zeros out the remaining bits. As another example, if two registers contain

(R1) = 10100101
(R2) = 11111111

then

(R1) XOR (R2) = 01011010

With one word set to all 1s, the XOR operation inverts all of the bits in the other word (1's complement).

In addition to bitwise logical operations, most machines provide a variety of shifting and rotating functions. The most basic operations are illustrated in Figure 8-4. With a *logical shift*, the bits of a word are shifted left or right. On one end, the bit shifted out is lost. On the other end, a 0 is shifted in. Logical shifts are useful primarily for isolating fields within a word. The 0s that are shifted into a word displace unwanted information which is shifted off the other end.

As an example, suppose we wish to transmit characters of data to an I/O device 1 character at a time. If each memory word is 16 bits in length and contains 2 characters, we must *unpack* the characters before they can be sent. To send the 2 characters in a word,

1. Load the word into a register.
2. AND with the value 1111111100000000. This masks out the character on the right.
3. Shift to the right eight times. This shifts the remaining character to the right half of the register.
4. Perform I/O. The I/O module will read the lower-order 8 bits from the data bus.

The preceding steps result in sending the left-hand character. To send the right-hand character,

1. Load the word again into the register.
2. AND with 0000000011111111.
3. Perform I/O.

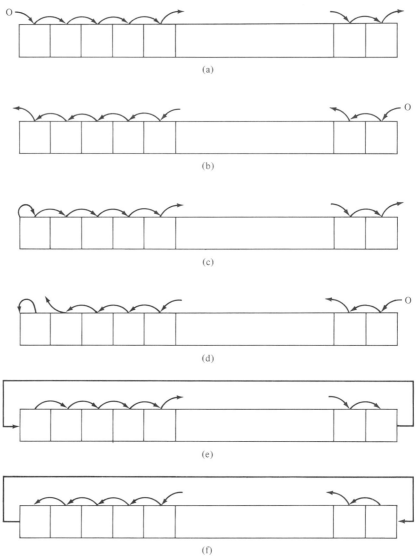

FIGURE 8-4. Shift and rotate operations: (a) logical right shift; (b) logical left shift; (c) arithmetic right shift; (d) arithmetic left shift; (e) right rotate; (f) left rotate

The *arithmetic shift* operation treats the data as a signed integer and does not shift the sign bit. On a right arithmetic shift, the sign bit is normally replicated into the bit position to its right. These operations can speed up certain arithmetic operations. With numbers in 2's-complement notation, a left or right shift corresponds to multiplication or division by 2, respectively, provided there is no overflow or underflow.

Rotate, or cyclic shift, operations preserve all of the bits being operated on. One possible use of a rotate is to bring each bit successively into the leftmost bit, where it can be identified by testing the sign of the data (treated as a number).

As with arithmetic operations, logical operations involve ALU activity and may involve data transfer operations.

Conversion

Conversion instructions are ones that change the format or operate on the format of data. An example is converting from decimal to binary.

An example of a more complex editing instruction is the S/370 Translate (TR) instruction. This instruction can be used to convert from one 8-bit code to another, and it takes three operands:

TR R1,R2,L

The operand R2 contains the address of the start of a table of 8-bit codes. The L bytes starting at the address specified in R1 are translated, each byte being replaced by the contents of a table entry indexed by that byte. For example, to translate from EBCDIC to ASCII, we first create a 256-byte table in storage locations, say, 1000–10FF hexadecimal. The table contains the characters of the ASCII code in the sequence of the binary representation of the EBCDIC code; that is, the ASCII code is placed in the table at the relative location equal to the binary value of the EBCDIC code of the same character. Thus locations 10F0 through 10F9 will contain the values 30 through 39, since F0 is the EBCDIC code for the digit 0, and 30 is the ASCII code for the digit 0, and so on through digit 9. Now suppose we have the EBCDIC for the digits 1984 starting at location 2100 and we wish to translate to ASCII. Assume the following:

Locations 2100–2103 contain F1 F9 F8 F4.
R1 contains 2100.
R2 contains 1000.

Then, if we execute

TR R1,R2,4

locations 2100–2103 will contain 31 39 38 34.

Input/Output

Input/Output instructions were discussed in some detail in Chapter 5. As we saw, there are a variety of approaches taken, including isolated programmed I/O, memory-mapped programmed I/O, DMA, and the use of an I/O processor. Many implementations provide only a few I/O instructions, with the specific actions specified by parameters, codes, or command words.

System Control

System control instructions are generally privileged instructions that can be executed only while the processor is in a certain privileged state or is executing a program in a special privileged area of memory. Typically, these instructions are reserved for the use of the operating system.

Some examples of system control operations are as follows. A system control instruction may read or alter a control register; we will discuss control registers in Chapter 10. Another example is an instruction to read or modify a storage protection key, such as is used in the S/370 memory system. Another example is access to process control blocks in a multiprogramming system.

Transfer of Control

For all of the operation types discussed so far, the instruction specifies the operation to be performed and the operands. Implicitly, the next instruction to be performed is the one that immediately follows, in memory, the current instruction. Thus, in the normal course of events, instructions are executed consecutively from memory. The CPU simply increments the program counter prior to fetching the next instruction.

However, a significant fraction of the instructions in any program have as their function changing the sequence of instruction execution. For these instructions, the operation performed by the CPU is to update the program counter to contain the address of some instruction in memory.

There are a number of reasons why transfer-of-control operations are required. Among the most important are

1. In the practical use of computers, it is essential to be able to execute each instruction more than once and perhaps many thousands of times. It may require thousands or perhaps millions of instructions to implement an application. This would be unthinkable if each instruction had to be written out separately. If a table or a list of items is to be processed, a program loop is needed. One sequence of instructions is executed repeatedly to process all the data.
2. Virtually all programs involve some decision making. We would like the computer to do one thing if one condition holds, and another thing if another condition holds. For example, a sequence of instructions computes the square root of a number. At the start of the sequence, the sign of the number is tested. If the number is negative, the computation is not performed, but an error condition is reported.
3. To correctly compose a large or even medium-size computer program is an exceedingly difficult task. It helps if there are mechanisms for breaking the task up into smaller pieces that can be worked on one at a time.

We now turn to a discussion of the most common transfer-of-control operations found in instruction sets:

- Branch
- Skip
- Subroutine Call

Branch Instructions

A branch instruction, also called a jump instruction, has as one of its operands the address of the next instruction to be executed. Most often, the instruction is a *conditional branch* instruction. That is, the branch is made (update program counter to equal address specified in operand) only if a certain condition is met. Otherwise, the next instruction in sequence is executed (increment program counter as usual).

There are two common ways of generating the condition to be tested in a conditional branch instruction. First, most machines provide a 1-bit or multiple-bit condition code that is set as the result of some operations. This code can be thought of as a short user-visible register. As an example, an arithmetic operation (ADD, SUBTRACT, and so on) could set a 2-bit condition code with one of the following four values: 0, positive, negative, overflow. On such a machine, there could be four different conditional branch instructions:

BRP X   Branch to location X if result is positive.
BRN X   Branch to location X if result is negative.
BRZ X   Branch to location X if result is zero.
BRO X   Branch to location X if overflow occurs.

In all of these cases, the result referred to is the result of the most recent operation that set the condition code.

Another approach that can be used with a three-address instruction format is to perform a comparison and specify a branch in the same instruction. For example,

BRE R1,R2,X   Branch to X if contents of R1 = contents of R2.

Figure 8-5 shows examples of these operations. Note that a branch can be either *forward* (an instruction with a higher address), or *backward* (lower address). The example shows how an unconditional and a conditional branch can be used to create a repeating loop of instructions. The instructions in locations 202 through 210 will be executed repeatedly until the result of subtracting Y from X is 0.

Skip Instructions

Another common form of transfer-of-control instruction is the skip instruction. The skip instruction includes an implied address. Typically, the skip implies that one instruction be skipped; thus the implied address equals the address of the next instruction plus one instruction-length.

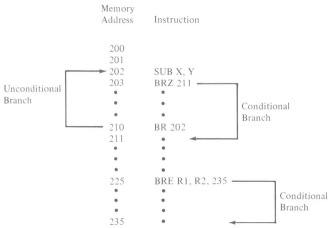

FIGURE 8-5. Branch instructions

Because the skip instruction does not require a destination address field, it is free to do other things. A typical example is the increment-and-skip-if-zero (ISZ) instruction. Consider the following program fragment:

```
301
    .
    .
    .
    .
309       ISZ    R1
310       BR     301
311
```

In this fragment, the two transfer-of-control instructions are used to implement an iterative loop. R1 is set with the negative of the number of iterations to be performed. At the end of the loop, R1 is incremented. If it is not 0, the program branches back to the beginning of the loop. Otherwise, the branch is skipped and the program continues with the next instruction after the end of the loop.

Subroutine Call Instructions

Perhaps the most important innovation in the development of programming languages is the *subroutine*. A subroutine is a self-contained computer program that is incorporated into a larger program. At any point in the program the subroutine may be invoked or *called*. That is, at that point, the computer is instructed to go and execute the entire subroutine and then return to the point from which the call took place.

The two principal reasons for the use of subroutines are economy and modularity. A subroutine allows the same piece of code to be used many times. This is important for economy in programming effort, and for making the most efficient use of storage space in the system (the program must be stored). Subroutines also allow large programming tasks to be subdivided into smaller units. This use of *modularity* greatly eases the programming task.

The subroutine mechanism involves two basic instructions: a call instruction that branches from the present location to the subroutine, and a return instruction that returns from the subroutine to the place from which it was called. Both of these are forms of branching instructions.

Figure 8-6 illustrates the use of subroutines to construct a program. In this example, there is a main program starting at location 4000. This program includes a call to subroutine SUB1, starting at location 4500. When this call instruction is encountered, the CPU suspends execution of the main program and begins execution of SUB1 by fetching the next instruction from location 4500. Within SUB1, there are two calls to SUB2 at location 4800. In each case the execution of SUB1 is suspended and SUB2 is executed. The RETURN statement causes the CPU to go back to the calling program and continue execution at the instruction after the corresponding CALL instruction. This behavior is illustrated in Figure 8-7.

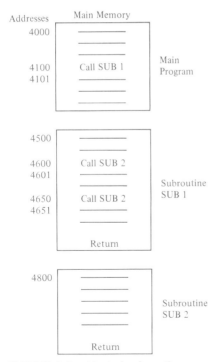

FIGURE 8-6.   Nested subroutines

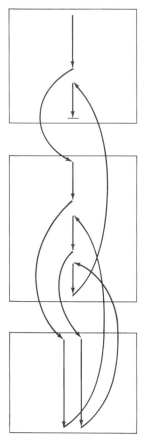

FIGURE 8-7.   Execution sequence for nested subroutines of Figure 8-6

Several points are worth noting:

1. A subroutine can be called from more than one location.
2. A subroutine call can appear in a subroutine. This allows the *nesting* of subroutines to an arbitrary depth.
3. Each subroutine call is matched by a return in the called program.

Since we would like to be able to call a subroutine from a variety of points, the CPU must somehow save the return address so that the return can take place appropriately. There are three common places for storing the return address:

- Register
- Start of Subroutine
- Top of Stack

Consider a machine-language instruction CALL X, which stands for *call subroutine at location X*. If the register approach is used, CALL X causes the following actions:

$$RN \leftarrow PC + \Delta$$
$$PC \leftarrow X$$

where RN is a register that is always used for this purpose, PC is the program counter, and Δ is the instruction length. The called subroutine can now save the contents of RN to be used for the later return.

A second possibility is to store the return address at the start of the subroutine. In this case, CALL X causes

$$X \leftarrow PC$$
$$PC \leftarrow X + 1$$

This is quite handy. The return address has been stored safely away.

Both of the preceding approaches work and have been used. The only limitation of these approaches is that they prevent the use of *reentrant* subroutines [HIGM67, POHL81]. A reentrant subroutine is one in which it is possible to have several calls open to it at the same time. A recursive procedure is an example of the use of this feature [BARR68, BURG75].

A more general and powerful approach is to use a stack (see Appendix 8A for a definition of the stack). When the CPU executes a call, it places the return address on the stack. When it executes a return, it uses the address on top of the stack. Figure 8-8 illustrates the use of the stack.

In addition to providing a return address, it is also often necessary to pass parameters with a subroutine call. These can be passed in registers. Another possibility is to store the parameters in memory just after the CALL instruction. In this case, the return must be to the location following the parameters. Again, both of these approaches have drawbacks. If registers are used, the called program and the calling program must be written to assure that the registers are used properly. The storing of parameters in memory makes it difficult to exchange a variable number of parameters. And both approaches prevent the use of reentrant subroutines.

A more flexible approach to parameter-passing is the stack. When the processor executes a call, it not only stacks the return address, it stacks parameters to be passed to the called procedure. The called procedure can access the parameters from the stack. Upon return, return parameters can also be placed on the

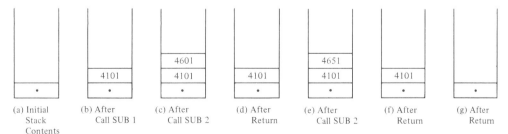

FIGURE 8-8. Use of stack to implement nested subroutines of Figure 8-6

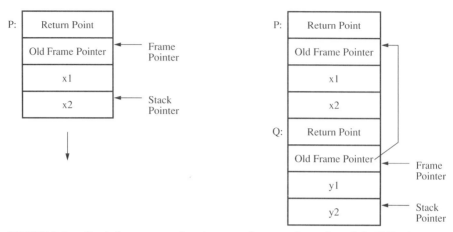

FIGURE 8-9. Stack frame growth using sample procedures P and Q [DEWA90]

stack, *under* the return address. The entire set of parameters, including return address, that is stored for a procedure invocation is referred to as a *stack frame*.

An example is provided in Figure 8-9. The example refers to procedure P in which the local variables x1 and x2 are declared, and procedure Q, which can be called by P and in which the local variables y1 and y2 are declared. In this figure, the return point for each procedure is the first item stored in the corresponding stack frame. Next is stored a pointer to the beginning of the previous frame. This is needed if the number or length of parameters to be stacked is variable.

IBM 370 Operation Types

The System/370 principles of operations manual [IBM83a] defines five broad classes of machine instructions:

- General
- Decimal
- Floating point
- Privileged I/O
- Privileged System Control

The first class is used by application programmers and may be augmented by the second and third for additional arithmetic operations. The last two classes contain instructions that execute only when the CPU is in a supervisor state and are generally used only by operating-system programs.

Following [LEBA84b], we find it more useful to divide machine instructions into 12 categories that better separate them according to function:

- *Fixed-Point Arithmetic Instructions:* For all fixed-point binary arithmetic instructions, one register is used to contain one of the operands and is also used to store the result, with the other operand being either in a register or in memory. Two types of operations are provided: those that treat the operands as 2's-complement numbers and those that treat them as unsigned integers. Operands may be either 16 or 32 bits long, as specified by the op code.

- *Logical Instructions:* Bitwise AND, OR, and XOR operations are provided.
- *General Register Shifting Instructions:* The eight shift instructions provide the following three pairs of alternatives: left or right, single or double register, and signed or logical. The amount of the shift left or right is specified in operand 2. The shift affects either a single register or an even-odd register pair. The arithmetic shift does not disturb the sign bit.
- *General Register Load and Store Instructions:* Used to transfer register to register, register to memory, or memory to register.
- *Compare Instructions:* These instructions perform comparison and testing functions. The result is to set a 2-bit condition code that can be tested by a subsequent conditional branch instruction.
- *Branch Instructions:* This set includes conditional branch instructions that branch based on the current value of the condition code. Also included is a branch-and-link (BAL) instruction, which stores the address of the next sequential instruction in a register, to be used for subroutine call and return purposes. The programmer must specify, in the BAL instruction, which register is to be used for saving the return address. The called subroutine must be written to accept the return address from that register, and subsequently use it in a branch or conditional branch instruction to return to the calling program.
- *Conversion Instructions:* This category contains a variety of instructions that involve some operations on the content of data. For example, CVB converts a decimal number to binary.
- *Decimal Instructions:* These instructions operate on packed decimal data. They include arithmetic operations, as well as shifting and unpacking operations.
- *Floating-Point Instructions:* Specific instructions are provided for 4-, 8-, and 16-byte floating-point numbers. For all three types, add, subtract, multiply, and divide instructions are provided.
- *Special-Purpose Control Instructions:* These are infrequently-used instructions that are available to application programs. The most common of these is Supervision Call (SVC). The SVC instruction causes an interrupt, which passes control to the operating system. A program request for system services, such as I/O functions, would issue SVC instructions.
- *Privileged I/O Instructions:* These are used to perform I/O operations using the I/O channels. These were discussed in Chapter 5. Start I/O (SIO) is an example.
- *Privileged System-Control Instructions:* This is another set of instructions that can be issued only by the operating system. It is used to control registers and data structures that are of concern to the operating system.

Table 8-7 gives an example of each instruction type. The operands are expressed in a notation to be explained in Chapter 9.

TABLE 8-7   Examples of IBM System/370 Instruction Types

Type	Example	Format	Description
Fixed-point arithmetic	AH R1, D2 (X2, B2)	RX	Add second operand to first. Second operand is 16 bits; the first operand and result are 32 bits.
Logical	XI D1(R1), I2	SI	The XOR of I2 and the byte at D1(R1) are stored at D1(R1)
General register shifting	SLDL R1, D2(R2)	RS	Shift left double logical. The 64-bit double register at R1 is shifted left the number of bits specified by the second operand.
General register load and store	LCR R1, R2	RR	The 2's complement of the second operand is placed in the first operand
Data moving, conversion, and translation	MVN D1(L, R1), D2(R2)	SS	The rightmost 4 bits of the L bytes beginning at D2(R2) are moved to the rightmost 4 bits of the corresponding bytes at D1(R1). The leftmost 4 bits are unchanged.
Decimal	AP D1(L1, R1), D2(L2, R2)	SS	The second operand is added to the first. Both are in packed decimal format of the lengths indicated.
Floating-point	AD R1, D2 (X2, R2)	RX	Add second operand to first. Normalize result.
Compare	CR R1, R2	RR	Compare two operands and set condition code (0; equal; 1: $(R1) < (R2)$; 2: $(R2) < (R1)$).
Branch	BXH R1, R3, D2(R2)	RS	Branch on index high. Add (R3) to (R1). Compare result with (R3) if R3 odd and (R3 + 1) if R3 even. Branch if sum is greater to D2(R2)
Special-purpose control	SVC I	RR	Causes an interrupt, with the I field providing part of the interruption code.
Privileged I/O	SIO D2(R2)	S	Start I/O. Bits 16-31, D2 (R2), identify the channel, subchannel, and device
Privileged system-control	IVSK R1, R2	RRE	Insert virtual storage key. The key associated with the location referenced by R2 is stored in R1.

VAX Operation Types

The VAX instruction set was not designed to be easy to program. Rather, the more compelling goal was to provide for effective compiler-generated code

[STRE78b, BHAN79]. The designers felt that the decreasing cost of hardware would allow the implementation of a complex instruction set architecture on a minicomputer and that the increasing cost of software dictated programmer use of high-level languages even for systems programming. Some of the effects of this viewpoint on the instruction set design are

- A regular and consistent treatment of operators. For example, because there is a divide longword instruction, there are also divide word and divide byte instructions.
- Inclusion of several forms of common operators. For example, there are three forms of integer add instructions: (1) one operand, which is incremented, (2) two operands, in which one operand is added to a second with the result stored in the second, and (3) three operands, in which two operands are added and the result stored in the third.

This generous approach to instruction definition is supported by a variable-length, variable-operand instruction format.

The bulk of VAX instructions fall into one of the following 9 categories:

- *Integer Logic and Arithmetic:* The usual arithmetic functions are provided for byte, word, and longword. A few special instructions support extended precision, such as Add With Carry. The general-purpose MOV instructions are also included in this category. Only a few logical and shift instructions are provided. It was felt that these are used primarily for field isolation and that the field instructions described in this list are more efficient for that purpose.
- *Floating-Point Arithmetic:* The same arithmetic operations are provided for floating-point as for integer numbers.
- *Address:* Two instructions are provided that make use of the address of the operand. Move address (MOVA) stores the address. This is useful for getting and then modifying the result of complex addressing-mode calculations. Push address (PUSHA) places an address on a stack and is useful in implementing a subroutine mechanism.
- *Field:* These instructions operate on variable-bit fields. Included are extract field, which extracts a 0- to 32-bit field; compare field, which compares a field against a longword operand; and find first, which finds the first occurrence of a 1 or 0 bit. These instructions provide a powerful and compact facility for manipulating bit-level data.
- *Control:* There is a complete set of conditional branch instructions. There are also subroutine call instructions that push the return address onto a stack. Two sets of instructions are provided by the VAX. The simplest set of operations does not provide any special support for parameter passing, but only provides the proper address linkage. The Jump to Subroutine (JSB) instruction causes the CPU to push the address of the next instruction onto a system stack and branch to the location specified by the JSB operand. To return, the subroutine contains a Return from Subroutine (RSB) instruction, which causes the CPU to load the program counter from the top of the stack. A more powerful, but

more time-consuming, call is provided by the CALL instruction. In this case, the CPU pushes onto the stack the return address plus the contents of some of the VAX CPU registers. The first word of the called program contains a bit pattern in which the bits set to 1 specify which registers are to be saved on the stack. Thus the called program can cause those registers that it will reuse to be saved. The Return (RET) instruction restores those registers from the stack and loads the program counter from the stack.

- *Queue:* The VAX provides instructions for manipulating linked lists of data. A queue, or linked list, consists of an ordered set of data items. Associated with each data item are the addresses of the predecessor and successor members of the list. Instructions for inserting and removing queue entries are provided. These facilitate list processing, which is a versatile form of programming often used in artificial-intelligence applications [FOST67].
- *Character String:* A versatile set of instructions for manipulating strings or sequences of characters is provided. It includes move string, with translation options; string compare; single-character search; and substring search. A string is identified by its starting address and length.
- *Packed Decimal:* Arithmetic, shifting, and unpacking operations are provided.
- *Privileged Instructions:* As with the S/370, these are instructions generally reserved for operating-system use.

The VAX instruction set is rich and contains a number of specialized instructions. The intent was to provide tools for the compiler writer to produce optimized machine language translations of high-level-language programs. There is evidence that this goal has succeeded. Several case studies [CLAR82, WIEC82] examined VAX instruction usage for a variety of high-level languages and applications. The studies looked at opcode distributions and addressing mode frequencies. The results showed that the usage of VAX features was highly skewed for a given program; that is, relatively few opcodes and addressing modes accounted for most of the instructions. However, this skewing differed for different programs, so that a wide range of VAX features found use when a range of programs was considered.

So, these studies indicate that the systems programmers do, in fact, take advantage of the rich set of features available on the VAX. Whether this instruction set architecture provides an actual benefit, however, is difficult to say. One careful study [HUCK83] compared the IBM 370 and the VAX machine instruction sets using a variety of applications and languages. The study found that the static memory requirements for the 370 and the VAX were about the same; the VAX programs contained fewer instructions, but the average instruction length was longer. This study also looked at dynamic instruction use, that is, the instructions actually executed during a program. Even though the VAX architecture executed fewer instructions, the instructions were, on average, much more complex, requiring the CPU to do more "work" to interpret and execute. The author concluded that, with CPUs of comparable power, the S/370 programs are faster to execute.

From the preceding, we can draw the conclusion that the older S/370 design at least holds its own with the sophisticated VAX design. This conclusion highlights the difficulties in designing and evaluating instruction sets.

Condition Codes

We have mentioned that condition codes are bits in special registers that may be set by certain operations and used in conditional branch instructions. These conditions are set by arithmetic and compare operations. The compare operation in most languages subtracts two operands, as does a subtract operation. The difference is that a compare operation only sets condition codes whereas a subtract operation also stores the result of the subtraction in the destination operand.

As an example, Table 8-8 lists the condition codes used on the 80386/80486 machines.

Each condition, or combinations of these conditions, can be tested for a conditional jump. Table 8-9 shows the combinations of conditions for which conditional jump opcodes have been defined.

Several interesting observations can be made about this list. First, we may wish to test two operands to determine if one number is bigger than another. But this will depend on whether the numbers are signed or unsigned. For example the 8-bit number 11111111 is bigger than 00000000 if the two numbers are interpreted as unsigned integers ($255 > 0$), but is less if they are considered as 8-bit 2's-complement numbers ($-1 < 0$). Many assembly languages therefore

TABLE 8-8   Intel 80386/80486 Condition Codes

Status Bit	Name	Description
C	Carry	Indicates carrying out or borrowing into the leftmost bit position following an arithmetic operation. Also modified by some of the shift and rotate operations.
P	Parity	Parity of the result of an arithmetic or logic operation. 1 indicates even parity; 0 indicates odd parity.
A	Auxiliary Carry	Represents carrying or borrowing between half-bytes of an 8-bit arithmetic or logic operation using the AL register.
Z	Zero	Indicates that the result of an arithmetic or logic operation is 0.
S	Sign	Indicates the sign of the result of an arithmetic or logic operation.
O	Overflow	Indicates an arithmetic overflow after an addition or subtraction.

TABLE 8-9   80386/80486 Conditions for Conditional Jump and SETcc Instructions

Symbol	Condition Tested	Comment
A, NBE	C = 0 AND Z = 0	Above; Not below or equal (greater than, unsigned)
AE, NB, NC	C = 0	Above or equal; Not below (greater than or equal, unsigned); Not carry
B, NAE, C	C = 1	Below; Not above or equal (less than, unsigned); Carry set
BE, NA	C = 1 OR Z = 1	Below or equal; Not above (less than or equal, unsigned)
E, Z	Z = 1	Equal; Zero (signed or unsigned)
G, NLE	[(S = 1 AND O = 0) OR (S = 0 AND O = 1)] AND [Z = 0]	Greater than; Not less than or equal (signed)
GE, NL	(S = 1 AND O = 1) OR (S = 0 AND O = 0)	Greater than or equal; Not less than (signed)
L, NGE	(S = 1 AND O = 0) OR (S = 0 AND O = 1)	Less than; Not greater than or equal (signed)
LE, NG	(S = 1 AND O = 1) OR (S = 0 AND O = 0) OR (Z = 1)	Less than or equal; Not greater than (signed)
NE, NZ	Z = 0	Not equal; Not zero (signed or unsigned)
NO	O = 0	No overflow
NS	S = 0	No sign
NP, PO	P = 0	Not parity; Parity odd
O	O = 1	Overflow
P	P = 1	Parity; Parity even
S	S = 1	Sign

introduce two sets of terms to distinguish the two cases: If we are comparing two numbers as signed integers, we use the terms *less than* and *greater than;* if we are comparing them as unsigned integers, we use the terms *below* and *above.*

A second observation concerns the complexity of comparing signed integers. A signed result is greater than or equal to zero if (a) the sign bit is zero and there is no overflow (S = 1 AND O = 0) or (b) the sign bit is one and there is an overflow. A study of Figure 7-3 should convince you that the conditions tested for the various signed operations are appropriate (see Problem 8.14).

Intel 80386/80486 Operation Types

As with the VAX architecture, the 80386/80486 provides a complex array of operation types. Table 8-10 lists the types and gives examples of each. Most of these are the conventional instructions found in most machine instruction sets, but several types of instructions are tailored to the 80X876 architecture and are of particular interest.

TABLE 8-10 Intel 80386/80486 Operation Types (with examples of typical operations)

Instruction	Description
	Arithmetic
ADD	Add operands
SUB	Subtract operands
MUL	Multiply Double/Single Precision
DIV	Divide unsigned
	Bit Manipulation
BTS	Bit test and set. Operates on a bit field operand. The instruction copies the current value of a bit to flag CF and sets the original bit to 1.
BSF	Bit scan forward. Scans a word or doubleword for a one-bit and stores the number of the first one-bit into a register.
	Data Transfer
General Purpose	
MOV	Move operand, between registers or between register and memory
PUSH	Push operand onto stack
PUSHA	Push all registers on stack
Conversion	
MOVSX	Move byte, word, dword, sign extended. Moves a byte to a word or a word to a doubleword with 2's-complement sign extension.
IN, OUT	Input, output operand from I/O space
Address Object	
LEA	Load effective address. Loads the offset of the source operand, rather than its value, to the destination operand.
LDS	Load pointer into D segment register
Flag Manipulation	
LAHF	Load A register from flags. Copies SF, ZF, AF, PF, and CF bits into A register.
STC	Set Carry flag
	High Level Language Support
BOUND	Check array bounds. Verifies that the value in operand 1 is within lower and upper limits. The limits are in two adjacent memory locations referenced by operand 2. An interrupt occurs if the value is out of bounds. This instruction is used to check an array index.
ENTER	Creates a stack frame that can be used to implement the rules of a block-structured high-level language.
LEAVE	Reverses the action of the previous ENTER.
SETcc	Sets a byte to zero or one depending on any of the 16 conditions defined by status flags.
	Logical Instructions and Shift/Rotate
AND	AND operands
SHL/SHR	Shift logical left or right
SAL/SAR	Shift arithmetic left or right
ROL/ROR	Rotate left or right

TABLE 8-10   Intel 80386/80486 Operation Types (continued)

Processor Control

ESC	Processor extension escape. An escape code that indicates the succeeding instructions are to be executed by a numeric coprocessor that supports high-precision integer and floating-point calculations.
HLT	Halt
LOCK	Asserts a hold on shared memory so that the 80386/80486 has exclusive use of it during the instruction which immediately follows the LOCK.
MOV	Move to/from control registers
WAIT	Wait until BUSY# negated. Suspends 80386/80486 program execution until the processor detects that the BUSY pin is inactive, indicating that the numeric coprocessor has finished execution.

Program Control

JE/JZ	Jump if equal/zero
CALL	Transfer control to another location. Before transfer, the address of the instruction following the CALL is placed on the stack.
JMP	Unconditional jump
LOOPE/LOOPZ	Loops if equal/zero. This is a conditional jump using a value stored in register ECX. The instruction first decrements ECX before testing ECX for the branch condition.
INT/INTO	Interrupt/Interrupt if overflow. Transfers control to an interrupt service routine.

Protection

SGDT	Store global descriptor table
LSL	Load segment limit. Loads a user-specified register with a segment limit.
VERR/VERW	Verify segment for reading/writing

String Manipulation

MOVS	Move byte, word, dword string. The instruction operates on one element of a string, indexed by registers ESI and EDI. After each string operation, the registers are automatically incremented or decremented to point to the next element of the string.
LODS	Load byte, word, dword of string
XLAT	Table look-up translation. Replaces a byte in AL with a byte from a user-coded translation table. When XLAT is executed, AL should have an unsigned index to the table. XLAT changes the contents of AL from the table index to the table entry.

Cache/TLB

INVD	Flushes the internal cache memory
WBINVD	Flushes the internal cache memory after writing dirty lines to memory.
INVLPG	Invalidates a translation lookaside buffer (TLB) entry

The 80386/80486 provides four instructions to support procedure call/return: CALL, ENTER, LEAVE, RETURN. It will be instructive to look at the support provided by these instructions[1]. Recall from Figure 8-9 that a common means of implementing the procedure call/return mechanism is via the use of stack frames. When a new procedure is called, the following must be performed upon entry to the new procedure:

- Push the return point on the stack
- Push current frame pointer on stack
- Copy stack pointer as new value of frame pointer
- Adjust stack pointer to allocate frame

The CALL instruction pushes the current instruction pointer value onto the stack and causes a jump to the entry point of the procedure by placing the address of the entry point in the instruction pointer. In the 8088 and 8086 machines, the typical procedure began with the sequence:

```
PUSH    EBP
MOV     EBP, ESP
SUB     ESP, space_for_locals
```

where EBP is the frame pointer and ESP is the stack pointer. In the 80286 and later machines, the ENTER instruction performs all of the above operations in a single instruction.

The ENTER instruction was added to the instruction set to provide direct support for the compiler. The instruction also includes a feature for support of what are called nested procedures in languages such as Pascal, COBOL, and Ada (not found in C or FORTRAN). It turns out that there are better ways of handling nested procedure calls for these languages. Furthermore, although the ENTER instruction saves a few bytes of memory compared to the PUSH, MOV, SUB sequence (4 bytes versus 6 bytes), it actually takes longer to execute (10 clock cycles versus 6 clock cycles). Thus, although it may have seemed a good idea to the instruction-set designers to add this feature, it complicates the implementation of the processor while providing little or no benefit. We will see in Part V that, in contrast, a RISC approach to processor design would avoid complex instruction such as ENTER and might produce a more efficient implementation with a sequence of simpler instructions.

Another set of specialized instructions deals with memory segmentation. These are privileged instructions that can be only executed from the operating system. They allow local and global segment tables (called descriptor tables) to be loaded and read, and for the privilege level of a segment to be checked and altered.

The special instructions for dealing with the on-chip cache were discussed in Chapter 4.

---

[1] This discussion is based on a treatment in [DEWA90], which should be consulted for a more detailed analysis.

8.4

ASSEMBLY LANGUAGE

A CPU can understand and execute machine instructions. Such instructions are simply binary numbers stored in the computer. If a programmer wished to program directly in machine language, then it would be necessary to enter the program as binary data.

Consider the simple BASIC statement

N = I + J + K

Suppose we wished to program this statement in machine language and to initialize I, J, and K to 2, 3, and 4, respectively. This is shown in Figure 8-10a. The program starts in location 101 (hexadecimal). Memory is reserved for the four variables starting at location 201. The program consists of four instructions:

1. Load the contents of location 201 into the AC.
2. Add the contents of location 202 to the AC.
3. Add the contents of location 203 to the AC.
4. Store the contents of the AC in location 204.

This is clearly a tedious and very error-prone process.

A slight improvement is to write the program in hexadecimal rather than binary notation (Figure 8-10b). We could write the program as a series of lines. Each line contains the address of a memory location and the hexadecimal code of the binary value to be stored in that location. Then we need a program that will accept this input, translate each line into a binary number, and store it in the specified location.

This is only a slight improvement. To do much better, we can make use of the symbolic name or mnemonic of each instruction. Let us use that instead of the actual op code. This results in the *symbolic program* shown in Figure 8-10c. Each line of input still represents one memory location. Each line consists of three fields, separated by spaces. The first field contains the address of a location. For an instruction, the second field contains the three-letter symbol for the op code. If it is a memory-referencing instruction, then a third field contains the address. To store arbitrary data in a location, we invent a *pseudoinstruction* with the symbol DAT. This is merely an indication that the third field on the line contains a hexadecimal number to be stored in the location specified in the first field.

For this type of input we need a slightly more complex program. The program accepts each line of input, generates a binary number based on the second and third (if present) fields, and stores it in the location specified by the first field.

The use of a symbolic program makes life much easier but is still awkward. In particular, we must give an absolute address for each word. This means that the program and data can be loaded into only one place in memory, and we must

Address	Contents
101	0010 0010 0000 0001
102	0001 0010 0000 0010
103	0001 0010 0000 0011
104	0011 0010 0000 0100
201	0000 0000 0000 0010
202	0000 0000 0000 0011
203	0000 0000 0000 0100
204	0000 0000 0000 0000

(a) Binary Program

Address			
101	LDA	201	
102	ADD	202	
103	ADD	203	
104	STA	204	
201	DAT	2	
202	DAT	3	
203	DAT	4	
204	DAT	0	

(c) Symbolic Program

Address	Contents
101	2 2 0 1
102	1 2 0 2
103	1 2 0 3
104	3 2 0 4
201	0 0 0 2
202	0 0 0 3
203	0 0 0 4
204	0 0 0 0

(b) Hexadecimal Program

Label	Operation	Opened
FORMUL	LDA	I
	ADD	J
	ADD	K
	STA	N
I	DATA	2
J	DATA	3
K	DATA	4
N	DATA	0

(d) Assembly Program

FIGURE 8-10. Computation of the formula N = I + J + K

know that place ahead of time. Worse, suppose we wish to change the program some day by adding or deleting a line. This will change the addresses of all subsequent words.

A much better system, and one commonly used, is to use symbolic addresses. This is illustrated in Figure 8-10d. Each line still consists of three fields. The first field is still for the address, but a symbol is used instead of an absolute numerical address. Some lines have no address, implying that the address of that line is one more than the address of the previous line. For memory-reference instructions, the third field also contains a symbolic address.

With this last refinement, we have invented an *assembly language*. Programs written in assembly language (assembly programs) are translated into machine language by an *assembler*. This program must not only do the symbolic translation discussed earlier, but also assign some form of memory addresses to symbolic addresses.

The development of assembly language was a major milestone in the evolution of computer technology. It was the first step to the high-level languages in use today. Although few programmers use assembly language, virtually all machines provide one. They are used, if at all, for systems programs such as compilers and I/O routines.

8.5

RECOMMENDED READING

A number of textbooks provide good coverage of machine language, including [HENN90], [TANE90], and [HAYE88]. The VAX machine instruction set is well covered by [DEC81], [LEVY89], and [ELAS84]. The IBM S/370 is covered in [IBM83] and [LEBA84a]. An excellent discussion of the 80X86 instruction set is continued in [DEWA90].

8.6

PROBLEMS

8.1 Many CPUs provide logic for performing arithmetic on packed decimal numbers. Although the rules for decimal arithmetic are similar to those for binary operations, the decimal results may require some corrections to the individual digits if binary logic is used.

Consider the decimal addition of two unsigned numbers. If each number consists of N digits, then there are $4N$ bits in each number. The two numbers are to be added using a binary adder. Suggest a simple rule for correcting the result. Perform addition in this fashion on the numbers 1698 and 1786.

8.2 The 10's complement of the decimal number X is defined to be $10^N - X$, where N is the number of decimal digits in the number. Describe the use of 10's-complement representation to perform decimal subtraction. Illustrate the procedure by subtracting $(0326)_{10}$ from $(0736)_{10}$.

8.3 It was stated that the instruction set defines many of the functions performed by the CPU. List some CPU functions not dependent on instruction set design.

8.4 Compare zero-, one-, two-, and three-address machines by writing programs to compute

$$X = (A + B \times C)/(D - E \times F)$$

for each of the four machines. The instructions available for use are

0 Address	1 Address	2 Address	3 Address
PUSH M	LOAD M	MOV(X ← Y)	MOVE(X ← Y)
POP M	STORE M	ADD(X ← X + Y)	ADD(X ← Y + Z)
ADD	ADD M	SUB(X ← X − Y)	SUB(X ← Y − Z)
SUB	SUB M	MUL(X ← X * Y)	MUL(X ← Y * Z)
MUL	MUL M	DIV(X ← X/Y)	DIV(X ← Y/Z)
DIV	DIV M		

8.5 Consider a hypothetical computer with an instruction set of only two n-bit instructions. The first bit specifies the op code, and the remaining bits specify one of the 2^{n-1} n-bit words of main memory. The two instructions are

SUBS X   Subtract the contents of location X from the accumulator, and store the result in location X and in the accumulator.

JUMP X   Place address X in the program counter.

A word in main memory may contain either an instruction or a binary number in 2's-complement notation. Demonstrate that this instruction repertoire is reasonably complete by specifying how the following operations can be programmed:

(a) Data Transfer: Location X to accumulator, accumulator to location X

(b) Addition: Add contents of location X to accumulator.

(c) Conditional Branching

(d) Logical OR

(e) I/O Operations

8.6   Many instruction sets contain the instruction NOOP, meaning no operation, which has no effect on the CPU state other than incrementing the program counter. Suggest some uses of this instruction.

8.7   Suppose a stack is to be used by the CPU to manage subroutine calls and returns. Can the program counter be eliminated by using the top of the stack as a program counter?

8.8   Appendix 8A points out that there are no stack-oriented instructions in an instruction set if the stack is to be used only by the CPU for such purposes as subroutine handling. How can the CPU use a stack for any purpose without stack-oriented instructions?

8.9   Convert the following formulas from reverse Polish to infix

(a) AB + C + D *

(b) AB/CD/ +

(c) ABCDE + * * /

(d) ABCDE + F/ + G − H/ * +

8.10 Convert the following formulas from infix to reverse Polish

(a) A + B + C + D + E

(b) (A + B) * (C + D) + E

(c) (A * B) + (C * D) + E

(d) (A − B) * (((C − D * E)/F)/G) * H

8.11 Convert the expression A + B − C to postfix notation using Dijkstra's algorithm. Show the steps involved. Is the result equivalent to (A + B) − C or A + (B − C)? Does it matter?

8.12 In the IBM S/360 and S/370 architectures, each byte of main memory has a unique address. The original IBM S/360 architecture requires that the operands in memory be *boundary aligned*; that is, a 2-byte operand has to start at an address that is a multiple of 2, a 4-byte operand has to start at an address that is a multiple of 4, and an 8-byte operand has to start at an address that is a multiple of 8. Starting with the IBM 360/85 and continuing in the IBM 370 series, this alignment restriction was removed. Later, paging was introduced in the S/370 with page sizes of 2,048 or 4,096 bytes (aligned on 2K or 4K address boundaries). Discuss how nonaligned operands and page-fault checking interact to slow down *all* memory references on these later machines.

8.13 The 80X86 architecture includes an instruction called Decimal Adjust after Addition (DAA). DAA performs the following sequence of instructions:

if ((AL AND 0FH) > 9) OR (AF = 1) **then**
    $AL \leftarrow AL + 6$;
    $AF \leftarrow 1$;
else
    $AF \leftarrow 0$;
endif:
if ((AL > 9FH) OR (CF = 1) **then**
    $AL \leftarrow AL + 60H$;
    $CF \leftarrow 1$;
else
    $CF \leftarrow 0$;
endif:

"H" indicates hexadecimal. AL is an 8-bit register that holds the result of addition of two unsigned 8-bit integers. AF is a flag set if there is a carry from bit 3 to bit 4 in the result of an addition. CF is a flag set if there is a carry from bit 7 to bit 8. Explain the function performed by the DAA instruction.

8.14 The 80X86 Compare instruction (CMP) subtracts the source operand from the destination operand; it updates the status flags (C, P, A, Z, S, O) but does not alter either of the operands. The CMP instruction may be followed by a conditional Jump (Jcc) or Set Condition (SETcc) instruction, where cc refers to one of the 16 conditions listed in Table 8-9. Demonstrate that the conditions tested for a signed number comparison are correct.

8.15 Most microprocessor instruction sets include an instruction that tests a condition and sets a destination operand if the condition is true. Examples include the SETcc on the 80X86, the Scc on the Motorola MC68000 and the Scond on the National NS32000.
  (a) There are a few differences among these instructions:
    • SETcc and Scc operate only on a byte, whereas Scond operates on byte, word, and doubleword operands.
    • SETcc and Scond set the operand to integer one if true and to zero if false. Scc sets the byte to all binary ones if true and all zeroes if false.
    What are the relative advantages and disadvantages of these differences?
  (b) None of these instructions set any of the condition code flags and thus an explicit test of the result of the instruction is required to determine its value. Discuss whether condition codes should be set as a result of this instruction.
  (c) A simple IF statement such as IF a > b THEN can be implemented

using a numerical representation method, that is, making the boolean value manifest, as opposed to a *flow of control* method, which represents the value of a boolean expression by a point reached in the program. A compiler might implement IF a > b THEN with the following 80X86 code:

```
        SUB   CX, CX      ;set register CX to 0
        MOV   AX, B       ;move contents of location B to register AX
        CMP   AX, A       ;compare contents of register AX and location A
        JLE   TEST        ;jump if A ≤ B
        INC   CX          ;add 1 to contents of register CX
TEST    JCXZ  OUT         ;jump if contents of CX equal 0
THEN

OUT
```

The result of (A > B) is a boolean value held in a register and available later on, outside the context of the flow of code shown above. It is convenient to use register CX for this, because many of the branch and loop opcodes have a built-in test for CX.

Show an alternative implementation using the SETcc instruction that saves memory and execution time (Hint: no additional new 80X86 instructions are needed, other than the SETcc).

(d) Now consider the high-level language statement:

A: = (B > C) OR (D = F)

A compiler might generate the following code

```
        MOV     EAX, B      ;move from location B to register EAX
        CMP     EAX, C
        MOV     BL, 0       ;0 represents false
        JLE     N1
        MOV     BL, 1       ;1 represents true
N1:     MOV     EAX, D
        CMP     EAX, F
        MOV     BH, 0
        JNE     N2
        MOV     BH, 1
N2:     OR      BL, BH
```

Show an alternative implementation using the SETcc instruction that saves memory and execution time.

APPENDIX 8A

Stacks

A *stack* is an ordered set of elements, only one of which can be accessed at a time. The point of access is called the *top* of the stack. The number of elements in the

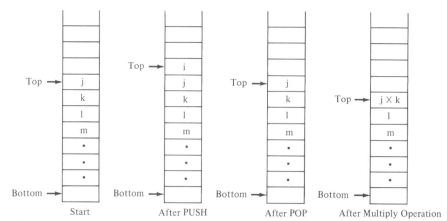

FIGURE 8-11. Basic stack operations

stack, or *length* of the stack, is variable. Items may only be added to or deleted from the top of the stack. For this reason, a stack is also known as a *pushdown list* or a *last-in-first-out (LIFO) list*.

The simplest way of explaining stack structure and operation is by illustration. Figure 8-11 shows the basic operations that can be performed. We begin at some point in time when the stack contains some number of elements. A PUSH operation appends one new item to the top of the stack. A POP operation removes the top item from the stack. In both cases, the top of the stack moves accordingly. In addition, binary operations, which require two operands (e.g., multiply, divide, add, subtract), use the top two stack items as operands, pop both items, and push the result back onto the stack. Unary operations, which require only one operand (e.g., logical NOT), use the item on the top of the stack. All of these operations are summarized in Table 8-11.

8A-1 Stack Implementation

The stack is a useful structure to provide as part of a CPU implementation. One use, discussed in Section 8-3, is to manage subroutine calls and returns. Stacks

TABLE 8-11   Stack-Oriented Operations

PUSH	Append a new element on the top of the stack
POP	Delete the top element of the stack
Unary operation	Perform operation on top element of stack. Replace top element with result
Binary operation	Perform operation on top two elements of stack. Delete top two elements of stack. Place result of operation on top of stack

may also be useful to the programmer. An example of this is expression evaluation, discussed later in this section.

The implementation of a stack depends in part on its potential uses. If it is desired to make stack operations available to the programmer, then the instruction set will include stack-oriented operations, including PUSH, POP, and operations that use the top one or two stack elements as operands. Since all of these operations refer to a unique location, namely the top of the stack, the address of the operand or operands is implicit and need not be included in the instruction. These are the zero-address instructions referred to in Section 8-1.

If the stack mechanism is to be used only by the CPU, for such purposes as subroutine handling, then there will not be explicit stack-oriented instructions in the instruction set. In either case, the implementation of a stack requires that there be some set of locations used to store the stack elements. A typical approach is illustrated in Figure 8-12a. A contiguous block of locations is reserved in main memory (or virtual memory) for the stack. Most of the time, the block is partially filled with stack elements and the remainder is available for stack growth. Three addresses are needed for proper operation, and these are often stored in CPU registers:

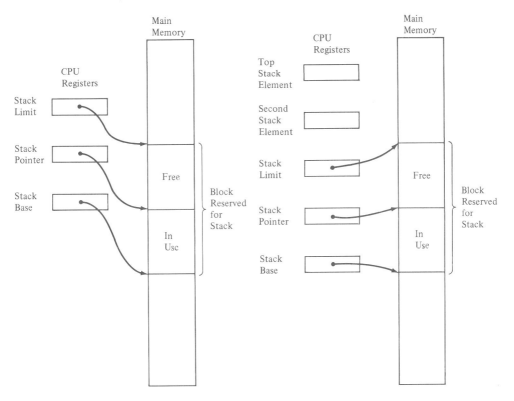

(a) All of Stack in Memory   (b) Top Two Elements in Registers

FIGURE 8-12. Typical stack organizations

- *Stack Pointer:* Contains the address of the top of the stack. If an item is appended to or deleted from the stack, the pointer is incremented or decremented to contain the address of the new top of the stack.
- *Stack Base:* Contains the address of the bottom location in the reserved block. If an attempt is made to POP when the stack is empty, an error is reported.
- *Stack Limit:* Contains the address of the other end of the reserved block. If an attempt is made to PUSH when the block is fully utilized for the stack, an error is reported.

To speed up stack operations, the top two stack elements are often stored in registers, as shown in Figure 8-12b. In this case, the stack pointer contains the address of the third element of the stack.

8A-2 Expression Evaluation

Mathematical formulas are usually expressed in what is known as *infix* notation. In this form, a binary operation appears between the operands (e.g., a + b). For complex expressions, parentheses are used to determine the order of evaluation of expressions. For example, a + (b × c) will yield a different result than (a + b) × c. To minimize the use of parentheses, operations have an implied precedence. Generally, multiplication takes precedence over addition, so that a + b × c is equivalent to a + (b × c).

An alternate technique is known as *reverse Polish* or postfix notation. In this notation, the operator follows its two operands. For example,

a + b   becomes ab +
a + (b × c) becomes abc × +
(a + b) × c becomes ab + c ×

Note that, regardless of the complexity of an expression, no parentheses are required when using reverse Polish.

The advantage of postfix notation is that an expression in this form is easily evaluated using a stack. An expression in postfix notation is scanned from left to right. For each element of the expression, the following rules are applied.

1. If the element is a variable or constant, push it onto the stack.
2. If the element is an operator, pop the top two items of the stack, perform the operation, and push the result.

After the entire expression has been scanned, the result is on the top of the stack.

The simplicity of this algorithm makes it a convenient one for evaluating expressions. Accordingly, many compilers will take an expression in a high-level language, convert it to postfix notation, and then generate the machine instructions from that notation. Figure 8-13 shows the sequence of machine instructions for evaluating $f = (a - b)/(c + d * e)$ using stack-oriented instructions. The fig-

Stack	General Registers	Single Register
Push a	Load G[1], a	Load d
Push b	Subtract G[1], b	Multiply e
Subtract	Load G[2], d	Add c
Push c	Multiply G[2], e	Store f
Push d	Add G[2], c	Load a
Push e	Divide G[1], G[2]	Subtract b
Multiply	Store G[1], f	Divide f
Add		Store f
Divide		
Pop f		
Number of Instructions		
10	7	8
Memory Access		
10 op + 6 d	7 op + 6 d	8 op + 8 d

FIGURE 8-13.   Comparison of three programs to calculate $f = (a - b)/(c + d \times e)$

ure also shows the use of one-address and two-address instructions. Note that, even though the stack-oriented rules were not used in the last two cases, the postfix notation served as a guide for generating the machine instructions. The sequence of events for the stack program is shown in Figure 8-14.

The process of converting an infix expression to a postfix expression is itself most easily accomplished using a stack. The following algorithm is due to

FIGURE 8-14.   Use of stack to compute $f = (a - b)/(d \times e + c)$

Dijkstra [DIJK63]. The infix expression is scanned from left to right, and the postfix expression is developed and output during the scan. The steps are as follows:

1. Examine the next element in the input.
2. If it is an operand, output it.
3. If it is an opening parenthesis, push it onto the stack.
4. If it is an operator, then

    If the top of the stack is an opening parenthesis, then push the operator.
    If it has higher priority than the top of the stack (multiply and divide have higher priority than add and subtract) then push the operator.
    Else, pop operation from stack to output, and repeat step 4.
5. If it is a closing parenthesis, pop operators to the output until an opening parenthesis is encountered. Pop and discard the opening parenthesis.
6. If there is more input, go to step 1.
7. If there is no more input, unstack the remaining operands.

Figure 8-15 illustrates the use of this algorithm. This example should give the reader some feel for the power of stack-based algorithms.

Input	Output	Stack (top on right)
A + B * C + (D + E) * F	empty	empty
+ B * C + (D + E) * F	A	empty
B * C + (D + E) * F	A	+
* C + (D + E) * F	A B	+
C + (D + E) * F	A B	+ *
+ (D + E) * F	A B C	+ *
(D + E) * F	A B C * +	+
D + E) * F	A B C * +	+ (
+ E) * F	A B C * + D	+ (
E) * F	A B C * + D	+ (+
) * F	A B C * + D E	+ (+
* F	A B C * + D E +	+
F	A B C * + D E +	+ *
empty	A B C * + D E + F	+ *
empty	A B C * + D E + F * +	

FIGURE 8-15. Conversion of an expression from infix to postfix notation

CHAPTER 9

Instruction Sets: Addressing Modes and Formats

In Chapter 8, we focused on *what* an instruction set does. Specifically, we examined the types of operands and operations that may be specified by machine instructions. This chapter turns to the question of *how* to specify the operands and operations of instructions. Two issues arise. First, how is the address of an operand specified, and second, how are the bits of an instruction organized to define the operand addresses and operation of that instruction.

9.1

ADDRESSING

As we have mentioned, the address field or fields in a typical instruction format are quite limited. We would like to be able to reference a large range of locations in main memory or, for some systems, virtual memory. To achieve this objective, a variety of addressing techniques have been employed. They all involve some tradeoff between address range and/or addressing flexibility on the one hand, and the number of memory references and/or the complexity of address calculation on the other. In this section, we examine the most common addressing techniques:

- Immediate
- Direct
- Indirect
- Register
- Register Indirect

375

- Displacement
- Stack

These modes are illustrated in Figure 9-1. In this section, we use the following notation:

A = contents of the (an) address field in the instruction
EA = actual (effective) address of the location containing
    the referenced operand
(X) = contents of location X

Table 9-1 indicates the address calculation performed for each addressing mode.

Before beginning this discussion, two comments need to be made. First, virtually all computer architectures provide more than one of these addressing modes. The question arises as to how the control unit can determine which address mode is being used in a particular instruction. Several approaches are taken. Often, different op codes will use different addressing modes. Also, one or more bits in the instruction format can be used as a *mode field*. The value of the mode field determines which addressing mode is to be used.

The second comment concerns the interpretation of the effective address (EA). In a system without virtual memory, the *effective address* will be either a main memory address or a register. In a virtual memory system, the effective address is a virtual address or a register. The actual mapping to a physical address is a function of the paging mechanism and is invisible to the programmer.

Immediate Addressing

The simplest form of addressing is immediate addressing, in which the operand is actually present in the instruction.

OPERAND = A

This mode can be used to define and use constants or set initial values of variables. Typically, the number will be stored in 2's-complement form; the leftmost bit of the operand field is used as a sign bit. When the operand is loaded into a data register, the sign bit is extended to the left to the full data word size.

TABLE 9-1   Basic Addressing Modes

Mode	Algorithm	Principal Advantage	Principal Disadvantage
Immediate	Operand = A	No memory reference	Limited operand magnitude
Direct	EA = A	Simple	Limited address space
Indirect	EA = (A)	Large address space	Multiple memory references
Register	EA = R	No memory reference	Limited address space
Register indirect	EA = (R)	Large address space	Extra memory reference
Displacement	EA = A + (R)	Flexibility	Complexity
Stack	EA = top of stack	No memory reference	Limited applicability

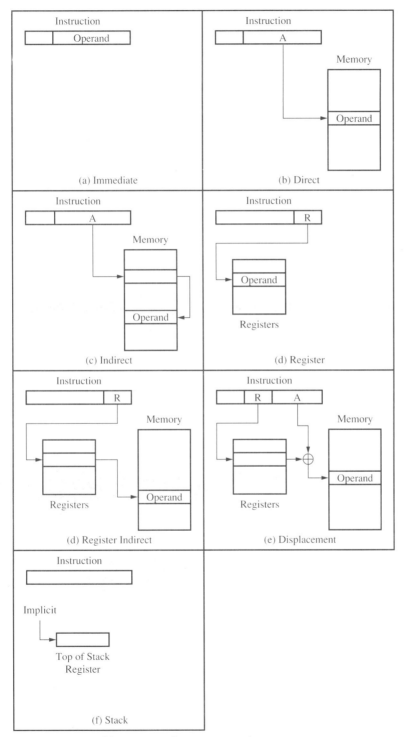

FIGURE 9-1. Addressing modes

The advantage of immediate addressing is that no memory reference other than the instruction fetch is required to obtain the operand, thus saving one memory or cache cycle in the instruction cycle. The disadvantage is that the size of the number is restricted to the size of the address field, which, in most instruction sets, is small compared to the word length.

Direct Addressing

A very simple form of addressing is direct addressing, in which the address field contains the effective address of the operand.

EA = A

The technique was common in earlier generations of computers and is still found on a number of small computer systems. It requires only one memory reference and no special calculation. The obvious limitation, mentioned earlier, is that it provides only a limited address space.

Indirect Addressing

The problem with direct addressing is that the length of the address field is usually less than the word length, thus limiting the address range. One solution is to have the address field refer to the address of a word in memory, which in turn contains a full-length address of the operand. This is known as *indirect addressing*.

EA = (A)

(As defined earlier, the parentheses are to be interpreted as meaning *contents of*.) The obvious advantage of this approach is that for the word length of N, an address space of 2^N is now available. The disadvantage is that instruction execution requires two memory references to fetch the operand, one to get its address and a second to get its value.

You will note that although the number of words that can be addressed is now equal to 2^N, the number of different effective addresses that may be referenced at any one time is limited to 2^K, where K is the length of the address field. Typically, this is not a burdensome restriction, and it can be an asset. In a virtual-memory environment, all of the effective address locations can be confined to page 0 of any process. Since the address field of an instruction is small, it will naturally produce low-numbered direct addresses, which would appear in page 0. (The only restriction is that the page size must be greater than or equal to 2^K.) When a process is active, there will be repeated references to page 0, causing it to remain in real memory. Thus, an indirect memory reference will involve, at most, one page fault rather than two.

A rarely used variant of indirect addressing is multilevel or cascaded indirect addressing.

$$EA = (. . . (A) . . .)$$

In this case, one bit of a full-word address is an indirect flag (I). If the I bit is 0, then the word contains the EA. If the I bit is 1, then another level of indirection is invoked. There does not appear to be any particular advantage to this approach, and its disadvantage is that three or more memory references could be required to fetch an operand.

Register Addressing

Register addressing is similar to direct addressing. The only difference is that the address field refers to a register rather than a main memory address.

$$EA = R$$

Typically, an address field that references registers will have 3 or 4 bits, so that a total of 8 or 16 general-purpose registers can be referenced.

The advantages of register addressing are that (1) only a small address field is needed in the instruction, and (2) no memory references are required. As was discussed in Chapter 4, the memory access time for a register internal to the CPU is much less than that for a main memory address. The disadvantage of register addressing is that the address space is very limited.

If register addressing is heavily used in an instruction set, this implies that the CPU registers will be heavily used. Because of the severely limited number of registers (compared to main memory locations), their use in this fashion makes sense only if they are employed efficiently. If every operand is brought into a register from main memory, operated on once, and then returned to main memory, then a wasteful intermediate step has been added. If, instead, the operand in a register remains in use for multiple operations, then a real savings is achieved. An example is the intermediate result in a calculation. In particular, suppose that the algorithm for 2's-complement multiplication were to be implemented in software. The location labeled A in the flowchart (Figure 7-10) is referenced many times and should be implemented in a register rather than a main memory location.

It is up to the programmer to decide which values should remain in registers and which should be stored in main memory. Most modern CPUs employ multiple general-purpose registers, placing a burden for efficient execution on the assembly-language programmer (e.g., compiler writer).

Register Indirect Addressing

Just as register addressing is analogous to direct addressing, register indirect addressing is analogous to indirect addressing. In both cases, the only difference is whether the address field refers to a memory location or a register. Thus, for register indirect address,

$$EA = (R)$$

The advantages and limitations of register indirect addressing are basically the same as for indirect addressing. In both cases, the address space limitation (limited range of addresses) of the address field is overcome by having that field refer to a word-length location containing an address. In addition, register indirect addressing uses one less memory reference than indirect addressing.

Displacement Addressing

A very powerful mode of addressing combines the capabilities of direct addressing and register indirect addressing. It is known by a variety of names depending upon the context of its use, but the basic mechanism is the same. We will refer to this as *displacement addressing.*

$$EA = A + (R)$$

Displacement addressing requires that the instruction have two address fields, at least one of which is explicit. The value contained in one address field (value = A) is used directly. The other address field, or an implicit reference based on op code, refers to a register whose contents are added to A to produce the effective address.

We will describe three of the most common uses of displacement addressing:

* Relative Addressing
* Base-Register Addressing
* Indexing

Relative Addressing

For relative addressing, the implicitly referenced register is the program counter (PC). That is, the current instruction address is added to the address field to produce the EA. Typically, the address field is treated as a 2's-complement number for this operation. Thus the effective address is a displacement relative to the address of the instruction.

Relative addressing exploits the concept of locality that was discussed in Chapters 4 and 6. If most memory references are relatively near to the instruction being executed, then the use of relative addressing saves address bits in the instruction.

Base-Register Addressing

For base-register addressing, the interpretation is the following: The referenced register contains a memory address and the address field contains a displacement (usually an unsigned integer representation) from that address. The register reference may be explicit or implicit.

Base-register addressing also exploits the locality of memory references. It is a convenient means of implementing segmentation, which was discussed in Chapter 6. In some implementations, a single segment-base register is employed and is used implicitly. In others, the programmer may choose a register to hold the base address of a segment, and the instruction must reference it explicitly. In this latter case, if the length of the address field is K and the number of possible registers is N, then one instruction can reference any one of N areas of 2^K words.

Indexing

For indexing, the interpretation is typically the following: The address field references a main memory address, and the referenced register contains a positive displacement from that address. Note that this usage is just the opposite of the interpretation for base-register addressing. Of course, it is more than just a matter of user interpretation. Because the address field is considered to be a memory address in indexing, it generally contains more bits than an address field in a comparable base-register instruction. Also, we shall see that there are some refinements to indexing that would not be as useful in the base-register context. Nevertheless, the method of calculating the EA is the same for both base-register addressing and indexing, and in both cases the register reference is sometimes explicit and sometimes implicit (for different CPU types).

An important use of indexing is to provide an efficient mechanism for performing iterative operations. Consider, for example, a list of numbers stored starting at location A. Suppose that we would like to add 1 to each element on the list. We need to fetch each value, add 1 to it, and store it back. The sequence of effective addresses that we need is A, A + 1, A + 2, . . . , up to the last location on the list. With indexing, this is easily done. The value A is stored in the instruction's address field, and the chosen register, called an *index register*, is initialized to 0. After each operation, the index register is incremented by 1.

Because index registers are commonly used for such iterative tasks, it is typical that there is a need to increment or decrement the index register after each reference to it. Since this is such a common operation, some systems will automatically do this as part of the same instruction cycle. This is known as *autoindexing*. If certain registers are devoted exclusively to indexing, then autoindexing can be invoked implicitly and automatically. If general-purpose registers are used, the autoindex operation may need to be signaled by a bit in the instruction. Autoindexing using increment can be depicted as follows.

$$EA = A + (R)$$
$$(R) \leftarrow (R) + 1$$

In some machines, both indirect addressing and indexing are provided, and it is possible to employ both in the same instruction. There are two possibilities: the indexing is performed either before or after the indirection.

If indexing is performed after the indirection, it is termed *postindexing*.

$$EA = (A) + (R)$$

First, the contents of the address field are used to access a memory location containing a direct address. This address is then indexed by the register value. This technique is useful for accessing one of a number of blocks of data of a fixed format. For example, it was described in Chapter 6 that the operating system needs to employ a process control block for each process. The operations performed are the same regardless of which block is being manipulated. Thus the addresses in the instructions that reference the block could point to a location (value = A) containing a variable pointer to the start of a process control block. The index register contains the displacement within the block.

With *preindexing*, the indexing is performed before the indirection.

$$EA = (A + (R))$$

An address is calculated as with simple indexing. In this case, however, the calculated address contains not the operand but the address of the operand. An example of the use of this technique is to construct a multiway branch table. At a particular point in a program, there may be a branch to one of a number of locations depending on conditions. A table of addresses can be set up starting at location A. By indexing into this table, the required location can be found.

Normally, an instruction set will not include both preindexing and postindexing.

Stack Addressing

The final addressing mode that we consider is stack addressing. As defined in Appendix 8A, a stack is a linear array of locations. It is sometimes referred to as a *pushdown list* or *last-in-first-out queue*. The stack is a reserved block of locations. Items are appended to the top of the stack so that, at any given time, the block is partially filled. Associated with the stack is a pointer whose value is the address of the top of the stack. Alternatively, the top two elements of the stack may be in CPU registers, in which case the stack pointer references the third element of the stack (Figure 8-12b). The stack pointer is maintained in a register. Thus, references to stack locations in memory are in fact register indirect addresses.

The stack mode of addressing is a form of implied addressing. The machine instructions need not include a memory reference but implicitly operate on the top of the stack. Stacks have not been common traditionally but are becoming quite common in microprocessors.

80386/80486 Addressing

Recall from Figure 6-29 that the 80386/80486 address translation mechanism produces an address, called a virtual or effective address, that is an offset into a segment. The sum of the starting address of the segment and the effective address produces a linear address. If paging is being used, this linear address must pass through a page-translation mechanism to produce a physical address. In what follows, we ignore this last step, since it is transparent to the instruction set and to the programmer.

The 80386/80486 is equipped with a variety of addressing modes intended to allow the efficient execution of high level languages such as C and FORTRAN. Figure 9-2 indicates the hardware involved. The segment that is the subject of

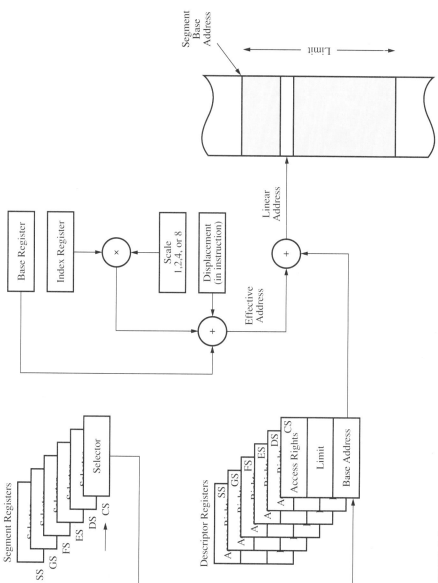

FIGURE 9-2. 80386/80486 addressing mode calculation [INTE90]

the reference is determined by the segment register. There are six segment registers; the one being used for a particular reference depends on the context of execution and the instruction. Each segment register holds the starting address of the corresponding segment. Associated with each user-visible segment register is a segment descriptor register (not programmer-visible) which records the access rights for the segment, as well as the starting address and limit (length) of the segment. In addition, there are two registers that may be used in constructing an address: the base register and the index register.

Table 9-2 lists the eleven addressing modes that may be used to specify operands. Let us consider each of these in turn.

For the **immediate mode,** the operand is included in the instruction.

The **register operand mode** specifies one of the 8-, 16-, or 32-bit registers.

In the **direct mode,** the operand's offset (the effective address of Figure 9-2) is contained as part of the instruction as an 8-, 16-, or 32-bit displacement. Keep in mind that the terminology used by Intel is not in keeping with accepted terminology if segmentation is provided. With segmentation, all addresses in instructions refer merely to an offset in a segment. Thus, direct addressing in a segmented 80386/80486 is similar to what we have called displacement addressing. In any case, the direct addressing mode is found on few machines because, as mentioned earlier, it leads to long instructions. In the case of the 80386 and 80486, the direct address can be as long as 32 bits, making for a 6-byte instruction. Direct addressing can be useful for referencing global variables.

TABLE 9-2   Intel 80386/80486 Addressing Modes

Mode	Algorithm
Immediate	Operand = A
Register Operand	LA = R
Direct Operand	LA = (SR) + A
Register Indirect	LA = (SR) + (B)
Based	LA + (SR) + (B) + A
Index	LA = (SR) + (I) + A
Scaled Index	LA = (SR) + (I) $\times$ S + A
Based Index	LA = (SR) + (B) + (I)
Based Scaled Index	LA = (SR) + (I) $\times$ S + (B)
Based Index with Displacement	LA = (SR) + (B) + (I) + A
Based Scaled Index with Displacement	LA = (SR) + (I) $\times$ S + (B) + A

LA = linear address
(X) = contents of X
SR = segment register
A = contents of an address field in the instruction
R   = register
B = base register
I   = index register
S = scaling factor

The remaining addressing modes are indirect, in the sense that the address portion of the instruction tells the processor where to look to find the address. The **register indirect mode** specifies that one of the 8-, 16-, or 32-bit registers contains the effective address.

With the **based mode,** the instruction includes a displacement to be added to a base register, which may be any of the general-purpose registers. A base register is generally used by a compiler to point to the start of a local variable area. For example, the base register could point to the beginning of a stack frame, which will contain the local variables for the corresponding procedure.

A very similar addressing mode is the **index mode.** Again the instruction includes a displacement to be added to a register, in this case called an index register. The index register may be any of the general-purpose registers except the one called ESP, which is generally used for stack processing. An index register is generally used by a compiler to access the elements of an array, or a string of characters. However, in its plain form, the index mode has the identical effect to the based mode, except that it is restricted not to use the ESP register.

In the **scaled index mode,** the contents of the index register are multiplied by a scaling factor of 2, 4, or 8, and then added to a displacement. This mode is very convenient for indexing arrays. A scaling factor of 2 can be used for an array of 16-bit integers. A scaling factor of 4 can be used for 32-bit integers or floating-point numbers. Finally, a scaling factor of 8 can be used for an array of double-precision floating-point numbers.

The **based index mode** adds the contents of the base and index registers to form the effective address. Again, the base register can be any general-purpose register and the index register can be any general-purpose register except ESP. The **based scaled index mode** sums the contents of the index register multiplied by a scaling factor and the contents of the base register.

The **based index with displacement mode** sums the contents of the base register, the index register, and a displacement. As an example, this addressing mode could be used for accessing a local array on a stack frame. The **based scaled index with displacement mode** is the same as the last mode, with the inclusion of scaling on the index register. Again, this is useful if an array is stored in a stack frame; in this case, the array elements would be 2, 4, or 8 bytes each in length.

IBM 370 Addressing

The addressing structure of the IBM System/370 and 370-XA is comparatively simple. Memory is addressable at the byte level, and all instruction memory references are virtual addresses. In System/370, a 24-bit virtual address is generated, and in 370-XA, a 31-bit virtual address is generated. The address is the address of a byte but may actually refer to one or more bytes depending on the op code.

Three basic addressing modes are supported: immediate, register, and storage. An *immediate operand* is a 1-byte value contained in some instructions. A *register operand* is generally contained in a general register or a floating-point register, depending on the instruction. There are 16 32-bit general registers and 4 64-bit floating-point registers; for consistency, 4 bits are always used to identify the register. A few instructions reference a control register. This will be discussed in Chapter 10.

A *storage operand* is contained in virtual memory. Each storage-operand reference consists of a 12-bit displacement and a 4-bit register identifier that designates one of the general registers. This is the displacement mode discussed earlier (see Table 9-1). If the register identifier is 0, this does not indicate register zero but, rather, indicates that the register component is not to be used. This results in a direct 12-bit address. When the register is used to compute the base address, only the rightmost 24 or 31 bits of the register are used for System/370 or 370-XA, respectively.

Some instructions also employ an index register, in addition to a base register. Again, one of the general registers is used, and a 4-bit index register reference is included in the instruction. Autoindexing is provided.

Table 9-3 summarizes the IBM addressing modes. This addressing structure is simple and relatively easy to use. The programmer must recognize the use of $2^{12} = 4,096$ segments in the address space.

VAX Addressing

The VAX provides one of the most complex arrays of addressing modes to be found on any machine. Before discussing these modes, we must describe the register structure of the VAX.

The VAX provides 16 32-bit general-purpose registers, numbered 0 through 15. In addition to being usable as general-purpose registers, a number of the registers have special uses:

- R15 is the program counter (PC) and contains the address of the next byte of the program. The PC is not used as a temporary accumulator or index register, but it can be used in addressing.
- R14 is the stack pointer (SP) and is usually assumed to point to the head of a stack in memory. Some instructions make implicit references to this register.
- R13 and R12 are the frame pointer (FP) and argument pointer (AP), respectively. These registers are used in the subroutine calling facility for passing parameters.

TABLE 9-3   IBM System/370 Addressing Modes

Mode	Algorithm	Size
Immediate	Operand = A	8 bits
Register	EA = R	4 bits
Displacement	EA = A + (R)	R = 4 bits; (R) = 32 bits; A = 12 bits
Indexed	EA = A + (R) + (X)	R, X = 4 bits; (R), (X) = 32 bits; A = 12 bits

- R0 through R5 are implicitly used by some instructions to store temporary results and, upon completion, final results.

  With the exception of the PC, all of these registers can be used for general programming purposes. This design creates the risk that the programmer will make inappropriate use of a register (e.g., destroy a needed value). On the other hand, this design provides a consistent means of addressing all registers, thus reducing the number and complexity of instructions. And, as you shall see, any help in that department is welcome indeed on the VAX.

  We can now provide a brief tour through the world of VAX addressing. Table 9-4 summarizes the available modes. These modes can be conveniently organized along two dimensions:

- General addressing versus program-counter relative addressing.
- Nonindexed versus indexed.

  The only difference between general addressing and program-counter addressing is that the latter makes use of R15 and the former of any other register. PC-addressing is convenient because it makes a program location independent. If all address references are relative to the PC, then the entire program can be loaded into any portion of memory. For clarity to the programmer, the R15 instructions are given different mnemonics.

  Indexed addressing is built onto some of the nonindexed addressing modes. We will first summarize the nonindexed modes and then explain the mechanism for indexing.

  In the following discussion, we will not make reference to the length of data referenced by an address. This depends on the op code and can be 1 byte, 2 bytes (word), or 4 bytes (longword). If an address refers to a register and a longword is required, the referenced register and the next one in sequence are used. We look first at general register addressing.

- *Literal:* This is an immediate addressing mode in which a 6-bit value appears in the operand field. Because this mode is limited to 6-bit values, another form of immediate addressing is also employed and is described presently. The literal mode is a space-saver for small numbers.
- *Register:* This is the simplest form of addressing. The content of a register is the operand. The PC should not be used in this mode because the results are unpredictable.
- *Register Deferred:* This is simple register indirect addressing. Multilevel indirect addressing is not allowed. We will see that indirect addressing can be combined with other modes.
- *Autoincrement:* This is similar to the autoindexing we discussed earlier. The difference is that we are not using displacement addressing. This mode is usefully employed, for example, by loading the address of a table into a register. With autoincrement, the register is incremented by the length of the operand, which in turn is determined by the op code.

TABLE 9-4   VAX Addressing Modes

(a) General Register Addressing (Nonindexed)

Code	Mode	Algorithm	Indexable?	Size (bits)
00XX	Literal	Operand = A	No	6
0101	Register	EA = R	No	4
0110	Register deferred	EA = (R)	Rx	4
0111	Autodecrement	$(R) \leftarrow (R) - \Delta$ EA = (R)	Rx $\neq$ n	4
1000	Autoincrement	EA = (R) $(R) \leftarrow (R) + \Delta$	Rx $\neq$ n	4
1001	Autoincrement deferred	EA = ((R)) $(R) \leftarrow (R) + 4$	Rx $\neq$ n	4
1010	Byte displacement	EA = A + (R)	Rx	R = 4; A = 8
1011	Byte displacement deferred	EA = (A + (R))	Rx	R = 4; A = 8
1100	Word displacement	EA = A + (R)	Rx	R = 4; A = 16
1101	Word displacement deferred	EA = (A + (R))	Rx	R = 4; A = 16
1110	Longword displacement	EA = A + (R)	Rx	R = 4; A = 32
1111	Longword displacement deferred	EA = (A + (R))	Rx	R = 4; A = 32

(b) Program Counter Addressing (Nonindexed)

Code	Mode	Algorithm	Indexable?	Size (bits)
1000	Immediate	EA = (PC) $(PC) \leftarrow (PC) + \Delta$	Rx	4
1001	Absolute	EA = ((PC)) $(PC) \leftarrow (PC) + 4$	Rx	4
1010	Byte relative	EA = A + (PC)	Rx	R = 4; A = 8
1011	Byte relative deferred	EA = (A + (PC))	Rx	R = 4; A = 8
1100	Word relative	EA = A + (PC)	Rx	R = 4; A = 16
1101	Word relative deferred	EA = (A + (PC))	Rx	R = 4; A = 16
1110	Longword relative	EA = A + (PC)	Rx	R = 4; A = 32
1111	Longword relative deferred	EA = (A + (PC))	Rx	R = 4; A = 32

(c) Indexed Addressing

Code	Mode	Algorithm	Indexable?	Size (bits)
0100	Indexed	EA = $EA_B + \Delta *$ (Rx)	No	R = 4; EA_B = 32

(d) Branch Addressing

Code	Mode	Algorithm	Indexable?	Size (bits)
None	Branch	EA = A + (PC)	No	A = 8 or 16

- *Autoincrement Deferred:* Here we have two levels of indirect addressing. The register contains the address of a location that contains the address of the operand. This unusual mode could be used to index into a table of addresses.
- *Autodecrement:* The content of the register is decremented before being used as an address, whereas in autoincrement it is incremented afterwards.
- *Displacement:* This is the same as the displacement mode discussed earlier, in the general discussion. The displacement can be 8, 16, or 32 bits and is added to the 32-bit register to obtain the address. In the terminology that we used earlier, VAX displacement addressing can be used for either base-register addressing or indexing. The programmer must specify whether the displacement is 8(B), 16(W), or 32(L) bits long.
- *Displacement Deferred:* Here we combine indirect and displacement addressing. The address computed by displacement refers to a location containing the address of the operand. This could be used to access a data structure containing addresses.

We now turn to the program counter (PC) addressing modes.

- *Immediate:* This is identical to autoincrement using R15. It in fact is used for immediate addressing, since literal addressing can be used only for 6-bit values. What is done is to store the operand immediately following the operand specifier. Since the operand is now embedded in the instruction, the PC must be incremented to point beyond the operand value. Thus the operand is not constrained by instruction-length considerations.
- *Absolute:* This is identical to autoincrement deferred using R15. It is, in fact, simple direct addressing as we define it in the general discussion. This mode requires the use of a fixed, constant address (embedded in the instruction). Its most common use is by the operating system to reference an address that is constant for all processes.
- *Relative:* This mode is the displacement mode using R15. It is useful for writing position-independent code, as mentioned earlier. As with the ordinary displacement mode, the displacement can be 8, 16, or 32 bits long. Note that the PC must be incremented to skip over the displacement field to continue fetching instruction bytes.
- *Relative Deferred:* This is the displacement deferred mode using R15.

Since all address references in the VAX instruction set are to virtual memory, the value of the PC addressing modes has been questioned. For example, [COOK82] proposes that references to R15 be prohibited and that the freed-up address mode codes be used for stack addressing. While these might be useful, it does further complicate an already complex addressing mode repertoire. Further, the immediate and absolute modes seem useful as a way of reducing the number of memory references. Finally, relative addressing makes it possible to provide a standard program that can be run in different areas of virtual memory for different users. In any case, this discussion demonstrates once more that there is no "right" instruction set design; there are only tradeoffs among attractive alternatives.

The *indexed addressing modes* available on the VAX combine one of the previous addressing modes with indexing in a rather innovative way. In effect, indexing is provided as an orthogonal (independent) capability to the other addressing modes. This approach yields a rich and powerful addressing facility.

The index mode requires two operand specifiers, known as the *primary* operand specifier and the *base* operand specifier. The base operand specifier refers to the starting location of a table of values in memory. The primary operand specifier refers to a register to be used as an index register. The actual address of the operand is determined by first multiplying the contents of the index register by the size of the operand in bytes; this value is then added to the base operand specifier to yield the operand address. The size of the operand in bytes is determined by the op code.

This technique provides a very general and efficient mechanism for accessing arrays. It has three advantages:

1. The index is scaled by the data size. Since VAX addressing is at the byte level, and a variety of data unit sizes are used, this is an important feature.
2. Indexing can be applied to almost any of the other addressing modes, resulting in a comprehensive set of indexed addressing modes.
3. As we shall see, the space required to specify indexing and the index register is used only when indexing is used.

There are a few restrictions on indexing. Indexing cannot be used with register, index, or literal mode. The index register cannot be the same as the base operand register if that latter register is modified during address computation.

There is one final addressing mode, known as branch addressing, that does not fit into the preceding scheme. All of the addressing modes discussed so far are independent of an op code and are identified by a 4-bit addressing mode code and a 4-bit register identifier (literal is a special case). Branch addressing, in contrast, is identified by certain branch instructions. The effective address consists of an 8- or 16-bit displacement added to the program counter. This address is used as the address of the next instruction rather than the address of a data operand.

A glance at Table 9-4 confirms that branch addressing is identical to byte relative or word relative addressing. The only difference is that branch addressing saves 1 byte in the instruction; the 4-bit mode code and 4-bit register identifier are not used. This special mode is justified by the developers by observing that (1) a large fraction of the program's instructions are branches and (2) most of these branches specify a location a short distance from the current instruction. Thus, this 1-byte savings results in a noticeable reduction in code size. This is an excellent example of the choice that the VAX designers have made to provide efficient coding at the expense of increased CPU complexity.

9.2

INSTRUCTION FORMATS

An instruction format defines the layout of the bits of an instruction, in terms of its constituent parts. An instruction format must include an op code and, implicitly or explicitly, one or more operands. Each explicit operand is referenced using one of the addressing modes described in Section 9.1. The format must, implicitly or explicitly, indicate the addressing mode for each operand. For most instruction sets, more than one instruction format is used.

The design of an instruction format is a complex art, and an amazing variety of designs have been implemented. In this section, we examine the key design issues, looking briefly at some designs to illustrate points, and then we examine the IBM 370 and VAX solutions in detail.

Instruction Length

The most basic design issue to be faced is the instruction format length. This decision affects, and is affected by, memory size, memory organization, bus structure, CPU complexity, and CPU speed. This decision determines the richness and flexibility of the machine as seen by the assembly-language programmer.

The most obvious tradeoff here is between the desire for a powerful instruction repertoire and a need to save space. Programmers want more op codes, more operands, more addressing modes, and greater address range. More op codes and more operands make life easier for the programmer, since shorter programs can be written to accomplish given tasks. Similarly, more addressing modes gives the programmer greater flexibility in implementing certain functions, such as table manipulations and multiple-way branching. And, of course, with the increase in main memory size and the increasing use of virtual memory, programmers want to be able to address larger memory ranges. All of these things (op codes, operands, addressing modes, address range) require bits and push in the direction of longer instruction lengths. But longer instruction length may be wasteful. A 32-bit instruction occupies twice the space of a 16-bit instruction but is probably much less than twice as useful.

Beyond this basic tradeoff, there are other considerations. Either the instruction length should be equal to the memory-transfer length (in a bus system, data-bus length) or one should be a multiple of the other. Otherwise, we will not get an integral number of instructions during a fetch cycle. A related consideration is the memory transfer rate. This rate has not kept up with increases in processor speed. Accordingly, memory can become a bottleneck if the processor can execute instructions faster than it can fetch them. One solution to this problem is the use of cache memory (see Section 4-3); another is to use shorter instructions. Again, 16-bit instructions can be fetched at twice the rate of 32-bit instructions but probably can be executed less than twice as fast.

A seemingly mundane but nevertheless important feature is that the instruction length should be a multiple of the character length, which is usually 8 bits, and of the length of fixed-point numbers. To see this, we need to make use of that unfortunately ill-defined word, "word" [FRAI83]. The word length of memory is, in some sense, the "natural" unit of organization. The size of a word usually determines the size of fixed-point numbers (usually the two are equal). Word size is also typically equal to, or at least integrally related to, the memory transfer size. Since a common form of data is character data, we would like a word to store an integral number of characters. Otherwise, there are wasted bits in each word when storing multiple characters, or a character will have to straddle a word boundary. The importance of this point is such that IBM, when it introduced the System/360 and wanted to employ 8-bit characters, made the wrenching decision to move from the 36-bit architecture of the scientific members of the 700/7000 series to a 32-bit architecture.

Allocation of Bits

We've looked at some of the factors that go into deciding the length of the instruction format. An equally difficult issue is how to allocate the bits in that format. The tradeoffs here are complex.

For a given instruction length, there is clearly a tradeoff between the number of op codes and the power of the addressing capability. More op codes obviously means more bits in the op code field. For an instruction format of a given length, this reduces the number of bits available for addressing. There is one interesting refinement to this trade-off, and that is the use of variable-length op codes. In this approach, there is a minimum op code length but, for some op codes, additional operations may be specified for using additional bits in the instruction. For a fixed-length instruction, this leaves fewer bits for addressing. Thus this feature is used for those instructions that require fewer operands and/or less powerful addressing. We will see examples of this strategy presently.

The following interrelated factors go into determining the use of the addressing bits.

- *Number of Addressing Modes:* Sometimes, an addressing mode can be indicated implicitly. For example, certain op codes might always call for indexing. In other cases, the addressing modes must be explicit, and one or more mode bits will be needed.
- *Number of Operands:* We have seen that fewer addresses can make for longer, more awkward programs (e.g., Figure 8-3). Typical instructions on today's machines provide for two operands. Each operand address in the instruction might require its own mode indicator, or the use of a mode indicator could be limited to just one of the address fields.
- *Register vs. Memory:* A machine must have registers so that data can be brought into the CPU for processing. With a single user-visible register (usually called the *accumulator*), one operand address is implicit and consumes no instruction

bits. However, single-register programming is awkward and requires many instructions. Even with multiple registers, only a few bits are needed to specify the register. The more that registers can be used for operand references, the fewer bits are needed. A number of studies indicate that a total of 8 to 32 user-visible registers is desirable [LUND77, HUCK83].

- *Number of Register Sets:* A number of machines have one set of general-purpose registers, with typically 8 or 16 registers in the set. These registers can be used to store data and can be used to store addresses for displacement addressing. The trend recently has been away from one bank of general-purpose registers and toward a collection of two or more specialized sets (such as data and displacement). This trend shows up everywhere from single-chip micropro-cessors to supercomputers. One advantage of this approach is that, for a fixed number of registers, a functional split requires fewer bits to be used in the instruction. For example, with two sets of eight registers, only 3 bits are re-quired to identify a register; the op code implicitly will determine which set of registers is being referenced. There seems to be little disadvantage to this approach [LUND77]. In systems such as the S/370, which has one set of gen-eral-purpose registers, programmers usually establish conventions that assign about half the registers to data and half to displacement and maintain a fixed assignment [MALL79].

- *Address Range:* For addresses that reference memory, the range of addresses that can be referenced is related to the number of address bits. Because this imposes a severe limitation, direct addressing is rarely used. With displace-ment addressing, the range is opened up to the length of the address register. Even so, it is still convenient to allow rather large displacements from the register address, which requires a relatively large number of address bits in the instruction.

- *Address Granularity:* For addresses that reference memory rather than registers, another factor is the granularity of addressing. In a system with 16- or 32-bit words, an address can reference a word or a byte at the designer's choice. Byte addressing is convenient for character manipulation but requires, for a fixed-size memory, more address bits.

Thus the designer is faced with a host of factors to consider and balance. How critical the various choices are is not clear. As an example, we cite one study [CRAG79] that compared various instruction format approaches, including the use of a stack, general-purpose registers, an accumulator, and only memory-to-register approaches. Using a consistent set of assumptions, no significant differ-ence in code space or execution time was observed.

Let us briefly look at how two machine designs balance these various factors.

PDP-8

One of the simplest instruction designs for a general-purpose computer was for the PDP-8 [BELL78b]. The PDP-8 uses 12-bit instructions and operates on 12-bit words. There is a single general-purpose register, the accumulator.

Despite the limitations of this design, the addressing is quite flexible. Each memory reference consists of 7 bits plus 2 1-bit modifiers. The memory is divided into fixed-length pages of $2^7 = 128$ words each. Address calculation is based on references to page 0 or the current page (page containing this instruction) as determined by the page bit. The second modifier bit indicates whether direct or indirect addressing is to be used. These two modes can be used in combination, so that an indirect address is a 12-bit address contained in a word of page 0 or the current page. In addition, 8 dedicated words on page 0 are autoindex "registers." When an indirect reference is made to one of these locations, preindexing occurs.

Figure 9-3 shows the PDP-8 instruction format. There are a 3-bit op code and 3 types of instructions. For op codes 0 through 5, the format is a single-address memory reference instruction including a page bit and an indirect bit. Thus there are only 6 basic operations. To enlarge the group of operations, op code 7 defines a register reference or *microinstruction*. In this format, the remaining bits are used to encode additional operations. In general, each bit defines a specific operation (e.g., clear accumulator), and these bits can be combined in a single instruction. The microinstruction strategy was used as far back as the PDP-1 by DEC and is, in a sense, a forerunner of today's microprogrammed machines, to be discussed in Part IV. Op code 6 is the I/O operation; 6 bits are used to select one of 64 devices, and 3 bits specify a particular I/O command.

The PDP-8 instruction format is remarkably efficient. It supports indirect addressing, displacement addressing, and indexing. With the use of the op code extension, it supports a total of approximately 35 instructions. Given the constraints of a 12-bit instruction length, the designers could hardly have done better.

PDP-10

A sharp contrast to the instruction set of the PDP-8 is that of the PDP-10. The PDP-10 was designed to be a large-scale time-shared system, with an emphasis on making the system easy to program, even if additional hardware expense was involved.

Among the design principles that were employed in designing the instruction set were [BELL78c].

- *Orthogonality:* Orthogonality is a principle by which two variables are independent of each other. In the context of an instruction set, the term indicates that other elements of an instruction are independent of (not determined by) the op code. The PDP-10 designers use the term to describe the fact that an address is always computed in the same way, independent of the op code. This is in contrast to many machines, where the address mode sometimes depends implicitly on the operator being used.
- *Completeness:* Each arithmetic data type (integer, fixed-point, real) should have a complete and identical set of operations.

Memory Reference Instructions

Input/Output Instructions

Register Reference Instructions

Group 1 Microinstructions

1 1 1 0	CLA	CLL	CMA	CML	RAR	RAL	BSW	IAC
0 1 2 3	4	5	6	7	8	9	10	11

Group 2 Microinstructions

1 1 1 1	CLA	SMA	SZA	SNL	RSS	OSR	HLT	0
0 1 2 3	4	5	6	7	8	9	10	11

Group 3 Microinstructions

1 1 1 1	CLA	MQA	0	MQL	0	0	0	1
0 1 2 3	4	5	6	7	8	9	10	11

Mnemonics

CLA = CLear Accumulator
CLL = CLear Link
CMA = CoMplement Accumulator
CML = CoMplement Link
RAR = Rotate Accumulator Right
RAL = Rotate Accumulator Left
BSW = Byte SWap
IAC = Increment ACcumulator

SMA = Skip on Minus Accumulator
SZA = Skip on Zero Accumulator
SNL = Skip on Nonzero Link
RSS = Reverse Skip Sense
OSR = Or with Switch Register
HLT = HaLT
MQA = Multiplier Quotient into Accumulator
MQL = Multiplier Quotient Load

FIGURE 9-3.   PDP-8 instruction formats

- *Direct Addressing:* Base plus displacement addressing, which places a memory organization burden on the programmer, was avoided in favor of direct addressing.

Each of these principles advances the main goal of ease of programming.

The PDP-10 has a 36-bit word length and a 36-bit instruction length. The fixed instruction format is shown in Figure 9-4. The op code occupies 9 bits, allowing up to 512 operations. In fact, a total of 365 different instructions are defined. Most instructions have two addresses, one of which is one of 16 general-purpose

FIGURE 9-4. PDP-10 instruction format

registers. Thus this operand reference occupies 4 bits. The other operand reference starts with an 18-bit memory address field. This can be used as an immediate operand or a memory address. In the latter usage, both indexing and indirect addressing are allowed. The same general-purpose registers are also used as index registers.

A 36-bit instruction length is true luxury. There is no need to do clever things to get more op codes; a 9-bit op code field is more than adequate. Addressing is also straightforward. An 18-bit address field makes direct addressing desirable. For memory sizes greater than 2^{18}, indirection is provided. For the ease of the programmer, indexing is provided for table manipulation and iterative programs. Also, with an 18-bit operand field, immediate addressing becomes attractive.

The PDP-10 instruction set design does accomplish the objectives listed earlier [LUND77]. It makes it comparatively easy for the programmer at the expense of an inefficient utilization of space. This was a conscious choice made by the designers and therefore cannot be faulted on the grounds of poor design.

Variable-Length Instructions

The examples we have looked at so far have used a single fixed instruction length, and we have implicitly discussed tradeoffs in that context. But the designer may choose instead to provide a variety of instruction formats of different lengths. This tactic makes it easy to provide a large repertoire of op codes, with different op code lengths. Addressing can be more flexible, with various combinations of register and memory references plus addressing modes. With variable-length instructions, these many variations can be provided efficiently and compactly.

The principal price to pay for variable-length instructions is an increase in the complexity of the CPU. Falling hardware prices, the use of microprogramming (discussed in Part IV), and a general increase in understanding the principles of CPU design have all contributed to making this a small price to pay.

The use of variable-length instructions does not remove the desirability of making all of the instruction lengths integrally related to the word length. Since the CPU does not know the length of the next instruction to be fetched, a typical strategy is to fetch a number of bytes or words equal to at least the longest possible instruction. This means that sometimes multiple instructions are fetched. However, as we shall see in Chapter 10, this is a good strategy to follow in any case.

Again, we look briefly at several variable-length designs. The IBM 370 and VAX, both of which are variable-length designs, are examined in some detail at the end of this section.

IBM 1401

The IBM 1401 was a popular second-generation, business-oriented system [BELL71b]. Memory in the 1401 is organized in 8-bit characters. For data, each character stores either a 6-bit character or a 4-bit code for a decimal digit. There is also a parity bit. The remaining bit is used as a delimiter, to indicate the start of an instruction or the end of a numeric or character string. Thus, not only instructions but data are of variable lengths.

Table 9-5 depicts the IBM 1401 instruction formats. Six different instruction lengths are possible. The first character contains a 6-bit opcode representing one of about 30 different instructions. Some operations, such as no-op, require only this single character. Other instructions may include zero, one, or two operand references, and zero or one op code extension.

All addressing is in the direct addressing mode. Operand references are 3 characters long. A clever way to save space is the use of *chained instructions.* With a chained instruction, the operands for the current operation are assumed to be at the same address as for the previous operation. This is the reason for needing an instruction delimiter in the op code character, since the length of an instruction can not fully be determined from the op code alone.

For some instructions, the op code is extended by an additional character positioned at the end of the instruction. An example is the particular test to be performed in a conditional branch instruction.

The instruction set design for the 1401 is straightforward and flexible. It appears to offer a remarkably compact way of representing a variety of instruction types.

PDP-11

The PDP-11 was designed to provide a powerful and flexible instruction set within the constraints of a 16-bit minicomputer [BELL70].

The PDP-11 employs a set of 8 16-bit general-purpose registers. Two of these registers have additional significance: one is used as a stack pointer for special-purpose stack operations, and one is used as the program counter, which contains the address of the next instruction. The unusual tactic of special purposes for general-purpose registers is repeated on the VAX and was discussed there.

Figure 9-5 shows the PDP-11 instruction formats. Thirteen different formats are used, encompassing zero-, one-, and two-address instruction types. The op code can vary from 4 to 16 bits in length. Register references are 6 bits in length. Three bits identify the register, and the remaining 3 bits identify the addressing

TABLE 9-5 IBM 1401 Instruction Formats

Length (char)	Location: M[1]	M[(1 + 1):(1 + 3)]	M[(1 + 4):(1 + 6)]	M[1 + 7]	Types
1	C[0]				No-op, halt, or single character to specify a chained instruction
2	C[0]	C[1]			The d character is used to specify additional instruction information (e.g., select, card stacker)
4	C[0]	C[1, 2, 3]			Unconditional branch instruction or single-address arithmetic; M[A] ← f(M[A])
5	C[0]	C[1, 2, 3]	C[4]		Conditional branch instruction; C[4] selects a specific test
7	C[0]	C[1, 2, 3]	C[4, 5, 6]		Two-address instruction; M[B] ← M[B] b M[A] (e.g., add, subtract)
8	C[0]	C[1, 2, 3]	C[4, 5, 6]	C[7]	Conditional branch based on Mp[B] character; d character is test character (e.g., branch if character equal)

Function of instruction characters:
C[0] opcode: always contains a word-mark flag or F bit.
C[1, 2, 3] = branch address for 1—Address register or first operand address for the A—Address register.
C[1] or C[4] or C[7] d—character; used as a single character for additional operation code information or a character for comparison, or to select a test.
C[4, 5, 6] primary operand (B—Address register specification).

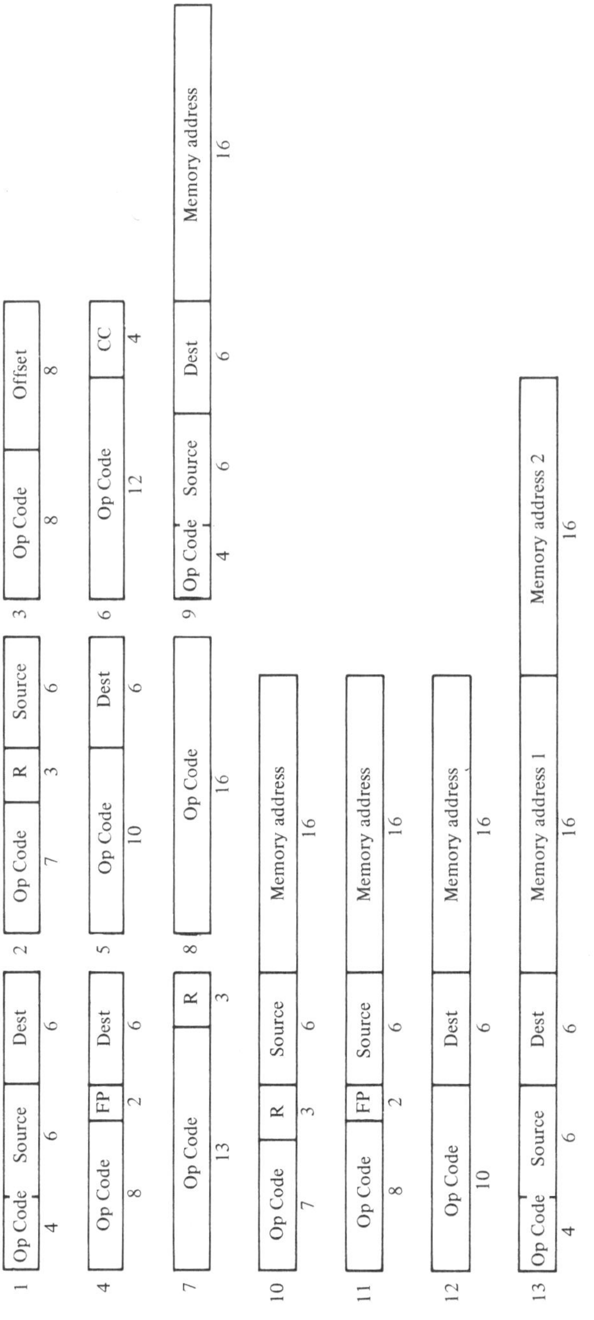

Source and dest each contain a 3-bit addressing mode field and a 3-bit register number;
FP is 1 of the floating point registers 0, 1, 2, or 3;
R is 1 of the general registers;
CC is the condition code field

FIGURE 9-5. Instruction formats used on the PDP-11; the numbers indicate the field lengths

mode. The PDP-11 is endowed with a rich set of addressing modes. As these are a subset of the VAX addressing modes, we refrain from a discussion here. One advantage of linking the addressing mode to the operand rather than the op code, as is sometimes done, is that any addressing mode can be used with any op code. As was mentioned, this independence is referred to as *orthogonality*.

PDP-11 instructions are usually 1 word (16 bits) long. For some instructions, one or two memory addresses are appended, so that 32-bit and 48-bit instructions are part of the repertoire. This provides for further flexibility in addressing.

The PDP-11 instruction set and addressing capability are complex. This increases both hardware cost and programming complexity. The advantage is that more efficient or compact programs can be developed.

80386/80486 Instruction Formats

The 80386/80486 is equipped with a variety of instruction formats. Of the elements described below, only the opcode field is always present. Figure 9-6 illustrates the general instruction format. Instructions are made up of optional instruction prefixes, a one- or two-byte opcode, an optional address specifier which consists of the Mod R/M byte and the Scale Index Byte, an optional displacement, and an optional immediate field.

Let us first consider the prefix bytes:

- *Repeat:* The REP prefixes specify repeated operation of a string, which enables the 80386/80486 to process strings much faster than with a regular software loop. There are five different REP prefixes: REP, REPE, REPZ, REPNE, and REPNZ. When the absolute REP prefix is present, the operation specified in the instruction is executed repeatedly on successive elements of the string; the number of repetitions is specified in register CX. The conditional REP prefix causes the instruction to repeat until the count in CX goes to zero or until the condition is met.
- *Address size:* Switches between 32-bit and 16-bit address generation.
- *Operand Size:* Switches between 32-bit and 16-bit operands.
- *Segment override:* Explicitly specifies which segment register an instruction should use, overriding the default segment-register selection generated by the 80386/80486 for that instruction.

The instruction itself includes the following fields:

- *Opcode:* one or two-byte opcode. The opcode may also include bits that specify if data is byte or full-size (16 or 32 bits depending on context), direction of data operation (to or from memory), and whether an immediate data field must be sign-extended.
- *Mod r/m:* This byte, and the next, provide addressing information. The Mod r/m byte specifies whether an operand is in a register or in memory; if it is in memory, then fields within the byte specify the addressing mode to be used. The Mod r/m byte consists of three fields: The Mod field (2 bits) combines with

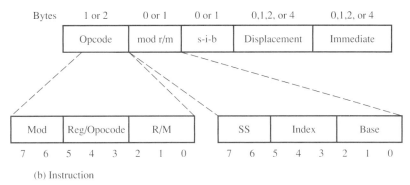

FIGURE 9-6. 80386/80486 instruction format

the r/m field to form 32 possible values, 8 registers and 24 indexing modes; the Reg/Opcode field (3 bits) specifies either a register number of three more bits of opcode information; the r/m field (3 bits) can specify a register as the location of an operand, or it can form part of the addressing-mode encoding in combination with the Mod field.

- *SIB:* Certain encoding of the Mod r/m byte specify the inclusion of the SIB byte to fully specify the addressing mode. The SIB byte consists of three fields: The SS field (2 bits) specifies the scale factor for scaled indexing; the Index field (3 bits) specifies the index register; the Base field (3 bits) specifies the base register.
- *Displacement:* When the addressing-mode specifier indicates that a displacement is used, an 8-, 16-, or 32-bit signed integer displacement field is added.
- *Immediate:* Provides the value of an 8-, 16-, or 32-bit operand.

Several comparisons may be useful here. In the 80386/80486 format, the addressing mode is provided as part of the opcode sequence, rather than with each operand. Since only one operand can have address-mode information, only one memory operand can be referenced in an instruction. In contrast, the VAX carries the address-mode information with each operand, allowing memory-to-memory operations. The 80386/80486 instructions are therefore more compact. However, if a memory-to-memory operation is required, the VAX can accomplish this in a single instruction.

The 80386/80486 format allows the use of not only 1-byte but 2-byte and 4-byte offsets for indexing. Although the use of the larger index offsets results in longer instructions, this feature provides needed flexibility. For example, it is useful in addressing large arrays or large stack frames. In contrast, the IBM S/370 instruction format allows offsets no greater than 4K bytes (12 bits of offset information), and the offset must be positive. When a location is not in reach of this offset, the compiler must generate extra code to generate the needed address. This problem is especially apparent in dealing with stack frames which have local variables occupying in excess of 4K bytes. As [DEWA90] puts it, "Generating code for the 370 is so painful as a result of that restriction that there have been compilers for the 370 that simply chose to limit the size of the stack frame to 4K bytes."

As can be seen, the encoding of the 80386/80486 instruction set is very complex. This has to do partly with the need to be backward compatible with the 8086 machine and partly with a desire on the part of the designers to provide every possible assistance to the compiler writer in producing efficient code. It is a matter of some debate whether an instruction set as complex as this is preferable to the opposite extreme of the RISC instruction sets that we examine later in this book.

IBM 370 Instruction Formats

The IBM 370 employs three instruction lengths: 2 bytes, 4 bytes, and 6 bytes. Two op code lengths are provided: 1 byte and 2 bytes. A total of ten different instruction formats are used. In most cases, an instruction includes two operands, but there are some one-operand and three-operand instructions.

Figure 9-7 illustrates the set of instructions for the 370. The first (leftmost) 2 bits of the op code specify the length and format of the instruction as follows:

- 00: 2 bytes, RR
- 01: 4 bytes, RX
- 10: 4 bytes, RRE/RS/RX/S/SI
- 11: 6 bytes, SS/SSE

We briefly describe each instruction format type:

- *Register and Register (RR):* All two-byte instructions are in this format. The two operand references are 4-bit register identifiers. Since many operations can be profitably performed with just the use of registers, this provides a very compact representation.
- *Register and Register Extended (RRE):* This format is used for a few special-purpose privileged instructions that are generally used only by the operating system. The extended op code allows additional operations.
- *Register and Indexed Storage (RX):* Most 4-byte instructions, such as the RX ones, reference one register and one virtual memory operand. The most common of these, the RX format, uses indexing. The first operand is a register. The second operand is referenced by the sum of the 12-bit displacement and the contents of a base and an index register, both of which are from the pool of general-purpose registers.
- *Register and Storage (RS):* This is the only 3-address format. As with RX, there are three register references, but in this case they refer to three different oper-

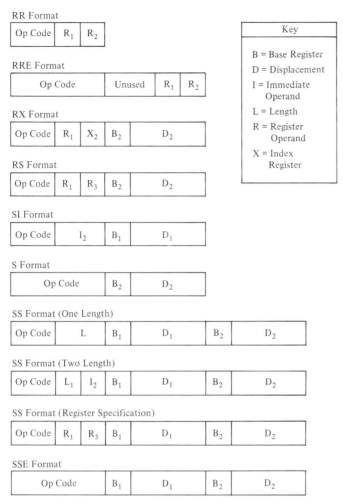

FIGURE 9-7.   IBM S/370 instruction formats

ands. The third register is used as a base register, associated with a 12-bit displacement; the others are pure register references.

- *Storage and Immediate (SI):* This is used for immediate addressing. One reference is a base plus displacement address. The other 8 bits are an immediate operand.
- *Storage (S):* These are privileged instructions used for I/O or system control functions. An extended 16-bit op code is used. The last 16 bits normally contain the base/displacement address of one operand. The other operand, if any, is implied by the op code.
- *Storage and Storage (SS):* This format occupies 6 bytes and references two virtual addresses. The remaining 8 bits can be used in one of three ways. In the one-length format, the 8-bit L field specifies the number of bytes to be oper-

ated on. For example, the Move Character (MVC) instruction moves a block of bytes from one location to another, with the start of each location specified as a base/displacement address. In the two-length format, two 4-bit L fields specify the size of the two operands in bytes. This format is used for decimal arithmetic instructions. For decimal arithmetic, decimal digits are stored in 4-bit fields, and the lengths of the two operands may differ. A few privileged instructions use the third variation, in which the second byte designates two general registers. The registers contain the length specification and/or other control information.

- *Storage and Storage Extended (SSE):* Some privileged instructions use an 8-bit op code and two 16-bit virtual memory address references.

Although the 370 instruction set is rich, the formats are straightforward and make reasonably efficient use of instruction length. Both register and memory references are used, in various combinations, and two op code lengths are employed. Three different instruction lengths are used. The results are difficult to criticize. Its strengths and weaknesses can perhaps be best understood by comparing it to a more flexible but more complex instruction set, that of the VAX.

VAX Instruction Formats

Most architectures provide a relatively small number of fixed instruction formats. This can cause two problems for the programmer. First, addressing mode and op code are not orthogonal. For example, for a given operation, one operand must come from a register and another from memory, or both from registers, and so on. Second, only a limited number of operands can be accommodated: typically, up to two. Since some operations inherently require more operands, various strategies must be used to achieve the desired result using two or more instructions.

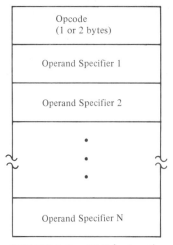

FIGURE 9-8. VAX instruction format

To avoid these problems, two criteria were used in designing the VAX instruction format [STRE78b]:

1. All instructions should have the "natural" number of operands.
2. All operands should have the same generality in specification.

The result is a highly variable instruction format, illustrated in Figure 9-8. An instruction consists of a 1- or 2-byte op code followed by from zero to six operand specifiers, depending on the op code. The minimum instruction length is 1 byte, and instructions of up to 37 bytes can be constructed! Figure 9-9 gives a few examples.

Hexidecimal Format		Explanation	Assembler Notation
0	5	Op Code for RSB	RSB Return from subroutine
D	4	Op Code for CLRL	CLRL R9
5	9	Register R9	Clear register R9
B	0	Op Code for MOVW	MOVW 356(R4), 25(R11)
C	4	Word Displacement Mode, Register R4	Move a word from address which is 356 plus contents of
6	4		R4 to address which is 25
0	1	356 in Hexadecimal	plus contents of R11
A	B	Byte Displacement Mode, Register R11	
1	9	25 in Hexadecimal	
C	1	Op Code for ADDL3	ADDL3 #5, RO, @ A[R2]
0	5	Short Literal 5	Add 5 to a 32-bit integer in RO and store the result in
5	0	Register Mode R0	address which is sum of A and 4 times the contents of
4	2	Index Prefix R2	R2
D	F	Indirect Word Relative (Displacement from PC)	
		Displacement from PC to Location A	

FIGURE 9-9. Examples of VAX instructions

Let us look at the parts of a VAX instruction. It begins with a 1-byte op code. This suffices to handle most VAX instructions. However, as there are over 300 different instructions, 8 bits are not enough. The hexadecimal codes FD and FF indicate an extended op code, with the remainder being specified in the second byte.

The remainder of the instruction consists of up to six operand specifiers. An operand specifier is, at minimum, a 1-byte format in which the leftmost 4 bits are the mode specifier (see Table 9-4) and the rightmost 4 bits specify one of 16 general-purpose registers. The only exception to this rule is the literal mode, which is signaled by the pattern 00 in the leftmost 2 bits, leaving space for a 6-bit literal. Because of this exception, a total of 12 different addressing modes can be specified.

An operand specifier often consists of just 1 byte, indicating an addressing mode and a register. The length of a specifier can be extended in two ways. First, a constant value of 1 or more bytes may immediately follow the first byte. An example of this is the displacement mode, in which an 8-, 16-, or 32-bit displacement is used. Second, an index mode of addressing may be used. In this case, the first byte of the operand specifier consists of the 4-bit mode code of 0100 and a 4-bit index register identifier. The remainder of the operand specifier consists of the base operand specifier, which may itself be 1 or more bytes in length.

The reader may be wondering, as the author did, what kind of instruction requires six operands. Surprisingly, the VAX has a number of such instructions. Consider

ADDP6 OP1, OP2, OP3, OP4, OP5, OP6

This instruction adds two packed decimal numbers. OP1 and OP2 specify the length and starting address of one BCD string; OP3 and OP4 specify a second string. These two are added, and the result is stored in the BCD string whose length and starting location are specified by OP5 and OP6.

The VAX instruction set provides for a wide variety of operations and addressing modes. This gives the programmer, such as the compiler writer, a very powerful and flexible tool for developing programs. In theory, this should lead to efficient machine-language compilations of high-level language programs and, in general, to effective and efficient use of CPU resources. The penalty to be paid for these benefits is the increased complexity of the CPU compared, say, to that of the S/370.

We will return to a consideration of these matters in Chapter 13, where we will examine the case for very simple instruction sets.

9.3

RECOMMENDED READING

The references cited in Chapter 8 are equally applicable to the material of this chapter. In addition, the reader may wish to consult [FLYN85] for a recent discussion and analysis of instruction set design issues, particularly those relating to formats.

9.4

PROBLEMS

9.1   Justify the assertion that a 32-bit instruction is probably much less than twice as useful as a 16-bit instruction.

9.2   Given the following memory values and a one-address machine with an accumulator, what values to the following instructions load into the accumulator?

- Word 20 contains 40.
- Word 30 contains 50.
- Word 40 contains 60.
- Word 50 contains 70.

(a) LOAD IMMEDIATE 20
(b) LOAD DIRECT 20
(c) LOAD INDIRECT 20
(d) LOAD IMMEDIATE 30
(e) LOAD DIRECT 30
(f) LOAD INDIRECT 30

9.3   Let the address stored in the program counter be designated by the symbol X1. The instruction stored in X1 has an address part (operand reference) X2. The operand needed to execute the instruction is stored in the memory word with address X3. An index register contains the value X4. What is the relationship between these various quantities of the addressing mode if the instruction is (a) direct; (b) indirect; (c) PC-relative; (d) indexed?

9.4   A PC-relative mode branch instruction is stored in memory at address 620_{10}. The branch is made to location 530_{10}. The address field in the instruction is 10 bits long. What is the binary value in the instruction?

9.5   How many times does the CPU need to refer to memory when it fetches and executes an indirect-address-mode instruction if the instruction is (a) a computation requiring a single operand; (b) a branch?

9.6   The IBM 370 does not provide indirect addressing. Assume that the address of an operand is in main memory. How would you access the operand?

9.7   Why was IBM's decision to move from 36 bits to 32 bits per word wrenching, and to whom?

9.8   Explain why the VAX PC addressing modes may have limited usefulness because of the use of virtual addresses on the VAX.

9.9   In [COOK82], the author proposes that the PC-relative addressing modes be eliminated in favor of other modes, such as the use of a stack. What is the disadvantage of this proposal?

9.10 The autodecrement addressing mode on the VAX may not be used with register 15. Why not?

9.11 What VAX addressing modes can be used to support stack operations?

9.12 Assume an instruction set that uses a fixed 16-bit instruction length. Operand specifiers are 6 bits in length. There are K two-operand instructions and L zero-operand instructions. What is the maximum number of one-operand instructions that can be supported?

9.13 Design a variable-length op code to allow all of the following to be encoded in a 36-bit instruction:

7   instructions with two 15-bit addresses and one 3-bit register number
500 instructions with one 15-bit address and one 3-bit register number
50   instructions with no addresses or registers

9.14 Consider the results of Problem 8.4. Assume that M is a 16-bit memory address and that X, Y, and Z are either 16-bit addresses or 4-bit register numbers. The 1-address machine uses an accumulator, and the 2- and 3-address machines have 16 registers and instructions operating on all combinations of memory locations and registers. Assuming 8-bit op codes and instruction lengths that are multiples of 4 bits, how many bits does each machine need to compute X?

9.15 The text states that the VAX *absolute* addressing mode is simple indirect addressing as defined in the general discussion. Table 9-4 defines this mode as EA = ((PC)). In this register indirect addressing?

9.16 Is there any possible justification for an instruction with two op codes?

9.17 At a certain point in time, the base and index registers in an IBM 370 contain 004AF6C0 and 0000164E, respectively.

(a) Find the effective address of an RX format instruction with displacement D equal to 2F2.

(b) What should the value of D be for the effective address to be (b1) 4B0D8D; (b2) 4B1F18?

9.18 The 80X86 includes the following instruction:

IMUL op1, op2, immediate

This instruction multiplies op2, which may be either register or memory, by the immediate operand value, and places the result in op1, which must be a register. There is no other three-operand instruction of this sort in the instruction set. What is the possible use of such an instruction? Hint: consider indexing.

CHAPTER 10

CPU Structure and Function

The purpose of this chapter is to discuss aspects of the CPU not yet covered in Part III, and then to pull all of the material of Part III together to give a complete picture of CPU structure and function.

Recall that the major components of a CPU are the ALU, the control unit, and registers (Figure 1-5). The functionality of the ALU was described in Chapter 7. The discussion of instruction set architecture in Chapters 8 and 9 describes, in large part, the functionality of the control unit.

This chapter begins with a summary of CPU organization. Registers, which form the internal memory of the CPU, are then analyzed. We are then in a position to return to the discussion (begun in Section 3.2) of the instruction cycle. A description of the instruction cycle and a common technique known as *instruction pipelining* complete our description of the functionality of the CPU's control unit. The internal structure and function of the control unit are described in Part IV.

The chapter concludes with an examination of the IBM S/370 and VAX CPU organizations.

10.1

PROCESSOR ORGANIZATION

To understand the organization of the CPU, let us consider the requirements placed on the CPU, the things that it must do:

- *Fetch Instructions:* The CPU must read instructions from memory.
- *Interpret Instructions:* The instruction must be decoded to determine what action is required.
- *Fetch Data:* The execution of an instruction may require reading data from memory or an I/O module.

- *Process Data:* The execution of an instruction may require performing some arithmetic or logical operation on data.
- *Write Data:* The results of an execution may require writing data to memory or an I/O module.

In order to be able to do these things, it should be clear that the CPU needs to temporarily store some data. It must remember the location of the last instruction so that it can know where to get the next instruction. It needs to store instructions and data temporarily while an instruction is being executed. In other words, the CPU needs a small internal memory.

Figure 10-1 is a simplified view of a CPU, indicating its connection to the rest of the system via the system bus. A similar interface would be needed for any of the interconnection structures described in Chapter 3. The reader will recall that the major components of the CPU are an *arithmetic and logic unit* (ALU) and a *control unit* (CU). The ALU does the actual computation or processing of data. The control unit controls the movement of data and instructions into and out of the CPU and controls the operation of the ALU. In addition, the figure shows a minimal internal memory, consisting of a set of storage locations, called *registers*.

Figure 10-2 is a slightly more detailed view of the CPU. The data transfer and logic control paths are indicated, including an element labeled *internal CPU bus*. This element is needed to transfer data between the various registers and the ALU, since the ALU in fact operates only on data in the internal CPU memory. The figure also shows typical basic elements of the ALU. Note the similarity between the internal structure of the computer as a whole and the internal structure of the CPU. In both cases, there is a small collection of major elements (computer: CPU, I/O, memory; CPU: control unit, ALU, registers) connected by data paths.

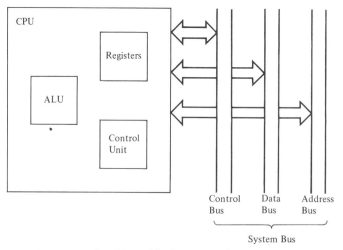

FIGURE 10-1. The CPU with the system bus

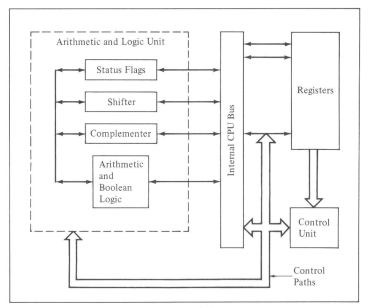

FIGURE 10-2.   Internal structure of the CPU

REGISTER ORGANIZATION

As we discussed in Chapter 4, a computer system employs a memory hierarchy. At higher levels of the hierarchy, memory is faster, smaller, and more expensive (per bit). Within the CPU, there is a set of registers that function as a level of memory above main memory and cache in the hierarchy. The registers in the CPU serve two functions:

* *User-Visible Registers:* These enable the machine- or assembly-language programmer to minimize main-memory references by optimizing use of registers.
* *Control and Status Registers:* These are used by the control unit to control the operation of the CPU and by privileged, operating-system programs to control the execution of programs.

There is not a clean separation of registers into these two categories. For example, on some machines the program counter is user visible (e.g., VAX), but on many it is not. For purposes of the following discussion, however, we will use these categories.

User-Visible Registers

A user-visible register is one that may be referenced by means of the machine language that the CPU executes. Virtually all contemporary CPU designs provide for a number of user-visible registers, as opposed to a single accumulator. We can characterize these in the following categories:

- General Purpose
- Data
- Address
- Condition Codes

General-purpose registers can be assigned to a variety of functions by the programmer. Sometimes, their use within the instruction set is orthogonal to the operation. That is, any general-purpose register can contain the operand for any op code. This provides true general-purpose register use. Often, however, there are restrictions. For example, there may be dedicated registers for floating-point operations.

In some cases, general-purpose registers can be used for addressing functions (e.g., register indirect, displacement). In other cases, there is a partial or clean separation between data registers and address registers. *Data registers* may be used only to hold data and cannot be employed in the calculation of an operand address. *Address registers* may themselves be somewhat general purpose, or they may be devoted to a particular addressing mode. Examples include

- *Segment Pointers:* In a machine with segmented addressing (see Section 6.3), a segment register holds the address of the base of the segment. There may be multiple registers: for example, one for the operating system and one for the current process.
- *Index Registers:* These are used for indexed addressing and may be auto-indexed.
- *Stack Pointer:* If there is user-visible stack addressing, then typically the stack is in memory and there is a dedicated register that points to the top of the stack. This allows implicit addressing; that is, push, pop, and other stack instructions need not contain an explicit stack operand.

There are several design issues to be addressed here. An important one is whether to use completely general-purpose registers or to specialize their use. We have already touched on this issue in the preceding chapter, since it affects instruction set design. With the use of specialized registers, it can generally be implicit in the op code which type of register a certain operand specifier refers to. The operand specifier must only identify one of a set of specialized registers rather than one out of all the registers, thus saving bits. On the other hand, this specialization limits the programmer's flexibility. There is no final and best solution to this design issue, but, as was mentioned, the trend seems to be toward the use of specialized registers.

Another design issue is the number of registers, either general purpose or data plus address, to be provided. Again, this affects instruction set design since more registers require more operand specifier bits. As we previously discussed, somewhere between 8 and 32 registers appears optimum [LUND77]. Fewer registers results in more memory references; more registers does not noticeably reduce memory references (e.g., see [WILL90]). However, a new approach, which finds advantage in the use of hundreds of registers, is exhibited in some RISC systems and is discussed in Chapter 13.

Finally, there is the issue of register length. Registers that must hold addresses obviously must be at least long enough to hold the largest address. Data registers should be able to hold values of most data types. Some machines allow two contiguous registers to be used as one for holding double-length values.

A final category of registers, which is at least partially visible to the user, holds *condition codes* (also referred to as *flags*). Condition codes are bits set by the CPU hardware as the result of operations. For example, an arithmetic operation may produce a positive, negative, zero, or overflow result. In addition to the result itself being stored in a register or memory, a condition code is also set. The code may subsequently be tested as part of a conditional branch operation.

Condition code bits are collected into one or more registers. Usually, they form part of a control register. Generally, machine instructions allow these bits to be read by implicit reference, but they cannot be altered by the programmer.

In some machines, a subroutine call will result in the automatic saving of all user-visible registers, to be restored on return. The saving and restoring is performed by the CPU as part of the execution of call and return instructions. This allows each subroutine to use the user-visible registers independently. On other machines, it is the responsibility of the programmer to save the contents of the relevant user-visible registers prior to a subroutine call, by including instructions for this purpose in the program.

Control and Status Registers

There are a variety of CPU registers that are employed to control the operation of the CPU. Most of these, on most machines, are not visible to the user. Some of them may be visible to machine instructions executed in a control or operating-system mode.

Of course, different machines will have different register organizations and use different terminology. We list here a reasonably complete list of register types, with a brief description.

Four registers are essential to instruction execution:

* *Program Counter (PC):* Contains the address of an instruction to be fetched.
* *Instruction Register (IR):* Contains the instruction most recently fetched.
* *Memory Address Register (MAR):* Contains the address of a location in memory.
* *Memory Buffer Register (MBR):* Contains a word of data to be written to memory or the word most recently read.

The program counter contains an instruction address. Typically, the program counter is updated by the CPU after each instruction fetch so that it always points to the next instruction to be executed. A branch or skip instruction will also modify the contents of the PC. The fetched instruction is loaded into an instruction register, where the op code and operand specifiers are analyzed.

Data are exchanged with memory using the MAR and MBR. In a bus organized system, the MAR connects directly to the address bus, and the MBR connects directly to the data bus. User-visible registers, in turn, exchange data with the MBR.

The four registers just mentioned are used for the movement of data between the CPU and memory. Within the CPU, data must be presented to the ALU for processing. The ALU may have direct access to the MBR and user-visible registers. Alternatively, there may be additional buffering registers at the boundary to the ALU; these registers serve as input and output registers for the ALU and exchange data with the MBR and user-visible registers.

All CPU designs include a register or set of registers, often known as the *program status word* (PSW), that contain status information. The PSW typically contains condition codes plus other status information. Common fields or flags include the following:

- *Sign:* Contains the sign bit of the result of the last arithmetic operation.
- *Zero:* Set when the result is 0.
- *Carry:* Set if an operation resulted in a carry (addition) into or borrow (subtraction) out of a high-order bit. Used for multiword arithmetic operations.
- *Equal:* Set if a logical compare result is equality.
- *Overflow:* Used to indicate arithmetic overflow.
- *Interrupt Enable/Disable:* Used to enable or disable interrupts.
- *Supervisor:* Indicates whether the CPU is executing in supervisor or user mode. Certain privileged instructions can be executed only in supervisor mode, and certain areas of memory can be accessed only in supervisor mode.

There are a number of other registers related to status and control that might be found in a particular CPU design. In addition to the PSW, there may be a pointer to a block of memory containing additional status information (e.g., process control blocks). In machines using vectored interrupts, an interrupt vector register may be provided. If a stack is used to implement certain functions (e.g., subroutine call), then a system stack pointer is needed. A page table pointer is used with a virtual memory system. Finally, registers may be used in the control of I/O operations.

A number of factors go into the design of the control and status register organization. One key issue is operating system support. Certain types of control information are of specific utility to the operating system. If the CPU designer has a functional understanding of the operating system to be used, then the register organization can to some extent be tailored to the operating system.

Another key design decision is the allocation of control information between registers and memory. It is common to dedicate the first (lowest) few hundred or thousand words of memory for control purposes. The designer must decide how much control information should be in registers and how much in memory. The usual tradeoff of cost versus speed arises.

Intel 8085 CPU Organization

As an example of the organization of CPU registers and their relationship to other CPU components, let us consider the relatively simply Intel 8085 [INTE81], which is an enhanced version of the Intel 8080.

The organization, in simplified form, of the 8085 is shown in Figure 10-3. The CPU is organized around a single 8-bit internal bus. Connected to the bus are the following:

- *Accumulator:* Used as a temporary buffer to store input to the ALU. It is also user visible and is addressed in some instructions.
- *Temporary Register:* The other ALU input.
- *Flags:* These are set as a result of ALU operations.
- *ALU Output:* The result of an ALU operation is placed on the bus.
- *Instruction Register (IR):* Loaded from the MBR via the bus.
- *Register Array:* Discussed presently.
- *Address/Data Buffer:* This buffer connects to multiplexed bus lines. Some of the time, this buffer acts as a memory buffer register (MBR) to exchange data with the system bus. At other times it acts as the low-order 8 bits of a memory address register (MAR). This multiplexing allows the 8085 package to have more pins available for control signals to the system bus.
- *Address Buffer:* Used as the high-order 8 bits of the MAR.

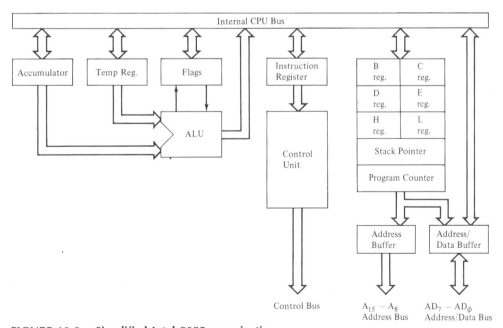

FIGURE 10-3. Simplified Intel 8085 organization

The 8085 connects to the external world via address, data, and control buses. The control unit controls the movement of data into, out of, and within the CPU. It also controls the functioning of the ALU. For clarity the signal lines emanating from the control unit are not depicted.

The register array contains five 16-bit registers. The B–C, D–E, and H–L registers are user visible, as is the stack pointer, which is used for stack-oriented machine instructions. The first three of the registers can be treated either as a single 16-bit register each or as two 8-bit registers each. Any of these registers may be loaded, 8 bits at a time, from the internal bus or transferred to the address buffer or address/data buffer. In addition, treated as 16-bit registers, any of the registers can be transferred to the memory address register that connects to the external address bus. The control unit activates internal data paths within the register array to effect a transfer to or from the internal bus or to the address buffer and/or address/data buffer.

The program counter is moved to the MAR (address plus address/data buffers) to begin the fetching of the next instruction. The instruction is brought in through the address/data buffer and internal CPU bus to the instruction register, from where it is decoded and executed by the control unit. Most 8085 instructions are 8 bits long. Some instructions are 2 or 3 bytes long, requiring multiple 8-bit fetches prior to execution.

Input to the ALU is provided by the accumulator and temporary register. The ALU also provides output to a 5-bit register of flags, which are

- Z: Result of ALU operation is zero(1) or nonzero(0).
- S: Sign of result of ALU operation.
- P: Parity of result of ALU operation is even(1)/odd(0).
- CY: ALU operation resulted in carry(1)/no-carry(0).
- AC: ALU operation resulted in carry(1)/no-carry(0) between the fourth and fifth bits.

As an example, the 8085 instruction ADD B causes the contents of register B to be added to the contents of the accumulator, with the result placed in the accumulator. To execute this instruction, the control unit moves the contents of register B to the temporary register. The ALU performs the add operation on its inputs. The result is placed on the internal CPU bus and copied into the accumulator. The ALU also updates the flags to reflect the results of the add.

Example Microprocessor Register Organizations

It is instructive to examine and compare the register organization of comparable systems. In this section, we look at three 16-bit microprocessors that were designed at about the same time: the Zilog Z8000 [PEUT79], the Intel 8086 [MORS78, HEYW83], and the Motorola MC68000 [STRI79]. Figure 10-4 depicts the register organization of each; purely internal registers, such as a memory address register, are not shown.

The Z8000 makes use of 16 16-bit general-purpose registers, which can be used

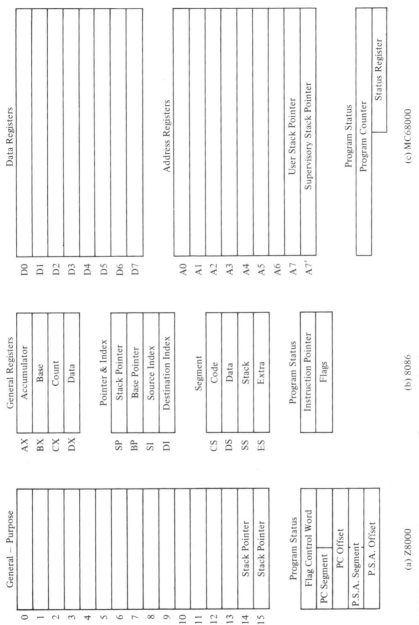

FIGURE 10-4. Microprocessor register organizations

for data, addresses, and indexing. The designers felt that it was more important to provide a regularized, general set of registers than to save instruction bits by using special-purpose registers. Further, they preferred to leave it to the programmer to assign functions to registers, assuming that there might be different functional breakdowns for different applications. The registers can also be used for 8-bit and 32-bit operations. A segmented address space is used (7-bit segment number, 16-bit offset), and two registers are needed to hold a single address. Two of the registers are also used as implied stack pointers for system mode and normal mode.

The Z8000 also includes five registers related to program status. Two registers hold the program counter and two the address of a Program Status Area in memory. A 16-bit flag register holds various status and control bits.

The Intel 8086 takes a different approach to register organization. Every register is special purpose, although some registers are also usable as general purpose. The 8086 contains four 16-bit data registers that are addressable on a byte or 16-bit basis, and four 16-bit pointer and index registers. The data registers can be used as general purpose in some instructions. In others, the registers are used implicitly. For example, a multiply instruction always uses the accumulator. The four pointer registers are also used implicitly in a number of operations; each contains a segment offset. There are also four 16-bit segment registers. Three of the four segment registers are used in a dedicated, implicit fashion, to point to the segment of the current instruction (useful for branch instructions), a segment containing data, and a segment containing a stack, respectively. These dedicated and implicit uses provide for compact encoding at the cost of reduced flexibility. The 8086 also includes an instruction pointer and a set of 1-bit status and control flags.

The Motorola MC68000 falls somewhere between the design philosophies of the Zilog and Intel microprocessors. The MC68000 partitions its 32-bit registers into eight data registers and nine address registers. The eight data registers are used primarily for data manipulation and are used in addressing only as index registers. The width of the registers allows 8-, 16-, and 32-bit data operations, determined by opcode. The address registers contain 32-bit (no segmentation) addresses; two of these registers are also used as stack pointers, one for users and one for the operating system, depending on the current execution mode. Both registers are numbered 7, since only one can be used at a time. The MC68000 also includes a 32-bit program counter and a 16-bit status register.

Like the Zilog designers, the Motorola team wanted a very regular instruction set, with no special-purpose registers. A concern for code efficiency led them to divide the registers into two functional components, saving one bit on each register specifier. This seems a reasonable compromise between complete generality and code compaction.

The point of this comparison should be clear. There is, as yet, no universally accepted philosophy concerning the best way to organize CPU registers [TOON81]. As with overall instruction set design and so many other CPU design issues, it is still a matter of judgment and taste.

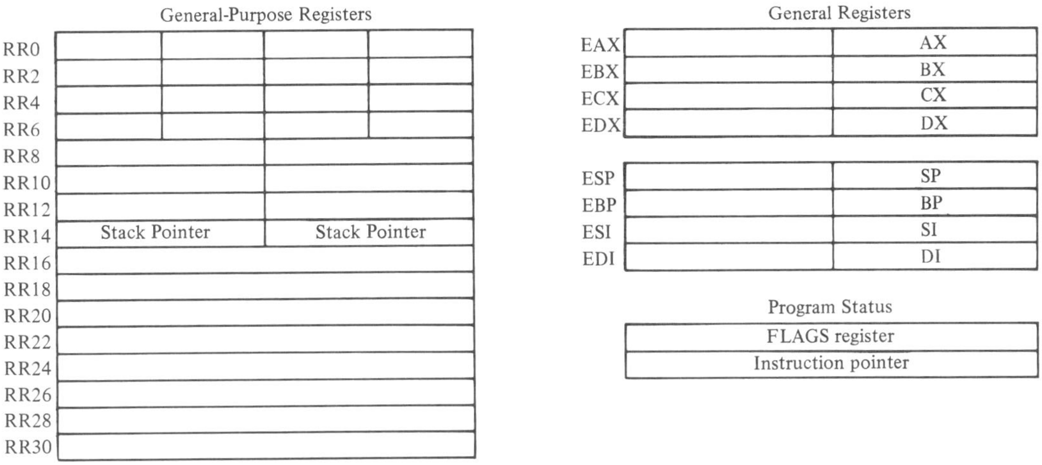

General-Purpose Registers

RR0				
RR2				
RR4				
RR6				
RR8			
RR10			
RR12			
RR14	Stack Pointer	Stack Pointer	
RR16		
RR18		
RR20		
RR22		
RR24		
RR26		
RR28		
RR30		

General Registers

EAX		AX
EBX		BX
ECX		CX
EDX		DX

ESP		SP
EBP		BP
ESI		SI
EDI		DI

Program Status

FLAGS register
Instruction pointer

(a) Z80,000   (b) 80386

FIGURE 10-5. Register organization extensions for 32-bit microprocessors

A second instructive point concerning register organization design is illustrated in Figure 10-5. This figure shows the user-visible register organization for the Zilog 80,000 [PHIL85] and the Intel 80386 [ELAY85], which are 32-bit microprocessors designed as extensions of the Z8000 and 8086, respectively[1]. Both of these new processors use 32-bit registers. However, to provide upward compatibility for programs written on the earlier machines, both of the new processors retain the original register organization embedded in the new organization. Given this design constraint, the architects of the 32-bit processors had limited flexibility in designing the register organization.

10.3

THE INSTRUCTION CYCLE

In Section 3.2, we described the CPU's instruction cycle. Figure 10-6 repeats one of the figures used in that description (Figure 3-9). To recall, an instruction cycle includes the following subcycles:

- *Fetch:* Read the next instruction from memory into the CPU.
- *Execute:* Interpret the op code and perform the indicated operation.
- *Interrupt:* If interrupts are enabled and an interrupt has occurred, save the current process state and service the interrupt.

We are now in a position to elaborate somewhat on the instruction cycle. First, we must introduce one additional subcycle, known as the indirect cycle.

[1]Since the MC68000 already uses 32-bit registers, the MC68020 [MACG84], which is a full 32-bit extension, uses the same register organization.

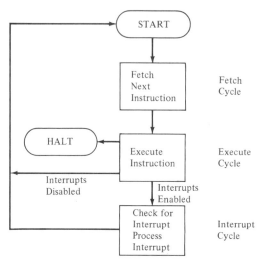

FIGURE 10-6. Instruction cycle with interrupts

The Indirect Cycle

We have seen, in Chapter 9, that the execution of an instruction may involve one or more operands in memory, each of which requires a memory access. Further, if indirect addressing is used, then additional memory accesses are required.

We can think of the fetching of indirect addresses as one more instruction subcycle. The result is shown in Figure 10-7. The main line of activity consists of alternating instruction fetch and instruction execution activities. After an instruction is fetched, it is examined to determine if any indirect addressing is involved. If so, the required operands are fetched using indirect addressing. Following execution, an interrupt may be processed before the next instruction fetch.

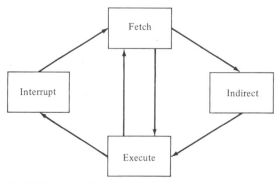

FIGURE 10-7. The instruction cycle

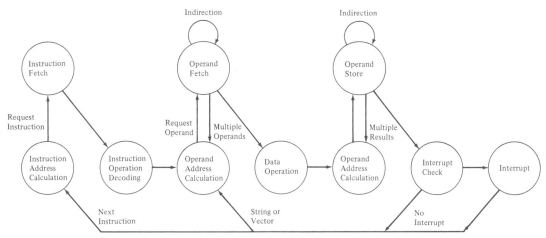

FIGURE 10-8.   Instruction cycle state diagram

Another way to view this process is shown in Figure 10-8, which is a revised version of Figure 3-12. This illustrates more correctly the nature of the instruction cycle. Once an instruction is fetched, its operand specifiers must be identified. Each input operand in memory is then fetched, and this process may require indirect addressing. Register-based operands need not be fetched. Once the op code is executed, a similar process may be needed to store the result in main memory.

Data Flow

The exact sequence of events during an instruction cycle depends on the design of the CPU. We can, however, indicate in general terms what must happen. Let us assume a CPU that employs a memory address register (MAR), a memory buffer register (MBR), a program counter (PC), and an instruction register (IR).

During the *fetch cycle,* an instruction is read from memory. Figure 10-9 shows the flow of data during this cycle. The PC contains the address of the next instruction to be fetched. This address is moved to the MAR and placed on the address bus. The control unit requests a memory read, and the result is placed on the data bus and copied into the MBR and then moved to the IR. Meanwhile, the PC is incremented by 1, preparatory for the next fetch.

Once the fetch cycle is over, the control unit examines the contents of the IR to determine if it contains an operand specifier using indirect addressing. If so, an *indirect cycle* is performed. As shown in Figure 10-10, this is a simple cycle. The rightmost N bits of the MBR, which contain the address reference, are transferred to the MAR. Then the control unit requests a memory read, to get the desired address of the operand into the MBR.

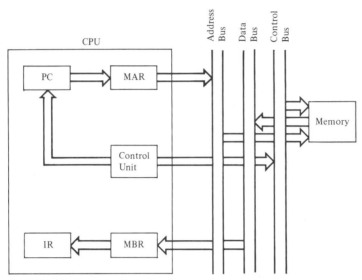

FIGURE 10-9. Data flow, fetch cycle

The fetch and indirect cycles are simple and predictable. The *instruction cycle* takes many forms since the form depends on which of the various machine instructions is in the IR. This cycle may involve transferring data among registers, read or write from memory or I/O, and/or the invocation of the ALU.

Like the fetch and indirect cycles, the *interrupt cycle* is simple and predictable

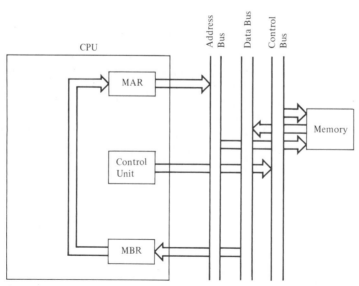

FIGURE 10-10. Data flow, indirect cycle

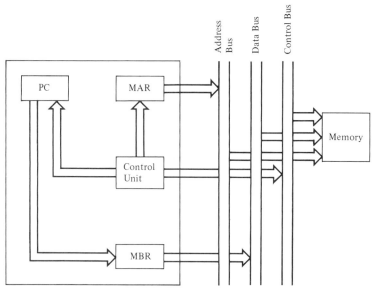

FIGURE 10-11.   Data flow, interrupt cycle

(Figure 10-11). The current contents of the PC must be saved so that the CPU can resume normal activity after the interrupt. Thus the contents of the PC are transferred to the MBR to be written into memory. The special memory location reserved for this purpose is loaded into the MAR from the control unit. It might, for example, be a stack pointer. The PC is loaded with the address of the interrupt routine. As a result, the next instruction cycle will begin by fetching the appropriate instruction.

10.4

INSTRUCTION PIPELINING

As computer systems evolve, greater performance can be achieved by taking advantage of improvements in technology, such as faster circuitry. In addition, organizational enhancements to the CPU can improve performance. We have already seen some examples of this, such as the use of multiple registers rather than a single accumulator, and the use of a cache memory. Another organizational approach, which is quite common, is instruction pipelining.

Pipelining Strategy

Instruction pipelining is similar to the use of an assembly line in a manufacturing plant. An assembly line takes advantage of the fact that a product goes through various stages of production. By laying the production process out in an assembly line, products at various stages can be worked on simultaneously. This process is also referred to as *pipelining,* because, as in a pipeline, new inputs are accepted at one end before previously accepted inputs appear as outputs at the other end.

To apply this concept to instruction execution, we must recognize that, in fact, an instruction has a number of stages. Figure 10-8, for example, breaks the instruction cycle up into ten tasks, which occur in sequence. Clearly, there should be some opportunity for pipelining.

As a simple approach, consider subdividing instruction processing into two stages: fetch instruction and execute instruction. There are times during the execution of an instruction when main memory is not being accessed. This time could be used to fetch the next instruction in parallel with the execution of the current one. Figure 10-12a depicts this approach. The pipeline has two independent stages. The first stage fetches an instruction and buffers it. When the second stage is free, the first stage passes it the buffered instruction. While the second stage is executing the instruction, the first stage takes advantage of any unused memory cycles to fetch and buffer the next instruction. This is called *instruction prefetch* or *fetch overlap.*

It should be clear that this process will speed up instruction execution. If the fetch and instruction stages were of equal duration, the instruction cycle time would be halved. However, if we look more closely at this pipeline (Figure 10-12b), we will see that this doubling of execution rate is unlikely for two reasons:

1. The execution time will generally be longer than the fetch time. Execution will involve reading and storing operands and the performance of some operation. Thus the fetch stage may have to wait for some time before it can empty its buffer.

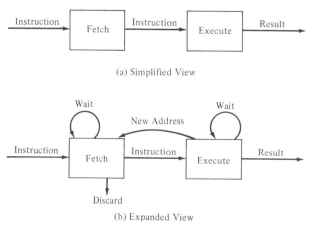

(a) Simplified View

(b) Expanded View

FIGURE 10-12. Two-stage instruction pipeline

2. A conditional branch instruction makes the address of the next instruction to be fetched unknown. Thus the fetch stage must wait until it receives the next instruction address from the execute stage. The execute stage may then have to wait while the next instruction is fetched.

The time loss from the second reason can be reduced by guessing. A simple rule is the following: When a conditional branch instruction is passed on from the fetch to the execute stage, the fetch stage fetches the next instruction in memory after the branch instruction. Then, if the branch is not taken, no time is lost. If the branch is taken, the fetched instruction must be discarded and a new instruction fetched.

While these factors reduce the potential effectiveness of the two-stage pipeline, some speedup occurs. To gain further speedup, the pipeline must have more stages. Let us consider the following decomposition of the instruction processing.

* *Fetch Instruction (FI):* Read the next expected instruction into a buffer.
* *Decode Instruction (DI):* Determine the opcode and the operand specifiers.
* *Calculate Operands (CO):* Calculate the effective address of each source operand. This may involve displacement, register indirect, indirect, or other forms of address calculation.
* *Fetch Operands (FO):* Fetch each operand from memory. Operands in registers need not be fetched.
* *Execute Instruction (EI):* Perform the indicated operation and store the result, if any, in the specified destination operand location.
* *Write Operand (WO):* Store the result in memory.

With this decomposition, the various stages will be of more nearly equal duration. For the sake of illustration, let us assume equal duration. Then, Figure 10-13 shows that a six-stage pipeline can reduce the execution time for 9 instructions from 54 time units to 14 time units.

Several comments: The diagram assumes that each instruction goes through all six stages of the pipeline. This will not always be the case. For example, a load instruction does not need the WO stage. However, to simplify the pipeline hardware, the timing is set up assuming that each instruction requires all six stages. Also, the diagram assumes that all of the stages can be performed in parallel. In particular, it is assumed that there are no memory conflicts. For example, the FI, FO, and WO stages involve a memory access. The diagram implies that all of these accesses can occur simultaneously. Most memory systems will not permit that. However, the desired value may be in cache, or the FO or WO stage may be null. Thus, much of the time, memory conflicts will not slow down the pipeline.

Several other factors serve to limit the performance enhancement. If the six stages are not of equal duration, there will be some waiting involved at various pipeline stages, as discussed before for the two-stage pipeline. Another difficulty is the conditional branch instruction, which can invalidate several instruction fetches. A similar unpredictable event is an interrupt. Figure 10-14 illus-

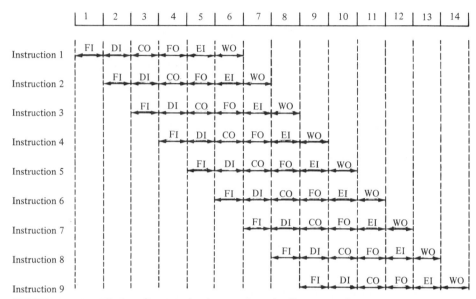

FIGURE 10-13. Timing diagram for instruction pipeline operation

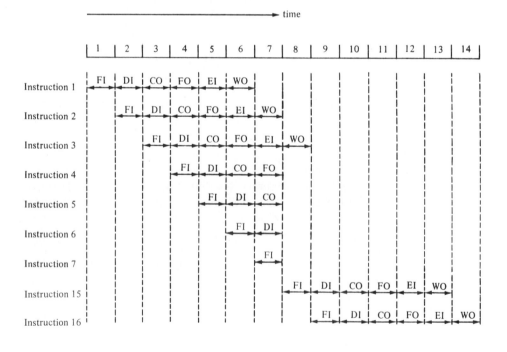

Branch Penalty

FIGURE 10-14. The effect of a conditional branch on instruction pipeline operation

trates the effects of the conditional branch, using the same program as Figure 10-13. Assume that instruction 3 is a conditional branch to instruction 15. Until the instruction is executed, there is no way of knowing which instruction will come next. The pipeline, in this example, simply loads the next instruction in sequence (instruction 4) and proceeds. In Figure 10-13, the branch is not taken, and we get the full performance benefit of the enhancement. In Figure 10-14, the branch is taken. This is not determined until the end of time unit 7. At this point, the pipeline must be cleared of instructions that are not useful. During time unit 8, instruction 15 enters the pipeline. No instructions complete during time units 9 through 12; this is the performance penalty incurred because we could not anticipate the branch. Figure 10-15 indicates the logic needed for pipelining to account for branches and interrupts.

Other problems arise that did not appear in our simple two-stage organization. The CO stage may depend on the contents of a register that could be altered by a previous instruction that is still in the pipeline. Other such register and memory conflicts could occur. The system must contain logic to account for this type of conflict.

From the preceding discussion, it might appear that the greater the number of stages in the pipeline, the faster the execution rate. Some of the IBM S/360 designers pointed out two factors that frustrate this seemingly simple pattern for high-performance design [ANDE67], and they remain true today:

1. At each stage of the pipeline, there is some overhead involved in moving data from buffer to buffer and in performing various preparation and delivery functions. This overhead can appreciably lengthen the total execution time of a single instruction. This is significant when sequential instructions are logically dependent, either through heavy use of branching or through memory access dependencies.
2. The amount of control logic required to handle memory and register dependencies and to optimize the use of the pipeline increases enormously with the number of stages. This can lead to a situation where the control logic controlling the gating between stages is more complex than the stages being controlled.

Instruction pipelining is a powerful technique for enhancing performance but requires careful design to achieve optimum results with reasonable complexity.

Dealing with Branches

One of the major problems in designing an instruction pipeline is assuring a steady flow of instructions to the initial stages of the pipeline. The primary impediment, as we have seen, is the conditional branch instruction. Until the instruction is actually executed, it is impossible to determine whether the branch will be taken or not.

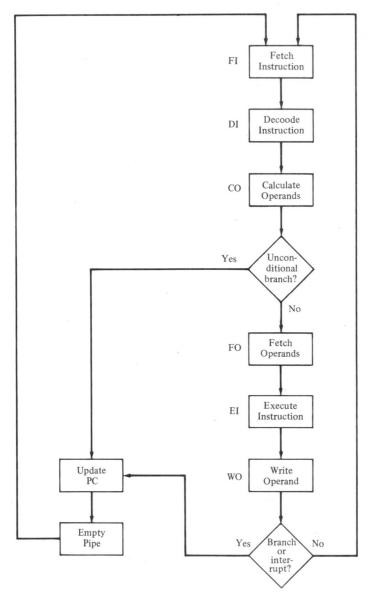

FIGURE 10-15. Six-stage CPU instruction pipeline

A variety of approaches have been taken for dealing with conditional branches:

- Multiple streams
- Prefetch branch target
- Loop buffer

- Branch prediction
- Delayed branch

Multiple Streams

A simple pipeline suffers a penalty for a branch instruction because it must choose one of two instructions to fetch next and may make the wrong choice. A brute-force approach is to replicate the initial portions of the pipeline and allow the pipeline to fetch both instructions, making use of two streams. There are several problems with this approach:

- With multiple pipelines there are contention delays for access to the registers and to memory.
- Additional branch instructions may enter the pipeline (either stream) before the original branch decision is resolved. Each such instruction needs an additional stream.

Despite these drawbacks, this strategy can improve performance. Examples of machines with two or more pipeline streams are the IBM 370/168 and the IBM 3033.

Prefetch Branch Target

When a conditional branch is recognized, the target of the branch is prefetched, in addition to the instruction following the branch. This target is then saved until the branch instruction is executed. If the branch is taken, the target has already been prefetched.
   The IBM 360/91 uses this approach.

Loop Buffer

A loop buffer is a small, very high-speed memory maintained by the instruction fetch stage of the pipeline, and containing the n most recently fetched instructions, in sequence. If a branch is to be taken, the hardware first checks whether the branch target is within the buffer. If so, the next instruction is fetched from the buffer. The loop buffer has three benefits:

1. With the use of prefetching, the loop buffer will contain some instruction sequentially ahead of the current instruction fetch address. Thus instructions fetched in sequence will be available without the usual memory access time.
2. If a branch occurs to a target just a few locations ahead of the address of the branch instruction, the target will already be in the buffer. This is useful for the rather common occurrence of IF-THEN and IF-THEN-ELSE sequences.
3. This strategy is particularly well suited to dealing with loops, or iterations, hence the name loop buffer. If the loop buffer is large enough to contain all of the instructions in a loop, then those instructions need to be fetched from

memory only once, for the first iteration. For subsequent iterations, all of the needed instructions are already in the buffer.

The loop buffer is similar in principle to a cache dedicated to instructions. The differences are that the loop buffer only retains instructions in sequence and is much smaller in size and hence lower in cost.

Figure 10-16 gives an example of a loop buffer. If the buffer contains 256 bytes, and byte addressing is used, then the least significant 8 bits are used to index the buffer. The remaining most significant bits are checked to determine if the branch target lies within the environment captured by the buffer.

Among the machines using a loop buffer are some of the CDC machines (Star-100, 6600, 7600) and the CRAY-1. A specialized form of loop buffer is available on the Motorola 68010, for executing a three-instruction loop involving the DBcc (decrement and branch on condition) instruction (see Problem 10.8). A three-word buffer is maintained and the processor executes these instructions repeatedly until the loop condition is satisfied.

Branch Prediction

Various techniques can be used to predict whether a branch will be taken. Among the more common are the following:

- Predict never taken
- Predict always taken
- Predict by opcode
- Taken/not taken switch
- Branch history table

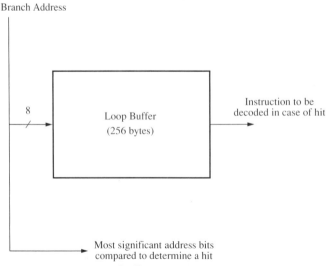

FIGURE 10-16. Loop buffer

The first three approaches are static: they do not depend on the execution history up to the time of the conditional branch instruction. The latter two approaches are dynamic: they depend on the execution history.

The first two approaches are the simplest. These either always assume that the branch will not be taken and continue to fetch instructions in sequence, or they always assume that the branch will be taken and always fetch from the branch target. The 68020 and the VAX 11/780 use the predict-never-taken approach. The VAX 11/780 also includes a feature to minimize the effect of a wrong decision. If the fetch of the instruction after the branch will cause a page fault or protection violation, the processor halts its prefetching until it is sure that the instruction should be fetched.

Studies analyzing program behavior have shown that branches are taken more than 50 percent of the time [LILJ88], so if the cost of prefetching from either path is the same, then always prefetching from the branch target address should give better performance than always prefetching from the sequential path. However, in a paged machine, prefetching the branch target is more likely to cause a page fault than prefetching the next instruction in sequence, so this performance penalty should be taken into account. An avoidance mechanism such as is used on the VAX may be employed to reduce this penalty.

The final static approach makes the decision based on the opcode of the branch instruction. The processor assumes that the branch will be taken for certain branch opcodes and not for others. [LILJ88] reports success rates of greater than 75 percent with this strategy.

Dynamic branch strategies attempt to improve the accuracy of prediction by recording the history of conditional branch instructions in a program. For example, one or more bits can be associated with each conditional branch instruction that reflect the recent history of the instruction. These bits are referred to as a taken/not taken switch that directs the processor to make a particular decision the next time the instruction is encountered. Typically, these history bits are not associated with the instruction in main memory. Rather, they are kept in temporary high-speed storage. One possibility is to associate these bits with any conditional branch instruction that is in a cache. When the instruction is replaced in the cache, its history is lost. Another possibility is to maintain a small table for recently executed branch instructions with one or more bits in each entry. The processor could access the table associatively, like a cache, or by using the low-order bits of the branch instruction's address.

With a single bit, all that can be recorded is whether the last execution of this instruction resulted in a branch or not. A shortcoming of using a single bit appears in the case of a conditional branch instruction that is almost always taken, such as a loop instruction. With only one bit of history, an error in prediction will occur twice for each use of the loop: once on entering the loop, and once on exiting.

If two bits are used, they can be used to record the result of the last two instances of the execution of the associated instruction, or to record a state in some other fashion. Figure 10-17 shows a typical approach (see Problem 10.7 for

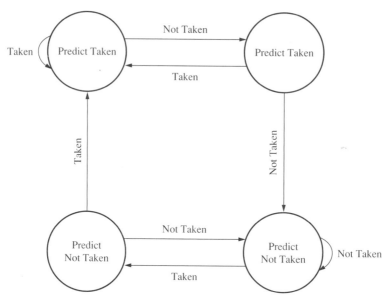

FIGURE 10-17. Branch prediction state diagram

other possibilities). The decision process can be represented by a finite-state machine with four states. If the last two branches of the given instruction have taken the same path, the prediction is to take that path again. If the prediction is wrong, it remains the same the next time the instruction is encountered. If the prediction is wrong again, however, the next prediction will be to select the opposite path. Thus, the algorithm requires two consecutive wrong predictions to change the prediction decision. If a branch executes an unusual direction once, such as for a loop, the prediction will be wrong only once.

An example of a system that uses the taken/not taken switch approach is the IBM 3090/400.

The use of history bits, as just described, has one drawback: If the decision is made to take the branch, the target instruction cannot be fetched until the target address, which is an operand in the conditional branch instruction, is decoded. Greater efficiency could be achieved if the instruction fetch could be initiated as soon as the branch decision is made. For this purpose, more information must be saved, in what is known as a branch target buffer, or a branch history table.

The branch history table is a small cache memory associated with the instruction fetch stage of the pipeline. Each entry in the table consists of three elements: the address of a branch instruction, some number of history bits that record the state of use of that instruction, and information about the target instruction. In most proposals and implementations, this third field contains the address of the target instruction. Another possibility is for the third field to actually contain the target instruction. The trade-off is clear: Storing the target address yields a smaller table but a greater instruction fetch time compared to storing the target instruction.

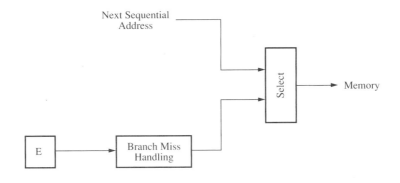

(a) Predict Never Taken Strategy

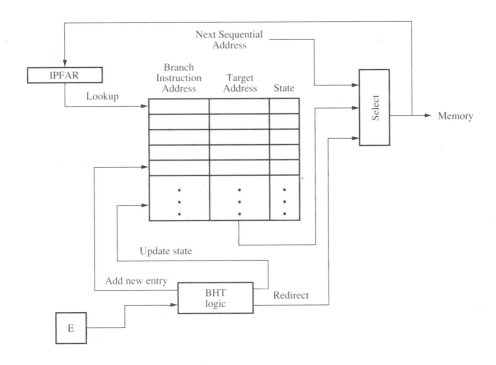

(b) Branch History Table Strategy

FIGURE 10-18.   Dealing with branches

Figure 10-18 contrasts this scheme with a predict never taken strategy. With the former strategy, the instruction fetch stage always fetches the next sequential address. If a branch is taken, some logic in the processor detects this and instructs that the next instruction be fetched from the target address (in addition to flushing the pipeline). The branch history table is treated as a cache. Each prefetch triggers a lookup in the branch history table. If no match is found, the next sequential address is used for the fetch. If a match is found, a prediction is made based on the state of the instruction: either the next sequential address or the branch target address is fed to the select logic.

When the branch instruction is executed, the execute stage signals the branch history table logic with the result. The state of the instruction is updated to reflect a correct or incorrect prediction. If the prediction is incorrect, the select logic is redirected to the correct address for the next fetch. When a conditional branch instruction is encountered that is not in the table, it is added to the table and one of the existing entries is discarded, using one of the cache replacement algorithms discussed in Chapter 4.

One example of an implementation of a branch history table is the Advanced Micro Device AMD29000 microprocessor.

Delayed Branch

It is possible to improve pipeline performance by automatically rearranging instructions within a program, so that branch instructions occur later than actually desired. This intriguing approach is examined in Chapter 13.

10.5

INTEL 80486 PIPELINING

The 80486 implements a five-stage pipeline with the following stages:

- *Fetch:* Instructions are fetched from the cache (see Chapter 4) or from external memory and placed into one of the two 16-byte prefetch buffers. The objective of the fetch stage is to fill the prefetch buffers with new data as soon as the old data has been consumed by the instruction decoder. Since instructions are of variable length (from one to eleven bytes not counting prefixes), the status of the prefetcher relative to the other pipeline stages varies from instruction to instruction. On average, about five instructions are fetched with each 16-byte load [CRAW90]. The fetch stage operates independently of the other stages to keep the prefetch buffers full.
- *Decode stage 1:* All opcode and addressing-mode information is decoded in the D1 stage. The required information, as well as instruction-length information, are included in at most the first three bytes of the instruction. Hence, three bytes are passed to the D1 stage from the prefetch buffers. The D1 decoder can then direct the D2 stage to capture the rest of the instruction (displacement and immediate data) which is not involved in the D1 decoding.
- *Decode stage 2:* The D2 stage expands each opcode into control signals for the ALU. It also controls the computation of the more complex addressing modes.
- *Execute:* This stage includes ALU operations, cache access, and register update.

• *Write back:* This stage, if needed, updates registers and status flags modified during the preceding execute stage. If the current instruction updates memory, the computed value is sent to the cache and to the bus-interface write buffers at the same time.

With the use of two decode stages, the pipeline can sustain a throughput of close to one instruction per clock cycle. Complex instructions and conditional branches can slow this rate down.

Figure 10-19 shows examples of the operation of the pipeline. Part (a) shows that there is no delay introduced into the pipeline when a memory access is required. However, as part (b) shows, there can be a delay for values used to compute memory addresses. That is, if a value is loaded from memory into a register and that register is then used as a base register in the next instruction, the processor will stall for one cycle. In this example, the processor accesses the cache in the EX stage of the first instruction and stores the value retrieved in the register during the WB stage. However, the next instruction needs this register in its D2 stage. When the D2 stage lines up with the WB stage of the previous

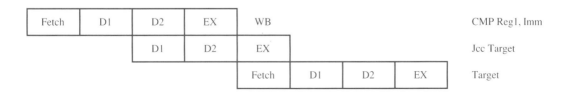

(a) No Data Load Delay in the Pipeline

(b) A Pointer Load Delay

(c) Branch Instruction Timing

FIGURE 10-19.   80486 instruction pipeline examples

instruction, bypass signal paths allow the D2 stage to have access to the same data being used by the WB stage for writing, saving one pipeline stage.

Figure 10-19c illustrates the timing of a branch instruction, assuming that the branch is taken. The compare instruction updates condition codes in the WB stage, and bypass paths make this available to the EX stage of the jump instruction at the same time. In parallel, the processor runs a speculative fetch cycle to the target of the jump during the EX stage of the jump instruction. If the processor determines a false branch condition, it discards this prefetch and continues execution with the next sequential instruction (already fetched and decoded).

10.6

IBM S/370 CPU ORGANIZATION

The IBM S/370 CPU organization is described in logical and functional terms in [IBM83a] and [IBM83b]. This organization is implemented on a variety of models, including the 370, 303X, 308X, and 309X models. Although the implementations vary, the logical function remains the same.

Register Organization

The register organization of the S/370 is summarized in Table 10-1.

- *General Registers:* There are 16 32-bit general-purpose registers, numbered 0 to 15. These may be used in arithmetic and logical operations. For some operations, two adjacent registers are used to form a 64-bit operand. Specifiers of 64-bit register operands must designate an even-numbered register, which contains the leftmost 32 bits of the operand. All but register 0 can also be used as base-address and index registers. This restriction is because, in the instruction formats, a base or index specifier of 0 indicates that no base or index is to be applied.
- *Floating-Point Registers:* There are four 64-bit floating-point registers, which are referenced by floating-point instructions. Two pairs of adjacent registers can be used for operation on 128-bit floating-point numbers.
- *Control Registers:* There are 16 32-bit control registers. These are not available for use by application programs. They are used to support specific system

TABLE 10-1   IBM S/370 CPU Registers

Type	Number	Length (bits)	Purpose
General	16	32	General-purpose user registers
Floating point	4	64	Floating-point operations
Control	16	32	Various control operations
Program status word (PSW)	1	64	Status bits plus program counter

functions and to store system parameters, such as addresses of segment tables, and mask bits for disabling certain types of interrupts.

- *Program Status Word (PSW):* The PSW includes the instruction address (program counter), condition code, and other information used to control instruction sequencing and to determine the state of the CPU.

The use of the general and floating-point registers is easily understood. Let us elaborate briefly on the others.

Program Status Word

The PSW contains information about the status of the program currently being executed. Additional control and status information is contained in control registers and permanently assigned storage locations. The status of the CPU can be changed by loading a new PSW or part of a PSW.

There are several PSW formats, each used with a different operating mode. Figure 10-20 depicts the two most important formats. The extended-control (EC) mode is the normal 370 mode of operation. The extended-architecture (XA) mode is used when 31-bit addresses are employed. Table 10-2 defines the fields of these two PSW formats.

Two of the fields in the PSW warrant elaboration.

PSW Key

The 4-bit PSW key is used in the operation of the storage protection function. Storage protection is necessary because multiple processes, through the virtual memory mechanism, may access real memory, and the real storage used by a process must be protected from violation by other processes.

The mechanism is as follows. Each 2K- or 4K-byte block of memory has associated with it a storage key, which includes a 4-bit access code and a fetch bit.

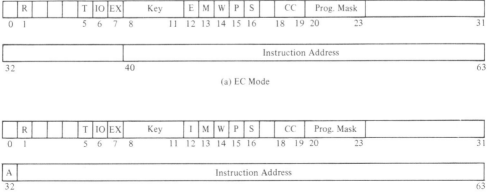

FIGURE 10-20. IBM S/370 program status word (PSW) formats

TABLE 10-2   IBM S/370 PSW Fields

PER Mask (R)
   Controls whether the CPU is enabled for interrupts associated with program-event recording (PER). When the bit is set, interruptions are permitted subject to the PER-event-mask bits in control register 9.

DAT Mode (T)
   Indicates whether addresses are real or virtual. In the latter case, dynamic address translation (DAT) is invoked.

I/O Mask (IO)
   Indicates whether I/O interrupts are enabled.

External Mask (EX)
   Indicates whether external interrupts are enabled.

PSW Key
   Forms the access key for storage references. If a memory reference is key-protected, then the PSW key must match the storage key to permit access.

EC Mode (E)
   In non-XA operation, specifies whether EC mode or an alternate 360-type mode is in use.

Machine-Check Mask (M)
   Indicates whether machine-check interrupts are enabled.

Wait State (W)
   Indicates whether CPU is in wait state.

Problem State (P)
   Indicates whether CPU is in problem state.

Address-Space Control (S)
   When virtual addresses are used, indicates whether the primary or secondary address space is to be used.

Condition Code (CC)
   Set by most arithmetic and logical instructions. The condition code may be tested by a conditional branch instruction.

Program Mask
   These four bits are used to enable/disable interrupts due to the following program exception events: fixed-point overflow, decimal overflow, exponent underflow, significance.

Addressing Mode (A)
   Determines whether effective addresses will be 24 or 31 bits.

Instruction Address
   The address of the leftmost byte of the next instruction to be executed.

When a program attempts to store data into one of the locations in a block, the current PSW key is compared to the access code, and a write operation is permitted only if the codes match. If the fetch bit is set, then the PSW key must also match the access code for read operations.

With 4 bits, up to 16 different keys may be employed. The operating system is responsible for setting the PSW key when a process is initiated.

Condition Code

The 2-bit condition code in the PSW is automatically set to reflect the result of a majority of the arithmetic, logical, and I/O instructions. Four condition-code settings are possible. Table 10-3 gives some examples of the interpretation of the condition code following some operations. Once set, the condition code remains unchanged until modified by another one of the instructions that set the condition code.

The condition code is used by the branch-on-condition instruction. This instruction includes a 4-bit mask with each bit corresponding to one of the four possible condition codes. The branch occurs if the condition code is equal to any one of the values specified in the mask.

Control Registers

The 16 control registers are used by the operating system to maintain control information relating to CPU operation. The control registers may be set and read by privileged machine instructions. In some cases, the contents of a control register are read under program control to determine the course of action to be taken. In other cases, the information is used directly by the CPU. Examples of control-register information are:

• Block-multiplexor channel status information
• Paging information
• Segmentation information
• Program-event-recording information (explained presently)

TABLE 10-3   Typical IBM S/370 Condition Code Settings

Instruction Type	Condition Code			
	0	1	2	3
Arithmetic	0	< 0	> 0	Overflow
Compare	Equal	Low	High	—
Connect channel	Successful	Connected to another CPU	—	Not operational
Load	0	< 0	> 0	—
Start I/O	Successful	CSW stored	Busy	Not operational

Interrupt Processing

Interrupt processing within the CPU is a facility provided to support the operating system. It allows an application program to be suspended, in order that a variety of interrupt conditions can be serviced, and later resumed.

Classes of Interrupt

Six classes of interrupts are defined for the S/370. These are listed in Table 10-4. A brief description follows:

- *Supervisor Call:* This type of interrupt is caused by the execution of the SVC instruction. It is a means whereby a program can invoke operating-system services, such as perform an I/O operation, obtain virtual storage, or pass control to another program. The specific service requested is indicated by an 8-bit parameter in the SVC instruction.
- *Program:* A program interrupt occurs when the CPU detects an error associated with program execution. An example is a page fault; the program is suspended until the needed page is loaded into memory. In most other cases, a program error results in the program being terminated and a dump of the user's virtual storage being generated. Examples of such conditions are (1) referencing a real address beyond actual memory, (2) attempting to access a location when the PSW key does not match the access code, (3) arithmetic overflow and underflow, and (4) attempt by an application program to execute a privileged instruction.
- *Machine Check:* A machine check interrupt occurs when a hardware error is detected in a channel, CPU, or storage. If it is possible to recover from the error, the operating system will attempt to do so and resume normal operation. Otherwise, the CPU is halted. An example of a recoverable error is a

TABLE 10-4   IBM S/370 Interrupt Classes

Class	Source of Interruption	Time of Interruption
I/O	Channel	On completion of channel operation, or the occurrence of certain I/O related events
External	Timers Malfunction alert External signal	On the occurrence of timer expiration, malfunction alert, etc.
SVC	Program	When SVC call is issued
Program check	Program	On overflow/underflow, virtual address translation error, address error, etc.
Machine check	Hardware	On hardware malfunction
Restart	Restart key	On pressing restart key

storage bit error that is corrected using the error-correcting code. An example of an unrecoverable error is a detected malfunction of a CPU mechanism, such as dynamic address translation, which did not correct itself upon automatic retry.

- *External:* This category covers a variety of types of interrupts, including clock, timer, and another CPU. (1) The CPU maintains a time-of-day clock. The operating system can schedule an interrupt to occur at a particular time to, for example, issue periodic operation commands. (2) Timers are used to measure intervals of time. A timer can be used by the operating system to define a *time slice* that limits program execution time. It can be used by an application program to time events. (3) A CPU-to-CPU signal is used in the coordination of a multiple processor configuration (see Chapter 15).

- *Input/Output:* An I/O interrupt is the means by which a channel communicates with the CPU. An interrupt is generated at the completion of an I/O operation and, optionally, at various stages of the operation. The latter are known as *program-controlled interrupts.*

- *Restart:* A restart interrupt provides a means for the operator or another CPU to invoke the execution of a specified program. The operator causes the interrupt by pressing the RESTART key on the system control panel. Another CPU may cause the interrupt by signaling a restart interrupt.

Point of Interrupt

Normally, an interrupt can occur only at the boundary between instructions. That is, while the CPU is in the process of executing an instruction, it does not check for interrupts. Only at the end of each instruction cycle is it possible to interrupt the CPU. In the case of three instructions that involve processing strings of data (COMPARE LOGICAL LONG, MOVE LONG, TEST BLOCK), an interrupt is permitted when the instruction is in a partial stage of completion. After the interrupt has been serviced, the execution of the interrupted instruction is resumed from the point of interruption.

Interrupt Handling

When an interrupt occurs and is recognized by the CPU, a sequence of events takes place.

1. The current PSW is saved in a dedicated location of main memory corresponding to the type of interrupt. Thus there are six 64-bit "old PSW" locations. Note that the stored PSW contains the address of the next instruction that would have been executed had no interrupt occurred.

2. The PSW is then loaded from another dedicated location corresponding to the type of interrupt. Again, since there are six types of interrupts, there are six 64-bit "new PSW" locations. The new PSW includes the address of the first instruction for the interrupt-handling routine for that type of interrupt.

These first two steps are performed by the CPU as part of the interrupt cycle of the instruction cycle. The remaining three steps are performed by the execution of instructions.

3. The interrupt handler begins by saving the contents of the 16 general registers. It is then free to use those registers in executing instructions that process the interrupt.
4. The actual processing of the interrupt occurs.
5. The interrupt handler reloads the general registers with the saved values and loads the PSW with the value stored in the old PSW location. This causes the interrupted program to be resumed as if it had not been interrupted.

PSW Mask Bits

It is possible, by means of the PSW, to disable certain types of interrupts. This is done by means of mask bits. There is a mask bit in the PSW for each of the following types of interrupts: external, I/O, and machine check. When the mask bit is set to 0, the corresponding type of interrupt is ignored by the CPU. The interrupt remains pending and may be processed later when the interrupt type is enabled.

The CPU cannot be disabled for supervisor call and restart interruptions. Certain program interrupts can be disabled. As Table 10-2 indicates, the Program Mask bits control four types of program interrupts. In addition, there is a subclass of program interrupts, known as *program event recording* (PER), that is useful for debugging purposes. When the PER mask bit in the PSW is set to zero, then PER interrupts are disabled. When the PER bit is set to one, then the following events may be enabled as interrupts.

- Successful execution of a branch instruction
- Alteration of the contents of designated general registers
- Fetching of an instruction from designated main storage locations
- Alteration of the contents of designated main storage locations.

Control words 9 through 11 contain mask bits for these four events, and the addresses of the designated registers and memory location ranges.

The ability to disable interrupts is an important one. It allows certain programs, such as interrupt-handling routines, to accomplish their work uninterrupted when interrupts would cause unwanted delays or would interfere with program operation.

Interrupt Priorities

It is possible for several different types of interrupts to occur during the execution of a single instruction. When this happens the CPU must decide, during the interrupt cycle, which interrupt to process.

If a nonrecoverable hardware error has occurred, the associated machine-check interrupt is honored, regardless of other conditions. Otherwise, the following descending priority of interrupts is followed:

- Supervisor Call
- Program
- Machine Check (recoverable)
- External
- I/O
- Restart

The CPU picks the highest-priority enabled interrupt to process. The remaining interrupts are left pending.

CPU States

The S/370 CPU functions in one of a number of states, which form a three-level hierarchy (Figure 10-21). At any given time, the CPU is in one of the following primary states:

- *Load:* The CPU enters this state in response to a console key input. During this state, an initializing program is read from disk. This program is used to bring in and initialize the operating system. Once the program is loaded, the CPU changes to the operating state.
- *Operating:* This is the state in which the CPU performs its normal role, by executing application and system programs, and by servicing interrupts.
- *Check-Stopped:* This state is entered in response to certain machine-check interrupts. In this state, the CPU does not accept instructions or interrupts. The CPU leaves this state when the operator presses a reset console key. Depending on configuration, the CPU then goes to the load or stopped state.
- *Stopped:* This state is entered under operator or other-CPU command. The CPU does not function in this state. It is returned to the operating state by a restart signal from the operator or other CPU.

The operating state consists of two substates:

- *Wait:* In this state the CPU is not executing instructions but will respond to interrupts. The CPU is in this state when there is no work to perform. Either

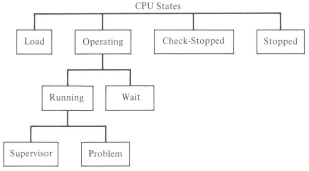

FIGURE 10-21.   IBM S/370 CPU states

there are no active processes, or all processes are waiting for the completion of events, such as I/O operations. An interrupt places the CPU in running state.
- *Running:* In this state, instructions are being executed.

When the processor is in the running state, it can be in one of two substates:

- *Problem:* In this state, the CPU is executing an application program and is restricted to a subset of machine instructions. If the CPU is presented with a privileged instruction while in this state, a program interrupt occurs.
- *Supervisor:* The CPU can execute any machine instruction. This state is employed when the CPU is executing operating-system instructions.

IBM 3033 Pipelining

The IBM 3033 was introduced in 1977 to provide a significant performance improvement over the available models in the System/370 product line [CONN79]. The system is compatible with the 370 processors; it executes the same instruction set and controls the same I/O channels. One of the key ways in which performance has been enhanced is the use of an improved instruction pipelining scheme. This scheme is also used in the later 308X and 3090 series of machines.

The Instruction Pre-Processing Function (IPPF) is the unit that performs the pipelining function and provides op codes and operands to the execution unit, as depicted in Figure 10-22. Three 32-byte instruction buffers are utilized, each of which can hold an average of eight instructions. At any one time, one of the buffers is active and the IPPF fetches instructions in sequence as rapidly as possible to keep the buffer full. At the other end of the buffer, instructions are removed one at a time and placed in an instruction register for processing. The IPPF performs the following operations on the instruction in this register:

- The op code is decoded to determine the number and size of operands, and also to determine if it is a branch instruction.
- Operand addresses are generated. These are placed in operand address registers.
- Source operands are fetched and placed in operand buffers.

The general registers in the IPPF are duplicates of those found in the execution unit and are used exclusively for address calculations by the IPPF. To sustain a high execution rate when instruction execution times vary, another buffer is placed between the instruction register and the execution unit. This buffer, called the *instruction queue,* holds four decoded instructions awaiting execution.

To account for branches, there are three instruction buffers, only one of which is active at a time. When no branches are encountered, the IPPF attempts to keep the active buffer full; the other instruction buffers are empty. When an unconditional branch is encountered, the remaining contents of the active instruction buffer are useless, and the IPPF begins again, filling an empty active buffer. When a conditional branch occurs, the IPPF makes a "guess," based on designer judgment, as to the most likely outcome of the branch instruction. The active

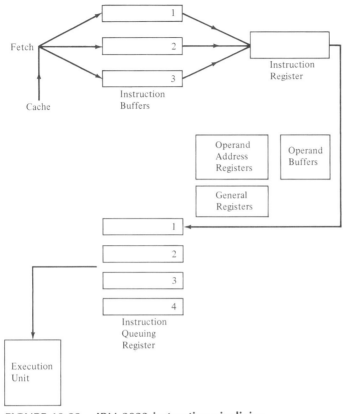

FIGURE 10-22. IBM 3033 instruction pipelining

buffer is deactivated, and the IPPF begins filling a new active buffer with instructions starting from the likely branch destination point. If the guess was right, then time has been saved. If the guess was wrong for a branch that changes the instruction stream, then the previously active buffer will still contain some of the instructions to be executed, again saving time.

To further enhance branch processing, the third instruction buffer is used for fetching instructions in the same manner as just described when a second conditional branch instruction is encountered prior to the resolution of the first one.

10.7

VAX CPU ORGANIZATION

Register Organization

The register organization of the VAX varies with the CPU model. Table 10-5 lists the registers common to all VAX CPUs.

TABLE 10-5   VAX CPU Registers

Type	Number	Length (bits)	Purpose
General	16	32	General-purpose plus special-purpose
Processor status longword (PSL)	1	32	Status and control bits
Console terminal	4	32	Communication with console terminal
Clock	4	32	Timing functions
Accelerator control/status	1	32	Controls floating-point accelerator function

- *General:* There are 16 32-bit registers, numbers 0 to 15. These are used as general-purpose registers for all types of VAX instructions. In addition, four of the registers have special uses, one of which serves as the program counter.
- *Processor Status Longword (PSL):* This contains control and status information. Its format and use are described presently.
- *Console Terminal:* The console terminal is used by the operator to control the system. Two registers are associated with input from the terminal and two with output. In addition to a field for buffering data, the registers include an interrupt enable bit and various status bits.
- *Clock:* One 32-bit register contains the current time and date to a resolution of 10 ms. Several other registers are used to control the use of an interval timer that provides interrupts at programmed intervals.
- *Accelerator Control/Status:* This 32-bit register actually contains only two useful bits. One bit indicates whether the floating-point accelerator exists. Another bit is used to enable or disable the floating-point accelerator. The floating-point accelerator is a special-purpose processor that executes the VAX floating-point instructions. When it is present and enabled, it executes these instructions at a higher speed than the CPU would, thus increasing performance.

Processor Status Longword

Processor state information is maintained in the 32-bit PSL (Figure 10-23). The upper 16 bits are protected and may not be modified by a user program. These bits are concerned with interrupt processing and the mode, or state, of the CPU.

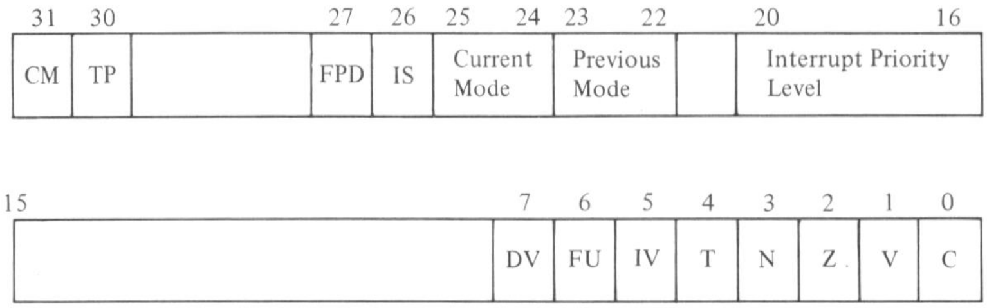

FIGURE 10-23.   VAX processor status longword

The lower 16 bits are referred to as the *Program Status Word* (PSW) and are accessible by user program. The PSW provides a 4-bit condition code and a 4-bit trap enable/disable code. Traps are similar to interrupts, as explained later in this section.

Table 10-6 explains the various PSL fields.

Interrupt Processing

Two classes of events will cause the VAX CPU to suspend execution of the current instruction stream and respond to the event: exceptions and interrupts. In both cases the CPU saves the context of the current process and transfers to a predefined routine to service the condition.

TABLE 10-6   VAX PSL Fields

CONDITION CODES (N, Z, V, C)
These bits reflect the result of the most recent instruction that affects them: N = negative, Z = zero, V = overflow, C = carry. These bits may be tested by a conditional branch instruction.

TRAP-ENABLE FLAGS (DV, FU, IV, T)
These bits are used to enable/disable a type of interrupt called a trap: DV = decimal overflow, FU = floating underflow, IV = integer overflow, T = trace.

INTERRUPT PRIORITY LEVEL (IPL)
The CPU's current priority level. Only interrupts of higher priority will be acknowledged.

PREVIOUS MODE
Value of the access mode prior to the current one.

CURRENT MODE
Current processor access mode. The four modes are kernel, executive, supervisor, and user.

INTERRUPT STACK (IS)
This bit indicates that the CPU is processing an interrupt. For this purpose, it makes use of a special stack called the interrupt stack.

FIRST PART DONE (FPD)
Used with instructions that may be interrupted during execution. If FPD = 1 when the CPU returns from an interrupt, it resumes the operation where it left off, rather than restarting the instruction.

TRACE PENDING (TP)
The trace facility allows a debugger to gain control following the execution of every instruction, using a trace interrupt. When trace interrupts are enabled, the TP bit ensures that only one trace interrupt can occur for each instruction.

COMPATIBILITY MODE (CM)
When the VAX-11 CPU is in compatibility mode, it executes PDP-11 instructions rather than VAX instructions. Other VAXes provide this function via software emulation.

Interrupts

An interrupt is defined in the VAX architecture in a somewhat more restrictive fashion than for most other systems. An interrupt is an event external to the current process that causes the CPU to change the flow of control. Typically, an interrupt is processed after the currently executing instruction is completed. The CPU also services interrupts at well-defined points during the execution of long, iterative instructions.

Two kinds of interrupts are used: hardware and software. Hardware interrupts include those generated by peripheral devices, the clock, and various machine errors. Software interrupts are generated upon request by means of a privileged instruction that can be used by the operating system and other system routines. To explain its use, we first need to discuss priorities.

At any given time, the VAX CPU is executing at a given priority level, as determined by the IPL field in the Processor Status Longword. There is also a priority level associated with each interrupt. When an interrupt occurs, the CPU will service the interrupt only if the interrupt priority is greater than the current CPU priority. Otherwise, the interrupt remains pending until the CPU priority drops below the interrupt priority.

When an interrupt is processed, the current PSL and general registers are saved, and a new PSL is loaded corresponding to the interrupt type. The CPU's priority is now equal to the priority of the interrupt it is servicing. Thus, when an interrupt is being serviced, only interrupts of higher priority can interrupt the CPU.

Table 10-7 shows the interrupt priority levels defined for the VAX VMS operating system. The lowest level, IPL 0, is used for all user processes and most operating-system programs. The next fifteen levels are used for software interrupts. The highest sixteen levels are used for hardware interrupts including, in ascending order, peripheral device, clock, and urgent processor error conditions.

Now we can explain the use of software interrupts. Software interrupts are used by the operating system to optimize the use of system resources and maintain system responsiveness. For example, as soon as an I/O transfer to or from a device is completed, a new transfer will be started if one is queued for the device.

To accomplish this, different I/O processing functions are performed at different levels. This is done as follows. When an I/O interrupt occurs, control is passed to an I/O device driver. The driver, executing at the device's hardware interrupt priority, executes just long enough to save essential status information. It then issues a software interrupt requesting that execution be resumed at a lower level. The result is that other hardware interrupts at the same or lower level are locked out for the minimum amount of time.

Exceptions

Exceptions are events that relate to the currently executing process and usually to the currently executing instruction. Examples include

TABLE 10-7   VAX Interrupt Priority Levels

Priority		Hardware Event
Hex	Decimal	
1F	31	Machine Check, Kernel Stack Not Valid
1E	30	Power Fail
1D	29	⎫ Processor,
1C	28	⎪
1B	27	⎬ Memory, or
1A	26	⎪
19	25	⎭ Bus Error
18	24	Clock
17	23	UNIBUS BR7
16	22	UNIBUS BR6
15	21	UNIBUS BR5
14	20	UNIBUS BR4 Device Interrupt
13	19	
12	18	
11	17	
10	16	

Priority		Software Event
OF	15	⎫ Reserved for
OE	14	⎬ DIGITAL
OD	13	⎪
OC	12	⎭
OB	11	⎫ Device
OA	10	⎬ Drivers
09	09	⎪
08	08	⎭
07	07	Timer Process
06	06	Queue Asynchronous System Trap (AST)
05	05	Reserved for DIGITAL
04	04	I/O Post
03	03	Process Scheduler
02	02	AST Delivery
01	01	Reserved for DIGITAL
00	00	User Process Level

- Page fault
- Arithmetic exceptions, such as overflow, underflow, and divide by 0
- Traps, such as those used to debug programs by allowing the debugger to gain control following the execution of every instruction

Unlike interrupts, exceptions do not have a predefined priority level. Rather, the priority of an exception is the same as the current priority. In most cases, exceptions are handled at the end of an instruction. In some cases, such as a page fault, they must be handled in the middle of an instruction. After the exception is handled, execution resumes unless some abort condition is detected, which halts the process.

System Control Block

When an interrupt or exception is serviced by the CPU, it saves the context of the current process in a process control block; this was described in general terms in Chapter 6. The CPU then transfers control to a handler routine to service the interrupt.

The address to which control is transferred is dictated by the System Control Block. For each exception and each interrupting device controller, there is a separate 32-bit entry in the System Control Block. The entry contains the address of the procedure to be invoked to handle the interrupt or exception. Figure 10-24 shows the overall organization of the block. The first 20 addresses relate to the various exceptions. Then comes a section that deals with various processor faults relating to the memory or bus. This is followed by software interrupts, interrupts relating to the clock and console, and device interrupts generated by I/O modules (external adapters). Up to 16 adapters can be handled at four priority levels. Table 10-8 lists the entries in the System Control Block.

Processor Access Mode

The VAX concept of processor access mode was introduced in Chapter 6. This concept facilitates the protection and sharing of system resources among processes. The access mode determines:

* *Instruction execution privilege:* What instructions the processor will execute.
* *Memory access privileges:* Which locations in memory the current instruction can access.

To recall, the four modes for the VMS operating system are:

* *Kernel:* Interrupt and exception handling, scheduling, paging, physical I/O.
* *Executive:* Record (file) management.
* *Supervisor:* User command language interpreter.
* *User:* User procedures and data.

The kernel is the most-privileged mode, decreasing to the user mode, which is the least-privileged mode.

A procedure executing in a less-privileged mode often needs to call a procedure that executes in a more-privileged mode; for example, a user program requires an operating-system service. This call is achieved by using a change mode instruction, which causes an exception that transfers control to a routine at the new access mode (by means of the System Control Block). A return is made by executing the REI (return from exception or interrupt) instruction.

VAX 8600 Pipelining

One of the most advanced members of the VAX family is the VAX 8600, introduced in 1985. The VAX 8600 is designed to provide improved performance for the same functionality as the VAX-11 series [FOSS85a]. Thus, the 8600 executes the same instruction set, runs the same operating system, and interfaces to the same I/O bus structure as the VAX-11.

One of the key factors in the high performance of the 8600 is the high degree of instruction pipelining. To explain, we first need to look at the overall organization of the VAX 8600, as depicted in Figure 10-25.

The CPU consists of five relatively independent subprocessors.

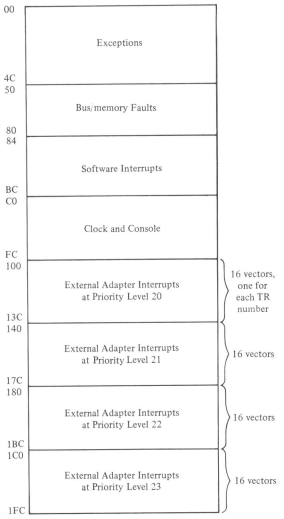

FIGURE 10-24.   VAX system control block (first page)

- *E Box:* Executes the VAX instruction set, and generally directs the system.
- *I Box:* Prefetches instructions and decodes the op codes and operands for later execution by the E box.
- *F Box:* Is a floating-point accelerator. When it is present, floating-point instructions are routed to it by the I box. The F box contains special hardware for fast unpacking, aligning, and arithmetic operations [FOSS85b].
- *M Box:* Controls access to main memory from the CPU and I/O devices. It contains a 16-KByte cache and a translation buffer for holding recently used translations of virtual to physical memory addresses.
- *Console:* Provides an interface to the operator, the boot device, and remote diagnostics.

TABLE 10-8   VAX System Control Block

Offset	Name
00	passive release
04	machine check
08	kernel stack not valid
0C	power fail
10	reserved or privileged instruction
14	customer reserved instruction
18	reserved or illegal operand
1C	reserved or illegal addressing mode
20	access-control violation
24	page fault
28	trace fault
2C	breakpoint instruction
30	compatibility mode exception
34	arithmetic exception
38-3C	unused
40	change mode to kernel
44	change mode to execute
48	change mode to supervisor
4C	change mode to user
50-60	bus or memory errors
64-80	unused
84-BC	software levels 1-F
C0	interval timer
C4	unused
C8	subset emulation
CC	suspended emulation
D0-EC	unused
F0	console storage receive
F4	console storage transmit
F8	console terminal receive
FC	console terminal transmit
100-1FC	adapter vectors
200-5FC	device vectors

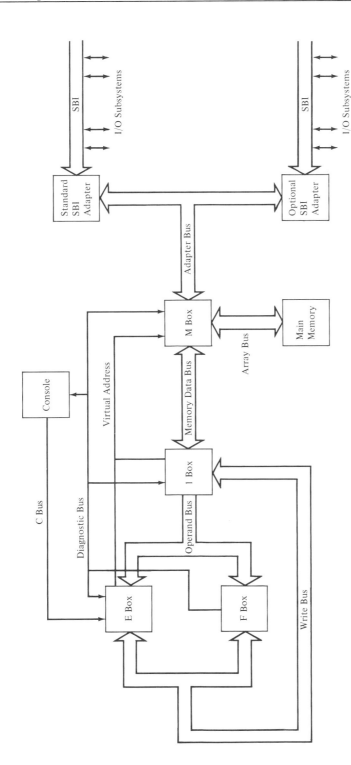

FIGURE 10-25.   VAX 8600 CPU architecture

The existence of separate I and E boxes provides the structure for pipelining. The I box is a separate subsystem that fetches instructions, decodes opcodes, fetches source operands, and stores results. The opcode and operands are presented to the E box (or F box) for execution. The sequence of events is as follows. The I box maintains an 8-byte buffer for the instruction stream. For each instruction, the opcode is examined to determine the number and size of operands. Each source operand is fetched. In some cases, this involves the use of a register. For this purpose, the I box maintains a duplicate set of the 16 general-purpose registers. Any update to a register by the E box automatically updates the I box copy. When the E box is ready for the next instruction, the I box supplies the operands and the opcode. When execution is complete, the I box supplies the address for storing the result.

The independence of the E and I boxes provides a means for pipelining. But the 8600 architecture goes further than simply fetching one instruction while executing another. The entire sequence of instruction activities is pipelined. The solid boxes on the diagonal in Figure 10-26 show the successive actions the CPU takes to perform a typical instruction. As indicated by the dashed lines above and below the solid ones, each of these six activities is performed separately and may be performed in parallel with the other activities. Of course, movement through the pipe cannot always be at top speed. Several possible reasons for slowdown are

• A conditional branch instruction invalidates an instruction fetch.
• A cache miss requires waiting for data from main storage (the basic cycle time is based on a cache hit).
• A multiplication or division ties up the E box for an extended period.

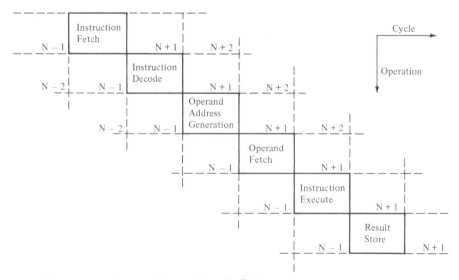

FIGURE 10-26. VAX 8600 instruction pipelining

10.8

RECOMMENDED READING

[STON90], [HENN91], and [HAYE88] contain detailed discussions of pipelining. [RAMA77] provides a logical and performance analysis of instruction pipelining as well as other uses of pipeline in processors. [SOHI90] provides an excellent, detailed discussion of the hardware design issues involved in an instruction pipeline. The following examine various branch prediction strategies that can be used to enhance the performance of instruction pipelining: [DUBE91], [LEE84], [MCFA86], and [LILJ88]. [KAEL91] examines the difficulty introduced into branch prediction by instructions whose target address is variable. [MILU91] examines the technology differences between silicon and gallium arsenide microprocessors as they relate to pipeline design.

The Intel 80486 instruction pipeline is described in [TABA91], [CRAW90], and [SLAT89].

10.9

PROBLEMS

10.1 Suggest a use for the Intel 8085 AC flag, defined in Section 10.2.

10.2 (a) If the last operation performed on a computer with an 8-bit word was an addition in which the two operands were 2 and 3, what would be the value of the following flags?

- Carry
- Zero
- Overflow
- Sign
- Even Parity
- Half-Carry

(b) What if the operands were −1 (2's complement) and +1?

10.3 Consider the timing diagram of Figure 10-13. Assume that there is only a two-stage pipeline (fetch, execute). Redraw the diagram to show how many time units are now needed for four instructions.

10.4 One limitation of the multiple-stream approach to dealing with branches in a pipeline is that additional branches will be encountered before the first branch is resolved. Suggest two additional limitations or drawbacks.

10.5 What properties should be designed into the op codes on a new system to allow future implementation of separate and pipelined, parallel circuitry for floating-point, fixed-point, and bit/byte string instructions?

10.6 When several different types of interrupts occur during the execution of an IBM S/370 instruction, what sequence of PSW stores and loads is needed to enforce the priority rules?

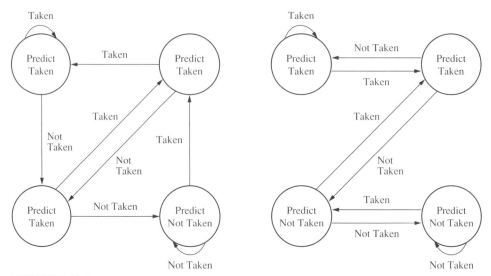

PROBLEM 10.7

10.7 Consider the above state diagrams.
   (a) Describe the behavior of each.
   (b) Compare these with the branch prediction state diagram in Section 10.4. Discuss the relative merits of each of the three approaches to branch prediction.

10.8 The Motorola 680X0 machines include the instruction Decrement and Branch According to Condition, which has the following form:

DBcc Dn, displacement

where cc is one of the testable conditions, Dn is a general-purpose register, and displacement specifies the target address relative to the current address. The instruction can be defined as follows:

if (cc = False)
then begin
    Dn := (Dn) − 1;
    if Dn ≠ −1 **then** PC := (PC) + displacement **end**
else PC := (PC) + 2;

When the instruction is executed, the condition is first tested to determine whether the termination condition for the loop is satisfied. If so, no operation is performed and execution continues at the next instruction in sequence. If the condition is false, the specified data register is decremented and checked to see if it is less than zero. If it is less than zero, the loop is terminated and execution continues at the next instruction in sequence. Otherwise the program branches to the specified location.

Now consider the following assembly-language program fragment:

```
AGAIN           CMPM.L      (A0)+,(A1)+
                DBNE        D1,AGAIN
                NOP
```

Two strings addressed by A0 and A1 are compared for equality; the string pointers are incremented with each reference. D1 initially contains the number of longwords (4 bytes) to be compared.

(a) The initial contents of the registers are A0 = $00004000, A1 = $00005000, and D1 = $000000FF (the $ indicates hexadecimal notation). Memory between $4000 and $6000 is loaded with words $AAAA. If the program above is run, specify the number of times the DBNE loop is executed and the contents of the three registers when the NOP instruction is reached.

(b) Repeat (a), but now assume that memory between $4000 and $4FEE is loaded with $0000 and between $5000 and $6000 is loaded with $AAA.

10.9 Redraw Figure 10-19c assuming that the conditional branch is not taken.

PART IV

THE CONTROL UNIT

The control unit is that portion of the CPU that actually causes things to happen. The control unit issues control signals external to the CPU to cause data exchange with memory and I/O modules. The control unit also issues control signals internal to the CPU to move data between registers, to cause the ALU to perform a specified function, and to regulate other internal operations. Input to the control unit consists of the instruction register, flags, and control signals from external sources (e.g., interrupt signals).

Chapter 11 examines the operation of the control unit, explaining in functional terms what the control unit does. It is seen that the basic responsibility of the control unit is to cause a sequence of elementary operations, called *micro-operations,* to occur during the course of an instruction cycle. Then, in Chapter 12, we see how the concept of micro-operation leads to an elegant and powerful approach to control unit implementation.

CHAPTER 11

Control Unit Operation

In Chapter 8, we pointed out that a machine instruction set goes a long way toward defining the CPU. If we know the machine instruction set, including an understanding of the effect of each op code and an understanding of the addressing modes, and if we know the set of user-visible registers, then we know the functions that the CPU must perform. This is not the complete picture. We must know the external interfaces, usually through a bus, and the way in which interrupts are handled. With this line of reasoning, the following list of those things needed to specify the function of a CPU emerges:

1. Operations (op codes)
2. Addressing Modes
3. Registers
4. I/O Module Interface
5. Memory Module Interface
6. Interrupt Processing Structure

This list, though general, is rather complete. Items 1 through 3 are defined by defining the instruction set. Items 4 and 5 are typically defined by defining the system bus. Item 6 is defined partially by the system bus and partially by the type of support the CPU offers to the operating system.

This list of six items might be termed the functional requirements for a CPU. They determine what a CPU must do. This is what occupied us in Parts II and III. Now, we turn to the question of how these functions are performed or, more specifically, how the various elements of the CPU are controlled to provide these functions. Thus we turn to a discussion of the control unit, which controls the operation of the CPU.

11.1

MICRO-OPERATIONS

The function of a computer is to execute programs. We have seen that the operation of a computer, in executing a program, consists of a sequence of instruction cycles, with one machine instruction per cycle. Of course, we must remember that this sequence of instruction cycles is not necessarily the same as the *written sequence* of instructions that make up the program, because of the existence of branching instructions. What we are referring to here is the execution *time sequence* of instructions.

We have further seen that each instruction cycle can be considered to be made up of a number of smaller units. One subdivision that we found convenient is fetch, indirect, execute, and interrupt, with only fetch and execute cycles always occurring.

To design a control unit, however, we need to break the description down further. In our discussion of pipelining in Chapter 10, we began to see that a further decomposition is possible. In fact, we will see that each of the smaller cycles involves a series of steps, each of which involves the CPU registers. We will refer to these steps as *micro-operations*. The prefix *micro* refers to the fact that each step is very simple and accomplishes very little. Figure 11-1 depicts the relationship among the various concepts we have been discussing. To summarize, the execution of a program consists of the sequential execution of instructions. Each instruction is executed during an instruction cycle made up of shorter subcycles (e.g., fetch, indirect, execute, interrupt). The performance of each subcycle involves one or more shorter operations, that is, micro-operations.

Micro-operations are the functional, or atomic, operations of a CPU. In this section, we will examine micro-operations, to gain an understanding of how the events of any instruction cycle can be described as a sequence of such micro-operations. A simple example, based on [MANO88], will be used. In the remainder of this chapter, we then show how the concept of micro-operations serves as a guide to the design of the control unit.

The Fetch Cycle

We begin by looking at the fetch cycle, which occurs at the beginning of each instruction cycle and causes an instruction to be fetched from memory. For purposes of discussion, we assume the organization depicted in Figure 10-9. Four registers are involved:

- *Memory Address Register (MAR):* Is connected to the address lines of the system bus. It specifies the address in memory for a read or write operation.
- *Memory Buffer Register (MBR):* Is connected to the data lines of the system bus. It contains the value to be stored in memory or the last value read from memory.
- *Program Counter (PC):* Holds the address of the next instruction to be fetched.
- *Instruction Register (IR):* Holds the last instruction fetched.

Let us look at the sequence of events for the fetch cycle from the point of view of its effect on the CPU registers. An example appears in Figure 11-2. At the beginning of the fetch cycle, the address of the next instruction to be executed is in the program counter (PC); in this case the address is 1100100. The first step is

Program Execution
Instruction Cycle
Instruction Cycle
Instruction Cycle
Fetch
Indirect
Execute
Interrupt
Fetch
Indirect
μOP
μOP
μOP
μOP
μOP

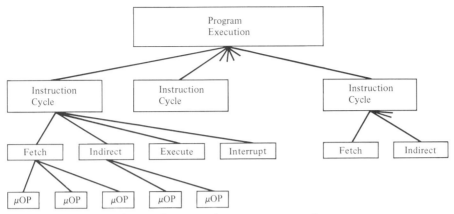

FIGURE 11-1. Constituent elements of a program execution

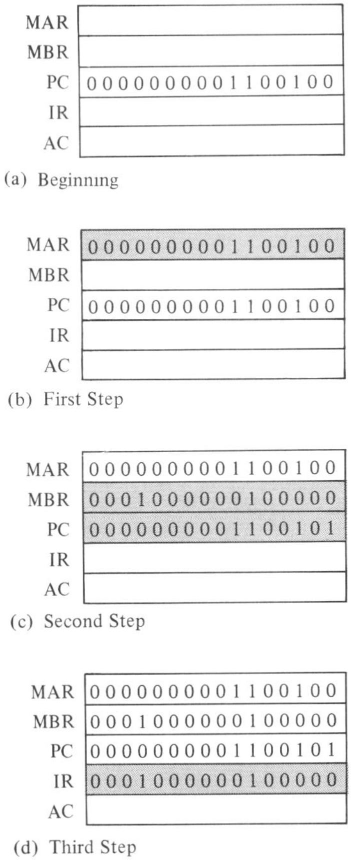

MAR
MBR
PC 0000000001100100
IR
AC
(a) Beginning
MAR 0000000001100100
MBR
PC 0000000001100100
IR
AC
(b) First Step
MAR 0000000001100100
MBR 0001000000100000
PC 0000000001100101
IR
AC
(c) Second Step
MAR 0000000001100100
MBR 0001000000100000
PC 0000000001100101
IR 0001000000100000
AC
(d) Third Step

FIGURE 11-2. Sequence of events, fetch cycle

to move that address to the memory address register (MAR), since this is the only register connected to the address lines of the system bus. The second step is to bring in the instruction. The desired address (in the MAR) is placed on the address bus, the control unit issues a READ command on the control bus, and the result appears on the data bus and is copied into the memory buffer register (MBR). We also need to increment the PC by 1 to get ready for the next instruction. Since these two actions (read word from memory, add 1 to PC) do not interfere with each other, we can do them simultaneously to save time. The third step is to move the contents of the MBR to the instruction register (IR). This frees up the MBR for use during a possible indirect cycle.

Thus, the simple fetch cycle actually consists of three steps and four micro-operations. Each micro-operation involves the movement of data into or out of a register. So long as these movements do not interfere with one another, several of them can take place during one step, saving time. Symbolically, we can write this sequence of events as follows:

t_1: MAR ← (PC)
t_2: MBR ← Memory
    PC   ← (PC) + 1
t_3: IR   ← (MBR)

We need to make several comments about this sequence. We assume that a clock is available for timing purposes, and that it emits regularly spaced clock pulses. Each clock pulse defines a time unit. Thus all time units are of equal duration. Each micro-operation can be performed within the time of a single time unit. The notation (t_1, t_2, t_3) represents successive time units. In words, we have

- First time unit: Move contents of PC to MAR
- Second time unit: Move contents of memory location specified by MAR to MBR. Increment by 1 the contents of the PC.
- Third time unit: Move contents of MBR to IR.

Note that the second and third micro-operations both take place during the second time unit. The third micro-operation could have been grouped with the fourth without affecting the fetch operation:

t_1: MAR ← (PC)
t_2: MBR ← Memory
t_3: PC   ← (PC) + 1
    IR   ← (MBR)

The groupings of micro-operations must follow two simple rules:

1. The proper sequence of events must be followed. Thus (MAR ← (PC)) must precede (MBR ← Memory) since the memory read operation makes use of the address in the MAR.
2. Conflicts must be avoided. One should not attempt to read to and write from the same register in one time unit, since the results would be unpredictable.

For example, the micro-operations (MBR ← Memory) and (IR ← MBR) should not occur during the same time unit.

A final point worth noting is that one of the micro-operations involves an addition. To avoid duplication of circuitry, this addition could be performed by the ALU. The use of the ALU may involve additional micro-operations, depending on the functionality of the ALU and the organization of the CPU. We defer a discussion of this point until later in this chapter.

It is useful to compare events described in this and the following subsections to Figure 3-5. Whereas micro-operations are ignored in that figure, this discussion shows the micro-operations needed to perform the subcycles of the instruction cycle.

The Indirect Cycle

Once an instruction is fetched, the next step is to fetch source operands. Continuing our simple example, let us assume a one-address instruction format, with direct and indirect addressing allowed. If the instruction specifies an indirect address, then an indirect cycle must precede the execute cycle. The data flow is indicated in Figure 10-10 and includes the following micro-operations:

t_1: MAR ← (IR(Address))
t_2: MBR ← Memory
t_3: IR(Address) ← (MBR(Address))

The address field of the instruction is transferred to the MAR. This is then used to fetch the address of the operand. Finally, the address field of the IR is updated from the MBR, so that it now contains a direct rather than an indirect address.

The IR is now in the same state as if indirect addressing had not been used, and it is ready for the execute cycle. We skip that cycle for a moment, to consider the interrupt cycle.

The Interrupt Cycle

At the completion of the execute cycle, a test is made to determine whether any enabled interrupts have occurred. If so, the interrupt cycle occurs. The nature of this cycle varies greatly from one machine to another. We present a very simple sequence of events, as illustrated in Figure 10-11. We have

t_1: MBR ← (PC)
t_2: MAR ← Save-address
    PC ← Routine-address
t_3: Memory ← (MBR)

In the first step, the contents of the PC are transferred to the MBR, so that they can be saved for return from the interrupt. Then the MAR is loaded with the address at which the contents of the PC are to be saved, and the PC is loaded with the address of the start of the interrupt-processing routine. These two actions may each be a single micro-operation. However, since most CPUs provide multiple types and/or levels of interrupts, it may take one or more additional micro-operations to obtain the save-address and the routine-address before they can be transferred to the MAR and PC, respectively. In any case, once this is done, the final step is to store the MBR, which contains the old value of the PC, into memory. The CPU is now ready to begin the next instruction cycle.

The Execute Cycle

The fetch, indirect, and interrupt cycles are simple and predictable. Each involves a small, fixed sequence of micro-operations and, in each case, the same micro-operations are repeated each time around.

This is not true of the execute cycle. For a machine with N different op codes, there are N different sequences of micro-operations that can occur. Let us consider several hypothetical examples.

First consider an add instruction:

ADD R1, X

which adds the contents of the location X to register R1. The following sequence of micro-operations might occur:

t_1: MAR ← (IR (address))
t_2: MBR ← Memory
t_3: RI ← (RI) + (MBR)

We begin with the IR containing the ADD instruction. In the first step, the address portion of the IR is loaded into the MAR. Then, the referenced memory location is read. Finally, the contents of R1 and MBR are added by the ALU. Again, this is a simplified example. Additional micro-operations may be required to extract the register reference from the IR and perhaps to stage the ALU inputs or outputs in some intermediate registers.

Let us look at two more-complex examples. A common instruction is increment and skip if zero:

ISZ X

The content of location X is incremented by 1. If the result is 0, the next instruction is skipped. A possible sequence of micro-operations is

t_1: MAR ← (IR (address))
t_2: MBR ← Memory
t_3: MBR ← (MBR) + 1
t_4: Memory ← (MBR)
    If (MBR = 0) then (PC ← (PC) + 1).

The new feature introduced here is the conditional action. The PC is incremented if MBR = 0. This test and action can be implemented as one micro-operation. Note also that this micro-operation can be performed during the same time unit during which the updated value in MBR is stored back to memory.

Finally, consider a subroutine call instruction. As an example, consider a branch-and-save-address instruction:

BSA X

The address of the instruction that follows the BSA instruction is saved in location X, and execution continues at location X + 1. The saved address will later be used for return. This is a straightforward technique for providing subroutine calls. The following micro-operations suffice:

t_1: MAR ← (IR (address))
    MBR ← (PC)
t_2:PC ← (IR (address))
    Memory ← (MBR)
t_3: PC ← (PC) + 1

The address in the PC at the start of the instruction is the address of the next instruction in sequence. This is saved at the address designated in the IR. The latter address is also incremented to provide the address of the instruction for the next instruction cycle.

The Instruction Cycle

We have seen that each phase of the instruction cycle can be decomposed into a sequence of elementary operations called micro-operations. In our example, there is one sequence each for the fetch, indirect, and interrupt cycles, and, for the execute cycle, there is one sequence of micro-operations for each op code.

To complete the picture, we need to tie sequences of micro-operations together, and this is done in Figure 11-3. We assume a new 2-bit register called the *instruction cycle code* (ICC). The ICC designates the state of the CPU in terms of which portion of the cycle it is in:

00: Fetch
01: Indirect
10: Execute
11: Interrupt

At the end of each of the four cycles, the ICC is set appropriately. The indirect cycle is always followed by the execute cycle. The interrupt cycle is always followed by the fetch cycle (see Figure 10-7). For both the execute and fetch cycles, the next cycle depends upon the state of the system.

Thus the flowchart of Figure 11-3 defines the complete sequence of micro-operations, depending only on the instruction sequence and the interrupt pattern. Of course, this is a simplified example. The flowchart for an actual CPU would be more complex. In any case, we have reached the point in our discussion in which the operation of the CPU is defined as the performance of a se-

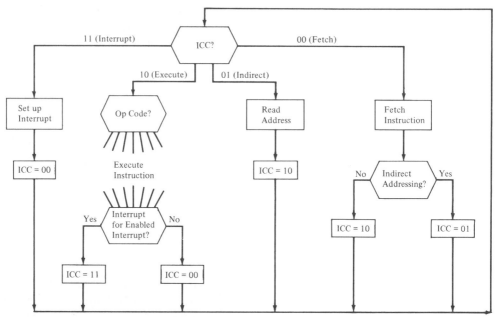

FIGURE 11-3.   Flowchart for instruction cycle

quence of micro-operations. We can now consider how the control unit causes this sequence to occur.

CONTROL OF THE CPU

Functional Requirements

As a result of our analysis in the preceding section, we have decomposed the behavior or functioning of the CPU into elementary operations, called micro-operations. Our motivation is this: We want to determine the nature of the control unit. By reducing the operation of the CPU to its most fundamental level, we are able to define exactly what it is that the control unit must cause to happen. Thus, we can define the *functional requirements* for the control unit: those functions that the control unit must perform. A definition of these functional requirements is the basis for the design and implementation of the control unit.

With the information at hand, the following three-step process leads to a characterization of the control unit:

1. Define the basic elements of the CPU.
2. Describe the micro-operations that the CPU performs.
3. Determine the functions that the control unit must perform to cause the micro-operations to be performed.

We have already performed steps 1 and 2. Let us summarize the results. First, the basic function elements of the CPU are the following:

- ALU
- Registers
- Internal Data Paths
- External Data Paths
- Control Unit

Some thought should convince the reader that this is a complete list. The ALU is the functional essence of the computer. Registers are used to store data internal to the CPU. Some registers contain status information needed to manage instruction sequencing (e.g., a program status word). Others contain data that go to or come from the ALU, memory, and I/O modules. Internal data paths are used to move data between registers and between register and ALU. External data paths link registers to memory and I/O modules, often by means of a system bus. The control unit causes operations to happen within the CPU.

The execution of a program consists of operations involving these CPU elements. As we have seen, these operations consist of a sequence of micro-operations. Upon review of Section 11.1, the reader should see that all micro-operations fall into one of the following categories:

- Transfer data from one register to another.
- Transfer data from a register to an external interface (e.g., system bus).
- Transfer data from external interface to a register.
- Perform an arithmetic or logic operation, using registers for input and output.

All of the micro-operations needed to perform one instruction cycle, including all of the micro-operations to execute every instruction in the instruction set, fall into one of these categories.

We can now be somewhat more explicit about the way in which the control unit functions. The control unit performs two basic tasks:

- *Sequencing:* The control unit causes the CPU to step through a series of micro-operations in the proper sequence, based on the program being executed.
- *Execution:* The control unit causes each micro-operation to be performed.

The preceding is a functional description of what the control unit does. The key to how the control unit operates is the use of control signals.

Control Signals

We have defined the elements that make up the CPU (ALU, registers, data paths) and the micro-operations that are performed. For the control unit to perform its function, it must have inputs that allow it to determine the state of the system and outputs that allow it to control the behavior of the system. These are the external specifications of the control unit. Internally, the control unit must have the logic required to perform its sequencing and execution functions. We defer a discussion of the internal operation of the control unit to Section 11.3 and

Chapter 12. The remainder of this section is concerned with the interaction between the control unit and the other elements of the CPU.

Figure 11-4 is a general model of the control unit, showing all of its inputs and outputs. The inputs are

- *Clock:* This is how the control unit "keeps time." The control unit causes one micro-operation (or a set of simultaneous micro-operations) to be performed for each clock pulse. This is sometimes referred to as the *processor cycle time,* or the *clock cycle time.*
- *Instruction Register:* The op code of the current instruction is used to determine which micro-operations to perform during the execute cycle.
- *Flags:* These are needed by the control unit to determine the status of the CPU and the outcome of previous ALU operations. For example, for the increment-and-skip-if-zero (ISZ) instruction, the control unit will increment the PC if the zero flag is set.
- *Control Signals from Control Bus:* The control bus portion of the system bus provides signals to the control unit, such as interrupt signals and acknowledgments.

The outputs are

- *Control Signals Within the CPU:* These are two types: those that cause data to be moved from one register to another, and those that activate specific ALU functions.
- *Control Signals to Control Bus:* These are also of two types: control signals to memory, and control signals to the I/O modules.

The new element that has been introduced in this figure is the control signal. Three types of control signals are used: those that activate an ALU function, those that activate a data path, and those that are signals on the external system

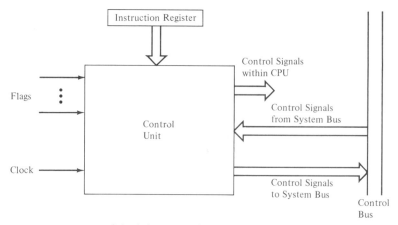

FIGURE 11-4. Model of the control unit

bus or other external interface. All of these signals are ultimately applied directly as binary inputs to individual logic gates.

Let us consider again the fetch cycle to see how the control unit maintains control. The control unit keeps track of where it is in the instruction cycle. At a given point, it knows that the fetch cycle is to be performed next. The first step is to transfer the contents of the PC to the MAR. The control unit does this by activating the control signal that opens the gates between bits of the PC and the bits of the MAR. The next step is to read a word from memory into the MBR and increment the PC. The control unit does this by sending the following control signals simultaneously:

1. A control signal that opens gates allowing the contents of the MAR onto the address bus.
2. A memory read control signal on the control bus.
3. A control signal that opens the gates allowing the contents of the data bus to be stored in the MBR.
4. Control signals to logic that adds 1 to the contents of the PC and stores the result back to the PC.

Following this, the control unit sends a control signal that opens gates between the MBR and the IR.

This completes the fetch cycle except for one thing: The control unit must decide whether to perform an indirect cycle or an execute cycle next. To decide this, it examines the IR to see if an indirect memory reference is made.

The indirect and interrupt cycles work similarly. For the execute cycle, the control unit begins by examining the op code and, on the basis of that, decides which sequence of micro-operations to perform for the execute cycle.

A Control Signals Example

To illustrate the functioning of the control unit, let us examine a simple example, adapted from one in [ANDR80]. Figure 11-5 illustrates the example. This is a simple CPU with a single accumulator. The data paths between elements are indicated. The control paths for signals emanating from the control unit are not shown, but the terminations of control signals are labeled C_i and indicated by a circle. The control unit receives inputs from the clock, the instruction register, and flags. With each clock cycle, the control unit reads all of its inputs and emits a set of control signals. Control signals go to three separate destinations:

- *Data Paths:* The control unit controls the internal flow of data. For example, on instruction fetch, the contents of the memory buffer register are transferred to the instruction register. For each path to be controlled, there is a gate (indicated by a circle in the figure). A control signal from the control unit temporarily opens the gate to let data pass.
- *ALU:* The control unit controls the operation of the ALU by a set of control signals. These signals activate various logic devices and gates within the ALU.

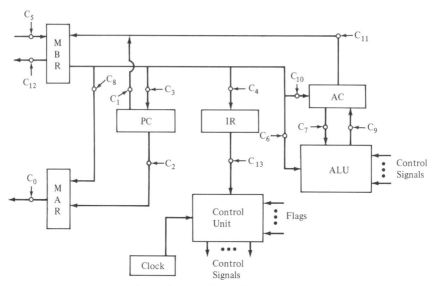

FIGURE 11-5. Data paths and control signals

- *System Bus:* The control unit sends control signals out onto the control lines of the system bus (e.g., memory READ).

The control unit must maintain knowledge of where it is in the instruction cycle. Using this knowledge, and by reading all of its inputs, the control unit emits a sequence of control signals that causes micro-operations to occur. It uses the clock pulses to time the sequence of events, allowing time between events for signal levels to stabilize. Table 11-1 indicates the control signals that are needed for some of the micro-operation sequences described earlier. For simplicity, the data and control paths for incrementing the PC and for loading the fixed addresses into the PC and MAR are not shown.

It is worth pondering the minimal nature of the control unit. The control unit is the engine that runs the entire computer. It does this based only on knowing the instructions to be executed and the nature of the results of arithmetic and logical operations (e.g., positive, overflow, etc.). It never gets to see the data being processed or the actual results produced. And it controls everything with a few control signals to points within the CPU and a few control signals to the system bus.

Internal CPU Organization

Figure 11-5 indicates the use of a variety of data paths. The complexity of this type of organization should be clear. More typically, some sort of internal bus arrangement, as was suggested in Figure 10-2, will be used.

TABLE 11-1 Micro-operations and Control Signals

Micro-Operations		Active Control Signals
Fetch:	t_1: MAR ← (PC)	C_2
	t_2: MBR ← Memory	C_5, C_R
	PC ← (PC) + 1	
	t_3: IR ← (MBR)	C_4
Indirect:	t_1: MAR ← (IR(Address))	C_8
	t_2: MBR ← Memory	C_5, C_R
	t_3: IR(Address) ←	C_4
	(MBR(Address))	
Interrupt:	t_1: MBR ← (PC)	C_1
	t_2: MAR ← Save-address	
	PC ← Routine-address	
	t_3: Memory ← (MBR)	C_{12}, C_W

C_R = Read control signal to system bus
C_W = Write control signal to system bus

Using an internal CPU bus, Figure 11-5 can be rearranged as shown in Figure 11-6. The ALU and all CPU registers are connected by a single internal bus. Gates and control signals are provided for movement of data onto and off the bus from each register. Additional control signals control data transfer to and from the system (external) bus and the operation of the ALU.

Two new registers, labeled Y and Z, have been added to the organization. These are needed for the proper operation of the ALU. When an operation involving two operands is performed, one can be obtained from the internal bus, but the other must be obtained from another source. The AC could be used for this purpose, but this limits the flexibility of the system and would not work with a CPU with multiple general-purpose registers. Register Y provides temporary storage for the other input. The ALU is a combinatorial circuit (see the appendix to this book) with no internal storage. Thus, when control signals activate an ALU function, the input to the ALU is transformed to the output. Thus, the output of the ALU cannot be directly connected to the bus since this output would feed back to the input. Register Z provides temporary output storage. With this arrangement, an operation to add a value from memory to the AC would have the following steps:

t_1: MAR ← (IR (address))
t_2: MBR ← Memory
t_3: Y ← (MBR)
t_4: Z ← (AC) + (Y)
t_5: AC ← (Z)

Other organizations are possible, but, in general, some sort of internal bus or set of internal buses is used. The use of common data paths simplifies the inter-

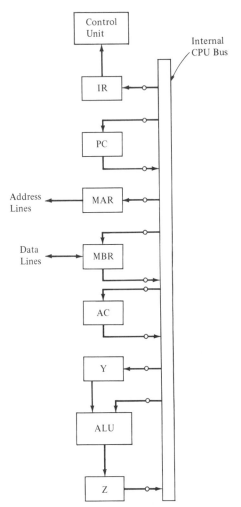

FIGURE 11-6. CPU with internal bus

connection layout and the control of the CPU. Another practical reason for the
use of an internal bus is to save space. Especially for microprocessors, which
may occupy only a 1/4-inch square piece of silicon, space occupied by inter-regis-
ter connections must be minimized.

The Intel 8085

To illustrate some of the concepts introduced thus far in this chapter, let us again
consider the Intel 8085. A more complete depiction of its organization is shown
in Figure 11-7. Several additions have been made to Figure 10-3.

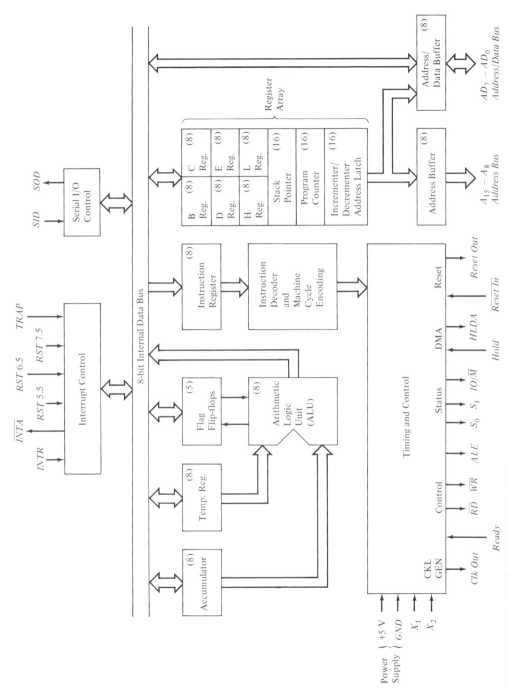

FIGURE 11-7. Intel 8085 CPU block diagram

- *Incrementer/Decrementer Address Latch:* Logic that can add 1 to or subtract 1 from the contents of the stack pointer or program counter. This saves time by avoiding the use of the ALU for this purpose.
- *Interrupt Control:* This module handles multiple levels of interrupt signals.
- *Serial I/O Control:* This module interfaces to devices that communicate 1 bit at a time.

Table 11-2 describes the external signals into and out of the 8085. These are linked to the external system bus. These signals are the interface between the 8085 processor and the rest of the system (Figure 11-8).

The control unit is identified as having two components labeled (1) instruction decoder and machine cycle encoding and (2) timing and control. A discussion of the first component is deferred until the next section. The essence of the control unit is the timing and control module. This module includes a clock and accepts as inputs the current instruction and some external control signals. Its output consists of control signals to the other components of the CPU plus control signals to the external system bus.

TABLE 11-2   INTEL 8085 External Signals

Address and Data Signals

High Address (A_{15}–A_8)
   The high-order 8 bits of a 16-bit address.

Address/Data (AD_7–AD_0)
   The lower-order 8 bits of a 16-bit address or 8 bits of data. This multiplexing saves on pins.

Serial Input Data (SID)
   A single-bit input to accommodate devices that transmit serially (one bit at a time).

Serial Output Data (SOD)
   A single-bit output to accommodate devices that receive serially.

Timing and Control Signals

CLK (OUT)
   The system clock. Each cycle represents one T state. The CLK signal goes to peripheral chips and synchronizes their timing.

X_1, X_2
   These signals come from an external crystal or other device to drive the internal clock generator.

Address Latch Enabled (ALE)
   Occurs during the first clock state of a machine cycle and causes peripheral chips to store the address lines. This allows the addressed module (e.g. memory, I/O) to recognize that it is being addressed.

Status (S_0, S_1)
   Control signals used to indicate whether a read or write operation is taking place.

TABLE 11-2 (continued)

IO/M
Used to enable either I/O or memory modules for read and write operations.

Read Control (RD)
Indicates that the selected memory or I/O module is to be read and that the data bus is available for data transfer.

Write Control (WR)
Indicates that data on the data bus is to be written into the selected memory or I/O location.

Memory and I/O Initiated Symbols

HOLD
Requests the CPU to relinquish control and use of the external system bus. The CPU will complete execution of the instruction presently in the IR and then enter a hold state, during which no signals are inserted by the CPU to the control, address, or data buses. During the hold state, the bus may be used for DMA operations.

Hold Acknowledge (HOLDA)
This control unit output signal acknowledges the HOLD signal and indicates that the bus is now available.

READY
Used to synchronize the CPU with slower memory or I/O devices. When an addressed device asserts READY, the CPU may proceed with an input (DBIN) or output (WR) operation. Otherwise, the CPU enters a wait state until the device is ready.

Interrupt-Related Signals

TRAP
Restart Interrupts (RST 7.5, 6.5, 5.5)
Interrupt Request (INTR)
These five lines are used by an external device to interrupt the CPU. The CPU will not honor the request if it is in the hold state or if the interrupt is disabled. An interrupt is honored only at the completion of an instruction. The interrupts are in descending order of priority.

Interrupt Acknowledge
Acknowledges an interrupt.

CPU Initialization

RESET IN
Causes the contents of the PC to be set to zero. The CPU resumes execution at location zero.

RESET OUT
Acknowledges that the CPU has been reset. The signal can be used to reset the rest of the system.

Voltage and Ground

V_{cc}
+5 volt power supply.
V_{ss}
Electrical ground.

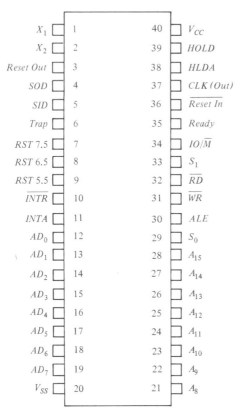

FIGURE 11-8. Intel 8085 pin configuration

The timing of CPU operations is synchronized by the clock and controlled by the control unit with control signals. Each instruction cycle is divided into from one to five *machine cycles;* each machine cycle is in turn divided into from three to five *states.* Each state lasts one clock cycle. During a state, the CPU performs one or a set of simultaneous micro-operations as determined by the control signals.

The number of machine cycles is fixed for a given instruction but varies from one instruction to another. Machine cycles are defined to be equivalent to bus accesses. Thus the number of machine cycles for an instruction depends on the number of times the CPU must communicate with external devices. For example, if an instruction consists of two 8-bit portions, then two machine cycles are required to fetch the instruction. If that instruction involves a 1-byte memory or I/O operation, then a third machine cycle is required for execution.

Figure 11-9 gives an example of 8085 timing, showing the value of external control signals. Of course, at the same time, internal control signals are being generated by the control unit to control internal data transfers. The diagram shows the instruction cycle for an OUT instruction. Three machine cycles (M_1, M_2, M_3) are needed. During the first, the OUT instruction is fetched. The second machine cycle fetches the second half of the instruction, which contains the

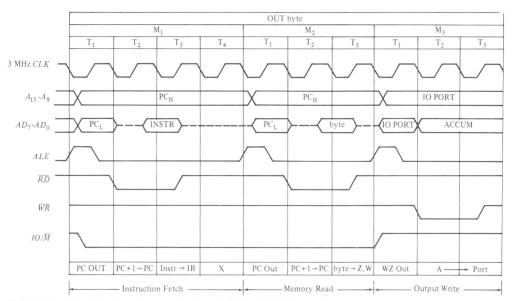

FIGURE 11-9. Timing diagram for Intel 8085 OUT instruction

number of the I/O device selected for output. During the third cycle, the contents of the AC are written out to the selected device over the data bus.

The start of each machine cycle is signaled by the Address Latch Enabled (ALE) pulse from the control unit. The ALE pulse alerts external circuits. During timing state T_1 of machine cycle M_1, the control unit sets the IO/M signal to indicate that this is a memory operation. Also, the control unit causes the contents of the PC to be placed on the address bus (A_{15}–A_8) and the address/data bus (AD_7–AD_0). With the falling edge of the ALE pulse, the other modules on the bus store the address.

During timing state T_2, the addressed memory module places the contents of the addressed memory location on the address/data bus. The control unit sets the Read Control (RD) signal to indicate a read, but it waits until T_3 to copy the data from the bus. This gives the memory module time to put the data on the bus and for the signal levels to stabilize. The final state, T_4, is a *bus idle* state during which the CPU decodes the instruction. The remaining machine cycles proceed in a similar fashion.

11.3

HARDWIRED IMPLEMENTATION

We have discussed the control unit in terms of its inputs, output, and functions. It is now time to turn to the topic of control unit implementation. A wide variety of techniques have been used. Most of these fall into one of two categories:

- Hardwired Implementation
- Microprogrammed Implementation

In a hardwired implementation, the control unit is essentially a combinatorial circuit. Its input logic signals are transformed into a set of output logic signals, which are the control signals. This approach is examined in this section. Microprogrammed implementation is the subject of Chapter 12.

Control Unit Inputs

Figure 11-4 depicts the control unit as we have so far discussed it. The key inputs are the instruction register, the clock, flags, and control bus signals. In the case of the flags and control bus signals, each individual bit typically has some meaning (e.g., overflow). The other two inputs, however, are not directly useful to the control unit.

First consider the instruction register. The control unit makes use of the op-code and will perform different actions (issue a different combination of control signals) for different instructions. To simplify the control unit logic, there should be a unique logic input for each op code. This function can be performed by a *decoder*, which takes an encoded input and produces a single output. In general, a decoder will have n binary inputs and 2^n binary outputs. Each of the 2^n different input patterns will activate a single unique output. Table 11-3 is an example. The decoder for a control unit will typically have to be more complex than that, to account for variable-length op codes. An example of the digital logic used to implement a decoder is presented in Appendix A.

TABLE 11-3 A Decoder With Four Inputs and Sixteen Outputs

I_1	I_2	I_3	I_4	O_1	O_2	O_3	O_4	O_5	O_6	O_7	O_8	O_9	O_{10}	O_{11}	O_{12}	O_{13}	O_{14}	O_{15}	O_{16}
0	0	0	0	0	0	0	0	0	0	0	0	0	0	0	0	0	0	0	1
0	0	0	1	0	0	0	0	0	0	0	0	0	0	0	0	0	0	1	0
0	0	1	0	0	0	0	0	0	0	0	0	0	0	0	0	0	1	0	0
0	0	1	1	0	0	0	0	0	0	0	0	0	0	0	0	1	0	0	0
0	1	0	0	0	0	0	0	0	0	0	0	0	0	0	1	0	0	0	0
0	1	0	1	0	0	0	0	0	0	0	0	0	0	1	0	0	0	0	0
0	1	1	0	0	0	0	0	0	0	0	0	0	1	0	0	0	0	0	0
0	1	1	1	0	0	0	0	0	0	0	0	1	0	0	0	0	0	0	0
1	0	0	0	0	0	0	0	0	0	0	1	0	0	0	0	0	0	0	0
1	0	0	1	0	0	0	0	0	0	1	0	0	0	0	0	0	0	0	0
1	0	1	0	0	0	0	0	0	1	0	0	0	0	0	0	0	0	0	0
1	0	1	1	0	0	0	0	1	0	0	0	0	0	0	0	0	0	0	0
1	1	0	0	0	0	0	1	0	0	0	0	0	0	0	0	0	0	0	0
1	1	0	1	0	0	1	0	0	0	0	0	0	0	0	0	0	0	0	0
1	1	1	0	0	1	0	0	0	0	0	0	0	0	0	0	0	0	0	0
1	1	1	1	1	0	0	0	0	0	0	0	0	0	0	0	0	0	0	0

The clock portion of the control unit issues a repetitive sequence of pulses. This is useful for measuring the duration of micro-operations. Essentially, the period of the clock pulses must be long enough to allow the propagation of signals along data paths and through CPU circuitry. However, as we have seen, the control unit emits different control signals at different time units within a single instruction cycle. Thus we would like a counter as input to the control unit, with a different control signal being used for T_1, T_2, and so forth. At the end of an instruction cycle, the control unit must feed back to the counter to re-initialize it at T_1.

With these two refinements, the control unit can be depicted as in Figure 11-10.

Control Unit Logic

To define the hardwired implementation of a control unit, all that remains is to discuss the internal logic of the control unit that produces output control signals as a function of its input signals.

Essentially, what must be done is, for each control signal, to derive a Boolean expression of that signal as a function of the inputs. This is best explained by example. Let us consider again our simple example illustrated in Figure 11-5. We saw in Table 11-1 the micro-operation sequences and control signals needed to control three of the four phases of the instruction cycle.

Let us consider a single control signal, C_5. This signal causes data to be read from the external data bus into the MBR. We can see that it is used twice in

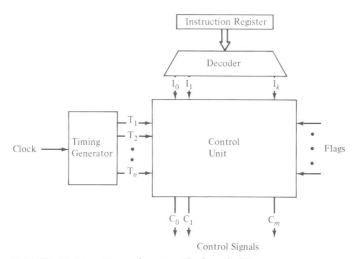

FIGURE 11-10.   Control unit with decoded inputs

Table 11-1. Let us define two new control signals, P and Q, that have the following interpretation:

PQ = 00   Fetch Cycle
PQ = 01   Indirect Cycle
PQ = 10   Execute Cycle
PQ = 11   Interrupt Cycle

Then the following Boolean expression defines C_5:

$$C_5 = \overline{P} \cdot \overline{Q} \cdot T_2 + \overline{P} \cdot Q \cdot T_2$$

That is, the control signal C_5 will be asserted during the second time unit of both the fetch and indirect cycles.

This expression is not complete. C_5 is also needed during the execute cycle. For our simple example, let us assume that there are only three instructions that read from memory: LDA, ADD, and AND. Now, we can define C_5 as

$$C_5 = \overline{P} \cdot \overline{Q} \cdot T_2 + \overline{P} \cdot Q \cdot T_2 + P \cdot \overline{Q} \cdot (LDA + ADD + AND) \cdot T_2$$

This same process could be repeated for every control signal generated by the CPU. The result would be a set of Boolean equations that define the behavior of the control unit and hence of the CPU.

To tie everything together, the control unit must control the state of the instruction cycle. As was mentioned, at the end of each subcycle (fetch, indirect, execute, interrupt), the control unit issues a signal that causes the timing generator to reinitialize and issue T_1. The control unit must also set the appropriate values of P and Q to define the next subcycle to be performed.

The reader should be able to appreciate that in a modern complex CPU, the number of Boolean equations needed to define the control unit is very large. The task of implementing a combinatorial circuit that satisfies all of these equations becomes extremely difficult. The result is that a far simpler approach, known as *microprogramming*, is usually used. This is the subject of the next chapter.

11.4

RECOMMENDED READING

A number of textbooks treat the basic principles of control unit function, including [HENN91], [WARD90], [HAYE88], and [MANO88]. The Intel 8085 CPU is examined in detail in [ROON84] and [MALV83].

11.5

PROBLEMS

11.1 Your ALU can add its two input registers, and it can logically complement the bits of either input register, but it cannot subtract. Numbers are to be stored in 2's-complement representation. List the micro-operations your control unit must perform to cause a subtraction.

11.2 Show the micro-operations and control signals in the same fashion as Table 11-1 for the CPU in Figure 11-5 for the following instructions:

- Load Accumulator
- Store Accumulator
- Add to Accumulator
- AND to Accumulator
- Jump
- Jump if AC = 0
- Complement Accumulator

11.3 Assume that propagation delay along the bus and through the ALU of Figure 11-6 are 20 and 100 ns, respectively. The time required for a register to copy data from the bus is 10 ns. What is the time that must be allowed for **(a)** transferring data from one register to another? **(b)** incrementing the program counter?

11.4 Write the sequence of micro-operations required for the bus structure of Figure 11-6 to add a number to the AC when the number is (a) an immediate operand, (b) a direct-address operand, and (c) an indirect-address operand.

11.5 Show diagrams similar to that of Figure 11-9 for the following 8085 instructions:

a. MOV reg1, reg2   reg1 ← (reg2)
b. MOV M, reg   M ← (reg)

11.6 Suggest an internal data path and control signal organization for the Intel 8085 register array.

11.7 A stack is implemented as shown in Figure 8-12. Show the sequence of micro-operations for (a) popping and (b) pushing the stack.

CHAPTER 12

Microprogrammed Control

The term *microprogram* was first coined by M. V. Wilkes in the early 1950s [WILK51]. Wilkes proposed an approach to control unit design that was organized and systematic and avoided the complexities of a hardwired implementation. The idea intrigued many researchers but appeared unworkable because it would require a fast, relatively inexpensive control memory.

The state of the microprogramming art was reviewed by *Datamation* in its February 1964 issue. No microprogrammed system was in wide use at that time, and one of the papers [HILL64] summarized the then-popular view that the future of microprogramming "...is somewhat cloudy. None of the major manufacturers has evidenced interest in the technique, although presumably all have examined it."

This situation changed dramatically within a very few months. IBM's System/360 was announced in April, and all but the largest models were microprogrammed. Although the 360 series predated the availability of semiconductor ROM, the advantages of microprogramming were compelling enough for IBM to make this move. Since then, microprogramming has become an increasingly popular vehicle for a variety of applications, one of which is the use of microprogramming to implement the control unit of a CPU. That application is examined in this chapter.

12.1

BASIC CONCEPTS

Microinstructions

The control unit, as just described, seems a reasonably simple device. Nevertheless, to implement a control unit as an interconnection of basic logic elements is no easy task. The design must include logic for sequencing through micro-operations, for executing micro-operations, for interpreting op codes, and for making decisions based on ALU flags. It is difficult to design and test such a piece of hardware. Furthermore, the design is relatively inflexible. For example, it is difficult to change the design if one wishes to add a new machine instruction.

There is an alternative, one that is quite common for computers made today, and that is to implement a microprogrammed control unit.

Consider again Table 11-1. In addition to the use of control signals, each micro-operation is described in symbolic notation. This notation looks suspiciously like a programming language! In fact it is a language, known as a *microprogramming language*. Each line describes a set of micro-operations occurring at one time and is known as a *microinstruction*. A sequence of instructions is known as a *microprogram*, or *firmware*. This latter term reflects the fact that a microprogram is midway between hardware and software. It is easier to design in firmware than hardware, but it is more difficult to write a firmware program than a software program.

How can we use the concept of microprogramming to implement a control unit? Consider that for each micro-operation, all that the control unit is allowed to do is generate a set of control signals. Thus, for any micro-operation, each control line emanating from the control unit is either on or off. This condition can, of course, be represented by a binary digit for each control line. So, we could construct a *control word* in which each bit represents one control line. Then, each micro-operation would be represented by a different pattern of 1s and 0s in the control word.

This begins to look promising. Suppose we string together a sequence of control words to represent the sequence of micro-operations performed by the control unit. Now we are almost there. Next, we must recognize that the sequence of micro-operations is not fixed. Sometimes we have an indirect cycle; sometimes we do not. So, let us put our control words in a memory, with each word having a unique address. Now, add an address field to each control word, indicating the location of the next control word to be executed if a certain condition is true (e.g., the indirect bit in a memory-reference instruction is 1). Also, add a few bits to specify the condition.

The result is known as a *horizontal microinstruction* and is shown in Figure 12-1a. The format of the microinstruction or control word is as follows. There are one bit for each internal CPU control line and one bit for each system bus control line. There is a condition field indicating the condition under which there should be a branch, and there is a field with the address of the microinstruction to be executed next when a branch is taken. Such a microinstruction is interpreted as follows:

1. To execute this microinstruction, turn on all the control lines indicated by a 1 bit; leave off all control lines indicated by a 0 bit. The resulting control signals will cause one or more micro-operations to be performed.

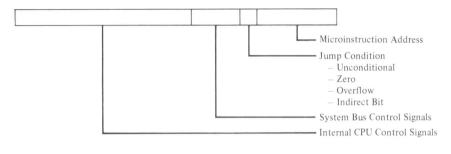

(a) Horizontal Microinstruction

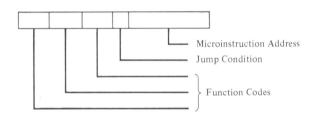

(b) Vertical Microinstruction

FIGURE 12-1. Typical microinstruction formats

2. If the condition indicated by the condition bits is false, execute the next microinstruction in sequence.
3. If the condition indicated by the condition bits is true, the next microinstruction to be executed is indicated in the address field.

Figure 12-2 shows how these control words or micro-instructions could be arranged in a *control memory*. The microinstructions in each routine are to be executed sequentially. Each routine ends with a branch or jump instruction indicating where to go next. There is a special execute cycle routine whose only purpose is to signify that one of the machine instruction routines (AND, ADD, and so on) is to be executed next, depending on the current op code.

The control memory of Figure 12-2 is a concise description of the complete operation of the control unit. It defines the sequence of micro-operations to be performed during each cycle (fetch, indirect, execute, interrupt), and it specifies the sequencing of these cycles. If nothing else, this notation would be a useful device for documenting the functioning of a control unit for a particular computer. But it is more than that. It is also a way of implementing the control unit.

Microprogrammed Control Unit

The control memory of Figure 12-2 contains a program that describes the behavior of the control unit. It follows that we could implement the control unit by simply executing that program.

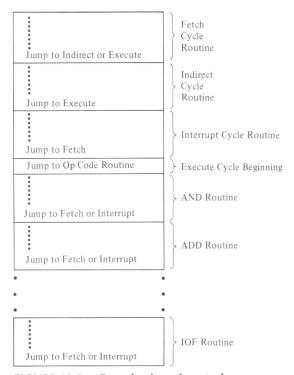

FIGURE 12-2. **Organization of control memory**

Figure 12-3 shows the key elements of such an implementation. The set of microinstructions is stored in the *control memory*. The *control address register* contains the address of the next microinstruction to be read. When a microinstruction is read from the control memory, it is transferred to a *control buffer register*.

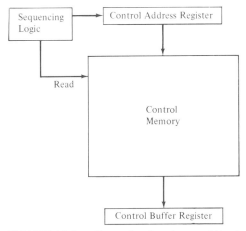

FIGURE 12-3. **Control unit microarchitecture**

The left-hand portion of that register (see Figure 12-1a) connects to the control lines emanating from the control unit. Thus, *reading* a microinstruction from the control memory is the same as *executing* that microinstruction! The third element shown in the figure is a sequencing unit that loads the control address register and issues a read command.

Let us examine this structure in greater detail, as depicted in Figure 12-4. Comparing this to Figure 11-4, we see that the control unit still has the same inputs (IR, ALU flags, clock) and outputs (control signals). The control unit functions as follows:

1. To execute an instruction, the sequencing logic unit issues a READ command to the control memory.
2. The word whose address is specified in the control address register is read into the control buffer register.

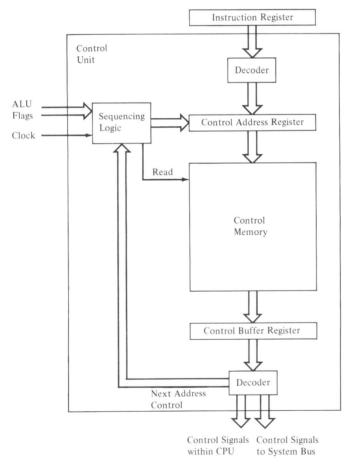

FIGURE 12-4. **Functioning of microprogrammed control unit**

3. The content of the control buffer register generates control signals and next-address information for the sequencing logic unit.
4. The sequencing logic unit loads a new address into the control address register based on the next-address information from the control buffer register and the ALU flags.

All of this happens during one clock pulse.

The last step just listed needs elaboration. At the conclusion of each microinstruction, the sequencing logic unit loads a new address into the control address register. Depending on the value of the ALU flags and the control buffer register, one of three decisions is made:

• Get the next instruction: Add 1 to the control address register.
• Jump to a new routine based on a jump microinstruction: Load the address field of the control buffer register into the control address register.
• Jump to a machine instruction routine: Load the control address register based on the op code in the IR.

A final point: Figure 12-4 shows two modules labeled *decoder*. The upper decoder translates the op code of the IR into a control memory address. The lower decoder is not used for horizontal microinstructions but is used for *vertical microinstructions* (Figure 12-1b). As was mentioned, in a horizontal microinstruction every bit in the control field attaches to a control line. In a vertical microinstruction, a code is used for each action to be performed, e.g., MAR ← (PC), and the decoder translates this code into individual control signals. The advantage of vertical microinstructions is that they are more compact (fewer bits) than horizontal microinstructions, at the expense of a small additional amount of logic and time delay.

Wilkes Control

As was mentioned, Wilkes first proposed the use of a microprogrammed control unit in 1951 [WILK51]. This proposal was subsequently elaborated into a more detailed design [WILK53]. It is instructive to examine this seminal proposal.

Wilkes was concerned with developing a systematic approach to the design of a control unit. The configuration that he proposed is depicted in Figure 12-5. The heart of the system is a matrix partially filled with diodes. During a machine cycle, one row of the matrix is activated with a pulse. This generates signals at those points where a diode is present (indicated by a dot in the diagram). The first part of the row generates the control signals that control the operation of the CPU. The second part generates the address of the row to be pulsed in the next machine cycle. Thus each row of the matrix is one microinstruction, and the layout of the matrix is the control memory.

At the beginning of the cycle, the address of the row to be pulsed is contained in Register I. This address is the input to the decoder, which, when activated by a clock pulse, activates one row of the matrix. Depending on the control signals,

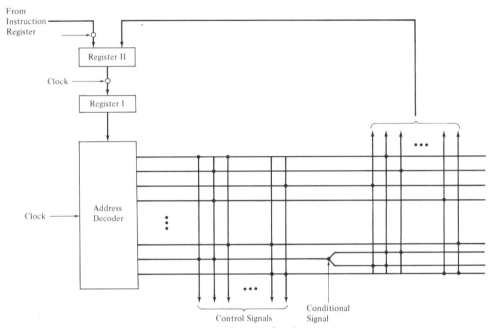

FIGURE 12-5. Wilkes's microprogrammed control unit

either the op code in the instruction register or the second part of the pulsed row is passed into Register II during the cycle. Register II is then gated to Register I by a clock pulse. Alternating clock pulses are used to activate a row of the matrix and to transfer from Register II to Register I. The two-register arrangement is needed since the decoder is simply a combinatorial circuit; with only one register, the output would become the input during a cycle, causing an unstable condition.

This scheme is very similar to the horizontal microprogramming approach described earlier (Figure 12-1a). The main difference is this: In the previous description, the control address register could be incremented by one to get the next address. In the Wilkes scheme, the next address is contained in the micro-instruction. To permit branching, a row must contain two address parts, controlled by a conditional signal (e.g., flag), as shown in the figure.

Having proposed this scheme, Wilkes provides an example of its use to implement the control unit of a simple machine. This example, the first known design of a microprogrammed CPU, is worth repeating here because it illustrates many of the contemporary principles of microprogramming.

The CPU of the hypothetical machine includes the following registers:

A multiplicand
B accumulator (least-significant half)
C accumulator (most-significant half)
D shift register

In addition, there are three registers and two 1-bit flags accessible only to the control unit. The registers are

E serves as both a memory address register (MAR) and temporary storage
F program counter
G another temporary register, used for counting

Table 12-1 lists the machine instruction set for this example. Table 12-2 is the complete set of microinstructions, expressed in symbolic form, that implements the control unit. Thus a total of 38 microinstructions is all that is required to completely define the system.

The first column gives the address (row number) of each microinstruction. Those addresses corresponding to op codes are labeled. Thus, when the op code for the add instruction (A) is encountered, the microinstruction at location 5 is executed. Columns 2 and 3 express the actions to be taken by the ALU and control unit, respectively. Each symbolic expression must be translated into a set of control signals (microinstruction bits). Columns 4 and 5 have to do with the setting and use of the two flags (flip-flops). Column 4 specifies the signal that sets the flag. For example, $(1)C_s$ means that flag number 1 is set by the sign bit of the number in register C. If column 5 contains a flag identifier, then columns 6 and 7 contain the two alternative microinstruction addresses to be used. Otherwise, column 6 specifies the address of the next microinstruction to be fetched.

Instructions 0 through 4 constitute the fetch cycle. Microinstruction 4 presents the op code to a decoder, which generates the address of a microinstruction corresponding to the machine instruction to be fetched. The reader should be able to deduce the complete functioning of the control unit from a careful study of Table 12-2.

TABLE 12-1 Machine Instruction Set for Wilkes Example

Notation: Acc = accumulator
Acc_1 = most significant half of accumulator
Acc_2 = least significant half of accumulator
n = storage location n
$C(X)$ = contents of X (X = register or storage location)

Order	Effect of Order
A n	$C(Acc) + C(n)$ to Acc
S n	$C(Acc) - C(n)$ to Acc
H n	$C(n)$ to Acc_2
V n	$C(Acc_2) \cdot C(n)$ to Acc, where $C(n) \geqslant 0$
T n	$C(Acc_1)$ to n, 0 to Acc
U n	$C(Acc_1)$ to n
R n	$C(Acc) \cdot 2^{-(n+1)}$ to Acc
L n	$C(Acc) \cdot 2^{n+1}$ to Acc
G n	IF $C(Acc) < 0$, transfer control to n; if $C(Acc) \geqslant 0$, ignore (i.e., proceed serially)
I n	Read next character on input mechanism into n
O n	Send $C(n)$ to output mechanism

TABLE 12-2   Microinstructions for Wilkes Example

Notation: $A, B, C, \ldots$ stand for the various registers in the arithmetical and control register units. 'C to D' indicates that the switching circuits connect the output of register C to the input of register D; '$(D + A)$ to C' indicates that the output of register A is connected to the one input of the adding unit (the output of D is permanently connected to the other input), and the output of the adder to register C.

A numerical symbol n in quotes (e.g., 'n') stands for the source whose output is the number n in units of the least significant digit.

	Arithmetical Unit	Control Register Unit	Conditional Flip-flop Set	Use	Next Micro-instruction 0	1
0		F to G and E			1	
1		$(G$ to '1'$)$ to F			2	
2		Store to G			3	
3		G to E			4	
4		E to decoder			—	
A 5	C to D				16	
S 6	C to D				17	
H 7	Store to B				0	
V 8	Store to A				27	
T 9	C to Store				25	
U 10	C to Store				0	
R 11	B to D	E to G			19	
L 12	C to D	E to G			22	
G 13		E to G	$(1)C_s$		18	
I 14	Input to Store				0	
O 15	Store to Output				0	
16	$(D + $ Store$)$ to C				0	
17	$(D - $ Store$)$ to C				0	
18				1	0	1
19	D to B (R)*	$(G - $ '1'$)$ to E			20	
20	C to D		$(1)E_s$		21	
21	D to C (R)			1	11	0
22	D to C (L)†	$(G - $ '1'$)$ to E			23	
23	B to D		$(1)E_s$		24	
24	D to B (L)			1	12	0
25	'0' to B				26	
26	B to C				0	
27	'0' to C	'18' to E			28	
28	B to D	E to G	$(1)B_l$		29	
29	D to B (R)	$(G - $ '1'$)$ to E			30	
30	C to D (R)		$(2)E_s$	1	31	32
31	D to C			2	28	33
32	$(D + A)$ to C			2	28	33
33	B to D		$(1)B_l$		34	
34	D to B (R)				35	

TABLE 12-2   *(Continued)*

	Arithmetical Unit	Control Register Unit	Conditional Flip-flop	Next Micro-instruction	
35	C to D (R)		1	36	37
36	D to C			0	
37	(D − A) to C			0	

*Right shift. The switching circuits in the arithmetic unit are arranged so that the least significant digit of register C is placed in the most significant place of register B during right shift micro-operations, and the most significant digit of register C (sign digit) is repeated (thus making the correction for negative numbers).

†Left shift. The switching circuits are similarly arranged to pass the most significant digit of register B to the least significant place of register C during left shift micro-operations.

Advantages and Disadvantages

The principal advantage of the use of microprogramming to implement a control unit is that it simplifies the design of the control unit. Thus it is both cheaper and less error-prone to implement. A *hardwired* control unit must contain complex logic for sequencing through the many micro-operations of the instruction cycle. On the other hand, the decoders and sequencing logic unit of a micro-programmed control unit are very simple pieces of logic.

The principal disadvantage of a microprogrammed unit is that it will be somewhat slower than a hardwired unit of comparable technology. Despite this, microprogramming is the dominant technique for implementing control units in contemporary computers, due to its ease of implementation. We now examine the microprogrammed approach in greater detail.

12.2

MICROINSTRUCTION SEQUENCING

The two basic tasks performed by a microprogrammed control unit are

- *Microinstruction Sequencing:* Get the next microinstruction from the control memory.
- *Microinstruction Execution:* Generate the control signals needed to execute the microinstruction.

In designing a control unit, these tasks must be considered together, since both affect the format of the microinstruction and the timing of the control unit. In this section, we will focus on sequencing and say as little as possible about format and timing issues. These issues are examined in more detail in the next section.

Design Considerations

Two concerns are involved in the design of a microinstruction sequencing technique: the size of the microinstruction and the address-generation time. The first concern is obvious; minimizing the size of the control memory reduces the cost of that component. The second concern is simply a desire to execute microinstructions as fast as possible.

In executing a microprogram, the address of the next microinstruction to be executed is in one of these categories:

- Determined by instruction register
- Next sequential address
- Branch

The first category occurs only once per instruction cycle, just after an instruction is fetched. The second category is the most common in most designs. However, the design cannot be optimized just for sequential access. Branches, both conditional and unconditional, are a necessary part of a microprogram. Furthermore,

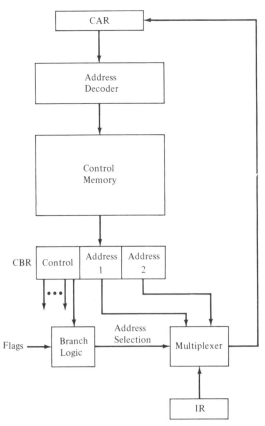

FIGURE 12-6. Branch control logic, two address fields

microinstruction sequences tend to be short; one out of every three or four microinstructions could be a branch [SIEW82a]. Thus it is important to design compact, time-efficient techniques for microinstruction branching.

Based on the current microinstruction, condition flags, and the contents of the instruction register, a control memory address must be generated for the next microinstruction. A wide variety of techniques have been used. We can group them into three general categories as illustrated in Figures 12-6 to 12-8 (based on [CLIN81]). These categories are based on the format of the address information in the microinstruction:

• Two address fields
• Single address field
• Variable format

The simplest approach is to provide two address fields in each microinstruction. Figure 12-6 suggests how this information is to be used. A multiplexer is provided that serves as a destination for both address fields plus the instruction

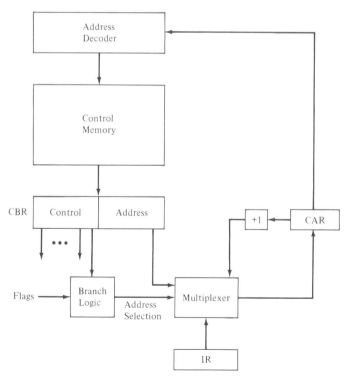

FIGURE 12-7. Branch control logic, single address field

register. Based on an address-selection input, the multiplexer transmits either the op code or one of the two addresses to the control address register (CAR). The CAR is subsequently decoded to produce the next microinstruction address. The address-selection signals are provided by a branch logic module whose input consists of control unit flags plus bits from the control portion of the microinstruction.

Although the two-address approach is simple, it requires more bits in the microinstruction than other approaches. With some additional logic, savings can be achieved. A common approach is to have a single address field (Figure 12-7). With this approach, the options for next address are

- Address field
- Instruction register code
- Next sequential address

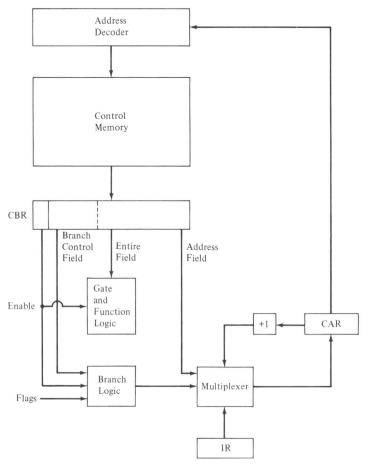

FIGURE 12-8. Branch control logic, variable format

The address-selection signals determine which option is selected. This approach reduces the number of address fields to one. Note, however, that the address field will often not be used. Thus, there is some inefficiency in the microinstruction coding scheme.

Another approach is to provide for two entirely different microinstruction formats (Figure 12-8). One bit designates which format is being used. In one format, the remaining bits are used to activate control signals. In the other format, some bits drive the branch logic module, and the remaining bits provide the address. With the first format, the next address is either the next sequential address or an address derived from the instruction register. With the second format, either a conditional or unconditional branch is being specified. One disadvantage of this approach, as just described, is that one entire cycle is consumed with each branch microinstruction. With the other approaches, address generation occurs as part of the same cycle as control signal generation, minimizing control memory accesses.

Of course, the approaches just described are general. Specific implementations will often involve a variation or combination of these techniques.

Address Generation

We have looked at the sequencing problem from the point of view of format considerations and general logic requirements. Another viewpoint is to consider the various ways in which the next address can be derived or computed.

Table 12-3 lists the various address generation techniques. These can be divided into explicit techniques, in which the address is explicitly available in the microinstruction, and implicit techniques, which require additional logic to generate the address.

We have essentially dealt with the explicit techniques. With a two-field approach, two alternative addresses are available with each microinstruction. Using either a single address field or a variable format, various branch instructions can be implemented. A conditional branch instruction depends on the following types of information:

- ALU flags
- Part of the op code or address mode fields of the machine instruction
- Parts of a selected register, such as the sign bit
- Status bits within the control unit

TABLE 12-3   Microinstruction Address
Generation Techniques

Explicit	Implicit
Two-Field	Mapping
Unconditional branch	Addition
Conditional branch	Residual control

Several implicit techniques are also commonly used. One of these, mapping, is required with virtually all designs. The op code portion of a machine instruction must be mapped into a microinstruction address. This occurs only once per instruction cycle.

A common implicit technique is one that involves combining or adding two portions of an address to form the complete address. This approach was taken for the IBM S/360 family [TUCK67] and used on many of the S/370 models. We will use the IBM 3033 as an example.

The control address register on the IBM 3033 is 13 bits long and is illustrated in Figure 12-9. Two parts of the address can be distinguished. The highest-order 8 bits (00–07) normally do not change from one microinstruction cycle to the next. During the execution of a microinstruction, these 8 bits are copied directly from an 8-bit field of the microinstruction (the BA field) into the highest-order 8 bits of the control address register. This defines a 32-bit block of microinstructions in control memory. The remaining 5 bits of the control address register are set to specify the specific address of the microinstruction to be fetched next. Each of these bits is determined by a 4-bit field (except one is a 7-bit field) in the current microinstruction; the field specifies the condition for setting the corresponding bit. For example, a bit in the control address register might be set to 1 or 0 depending on whether a carry occurred on the last ALU operation.

The final approach listed in Table 12-3 is termed *residual control*. This approach involves the use of a microinstruction address that has previously been saved in temporary storage within the control unit. For example, some microinstruction sets come equipped with a subroutine facility. An internal register or stack of registers is used to hold return addresses. An example of this approach is taken on the LSI-11, which we now examine.

LSI-11 Microinstruction Sequencing

The LSI-11 is a microcomputer version of a PDP-11, with the main components of the system residing on a single board. The LSI-11 is implemented using a microprogrammed control unit [SEBE76, CLIN81, DEC78b].

The LSI-11 makes use of a 22-bit microinstruction and a control memory of 2K 22-bit words. The next microinstruction address is determined in one of five ways:

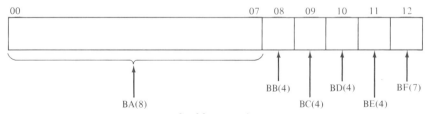

FIGURE 12-9. IBM 3033 control address register

- *Next Sequential Address:* In the absence of other instructions, the control unit's control address register is incremented by 1.
- *Op code Mapping:* At the beginning of each instruction cycle, the next microinstruction address is determined by the op code.
- *Subroutine Facility:* Explained presently.
- *Interrupt Testing:* Certain microinstructions specify a test for interrupts. If an interrupt has occurred, this determines the next microinstruction address.
- *Branch:* Conditional and unconditional branch microinstructions are used.

A one-level subroutine facility is provided. One bit in every microinstruction is dedicated to this task. When the bit is set, an 11-bit return register is loaded with the updated contents of the control address register. A subsequent microinstruction that specifies a return will cause the control address register to be loaded from the return register.

The return is one form of unconditional branch instruction. Another form of unconditional branch causes the bits of the control address register to be loaded from 11 bits of the microinstruction. The conditional branch instruction makes use of a 4-bit test code within the microinstruction. This code specifies testing of various ALU condition codes to determine the branch decision. If the condition is not true, the next sequential address is selected. If it is true, the 8 lowest-order bits of the control address register are loaded from 8 bits of the microinstruction. This allows branching within a 256-word page of memory.

As can be seen, the LSI-11 includes a powerful address sequencing facility within the control unit. This allows the microprogrammer considerable flexibility and can ease the microprogramming task. On the other hand, this approach requires more control unit logic than simpler capabilities.

12.3

MICROINSTRUCTION EXECUTION

The microinstruction cycle is the basic event on a microprogrammed CPU. Each cycle is made up of two parts: fetch and execute. The fetch portion is determined by the generation of a microinstruction address, and this was dealt with in the preceding section. This section deals with the execution of a microinstruction.

Let us recall what the execution of a microinstruction causes to happen. In essence, the effect of execution is to generate control signals. Some of these signals control points internal to the CPU. The remaining signals go to the external control bus or other external interface. As an incidental function, the address of the next microinstruction is determined.

The preceding description suggests the organization of a control unit shown in Figure 12-10. This slightly revised version of Figure 12-4 emphasizes the focus of this section. The major modules in this diagram should by now be clear. The sequencing logic module contains the logic to perform the functions discussed in the preceding section. It generates the address of the next microinstruction,

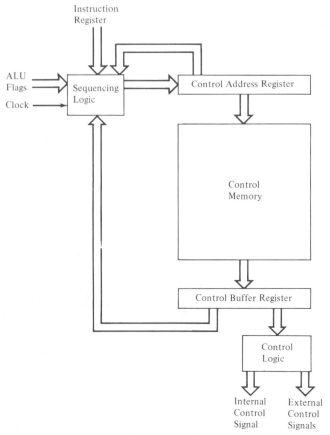

FIGURE 12-10. Control unit organization

using as inputs the instruction register, ALU flags, the control address register (for incrementing), and the control buffer register. The last may provide an actual address, control bits, or both. The module is driven by a clock that determines the timing of the microinstruction cycle.

The control logic module generates control signals as a function of some of the bits in the microinstruction. It should be clear that the format and content of the microinstruction will determine the complexity of the control logic module.

A Taxonomy of Microinstructions

Microinstructions can be classified in a variety of ways. Distinctions that are commonly made in the literature include

- Vertical/Horizontal
- Packed/Unpacked

- Hard/Soft Microprogramming
- Direct/Indirect Encoding

All of these bear on the format of the microinstruction. None of these terms has been used in a consistent, precise way in the literature. However, an examination of these pairs of qualities serves to illuminate microinstruction design alternatives. In the following paragraphs, we first look at the key design issue underlying all of these pairs of characteristics, and then we look at the concepts suggested by each pair.

In the original proposal by Wilkes [WILK51], each bit of a microinstruction either directly produced a control signal or directly produced one bit of the next address. We have seen, in the preceding section, that more-complex address sequencing schemes, using fewer microinstruction bits, are possible. These schemes require a more-complex sequencing logic module. A similar sort of tradeoff exists for the portion of the microinstruction concerned with control signals. By encoding control information, and subsequently decoding it to produce control signals, control word bits can be saved.

How can this encoding be done? To answer that, consider that there are a total of K different internal and external control signals to be driven by the control unit. In Wilkes's scheme, K bits of the microinstruction would be dedicated to this purpose. This allows all of the 2^K possible combinations of control signals to be generated during any instruction cycle. But we can do better than this if we observe that not all of the possible combinations will be used. Examples include the following:

- Two sources cannot be gated to the same destination (e.g., C_2 and C_8 in Figure 11-5).
- A register cannot be both source and destination (e.g., C_5 and C_{12} in Figure 11-5).
- Only one pattern of control signals can be presented to the ALU at a time.
- Only one pattern of control signals can be presented to the external control bus at a time.

So, for a given CPU, all possible allowable combinations of control signals could be listed, giving some number $Q < 2^K$ possibilities. These could be encoded with $\log_2 Q$ bits, with $(\log_2 Q) < K$. This would be the tightest possible form of encoding that preserves all allowable combinations of control signals. In practice, this form of encoding is not used, for two reasons:

- It is as difficult to program as a pure decoded (Wilkes) scheme. This point is discussed further presently.
- It requires a complex and therefore slow control logic module.

Instead, some compromises are made. These are of two kinds.

- More bits than are strictly necessary are used to encode the possible combinations.
- Some combinations that are physically allowable are not possible to encode.

The latter kind has the effect of reducing the number of bits. The net result, however, is to use more than $\log_2 Q$ bits.

In the next subsection, we will discuss specific encoding techniques. The remainder of this subsection deals with the effects of encoding and the various terms used to describe it.

Based on the preceding, we can see that the control signal portion of the microinstruction format falls on a spectrum. At one extreme, there is one bit for each control signal; at the other extreme, a highly encoded format is used. Table 12-4 shows that other characteristics of a microprogrammed control unit also fall along a spectrum and that these spectra are, by and large, determined by the degree-of-encoding spectrum.

The second pair of items in the table is rather obvious. The pure Wilkes scheme will require the most bits. It should also be apparent that this extreme presents the most detailed view of the hardware. Every control signal is individually controllable by the microprogrammer. Encoding is done in such a way as to aggregate functions or resources, so that the microprogrammer is viewing the CPU at a higher, less detailed level. Furthermore, the encoding is designed to ease the microprogramming burden. Again, it should be clear that the task of understanding and orchestrating the use of all the control signals is a difficult one. As was mentioned, one of the consequences of encoding, typically, is to prevent the use of certain otherwise allowable combinations.

The preceding paragraph discusses microinstruction design from the microprogrammer's point of view. But the degree of encoding also can be viewed from its hardware effects. With a pure unencoded format, little or no decode logic is needed; each bit generates a particular control signal. As more-compact and more-aggregated encoding schemes are used, more-complex decode logic is needed. This in turn may affect performance. More time is needed to propagate signals through the gates of the more-complex control logic module. Thus, the execution of encoded microinstructions takes longer than the execution of unencoded ones.

TABLE 12-4 The Microinstruction Spectrum

Characteristics	
Unencoded	Highly Encoded
Many Bits	Few Bits
Detailed View of Hardware	Aggregated View of Hardware
Difficult to Program	Easy to Program
Concurrency Fully Exploited	Concurrency Not Fully Exploited
Little or No Control Logic	Complex Control Logic
Fast Execution	Slow Execution
Optimize Performance	Optimize Programming
Terminology	
Unpacked	Packed
Horizontal	Vertical
Hard	Soft

Thus all of the characteristics listed in Table 12-4 fall along a spectrum of design strategies. In general, a design that falls towards the left end of the spectrum is intended to optimize the performance of the control unit. Designs towards the right end are more concerned with optimizing the process of micro-programming. Indeed, microinstruction sets near the right end of the spectrum look very much like machine instruction sets. A good example of this is the LSI-11 design, described later in this section. Typically, when the objective is simply to implement a control unit, the design will be near the left end of the spectrum. The IBM 3033 design, discussed presently, is in this category. As we shall discuss later, some systems permit a variety of users to construct different microprograms using the same microinstruction facility. In the latter cases, the design is likely to fall near the right end of the spectrum.

We can now deal with some of the terminology introduced earlier. Table 12-4 indicates how three of these pairs of terms relate to the microinstruction spectrum. In essence, all of these pairs describe the same thing but emphasize different design characteristics.

The degree of packing relates to the degree of identification between a given control task and specific microinstruction bits. As the bits become more *packed*, a given number of bits contains more information. Thus packing connotes encoding. The terms *horizontal* and *vertical* relate to the relative width of microinstructions. [SIEW82a] suggests as a rule of thumb that vertical microinstructions have lengths in the range of 16 to 40 bits, and that horizontal microinstructions have lengths in the range of 40 to 100 bits. The terms *hard* and *soft* microprogramming are used to suggest the degree of closeness to the underlying control signals and hardware layout. Hard microprograms are generally fixed and committed to read-only memory. Soft microprograms are more changeable and are suggestive of user microprogramming.

The other pair of terms mentioned at the beginning of this subsection refers to direct versus indirect encoding, a subject to which we now turn.

Microinstruction Encoding

In practice, microprogrammed control units are not designed using a pure unen-coded or horizontal microinstruction format. At least some degree of encoding is used to reduce control memory width and to simplify the task of microprogram-ming.

The basic technique for encoding is illustrated in Figure 12-11a. The microin-struction is organized as a set of fields. Each field contains a code, which, upon decoding, activates one or more control signals.

Let us consider the implications of this layout. When the microinstruction is executed, every field is decoded and generates control signals. Thus, with N fields, N simultaneous actions are specified. Each action results in the activation of one or more control signals. Generally, but not always, we will want to design the format so that each control signal is activated by no more than one field. Clearly, however, it must be possible for each control signal to be activated by at least one field.

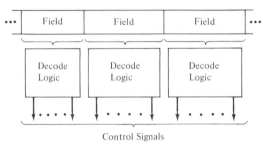

(a) Direct Encoding

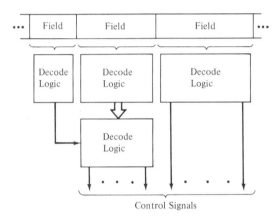

(b) Indirect Encoding

FIGURE 12-11.   **Microinstruction encoding**

Now consider the individual field. A field consisting of L bits can contain one of 2^L codes, each of which can be encoded to a different control signal pattern. Since only one code can appear in a field at a time, the codes are mutually exclusive, and, therefore, the actions they cause are mutually exclusive.

The design of an encoded microinstruction format can now be stated in simple terms:

• Organize the format into independent fields. That is, each field depicts a set of actions (pattern of control signals) such that actions from different fields can occur simultaneously.
• Define each field such that the alternative actions that can be specified by the field are mutually exclusive. That is, only one of the actions specified for a given field could occur at a time.

Two approaches can be taken to organizing the encoded microinstruction into fields: functional and resource. The *functional encoding* method identifies functions within the machine and designates fields by function type. For example, if various sources can be used for transferring data to the accumulator, one field can be designated for this purpose, with each code specifying a different source. *Resource encoding* views the machine as consisting of a set of independent resources and devotes one field to each (e.g., I/O, memory, ALU).

Another aspect of encoding is whether it is direct or indirect (Figure 12-11b). With indirect encoding, one field is used to determine the interpretation of another field. For example, consider an ALU that is capable of performing eight different arithmetic operations and eight different shift operations. A 1-bit field could be used to indicate whether a shift or arithmetic operation is to be used; a 3-bit field would indicate the operation. This technique generally implies two levels of decoding, increasing propagation delays.

Figure 12-12, from [RAUS80], is a simple example of these concepts. Assume a CPU with a single accumulator and several internal registers, such as a program counter and a temporary register for ALU input. Figure 12-12a shows a highly vertical format. The first 3 bits indicate the type of operation, the next 3 encode the operation, and the final 2 select an internal register. Figure 12-12b is a more horizontal approach, although encoding is still used. In this case different functions appear in different fields.

LSI-11 Microinstruction Execution

The LSI-11 [SEBE76, CLIN81, DEC78b] is a good example of a vertical microinstruction approach. We look first at the organization of the control unit, then at the microinstruction format.

LSI-11 Control Unit Organization

The LSI-11 is the first member of the PDP-11 family that was offered as a single-board processor. The board contains three LSI chips, an internal bus known as the *microinstruction bus* (MIB), and some additional interfacing logic.

Figure 12-13 depicts, in simplified form, the organization of the LSI-11 CPU. The three chips are the data, control, and control store chips. The data chip contains an 8-bit ALU, 26 8-bit registers, and storage for several condition codes. Sixteen of the registers are used to implement the eight 16-bit general-purpose registers of the PDP-11. Others include a program status word, memory address register (MAR), and memory buffer register. Because the ALU deals with only 8 bits at a time, two passes through the ALU are required to implement a 16-bit PDP-11 arithmetic operation. This is controlled by the microprogram.

The control store chip or chips contain the 22-bit-wide control memory. The control chip contains the logic for sequencing and executing microinstructions. It contains the control address register, the control data register, and a copy of the machine instruction register.

The MIB ties all of the components together. During microinstruction fetch, the control chip generates an 11-bit address onto the MIB. Control store is accessed, producing a 22-bit microinstruction, which is placed on the MIB. The

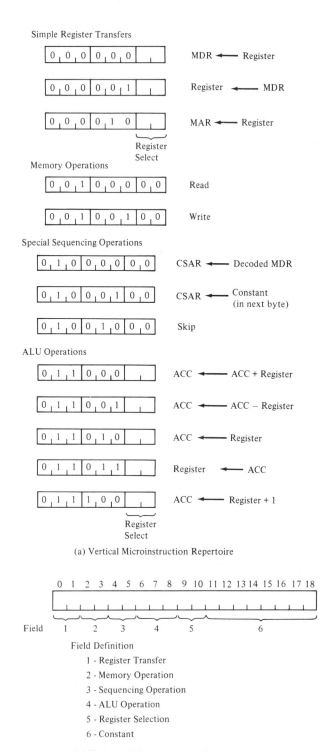

(a) Vertical Microinstruction Repertoire

Field Definition

1 - Register Transfer
2 - Memory Operation
3 - Sequencing Operation
4 - ALU Operation
5 - Register Selection
6 - Constant

(b) Horizontal Microinstruction Format

FIGURE 12-12. Alternative microinstruction formats for a simple machine

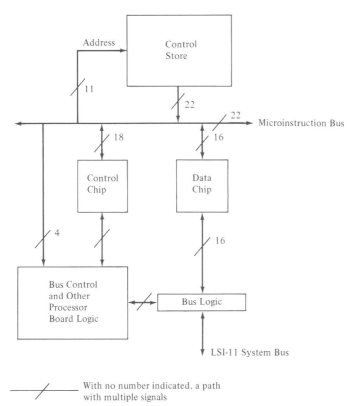

FIGURE 12-13.   Simplified block diagram of the LSI-11 processor

low-order 16 bits go to the data chip, while the low-order 18 bits go to the control chip. The high-order four bits control special CPU board functions.

Figure 12-14 provides a still simplified but more detailed look at the LSI-11 control unit: the figure ignores individual chip boundaries. The address sequencing scheme described in Section 12.2 is implemented in two modules. Overall sequence control is provided by the microprogram sequence control module, which is capable of incrementing the microinstruction address register and of performing unconditional branches. The other forms of address calculation are carried out by a separate translation array. This is a combinatorial circuit that generates an address based on the microinstruction, the machine instruction, the microinstruction program counter, and an interrupt register.

The translation array comes into play on the following occasions:

- The op code is used to determine the start of a microroutine.
- At appropriate times, address mode bits of the macroinstruction are tested to perform appropriate addressing.
- Interrupt conditions are periodically tested.
- Conditional branch microinstructions are evaluated.

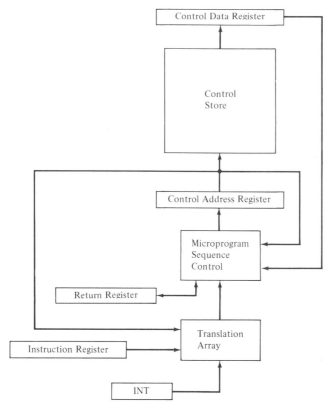

FIGURE 12-14. Organization of the LSI-11 control unit

LSI-11 Microinstruction Format

The LSI-11 uses an extremely vertical microinstruction format, which is only 22 bits wide. The microinstruction set strongly resembles the PDP-11 machine instruction set that it implements. This design was intended to optimize the performance of the control unit within the constraint of a vertical, easily-programmed design. Table 12-5 lists some of the LSI-11 microinstructions.

Figure 12-15 shows the 22-bit LSI-11 microinstruction format. The high-order 4 bits control special functions on the CPU board. The translate bit enables the translation array to check for pending interrupts. The load return register bit is used at the end of a microroutine to cause the next microinstruction address to be loaded from the return register.

The remaining 16 bits are used for highly encoded micro-operations. The format is much like a machine instruction, with a variable-length op code and one or more operands.

IBM 3033 Microinstruction Execution

The standard IBM 3033 control memory consists of 4K words. The first half of these (0000-07FF) contain 108-bit microinstructions, while the remainder (0800-

TABLE 12-5   Some LSI-11 Microinstructions

Arithmetic Operations	Shift word (byte) right (left) with (without) carry
Add Word (byte, literal)	Complement word (byte)
Test word (byte, literal)	*General Operations*
Increment word (byte) by 1	MOV word (byte)
Increment word (byte) by 2	Jump
Negate word (byte)	Return
Conditionally increment (decrement) byte	Conditional jump
Conditionally add word (byte)	Set (reset) flags
Add word (byte) with carry	Copy (load) condition flags
Conditionally add digits	Load G low
Subtract word (byte)	Conditionally MOV word (byte)
Compare word (byte, literal)	*Input/Output Operations*
Subtract word (byte) with carry	Input word (byte)
Decrement word (byte) by 1	Input status word (byte)
Logical Operations	Read
And word (byte, literal)	Write
Test word (byte)	Read (write) and increment word (byte) by 1
Or word (byte)	Read (write) and increment word (byte) by 2
Exclusive-Or word (byte)	Read (write) acknowledge
Bit clear word (byte)	Output word (byte, status)

TABLE 12-6   IBM 3033 Microinstruction Control Fields

	ALU Control Fields
AA(3)	Load A register from one of data registers
AB(3)	Load B register from one of data registers
AC(3)	Load C register from one of data registers
AD(3)	Load D register from one of data registers
AE(4)	Route specified A bits to ALU
AF(4)	Route specified B bits to ALU
AG(5)	Specifies ALU arithmetic operation on A input
AH(4)	Specifies ALU arithmetic operation on B input
AJ(1)	Specifies D or B input to ALU on B side
AK(4)	Route arithmetic output to shifter
CB(1)	Activate shifter
CC(5)	Specifies logical and carry functions
CE(7)	Specifies shift amount
CA(3)	Load F register
	Sequencing and Branching Fields
AL(1)	End operation and perform branch
BA(8)	Set high-order bits (00-07) of control address register
BB(4)	Specifies condition for setting bit 8 of control address register
BC(4)	Specifies condition for setting bit 9 of control address register
BD(4)	Specifies condition for setting bit 10 of control address register
BE(4)	Specifies condition for setting bit 11 of control address register
BF(4)	Specifies condition for setting bit 12 of control address register

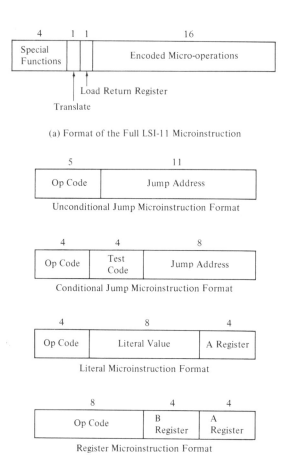

(a) Format of the Full LSI-11 Microinstruction

(b) Format of the Encoded Part of the LSI-11 Microinstruction

FIGURE 12-15. LSI-11 microinstruction format

0FFF) are used to store 126-bit microinstructions. The format is depicted in Figure 12-16. Although this is a rather horizontal format, encoding is still extensively used. The key fields of that format are summarized in Table 12-6.

The ALU operates on inputs from four dedicated, non-user-visible registers, A, B, C, and D. The microinstruction format contains fields for loading these registers from user-visible registers, performing an ALU function, and specifying a user-visible register for storing the result. There are also fields for loading and storing data between registers and memory.

The sequencing mechanism for the IBM 3033 was discussed in Section 12.2.

12.4

TI 8800

The Texas Instruments 8800 Software Development Board (SDB) is a microprogrammable 32-bit computer card. The system has a writeable control

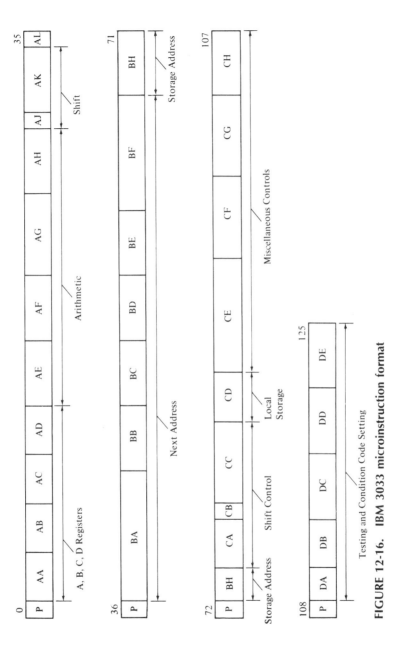

FIGURE 12-16.   IBM 3033 microinstruction format

store, implemented in RAM rather than ROM. Such a system does not achieve the speed or density of a microprogrammed system with a ROM control store. However, it is useful for developing prototypes and for educational purposes.

The 8800 SDB consists of the following components (Figure 12-17):

- Microcode Memory
- Microsequencer
- 32-bit ALU
- Floating Point and Integer Processor
- Local Data Memory

Two buses link the internal components of the system. The DA bus provides data from the microinstruction data field to the ALU, the floating-point proces-

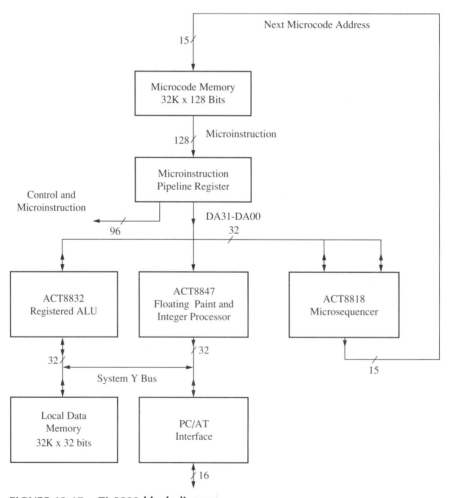

FIGURE 12-17. TI 8800 block diagram

sor, or the microsequencer. In the latter case, the data consists of an address to be used for a branch instruction. The bus can also be used for the ALU or microsequencer to provide data to other components. The System Y bus connects the ALU and floating-point processor to local memory and to external modules via the PC interface.

The board fits into an IBM PC-compatible host computer. The host computer provides a suitable platform for microcode assembly and debug.

Microinstruction Format

The microinstruction format for the 8800 consists of 128 bits broken down into 30 functional fields, as indicated in Table 12-7. Each field consists of one or more bits, and the fields are grouped into five major categories:

- Control of Board
- 8847 Floating Point and Integer Processor Chip
- 8832 Registered ALU
- 8818 Microsequencer
- WCS Data Field

As indicated in Figure 12-17, the 32 bits of the WCS data field are fed into the DA bus to be provided as data to the ALU, floating-point processor, or microsequencer. The other 96 bits (fields 1–27) of the microinstruction are control signals that are fed directly to the appropriate module. For simplicity, these other connections are not shown in Figure 12-17.

The first six fields deal with operations that pertain to the control of the board, rather than controlling an individual component. Control operations include:

1. Selection of condition codes for sequencer control. The first bit of field 1 indicates whether the condition flag is to be set to 1 or 0, and the remaining 4 bits indicate which flag is to be set.
2. Sending an I/O request to the PC/AT.
3. Enabling local data memory read/write operations.
4. Determination of the unit driving the system Y bus. One of the four devices attached to the bus (Figure 12-17) is selected.

The last 32 bits are the data field, which contain information specific to a particular microinstruction.

The remaining fields of the microinstruction are best discussed in the context of the device that they control. In the remainder of this section, we discuss the microsequencer and the registered ALU. The floating-point unit introduces no new concepts and is skipped.

Microsequencer

The principal function of the 8818 microsequencer is to generate the next microinstruction address for the microprogram. This 15-bit address is provided to the microcode memory (Figure 12-17).

TABLE 12-7   TI 8800 Microinstruction Format

Field Number	Number of Bits	Description
		Control of Board
1	5	Select condition code input
2	1	Enable/disable external I/O request signal
3	2	Enable/disable local data memory read/write operations
4	1	Load status/do not load status
5	2	Determine unit driving Y bus
6	2	Determine unit driving DA bus
		8847 Floating Point and Integer Processing Chip
7	1	C register control: clock, do not clock
8	1	Select most significant or least significant bits for Y bus
9	1	C register data source: ALU, multiplexer
10	4	Select IEEE or FAST mode for ALU and MUL
11	8	Select sources for data operands: RA registers, RB registers, P register, S register, C register
12	1	RB register control: clock, do not clock
13	1	RA register control: clock, do not clock
14	2	Data source confirmation
15	2	Enable/disable pipeline registers
16	11	8847 ALU function
		8832 Registered ALU
17	2	Write enable/disable data output to selected register: most significant half, least significant half
18	2	Select register file data source: DA bus, DB bus, ALU Y MUX output, system Y bus
19	3	Shift instruction modifier
20	1	Carry in: force, do not force
21	2	Set ALU configuration mode: 32, 16, or 8 bits
22	2	Select input to S multiplexer: register file, DB bus, MQ register
23	1	Select input to R multiplexer: register file, DA bus
24	6	Select register in file C for write
25	6	Select register in file B for read
26	6	Select register in file A for write
27	8	ALU function
		8818 Microsequencer
28	12	Control input signals to the 8818
		WCS Data Field
29	16	Most significant bits of writeable control store data field
30	16	Least significant bits of writeable control store data field

The next address can be selected from one of five sources:

1. The microprogram counter (MPC) register, used for repeat (re-use same address) and continue (increment address by 1) instructions.
2. The stack, which supports microprogram subroutine calls as well as iterative loops and returns from interrupts.
3. The DRA and DRB ports which provide two additional paths from external hardware by which microprogram addresses can be generated. These two ports are connected to the most significant and least significant 16 bits of the DA bus, respectively. This allows the microsequencer to obtain the next instruction address from the WCS data field of the current microinstruction or from a result calculated by the ALU.
4. Register counters RCA and RCB, which can be used for additional address storage.
5. An external input onto the bidirectional Y port to support external interrupts.

Figure 12-18 is a logical block diagram of the 8818. The device consists of the following principal functional groups:

- A 16-bit microprogram counter (MPC) consisting of a register and an incrementer.
- Two register counters, RCA and RCB, for counting loops and iterations, storing branch addresses, or driving external devices.
- A 65-word by 16-bit stack, which allows microprogram subroutine calls and interrupts.
- An interrupt return register and Y output enable for interrupt processing at the microinstruction level.
- A Y output multiplexer by which the next address can be selected from MPC, RCA, RCB, external buses DRA and DRB, or the stack.

Registers/Counters

The registers RCA and RCB may be loaded from the DA bus, either from the current microinstruction or from the output of the ALU. The values may be used as counters to control the flow of execution and may be automatically decremented when accessed. The values may also be used as microinstruction addresses to be supplied to the Y output multiplexer. Independent control of both registers during a single microinstruction cycle is supported with the exception of simultaneous decrement of both registers.

Stack

The stack allows multiple levels of nested calls or interrupts, and can be used to support branching and looping. Keep in mind that these operations refer to the control unit, not the overall processor, and that the addresses involved are those of microinstructions in the control memory.

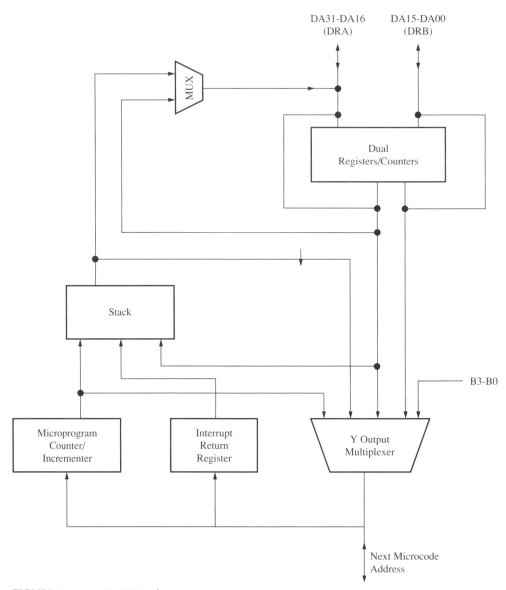

FIGURE 12-18. TI 8818 microsequencer

Six stack operations are possible:

1. Clear, which sets the stack pointer to zero, emptying the stack.
2. Pop, which decrements the stack pointer.
3. Push, which puts the contents of the MPC, interrupt return register, or DRA bus onto the stack and increments the stack pointer.

4. Read, which makes the address indicated by the read pointer available at the Y output multiplexer.
5. Hold, which causes the address of the stack pointer to remain unchanged.
6. Load stack pointer, which inputs the seven least significant bits of DRA to the stack pointer.

Control of Microsequencer

The microsequencer is controlled primarily by the 12-bit field of the current microinstruction, field 28 (Table 12-7). This field consists of the following sub-fields:

- OSEL (1 bit): Output select. Determines which value will be placed on the output of the multiplexer that feeds into the DRA bus (upper left-hand corner of Figure 12-18). The output is selected to come from either the stack or from register RCA. DRA then serves as input to either the Y output multiplexer or to register RCA.
- SELDR (1 bit): Select DR bus. If set to 1, this bit selects the external DA bus as input to the DRA/DRB buses. If set to 0, selects the output of the DRA multiplexer to the DRA bus (controlled by OSEL) and the contents of RCB to the DRB bus.
- ZEROIN (1 bit): Used to indicate a conditional branch. The behavior of the microsequencer will then depend on the condition code selected in field 1 (Table 12-7).
- RC2-RC0 (3 bits): Register controls. These bits determine the change in the contents of registers RCA and RCB. Each register can either remain the same, decrement, or load from the DRA/DRB buses.
- S2-S0 (3 bits): Stack controls. These bits determine which stack operation is to be performed.
- MUX2-MUX0: Output controls. These bits, together with the condition code if used, control the Y output multiplexer and therefore the next microinstruction address. The multiplexer can select its output from the stack, DRA, DRB, or MPC.

These bits can be set individually by the programmer. However, this is typically not done. Rather, the programmer uses mnemonics that equate to the bit patterns that would normally be required. Table 12-8 lists the 15 mnemonics for field 28. A microcode assembler converts these into the appropriate bit patterns.

As an example, the instruction INC88181 is used to cause the next microinstruction in sequence to be selected, if the currently selected condition code is 1. From Table 12-8, we have

INC88181 = 000000111110

which decodes directly into

- OSEL = 0: selects RCA as output from DRA output MUX; in this case the selection is irrelevant.

TABLE 12-8   TI 8818 Microsequencer Microinstruction Bits (Field 28)

Mnemonic	Value	Description
RST8818	000000000110	Reset Instruction
BRA88181	011000111000	Branch to DRA Instruction
BRA88180	010000111110	Branch to DRA Instruction
INC88181	000000111110	Continue Instruction
INC88180	001000001000	Continue Instruction
CAL88181	010000110000	Jump to Subroutine at Address Specified by DRA
CAL88180	010000101110	Jump to Subroutine at Address Specified by DRA
RET8818	000000011010	Return from Subroutine
PUSH8818	000000110111	Push Interrupt Return Address onto Stack
POP8818	100000010000	Return from Interrupt
LOADDRA	000010111110	Load DRA counter from DA Bus
LOADDRB	000110111110	Load DRB counter from DA Bus
LOADDRAB	000110111100	Load DRA/DRB
DECRDRA	010001111100	Decrement DRA Counter and Branch if not zero
DECRDRB	010101111100	Decrement DRB Counter and Branch if not zero

- SELDR = 0: as defined above; again, this is irrelevant for this instruction.
- ZEROIN = 0: combined with the value for MUX, indicates no branch should be taken.
- R = 000: retain current value of RA and RC.
- S = 111: retain current state of stack.
- MUX = 110: Choose MPC when condition code = 1, DRA when condition code = 0.

Registered ALU

The 8832 is a 32-bit ALU with 64 registers that can be configured to operate as four 8-bit ALUs, two 16-bit ALUs, or a single 32-bit ALU.

The 8832 is controlled by the 39 bits that make up fields 17 through 27 of the microinstruction (Table 12-7); these are supplied to the ALU as control signals. In addition, as indicated in Figure 12-17, the 8832 has external connections to the 32-bit DA bus and the 32-bit system Y bus. Inputs from the DA can be provided simultaneously as input data to the 64-word register file and to the ALU logic module. Input from the system Y bus is provided to the ALU logic module. Results of the ALU and shift operations are output to the DA bus or the system Y bus. Results can also be fed back to the internal register file.

Three 6-bit address ports allow a two-operand fetch and an operand write to be performed within the register file simultaneously. An MQ shifter and MQ register can also be configured to function independently to implement double-precision 8-bit, 16-bit, and 32-bit shift operations.

Fields 17 through 26 of each microinstruction control the way in which data flows within the 8832 and between the 8832 and the external environment. The fields are:

17. Write enable. These two bits specify write 32 bits, or 16 most significant bits, or 16 least significant bits, or do not write into register file. The destination register is defined by field 24.

18. Select register file data source. If a write is to occur to the register file, these two bits specify the source: DA bus, DB bus, ALU output, or system Y bus.

19. Shift instruction modifier. Specifies options concerning supplying end fill bits and reading bits that are shifted during shift instructions.

20. Carry in. This bit indicates whether a bit is carried into the ALU for this operation.

21. ALU configuration mode. The 8832 can be configured to operate as a single 32-bit ALU, two 16-bit ALUs, or four 8-bit ALUs.

22. S input. The ALU logic module inputs are provided by two internal multiplexers referred to as the S and R multiplexers. This field selects the input to be provided by the S multiplexer: register file, DB bus, or MQ register. The source register is defined by field 25.

23. R input. Selects input to be provided by the R multiplexer: register file or DA bus.

24. Destination register. Address of register in register file to be used for the destination operand.

25. Source register. Address of register in register file to be used for the source operand, provided by the S multiplexer.

26. Source register. Address of register in register file to be used for the source operand, provided by the R multiplexer.

Finally, field 27 is an 8-bit opcode that specifies the arithmetic or logical function to be performed by the ALU. Table 12-9 lists the different operations that can be performed.

As an example of the coding used to specify fields 17 through 27, consider the instruction to add the contents of register 1 to register 2 and place the result in register 3. The symbolic instruction is:

CONT11 [17], WELH, SELRFYMX, [24], R3, R2, R1, PASS+ADD

The assembler will translate this into the appropriate bit pattern. The individual components of the instruction can be described as follows:

- CONT11 is the basic NOP instruction
- Field [17] is changed to WELH (write enable, low and high) so that a 32-bit register is written into
- Field [18] is changed to SELRFYMX to select the feedback from the ALU Y MUX output
- Field [24] is changed to designate register R3 for the destination register
- Field [25] is changed to designate register R2 for one of the source registers

TABLE 12-9   TI 8832 Registered ALU Instruction Field (Field 27)

Group 1		Function
ADD	H#01	R + S + Cn
SUBR	H#02	(NOT R) + S + Cn
SUBS	H#03	R + (NOT S) + Cn
INCS	H#04	S + Cn
INCNS	H#05	(NOT S) + Cn
INCR	H#06	R + Cn
INCNR	H#07	(NOT R) + Cn
XOR	H#09	R XOR S
AND	H#0A	R AND S
OR	H#0B	R OR S
NAND	H#0C	R NAND S
NOR	H#0D	R NOR S
ANDNR	H#0E	(NOT R) AND S
Group 2		**Function**
SRA	H#00	Arithmetic right single precision shift
SRAD	H#10	Arithmetic right double precision shift
SRL	H#20	Logical right single precision shift
SRLD	H#30	Logical right double precision shift
SLA	H#40	Arithmetic left single precision shift
SLAD	H#50	Arithmetic left double precision shift
SLC	H#60	Circular left single precision shift
SLCD	H#70	Circular left double precision shift
SRC	H#80	Circular right single precision shift
SRCD	H#90	Circular right double precision shift
MQSRA	H#A0	Arithmetic right shift MQ register
MQSRL	H#B0	Logical right shift MQ register
MQSLL	H#C0	Logical left shift MQ register
MQSLC	H#D0	Circular left shift MQ register
LOADMQ	H#E0	Load MQ register
PASS	H#F0	Pass ALU to Y (no shift operation)
Group 3		**Function**
SET1	H#08	Set bit 1
SET0	H#18	Set bit 0
TB1	H#28	Test bit 1
TB0	H#38	Test bit 0
ABS	H#48	Absolute value
SMTC	H#58	Sign magnitude/two's complement
ADDI	H#68	Add immediate
SUBI	H#78	Subtract immediate
BADD	H#88	Byte add R to S
BSUBS	H#98	Byte subtract S from R
BSUBR	H#A8	Byte subtract R from S
BINCS	H#B8	Byte increment S
BINCNS	H#C8	Byte increment negative S
BXOR	H#D8	Byte XOR R and S
BAND	H#E8	Byte AND R and S
BOR	H#F8	Byte OR R and S

TABLE 12-9 (*Continued*)

Group 4		Function
CRC	H#00	Cyclic redundancy character accum.
SEL	H#10	Select S or R
SNORM	H#20	Single length normalize
DNORM	H#30	Double length normalize
DIVRF	H#40	Divide remainder fix
SDIVQF	H#50	Signed divide quotient fix
SMULI	H#60	Signed multiply iterate
SMULT	H#70	Signed multiply terminate
SDIVIN	H#80	Signed divide initialize
SDIVIS	H#90	Signed divide start
SDIVI	H#A0	Signed divide iterate
UDIVIS	H#B0	Unsigned divide start
UDIVI	H#C0	Unsigned divide iterate
UMULI	H#D0	Unsigned multiply iterate
SDIVIT	H#E0	Signed divide terminate
UDIVIT	H#F0	Unsigned divide terminate
Group 5		**Function**
LOADFF	H#0F	Load divide/BCD flip-flops
CLR	H#1F	Clear
DUMPFF	H#5F	Output divide/BCD flip-flops
BCDBIN	H#7F	BCD to binary
EX3BC	H#8F	Excess -3 byte correction
EX3C	H#9F	Excess -3 word correction
SDIVO	H#AF	Signed divide overflow test
BINEX3	H#DF	Binary to excess -3
NOP32	H#FF	No operation

- Field [26] is changed to designate register R1 for one of the source registers
- Field [27] is changed to specify an ALU operation of ADD. The ALU shifter instruction is PASS; therefore the ALU output is not shifted by the shifter.

Several points can be made about the symbolic notation. It is not necessary to specify the field number for consecutive fields. That is,

CONT11 [17], WELH, [18], SELRFYMX

can be written as

CONT11 [17], WELH, SELRFYMX

since SELRFYMX is in field 18.

ALU instructions from Group 1 of Table 12-9 must always be used in conjunction with Group 2. ALU instructions from Groups 3-5 must not be used with Group 2.

APPLICATIONS OF MICROPROGRAMMING

Since the introduction of microprogramming, and especially since the late 1960s, the applications of microprogramming have become increasingly varied and widespread. As early as 1971, most if not all of the contemporary uses of microprogramming were in evidence [FLYN71, HAAV71]. More recent surveys discuss essentially the same set of applications [RAVS80]. The set of current applications for microprogramming includes

• Realization of Computers
• Emulation
• Operating-System Support
• Realization of Special-Purpose Devices
• High-Level Language Support
• Microdiagnostics
• User Tailoring

This chapter has been devoted to a discussion of *realization of computers*. The microprogrammed approach offers a systematic technique for control unit implementation. A related technique is *emulation* [MALL75]. Emulation refers to the use of a microprogram on one machine to execute programs originally written for another. The most common use of emulation is to aid users in migrating from one computer to another. This is frequently done by a vendor to make it easier for existing customers to trade in older machines for newer ones, thus making a switch to another vendor unattractive. Users are often surprised to find out how long this transition tool stays around. One observer [MALL83] noted that it was still possible in 1983 to find an IBM System/370 emulating an IBM 1401 that was physically replaced over a decade and a half earlier!

Another fruitful use of microprogramming is in the area of *operating-system support*. Microprograms can be used to implement primitives that replace important portions of operating system software. This technique can simplify the task of operating system implementation and improve operating system performance.

Microprogramming is useful as a vehicle for implementing *special-purpose devices* that may be incorporated into a host computer. A good example of this is a data communications board. The board will contain its own microprocessor. Since it is being used for a special purpose, it makes sense to implement some of its functions in firmware rather than software to enhance performance.

High-level language support is another fruitful area for the application of microprogramming techniques. Various functions and data types can be implemented directly in firmware. The result is that it is easier to compile the program into an efficient machine language form. In effect, the machine language is tailored to meet the needs of the high-level language (e.g., FORTRAN, COBOL, Ada).

Microprogramming can be used to support the monitoring, detection, isolation, and repair of system errors. These features are known as *microdiagnostics* and can significantly enhance the system maintenance facility. This approach allows the system to reconfigure itself when failure is detected; for example, if a high-speed multiplier is malfunctioning, a microprogrammed multiplier can take over.

A general category of application is *user tailoring*. A number of machines provide a *writable control store*, that is, a control memory implemented in RAM rather than ROM, and allow the user to write microprograms. Generally, a very vertical, easy-to-use microinstruction set is provided. This allows the user to tailor the machine to the desired application.

12.6

RECOMMENDED READING

There are a number of books devoted to microprogramming. [SEGE91] presents the fundamentals of microcoding and the design of microcoded systems by means of a step-by-step design of a simple 16-bit processor. [ANDR80] and [CLIN81] provide quite good coverage of control unit implementations. Other books that cover this topic as well as other applications of microprogramming are [BANE82] and [AGRA76]. [KRAF81] uses an AT&T-developed minicomputer as a detailed case study. [SALI76] concentrates on user-microprogrammable machines and includes a number of systems that were commercially available at the time. [PARK89] and [TI90] provide a detailed description of the TI 8800 Software Development Board.

[MILU89], [MALL83], and [GALE75] contain reprints of a number of key papers on microprogramming. [KING88] also includes a number of papers.

12.7

PROBLEMS

12.1 Describe the implementation of the multiply instruction in the hypothetical machine designed by Wilkes. Use narrative and a flowchart.

12.2 Assume a microinstruction set that includes a microinstruction with the following symbolic form:

$$I(AC_0 = 1) \text{ THEN CAR} \leftarrow (C_{0-6}) \text{ ELSE CAR} \leftarrow (\text{CAR}) + 1$$

where AC_0 is the sign bit of the accumulator and C_{0-6} are the first seven bits of the microinstruction. Using this microinstruction, write a microprogram that implements a Branch Register Minus (BRM) machine instruction, which branches if the AC is negative. Assume that bits C_1–C_n of the microinstruction specify a parallel set of micro-operations. Express the program symbolically.

12.3 A simple CPU has four major phases to its instruction cycle: fetch, indirect, execute, and interrupt. Two 1-bit flags designate the current phase in a hardwired implementation.
(a) Why are these flags needed?
(b) Why are they not needed in a microprogrammed control unit?

12.4 Consider the control unit of Figure 12-7. Assume that the control memory is 24 bits wide. The control portion of the microinstruction format is divided into two fields. A micro-operation field of 13 bits specifies the micro-operations to be performed. An address selection field specifies a condition, based on the flags, that will cause a microinstruction branch. There are eight flags.
(a) How many bits are in the address selection field?
(b) How many bits are in the address field?
(c) What is the size of the control memory?

12.5 How can unconditional branching be done under the circumstances of the previous problem? How can branching be avoided; that is, describe a microinstruction that does not specify any branch, conditional or unconditional?

12.6 We wish to provide 8 control words for each machine instruction routine. Machine instruction op codes have 5 bits, and control memory has 1,024 words. Suggest a mapping from the instruction register to the control address register.

12.7 The machine instruction BPNZ causes a branch if the AC is positive and nonzero. The branch address may be expressed directly or indirectly, depending on an indirect (I) bit in the instruction. Suggest a microprogram routine, based on the organization of Figure 12-7, to implement this instruction.

12.8 An encoded microinstruction format is to be used. Show how a 9-bit micro-operation field can be divided into subfields to specify 46 different actions.

12.9 A CPU has 16 registers, an ALU with 16 logic and 16 arithmetic functions, and a shifter with 8 operations, all connected by an internal CPU bus. Design a microinstruction format to specify the various micro-operations for the CPU.

12.10 Analyze each of the microsequencer mnemonics in Table 12-9. Indicate why each bit is set to the indicated value, to achieve the desired function.

PART V

PERFORMANCE ENHANCEMENT

The final part of the book explores areas that go beyond the fundamentals of organization and architecture presented so far. All of the topics explored in this chapter deal with innovative architectural and organizational methods of enhancing the performance of the processor.

Chapter 13 examines one of the most significant innovations in recent years: the reduced instruction set computer (RISC). The RISC approach is a dramatic departure from the historical trend in processor design and brings into focus many of the important issues in computer organization and architecture.

Chapter 14 examines an even more recent and equally important design innovation: the superscalar processor. Although superscalar technology can be used on any processor, it is especially well suited to a RISC architecture.

Finally, as computer technology has evolved, and as the cost of hardware has dropped, computer designers have sought to use parallel processing schemes to enhance performance, reliability, or both. Chapter 15 looks at two of the most prominent and successful applications of parallel organization.

CHAPTER 13

Reduced Instruction Set Computers

Since the development of the stored-program computer around 1950, there have been remarkably few true innovations in the areas of computer organization and architecture. The following, though not constituting a complete list, are some of the major advances since the birth of the computer.

- *The Family Concept:* Introduced by IBM with its System/360 in 1964, followed shortly thereafter by DEC, with its PDP-8. The family concept decouples the architecture of a machine from its implementation. A set of computers are offered, with different price/performance characteristics, that present the same architecture to the user. The differences in price and performance are due to different implementations of the same architecture.
- *Microprogrammed Control Unit:* Suggested by Wilkes in 1951, and introduced by IBM on the S/360 line in 1964. Microprogramming eases the task of designing and implementing the control unit and provides support for the family concept.
- *Cache Memory:* First introduced commercially on IBM S/360 Model 85 in 1968. The insertion of this element into the memory hierarchy dramatically improves performance.
- *Pipelining:* A means of introducing parallelism into the essentially sequential nature of a machine-instruction program. Examples are instruction pipelining and vector processing.
- *Multiple Processors:* This category covers a number of different organizations and objectives.

To this list must now be added one of the most interesting and, potentially, one of the most important innovations: reduced instruction set computer (RISC) architecture. The RISC architecture is a dramatic departure from the historical trend in CPU architecture and challenges the conventional wisdom expressed in words and deeds by most computer architects. An analysis of the RISC architecture brings into focus many of the important issues in computer organization and architecture, and thus is a fitting close to this text.

Although RISC systems have been defined and designed in a variety of ways by different groups, the key elements shared by most (not all) designs are these:

• A limited and simple instruction set.
• A large number of general-purpose registers, or the use of compiler technology to optimize register usage.
• An emphasis on optimizing the instruction pipeline.

Table 13-1 compares several RISC and non-RISC systems.

We begin this chapter with a brief survey of some results on instruction sets, then examine each of the three topics just listed. This is followed by a description of two of the best-documented RISC designs.

13.1

INSTRUCTION EXECUTION CHARACTERISTICS

One of the most visible forms of evolution associated with computers is that of programming languages. As the cost of hardware has dropped, the relative cost of software has risen. Along with that, a chronic shortage of programmers has driven up software costs in absolute terms. Thus the major cost in the life cycle of a system is software, not hardware. Adding to the cost, and to the inconvenience, is the element of unreliability: it is common for programs, both system and application, to continue to exhibit new bugs after years of operation.

The response from researchers and industry has been to develop ever more powerful and complex high-level programming languages (compare FORTRAN to Ada). These high-level languages (HLL) allow the programmer to express algorithms more concisely, take care of much of the detail, and often support naturally the use of structured programming.

Alas, this solution gave rise to another problem, known as the *semantic gap,* the difference between the operations provided in HLLs and those provided in computer architecture. Symptoms of this gap are alleged to include execution inefficiency, excessive machine program size, and compiler complexity. Designers responded with architectures intended to close this gap. Key features include large instruction sets, dozens of addressing modes, and various HLL statements implemented in hardware. An example of the latter is the CASE machine instruction on the VAX. Such complex instruction sets are intended to

• Ease the task of the compiler writer.
• Improve execution efficiency, since complex sequences of operations can be implemented in microcode.
• Provide support for even more complex and sophisticated HLLs.

Meanwhile, a number of studies have been done over the years to determine the characteristics and patterns of execution of machine instructions generated

TABLE 13-1   Characteristics of Some CISCs, RISCs, and Superscalar Processors

Characteristic	Complex Instruction Set Computer (CISC)			Reduced Instruction Set Computer (RISC)		Superscalar	
	IBM 370/168	VAX 11/780	Intel 80486	Motorola 88000	MIPS R4000	IBM RS/System 6000	Intel 80960
Year developed	1973	1978	1989	1988	1991	1990	1989
Number of instructions	208	303	235	51	94	184	62
Instruction size (bytes)	2–6	2–57	1–11	4	32	4	4, 8
Addressing modes	4	22	11	3	1	2	11
Number of general-purpose registers	16	16	8	32	32	32	32–256
Control memory size (Kbits)	420	480	246	—	—	—	—
Cache size (KBytes)	64	64	8	16	128	32–64	0.5

from HLL programs. The results of these studies inspired some researchers to look for an altogether different approach: namely, to make the architecture that supports the HLL simpler, rather than more complex.

So, to understand the line of reasoning of the RISC advocates, we begin with a brief review of instruction execution characteristics. The aspects of computation of interest are

- *Operations Performed:* These determine the functions to be performed by the CPU and its interaction with memory.
- *Operands Used:* The types of operands and the frequency of their use determine the memory organization for storing them and the addressing modes for accessing them.
- *Execution Sequencing:* This determines the control and pipeline organization.

In the remainder of this section, we summarize the results of a number of studies of high-level-language programs. All of the results are based on dynamic measurements. That is, measurements are collected by executing the program and counting the number of times some feature has appeared or a particular property has held true. In contrast, static measurements merely perform these counts on the source text of a program. They give no useful information on performance, because they are not weighted relative to the number of times each statement is executed.

Operations

A variety of studies have been made to analyze the behavior of HLL programs. Table 4-9, discussed in Chapter 4, includes key results from a number of studies. There is quite good agreement in the results of this mixture of languages and applications. Assignment statements predominate, suggesting that the simple movement of data is of high importance. There is also a preponderance of conditional statements (IF, LOOP). These statements are implemented in machine language with some sort of compare and branch instruction. This suggests that the sequence control mechanism of the instruction set is important.

These results are instructive to the machine instruction set designer, indicating which types of statements occur most often and therefore should be supported in an "optimal" fashion. However, these results do not reveal which statements use the most time in the execution of a typical program. That is, given a compiled machine language program, which statements in the source language cause the execution of the most machine-language instructions?

To get at this underlying phenomenon, the Patterson programs [PATT82a] were compiled on the VAX, PDP-11, and Motorola 68000 to determine the average number of machine instructions and memory references per statement type. By multiplying the frequency of occurrence of each statement type by these averages, Table 13-2 is obtained. Columns 2 and 3 provide surrogate measures of the actual time spent executing the various statement types. The results suggest that the procedure call/return is the most time-consuming operation in typical HLL programs.

TABLE 13-2   Weighted Relative Dynamic Frequency of HLL Operations

	Dynamic Occurrence		Machine-Instruction Weighted		Memory-Reference Weighted	
	Pascal	C	Pascal	C	Pascal	C
ASSIGN	45	38	13	13	14	15
LOOP	5	3	42	32	33	26
CALL	15	12	31	33	44	45
IF	29	43	11	21	7	13
GOTO	—	3	—	—	—	—
OTHER	6	1	3	1	2	1

Source: [PATT82a].

The reader should be clear on the significance of Table 13-2. This table indicates the relative significance of various statement types in an HLL, when that HLL is compiled for a typical contemporary instruction set architecture. Some other architecture could conceivably produce different results. However, this study produces results that are representative for contemporary complex instruction set computer (CISC) architectures. Thus, they can provide guidance to those looking for more efficient ways to support HLLs.

Operands

Much less work has been done on the occurrence of types of operands, despite the importance of this topic. There are several aspects that are significant.

The Patterson study already referenced [PATT82a] also looked at the dynamic frequency of occurrence of classes of variables (Table 13-3). The results, consistent between Pascal and C programs, show that the majority of references are to simple scalar variables. Further, over 80% of the scalars were local (to the procedure) variables. In addition, references to arrays/structures require a previous reference to their index or pointer, which again is usually a local scalar. Thus, there is a preponderance of references to scalars, and these are highly localized.

The Patterson study examined the dynamic behavior of HLL programs, independent of the underlying architecture. As discussed before, it is necessary to deal with actual architectures to examine program behavior more deeply. One study, [LUND77], examined DEC-10 instructions dynamically and found that

TABLE 13-3   Dynamic Percentage of Operands

	Pascal	C	Average
Integer Constant	16	23	20
Scalar Variable	58	53	55
Array/Structure	26	24	25

each instruction on the average references 0.5 operand in memory and 1.4 registers. Similar results are reported in [HUCK83] for C, Pascal, and FORTRAN programs on S/370, PDP-11, and VAX. Of course, these figures depend highly on both the architecture and the compiler, but they do illustrate the frequency of operand accessing.

These latter studies suggest the importance of an architecture that lends itself to fast operand accessing, since this operation is performed so frequently. The Patterson study suggests that a prime candidate for optimization is the mechanism for storing and accessing local scalar variables.

Procedure Calls

We have seen that procedure calls and returns are an important aspect of HLL programs. The evidence (Table 13-2) suggests that these are the most time-consuming operations in compiled HLL programs. Thus, it will be profitable to consider ways of implementing these operations efficiently. Two aspects are significant: the number of parameters and variables that a procedure deals with, and the depth of nesting.

In Tanenbaum's study [TANE78], he found that 98% of dynamically called procedures were passed fewer than six arguments, and that 92% of them used fewer than six local scalar variables. Similar results were reported by the Berkeley RISC team [KATE83], as shown in Table 13-4. These results show that the number of words required per procedure activation is not large. The studies reported earlier indicated that a high proportion of operand references are to local scalar variables. These studies show that those references are in fact confined to relatively few variables.

The same Berkeley group also looked at the pattern of procedure calls and returns in HLL programs. They found that it is rare to have a long uninterrupted sequence of procedure calls followed by the corresponding sequence of returns. Rather, they found that a program remains confined to a rather narrow window of procedure-invocation depth. This is illustrated in Figure 4-32, which was discussed in Chapter 4. These results reinforce the conclusion that operand references are highly localized.

TABLE 13-4   Procedure Arguments and Local Scalar Variables

Percentage of Executed Procedure Calls With	Compiler, Interpreter and Typesetter	Small Nonnumeric Programs
> 3 arguments	0–7%	0–5%
> 5 arguments	0–3%	0%
> 8 words of arguments and local scalars	1–20%	0–6%
> 12 words of arguments and local scalars	1–6%	0–3%

Implications

A number of groups have looked at results such as those just reported and have concluded that the attempt to make the instruction set architecture close to HLLs is not the most effective design strategy. Rather, the HLLs can best be supported by optimizing performance of the most time-consuming features of typical HLL programs.

Generalizing from the work of a number of researchers, three elements emerge that, by and large, characterize RISC architectures. First, use a large number of registers. This is intended to optimize operand referencing. The studies just discussed show that there are several references per HLL instruction, and that there is a high proportion of move (assignment) statements. This, coupled with the locality and predominance of scalar references, suggests that performance can be improved by reducing memory references at the expense of more register references. Because of the locality of these references, an expanded register set seems practical.

Second, careful attention needs to be paid to the design of instruction pipelines. Because of the high proportion of conditional branch and procedure call instructions, a straightforward instruction pipeline will be inefficient. This manifests itself as a high proportion of instructions that are prefetched but never executed.

Finally, a simplified (reduced) instruction set is indicated. This point is not as obvious as the others, but should become clearer in the ensuing discussion. In addition, we will see that the desire to implement an entire CPU on a single chip suggests a reduced instruction set solution.

13.2

THE USE OF A LARGE REGISTER FILE

The results summarized in Section 13.1 point out the desirability of quick access to operands. We have seen that there is a large proportion of assignment statements in HLL programs, and many of these are of the simple form A = B. Also, there are a significant number of operand accesses per HLL statement. If we couple these results with the fact that most accesses are to local scalars, heavy reliance on register storage is suggested.

The reason that register storage is indicated is that it is the fastest available storage device, faster than both main memory and cache. The register file is physically small, generally on the same chip as the ALU and control unit, and employs much shorter addresses than addresses for cache and memory. Thus a strategy is needed that will allow the most frequently accessed operands to be kept in registers and to minimize register-memory operations.

Two basic approaches are possible, one based on software and the other on hardware. The software approach is to rely on the compiler to maximize register usage. The compiler will attempt to allocate registers to those variables that will be used the most in a given time period. This approach requires the use of sophisticated program-analysis algorithms. The hardware approach is simply to use more registers so that more variables can be held in registers for longer periods of time.

In this section, we will discuss the hardware approach. This approach has been pioneered by the Berkeley RISC group [PATT82a] and is used in the first commercial RISC product, the Pyramid [RAGA83].

Register Windows

On the face of it, the use of a large set of registers should decrease the need to access memory. The design task is to organize the registers in such a fashion that this goal is realized.

Since most operand references are to local scalars, the obvious approach is to store these in registers, with perhaps a few registers reserved for global variables. The problem is that the definition of *local* changes with each procedure call and return, operations that occur frequently. On every call, local variables must be saved from the registers into memory, so that the registers can be reused by the called program. Furthermore, parameters must be passed. On return, the variables of the parent program must be restored (loaded back into registers) and results must be passed back to the parent program.

The solution is based on two other results reported in Section 13.1. First, a typical procedure employs only a few passed parameters and local variables. Second, the depth of procedure activation fluctuates within a relatively narrow range (Figure 4-32). To exploit these properties, multiple small sets of registers are used, each assigned to a different procedure. A procedure call automatically switches the CPU to use a different fixed-size window of registers, rather than saving registers in memory. Windows for adjacent procedures are overlapped to allow parameter passing.

The concept is illustrated in Figure 13-1. At any time, only one window of registers is visible and is addressable as if it were the only set of registers (e.g., addresses 0 through $N - 1$). The window is divided into three fixed-size areas. Parameter registers hold parameters passed down from the procedure that

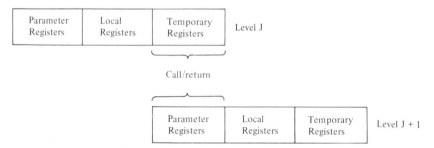

FIGURE 13-1.   Overlapping register windows

called the current procedure and results to be passed back up. Local registers are used for local variables, as assigned by the compiler. Temporary registers are used to exchange parameters and results with the next lower level (procedure called by current procedure). The temporary registers at one level are physically the same as the parameter registers at the next lower level. This overlap permits parameters to be passed without the actual movement of data.

To handle any possible pattern of calls and returns, the number of register windows would have to be unbounded. Instead, the register windows can be used to hold the few most recent procedure activations. Older activations must be saved in memory and later restored when the nesting depth decreases. Thus, the actual organization of the register file is as a circular buffer of overlapping windows.

This organization is shown in Figure 13-2, which depicts a circular buffer of six windows. The buffer is filled to a depth of 4 (A called B; B called C; C called D) with procedure D active. The current-window pointer (CWP) points to the win-

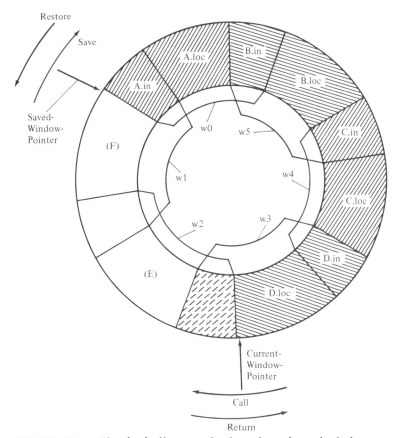

FIGURE 13-2. Circular-buffer organization of overlapped windows

dow of the currently active procedure. Register references by a machine instruction are offset by this pointer to determine the actual physical register. The saved-window pointer identifies the window most recently saved in memory. If procedure D now calls procedure E, arguments for E are placed in D's temporary registers (the overlap between w3 and w2) and the CWP is advanced by one window.

If procedure E then makes a call to procedure F, the call cannot be made with the current status of the buffer. This is because F's window overlaps A's window. If F begins to load its temporary registers, preparatory to a call, it will overwrite the parameter registers of A (A.In). Thus when CWP is incremented (modulo 6) so that it becomes equal to SWP, an interrupt occurs and A's window is saved. Only the first two portions (A.In and A.loc) need be saved. Then the SWP is incremented and the call to F proceeds. A similar interrupt can occur on returns. For example, subsequent to the activation of F, when B returns to A, CWP is decremented and becomes equal to SWP. This causes an interrupt that results in the restoral of A's window.

From the preceding, it can be seen that an N-window register file can hold only $N - 1$ procedure activations. The value of N need not be large. As was mentioned earlier, one study [TAMI83] found that, with eight windows, a save or restore is needed on only 1% of the calls or returns. The Berkeley RISC computers use 8 windows of 16 registers each. The Pyramid computer employs 16 windows of 32 registers each.

Global Variables

The window scheme just described provides an efficient organization for storing local scalar variables in registers. However, this scheme does not address the need to store global variables, those accessed by more than one procedure (e.g., COMMON variables in FORTRAN). Two options suggest themselves. First, variables declared as global in an HLL can be assigned memory locations by the compiler, and all machine instructions that reference these variables will use memory-reference operands. This is straightforward, from both the hardware and software (compiler) points of view. However, for frequently-accessed global variables, this scheme is inefficient.

An alternative is to incorporate a set of global registers in the CPU. These registers would be fixed in number and available to all procedures. A unified numbering scheme can be used to simplify the instruction format. For example, references to registers 0 through 7 could refer to unique global registers, and references to registers 8 through 31 could be offset to refer to physical registers in the current window. Thus, there is an increased hardware burden to accommodate the split in register addressing. In addition, the compiler must decide which global variables should be assigned to registers.

Large Register File Versus Cache

The register file, organized into windows, acts as a small, fast buffer for holding a subset of all variables that are likely to be used the most heavily. From this point of view, the register file acts much like a cache memory. The question therefore arises as to whether it would be simpler and better to use a cache and a small traditional register file.

Table 13-5 compares characteristics of the two approaches. The window-based register file holds all of the local scalar variables (except in the rare case of window overflow) of the most recent $N - 1$ procedure activations. The cache holds a selection of recently used scalar variables. The register file should save time, since all local scalar variables are retained. On the other hand, the cache may make more efficient use of space, since it is reacting to the situation dynamically. Furthermore, caches generally treat all memory references alike, including instructions and other types of data. Thus, savings in these other areas are possible with a cache and not a register file.

A register file may make inefficient use of space, since not all procedures will need the full window space allotted to them. On the other hand, the cache suffers from another sort of inefficiency: Data are read in in blocks. Whereas the register file contains only those variables in use, the cache reads in a block of data, some or much of which will not be used.

The cache is capable of handling global as well as local variables. There are usually many global scalars, but only a few of them are heavily used [KATE83]. A cache will dynamically discover these variables and hold them. If the window-based register file is supplemented with global registers, it too can hold some global scalars. However, it is difficult for a compiler to determine which globals will be heavily used.

With the register file, the movement of data between registers and memory is determined by the procedure nesting depth. Since this depth usually fluctuates within a narrow range, the use of memory is relatively infrequent. Most cache memories are set-associative with a small set size. Thus, there is the danger that other data or instructions will overwrite frequently used variables.

Based on the discussion so far, the choice between a large window-based register file and a cache is not clear cut. There is one characteristic, however, in which the register approach is clearly superior and which suggests that a cache-based system will be noticeably slower. This distinction shows up in the amount of addressing overhead experienced by the two approaches.

Figure 13-3 illustrates the difference. To reference a local scalar in a window-

TABLE 13-5 Characteristics of Large-Register-File and Cache Organizations

Large Register File	Cache
All local scalars	Recently-used local scalars
Individual variables	Blocks of memory
Compiler-assigned global variables	Recently-used global variables
Save/Restore based on procedure nesting depth	Save/Restore based on cache replacement algorithm
Register addressing	Memory addressing

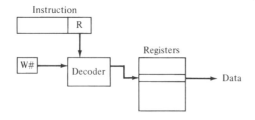

(a) Window-Based Register File

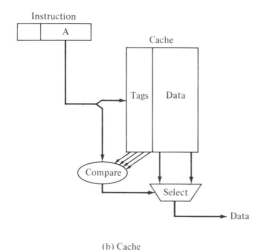

(b) Cache

FIGURE 13-3. Referencing a local scalar

based register file, a "virtual" register number and a window number are used. These can pass through a relatively simple decoder to select one of the physical registers. To reference a memory location in cache, a full-width memory address must be generated. The complexity of this operation depends on the addressing mode. In a set-associative cache, a portion of the address is used to read a number of words and tags equal to the set size. Another portion of the address is compared to the tags, and one of the words that were read is selected. It should be clear that even if the cache is as fast as the register file, the access time will be considerably longer. Thus, from the point of view of performance, the window-based register file is superior for local scalars. Further performance improvement could be achieved by the addition of a cache for instructions only.

13.3

COMPILER-BASED REGISTER OPTIMIZATION

Let us assume now that only a small number (e.g., 16–32) of registers is available on the target RISC machine. In this case, optimized register usage is the responsibility of the compiler. A program written in a high-level language has, of course, no explicit references to registers. Rather, program quantities are referred to symbolically. The objective of the compiler is to keep the operands for as many computations as possible in registers rather than main memory, and to minimize load-and-store operations.

In general, the approach taken is as follows. Each program quantity that is a candidate for residing in a register is assigned to a symbolic or virtual register. The compiler then maps the unlimited number of symbolic registers into a fixed number of real registers. Symbolic registers whose usage does not overlap can share the same real register. If, in a particular portion of the program, there are more quantities to deal with than real registers, then some of the quantities are assigned to memory locations. Load-and-store instructions are used to temporarily position quantities in registers for computational operations.

The essence of the optimization task is to decide which quantities are to be assigned to registers at any given point in the program. The technique most commonly used in RISC compilers is known as graph coloring, which is a technique borrowed from the discipline of topology [CHAI82, CHOW86, COUT86, CHOW90].

The graph coloring problem is this. Given a graph consisting of nodes and edges, assign colors to nodes such that adjacent nodes have different colors, and do this in such a way as to minimize the number of different colors. This problem is adapted to the compiler problem in the following way. First, the program is analyzed to build a register interference graph. The nodes of the graph are the symbolic registers. If two symbolic registers are "live" during the same program fragment, then they are joined by an edge to depict interference. An attempt is then made to color the graph with n colors, where n is the number of registers. If this process does not fully succeed, then those nodes that cannot be colored must be placed in memory, and loads and stores must be used to make space for the affected quantities when they are needed.

Figure 13-4 is a simple example of the process. Assume a program with six symbolic registers to be compiled into three actual registers. Figure 13-4a shows

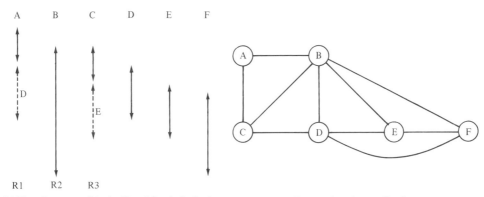

(a) Time Sequence of Active Use of Symbolic Registers   (b) Register Interference Graph

FIGURE 13-4.   The graph coloring approach

the time sequence of active use of each symbolic register, and part b shows the register interference graph. A possible coloring with three colors is indicated. One symbolic register, F, is left uncolored and must be dealt with using loads and stores.

In general, there is a trade-off between the use of a large set of registers and compiler-based register optimization. For example, [BRAD91a] reports on a study that modeled a RISC architecture with features similar to the Motorola 88000 and the MIPS R2000. They varied the number of registers from 16 to 128, and considered both the use of all general-purpose registers and registers split between integer and floating-point use. Their study showed that with even simple register optimization, there is little benefit to the use of more than 64 registers. With reasonably sophisticated register optimization techniques, there is only marginal performance improvement with above 32 registers. Finally, they noted that with a small number of registers (e.g., 16), a machine with a shared register organization executes faster than one with a split organization. Similar conclusions can be drawn from [HUGU91], which reports on a study that is primarily concerned with optimizing the use of a small number of registers, rather than comparing the use of large register sets to optimization efforts.

13.4

REDUCED INSTRUCTION SET ARCHITECTURE

In this section, we look at some of the general characteristics of and the motivation for a reduced instruction set architecture. Specific examples will be seen later in this chapter. We begin with a discussion of motivations for contemporary complex instruction set architectures.

Why CISC

We have noted the trend to richer instruction sets, which include a larger number of instructions and more-complex instructions. Two principal reasons have motivated this trend: a desire to simplify compilers and a desire to improve performance. Underlying both of these reasons was the shift to high-level languages (HLL) on the part of programmers; architects attempted to design machines that provided better support for HLLs.

It is not the intent of this chapter to say that the CISC designers took the wrong direction. RISC technology is very new and so the CISC versus RISC debate cannot now be settled. Indeed, because technology continues to evolve and because architectures exist along a spectrum rather than in two neat categories, a black-and-white assessment is unlikely ever to emerge. Thus, the comments that follow are simply meant to point out some of the potential pitfalls in the CISC approach and to provide some understanding of the motivation of the RISC adherents.

The first of the reasons cited, compiler simplification, seems obvious. The task of the compiler writer is to generate a sequence of machine instructions for each HLL statement. If there are machine instructions that resemble HLL statements, this task is simplified. This reasoning has been disputed by the RISC researchers ([HENN82], [RADI82], [PATT82b]). They have found that complex machine instructions are often hard to exploit since the compiler must find those cases that exactly fit the construct. The task of optimizing the generated code to minimize code size, reduce instruction execution count, and enhance pipelining is much more difficult with a complex instruction set. As evidence of this, studies cited earlier in this chapter indicate that most of the instructions in a compiled program are the relatively simple ones.

The other major reason cited is the expectation that a CISC will yield smaller, faster programs. Let us examine both aspects of this assertion: that programs will be smaller and that they will execute faster.

There are two advantages to smaller programs. First, because the program takes up less memory, there is a savings in that resource. With memory today being so inexpensive, this potential advantage is no longer compelling. More importantly, smaller programs should improve performance, and this will happen in two ways. First, fewer instructions means fewer instruction bytes to be fetched. And second, in a paging environment, smaller programs occupy fewer pages, reducing page faults.

The problem with this line of reasoning is that it is far from certain that a CISC program will be smaller than a corresponding RISC program. In many cases, the CISC program, expressed in symbolic machine language, may be *shorter* (i.e., fewer instructions), but the number of bits of memory occupied may not be noticeably *smaller*. Table 13-6 shows results from three studies that compared the size of compiled C programs on a variety of machines, including RISC I, which has a reduced instruction set architecture. Note that there is little or no savings using a CISC over a RISC. It is also interesting to note that the VAX, which has a much more complex instruction set than the PDP-11, achieves very little savings over the latter. These results were confirmed by IBM researchers [RADI82], who found that the IBM 801 (a RISC) produced code that was 0.9 times the size of code on an IBM S/370. The study used a set of PL/I programs.

There are several reasons for these rather surprising results. We have already

TABLE 13-6 Code Size Relative to RISC I

	[PATT82a] 11 C Programs	[KATE83] 12 C Programs	[HEAT84] 5 C Programs
RISC I	1.0	1.0	1.0
VAX-11/780	0.8	0.67	
M68000	0.9		0.9
Z8002	1.2		1.12
PDP-11/70	0.9	0.71	

noted that compilers on CISCs tend to favor simpler instructions, so that the conciseness of the complex instructions seldom comes into play. Also, since there are more instructions on a CISC, longer op codes are required, producing longer instructions. Finally, RISCs tend to emphasize register rather than memory references, and the former require fewer bits. An example of this last effect is discussed presently (see Figure 13-5).

So, the expectation that a CISC will produce smaller programs, with the attendant advantages, may not be realized. The second motivating factor for increasing complex instruction sets was that instruction execution would be faster. It seems to make sense that a complex HLL operation will execute more quickly as a single machine instruction rather than as a series of more-primitive instructions. However, because of the bias towards the use of those simpler instructions, this may not be so. The entire control unit must be made more complex, and/or the microprogram control store must be made larger, to accommodate a richer instruction set. Either factor increases the execution time of the simple instructions.

In fact, some researchers have found that the speedup in the execution of complex functions is due not so much to the power of the complex machine instructions as to their residence in high-speed control store [RADI82]. In effect, the control store acts as an instruction cache. Thus, the hardware architect is in the position of trying to determine which subroutines or functions will be used most frequently and assigning those to the control store by implementing them in microcode. The results have been less than encouraging. Thus on S/370 systems, instructions such as Translate and Extended-Precision-Floating-Point-

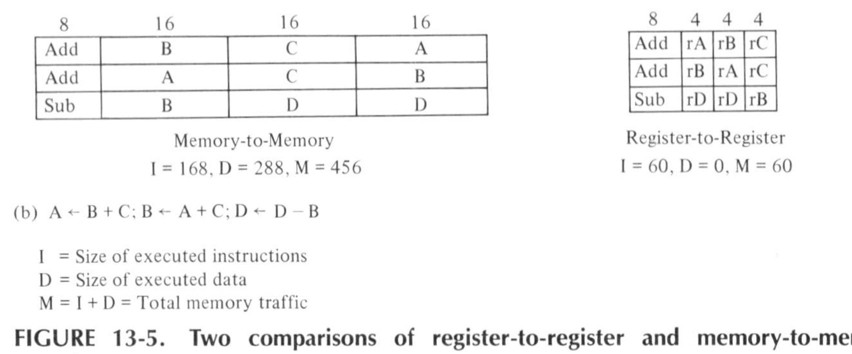

I = Size of executed instructions
D = Size of executed data
M = I + D = Total memory traffic

FIGURE 13-5. Two comparisons of register-to-register and memory-to-memory approaches

Divide reside in high-speed storage, while the sequence involved in setting up procedure calls or initiating an interrupt handler are in slower main memory.

Thus, it is far from clear that the trend to increasingly complex instruction sets is appropriate. This has led a number of groups to pursue the opposite path.

Characteristics of Reduced Instruction Set Architectures

Although a variety of different approaches to reduced instruction set architecture have been taken, certain characteristics are common to all of them. These characteristics are listed in Table 13-7 and described here. Specific examples are explored later in this chapter.

The first characteristic listed in Table 13-7 is that there is one machine instruction per machine cycle. A *machine cycle* is defined to be the time it takes to fetch two operands from registers, perform an ALU operation, and store the result in a register. Thus, RISC machine instructions should be no more complicated, than, and execute about as fast as, microinstructions on CISC machines. With simple, one-cycle instructions, there is little or no need for microcode; the machine instructions can be hardwired. Such instructions should execute faster than comparable machine instructions on other machines, since it is not necessary to access a microprogram control store during instruction execution.

A second characteristic is that most operations should be register-to-register, with only simple LOAD and STORE operations accessing memory. This design feature simplifies the instruction set and therefore the control unit. For example, a RISC instruction set may include only one or two ADD instructions (e.g., integer add, add with carry); the VAX has 25 different ADD instructions. Another benefit is that such an architecture encourages the optimization of register use, so that frequently accessed operands remain in high-speed storage.

This emphasis on register-to-register operations is unique to RISC designs. Other contemporary machines provide such instructions but also include memory-to-memory and mixed register/memory operations. Attempts to compare these approaches were made in the 1970s, before the appearance of RISCs. Figure 13-5a illustrates the approach taken. Hypothetical architectures were evaluated on program size and the number of bits of memory traffic. Results such as this one led one researcher to suggest that future architectures should

TABLE 13-7
Characteristics of Reduced Instruction Set Architectures

One Instruction Per Cycle
Register-to-Register Operations
Simple Address Modes
Simple Instruction Formats

contain no registers at all [MYER78]. One wonders what he would have thought, at the time, of the RISC machine marketed by Pyramid, which contains no less than 528 registers!

What was missing from those studies was a recognition of the frequent access to a small number of local scalars and that, with a large bank of registers or an optimizing compiler, most operands could be kept in registers for long periods of time. Thus Figure 13-5b may be a fairer comparison.

Returning to Table 13-7, a third characteristic is the use of simple addressing modes. Almost all instructions use simple register addressing. Several additional modes, such as displacement and PC-relative, may be included. Other, more-complex modes can be synthesized in software from the simple ones. Again, this design feature simplifies the instruction set and the control unit.

A final common characteristic is the use of simple instruction formats. Generally, only one or a few formats are used. Instruction length is fixed and aligned on word boundaries. Field locations, especially the op code, are fixed. This design feature has a number of benefits. With fixed fields, op code decoding and register operand accessing can occur simultaneously. Simplified formats simplify the control unit. Instruction fetching is optimized since word-length units are fetched. This also means that a single instruction does not cross page boundaries.

Taken together, these characteristics can be assessed to determine the potential benefits of the RISC approach. These benefits fall into two main categories: those related to performance and those related to VLSI implementation.

With respect to performance, a certain amount of "circumstantial evidence" can be presented. First, more-effective optimizing compilers can be developed. With more-primitive instructions, there are more opportunities for moving functions out of loops, reorganizing code for efficiency, maximizing register utilization, and so forth. It is even possible to compute parts of complex instructions at compile time. For example, the S/370 Move Characters (MVC) instruction moves a string of characters from one location to another. Each time it is executed, the move will depend on the length of the string, whether and in which direction the locations overlap, and what the alignment characteristics are. In most cases, these will all be known at compile time. Thus the compiler could produce an optimized sequence of primitive instructions for this function.

A second point, already noted, is that most instructions generated by a compiler are relatively simple anyway. It would seem reasonable that a control unit built specifically for those instructions and using little or no microcode could execute them faster than a comparable CISC.

A third point relates to the use of instruction pipelining. RISC researchers feel that the instruction pipelining technique can be applied much more effectively with a reduced instruction set. We examine this point in some detail presently.

A final, and somewhat less significant point, is that RISC programs should be more responsive to interrupts since interrupts are checked between rather elementary operations. Architectures with complex instructions either restrict interrupts to instruction boundaries or must define specific interruptible points and implement mechanisms for restarting an instruction.

The case for improved performance for a reduced instruction set architecture is far from proven. A number of studies have been done but not on machines of comparable technology and power. Further, most studies have not attempted to separate the effects of a reduced instruction set and the effects of a large register file. The "circumstantial evidence," however, is suggestive.

The second area of potential benefit, which is more clear-cut, relates to VLSI implementation. When VLSI is used, the design and implementation of the CPU are fundamentally changed. Traditional CPUs, such as the IBM S/370 and the VAX, consist of one or more printed circuit boards containing standardized SSI and MSI packages. With the advent of LSI and VLSI, it is possible to put an entire CPU on a single chip. For a single-chip CPU, there are two motivations for following a RISC strategy. First, there is the issue of performance. On-chip delays are of much shorter duration than inter-chip delays. Thus it makes sense to devote scarce chip real estate to those activities that occur frequently. We have seen that simple instructions and access to local scalars are, in fact, the most frequent activities. The Berkeley RISC chips were designed with this consideration in mind. Whereas a typical single-chip microprocessor dedicates about half of its area to the microcode control store, the RISC I chip devotes only about 6% of its area to the control unit [SHER84].

A second VLSI-related issue is design-and-implementation time. A VLSI processor is difficult to develop. Instead of relying on available SSI/MSI parts, the designer must perform circuit design, layout, and modeling at the device level. With a reduced instruction set architecture, this process is far easier, as evidenced by Table 13-8 [FITZ81]. If, in addition, the performance of the RISC chip is equivalent to comparable CISC microprocessors, then the advantages of the RISC approach become evident.

13.5

RISC PIPELINING

Pipelining with Regular Instructions

As we discussed in Section 10.4, instruction pipelining is often used to enhance performance. Let us reconsider this in the context of a RISC architecture. Most

TABLE 13-8 Design and Layout Effort For Some Microprocessors

CPU	Transistors (thousands)	Design (Person-Months)	Layout (Person-Months)
RISC I	44	15	12
RISC II	41	18	12
M68000	68	100	70
Z8000	18	60	70
Intel iAPx-432	110	170	90

instructions are register-to-register, and an instruction cycle has the following two phases:

- I: Instruction fetch.
- E: Execute. Performs an ALU operation with register input and output.

For load and store operations, three phases are required:

- I: Instruction fetch.
- E: Execute. Calculates memory address
- D: Memory. Register-to-memory or memory-to-register operation.

Figure 13-6 depicts the timing of a sequence of instructions using no pipelining. Clearly, this is a wasteful process. Even very simple pipelining can substantially improve performance. Figure 13-7 shows a two-way pipelining scheme, in which the I and E phases of two different instructions are performed simultaneously. This scheme can yield up to twice the execution rate of a serial scheme. Two problems prevent the maximum speed-up from being achieved. First, we assume that a single-port memory is used and that only one memory access is possible per phase. This requires the insertion of a wait state in some instructions. Second, a branch instruction interrupts the sequential flow of execution. To accommodate this with minimum circuitry, a NOOP instruction can be inserted into the instruction stream by the compiler or assembler.

Pipelining can be improved further by permitting two memory accesses per phase. This yields the sequence shown in Figure 13-8. Now, up to three instructions can be overlapped, and the improvement is as much as a factor of three. Again, branch instructions cause the speed-up to fall short of the maximum possible. Also, note that data dependencies have an effect. If an instruction needs an operand that is altered by the preceding instruction, a delay is required. Again, this can be accomplished by a NOOP.

The pipelining discussed so far works best if the three phases are of approximately equal duration. Because the E phase usually involves an ALU operation, it may be longer. In this case, we can divide into two subphases:

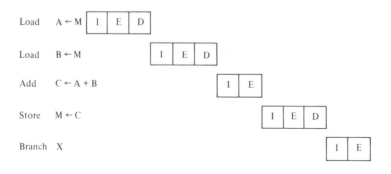

FIGURE 13-6. **Timing of sequential execution**

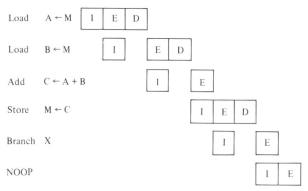

FIGURE 13-7. Two-way pipelined timing

- E_1: Register file read
- E_2: ALU operation and register write.

Because of the simplicity and regularity of the instruction set, the design of the phasing into three or four phases is easily accomplished. Figure 13-9 shows the result with a four-way pipeline. Up to four instructions at a time can be under way, and the maximum potential speed-up is a factor of four. Note again the use of NOOPs to account for data and branch delays.

Optimization of Pipelining

Because of the simple and regular nature of RISC instructions, pipelining schemes can be efficiently employed. There are few variations in instruction execution duration, and the pipeline can be tailored to reflect this. However, we have seen that data and branch dependencies reduce the overall execution rate.

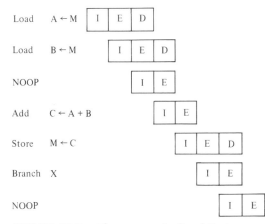

FIGURE 13-8. Three-way pipelined timing

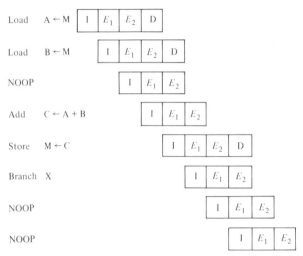

FIGURE 13-9. Four-way pipelined timing

To compensate for these dependencies, code reorganization techniques have been developed. First, let us consider branching instructions. *Delayed branch*, a way of increasing the efficiency of the pipeline, makes use of a branch that does not take effect until after the following instruction. This strange procedure is illustrated in Table 13-9. In the first column, we see a normal symbolic instruction machine-language program. After 102 is executed, the next instruction to be executed is 105. In order to regularize the pipeline, a NOOP is inserted after this branch. However, increased performance is achieved if the instructions at 101 and 102 are interchanged. Figure 13-10 shows the result. The JUMP instruction is fetched before the ADD instruction. Note, however, that the ADD instruction is fetched before the execution of the JUMP instruction has a chance to alter the program counter. Thus, the original semantics of the program are retained.

This interchange of instructions will work successfully for unconditional branches, calls, and returns. For conditional branches, this procedure cannot be blindly applied. If the condition that is tested for the branch can be altered by the

TABLE 13-9   Normal And Delayed Branch

Address	Normal Branch		Delayed Branch		Optimized Delayed Branch	
100	LOAD	X,A	LOAD	X,A	LOAD	X,A
101	ADD	1,A	ADD	1,A	JUMP	105
102	JUMP	105	JUMP	106	ADD	1,A
103	ADD	A,B	NOOP		ADD	A,B
104	SUB	C,B	ADD	A,B	SUB	C,B
105	STORE	A,Z	SUB	C,B	STORE	A,Z
106			STORE	A,Z		

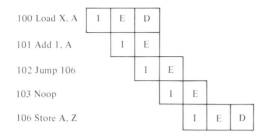

(a) Inserted NOOP

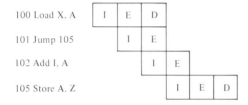

(b) Reversed Instructions

FIGURE 13-10.   Use of the delayed branch

immediately preceding instruction, then the compiler must refrain from doing the interchange and instead insert a NOOP. The experience with both the Berkeley RISC and IBM 801 systems is that the majority of conditional branch instructions can be optimized in this fashion ([PATT82a], [RADI82]).

A similar sort of tactic, called the delayed load, can be used on LOAD instructions. On LOAD instructions, the register that is to be the target of the load is locked by the CPU. The CPU then continues execution of the instruction stream until it reaches an instruction requiring that register, at which point it idles until the load is complete. If the compiler can rearrange instructions so that useful work can be done while the load is in the pipeline, efficiency is increased.

As a final note, we should point out that the design of the instruction pipeline should not be carried out in isolation from other optimization techniques applied to the system. For example, [BRAD91b] shows that the scheduling of instructions for the pipeline and the dynamic allocation of registers should be considered together to achieve the greatest efficiency.

13.6

MOTOROLA 88000

The 88000 is the first RISC processor from Motorola. Although the part number might seem to indicate some relationship with the MC68000 family of CISCs, the differences are profound. The MC68000 is representative of recent CISCs, whereas the 88000 is a rather pure example of a RISC system.

Instruction Set

Table 13-10 lists the instructions for the 88000, and Figure 13-11 shows the instruction formats. Like virtually all RISC systems, the 88000 employs a fixed 32-bit instruction length. The first 6 bits constitute the opcode for the instruction. In most instructions, the opcode is followed by two 5-bit register fields (result and first operand). The remaining 16 bits can contain an immediate operand or an offset for a conditional branch instruction. For instructions involving 3 regis-

TABLE 13-10   Motorola 88000 Instruction Set

Integer Arithmetic

ADD	Add
ADDU	Add Unsigned
SUB	Subtract
SUBU	Subtract Unsigned
MUL	Multiply
DIV	Divide
DIVU	Divide Unsigned
CMP	Compare

Floating-Point Arithmetic

FADD	Floating-Point Add
FSUB	Floating-Point Subtract
FMUL	Floating-Point Multiply
FDIV	Floating-Point Divide
FCMP	Floating-Point Compare
FLT	Convert Integer to Floating Point
INT	Round Floating Point to Integer
NINT	Round Floating Point to Nearest Integer
TRNC	Truncate Floating Point to Integer
FLDCR	Load From Floating-Point Control Register
FSTCR	Store to Floating-Point Control Register
FXCR	Exchange Floating-Point Control Register

Logical Instructions

AND	And
MASK	Logical Mask Immediate
OR	Or
XOR	Exclusive Or

Bit-Field Instructions

CLR	Clear Bit Field
SET	Set Bit Field
EXT	Extract Signed Bit Field
EXTU	Extract Unsigned Bit Field
MAKE	Make Bit Field
ROT	Rotate Bit Field
FF0	Find First Bit Clear
FF1	Find First Bit Set

Flow Control Instructions

BB0	Branch on Bit Clear
BB1	Branch on Bit Set
Bcnd	Conditional Branch
BR	Unconditional Branch
BSR	Branch to Subroutine
JMP	Unconditional Jump
JSR	Jump to Subroutine
TB0	Trap on Bit Clear
TB1	Trap on Bit Set
TBND	Trap on Bounds Check
Tcnd	Conditional Trap
RTE	Return from Exception

Load/Store/Exchange Instructions

LD	Load Register from Memory
LDA	Load Address
LDCR	Load from Control Register
ST	Store Register to Memory
STCR	Store to Control Register
XMEM	Exchange Register with Memory
XCR	Exchange Control Register

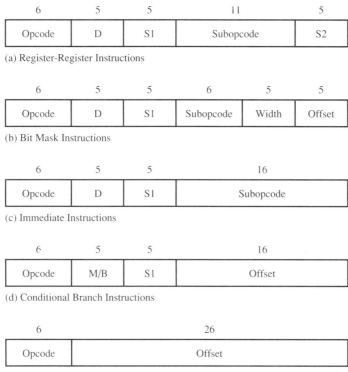

FIGURE 13-11.   Motorola 88000 instruction formats

ters (2 source and one result, or destination), 11 bits remain for an extension to the opcode to specify particular operations.

Note that in all of the formats, the positions of the key fields line up. Thus, the instruction decoder logic of the processor always accesses source and destination registers from the same relative location within the instruction. This speeds up instruction decoding and simplifies pipeline design.

Most of the instructions reference only register operands. Only a few simple load/store instructions reference memory. Bits in the subopcode indicate load and store of word (32 bits), halfword, and byte. For the latter two cases, a load into a register can be treated as signed or unsigned. Signed numbers are sign-extended to fill out the 32-bit destination register in 2's-complement notation. Unsigned numbers are padded with 0s.

All memory references are formed by adding the contents of a base register to a second operand. To maintain the simplicity and uniformity of the instruction operations, the same logic that is provided for integer arithmetic instructions is re-used for memory referencing. In the case of integer addition, the second operand can be either a 16-bit immediate quantity or a 32-bit register. The corresponding addressing modes are register indirect with unsigned immediate and register indirect with index. In addition, scaled indexing is provided to support the manipulation of arrays.[1]

One unique aspect of the instruction set is the inclusion of eight bit-field instructions, which are defined in Table 13-11. The fields on which these instructions operate can be of any width and located anywhere in the word. Bit-field hardware can clear, set, extract, and insert fields into registers. This hardware can essentially perform a single-cycle shift of any number of bits to a field of any width. The only limitation is that the amount of the shift plus the width of the affected field must be less than the width of the 32-bit register. This capability is handy for operations such as extracting the exponent from a floating-point number or Boolean data from a register that contains a set of flags.

Architecture

Figure 13-12 shows the overall architecture of the 88000. The main processor chip consists of multiple independent function units connected to a multiported register file. The function units can operate independently and concurrently, providing a very efficient means of processing instructions.

- *Integer unit:* Executes all integer arithmetic, bit field, boolean, and control register accesses.
- *Floating-point unit:* Provides IEEE 754 functions. It consists of a five-stage adder pipeline and a separate six-stage multiplier pipeline. These pipelines allow for multiple floating-point operations to be performed concurrently.
- *Instruction unit:* Responsible for fetching instructions and dispatching the decoded opcode via control signals to the appropriate execution units contained in the processor.
- *Data memory unit:* Responsible for loading and storing operands between the processor and external memory.

The memory bus (M bus) interfaces two cache memory management units to the memory system, one for data and one for instructions. This feature is implemented on a number of recent RISC systems. This architecture allows instructions to be fetched while transferring operands between the processor and memory, thus providing a speed-up.[2]

---

[1] See the discussion of 80386/80486 addressing modes in Chapter 9 for a description of scaled indexing.

[2] Manufacturers often refer to this configuration as a Harvard architecture. The original use of that term referred to the separation of instructions and data in main memory, not in caches.

TABLE 13-11 Motorola 88000 Bit-Field Instructions

Name	Instruction	Function
CLR	Clear bit field to zeros	$D \leftarrow S$; $D[(o + w - 1) \ldots o] \leftarrow 0s$
SET	Set bit field to ones	$D \leftarrow S$; $D[(o + w - 1) \ldots o] \leftarrow 1s$
EXT	Extract signed bit field	**if** $(w = 0)$ **then begin** $D[31 \ldots (32 - o)] \leftarrow S[31]$; $D[(31 - o) \ldots 0] \leftarrow S[31 \ldots o]$ **end** **else begin** $D[31 \ldots w] \leftarrow S[o + w - 1]$; $D[(w - 1) \ldots 0] \leftarrow S[(o + w - 1) \ldots o]$ **end**
EXTU	Extract unsigned bit field	**if** $(w = 0)$ **then begin** $D[31 \ldots (32 - o)] \leftarrow 0$; $D[(31 - o) \ldots 0] \leftarrow S[31 \ldots o]$ **end** **else begin** $D[31 \ldots w] \leftarrow 0$; $D[(w - 1) \ldots 0] \leftarrow S[(o + w - 1) \ldots o]$ **end**
MAK	Make a bit field	**if** $(w = 0)$ **then** $D \leftarrow shiftL(S,o)$ **else begin** $D \leftarrow 0$; $D[(o + w - 1) \ldots o] \leftarrow S[(w - 1) \ldots (0)]$ **end**
ROT	Rotate bit field right	$D \leftarrow rotateR(S,o)$
FF0	Find first zero bit	$i \leftarrow 31$; **while** $(i \geq 0$ **and** $S2[i] = 1)$ **do** $i \leftarrow i - 1$; **if** $(i < 0)$ **then** $D \leftarrow 32$ **else** $D \leftarrow i$;
FF1	Find first one bit	$i \leftarrow 31$; **while** $(i \geq 0$ **and** $S2[i] = 0)$ **do** $i \leftarrow i - 1$; **if** $(i < 0)$ **then** $D \leftarrow 32$ **else** $D \leftarrow i$;

D = destination register   o = offset
S = source register   w = width

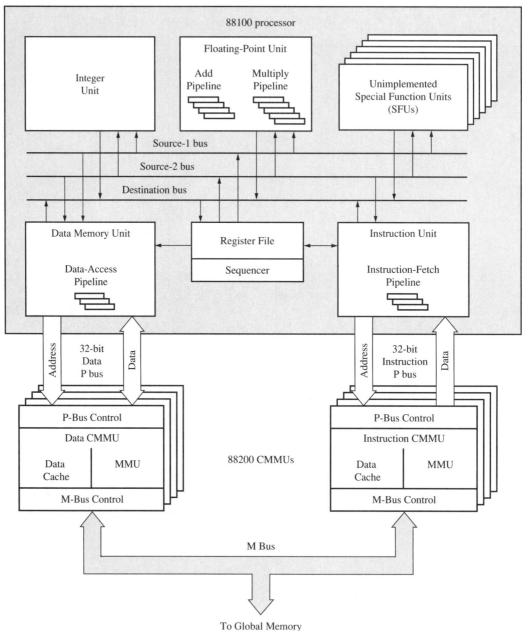

FIGURE 13-12.   The 88000 system block diagram

Register Management

The register file consists of thirty-two 32-bit general-purpose registers. Register 0 is hardwired with the value 0. This is convenient for storing zero in other registers or memory. The R1 register is used to automatically store the return address for a Branch or Jump to Subroutine instruction.

With the 88000 architecture, some means is needed to allow all of the function units to share the register file without destroying one another's register-based data. The mechanism used in the 88000 is known as register scoreboarding. The processor includes a scoreboard register, with one bit corresponding to each of the 31 registers (R0 is excluded since it cannot be updated). Any time that the instruction unit dispatches an instruction that takes more than one clock cycle to execute, the bit in the scoreboard register that corresponds to the destination register for that instruction is set. The bit is cleared when the result is stored in the destination register. All of the function units are free to access registers independently and proceed until they get to a point where they must fetch data from a register whose bit is set. At that point, the function unit must stall until the desired register is released.

Instruction Unit Pipeline

Each of the function units in the 88000 has a pipelined architecture to provide as high a degree of parallelism as possible. Figure 13-13 shows the 3-stage pipeline in the instruction unit. The unit fetches instructions from the instruction cache via a bus referred to as the PBUS.

The fetch stage consists of a Fetch Instruction Pointer (FIP) register that contains the address of the instruction to be fetched. At the beginning of each clock cycle, if there are no pipeline stalls or memory wait states, the FIP issues an address to the instruction cache.

During the next stage, the address in the FIP is transferred to the Next Instruction Pointer (NIP) register and the instruction is fetched from memory and placed in the Next Instruction register. During this stage, the instruction is partially decoded and any needed operands from the register file are prefetched and prepared for transfer to the appropriate function unit.

During the execute stage, the address in the NIP is transferred to the Execute Instruction Pointer (XIP) register and the instruction is transferred to the Executing Instruction register. During this stage, the instruction is dispatched to the appropriate function unit.

For each of the instruction pointers, a shadow register is maintained. If an exception occurs during a cycle, the shadow registers are frozen to save the values at the time of the exception. These are restored after exception processing.

13.7

MIPS R4000

One of the first commercially available chip sets was developed by MIPS Computer Systems. The system was inspired by an experimental system, also using the name MIPS, developed at Stanford [HENN84]. The most recent member of

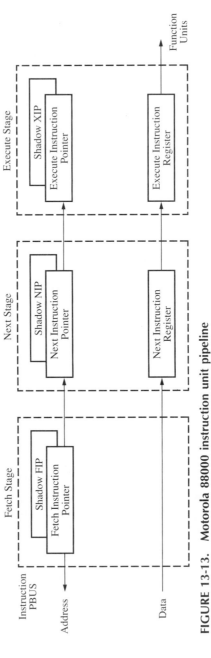

FIGURE 13-13. Motorola 88000 instruction unit pipeline

the MIPS family is the R4000. It has substantially the same architecture and instruction set of the earlier MIPS designs: the R2000, R3000, and R6000. The most significant difference is that the R4000 uses 64 rather than 32 bits for all internal and external data paths and for addresses, registers, and the ALU.

The use of 64 bits has a number of advantages over a 32-bit architecture. It allows a bigger address space—large enough for an operating system to map more than a terabyte of files directly into virtual memory for easy access. With one-gigabyte and larger disk drives now common, the 4-gigabyte address space of a 32-bit machine becomes limiting. Also, the 64-bit capacity allows the R4000 to process data such as IEEE single-precision floating-point numbers and character strings up to 8 characters in a single action.

The R4000 processor chip is partitioned into two sections, one containing the CPU, and the other containing a coprocessor for memory management. The CPU has a very simple architecture. The intent was to design a system in which the instruction execution logic was as simple as possible, leaving space available for logic to enhance performance (e.g., the entire memory management unit).

The processor supports thirty-two 64-bit registers. It also provides for up to 128 kbytes of high-speed cache, half each for instructions and data. The relatively large cache (the IBM 3090 provides 128-256 kbytes of cache) enables the system to keep large sets of program code and data local to the processor, off-loading the main memory bus and avoiding the need for a large register file with the accompanying windowing logic.

Instruction Set

Table 13-12 lists the basic instruction set for all MIPS R series processors. Table 13-13 lists the additional instructions implemented in the R4000. All processor instructions are encoded in a single 32-bit word format. All data operations are register-to-register; the only memory references are pure load/store operations.

The R4000 makes no use of condition codes. If an instruction generates a condition, the corresponding flags are stored in a general-purpose register. This avoids the need for special logic to deal with condition codes as they affect the pipelining mechanism and the reordering of instructions by the compiler. Instead, the mechanisms already implemented to deal with register-value dependencies are employed. Further, conditions mapped onto the register files are subject to the same compile-time optimizations in allocation and reuse as other values stored in registers.

As with most RISC-based machines, the MIPS uses a single 32-bit instruction length. This single instruction length simplifies instruction fetch and decode, and also simplifies the interaction of instruction fetch with the virtual memory management unit (i.e., instructions do not cross word or page boundaries). The three instruction formats (Figure 13-14) share common formatting of opcodes and register references, simplifying instruction decode. The effect of more complex instructions can be synthesized at compile time.

TABLE 13-12 MIPS R-Series Instruction Set

OP	Description	OP	Description
	Load/Store Instructions		**Multiply/Divide Instructions**
LB	Load Byte	MULT	Multiply
LBU	Load Byte Unsigned	MULTU	Multiply Unsigned
LH	Load Halfword	DIV	Divide
LHU	Load Halfword Unsigned	DIVU	Divide Unsigned
LW	Load Word	MFHI	Move From HI
LWL	Load Word Left	MTHI	Move To HI
LWR	Load Word Right	MFLO	Move From LO
SB	Store Byte	MTLO	Move To LO
SH	Store Halfword		
SW	Store Word		**Jump and Branch Instructions**
SWL	Store Word Left	J	Jump
SWR	Store Word Right	JAL	Jump and Link
		JR	Jump to Register
	Arithmetic Instructions	JALR	Jump and Link Register
	(ALU Immediate)	BEQ	Branch on Equal
ADDI	Add Immediate	BNE	Branch on Not Equal
ADDIU	Add Immediate Unsigned	BLEZ	Branch on Less Than or Equal to Zero
SLTI	Set on Less Than Immediate	BGTZ	Branch on Greater Than Zero
SLTIU	Set on Less Than Immediate	BLTZ	Branch on Less Than Zero
	Unsigned	BGEZ	Branch on Greater Than or
ANDI	AND Immediate		Equal to Zero
ORI	OR Immediate	BLTZAL	Branch on Less Than Zero And Link
XORI	Exclusive OR Immediate	BGEZAL	Branch on Greater Than or Equal to
LUI	Load Upper Immediate		Zero And Link
	Arithmetic Instructions		**Coprocessor Instructions**
	(3-operand, R-type)	LWCz	Load Word to Coprocessor
ADD	Add	SWCz	Store Word from Coprocessor
ADDU	Add Unsigned	MTCz	Move To Coprocessor
SUB	Subtract	MFCz	Move From Coprocessor
SUBU	Subtract Unsigned	CTCz	Move Control to Coprocessor
SLT	Set on Less Than	CFCz	Move Control From Coprocessor
SLTU	Set on Less Than Unsigned	COPz	Coprocessor Operation
AND	AND	BCzT	Branch on Coprocessor z True
OR	OR	BCzF	Branch on Coprocessor z False
XOR	Exclusive OR		
NOR	NOR		**Special Instructions**
	Shift Instructions	SYSCALL	System Call
SLL	Shift Left Logical	BREAK	Break
SRL	Shift Right Logical		
SRA	Shift Right Arithmetic		
SLLV	Shift Left Logical Variable		
SRLV	Shift Right Logical Variable		
SRAV	Shift Right Arithmetic Variable		

TABLE 13-13 Additional R4000 Instructions

OP	Description	OP	Description
	Load/Store Instructions		**Exception Instructions**
LL	Load Linked	TGE	Trap if Greater Than or Equal
SC	Store Conditional	TGEU	Trap if Greater Than or Equal Unsigned
SYNC	Sync	TLT	Trap if Less Than
		TLTU	Trap if Less Than Unsigned
	Jump and Branch Instructions	TEQ	Trap if Equal
BEQL	Branch on Equal Likely	TNE	Trap if Not Equal
BNEL	Branch on Not Equal Likely	TGEI	Trap if Greater Than or Equal Immediate
BLEZL	Branch on Less Than or Equal to Zero Likely	TGEIU	Trap if Greater Than or Equal Unsigned Immediate
BGTZL	Branch on Greater Than Zero Likely	TLTI	Trap if Less Than Immediate
BLTZL	Branch on Less Than Zero Likely	TLTIU	Trap if Less Than Unsigned Immediate
BGEZL	Branch on Greater Than or Equal to Zero Likely	TEQI	Trap if Equal Immediate
		TNEI	Trap if Not Equal Immediate
BLTZALL	Branch on Less Than Zero And Link Likely		
BGEZALL	Branch on Grater Than or Equal to Zero and Link Likely		**Coprocessor Instructions**
BCzTL	Branch on Coprocessor z True Likely	LDCz	Load Double Coprocessor
CDzFL	Branch on Coprocessor z False Likely	SDCz	Store Double Coprocessor

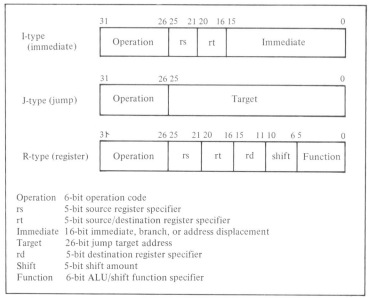

FIGURE 13-14. MIPS instruction formats

Only the simplest and most frequently used memory-addressing mode is implemented in hardware. All memory references consist of a 16-bit offset from a 32-bit register. For example, the "load word" instruction is of the form:

lw r2, 128(r3)   load word at address 128 offset from register 3 into register 2

Each of the 32 general-purpose registers can be used as the base register. One register, r0, always contains zero.

The compiler makes use of multiple machine instructions to synthesize typical addressing modes in conventional machines. Some examples are provided in Table 13-14 [CHOW87]. The table shows the use of the instruction **lui** (load upper immediate). This instruction loads the upper half of a register with a 16-bit immediate value, setting the lower half to zero.

TABLE 13-14 Synthesizing Other Addressing Modes with the MIPS Addressing Mode

Apparent Instruction	Actual Instruction
lw r2, <16-bit offset >	lw r2, <16-bit offset > (r0)
lw r2, <32-bit offset >	lui r1, <high 16 bits of offset > lw r2, <low 16 bits of offset > (r1)
lw r2, <32-bit offset > (r4)	lui r1, <high 16 bits of offset > addu r1, r1, r4 lw r2, <low 16 bits of offset > (r1)

Instruction Pipeline

With its simplified instruction architecture, the MIPS can achieve very efficient pipelining. It is instructive to look at the evolution of the MIPS pipeline, as it illustrates the evolution in RISC pipelining in general.

The initial experimental RISC systems and the first generation of commercial RISC processors achieve execution speeds that approach one instruction per system clock cycle. To improve on this performance, two classes of processors have evolved to offer execution of multiple instructions per clock cycle: superscalar and superpipelined architectures. In essence, a **superscalar architecture** replicates each of the pipeline stages so that two or more instructions at the same stage of the pipeline can be processed simultaneously. A **superpipelined** architecture is one which makes use of more, and more fine-grained, pipeline stages. With more stages, more instructions can be in the pipeline at the same time, increasing parallelism.

Both approaches have limitations. With superscalar pipelining, dependencies between instructions in different pipelines can slow down the system. Also, overhead logic is required to coordinate these dependencies. With superpipelining, there is overhead associated with transferring instructions from one stage to the next.

Chapter 14 is devoted to a study of superscalar architecture. The MIPS R4000 is a good example of a RISC-based superpipeline architecture.

Figure 13-15a shows the instruction pipelines of the R3000. In the R3000, the pipeline advances once per clock cycle. The MIPS compiler is able to reorder instructions to fill delay slots with code 70–90 percent of the time. All instructions follow the same sequence of five pipeline stages:

* instruction fetch
* source operand fetch from register file
* ALU operation or data operand address generation
* data memory reference
* write back into register file

As illustrated in Figure 13-15a, there is not only parallelism due to pipelining but also parallelism within the execution of a single instruction. The 60-ns clock cycle is divided into two 30-ns phases. The external instruction and data access operations to the cache each require 60 ns, as do the major internal operations (OP, DA, IA). Instruction decode is a simpler operation, requiring only a single 30-ns phase, overlapped with register fetch in the same instruction. Calculation of an address for a branch instruction also overlaps instruction decode and register fetch, so that a branch at instruction i can address the ICACHE access of instruction $i + 2$. Similarly, a load at instruction i fetches data that are immediately used by the OP of instruction $i + 1$, while an ALU/shift result gets passed directly into instruction $i + 1$ with no delay. This tight coupling between instructions makes for a highly efficient pipeline.

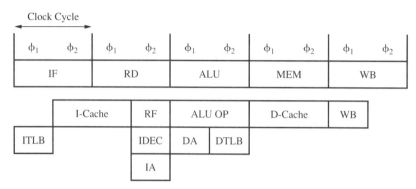

(a) Detailed R3000 Pipeline

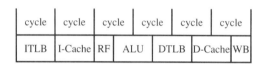

(b) Modified R3000 Pipeline with Reduced Latencies

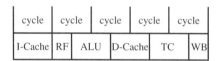

(c) Optimiized R3000 Pipeline with Parallel TLB and Cache Accesses

FIGURE 13-15. Enhancing the R3000 pipeline

IF = Instruction fetch
RD = Read
MEM = Memory access
WB = Write back
I-Cache = Instruction cache access
RF = Fetch operand from register
D-Cache = Data cache access
ITLB = Instruction address translation
IDEC = Instruction decode
IA = Compute instruction address
DA = Calculate data virtual address
DTLB = Data address translation
TC = Data cache tag check

In detail, then, each clock cycle is divided into separate phases, denoted as $\phi1$ and $\phi2$. The functions performed in each phase are summarized in Table 13-15.

The R4000 incorporates a number of technical advances over the R3000. The use of more advanced technology allows the clock cycle time to be cut in half, to 30 ns, and for the access time to the register file to be cut in half. In addition, there is greater density on the chip, which enables the instruction and data caches to be incorporated on the chip. Before looking at the final R4000 pipeline, let us consider how the R3000 pipeline can be modified to improve performance using R4000 technology.

Figure 13-15b shows a first step. Remember that the cycles in this figure are half as long as those in Figure 13-15a. Because they are on the same chip, the instruction and data cache stages take only half as long; so they still occupy only one clock cycle. Again, because of the speed-up of the register file access, register read and write still occupy only half of a clock cycle.

Because the R4000 caches are on-chip, the virtual-to-physical address translation can delay the cache access. This delay is reduced by implementing virtually-indexed caches and going to a parallel cache access and address translation.

TABLE 13-15   R3000 Pipeline Stages

Pipeline Stage	Phase	Function
IF	$\phi 1$	Using the TLB, translate an instruction virtual address to a physical address (after a branching decision).
IF	$\phi 2$	Send the physical address to the instruction address.
RD	$\phi 1$	Return instruction from instruction cache. Compare tags and validity of fetched instruction.
RD	$\phi 2$	Decode instruction. Read register file. If branch, calculate branch target address.
ALU	$\phi 1 + \phi 2$	If register-to-register operation, the arithmetic or logical operation is performed.
ALU	$\phi 1$	If a branch, decide whether the branch is to be taken or not. If a memory reference (load or store), calculate data virtual address.
ALU	$\phi 2$	If a memory reference, translate data virtual address to physical using TLB
MEM	$\phi 1$	If a memory reference, send physical address to data cache.
MEM	$\phi 2$	If a memory reference, return data from data cache, and check tags.
WB	$\phi 1$	Write to register file.

Figure 13-15c shows the optimized R3000 pipeline with this improvement. Because of the compression of events, the data cache tag check is performed separately on the next cycle after cache access.

In a superpipelined system, existing hardware is used several times per cycle by inserting pipeline registers to split up each pipe stage. Essentially, each superpipeline stage operates at a multiple of the base clock frequency, the multiple depending on the degree of superpipelining. The R4000 technology has the speed and density to permit superpipelining of degree 2. Figure 13-16a shows the optimized R3000 pipeline using this superpipelining. Note that this is essentially the same dynamic structure as Figure 13-15c.

Further improvements can be made. For the R4000, a much larger and specialized adder was designed. This makes it possible to execute ALU operations at twice the rate. Other improvements allow the execution of loads and stores at twice the rate. The resulting pipeline is shown in Figure 13-16b.

The R4000 has eight pipeline stages, meaning that as many as eight instructions can be in the pipeline at the same time. The pipeline advances at the rate of two stages per clock cycle. The eight pipeline stages are:

- *Instruction fetch first half:* Virtual address is presented to the instruction cache and the translation lookaside buffer.
- *Instruction fetch second half:* Instruction cache outputs the instruction and the TLB generates the physical address.
- *Register file:* Three activities occur in parallel:
  —instruction is decoded and check made for interlock conditions (i.e., this instruction depends on the result of a preceding instruction)

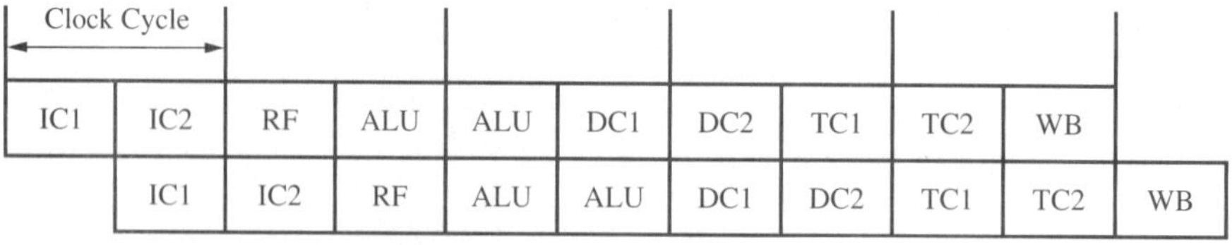

Clock Cycle										
IC1	IC2	RF	ALU	ALU	DC1	DC2	TC1	TC2	WB	
	IC1	IC2	RF	ALU	ALU	DC1	DC2	TC1	TC2	WB

(a) Superpipelined Implementation of the Optimized R3000 Pipeline

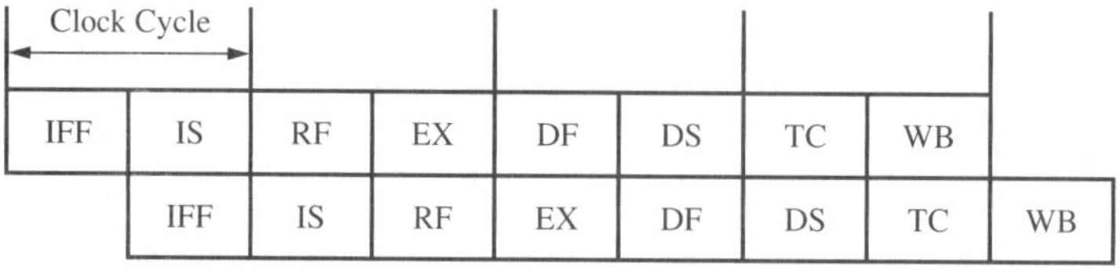

Clock Cycle								
IFF	IS	RF	EX	DF	DS	TC	WB	
	IFF	IS	RF	EX	DF	DS	TC	WB

(b) R4000 Pipeline

IFF = Instruction fetch first half
IS = Instruction fetch second half
RF = Fetch operands from register
EX = Instruction execute
DF = Data cache first half
DS = Data cache second half
TC = Tag check

FIGURE 13-16.   Theoretical R3000 and actual R4000 superpipelines

—instruction cache tag check is made
—operands are fetched from the register file
• *Instruction execute:* One of three activities can occur
    —if the instruction is a register-to-register operation, the ALU performs the arithmetic or logical operation
    —if the instruction is a load or store, the data virtual address is calculated
    —if the instruction is a branch, the branch target virtual address is calculated and branch conditions are checked
• *Data cache first:* Virtual address is presented to the data cache and TLB.
• *Data cache second:* Data cache outputs the instruction and the TLB generates the physical address.
• *Tag check:* Cache tag checks are performed for loads and stores.
• *Write back:* Instruction result is written back to register file.

13.8

THE RISC VERSUS CISC CONTROVERSY

For many years, the general trend in computer architecture and organization has been toward increasing CPU complexity: more instructions, more addressing modes, more specialized registers, and so on. The RISC movement represents a fundamental break with the philosophy behind that trend. Naturally, the appearance of RISC systems and the publication of papers by its proponents extolling RISC virtues, has led to a reaction from what might be called the mainstream of computer architecture.

The work that has been done on assessing merits of the RISC approach can be grouped into two categories:

- *Quantitative:* attempts to compare program size and execution speed of programs on RISC and CISC machines that use comparable technology.
- *Qualitative:* examination of issues such as high-level language support and optimum use of VLSI real estate.

Most of the work on quantitative assessment has been done by those working on RISC systems [PATT82b, HEAT84, PATT84], and has been, by and large, favorable to the RISC approach. Others have examined the issue and come away unconvinced [COLW85, FLYN87, DAVI87]. There are several problems with attempting such comparisons [SERL86]:

- There is no pair of RISC and CISC machines that are comparable in life-cycle cost, level of technology, gate complexity, sophistication of compiler, operating-system support, and so on.
- No definitive test set of programs exists. Performance varies with the program.
- It is difficult to sort out hardware effects from effects due to skill in compiler writing.
- Most of the comparative analysis on RISC has been done on "toy" machines rather than commercial products. Furthermore, most commercially-available machines advertised as RISC possess a mixture of RISC and CISC characteristics [MOKH86]. Thus a fair comparison with a commercial, "pure-play" CISC machine (e.g., VAX, Intel 80386) is difficult.

The qualitative assessment is, almost by definition, subjective. Several researchers have turned their attention to such an assessment [COLW85a, BERN81, WALL85], but the results are, at best, ambiguous, and certainly subject to rebuttal [PATT85b] and, of course, counter-rebuttal [COLW85b].

The success of the RISC approach in the marketplace remains to be seen. As research, development, and product introduction continue, the assessment goes on.

13.9

RECOMMENDED READING

Surveys of RISC technology include [TABA87], [WALL85], and [PATT85a]. [TABA91] and [DEWA90] provide extensive coverage of RISC systems. Two textbooks with good coverage of RISC concepts are [WARD90] and [HENN91]. Good surveys of RISC products are [MEND91], [WILS90], [ALLI88], [GIMA87], and [WEIS87]. [FLYN87] and [COLW85a] provide a critical look at the RISC versus CISC controversy. [STAL89] contains original material, reprints of key articles, and an annotated bibliography on the subject.

[TAMI83] examines various strategies for making use of a large set of registers. [HITC85] reports results that suggest that the performance improvements due to a large register set and to a reduced instruction set are independent.

The Motorola 88000 receives very detailed coverage in [ALSU90]. Other good articles are [MELE89] and [GOSS89]. [TABA91] devotes a chapter to this microprocessor. [KANE92] covers the commercial MIPS machine in detail. [GLAS91] provides a good overview of the MIPS R4000. [BASH91] discusses the evolution from the R3000 pipeline to the R4000 superpipeline.

[KATE83] contains a detailed description of the Berkeley RISC I and RISC II, which were very influential in the early development of RISC technology. Although this is a PhD thesis, it contains an excellent tutorial on RISC technology. [HENN84] describes the Stanford MIPS machine, another highly influential research system, and provides an excellent comparison with CISC approaches.

13.10

PROBLEMS

13.1 Considering the call-return pattern in Figure 4-32, how many overflows and underflows (each of which causes a register save/restore) will occur with a window size of

    (a) 5?

    (b) 8?

    (c) 16?

13.2 Assume an architecture in which 100 registers are to be used for a circular buffer of the type illustrated in Figure 13-2. In each window, five registers are used for parameters. Assume that the number of local variables used by a procedure obeys a uniform distribution from 5 to 14; that is, 10% use 5 variables, 10% use 6 variables, and so on. Finally, assume that the call-return pattern follows Figure 4-32. What combination of window size and number of windows is optimum?

13.3 In the discussion of Figure 13-2, it was stated that only the first two portions of a window are saved or restored. Why is it not necessary to save the temporary registers?

13.4 We wish to determine the execution time for a given program using the various pipelining schemes discussed in Section 13-5. Let

N = number of executed instructions
D = number of memory accesses
J = number of jump instructions

For the simple sequential scheme (Figure 13-6), the execution time is 2N + D phases. Derive formulas for two-way, three-way, and four-way pipelining.

13.5 Redraw Figure 13-9, taking into account delayed branch load techniques.

13.6 For those VAX addressing modes (Table 9-4) that can be synthesized in MIPS, show the MIPS equivalent.

13.7 In many cases, common machine instructions that are not listed as part of the MIPS instruction set can be synthesized with a single MIPS instruction. Show this for the following:

  Register-to-Register Move
  Increment, Decrement
  Complement
  Negate
  Clear

13.8 Consider the following code fragment in a high-level language:

for I in 1 . . . 100 **loop**
   S ← S + Q(I).VAL
end loop;

Assume that Q is an array of 32-byte records and the VAL field is in the first 4 bytes of each record. Using 80X36 code, we can compile this program fragment as follows:

```
        MOV   ECX, 1              ;use register ECX to hold 1
LP:     IMUL  EAX, ECX, 32       ;get offset in EAX
        MOV   EBX, Q[EAX]        :load VAL field
        ADD   S, EBX             ;add to S
        INC   ECX               ;increment I
        CMP   ECX, 100          :test against limit
        JNE   LP                :loop until I = 100
```

This program makes use of the IMUL instruction, which multiplies the second operand by the immediate value in the third operand and places the result in the first operand (see Problem 9.18). A RISC advocate would like to demonstrate that a clever compiler can eliminate unnecessarily complex instructions such as IMUL. Provide the demonstration by rewriting the above 80X36 program without using the IMUL instruction.

13.9 The 88000 instruction set includes both a Branch to Subroutine instruction and a Jump to Subroutine instruction. Speculate on what might be the difference between the two and why both would be desired in an instruction set that is so limited.

CHAPTER 14

Superscalar Processors

A superscalar implementation of a processor architecture is one in which common instructions—integer and floating-point arithmetic, loads, stores, and conditional branches—can be initiated simultaneously and executed independently. Such implementations raise a number of complex design issues related to the instruction pipeline.

Superscalar design arrives on the scene hard on the heels of RISC architecture. Although the simplified instruction set architecture of a RISC machine lends itself readily to superscalar techniques, the superscalar approach can be used on either a RISC or CISC architecture. However, virtually all of the superscalar implementations have been based on a RISC architecture.

Whereas the gestation period for the arrival of commercial RISC machines from the beginning of true RISC research with the IBM 801 and the Berkeley RISC I was seven or eight years, the first superscalar machines became commercially available within just a year or two of the coining of the term superscalar. Superscalar implementation, in conjunction with RISC or near-RISC architecture, looks to be one of the most exciting areas of research and development in computer organization and architecture over the next few years.

In this chapter, we begin with an overview of the superscalar approach, contrasting it with superpipelining. Next, the key design issues associated with superscalar implementation are presented. Finally, two of the most significant commercial superscalar processors are summarized.

14.1

OVERVIEW

The term *superscalar*, first coined in 1987 [AGER87], refers to a machine that is designed to improve the performance of the execution of scalar instructions. The name contrasts the intent of this effort with vector processors, discussed in Chapter 15. In most applications, the bulk of the operations are on scalar quantities. Accordingly, the superscalar approach represents the next step in the evolution of high-performance general-purpose processors.

Many researchers have investigated superscalar-like processors, and their research indicates that some degree of performance improvement is possible. Table 14-1 presents the reported performance advantages. The differences in the results arise from differences both in the hardware of the simulated machine and in the applications being simulated.

Superscalar versus Superpipelined

An alternative approach to achieving greater performance is referred to as superpipelining, a term first coined in 1988 [JOUP88]. Superpipelining exploits the fact that many pipeline stages perform tasks that require less than half a clock cycle. Thus, a doubled internal clock speed allows the performance of two tasks in one external clock cycle. We have seen one example of this approach with the MIPS R4000.

Figure 14-1 compares the two approaches. The upper part of the diagram illustrates an ordinary pipeline, used as a base for comparison. The base pipeline issues one instruction per clock cycle and can perform one pipeline stage per clock cycle. The pipeline has four stages: instruction fetch, operation decode, operation execution, and result write back. The execution stage is crosshatched for clarity. Note that although several instructions are executing concurrently, only one instruction is in its execution stage at any one time.

The next part of the diagram shows a superpipelined implementation that is capable of performing two pipeline stages per clock cycle. An alternative way of looking at this is that the functions performed in each stage can be split into two nonoverlapping parts and each can execute in half a clock cycle. A superpipeline implementation that behaves in this fashion is said to be of degree 2. Finally, the lowest part of the diagram shows a superscalar implementation capable of executing two instances of each stage in parallel. Higher-degree superpipeline and superscalar implementations are of course possible.

TABLE 14-1 Reported
Speedups of Superscalar-
Like Machines

Reference	Speedup
[TJAD70]	1.8
[KUCK72]	8
[WEIS84]	1.58
[ACOS86]	2.7
[SOHI87]	1.8
[SMIT89]	2.3
[JOUP89]	2.2
[LEE91]	7

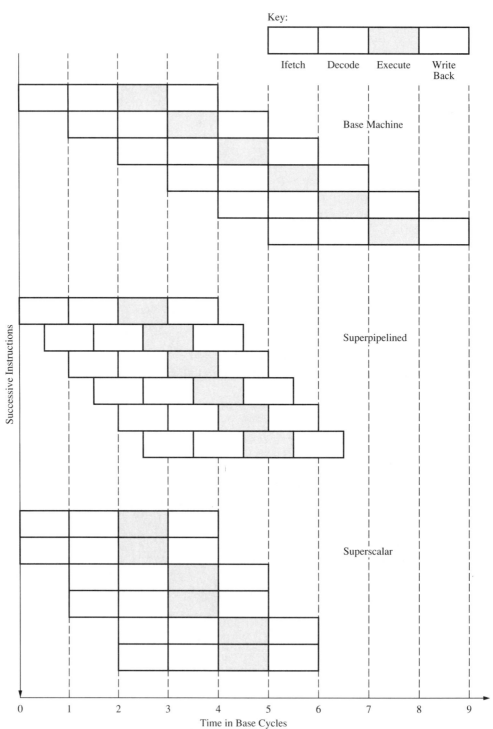

FIGURE 14-1. Comparison of superscalar and superpipeline approaches

Both the superpipeline and the superscalar implementations depicted in Figure 14-1 have the same number of instructions executing at the same time in the steady state. The superpipelined processor falls behind the superscalar processor at the start of the program and at each branch target.

Limitations

The superscalar approach depends on the ability to execute multiple instructions in parallel. The term **instruction-level parallelism** refers to the degree to which, on average, the instructions of a program can be executed in parallel. A combination of compiler-based optimization and hardware techniques can be used to maximize instruction-level parallelism. Before examining the design techniques used in superscalar machines to increase instruction-level parallelism, we need to look at the fundamental limitations to parallelism with which the system must cope. [JOHN91] lists five limitations:

- True data dependency
- Procedural dependency
- Resource conflicts
- Output dependency
- Antidependency

We examine the first three of these limitations in the remainder of this section. A discussion of the last two must await some of the developments in the next section.

True Data Dependency

Consider the following sequence:

add   r1, r2 ;load register r1 with the contents of r2 plus the contents of r1
move r3, r1 ;load register r3 with the contents of r1

The second instruction can be fetched and decoded, but cannot execute until the first instruction executes. The reason is that the second instruction needs data produced by the first instruction. This situation is referred to as a true data dependency (also called **flow dependency** or **write-read dependency**).

Figure 14-2 illustrates this dependency in a superscalar machine of degree 2. With no dependency, two instructions can be fetched and executed in parallel. If there is a data dependency between the first and second instructions, then the second instruction is delayed as many clock cycles as required to remove the dependency. In general, any instruction must be delayed until all of its input values have been produced.

True data dependencies limit the performance of any type of pipeline. For example, in a simple scalar pipeline, the above sequence of instructions would cause no delay. However, consider the following:

load   r1, eff ;load register r1 with the contents of effective memory address eff
move r3, r1 ;load register r3 with the contents of r1

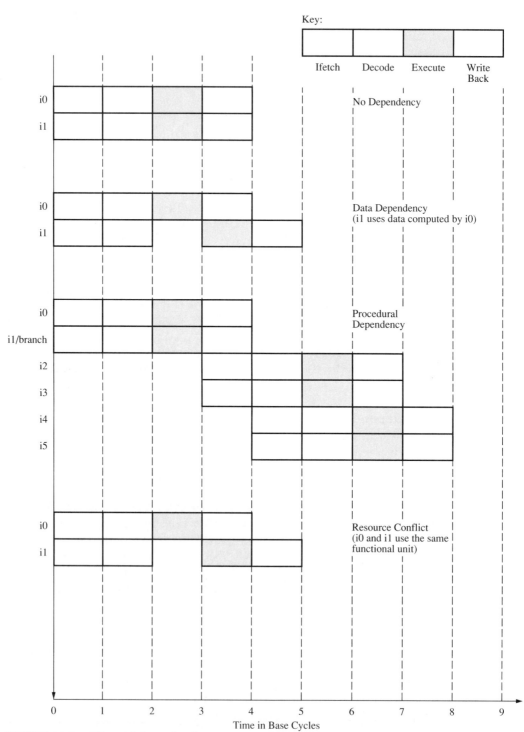

FIGURE 14-2. Effect of dependencies

A typical RISC processor takes two or more cycles to perform a load from memory, because of the delay of an off-chip memory or cache access. One way to compensate for this delay is for the compiler to reorder instructions so that one or more subsequent instructions that do not depend on the memory load can begin flowing through the pipeline. This scheme is less effective in the case of a superscalar pipeline: The independent instructions executed during the load are likely to be executed on the first cycle of the load, leaving the processor with nothing to do until the load completes.

Procedural Dependencies

As was discussed in Chapter 10, the presence of branches in an instruction sequence complicates the pipeline operation. The instructions following a branch (taken or not taken) have a procedural dependency on the branch and cannot be executed until the branch is executed. Figure 14-2 illustrates the effect of a branch on a superscalar pipeline of degree 2.

As we have seen, this type of procedural dependency also affects a scalar pipeline. Again, the consequence for a superscalar pipeline is more severe, since a greater magnitude of opportunity is lost with each delay.

If variable-length instructions are used, then another sort of procedural dependency arises. Because the length of any particular instruction is not known, it must be at least partially decoded before the following instruction can be fetched. This prevents the simultaneous fetching required in a superscalar pipeline. This is one of the reasons that superscalar techniques are more readily applicable to a RISC or RISC-like architecture, with its fixed instruction length.

Resource Conflict

A resource conflict is a competition of two or more instructions for the same resource at the same time. Examples of resources include memories, caches, buses, register-file ports, and functional units (e.g., ALU adder).

In terms of the pipeline, a resource conflict exhibits similar behavior to a data dependency (Figure 14-2). There are some differences, however. For one thing, resource conflicts can be overcome by duplication of resources, whereas a true data dependency cannot be eliminated. Also, when an operation takes a long time to complete, resource conflicts can be minimized by pipelining the appropriate functional unit. For example, all of the functional units in the Motorola 88000 are pipelined.

14.2

DESIGN ISSUES

Instruction-Level Parallelism and Machine Parallelism

[JOUP89a] makes an important distinction between the two related concepts of instruction-level parallelism and machine parallelism. **Instruction-level parallel-**

ism exists when instructions in a sequence are independent and thus can be executed in parallel by overlapping.

As an example of the concept of instruction-level parallelism, consider the following two code fragments [JOUP89b]:

Load R1 ← R2(23)   Add   R3 ← R3, "1"
Add   R3 ← R3, "1"   Add   R4 ← R3, R2
Add   R4 ← R4, R3   Store [R4] ← R0

(a) parallelism = 3   (b) parallelism = 1

The three instructions in (a) are independent and in theory all three could be executed in parallel. In contrast, the three instructions in (b) cannot be executed in parallel because the second instruction uses the result of the first, and the third instruction uses the result of the second.

Instruction-level parallelism is determined by the frequency of true data dependencies and procedural dependencies in the code. These factors, in turn, are dependent on the instruction set architecture and on the application. Instruction-level parallelism is also determined by what [JOUP89a] refers to as operation latency: the time until the result of an instruction is available for use as an operand in a subsequent instruction. The latency determines how much of a delay a data or procedural dependency will cause.

Machine parallelism is a measure of the ability of the processor to take advantage of instruction-level parallelism. Machine parallelism is determined by the number of instructions that can be fetched and executed at the same time (the number of parallel pipelines) and by the speed and sophistication of the mechanisms that the processor uses to find independent instructions.

Both instruction-level and machine parallelism are important factors in enhancing performance. A program may not have enough instruction-level parallelism to take full advantage of machine parallelism. The use of a fixed-length instruction set architecture, as in a RISC, enhances instruction-level parallelism. On the other hand, limited machine parallelism will limit performance no matter what the nature of the program.

Instruction Issue Policy

As was mentioned, machine parallelism is not simply a matter of having multiple instances of each pipeline stage. The processor must also be able to identify instruction-level parallelism and orchestrate the fetching, decoding, and execution of instructions in parallel. [JOHN91] uses the term **instruction issue** to refer to the process of initiating instruction execution in the processor's functional units and the term **instruction-issue policy** to refer to the protocol used to issue instructions.

In essence, the processor is trying to look ahead of the current point of execution to locate instructions that can be brought into the pipeline and executed. Three types of orderings are important in this regard:

- The order in which instructions are fetched
- The order in which instructions are executed
- The order in which instructions change register and memory locations

The more sophisticated the processor, the less it is bound by a strict relationship between these orderings. To achieve maximum utilization of the various pipeline elements, the processor will need to alter one or more of the above orderings with respect to the ordering to be found in a strict sequential execution. The one constraint on the processor is that the result must be correct. Thus, the processor must accommodate the various dependencies and conflicts discussed earlier.

In general terms, we can group superscalar instruction issue policies into the following categories:

- In-order issue with in-order completion
- In-order issue with out-of-order completion
- Out-of-order issue with out-of-order completion

In-Order Issue with In-Order Completion

The simplest instruction-issue policy is to issue instructions in the exact order that would be achieved by sequential execution (in-order issue) and to write results in that same order (in-order completion). Not even scalar pipelines follow such a simple-minded policy. However, it is useful to consider this policy as a baseline for comparing more sophisticated approaches.

Figure 14-3a gives an example of this policy. We assume a superscalar pipeline capable of fetching and decoding two instructions at a time, having three separate functional units (e.g., integer arithmetic, floating-point arithmetic), and having two instances of the writeback pipeline stage. The example assumes the following constraints on a six-instruction code fragment:

- I1 requires two cycles to execute
- I3 and I4 conflict for the same functional unit
- I5 depends on the value produced by I4
- I5 and I6 conflict for a functional unit

Instructions are fetched two at a time and passed to the decode unit. Since instructions are fetched in pairs, the next two instructions must wait until the pair of decode pipeline stages has cleared. To guarantee in-order completion, instruction issuing stalls when there is a conflict for a functional unit or when a functional unit requires more than one cycle to generate a result.

In this example, the elapsed time from decoding the first instruction to writing the last results is eight cycles.

In-Order Issue with Out-of-Order Completion

Out-of-order completion is used in scalar RISC processors to improve the performance of instructions that require multiple cycles. For example, floating-point operations on the Motorola 88000 are handled in this fashion.

(a) In-Order Issue and In-Order Completion

Decode		Execute				Writeback		Cycle
I1	I2							1
I3	I4	I1	I2					2
I3	I4	I1						3
	I4			I3		I1	I2	4
I5	I6			I4				5
	I6		I5			I3	I4	6
			I6					7
						I5	I6	8

(b) In-Order Issue and Out-of-Order Completion

Decode		Execute				Writeback		Cycle
I1	I2							1
I3	I4	I1	I2					2
	I4	I1		I3		I2		3
I5	I6			I4		I1	I3	4
	I6		I5			I4		5
			I6			I5		6
						I6		7

(c) Out-of-Order Issue and Out-of-Order Completion

Decode		Window	Execute				Writeback		Cycle
I1	I2								1
I3	I4	I1, I2	I1	I2					2
I5	I6	I3, I4	I1		I3		I2		3
		I4, I5, I6		I6	I4		I1	I3	4
		I5		I5			I4	I6	5
							I5		6

FIGURE 14-3. Superscalar instruction issue and completion policies

Figure 14-3b illustrates its use on a superscalar processor. Instruction I2 is allowed to run to completion prior to I1. This allows I3 to be completed earlier, with the net result of a savings of one cycle.

With out-of-order completion, any number of instructions may be in the execution stage at any one time, up to the maximum degree of machine parallelism across all functional units. Instruction issuing is stalled by a resource conflict, a data dependency, or a procedural dependency.

In addition to the above limitations, a new dependency, which we referred to earlier as an **output dependency** (also called **read-write dependency**), arises. The following code fragment illustrates this dependency (op represents any operation):

R3 := R3 op R5   (I1)
R4 := R3 + 1   (I2)
R3 := R5 + 1   (I3)
R7 := R3 op R4   (I4)

Instruction I2 cannot execute before instruction I1, because it needs the result in register R3 produced in I1; this is an example of a true data dependency, as described in Section 14.1. Similarly, I4 must wait for I3, because it uses a result produced by I3. What about the relationship between I1 and I3? There is no data dependency here, as we have defined it. However, if I3 executes to completion prior to I1, then the wrong value of the contents of R3 will be fetched for the execution of I4. Consequently, I3 must complete after I1 to produce the correct output values. To ensure this, the issuing of the third instruction must be stalled if its result might later be overwritten by an older instruction which takes longer to complete.

Out-of-order completion requires more complex instruction-issue logic than in-order completion. In addition, it is more difficult to deal with instruction interrupts and exceptions. When an interrupt occurs, instruction execution at the current point is suspended, to be resumed later. The processor must assure that the resumption takes into account that, at the time of interruption, instructions ahead of the instruction that caused the interrupt may already have completed.

Out-of-Order Issue with Out-of-Order Completion

With in-order issue, the processor will only decode instructions up to the point of a dependency or conflict. No additional instructions are decoded until the conflict is resolved. As a result, the processor cannot look ahead of the point of conflict to subsequent instructions that may be independent of those already in the pipeline and that may be usefully introduced into the pipeline.

To allow out-of-order issue, it is necessary to decouple the decode and execute stages of the pipeline. This is done with a buffer referred to as an **instruction window.** With this organization, after a processor has finished decoding an instruction, it is placed in the instruction window. As long as this buffer is not full, the processor can continue to fetch and decode new instructions. When a functional unit becomes available in the execute stage, an instruction from the instruction window may be issued to the execute stage. Any instruction may be issued, provided that (a) it needs the particular functional unit that is available and (b) no conflicts or dependencies block this instruction.

The result of this organization is that the processor has a lookahead capability, allowing it to identify independent instructions that can be brought into the execute stage. Instructions are issued from the instruction window with little regard for their original program order. As before, the only constraint is that the program execution behaves correctly.

Figure 14-3c illustrates this policy. On each cycle, two instructions are fetched into the decode stage. On each cycle, subject to the constraint of the buffer size, two instructions move from the decode stage to the instruction window. In this example, it is possible to issue instruction I6 ahead of I5 (recall that I5 depends on I4, but I6 does not). Thus one cycle is saved in both the execute and writeback stages, and the end-to-end savings, compared to Figure 14-3b, is one cycle.

The instruction window is depicted in Figure 14-3c to illustrate its role. However, this window is not an additional pipeline stage. The fact that an instruction is in the window simply implies that the processor has sufficient information about that instruction to decide when it can be issued.

The out-of-order issue, out-of-order completion policy is subject to the same constraints described earlier. An instruction cannot be issued if it violates a dependency or conflict. The difference is that more instructions are available for issuing, reducing the probability that a pipeline stage will have to stall. In addition, a new dependency, which we referred to earlier as an **antidependency** (also called **write-write dependency**), arises. The code fragment considered earlier illustrates this dependency:

R3 := R3 op R5   (I1)
R4 := R3 + 1   (I2)
R3 := R5 + 1   (I3)
R7 := R3 op R4   (I4)

Instruction I3 cannot complete execution before instruction I2 begins execution and had fetched its operands. This is so because I3 updates register R3, which is a source operand for I2. The term *antidependency* refers to the fact that the constraint is similar to that of a true data dependency, but reversed: instead of the first instruction producing a value that the second instruction uses, the second instruction destroys a value that the first instruction uses.

Register Renaming

When out-of-order instruction issuing and/or out-of-order instruction completion are allowed, we have seen that this gives rise to the possibility of output dependencies and antidependencies. These dependencies differ from true data dependencies and resource conflicts, which reflect the flow of data through a program and the sequence of execution. Output dependencies and antidependencies, on the other hand, arise because the values in registers may no longer reflect the sequence of values dictated by the program flow.

When instructions are issued in sequence and complete in sequence, it is possible to specify the contents of each register at each point in the execution. When out-of-order techniques are used, the values in registers cannot be fully known at each point in time just from a consideration of the sequence of instructions dictated by the program. In effect, values are in conflict for the use of registers, and the processor must resolve those conflicts by occasionally stalling a pipeline stage.

Antidependencies and output dependencies are both examples of storage conflicts. Multiple instructions are competing for the use of the same register locations, generating pipeline constraints that retard performance. The problem is made more acute when register optimization techniques are used (as discussed in Chapter 13), because these compiler techniques attempt to maximize the use of registers, hence maximizing the number of storage conflicts.

One method for coping with these types of storage conflicts is based on a traditional resource-conflict solution: duplication of resources. In this context, the technique is referred to as **register renaming.** In essence, registers are allocated dynamically by the processor hardware, and are associated with the values needed by instructions at various points in time. When a new register value is created (i.e., when an instruction executes that has a register as a destination operand), a new register is allocated for that value. Subsequent instructions that access that value as a source operand in that register must go through a renaming process: the register references in those instructions must be revised to refer to the register containing the needed value. Thus, the same original register reference in several different instructions may refer to different actual registers, if different values are intended.

Let us consider how register renaming could be used on the code fragment we have been examining:

$R3_b := R3_a$ op $R5_a$ (I1)
$R4_b := R3_b + 1$ (I2)
$R3_c := R5_a + 1$ (I3)
$R7_b := R3_c$ op $R4_b$ (I4)

The register reference without the subscript refers to the logical register reference found in the instruction. The register reference with the subscript refers to a hardware register allocated to hold a new value. When a new allocation is made for a particular logical register, subsequent instruction references to that logical register as a source operand are made to refer to the most recently allocated hardware register (recent in terms of the program sequence of instructions).

In this example, the creation of register $R3_c$ in instruction I3 avoids the anti-dependency on the second instruction and the output dependency on the first instruction, and does not interfere with the correct value being accessed by I4. The result is that I3 can be issued immediately; without renaming I3 cannot be issued until the first instruction is complete and the second instruction is issued.

Machine Parallelism

In the preceding, we have looked at three hardware techniques that can be used in a superscalar processor to enhance performance: duplication of resources, out-of-order issue, and renaming. One study that illuminates the relationship among these techniques was reported in [SMIT89]. The study made use of a simulation that modeled a machine with the characteristics of the MIPS R2000, augmented with various superscalar features. A number of different program sequences were simulated.

Figure 14-4 shows the results. In each of the graphs, the vertical axis corresponds to the mean speed-up of the superscalar machine over the scalar machine. The horizontal axis shows the results for four alternative processor organizations. The base machine does not duplicate any of the functional units, but can issue instructions out of order. The second configuration duplicates the load/store functional unit which accesses a data cache. The third configuration duplicates the ALU, and the fourth configuration duplicates both load/store and ALU. In each graph, results are shown for instruction window sizes of 8, 16, and 32 instructions, which dictates the amount of lookahead the processor can do. The difference between the two graphs is that, in the second, register renaming is allowed. This is equivalent to saying that the first graph reflects a machine that is limited by all dependencies, whereas the second graph corresponds to a machine that is limited only by true dependencies.

The two graphs, combined, yield some important conclusions. The first is that it is probably not worth it to add functional units without register renaming. There is some slight improvement in performance, but at the cost of increased hardware complexity. With register renaming, which eliminates antidependencies and output dependencies, noticeable gains are achieved by adding more functional units. Note, however, that there is a significant difference in the amount of gain achievable between using an instruction window of 8 versus a larger instruction window. This indicates that if the instruction window is too small, data dependencies will prevent effective utilization of the extra functional

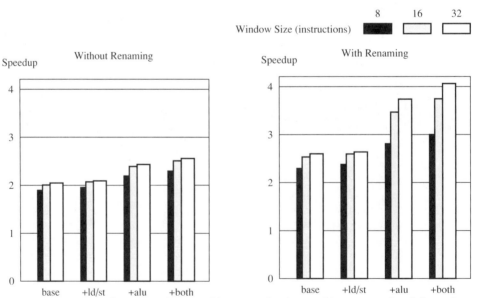

FIGURE 14-4.   Speedups of various machine organizations, without procedural dependencies

units; the processor must be able to look quite far ahead to find independent instructions in order to more fully utilize the hardware.

14.3

INTEL 80960

The Intel 80960, unlike the other processors that have been discussed in this book, is intended specifically for embedded applications. An embedded processor is one which is integrated as part of another piece of equipment and is programmed specifically to control that equipment. Thus, it is not intended for general-purpose applications, the way that a processor in a workstation or personal computer is.

Embedded processors must address a somewhat different set of requirements than general-purpose processors. Cost is especially important, since the processor is just one component in the overall product. Response time is also more critical in an embedded system. Many embedded systems must meet real-time requirements. Whereas a workstation is typically designed to deliver high average performance, in the case of a real-time system you have deterministic requirements: performance is measured by the worst case.

These differences drive the design of the processor. The embedded processor needs relatively sophisticated interrupt hardware, and must have provision for sharing the local bus with other devices. Cache design is critical, with on-chip caches typical so that performance is not held up by external memory accesses. Integrated peripherals, like DMA controllers, can cut external parts count and increase I/O performance.

The Intel 80960 is a RISC-based design intended to satisfy embedded requirements. The architecture was designed to be optimized for high-performance implementations. Specifically, the architecture lends itself to a superscalar implementation. The 80960CA, introduced in 1989, was the first commercially available superscalar processor.

Architecture and Organization

Figure 14-5 shows a logical block diagram of the 80960 architecture. It is a register-rich architecture designed to let implementations exploit pipelining and parallel execution strategies. Processing elements surround a multiport register file and receive their instructions from the instruction sequencer. The instruction sequencer fetches multiple instructions from memory and maintains these in an instruction cache. Instructions may be presented in parallel to processing elements.

Intel intends a number of different implementations of this basic architecture. To date, the following implementations have been produced:

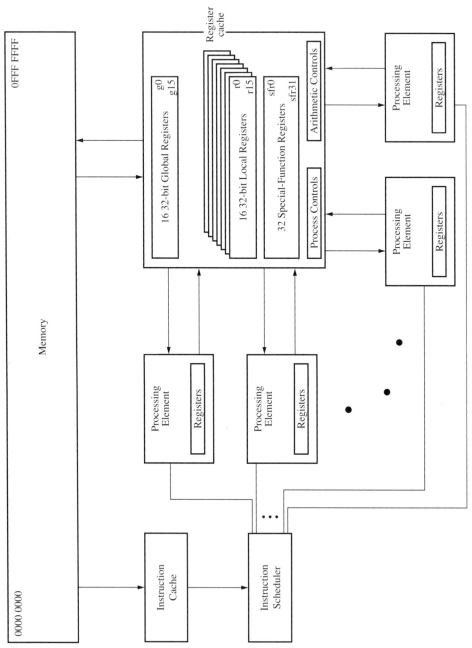

FIGURE 14-5. Logical block diagram of 80960 architecture

- 80960KA: includes a 512-byte instruction cache and an interrupt controller on chip.
- 80960KB: the features of the KA, plus an on-chip floating-point processing element.
- 80960MC: a military-qualified version of the KB that includes Ada tasking support and a memory management unit.
- 80960CA: the first member of the family to provide a superscalar pipeline. It also includes an on-chip DMA controller and a 1-KByte instruction cache.
- 80960MM: an enhanced version of the CA. It includes a second integer arithmetic unit, an on-chip data cache, a 2-KByte instruction cache, and additional logic in the address generation unit and instruction decoder to increase parallelism.

Figure 14-6 shows the 80960CA superscalar implementation of the architecture. The following are the key components.

- *Register file:* Provides 6 ports. Three ports are used for register-to-register function units: two for source operands and one for destination operands. Three ports are also provided to the memory-access function units: a 128-bit-wide load port, a 128-bit-wide store port, and a 32-bit-wide base-register access port to the address generation unit.
- *Instruction scheduler:* Can issue two instructions during each clock cycle and execute a branch instruction internally, for a maximum instruction dispatch rate of three instructions per clock cycle. Register scoreboarding is used to reduce dependencies.
- *Register execution units:* The integer execution unit performs integer addition and subtraction, and logical and shift functions, all performed in one clock cycle. The multiply/divide unit takes from 4 to 39 cycles per operation.
- *Address generation unit:* Produces a complete address from any of the addressing modes. It can fetch a base or scale register from the register file and a 12- or 32-bit offset from the instruction scheduler and compute the effective address in a single cycle. When two registers are required, two cycles are used.
- *Local register cache and on-chip RAM:* This high-speed static RAM module is used to hold a user-selectable number (between 5 and 15) of sets (16 32-bit registers per set) of local registers. Any memory not used for registers is available as a data cache, reducing average load/store time.
- *Multi-function bus controller:* Allows easy interface to a wide variety of I/O devices and external memory types. The bus controller includes an on-chip bus buffer that allows store operations to complete in a single clock cycle, by decoupling the execution of the instruction from reference to external memory.
- *DMA controller:* A four-channel DMA controller and I/O processor is autonomous from the main processor, allowing memory transfers to occur independently of program execution.
- *Interrupt controller:* Unlike many RISC chips, which provide only a single interrupt, the 80960CA supports up to 248 separate interrupt vectors at 31 different priorities using an on-chip interrupt controller.

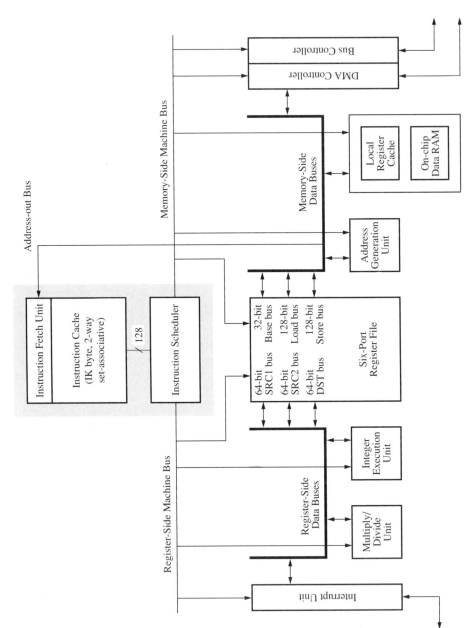

FIGURE 14-6. Block diagram of the 8096CA internal organization

Register Structure

At any time, 32 32-bit registers are visible to user programs. These are divided into two categories: global and local. The 16 global registers are available at all times; 15 of these are general purpose, and one is used to contain a frame pointer to the call/return stack (see Figure 8-9). The 16 local registers are only visible to the current routine, 13 of these are general purpose, and three are also dedicated to the call/return stack: r0, previous frame pointer; r1, stack pointer; r2, return instruction pointer. Also defined by the architecture are special function registers. There can be up to 32 of these, each from one to 32 bits in length. Typically, these registers are used to control on-chip peripherals such as DMA or interrupt controllers.

The data in the 16 global registers remain visible and unchanged when crossing procedure boundaries. The 16 local registers are tied to a particular procedure incarnation. When a CALL instruction is executed, the current contents of the local registers are moved to the register cache, to be restored with the matching RET instruction execution. Thus, the procedure is not required to save the local values. The global registers can be used to pass parameters and to maintain global variables.

Instruction Set

Table 14-2 lists the 62 instructions in the 80960 instruction set and Figure 14-7 shows the five instruction formats. As can be, the format is simple, fixed length, and designed with an efficient and logical encoding scheme. There are five distinct categories:

- REG: Instructions which operate on register data. The format includes three registers/literals (one of 32 registers or a constant value in the range 0 to 31). The mode bits dictate the addressing mode, and the special-purpose flag bits indicate whether special-purpose flags are to be accessed.
- COBR: Compare and branch instructions. The t bit is used by the processor for static branch prediction (see Chapter 10). It gives the compiler the ability to tell the processor whether the branch is likely to occur.
- CTRL: Control instructions, including unconditional branch, call, and return.
- MEMA: Includes loads, stores, and effective address calculations. Transfers can be in increments of size from 8 bits to 128 bits.
- MEMB: This format allows for addressing modes that include a 32-bit optional displacement value.

The first 2 bits of the 8-bit opcode determine whether the instruction is register, branch, or memory. This allows for rapid routing to separate execution units: an ALU for register operations, a bus or memory unit for memory operations, and a branch unit for change in execution flow.

TABLE 14-2 80960 Instruction Summary

REGISTER OPERATIONS

ARITHMETICS

add[i | o]	Add
addc	Add with Carry
sub[i | o]	Subtract
subc	Subtract with Borrow
mul[i | o]	Multiply
emul	Extended Multiply
div[i | o]	Divide
ediv	Extended Divide
rem[i | o]	Remainder
modi	Modulo Integer
sh[lo | ro | li | ri | di]	Shift

MOVEMENT

mov[l | t | q]	Move registers to registers
lda	Load Address

COMPARISON

cmp[i | o]	Compare
cmpdec[i | o]	Compare and Decrement
cmpinc[i | o]	Compare and Increment
concmp[i | o]	Conditional Compare
test [*]	Test for Condition
scanbyte	Scan for matching byte

CONTROL OPERATIONS

BRANCH

b	Branch (±2 MByte relative offset)
bx	Branch Extended (32-Bit Indirect Branch)
bal[x]	Branch and Link ("RISC Branch")
b[*]	Branch on Condition
cmpib[*]	Compare Integer and Branch on Condition
cmpob[*]	Compare Ordinal and Branch on Condition

FAULT

fault[*]	Fault on Condition
syncf	Synchronize Faults

PROCEDURE

call	Procedure Call (±2 MByte relative offset)
callx	Call Extended (32-Bit Indirect Call)
calls	System Procedure Call
ret	Return

ENVIRONMENT

modpc	Modify Process Controls
modac	Modify Arithmetic Controls
modtc	Modify Trace Controls
flushregs	Flush Local Register Cache to Memory

DEBUG

mark	Conditionally generate Trace Fault
fmark	Unconditionally generate Trace Fault

TABLE 14-2   80960 Instruction Summary (*continued*)

LOGICAL

and	dst := src1 & src2
andnot	dst := src2 & (~src1)
notand	dst := (~src2) & src1
nand	dst := ~(src2 & src1)
or	dst := src1 | src2
nor	dst := ~(src2 | src1)
ornot	dst := src2 | (~src1)
notor	dst := (~src2) | src1
xor	dst := (src2 | src1) & ~(src2 & src1)
xor	dst := ~(src2 | src1) | (src2 & src1)
not	dst := ~src
rotate	Rotate Bits

BIT AND BIT FIELD

setbit	Set a Bit
clrbit	Clear a Bit
notbit	Toggle (invert) a Bit
chkbit	Check a Bit and set condition code
alterbit	Change a Bit according to an operand
scanbit	Search src for most significant set bit
spanbit	Search src for most significant cleared bit
extract	Extract specified bit pattern from a word
modify	Modify selected bits in dst with src

MEMORY OPERATIONS

LOAD/STORE

ld[b | s | l | t | q]	Load
st[b | s | l | t | q]	Store

READ/MODIFY/WRITE

atadd	Atomic Add (Locked RMW Cycles)
atmod	Atomic Modify (Locked RMW Cycles)

i = integer, o = ordinal, b = byte, s = short, w = word (32-bits), l = long, t = triple, q = quad, lo = left ordinal, li = left integer, ro = right ordinal, ri = right integer, di = right dividing integer, dst = destination, src = source, x = extended,
* = Conditions: If [equal \| not equal \| less \| less or equal \| greater \| greater or equal \| ordered \| unordered]

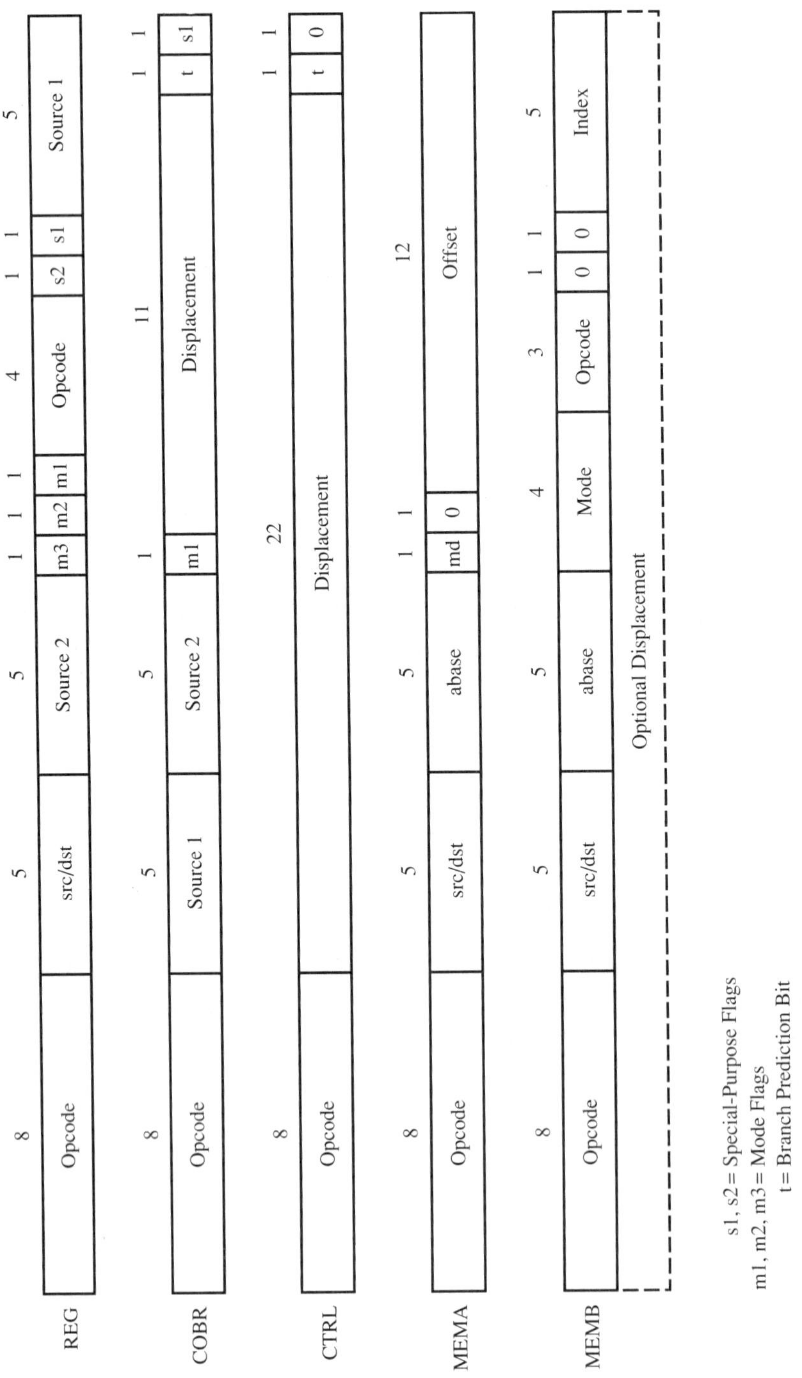

s1, s2 = Special-Purpose Flags
m1, m2, m3 = Mode Flags
t = Branch Prediction Bit

FIGURE 14-7. 80960 instruction formats

The instruction set includes some rather CISC-like instructions not found in most other RISC systems. These, plus some traditional RISC instructions, require multiple cycles to complete. Examples:

muli, mulo   ≈ 32-bit integer multiply
divi, divo   ≈ 32-bit integer divide
call, ret   ≈ call/return sequence
atadd, atmod   ≈ atomic operations to memory (change memory while location is locked)
ld, st   ≈ load, store; allow the use of complex addressing modes
extract, modify ≈ bit manipulation

A more purely RISC processor would implement few of these instructions in hardware, but rather emulate them through a series of simpler RISC instructions. These instructions were included in the 80960 for two key reasons:

1. The processor must fetch, decode, and execute fewer instructions. Thus, although it uses a simple, fixed format, the 80960 instruction set achieves code density (number of instructions needed to implement a given program) within 15 to 25 percent of a VAX, as compared with 40 percent or more for other RISC instruction sets [MCGA89]. Code density and instruction fetch bandwidth are two important issues in lower-end embedded system designs, where memory sizes are limited and memory subsystems may be unsophisticated and perform at less than ideal speeds.

2. In a minimal 80960 implementation, microcode can provide emulation for the given function at the same speed as equivalently-executed RISC instructions from memory. The benefit is that bus bandwidth is conserved. A higher performance 80960 implementation can replace some or all of the microcode with dedicated hardware. As an example, the 80960KA, using primarily a microcoded sequence, completes a subroutine call in 9 clock cycles. The 80960CA, by implementing the call in hardware, reduces this to 4 cycles. By widening the internal bus, the 80960MM gets this down to 2 cycles.

The 80960 architecture supports 11 different addressing modes (Table 14-3). This is perhaps the most obvious difference between the 80960 and a pure RISC machine, which typically has only 1 to 3 modes. The large number of modes achieves code density and higher speed. In a lower performance implementation, microcode and a simple effective-address calculation unit can calculate effective addresses at a rate greater than or equal to the equivalent RISC instruction, while also lowering the number of instruction fetches. In high performance implementation, the 80960 moves more of this function to hardware, allowing address calculations in one to two clock cycles.

The large variety of addressing modes is supported by a separate address generation unit (AGU) on the 80960CA. The AGU can fetch a base or scale register from the register file and a 12- or 32-bit offset from the instruction scheduler and compute the effective address in a single cycle. For addressing modes that require two registers be fetched, an additional cycle is required. To accomplish all this, the AGU must have the same capabilities as the integer execution

TABLE 14-3   80960 Addressing Modes

Mode	Value	Assembler Example	Description
Literal	value	12	Immediate 5-bit number in the range 0 to 31.
Register	register	r6	Contents of a register.
Absolute offset	offset	3	Absolute address of the target as an offset from byte 0 of the current process address space; offset value ranges from 0 to 2047.
Absolute displacement	displacement	−5208	Same as absolute offset, but the offset, called a displacement, is 32-bit 2's-complement number.
Register indirect	abase	(r6)	Address (referred to as an *address base*) is contained in a register.
Register indirect with offset	abase + offset	3 (r6)	Absolute offset in the range 0 to 2047 added to contents of register.

unit (Figure 14-6). Therefore, the AGU can be used as a second ALU when non-memory operation can be issued to the memory side and there are two independent integer arithmetic operations available for execution on the register side.

Instruction Pipeline

The basic 80960CA pipeline is three stages: a fetch/decode stage in which four instructions are fetched; an issue stage in which instructions are issued to various execution units and during which they fetch their operands from the register file; and a result-return stage during which results are written back into the register file.

The latency of a load operation will depend on whether the source of data is the on-chip data cache or external memory. Figure 14-8a shows an on-chip load. There is no delay in the return of this data to the register file, so the load is no

TABLE 14-3   80960 Addressing Modes (*continued*)

Mode	Value	Assembler Example	Description
Register indirect with displacement	abase + displacement	5208 (r6)	32-bit 2's-complement displacement added to contents of register.
Register indirect with index	abase + (index × scale)	(r6) [r7 * 4]	Index value in register, multiplied by a scale of 2, 4, 8, or 16, added to contents of register.
Register indirect with index and displacement	abase + (index × scale) + displacement	17 (r6) [r7 * 4]	32-bit 2's-complement displacement added to register indirect with index.
Index with displacement	(index × scale) + displacement	63 [r7 * 4]	Index value in register, multiplied by a scale, plus a 32-bit displacement.
IP with displacement	IP + displacement + 8	79 (IP)	Displacement plus a constant of 8 added to current value of instruction pointer.

slower than register-to-register moves. However, load operations from external memory may add two or more additional cycles into the pipeline, as shown in Figure 14-8b. The third cycle issues an address to the external bus, and external memory (here assumed to incur no wait states) returns the data to the bus controller in the fourth clock cycle. The data is written back to the register file in the fifth cycle.

14.4

IBM RS/6000

In 1975, the 801 minicomputer project at IBM pioneered many of the architecture concepts used in RISC systems. The 801, together with the Berkeley RISC I processor, launched the RISC movement. The 801, however, was simply a prototype intended to demonstrate design concepts. The success of the 801 project

	1	2	3	4	5
addi g0, g1, g2	Fetch	Issue	Result		
st g2, (g3)		Fetch	Issue	Return	
shlo g4, g5, g6			Fetch	Issue	Result
ld 100(g4), g5			Fetch	Issue	Result

(a) Basic Pipeline

	1	2	3	4	5
ld (g0), g1	Fetch	Issue	Addr	DataIn	
addi g2, g3, g4		Fetch	Issue	Result	
st g4, (g4)			Fetch	Issue	Return

(b) External Memory Load Pipeline

FIGURE 14-8.   80960 pipeline examples

led IBM to develop a commercial RISC workstation product, the RT PC. The RT PC, introduced in 1986, adapted the architectural concepts of the 801 to an actual product. The RT PC was not a commercial success, and had many rivals with comparable or better performance. In 1990, IBM produced a third system, which built on the lessons of the 801 and the RT PC. The IBM RISC System/6000 is a RISC-like superscalar machine marketed as a high-performance workstation.

RS/6000 Architecture

Figure 14-9 is a general view of the RS/6000 organization. As we have seen in the Motorola 88000 and the Intel 80960, the RS/6000 is broken up into independent functional units to enhance the opportunities for overlapped execution.

Figure 14-10 shows a logical view of the RS/6000 architecture, emphasizing the flow of data between memory, registers, and functional units. The shaded boxes indicate separate chips. Thus the branch processing unit, the fixed-point unit, the floating-point unit, and the data cache are each on a separate chip.

Branch Unit

The branch unit fetches instructions from the instruction cache four at a time. It processes this stream of instructions to feed a steady flow of instructions to the fixed- and floating-point processors. The branch unit itself, in addition to fetching and decoding instructions, provides all of the branching, interrupt, and condition code functions within the system.

The branch processor divides instructions into four categories:

• Branch instructions: These are processed entirely in the branch unit.
• Condition flag instructions: A complete set of logical instructions for manipulating condition flags is provided; these are also processed in the branch unit.

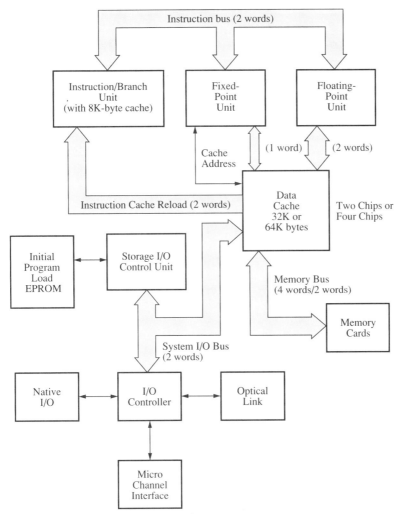

FIGURE 14-9.   RS/6000 organization

- Fixed-point instructions: These are dispatched to the fixed-point unit.
- Floating-point instructions: These are dispatched to the floating-point unit.

   To support its operations, six 32-bit registers are incorporated into the branch unit:

- *Condition flags:* The condition register contains eight independent condition code fields that are managed by the compiler as a special set of eight registers, as described below.
- *Link register:* Used to contain the target and/or return instruction address for subroutine linkage.

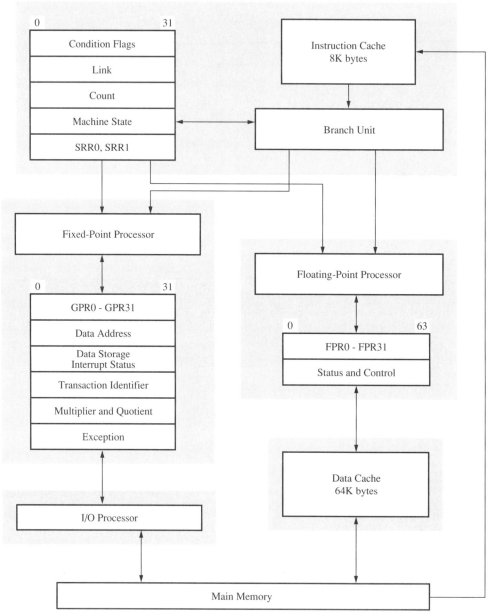

FIGURE 14-10. Logical view of RS/6000 architecture

- *Count register:* Used to control loop iteration.
- *Machine state register (MSR):* Contains the system information, such as user or supervisor mode, interrupt enable or disable, and address relocate enable or disable.

- *Save and restore registers (SSR):* Used to retain the old value of the MSR and the address of the instruction where an interrupt occurred.

Several additional points concerning these registers are worth noting. The condition register contains eight independent 4-bit condition code fields. This allows multiple condition codes to be retained, which reduces the interlock or dependency between instructions. For example, the compiler can transform this sequence:

compare
branch
compare
branch
   .
   .
   .

to this sequence:

compare
compare
   .
   .
   .

branch
branch
   .
   .
   .

Since each functional unit can send its condition codes to different fields in the condition register, interlocks between instructions caused by sharing of condition codes can be avoided.

The presence of the SRR registers in the branch processor allows it to handle simple interrupts and software interrupts without involving logic in the other functional units. Thus, simple operating-system services can be performed rapidly without complicated state manipulation or synchronization between the functional units.

Fixed-Point Unit

The fixed-point unit supports all 79 of the fixed-point arithmetic and logical operations as well as all 55 of the data reference instructions. The following registers are part of the fixed-point unit:

- *General-purpose:* There are 32 32-bit general-purpose registers that can be used for addresses, signed or unsigned integers, or logical values. In contrast to many other RISC processors, register 0 is not hardwired to the value 0. However, GPR0 cannot be used as a base or index register. Specifying GPR0 in an address indicates that there is no base or index component to the address; this is similar to the convention in the 370 architecture.

* *Data address and Data storage interrupt status:* Records information following a virtual memory page fault that allows the trap routine to recover and retry the instruction causing the problem.
* *Transaction identifier:* Contains the identifier of the currently executing process. This is used to support a hardware locking mechanism: a process may lock pages in virtual memory to prevent write or read/write access by other processes. When an access is attempted, the processor makes sure that there is a match between the lock on the page and the id in the register.
* *Multiplier and quotient:* Use for double-length multiply and divide and extended shift instructions.
* *Exception:* A status register that contains special flags, such as Carry and Overflow, that are set by arithmetic operations. It also contains the byte count and comparison byte used in string instructions.

Floating-Point Unit

The floating-point unit conforms to the IEEE 754 floating-point arithmetic standard, and employs 32 64-bit registers. The unit uses register renaming to minimize dependencies and therefore increase the efficiency of the execution pipeline. Six additional 64-bit registers are provided for this purpose.

The floating-point unit is only responsible for floating-point calculations. Loads from and stores to memory of floating-point numbers is the responsibility of the fixed-point unit. This allows all of the data cache directories and controls to be located in the fixed-point unit. Thus an instruction stream of intermixed floating-point operations and floating-point loads and stores will achieve higher throughput, since address calculations and memory operations can overlap computations.

Branch Processing

The key to the high performance of a RISC or superscalar machine is its ability to optimize the use of the pipeline. Typically, the most critical element in the design is the way in which branches are handled. In the RS/6000, branch processing is the responsibility of the branch unit. The unit is designed so that in many cases, it is able to provide a steady stream of instructions to the fixed- and floating-point units while dealing with branch instructions. Many branches, therefore, have no effect on the pace of execution in the other units; these types of branches are referred to as zero-cycle branches. To achieve zero-cycle branching, the following strategies are employed:

1. Logic is provided to scan through the instruction buffer for branches. Branch target addresses are generated when a branch first appears within five instructions of the top of the buffer, and no prior branches are pending execution.

2. An attempt is made to determine the outcome of conditional branches. If the condition code has been set sufficiently far in advance, this can be determined. In any case, as soon as a branch instruction is encountered within the top five instructions in the buffer, logic determines if the branch:

   a. Will be taken; this is the case for unconditional branches, for conditional branches whose condition code is known and indicates no branch, and for loop instructions that have not reached the final iteration.

   b. Will not be taken; this is the case for conditional branches whose condition code is known and indicates branch, and for loop instructions on the final iteration.

   c. Outcome cannot yet be determined.

   In the latter case, the target is fetched, but the branch is guessed not to be taken. Sequential instructions past the branch instruction are passed to the execution units in a conditional fashion. Once the condition code value is produced in the execution unit, the branch unit either cancels the instructions in the pipeline and proceeds with the fetched target if the branch is taken, or signals for the conditional instructions to be executed.

This reasonably simple strategy is based on statistics gathered from 801 instruction studies. These studies showed that about one-third of executed branch instructions were unconditional, one-third were used to terminate iteration loops, and one-third were conditional. Of the conditional branch instructions, the split between taken and not-taken outcomes was about 50-50. With the strategy outlined above, there is no clock cycle loss except for conditional branch instructions that are taken and, in that case, the loss averages about two cycles. Thus, the average overhead for branch processing is:

$$\frac{1}{3} \times 0 + \frac{1}{3} \times 0 + \frac{1}{6} \times 0 + \frac{1}{6} \times 2 = 0.33 \text{ cycles}$$

The incorporation of a branch prediction strategy based on static branch prediction or branch history was rejected because of the minimal payoff that could be achieved.

Figure 14-11 illustrates the RS/6000 pipeline delays for several branch-execution examples. The left-hand portion of each example shows a code fragment and the right-hand portion shows the associated pipeline behavior. The pipeline stages are:

- IF: Instruction fetch. Four instructions are fetched from the cache and placed into instruction buffers.
- Disp: Up to four instructions are examined for dispatching. The target addresses for branch instructions are generated.
- FXD: The fixed-point unit decodes fixed-point instructions and accesses the register file for operands.
- FXE: The fixed-point unit executes instructions. At the end of the FXE cycle, condition-code results are transmitted to the branch unit so that conditional branches can be resolved in the following cycle.

X1 ; single-cycle fixed-point			1	2	3	4	5	6	7
X2 ; instructions									
BRU ; unconditional branch to T1	IF	X1 X2 BRU S1	S2 S3	T1 T2 T3 T4	T5 T6	T7	T8	
S1									
S2	Disp		X1 X2 BRU		T1 T2	T3 T4	T5 T6	
S3									
T1 ; target instructions	FXD			X1	X2	T1	T2	T3
T2									
T3	FXE				X1	X2	T1	T2

Branch takes no execution cycles
and causes no execution delay

(a)

C ; fixed-point compare			1	2	3	4	5	6	7
BRC ; conditional branch	IF	C BRC S1 S2	S3 S4 S5 S6	T1 T2 T3 T4	T5 T6 T7 T8		S7 S8 S9 S10	
dependent on C									
S1 ; sequential fixed-point	Disp		C BRC S1'	S2' S3'	S4'S5'			
instructions									
S2	FXD			C	S1'	S2'	S3	S4
S3									
•	FXE				C	S1'	S2	S3
•									
T1 ; target instructions									
T2									
T3									

Branch takes no execution cycles
and causes no execution delay

(b)

C ; fixed-point compare			1	2	3	4	5	6	7	8
X1										
X2	IF	C X1 X2 BRC	S1 S2 S3 S4	T1 T2 T3 T4	T5 T6	T7	T8		
BRC ; conditional branch										
dependent on C	Disp		C X1	X2 BRU S1'	S2' S3'		T1 T2	T3 T4	
S1 ; sequential fixed-point										
instructions	FXD			C	X1	X2		T1	
S2										
S3	FXE				C	X1	X2		T1
•										
•										
T1 ; target instructions										
T2										
T3										
T4										

Branch causes one-cycle delay ($i = 2$);
maximum delay is $3 - i$ cycles, where i
is the number of fixed-point operations
between C and BRC

(c)

C ; fixed-point compare			1	2	3	4	5	6	7	8
X1										
X2	IF	C X1 X2 X3	BRC S1 S2 S3		T1 T2 T3 T4	T5 T6 T7 T8			
X3										
BRC ; conditional branch										
dependent on C										
S1 ; sequential fix-point	Disp		C X1	X2 X3 BRC	S1' S2'	X2	T1 T2	T3 T4	
instructions										
S2	FXD			C	X1	X1	X3	T1	T2
S3										
•	FXE				C		X2	X3	T1
•										
T1 ; target instructions										
T2										
T3										
T4										

Branch causes zero-cycle delay
($i = 3$); maximum delay is $3 - i$
cycles, where i is the number of
fixed-point operations between
C and BRC

(d)

FIGURE 14-11.   RS/6000 pipeline examples

Part (a) depicts the effect of an unconditional branch. Part (b) shows a conditional branch that is not taken. Part (c) shows a taken conditional branch whose condition is set two fixed-point instructions before the branch causing a one-cycle pipeline delay. Finally, part (d) shows a taken conditional branch that causes no pipeline delay. Note that the only branches that typically cause any pipeline delay are taken conditional branches that depend upon a fixed-point compare that cannot be scheduled with three or more instructions between it and the branch.

14.5

RECOMMENDED READING

[JOHN91] is an excellent book-length treatment of superscalar design. [JOUP89a] examines instruction-level parallelism, looks at various techniques for maximizing parallelism, and compares superscalar and superpipelined approaches using simulation.

[POPE91] provides a detailed look at a proposed superscalar machine. It also provides an excellent tutorial on the design issues related to out-of-order instruction policies. Another look at a proposed system is found in [KUGA91]; this article raises and considers most of the important design issues for superscalar implementation. [LEE91] examines software techniques that can be used to enhance superscalar performance. [WALL91] is an interesting study of the extent to which instruction-level parallelism can be exploited in a superscalar processor. [WAYN92] provides an instructive comparison of the instruction pipelines of the Intel 80486, the MIPS R4000, and the IBM RS/6000.

[MYER88] provides a comprehensive treatment of the 80960 family of processors. Good overview articles include [BAKE90] and [RYAN88]. The superscalar design aspects of the 80960 are covered in [MCGE91] and [MCGE90].

[RADI83] and [HOPK87] describe the IBM 801 system. The IBM RT is described in [WATE86] and [SIMP87]. [IBM90a] is a special issue devoted to the RS/6000, and [IBM90b] is a special publication also devoted to the RS/6000; together they provide a broad and in-depth look at the RS/6000. The RS/6000 receives chapter-length treatment in [DEWA90] and [TABA91]. Performance studies of the RS/6000 are reported in [OEHL91], [STEP91], and [HALL91]; these articles assess the performance implications of various design features of the RS/6000.

14.6

PROBLEMS

14.1 When out-of-order completion is used in a superscalar processor, resumption of execution after interrupt processing is complicated, because the exceptional condition may have been detected as an instruction that produced its result out of order. The program cannot be restarted at the instruction following the exceptional instruction, because subsequent instructions have already completed, and doing so would cause these instructions to be executed twice. Suggest a mechanism or mechanisms for dealing with this situation.

14.2 Consider the following sequence of instructions, where the syntax consists of an opcode followed by the destination register followed by one or two source registers:

0	ADD	r3, r1, r2
1	LOAD	r6, [r3]
2	AND	r7, r5, 3
3	ADD	r1, r6, r7
4	SRL	r7, r0, 8
5	OR	r2, r4, r7
6	SUB	r5, r3, r4
7	ADD	r0, r1, 10
8	LOAD	r6, [r5]
9	SUB	r2, r1, r6
10	AND	r3, r7, 15

Assume the use of a four-stage pipeline: fetch, decode/issue, execute, writeback. Assume that all pipeline stages take one clock cycle except for the execute stage. For simple integer arithmetic and logical instructions, the execute stage takes one cycle, but for a LOAD from memory, five cycles are consumed in the execute stage.

If we have a simple scalar pipeline but allow out-of-order execution, we can construct the following table for the execution of the first seven instructions:

Instruction	Fetch	Decode	Execute	Writeback
0	0	1	2	3
1	1	2	4	9
2	2	3	5	6
3	3	4	10	11
4	4	5	6	7
5	5	6	8	10
6	6	7	9	12

The entries under the four pipeline stages indicate the clock cycle at which each instruction begins each phase. In this program, the second ADD instruction (instruction 3) depends on the LOAD instruction (instruction 1) for one of its operands, r6. Because the LOAD instruction takes five clock cycles, and the issue logic encounters the dependent ADD instruction after two clocks, the issue logic must delay the ADD instruction for three clock cycles. With an out-of-order capability, the processor can stall instruction 3 at clock cycle 4, and then move on to issue the following three independent instructions, which enter execution at clocks 6, 8, and 9. The LOAD finishes execution at clock 9, so the dependent ADD can be launched into execution on clock 10.

a. Complete the above table.

b. Redo the table assuming no out-of-order capability. What is the savings using the capability?

c. Redo the table assuming a superscalar implementation that can handle two instructions at a time at each stage.

14.3 In the 80960 *IP with displacement* addressing mode, the displacement plus 8 is added to the address of the current instruction. Since instructions are 32 bits long, shouldn't the constant value be 4?

14.4 Unlike the 80960 and a number of other RISC and superscalar implementations, the RS/6000 does not have a central, multi-port register file. Contrast the register organization strategies of the 80960 and the RS/6000 and discuss the performance implications.

CHAPTER 15

Parallel Organization

Traditionally, the computer has been viewed as a sequential machine. Most computer programming languages require the programmer to specify algorithms as sequences of instructions. CPUs execute programs by executing machine instructions in a sequence and one at a time. Each instruction is executed in a sequence of operations (fetch instruction, fetch operands, perform operation, store results).

This view of the computer has never been entirely true. At the micro-operation level, multiple control signals are generated at the same time. Instruction pipelining, at least to the extent of overlapping fetch and execute operations, has been around for a long time. Both of these are examples of performing functions in parallel.

As computer technology has evolved, and as the cost of computer hardware has dropped, computer designers have sought more and more opportunities for parallelism, usually to improve performance and, in some cases, to improve reliability. In this chapter, we will look at three of the most prominent and successful approaches to parallel organization. First, the chapter examines multiprocessing, which is one of the earliest and still the most common example of parallel organization. Typically, multiprocessing involves the use of multiple CPUs sharing a common memory. Next, we look at hardware organizational approaches to vector computation. These approaches optimize the ALU for processing vectors or arrays of floating-point numbers. They have been used to implement the class of systems known as *supercomputers*.

These two topics by no means exhaust the field of parallel organization. A significant amount of research on both the hardware and software fronts is ongoing and will lead to additional approaches for commercially available, parallel-organized computers.

15.1

MULTIPROCESSING

The use of multiple processors is motivated by considerations of performance and/or reliability. We can classify such systems as follows:

- *Loosely Coupled Multiprocessing:* Consists of a collection of relatively autonomous systems, each CPU having its own main memory and I/O channels. The term *multicomputer* is often used in this context.
- *Functionally Specialized Processors:* Such as an I/O processor. In this case, there is a master, general-purpose CPU, and specialized processors are controlled by the master CPU and provide services to it.
- *Tightly Coupled Multiprocessing:* Consists of a set of processors that share a common main memory and are under the integrated control of an operating system.
- *Parallel Processing:* Tightly coupled multiprocessors that can cooperatively work on one task or job in parallel.

As this book is concerned with the organization and architecture of a single computer system, the first category in the preceding list is beyond its scope; the interested reader can consult [STAL90] and [STAL91]. We have already dealt with the concept of functionally specialized processors, primarily in Chapter 5. Parallel processing is primarily a software design problem and, although much research has been and is being done, is still beyond the state of practical application ([HABE85], [FOX87], [KARP87], [OBER88]). Thus this section focuses on tightly coupled multiprocessing.

We begin by elaborating somewhat on the definition of a tightly coupled multiprocessing system, to which we refer as a *multiprocessor.* Following [ENSL77], the key characteristics of a multiprocessor are

1. It contains two or more similar general-purpose processors of comparable capability.
2. All processors share access to global (common) memory. Some local (private) memory may also be used.
3. All processors share access to I/O devices, either through the same channels or through different channels that provide paths to the same devices.
4. The system is controlled by an integrated operating system that provides interaction between processors and their programs at the job, task, file, and data element levels.

Points 1 to 3 should be self-explanatory. Point 4 illustrates one of the contrasts with a loosely coupled multiprocessing system. In the latter, the physical unit of interaction is usually the complete file. In a multiprocessor, individual data elements can constitute the level of interaction, and there can be a high degree of cooperation between processes.

Organization

Figure 15-1 depicts in general terms the organization of a multiprocessor system. There are two or more CPUs. Each CPU is self-contained, including a control unit, ALU, registers, and, possibly, cache. Each CPU has access to a shared main memory and the I/O devices through some form of interconnection mechanism. The processors can communicate with each other through memory (messages and status information left in common data areas). It may also be possible for

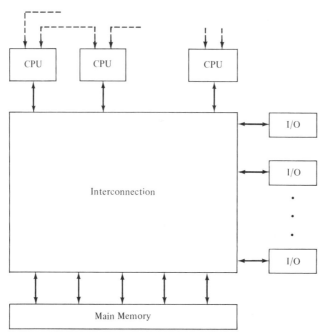

FIGURE 15-1. Generic block diagram, tightly coupled multiprocessor system

CPUs to directly exchange signals, as indicated by the dotted lines. The memory is often organized so that multiple simultaneous accesses to separate blocks of memory are possible. In some configurations, each CPU may also have its own private main memory and I/O channels in addition to the shared resources.

The organization of a multiprocessor system can be classified as follows:

- Time-Shared or Common Bus
- Multiport Memory
- Central Control Unit

These configurations were introduced in Section 3.3, which the reader may wish to review.

Time-Shared Bus

The time-shared bus is the simplest mechanism for constructing a multiprocessor system (Figure 15-2a). The structure and interfaces are basically the same as for a single-processor system that uses a bus interconnection. The bus consists of control, address, and data lines. To facilitate DMA transfers from I/O processors, the following features are provided:

- *Addressing:* It must be possible to distinguish modules on the bus to determine the source and destination of data.

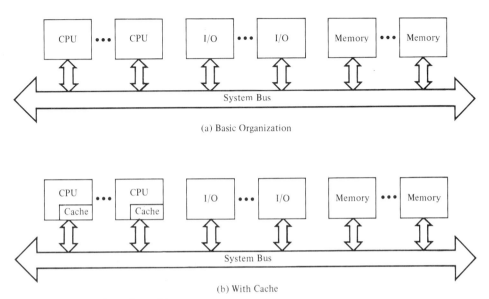

FIGURE 15-2. Time-shared bus

- *Arbitration:* Any I/O module can temporarily function as "master." A mechanism is provided to arbitrate competing requests for bus control, using some sort of priority scheme.
- *Time sharing:* When one module is controlling the bus, other modules are locked out and must, if necessary, suspend operation until bus access is achieved.

These features are directly usable in a multiprocessor configuration. In this latter case there are now multiple CPUs as well as multiple I/O processors all attempting to gain access to one or more memory modules via the bus.

The bus organization has several advantages compared to other approaches.

- *Simplicity:* This is the simplest approach to multiprocessor organization. The physical interface and the addressing, arbitration, and time-sharing logic of each processor remain the same as in a single-processor system.
- *Flexibility:* It is generally easy to expand the system by attaching more CPUs to the bus.
- *Reliability:* The bus is essentially a passive medium, and the failure of any attached device should not cause failure of the whole system.

The main drawback to the bus organization is performance. All memory references pass through the common bus. Thus the speed of the system is limited by the cycle time. To improve performance, it is desirable to equip each CPU with a cache memory (Figure 15-2b). This should reduce the number of bus accesses dramatically.

The use of caches introduces some new design considerations. Since each local cache contains an image of a portion of memory, if a word is altered in one cache, it could conceivably invalidate a word in another cache. To prevent this, the other CPUs must be alerted that an update has taken place. To meet this requirement, two techniques are possible: write through and write once [MAYB84]. These were introduced in Section 4.3, and the discussion is recapitulated here. The simpler technique is *write through*. All write operations are made to main memory as well as to the local cache, ensuring that main memory is always valid. Any other CPU-cache module monitors the bus to maintain consistency within its own cache.

The write-through technique is effective but involves an unnecessarily high rate of memory writes. With *write once* [GOOD83], the first time a CPU writes to a particular cache block, the cache controller also writes the block to main memory. This first write acts as a signal to all other cache controllers to make their corresponding blocks invalid and inaccessible. Subsequent writes by the CPU that performed the first write go only to its local cache. The block is written out again only when it is replaced.

Multiport Memory

The multiport memory approach allows the direct, independent access of main memory modules by each CPU and I/O module (Figure 15-3). Logic associated with memory is required for resolving conflicts. The method often used to resolve conflicts is to assign permanently designated priorities to each memory port. Typically, the physical and electrical interface at each port is identical to what would be seen in a single-port memory module. Thus, little or no modi-

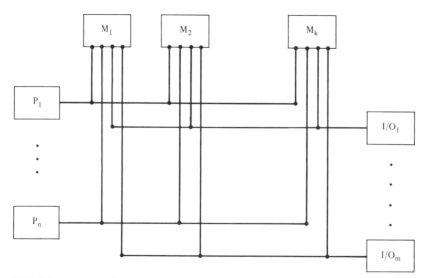

FIGURE 15-3. Multiport memory

fication is needed for either CPU or I/O modules to accommodate multiport memory.

The multiport memory approach is more complex than the bus approach, requiring a fair amount of logic to be added to the memory system. It should, however, provide better performance since each processor has a dedicated path to each memory module. Another advantage of multiport is that it is possible to configure portions of memory as "private" to one or more CPUs and/or I/O modules. This feature allows for increasing security against unauthorized access and for the storage of recovery routines in areas of memory not susceptible to modification by other processors.

One other point: A write-through policy should be used for cache control since there is no other means to alert other processors to a memory update.

An example of a commercial system using multiport memory is the Unisys 1100/20 (Figure 3-17).

Central Control Unit

The central control unit is an extension of the system controller concept introduced in Section 3.3 (e.g., see Figure 3-18). The central control unit funnels separate data streams back and forth between independent modules: CPU, memory, I/O. The controller can buffer requests and perform arbitration and timing functions. It can also pass status and control messages between CPUs and perform cache update alerting.

Because all of the logic for coordinating the multiprocessor configuration is concentrated in the central control unit, interfaces from I/O, memory, and CPU remain essentially undisturbed. This provides the flexibility and simplicity of interfacing of the bus approach. The key disadvantages of this approach are that the control unit is quite complex and that it is a potential performance bottleneck.

The central control unit structure is quite common for multiple processor mainframe systems, such as large-scale members of the IBM S/370 family.

Multiprocessor Operating Systems

In a tightly-coupled multiprocessor system, the user perceives a single operating system controlling system resources. In fact, such a configuration should appear as a single-processor multiprogramming system. In both cases multiple jobs or processes may be active at one time, and it is the responsibility of the operating system to schedule their execution and to allocate resources.

Enslow [ENSL77] identifies the following seven functions for a multiprocessor operating system:

- Resource allocation and management
- Table and data protection
- Prevention of system deadlock
- Abnormal termination

- I/O load balancing
- Processor load balancing
- Reconfiguration

Only the last three are unique or substantially different for multiprocessing systems compared to uniprocessor, multiprogramming systems. It is the responsibility of the multiprocessor operating system to see that resources are used efficiently; otherwise the investment in multiple CPUs is wasted. It must also reconfigure the system when a processor fails, to continue operation at a reduced performance level.

Tightly-coupled multiprocessors can be characterized by the way in which jobs are scheduled. There are two dimensions to the scheduling function [PETE85]:

- Whether processes are dedicated to processors
- How processes are scheduled on processors

If a separate short-term queue (see Figure 6-14) is kept for each processor, then once a process is activated, it is permanently assigned to one processor until its completion. In this case, one processor can be idle, with an empty queue, while another processor has a backlog. To prevent this situation, a common queue can be used. All processes go into one queue and are scheduled to any available processor. Thus, over the life of a job, the job may be executed on different processors at different times.

Regardless of whether processes are dedicated to processors, some means is needed to assign processes to processors. Two approaches have been used: master/slave and peer. With a *master/slave* architecture, the operating system always runs on a particular processor. The other processors may only execute user programs. The master is responsible for scheduling jobs. Once a process is active, if the slave needs service (e.g., an I/O call), it must send a request to the master and wait for the service to be performed. This approach is quite simple and requires little enhancement to a uniprocessor multiprogramming operating system. Conflict resolution is simplified since one processor has control of all memory and I/O resources. The disadvantages of this approach are two: (1) a failure of the master brings down the whole system, and (2) the master can become a performance bottleneck.

In a *peer* architecture, the operating system can execute on any processor, and each processor does self-scheduling from the pool of available processes. This approach complicates the operating system. The operating system must ensure that two processors do not choose the same process, and that the processes are not somehow lost from the queue. Techniques must be employed to resolve and synchronize competing claims to resources.

IBM System/370 Multiprocessing

The 370 architecture provides the capability for multiple CPUs to share main storage and to communicate with each other to coordinate activities. One copy of the operating system is shared by the CPUs, and the workload is dynamically balanced among them. Each CPU has its own set of I/O channels attached to it, but all CPUs have access to all I/O devices. If one CPU requires access to a device attached to another CPU, it asks the other CPU to execute the I/O operation for it.

Key characteristics of the S/370 multiprocessing capability are

- *Prefixing:* Used to share critical areas of main memory.
- *Signaling:* Used for processor-to-processor communication.
- *Synchronization:* Used to coordinate potentially conflicting CPU operations.

Prefixing

Certain dedicated locations in main memory are used to store control and status information. For example, Section 10.6 describes the six sets of old and new PSWs used to control interrupt processing. In a single CPU system, the first 4K bytes of storage are reserved for this purpose. Clearly, this arrangement cannot work in a multiple processor configuration, since all CPUs would attempt to use the same locations.

To overcome this problem, a distinction is made between *real storage* and *absolute storage*. Real storage refers to a memory reference made by a CPU. In a multiprocessor configuration, real addresses are translated into absolute addresses by hardware. The effect is illustrated in Figure 15-4. Each CPU is

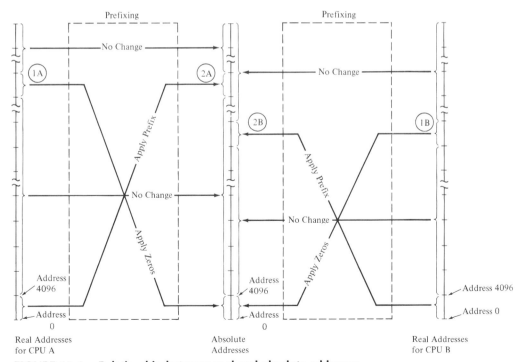

FIGURE 15-4. Relationship between real and absolute addresses

equipped with a Prefix Value Register (PVR), which contains the starting address P of a 4K-byte block of memory. Thus, the lower-order 12 bits of the PVR are always 0. When a real address R is generated by the CPU, an absolute address A is constructed using the following rules:

1. If $R < 4K$, then $A = R + P$.
2. If $P < R < P + 4K$, then $A = R - P$.
3. Otherwise, $A = R$.

The result is that references to the first 4K bytes of memory are translated to another, predetermined 4K-byte block of memory. Each CPU is given a separate 4K-byte block to use as its dedicated area. The algorithm also maps real references to that dedicated area into absolute references to the first 4K-byte block of memory. This allows that first block to be used in coordinating the activities of the CPUs and provides an individual block for each CPU to use in controlling its own activities.

The prefixing function is peformed after the virtual memory function. The sequence of events is

1. A virtual address is converted to a real address by means of dynamic address translation, as explained in Section 6.3.
2. The real address is converted to an absolute address by means of prefixing.

Signaling

Inter-CPU communication is provided by the Signal Processor Instruction (SIGP). This machine instruction has three operands: CPU address, order code, and status. The CPU address identifies the CPU to which the signal is being sent. The order code specifies the requested action, and the status operand specifies a register in which the status or result of the SIGP instruction is stored.

Table 15-1 lists some of the order codes used with the SIGP instruction. When the SIGP is executed on one CPU, the 2-bit condition code in the PSW indicates the result of the operation:

• Order Code Accepted
• Status Stored
• Busy
• Not Operational

The first two conditions indicate that the signal was successfully transmitted to the other CPU; some orders involve the return of status information, and others do not. A busy condition indicates that the access path to the other CPU is busy, or that the other CPU, though operational, cannot respond to the order code. Finally, the other CPU may not be operational.

The status bits indicate the response to the designated order. For example, the result of a successful STOP order is indicated by setting the appropriate status bit.

TABLE 15-1   IBM S/370 Interprocessor Orders

SENSE
  The addressed CPU sends its status to the issuing CPU.

START
  The addressed CPU enters the Operating state if it is in the Stopped state.

STOP
  The addressed CPU enters the Stopped state if it is in the Operating state.

STOP AND STORE STATUS
  The addressed CPU enters the Stopped state and its status is saved in absolute locations 216 to 512. Status includes the PSW and general, control, and floating-point registers.

EXTERNAL CALL
  An external interrupt is sent by one CPU to another as a request to provide services.

Synchronization

The S/370 architecture provides a set of mechanisms to facilitate cooperation among processes and processors.

One means of cooperation is for multiple processes to be able to access the same common area of memory. This area can be used for the exchange of status information. Conventions are needed to avoid conflicts in reading and updating common areas. For this purpose, the S/370 supports what amounts to a software locking arrangement. One word of the common storage is designated as the lock. Each CPU checks the lockword before attempting to access the common data areas. If the lockword is 0, the CPU stores its identifier in the word, and other CPUs must wait until the first CPU is done and resets the lockword.

For this convention to work, it must be possible to examine and update the lockword without the possibility that another process will access the storage area between the examination and updating operations. The machine instruction for this is Compare and Swap (CS). CS takes three operands. The first and second operands are compared. If they are equal, the third operand is stored at the second operand location. If they are not equal, the second operand is loaded into the first-operand location. To achieve the desired result, the first, second, and third operands should be 0, the lockword, and the CPU identifier, respectively. During the execution of the CS, no other CPU can access the specified location (second operand).

The architecture also specifies an interrupt mechanism and instructions for setting and synchronizing time-of-day (TOD) clocks in CPUs.

IBM 3033 Multiprocessor Organization

The discussion so far has concerned the architecture of multiprocessing on the S/370 family. We now look briefly at the organization of multiprocessing on a specific machine, the IBM 3033 [IBM82, CONN79].

The IBM 3033 can be configured with two tightly-coupled CPUs. Each CPU has its own set of channels that can be switched from a failing processor to the functioning processor. The two CPUs are connected by a specialized hardware module called the *Multiprocesor Communications Unit* (MCU), as depicted in Figure 15-5. The MCU can communicate with each CPU and also has direct communication with the channels and cache of each CPU. The MCU performs the following functions for both processors:

- Prefixing
- Interprocessor Communication
- Storage Access
- Broadcast of Storage Update

The first two functions have already been described. The MCU controls *storage access* to coordinate and resolve memory access conflicts between the two CPUs. Requests are buffered in the MCU and handled on a first-come-first-served basis when there is no conflict. When both CPUs attempt access to the same block of memory, a simple priority mechanism is used to resolve conflicts.

As was mentioned in Section 4.3, the IBM 3033 uses a write-through policy for its cache. That is, a write causes the corresponding word to be updated in both main memory and the cache. Since each CPU has its own cache, it is necessary for both caches to be updated. When a write takes place, the MCU automatically *broadcasts* this to the other processor, and, if that processor's cache contains the affected data, the data are automatically invalidated. I/O channel transfers are handled in the same way.

15.2

VECTOR COMPUTATION

Although the performance of mainframe general-purpose computers continues to improve relentlessly, there continue to be applications that are beyond the reach of the contemporary mainframe. There is a need for computers to solve

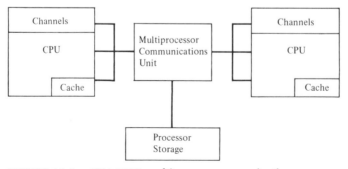

FIGURE 15-5.   IBM 3033 multiprocessor organization

mathematical problems of real processes, such as occur in disciplines including aerodynamics, seismology, meteorology, and atomic, nuclear, and plasma physics [WILS84].

Typically, these problems are characterized by the need for high precision and a program that repetitively performs floating-point arithmetic operations on large arrays of numbers. Most of these problems fall into the category known as *continuous-field simulation*. In essence, a physical situation can be described by a surface or region in three dimensions (e.g., the flow of air adjacent to the surface of a rocket). This surface is approximated by a grid of points. A set of differential equations defines the physical behavior of the surface at each point. The equations are represented as an array of values and coefficients, and the solution involves repeated arithmetic operations on the arrays of data.

To handle these types of problems, the supercomputer has been developed. These machines are typically capable of hundreds of millions of floating-point operations per second and cost in the 10 to 15 million-dollar range. In contrast to mainframes, which are designed for multiprogramming and intensive I/O, the supercomputer is optimized for the type of numerical calculation just described.

The supercomputer has limited use and, because of its price tag, a limited market. Comparitively few of these machines are operational, mostly at research centers and some government agencies with scientific or engineering functions. As with other areas of computer technology, there is a constant demand to increase the performance of the supercomputer. In some current applications in aerodynamics and nuclear physics, as many as 10^{13} arithmetic operations, absorbing more than two days of computing time on a contemporary supercomputer, are needed for a single problem [LEVI82]. Thus the technology and performance of the supercomputer continues to evolve.

There is another type of system that has been designed to address the need for vector computation, referred to as the *array processor*. Although a supercomputer is optimized for vector computation, it is a general-purpose computer, capable of handling scalar processing and general data processing tasks. Array processors do not include scalar processing; they are configured as peripheral devices by both mainframe and minicomputer users to run the vectorized portions of programs.

Approaches to Vector Computation

The key to the design of a supercomputer or array processor is to recognize that the main task is to perform arithmetic operations on arrays or vectors of floating-point numbers. In a general-purpose computer, this will require iteration through each element of the array. For example, consider two vectors (one-dimensional arrays) of numbers, A and B. We would like to add these and place the result in C. In the example of Figure 15-6, this requires six separate additions. How could we speed up this computation? The answer is to introduce some form of parallelism.

Several approaches have been taken to achieving parallelism in vector compu-

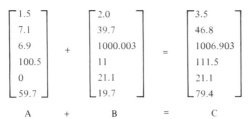

$$
\begin{bmatrix} 1.5 \\ 7.1 \\ 6.9 \\ 100.5 \\ 0 \\ 59.7 \end{bmatrix}
+
\begin{bmatrix} 2.0 \\ 39.7 \\ 1000.003 \\ 11 \\ 21.1 \\ 19.7 \end{bmatrix}
=
\begin{bmatrix} 3.5 \\ 46.8 \\ 1006.903 \\ 111.5 \\ 21.1 \\ 79.4 \end{bmatrix}
$$

$$
\text{A} \qquad + \qquad \text{B} \qquad = \qquad \text{C}
$$

FIGURE 15-6. Example of vector addition

tation. We illustrate this with an example based on one in [STON80]. Consider the vector multiplication $C = A \times B$, where A, B, and C are $N \times N$ matrices. The formula for each element of C is:

$$
c_{i,j} = \sum_{k=1}^{N} a_{i,k} \cdot b_{k,j}
$$

where A, B, and C have elements $a_{i,j}$, $b_{i,j}$, and $c_{i,j}$, respectively. Figure 15-7a shows a FORTRAN program for this computation that can be run on an ordinary scalar CPU.

One approach to improving performance can be referred to as *vector processing*. This assumes that it is possible to operate on a one-dimensional vector of data. Figure 15-7b is a FORTRAN program with a new form of instruction that allows vector computation to be specified. The notation (J = 1, N) indicates that operations on all indices J in the given interval are to be carried out as a single operation. How this can be achieved is addressed shortly.

The program in Figure 15-7b indicates that all the elements of the *i*th row are to be computed in parallel. Each element in the row is a summation, and the summations (across K) are done serially rather than in parallel. Even so, only N^2 vector multiplications are required for this algorithm as compared to N^3 scalar multiplications for the scalar algorithm.

Another approach, *parallel processing*, is illustrated in Figure 15-7c. This approach assumes that we have N independent CPUs that can function in parallel. To utilize processors effectively, we must somehow parcel out the computation to the various processors. Two primitives are used. The primitive FORK *n* causes an independent process to be started at location *n*. In the meantime, the original process continues execution at the instruction immediately following the FORK. Every execution of a FORK spawns a new process. The JOIN instruction is essentially the inverse of the FORK. The statement JOIN N causes N independent processes to be merged into one that continues execution at the instruction following the JOIN. The operating system must coordinate this merger, so the execution does not continue until all N processes have reached the JOIN instruction.

The program in Figure 15-7c is written to mimic the behavior of the vector processing program. In the parallel processing program, each column of C is

```
        DO 100  I = 1, N
        DO 100  J = 1, N
        C(I, J) = 0.0
        DO 100  K = 1, N
        C(I, J) = C(I, J) + A(I, K) * B(K, J)
100     CONTINUE
```

(a) Scalar Processing

```
        DO 100  I = 1, N
        C(I, J) = 0.0  (J = 1, N)
        DO 100  K = 1, N
        C(I, J) = C(I, J) + A(I, K) * B(K, J)  (J = 1, N)
100     CONTINUE
```

(b) Vector Processing

```
        DO 50  J = 1, N
        FORK 100
50      CONTINUE
        J = N
100     DO  I = 1, N
        C (I, J) = 0.0
        DO 200  K = 1, N
        C(I, J) = C (I, J) + A(I, K) * B(K, J)
200     CONTINUE
        JOIN N
```

(c) Parallel Processing

FIGURE 15-7. Matrix multiplication (C = A × B)

computed by a separate process. Thus the elements in a given row of C are computed in parallel.

The preceding discussion describes approaches to vector computation in logical or architectural terms. Let us turn now to a consideration of types of CPU organization that can be used to implement these approaches. A wide variety of organizations have been and are being pursued. Three main categories stand out:

- Pipelined ALU
- Parallel ALUs
- Parallel Processors

Figure 15-8 illustrates the first two of these approaches. We have already discussed pipelining in Chapter 10. Here the concept is extended to the operation of the ALU. Since floating-point operations are rather complex, there is opportunity for decomposing a floating-point operation into stages, so that different stages can operate on different sets of data concurrently. This is illustrated in Figure 15-9a. Floating-point addition is broken up into four stages (see Figure 7-20): compare, shift, add, and normalize. A vector of numbers is presented sequentially to the first stage. As the processing proceeds, four different sets of numbers will be operated on concurrently in the pipeline.

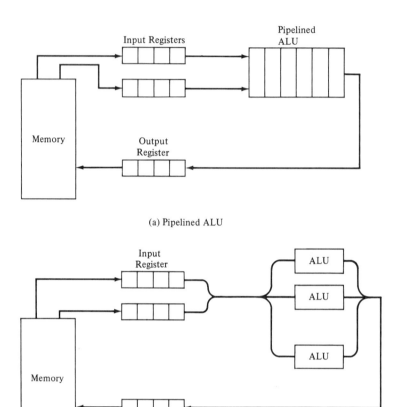

(a) Pipelined ALU

(b) Parallel ALUs

FIGURE 15-8. Approaches to vector computation

It should be clear that this organization is suitable to vector processing. To see this, consider the instruction pipelining described in Chapter 10. The CPU goes through a repetitive cycle of fetching and processing instructions. In the absence of branches, the CPU is continuously fetching instructions from sequential locations. Consequently, the pipeline is kept full and a savings in time is achieved. Similarly, a pipelined ALU will save time only if it is fed a stream of data from sequential locations. A single, isolated floating-point operation is not speeded up by a pipeline. The speed-up is achieved when a vector of operands is presented to the ALU. The control unit cycles the data through the ALU until the entire vector is processed.

The pipeline operation can be further enhanced if the vector elements are available in registers rather than from main memory. This is in fact suggested by Figure 15-8a. The elements of each vector operand are loaded as a block into a **vector register,** which is simply a large bank of identical registers. The result is

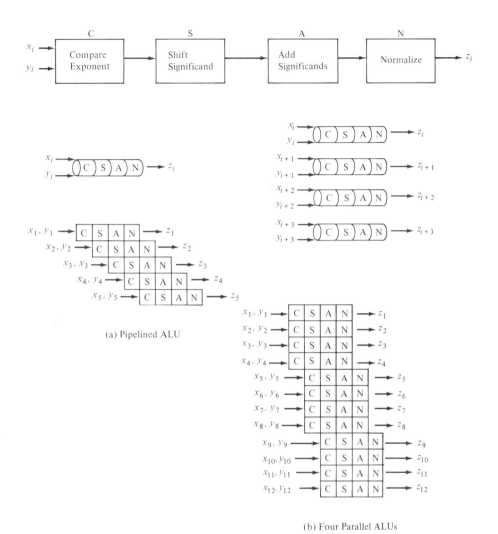

FIGURE 15-9. Pipelined processing

also placed in a vector register. Thus, most operations involve only the use of registers, and only load and store operations and the beginning and end of a vector operation require access to memory.

The mechanism illustrated in Figure 15-9 could be referred to as *pipelining within an operation*. That is, we have a single arithmetic operation (e.g., C = A + B) which is to be applied to vector operands, and pipelining allows multiple vector elements to be processed in parallel. This mechanism can be augmented with *pipelining across operations*. In this latter case, there are a sequence of arithmetic vector operations, and instruction pipelining is used to speed up processing. One approach to this, referred to as **chaining,** is found on the Cray supercomputers. The basic rule for chaining is this: A vector operation may start as soon as the first element of the operand vector(s) is available and the functional unit (e.g., add, subtract, multiply, divide) is free. Essentially, chaining causes results issuing from one functional unit to be fed immediately into another functional unit and so on. If vector registers are used, intermediate results do not have to be stored into memory and can be used even before the vector operation that created them runs to completion.

For example, when computing $C = (s \times A) + B$, where A, B, and C are vectors and s is a scalar, the Cray may execute three instructions at once. Elements fetched for a load immediately enter a pipelined multiplier, the products are sent to a pipelined adder, and the sums are placed in a vector register as soon as the adder completes them:

1. Vector Load $A \rightarrow$ Vector Register (VR1)
2. Vector Load $B \rightarrow$ VR2
3. Vector Multiply $s \times$ VR1 $\rightarrow$ VR3
4. Vector Add   VR3 + VR2 $\rightarrow$ VR4
5. Vector Store   VR4 $\rightarrow$ C

Instructions 2 and 3 can be chained (pipelined) since they involve different memory locations and registers. Instruction 4 needs the results of instructions 2 and 3, but it can be chained with them as well. As soon as the first element of vector registers 2 and 3 are available, the operation in instruction 4 can begin.

Another way in which vector processing can be achieved is by the use of multiple ALUs in a single CPU, under the control of a single control unit. In this case, the control unit routes data to ALUs so that they can function in parallel. It is also possible to use pipelining on each of the parallel ALUs. This is illustrated in Figure 15-9b. The example shows a case in which four ALUs operate in parallel.

As with pipelined organization, a parallel ALU organization is suitable for vector processing. The control unit routes vector elements to ALUs in a round-robin fashion until all elements are processed. This type of organization is more complex than a single-ALU CPI.

Finally, vector processing can be achieved by using multiple parallel CPUs. In this case, it is necessary to break the task up into multiple processes to be executed in parallel. This organization is effective only if the software and hardware for effective coordination of parallel processors is available. This is still an active research area, although some products have appeared [GEHR88].

We can expand our taxonomy of Section 15.1 to reflect these new structures, as shown in Figure 15-10. Computer organizations can be distinguished by the presence of one or more control units. Multiple control units imply multiple processors. Following our previous discussion, if the multiple processors can function cooperatively on a given task, they are termed *parallel processors.*

The reader should be aware of some unfortunate terminology likely to be encountered in the literature. The term *vector processor* is often equated with a pipelined ALU organization, although a parallel ALU organization is also designed for vector processing, and, as we have discussed, a parallel processor

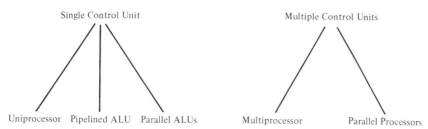

FIGURE 15-10.   A taxonomy of computer organizations

organization may also be designed for vector processing. *Array processing* is sometimes used to refer to a parallel ALU, although, again, any of the three organizations is optimized for the processing of arrays. To make matters worse, *array processor* usually refers to an auxiliary processor attached to a general-purpose CPU and used to perform vector computation. An array processor may use either the pipelined or parallel ALU approach.

At present, the pipelined ALU organization dominates the marketplace [KOZD80, RIGA84]. Pipelined systems are less complex than the other two approaches. Their control unit and operating-system design are well developed to achieve efficient resource allocation and high performance. The remainder of this section is devoted to a more detailed examination of this approach, using a specific example.

IBM 3090 Vector Facility

A good example of a pipelined ALU organization for vector processing is the vector facility developed for the IBM 370 architecture and implemented on the high-end 3090 series [PADE88, MOOR87, TUCK87, CLAR86]. This facility is an optional add-on to the basic system but is highly integrated with it. It resembles vector facilities found on supercomputers, such as the Cray family.

The IBM facility makes use of a number of vector registers. Each register is actually a bank of scalar registers. To compute the vector sum C = A + B, the vectors A and B are loaded into two vector registers. The data from these registers are passed through the ALU as fast as possible and the results are stored in a third vector register. The computation overlap, and the fact that the input data can be loaded into the registers in a block, results in a significant speeding up over an ordinary ALU operation.

Organization

The IBM vector architecture, and similar pipelined vector ALUs, provides increased performance over loops of scalar arithmetic instructions in three ways:

The fixed and predetermined structure of vector data permits housekeeping instructions inside the loop to be replaced by faster internal (hardware or microcoded) machine operations.

- Data-access and arithmetic operations on several successive vector elements can proceed concurrently by overlapping such operations in a pipelined design or by performing multiple-element operations in parallel.
- The use of vector registers for intermediate results avoids additional storage reference.

Figure 15-11 shows the general organization of the vector facility. Although the vector facility is seen to be a physically separate add-on to the CPU, its architecture is an extension of the System/370 architecture and is compatible with it. The vector facility is integrated into the System/370 architecture in the following ways:

- Existing System/370 instructions are used for all scalar operations.
- Arithmetic operations on individual vector elements produce exactly the same result as do corresponding System/370 scalar instructions. For example, one design decision concerned the definition of the result in a floating-point DIVIDE operation. Should the result be exact, as it is for scalar floating-point division, or should an approximation be allowed that would permit higher-speed implementation but could sometimes introduce an error in one or more low-order bit positions? The decision was made to uphold complete compatibility with the System/370 architecture at the expense of a minor performance degradation.
- Vector instructions are interruptible, and their execution can be resumed from the point of interruption after appropriate action has been taken, in a manner compatible with the System/370 program-interruption scheme.
- Arithmetic exceptions are the same as, or extensions of, exceptions for the scalar arithmetic instructions of System/370, and similar fix-up routines can be used. To accommodate this, a vector interruption index is employed which indicates the location in a vector register that is affected by an exception (e.g., overflow). Thus, when execution of the vector instruction resumes, the proper place in a vector register is accessed.
- Vector data resides in virtual storage, with page faults being handled in a standard manner.

This level of integration provides a number of benefits. Existing operating systems can support the vector facility with minor extensions. Existing application programs, language compilers, and other software can be run unchanged. Software that could take advantage of the vector facility can be modified as desired.

Registers

A key issue in the design of a vector facility is whether operands are located in registers or memory. The IBM organization is referred to as *register-to-register*, since the vector operands, both input and output, can be staged in vector registers. This approach is also used on the Cray supercomputer. An alternative

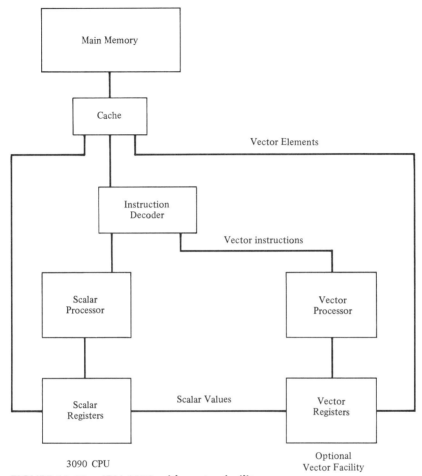

FIGURE 15-11. IBM 3090 with vector facility

approach, used on Control Data machines, is to obtain operands directly from memory. The main disadvantage of the use of vector registers is that the programmer or compiler must take them into account. For example, suppose that the length of the vector registers is K and the length of the vectors to be processed is $N > K$. In this case, a vector loop must be performed, in which the operation is performed on K elements at a time and the loop is repeated N/K times. The main advantage of the vector register approach is that the operation is decoupled from slower main memory and instead takes place primarily with registers.

The speed-up that can be achieved using registers is demonstrated in Figure 15-12 [PADE88]. The FORTRAN routine multiplies vector A by vector B to produce vector C, where each vector has a real part (AR, BR, CR) and an imaginary part (AI, BI, CI). The 3090 can perform one main-storage access per processor, or

FORTRAN ROUTINE:

```
        DO 100 J=1, 50
        CR(J) = AR(J)*BR(J)-AI(J)*BI(J)
100     CI(J) = AR(J)*BI(J)-AI(J)*BR(J)
```

Operation		Cycles
AR(J)*BR(J)	→ T1(J)	3
AI(J)*BI(J)	→ T2(J)	3
T1(J)-T2(J)	→ CR(J)	3
AR(J)*BI(J)	→ T3(J)	3
AI(J)*BR(J)	→ T4(J)	3
T3(J)+T4(J)	→ CI(J)	3
TOTAL		18

(a) Storage to Storage

Operation		Cycles
AR(J)	→ V1(J)	1
BR(J)	→ V2(J)	1
V1(J)*V2(J)	→ V3(J)	1
AI(J)	→ V4(J)	1
BI(J)	→ V5(J)	1
V4(J)*V5(J)	→ V6(J)	1
V3(J)-V6(J)	→ V7(J)	1
V7(J)	→ CR(J)	1
V1(J)*V5(J)	→ V8(J)	1
V4(J)*V2(J)	→ V9(J)	1
V8(J)+V9(J)	→ V0(J)	1
V0(J)	→ CI(J)	1
TOTAL		12

(b) Register to Register

Operation		Cycles
AR(J)	→ V1(J)	1
V1(J)*BR(J)	→ V2(J)	1
AI(J)	→ V3(J)	1
V3(J)*BI(J)	→ V4(J)	1
V2(J)-V4(J)	→ V5(J)	1
V5(J)	→ CR(J)	1
V1(J)*BI(J)	→ V6(J)	1
V3(J)*BR(J)	→ V7(J)	1
V6(J)+V7(J)	→ V8(J)	1
V8(J)	→ CI(J)	1
TOTAL		10

(c) Storage to Register

```
Vi = Vector registers
AR, BR, AI, BI = operands in
    memory
Ti = temporary locations in
    memory
```

Operation		Cycles
AR(J)	→ V1(J)	1
V1(j)*BR(J)	→ V2(J)	1
AI(J)	→ V3(J)	1
V2(J)-V3(J)*BI(J)	→ V2(J)	1
V2(J)	→ CR(J)	1
V1(J)*BI(J)	→ V4(J)	1
V4(J)+V3(J)*BR(J)	→ V4(J)	1
V4(J)	→ CI(J)	1
TOTAL		8

(d) Compound Instructions

FIGURE 15-12. Alternative programs for vector calculation

clock, cycle (either read or write), has registers that can sustain two accesses for reading and one for writing per cycle, and produces one result per cycle in its arithmetic unit. Let us assume the use of instructions that can specify two source operands and a result.[1] Part a of the figure shows that, with memory-to-memory instructions, each iteration of the computation requires a total of 18 cycles. With a pure register-to-register architecture (part b), this time is reduced to 12 cycles.

[1] For the 370 architecture, as we have seen in Section 3-2, the only three-operand instructions (register and storage instructions, RS) specify two operands in registers and one in memory. In part a of this example, we assume the existence of three-operand instructions in which all operands are in main memory. This is done for purposes of comparison and, in fact, such an instruction format could have been chosen for the vector architecture.

Of course, with register-to-register operation, the vector quantities must be loaded into the vector registers prior to computation and stored in memory afterward. For large vectors, this fixed penalty is relatively small. Figure 15-12c shows that the ability to specify both storage and register operands in one instruction further reduces the time to 10 cycles per iteration. This latter type of instruction is included in the vector architecture.[2]

Figure 15-13 illustrates the registers that are part of the IBM 3090 vector facility. There are 16 32-bit vector registers. The vector registers can also be coupled to form eight 64-bit vector registers. Any register element can hold an integer or

[2]Compound instructions, discussed below, afford a further reduction.

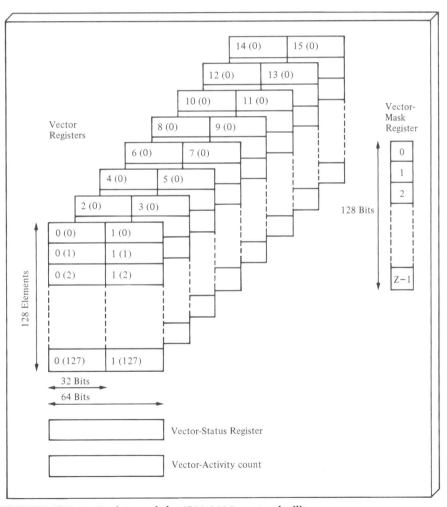

FIGURE 15-13.   Registers of the IBM 3090 vector facility

floating-point value. Thus, the vector registers may be used for 32-bit and 64-bit integer values, and 32-bit and 64-bit floating-point values.

The architecture specifies that each register contains from 8 to 512 scalar elements. The choice of actual length involves a design trade-off. The time to do a vector operation consists essentially of the overhead for pipeline startup and register filling plus one cycle per vector element. Thus, the use of a large number of register elements reduces the relative start-up time for a computation. However, this efficiency must be balanced against the added time required for saving and restoring vector registers on a process switch and the practical cost and space limits. These considerations led to the use of 128 elements per register in the current 3090 implementation.

Three additional registers are needed by the vector facility. The vector-mask register contains mask bits that may be used to select which elements in the vector registers are to be processed for a particular operation. The vector-status register contains control fields, such as the vector count that determines how many elements in the vector registers are to be processed. The vector-activity count keeps track of the time spent executing vector instructions.

Compound Instructions

As was discussed above, instruction execution can be overlapped using chaining to improve performance. The designers of the IBM vector facility chose not to include this capability for several reasons. The System/370 architecture would have to be extended to handle complex interruptions (including their effect on virtual memory management), and corresponding changes would be needed in the software. A more basic issue was the cost of including the additional controls and register access paths in the vector facility for generalized chaining.

Instead, three operations are provided that combine into one instruction (one opcode) the most common sequences in vector computation, namely multiplication followed by addition, subtraction, or summation. The storage-to-register MULTIPLY-AND-ADD instruction, for example, fetches a vector from storage, multiplies it by a vector from a register, and adds the product to a third vector in a register. By use of the compound instructions MULTIPLY-AND-ADD and MULTIPLY-AND-SUBTRACT in the example of Figure 15-12, the total time for the iteration is be reduced from 10 to eight cycles.

Unlike chaining, compound instructions do not require the use of additional registers for temporary storage of intermediate results, and they require one less register access. For example, consider the following chain:

$A \rightarrow VR1$
$VR1 + VR2 \rightarrow VR1$

In this case, two stores to the vector regiser VR1 are required. In the IBM architecture there is a storage-to-register ADD instruction. With this instruction, only the sum is placed in VR1. The compound instruction also avoids the need to reflect in the machine-state description the concurrent execution of a number of instructions, which simplifies status saving and restoring by the operating system and the handling of interrupts.

The Instruction Set

Table 15-2 on the next page summarizes the arithmetic and logical operations that are defined for the vector architecture. In addition, there are memory-to-register load and register-to-memory store instructions. Note that many of the instructions use a three-operand format. Also, many instructions have a number of variants, depending on the location of the operands. A source operand may be a vector register (V), storage (S), or a scalar register (Q). The target is always a vector register, except for comparison, the result of which goes into the vector-mask register. With all of these variants, the total number of opcodes (distinct instructions) is 171. This rather large number, however, is not as expensive to implement as might be imagined. Once the machine provides the arithmetic units and the data paths to feed operands from storage, scalar registers, and vector registers to the vector pipelines, the major hardware cost has been incurred. The architecture can, with little difference in cost, provide a rich set of variants on the use of those registers and pipelines.

Most of the instructions in Table 15-2 are self-explanatory. The two summation instructions warrant further explanation. The accumulate operation adds together the elements of a single vector (ACCUMULATE) or the elements of the product of two vectors (MULTIPLY-AND-ACCUMULATE). These instructions present an interesting design problem. We would like to perform this operation as rapidly as possible, taking full advantage of the ALU pipeline. The difficulty is that the sum of two numbers put into the pipeline is not available until several cycles later. Thus, the third element in the vector cannot be added to the sum of the first two elements until those two elements have gone through the entire pipeline. To overcome this problem, the elements of the vector are added in such a way as to produce four partial sums. In particular, elements 0, 4, 8, 12, . . . , 124 are added in that order to produce partial sum 0; elements 1, 5, 9, 13, . . . , 125 to partial sum 1; elements 2, 6, 10, 14, . . . , 126 to partial sum 2; and elements 3, 7, 11, 15, . . . , 127 to partial sum 4. Each of these partial sums can proceed through the pipeline at top speed, since the delay in the pipeline is roughly four cycles. A separate vector register is used to hold the partial sums. When all elements of the original vector have been processed, the four partial sums are added together to produce the final result. The performance of this second phase is not critical since only four vector elements are involved.

15.3

RECOMMENDED READING

[DESR87] is a broad but not very deep survey of the topics of this chapter. [ENSL77] is an excellent treatment of many of the issues discussed in Section

TABLE 15-2 IBM 3090 Vector Facility: Arithmetic and Logical Instructions

Operation	Long	Short	Binary or Logical	Operand Locations			
Add	FL	FS	BI	$V+V \rightarrow V$	$V+S \rightarrow V$	$Q+V \rightarrow V$	$Q+S \rightarrow V$
Subtract	FL	FS	BI	$V-V \rightarrow V$	$V-S \rightarrow V$	$Q-V \rightarrow V$	$Q-S \rightarrow V$
Multiply	FL	FS	BI	$V^*V \rightarrow V$	$V^*V \rightarrow V$	$Q^*V \rightarrow V$	$Q^*S \rightarrow V$
Divide	FL	FS	—	$V/V \rightarrow V$	$V/S \rightarrow V$	$Q/V \rightarrow V$	$Q/S \rightarrow V$
Compare	FL	FS	BI	$V \cdot V$	$V \cdot S$	$Q \cdot V$	$Q \cdot S$
Multiply and Add	FL	FS	—		$V+V^*S \rightarrow V$	$V+Q^*V \rightarrow V$	$V+Q^*S \rightarrow V$
Multiply and Subtract	FL	FS	—		$V-V^*S \rightarrow V$	$V-Q^*V \rightarrow V$	$V-Q^*S \rightarrow V$
Multiply and Accumulate	FL	FS	—	$P+V \cdot V \rightarrow P$	$P+V \cdot S \rightarrow P$		
Accumulate	FL	FS	—	$P+ \cdot V \rightarrow P$	$P+ \cdot S \rightarrow P$		
Complement	FL	FS	BI	$-V \rightarrow V$			
Positive Absolute	FL	FS	BI	$|V| \rightarrow V$			
Negative Absolute	FL	FS	BI	$-|V| \rightarrow V$			
Maximum	FL	FS	—			$Q \cdot V \rightarrow Q$	
Maximum Absolute	FL	FS	—			$Q \cdot V \rightarrow Q$	
Minimum	FL	FS	—			$Q \cdot V \rightarrow Q$	
Shift Left Logical	—	—	LO	$\cdot V \rightarrow V$			
Shift Right Logical	—	—	LO	$\cdot V \rightarrow V$			
And	—	—	LO	$V \& V \rightarrow V$	$V \& S \rightarrow V$	$Q \& V \rightarrow V$	$Q \& S \rightarrow V$
Or	—	—	LO	$V|V \rightarrow V$	$V|S \rightarrow V$	$Q|V \rightarrow V$	$Q|S \rightarrow V$
Exclusive Or	—	—	LO	$V \neq V \rightarrow V$	$V \neq S \rightarrow V$	$Q \neq V \rightarrow V$	$Q \neq S \rightarrow V$

Explanation:

Data Types
FL   Long floating-point
FS   Short floating-point
BI   Binary integer
LO   Logical

Operand Locations
V   Vector register
S   Storage
Q   Scalar (general or floating-point register)
P   Parital sums in vector register
·   Special Operation

15.1. [SIEW82b] is a systematic analysis of the various characteristics of multi-processor systems. [SATY80] examines the multiprocessing approach on the IBM S/370 and several other commercially available systems. Detailed analyses of the design issues associated with having local caches in a multiprocessor system are presented in [DUBO82] and [YEN85].

Good discussions of vector computation can be found in [STON87], [STON80], and [BAER80]. [RAMA78] examines pipelined ALUs in some detail. [HWAN85] looks at multiple processor approaches.

A number of case studies and other papers on multiprocessing and parallel processing can be found in [KUHN81], [LARS82], [LIEB81], [THUR80], and [THUR79].

15.4

PROBLEMS

15.1 In a multiprocessor IBM S/370 configuration, each CPU is assigned a separate 4K-byte block of absolute memory to hold its first 4K-byte block of real memory. Note that the prefixing mechanism does not prevent CPU X from writing into CPU Y's dedicated area. What other mechanism can be used to provide this protection?

15.2 Can you foresee any problem with the write-once cache approach on bus-based multiprocessors? If so, suggest a solution.

15.3 Produce a vectorized version of the following program:

```
        DO 20 I = 1, N
        B(I, 1) = 0
        DO 10 J = 1, M
        A(I) = A(I) + B(I, J) · C(I, J)
10 CONTINUE
        D(I) = E(I) + A(I)
20 CONTINUE
```

15.4 Consider the following method of sorting N items.
Procedure QUICKSORT (LOW, HIGH, A);
Array A[1:N], integer LOW, HIGH;
begin integer PIVOTPOINT;
    comment QUICKSORT sorts the portion of A from A[LOW] to A[HIGH];
    call PARTITION (LOW, HIGH, A, PIVOTPOINT);
    comment PARTITION is a procedure that moves around the elements in A between A[LOW] and A[HIGH] so that for all I in the range LOW ≤ I < PIVOTPOINT, A[I] ≤ A[PIVOTPOINT], and for all J in the range PIVOTPOINT < J ≤ HIGH, A[PIVOTPOINT] ≤ A[J]. PIVOTPOINT is an index selected by PARTITION and returned by PIVOTPOINT;
    if PIVOTPOINT > LOW + 1 then QUICKSORT (LOW, PIVOTPOINT − 1, A);

if PIVOTPOINT < HIGH − 1 then QUICKSORT (PIVOTPOINT + 1, HIGH, A);
end of QUICKSORT;

(a) Give a brief explanation of QUICKSORT to indicate that you understand that it sorts A when called initially with the statement QUICKSORT (1, N, A).

(b) Revise QUICKSORT by inserting FORK statements as necessary and corresponding JOIN statements. Indicate precisely what information has to be carried forth for each new branch of the fork from global data, and what information has to be handled in a private fashion for the fork.

(c) Assume that the overhead of a FORK and a JOIN is about the same as the time it takes to QUICKSORT an array of length 7 on a serial computer. Estimate the relative running times for a sort of 1,023 items for a serial computer, and for multiprocessors 2, 3, 4, 8, and 16 processors. (Assume that, by some miracle, PARTITION always manages to find a PIVOTPOINT exactly in the middle of the range.) The time for PIVOTPOINT is proportional to HIGH − LOW.

(d) Describe how to modify QUICKSORT so that it can interrogate to determine how many processors are in the total system and how many are idle via system calls, and then use this information to optimize its performance.

15.5 The inner loop of a matrix computation uses the statement

for J: = K step 1 until N do

A[I, J]: = A[I, J] × Q − A[K, J];

Assume that this statement is parceled out among the processors of a multiprocessor system so that each processor executes the statement for a different value of J. Assume also that the multiprocessor system has a central shared memory. When two different processors access the same memory module simultaneously, the module responds immediately to one processor, and the second processor has to wait one memory cycle, at which time it repeats its request.

(a) Assume that the array is stored by rows across the memories, so that at ascending addresses are elements with index pairs, (1, 1), (1, 2), . . . , (1, N), (2, 1), . . . , (2, N), . . . , (N, N), as ascending addresses cycle across the memories.

Diagram the cycle-by-cycle execution of the first five computation parcels under the assumption that all are initiated simultaneously, and that the number of memories is N.

(b) Now assume that the array is stored so that each row of A lies in a distinct memory module. Repeat part (a).

(c) Comment on the problem of data contention in this type of shared memory system, based on your observations.

Digital Logic

The operation of the digital computer is based on the storage and processing of binary data. Throughout this book, we have assumed the existence of storage elements that can exist in one of two stable states and of circuits than can operate on binary data under the control of control signals to implement the various computer functions. In this appendix, we suggest how these storage elements and circuits can be implemented in digital logic, specifically with combinational and sequential circuits. The appendix begins with a brief review of boolean algebra, which is the mathematical foundation of digital logic. Next, the concept of a gate is introduced. Finally, combinational and sequential circuits, which are constructed from gates, are described.

A.1

BOOLEAN ALGEBRA

The digital circuitry in digital computers and other digital systems is designed, and its behavior is analyzed, with the use of a mathematical discipline known as *boolean algebra*. The name is in honor of an English mathematician George Boole, who proposed the basic principles of this algebra in 1854 in his treatise, *An Investigation of the Laws of Thought on Which to Found the Mathematical Theories of Logic and Probabilities*. In 1938, Claude Shannon, a research assistant in the Electrical Engineering Department at M.I.T., suggested that boolean algebra could be used to solve problems in relay-switching circuit design [SHAN38]. Shannon's techniques were subsequently used in the analysis and design of electronic digital circuits. Boolean algebra turns out to be a convenient tool in two areas:

- *Analysis:* It is an economical way of describing the function of digital circuitry.
- *Design:* Given a desired function, boolean algebra can be applied to develop a simplified implementation of that function.

As with any algebra, boolean algebra makes use of variables and operations. In this case, the variables and operations are logical variables and operations. Thus, a variable may take on the value 1 (TRUE) or 0 (FALSE). The basic logical operations are AND, OR, and NOT, which are symbolically represented by dot, plus sign, and overbar.

A AND B = A · B
A OR B = A + B
NOT A = $\overline{A}$

The operation AND yields true (binary value 1) if and only if both of its operands are true. The operation OR yields true if either or both of its operands are true. The unary operation NOT inverts the value of its operand. For example, consider the equation

D = A + ($\overline{B}$ · C)

D is equal to 1 if A is 1 or if both B = 0 and C = 1. Otherwise D is equal to 0.

Several points concerning the notation are needed. In the absence of parentheses, the AND operation takes precedence over the OR operation. Also, when no ambiguity will occur, the AND operation is represented by simple concatenation instead of the dot operator. Thus

A + B · C = A + (B · C) = A + BC

all mean: Take the AND of B and C; then take the OR of the result and A.

Table A-1 defines the basic logical operations in a form known as a *truth table*, which simply lists the value of an operation for every possible combination of values of operands. The table also lists three other useful operators: XOR, NAND, and NOR. The exclusive-or (XOR) of two logical operands is 1 if and only if exactly one of the operands has the value 1. The NAND function is the complement (NOT) of the AND function, and the NOT is the complement of OR:

A NAND B = NOT (A AND B) = $\overline{AB}$
A NOR B = NOT (A OR B) = $\overline{A + B}$

As we shall see, these three new operations can be useful in implementing certain digital circuits.

Table A-2 summarizes key identities of boolean algebra. The equations have been arranged in two columns to show the complementary, or dual, nature of

TABLE A-1   Boolean Operators

P	Q	NOT P	P AND Q	P OR Q	P XOR Q	P NAND Q	P NOR Q
0	0	1	0	0	0	1	1
0	1	1	0	1	1	1	0
1	0	0	0	1	1	1	0
1	1	0	1	1	0	0	0

TABLE A-2   Basic Identities of Boolean Algebra

Basic Postulates		
$A \cdot B = B \cdot A$	$A + B = B + A$	Commutative Laws
$A \cdot (B + C) = (A \cdot B) + (A \cdot C)$	$A + (B \cdot C) = (A + B) \cdot (A + C)$	Distributive Laws
$1 \cdot A = A$	$0 + A = A$	Identity Elements
$A \cdot \bar{A} = 0$	$A + \bar{A} = 1$	Inverse Elements
Other Identities		
$0 \cdot A = 0$	$1 + A = 1$	
$A \cdot A = A$	$A + A = A$	
$A \cdot (B \cdot C) = (A \cdot B) \cdot C$	$A + (B + C) = (A + B) + C$	Associative Laws
$\overline{A \cdot B} = \bar{A} + \bar{B}$	$\overline{A + B} = \bar{A} \cdot \bar{B}$	DeMorgan's Theorem

the AND and OR operations. There are two classes of identities; basic rules (or *postulates*), which are stated without proof, and other identities that can be derived from the basic postulates. The postulates define the way in which boolean expressions are interpreted. One of the two distributive laws is worth noting because it differs from what we would find in ordinary algebra:

$$A + (B \cdot C) = (A + B) \cdot (A + C)$$

The two bottommost expressions are referred to as DeMorgan's theorem. We can restate them as follows:

$$A \text{ NOR } B = \bar{A} \text{ AND } \bar{B}$$
$$A \text{ NAND } B = \bar{A} \text{ OR } \bar{B}$$

The reader is invited to verify the expressions in Table A-2 by substituting actual values (1s and 0s) for the variables A, B, and C.

A.2

GATES

The fundamental building block of all digital logic circuits is the gate. Logical functions are implemented by the interconnection of gates.

A gate is an electronic circuit that produces an output signal that is a simple boolean operation on its input signals. The basic gates used in digital logic are AND, OR, NOT, NAND, and NOR. Figure A-1 depicts these five gates. Each gate is defined in three ways: graphic symbol, algebraic notation, and truth table. The symbology used here and throughout the appendix is the IEEE standard, IEEE Std 91 [IEEE84]. Note that the inversion (NOT) operation is indicated by a circle.

Each gate has one or two inputs and one output. When the values at the input are changed, the correct output signal appears almost instantaneously, delayed

Name	Graphic Symbol	Algebraic Function	Truth Table
AND	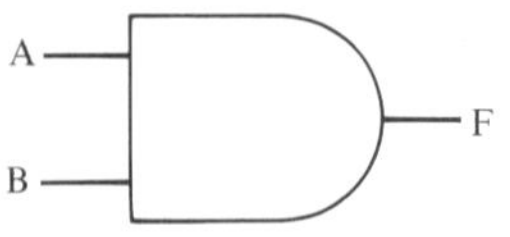 A ─┐ ⟩─ F B ─┘	$F = A \cdot B$ or $F = AB$	A B | F 0 0 | 0 0 1 | 0 1 0 | 0 1 1 | 1
OR	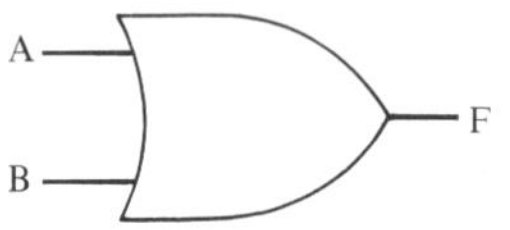 A ─┐ ⟩─ F B ─┘	$F = A + B$	A B | F 0 0 | 0 0 1 | 1 1 0 | 1 1 1 | 1
NOT	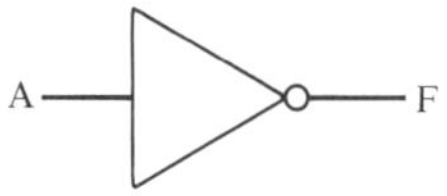 A ─▷o─ F	$F = \overline{A}$ or $F = A'$	A | F 0 | 1 1 | 0
NAND	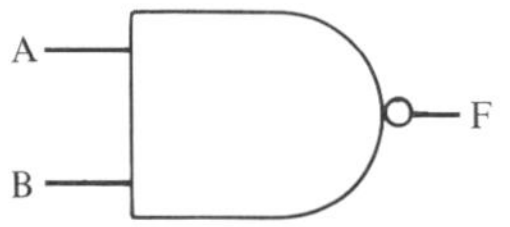 A ─┐ ⟩o─ F B ─┘	$F = (\overline{AB})$	A B | F 0 0 | 1 0 1 | 1 1 0 | 1 1 1 | 0
NOR	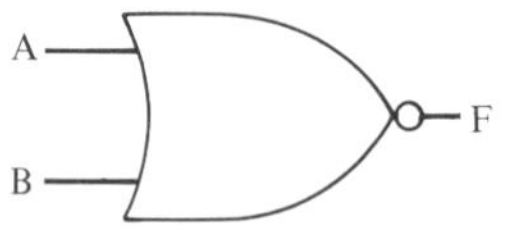 A ─┐ ⟩o─ F B ─┘	$F = (\overline{A + B})$	A B | F 0 0 | 1 0 1 | 0 1 0 | 0 1 1 | 0

FIGURE A-1.   Basic logic gates

only by the propagation time of signals through the gate (known as the *gate delay*). The significance of this is discussed in Section A.3.

In addition to the gates depicted in Figure A-1, gates with 3, 4, or more inputs can be used. Thus, $X + Y + Z$ can be implemented with a single OR gate with three inputs.

Typically, not all gate types are used in implementation. Design and fabrication are simpler if only one or two types of gates are used. Thus, it is important to identify *functionally complete* sets of gates. This means that any boolean function can be implemented using only the gates in the set. The following are functionally complete sets:

• AND, OR, NOT
• AND, NOT
• OR, NOT

• NAND
• NOR

It should be clear that AND, OR, and NOT gates constitute a functionally complete set, since they represent the three operations of boolean algebra. For the AND and NOT gates to form a functionally complete set, there must be a way to synthesize the OR operation from the AND and NOT operations. This can be done by applying DeMorgan's theorem:

$A + B = \overline{\overline{A} \cdot \overline{B}}$
A OR B = NOT((NOT A) AND (NOT B))

Similarly, the OR and NOT operations are functionally complete because they can be used to synthesize the AND operation.

Figure A-2 shows how the AND, OR, and NOT functions can be implemented solely with NAND gates, and Figure A-3 shows the same thing for NOR gates. For this reason, digital circuits can be, and frequently are, implemented solely with NAND gates or solely with NOR gates.

With gates, we have reached the most primitive level of computer science and engineering. An examination of the transistor combinations used to construct gates departs from that realm and enters the realm of electrical engineering. For the interested reader, [CLAR80] is an entertaining yet informative description of

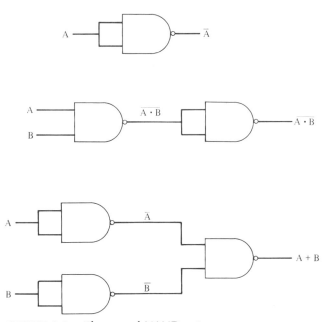

FIGURE A-2.   The use of NAND gates

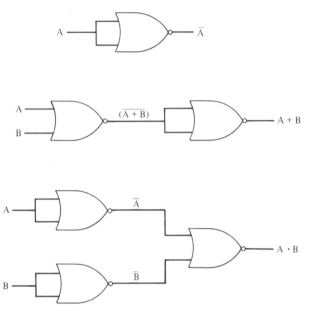

FIGURE A-3. The use of NOR gates

these matters for the computer scientist. For our purposes, however, we are content to describe how gates can be used as building blocks to implement the essential logical circuits of a digital computer.

A.3

COMBINATIONAL CIRCUITS

A combinational circuit is an interconnected set of gates whose output at any time is a function only of the input at that time. As with a single gate, the appearance of the input is followed almost immediately by the appearance of the output, with only gate delays.

In general terms, a combinational circuit consists of n binary inputs and m binary outputs. As with a gate, a combinational circuit can be defined in three ways:

- *Truth Table:* For each of the 2^n possible combinations of input signals, the binary value of each of the m output signals is listed.
- *Graphical Symbols:* The interconnected layout of gates is depicted.
- *Boolean Equations:* Each output signal is expressed as a boolean function of its input signals.

Implementation of Boolean Functions

Any boolean function can be implemented in electronic form as a network of gates. For any given function, there are a number of alternative realizations. Consider the boolean function represented by the truth table in Table A-3. We can express this function by simply itemizing the combinations of values of A, B, and C that cause F to be 1:

$$F = \overline{A}B\overline{C} + \overline{A}BC + AB\overline{C} \tag{A-1}$$

There are three combinations of input values that cause F to be 1, and if any one of these combinations occurs, the result is 1. This form of expression, for self-evident reasons, is known as the *sum of products* (SOP) form. Figure A-4 shows a straightforward implementation with AND, OR, and NOT gates.

Another form can also be derived from the truth table. The SOP form expresses that the output is 1 if any of the input combinations that produce 1 is true. We can also say that the output is 1 if none of the input combinations that produce 0 is true. Thus:

$$F = (\overline{\overline{A}\,\overline{B}\,\overline{C}}) \cdot (\overline{\overline{A}\,\overline{B}C}) \cdot (\overline{A\overline{B}\,\overline{C}}) \cdot (\overline{A\overline{B}C}) \cdot (\overline{ABC})$$

This can be rewritten using a generalization of deMorgan's theorem:

$$(\overline{X \cdot Y \cdot Z}) = \overline{X} + \overline{Y} + \overline{Z}$$

Thus,

$$
\begin{aligned}
F &= (\overline{\overline{A}} + \overline{\overline{B}} + \overline{\overline{C}}) \cdot (\overline{\overline{A}} + \overline{\overline{B}} + \overline{C}) \cdot (\overline{A} + \overline{\overline{B}} + \overline{\overline{C}}) \\
&\quad \cdot (\overline{A} + \overline{\overline{B}} + \overline{C}) \cdot (\overline{A} + \overline{B} + \overline{C}) \\
&= (A + B + C) \cdot (A + B + \overline{C}) \cdot (\overline{A} + B + C) \\
&\quad \cdot (\overline{A} + B + \overline{C}) \cdot (\overline{A} + \overline{B} + \overline{C})
\end{aligned}
\tag{A-2}
$$

This is in the *product of sums* (POS) form, which is illustrated in Figure A-5. For clarity, NOT gates are not shown. Rather, it is assumed that each input signal

TABLE A-3   A Boolean Function of Three Variables

A	B	C	F
0	0	0	0
0	0	1	0
0	1	0	1
0	1	1	1
1	0	0	0
1	0	1	0
1	1	0	1
1	1	1	0

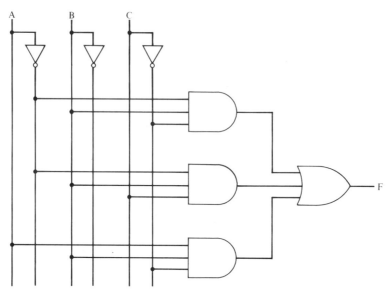

FIGURE A-4. Sum-of-products implementation of Table A-3

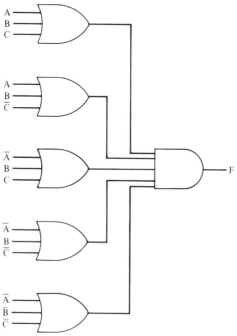

FIGURE A-5. Product-of-sums implementation of Table A-3

and its complement are available. This simplifies the logic diagram and makes the inputs to the gates more readily apparent.

Thus, a boolean function can be realized in either SOP or POS form. At this point, it would seem that the choice would depend on whether the truth table contains more 1s or 0s for the output function: The SOP has one term for each 1, and the POS has one term for each 0. However, there are other considerations:

- It is generally possible to derive a simpler boolean expression from the truth table than either SOP or POS.
- It may be preferable to implement the function with a single gate type (NAND or NOR).

The significance of the first point is that, with a simpler boolean expression, fewer gates will be needed to implement the function. Three methods that can be used to achieve simplification are

- Algebraic simplification
- Karnaugh maps
- Quine-McKluskey tables

Algebraic Simplification

Algebraic simplification involves the application of the identities of Table A-2 to reduce the boolean expression to one with fewer elements. For example, consider again Equation A-1. Some thought should convince the reader that an equivalent expression is

$$F = \overline{A}B + B\overline{C} \tag{A-3}$$

Or, even simpler,

$$F = B(\overline{A} + \overline{C})$$

This expression can be implemented as shown in Figure A-6. The simplification of Equation A-1 was done essentially by observation. For more complex expression, some more systematic approach is needed.

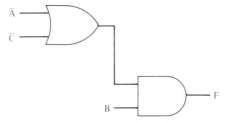

FIGURE A-6.   Simplified implementation of Table A-3

Karnaugh Maps

For purposes of simplification, the Karnaugh map is a convenient way of representing a boolean function of a small number (up to 4 to 6) of variables. The map is an array of 2^n squares, representing the possible combinations of values of n binary variables. Figure A-7a shows the map of four squares for a function of two variables. It is convenient for later purposes to list the combinations in the order 00, 01, 11, 10. Since the squares corresponding to the combinations are to be used for recording information, the combinations are customarily written above the squares. In the case of three variables, the representation is an arrangement of 8 squares (Figure A-7b), with the values for one of the variables to the left and for the other two variables above the squares. For four variables, 16 squares are needed, with the arrangement indicated in Figure A-7c.

The map can be used to represent any boolean function in the following way. Each square corresponds to a unique product in the sum-of-products form, with a 1 value corresponding to the variable and a 0 value corresponding to the NOT of that variable. Thus, the product $A\overline{B}$ corresponds to the fourth square in Figure A-7a. For each such product in the function, 1 is placed in the corresponding square. Thus, for the two-variable example, the map corresponds to $A\overline{B} + \overline{A}B$. Given the truth table of a boolean function, it is an easy matter to construct the map: for each combination of values of variables that produce a result of 1 in the truth table, fill in the corresponding square of the map with 1. Figure A-7b shows the result for the truth table of Table A-3. To convert from a boolean

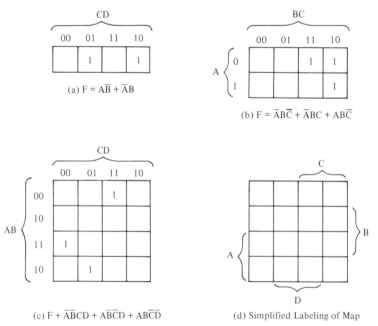

(a) $F = A\overline{B} + \overline{A}B$

(b) $F = \overline{A}B\overline{C} + \overline{A}BC + AB\overline{C}$

(c) $F + \overline{A}\overline{B}CD + AB\overline{C}D + AB\overline{C}\overline{D}$

(d) Simplified Labeling of Map

FIGURE A-7. The use of Karnaugh maps to represent boolean functions

expression to a map, it is first necessary to put the expression into what is referred to as *canonical* form: each term in the expression must contain each variable. So, for example, if we have Equation A-3, we must first expand it into the full form of Equation A-1, and then convert this to a map.

The labeling used in Figure A-7d emphasizes the relationship between variables and the rows and columns of the map. Here the two rows embraced by the symbol A are those in which the variable A has the value 1; the rows not embraced by the symbol A are those in which A is 0. Similarly for B, C, and D.

Once the map of a function is created, we can often write a simple algebraic expression for it by noting the arrangement of the 1s on the map. The principle is as follows. Any two squares that are adjacent differ in only one of the variables. If two adjacent squares both have an entry of one, then the corresponding product terms differ in only one variable. In such a case, the two terms can be merged by eliminating that variable. For example, in Figure A-8a, the two adjacent squares correspond to the two terms $\overline{A}B\overline{C}D$ and $\overline{A}BCD$. Thus the function expressed is

$$\overline{A}B\overline{C}D + \overline{A}BCD = \overline{A}BD$$

This process can be extended in several ways. First, the concept of adjacency can be extended to include wrapping around the edge of the map. Thus the top square of a column is adjacent to the bottom square, and the leftmost square of a row is adjacent to the rightmost square. These conditions are illustrated in Figure A-8b and c. Secondly, we can group not just 2 squares but 2^n adjacent squares, that is, 4, 8, etc. The next three examples in Figure A-8 show groupings of 4 squares. Note that in this case, two of the variables can be eliminated. The last three examples show groupings of 8 squares, which allows three variables to be eliminated.

In attempting to simplify, first look for the largest grouping possible (eight in a four-variable map). If any squares with a 1 remain uncircled, then look for successively smaller groupings. When you are encircling groups, you are allowed to use the same 1 more than once. Figure A-9a, based on Table A-3, illustrates this. If any isolated ones remain after the groupings, then each of these is circled as a group of one. Finally, before going from the map to a simplified boolean expression, any group of 1s that is completely overlapped by other groups can be eliminated. This is shown in Figure A-9b. In this case, the horizontal group is redundant and may be ignored in creating the boolean expression.

One additional feature of Karnaugh maps needs to be mentioned. In some cases, certain combinations of values of variables never occur and therefore the corresponding output never occurs. These are referred to as "don't care" conditions. For each such condition, the letter "d" is entered into the corresponding square of the map. In doing the grouping and simplification, each "d" can be treated as a 1 or not, whichever leads to the simplest expression.

An example, presented in [HAYE88], illustrates the points we have been discussing. We would like to develop the boolean expressions for a circuit that adds

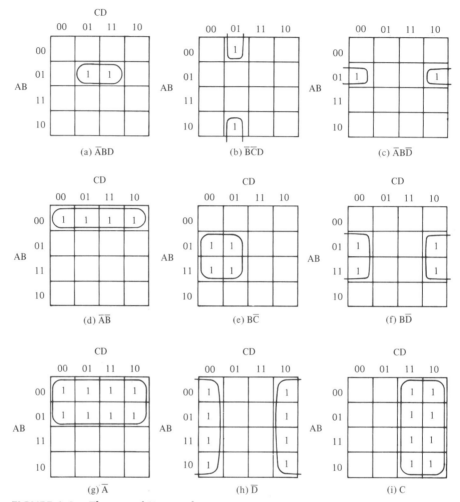

FIGURE A-8. The use of Karnaugh maps

1 to a packed decimal digit. Recall from Section 8.2, that with packed decimal, each decimal digit is represented by a 4-bit code, in the obvious way. Thus 0 = 0000, 1 = 0001, . . . , 8 = 1000, and 9 = 1001. The remaining 4-bit values, from 1010 to 1111, are not used. This code is also referred to as Binary Coded Decimal (BCD).

Table A-4 shows the truth table for producing a 4-bit result that is one more than a 4-bit BCD input. The addition is modulo 10. Thus 9 + 1 = 0. Also, note that six of the input codes produce "don't care" results, since those are not valid BCD inputs. Figure A-10 shows the resulting Karnaugh maps for each of the output variables. The d squares are used to achieve the best possible groupings.

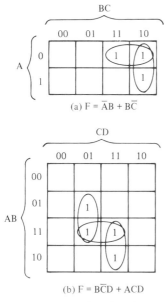

(a) F = $\overline{A}B + B\overline{C}$

(b) F = $B\overline{C}D + ACD$

FIGURE A-9.   Overlapping groups

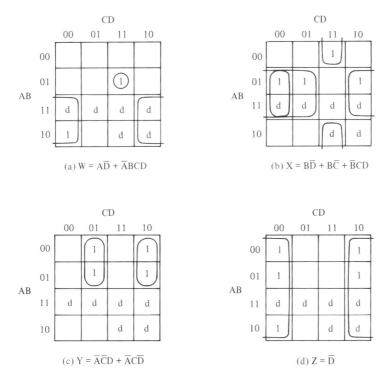

(a) W = $A\overline{D} + \overline{A}BCD$

(b) X = $B\overline{D} + B\overline{C} + \overline{B}CD$

(c) Y = $\overline{A}\overline{C}D + \overline{A}C\overline{D}$

(d) Z = $\overline{D}$

FIGURE A-10.   Karnaugh maps for the incrementer

TABLE A-4 Truth Table for the One-Digit Packed Decimal Incrementer

	Input					Output			
Number	A	B	C	D	Number	W	X	Y	Z
0	0	0	0	0	1	0	0	0	1
1	0	0	0	1	2	0	0	1	0
2	0	0	1	0	3	0	0	1	1
3	0	0	1	1	4	0	1	0	0
4	0	1	0	0	5	0	1	0	1
5	0	1	0	1	6	0	1	1	0
6	0	1	1	0	7	0	1	1	1
7	0	1	1	1	8	1	0	0	0
8	1	0	0	0	9	1	0	0	1
9	1	0	0	1	0	0	0	0	0
Don't-care Conditions	1	0	1	0		d	d	d	d
	1	0	1	1		d	d	d	d
	1	1	0	0		d	d	d	d
	1	1	0	1		d	d	d	d
	1	1	1	0		d	d	d	d
	1	1	1	1		d	d	d	d

The Quine-McKluskey Method

For more than four variables, the Karnaugh map method becomes increasingly cumbersome. With five variables, two 16×16 maps are needed, with one map considered to be on top of the other in three dimensions to achieve adjacency. Six variables requires the use of four 16×16 tables in four dimensions! An alternative approach is a tabular technique, referred to as the Quine-McKluskey method. The method is suitable for programming on a computer to give an automatic tool for producing minimized boolean expressions.

The method is best explained by means of an example. Consider the following expression:

$$ABCD + AB\overline{C}D + AB\overline{C}\,\overline{D} + A\overline{B}CD + \overline{A}BCD + \overline{A}BC\overline{D} + \overline{A}B\overline{C}D + \overline{A}\,\overline{B}\,\overline{C}D$$

Let us assume that this expression was derived from a truth table. We would like to produce a minimal expression suitable for implementation with gates.

The first step is to construct a table in which each row corresponds to one of the product terms of the expression. The terms are grouped according to the number of complemented variables. That is, we start with the term with no complements, if it exists, then all terms with one complement, and so on. Table A-5 shows the list for our example expression, with horizontal lines used to indicate the grouping. For clarity, each term is represented by a 1 for each un-complemented variable and a 0 for each complemented variable. Thus, we group terms according to the number of 1s they contain. The index column is simply the decimal equivalent and is useful in what follows.

TABLE A-5 First Stage of Quine-McKluskey Method for $F = ABCD + AB\overline{C}D + AB\overline{C}\,\overline{D} + \overline{A}BCD + \overline{A}BC\overline{D} + \overline{A}\,\overline{B}CD + \overline{A}\,\overline{B}\,\overline{C}D + \overline{A}\,\overline{B}CD$

Product Term	Index	A	B	C	D	
$\overline{A}\,\overline{B}\,\overline{C}D$	1	0	0	0	1	✓
$\overline{A}B\overline{C}D$	5	0	1	0	1	✓
$\overline{A}BC\overline{D}$	6	0	1	1	0	✓
$AB\overline{C}\,\overline{D}$	12	1	1	0	0	✓
$\overline{A}BCD$	7	0	1	1	1	✓
$A\overline{B}CD$	11	1	0	1	1	✓
$AB\overline{C}D$	13	1	1	0	1	✓
$ABCD$	15	1	1	1	1	✓

The next step is to find all pairs of terms that differ in only one variable, that is, all pairs of terms that are the same except that one variable is 0 in one of the terms and 1 in the other. Because of the way in which we have grouped the terms, we can do this by starting with the first group and comparing each term of the first group with every term of the second group. Then, compare each term of the second group with all of the terms of the third group, and so on. Whenever a match is found, place a check next to each term, combine the pair by eliminating the variable which differs in the two terms, and add that to a new list. Thus, for example, the terms $\overline{A}BC\overline{D}$ and $\overline{A}BCD$ are combined to produce $\overline{A}BC$. This process continues until the entire original table has been examined. The result is a new table with the following entries:

$\overline{A}\,\overline{C}D$

$AB\overline{C}$
$B\overline{C}D$ ✓
$\overline{A}BC$
$\overline{A}BD$ ✓

ABD ✓
ACD
BCD ✓

The new table is organized into groups, as indicated above, in the same fashion as the first table. The second table is then processed in the same manner as the first. That is, terms that differ in only one variable are checked and a new term produced for a third table. In this example, the third table that is produced contains only one term:

BD

In general, the process would proceed through successive tables until a table with no matches was produced. In this case, this has involved three tables.

Once the process described above is completed, we have eliminated many of the possible terms of the expression. Those terms that have not been eliminated are used to construct a matrix, as illustrated in Table A-6. Each row of the matrix corresponds to one of the terms that has not been eliminated (has no check) in any of the tables used so far. Each column corresponds to one of the terms in the original expression. An X is placed at each intersection of a row and a column such that the row element is "compatible" with the column element. That is, the variables present in the row element have the same value as the variables present in the column element. Next, circle each X that is alone in a column. Then, place a square around each X in any row in which there is an encircled X. If every column now has either a squared or a circled X, then we are done, and those row elements whose X's have been marked constitute the minimal expression. Thus, in our example, the final expression is:

$$AB\overline{C} + ACD + \overline{A}BC + \overline{A}\,CD$$

In cases in which some columns have neither a circle or a square, additional processing is required. Essentially, we keep adding row elements until all columns are covered.

Let us summarize the Quine-McKluskey method to try to justify intuitively why it works. The first phase of the operation is reasonably straightforward. The process eliminates unneeded variables in product terms. Thus, the expression $ABC + AB\overline{C}$ is equivalent to AB, since

$$ABC + AB\overline{C} = AB(C + \overline{C}) = AB1 = AB$$

After the elimination of variables, we are left with an expression which is clearly equivalent to the original expression. However, there may be redundant terms in this expression, just as we found redundant groupings in Karnaugh maps. The matrix layout assures that each term in the original expression is covered and does so in a way that minimizes the number of terms in the final expression.

NAND and NOR Implementations

Another consideration in the implementation of boolean functions concerns the types of gates used. It is often felt desirable to implement a boolean function

TABLE A-6 Last Stage of Quine-McKluskey Method for $F = ABCD + AB\overline{C}D + AB\overline{C}\,\overline{D} + A\overline{B}CD + \overline{A}BCD + \overline{A}BC\overline{D} + \overline{A}\overline{B}CD + \overline{A}\,\overline{B}\,CD$

	$ABCD$	$AB\overline{C}D$	$AB\overline{C}\,\overline{D}$	$A\overline{B}CD$	$\overline{A}BCD$	$\overline{A}BC\overline{D}$	$\overline{A}\overline{B}CD$	$\overline{A}\,\overline{B}\,CD$
BD	X	X			X		X	
$\overline{A}\,CD$							[X]	(X)
$\overline{A}BC$					[X]	(X)		
$AB\overline{C}$		[X]	(X)					
ACD	[X]			(X)				

solely with NAND gates or solely with NOR gates. Although this may not be the minimum-gate implementation, it has the advantage of regularity, which can simplify the manufacturing process. Consider again Equation A-3:

$$F = B(\overline{A} + \overline{C})$$

Since the complement of the complement of a value is just the value,

$$F = B(\overline{A} + \overline{C})$$
$$= \overline{\overline{(\overline{AB})} + \overline{(B\overline{C})}}$$

Applying deMorgan's theorem,

$$F = \overline{(\overline{AB})} \cdot \overline{(B\overline{C})}$$

which has three NAND forms, as illustrated in Figure A-11.

Multiplexers

The multiplexer connects multiple inputs to a single output. At any time, one of the inputs is selected to be passed to the output. A general block diagram representation is shown in Figure A-12. This represents a 4-to-1 multiplexer. There are four input lines, labeled D0, D1, D2, and D3. One of these lines is selected to provide the output signal F. To select one of the four possible inputs, a 2-bit

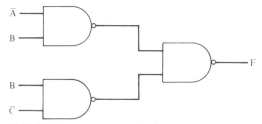

FIGURE A-11.   NAND implementation of Table A-3

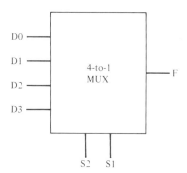

FIGURE A-12.   4-to-1 multiplexer representation

TABLE A-7
4-to-1 Multiplexer
Truth Table

S2	S1	F
0	0	D0
0	1	D1
1	0	D2
1	1	D3

selection code is needed, and this is implemented as two select lines labeled S1 and S2.

An example 4-to-1 multiplexer is defined by the truth table in Table A-7. This is a simplified form of truth table. Instead of showing all possible combinations of input variables, it shows the output as data from line D0, D1, D2, or D3. Figure A-13 shows an implementation using AND, OR, and NOT gates. S1 and S2 are connected to the AND gates in such a way that, for any combination of S1 and S2, three of the AND gates will output 0. The fourth AND gate will output the value of the selected line, which is either 0 or 1. Thus, three of the inputs to

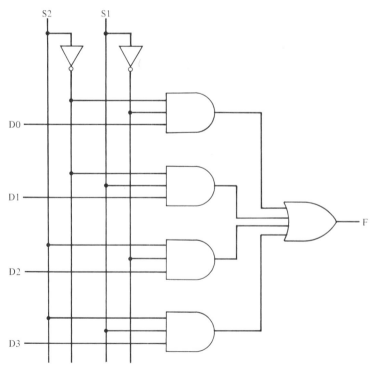

FIGURE A-13.   Multiplexer implementation

the OR gate are always 0, and the output of the OR gate will equal the value of the selected input gate. Using this regular organization, it is easy to construct multiplexers of size 8-to-1, 16-to-1, and so on.

Multiplexers are used in digital circuits to control signal and data routing. An example is the loading of the program counter (PC). The value to be loaded into the program counter may come from one of several different sources:

- A binary counter, if the PC is to be incremented for the next instruction.
- The instruction register, if a branch instruction using a direct address has just been executed.
- The output of the ALU, if the branch instruction specifies the address using a displacement mode.

These various inputs could be connected to the input lines of a multiplexer, with the PC connected to the output line. The select lines determine which value is loaded into the PC. Since the PC contains multiple bits, multiple multiplexers are used, one per bit. Figure A-14 illustrates this for 16-bit addresses.

Decoders

A decoder is a combinational circuit with a number of output lines, only one of which is asserted at any time, dependent on the pattern of input lines. In general, a decoder has n inputs and 2^n outputs. Figure A-15 shows a decoder with three inputs and eight outputs.

Decoders find many uses in digital computers. One example is address decoding. Suppose we wish to construct a 1K-byte memory using four 256×8 bit RAM chips. We want a single unified address space, which can be broken down as follows:

Address	Chip
0000–00FF	0
0100–01FF	1
0200–02FF	2
0300–03FF	3

Each chip requires 8 address lines, and these are supplied by the lower-order 8 bits of the address. The higher-order 2 bits of the 10-bit address are used to select

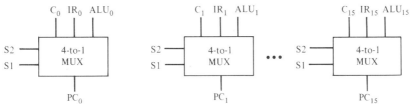

FIGURE A-14.   Multiplexer input to program counter

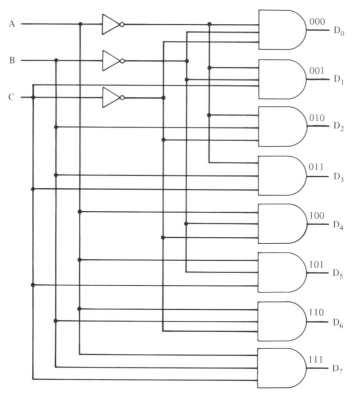

FIGURE A-15.   Decoder with 3 inputs and $2^3 = 8$ outputs

one of the four RAM chips. For this purpose, a 2-to-4 decoder is used whose output enables one of the four chips, as shown in Figure A-16.

With an additional input line, a decoder can be used as a demultiplexer. The demultiplexer performs the inverse function of a multiplexer; it connects a single

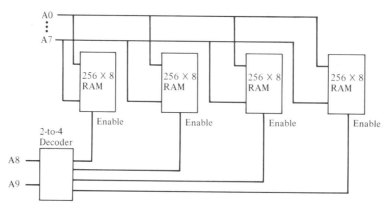

FIGURE A-16.   Address decoding

input to one of several outputs. This is shown in Figure A-17. As before, n inputs are decoded to produce a single one of 2^n outputs. All of the 2^n output lines are ANDed with a data input line. Thus the n inputs act as an address to select a particular output line, and the value on the data input line (0 or 1) is routed to that output line.

The configuration in Figure A-17 can be viewed in another way. Change the label on the new line from *Data Input* to *Enable*. This allows for the control of the timing of the decoder. The decoded output appears only when the encoded input is present *and* the enable line has a value of 1.

Programmable Logic Array (PLA)

Thus far, we have treated individual gates as building blocks, from which arbitrary functions can be realized. The designer could pursue a strategy of minimizing the number of gates to be used by manipulating the corresponding boolean expressions.

As the level of integration provided by integrated circuits increases, other considerations apply. Early integrated circuits, using small-scale integration (SSI), provided from one to ten gates on a chip. Each gate is treated independently, in the building-block approach described so far. Figure A-18 is an example of some SSI chips. To construct a logic function, a number of these chips are laid out on a printed-circuit board and the appropriate pin interconnections are made.

Increasing levels of integration made it possible to put more gates on a chip and to make gate interconnections on the chip as well. This yields the advantages of decreased cost, decreased size, and increased speed (since on-chip delays are of shorter duration than off-chip delays). A design problem arises, however. For each particular logic function or set of functions, the layout of gates and interconnections on the chip must be designed. The cost and time involved in such custom chip design is high. Thus it becomes attractive to develop a general-purpose chip that can be readily adapted to specific purposes. This is the intent of the *programmable logic array* (PLA).

The PLA is based on the fact that any boolean function (truth table) can be expressed in a sum-of-products (SOP) form, as we have seen. The PLA consists

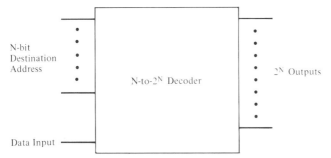

FIGURE A-17.   Implementation of a demultiplexer using a decoder

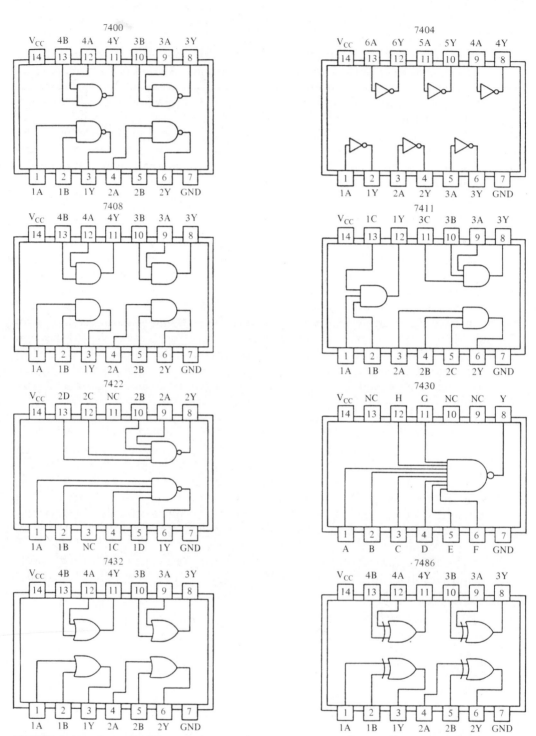

FIGURE A-18. Some SSI chips. Pin layouts from *The TTL Data Book for Design Engineers,* copyright © 1976 Texas Instruments Incorporated

of a regular arrangement of NOT, AND, and OR gates on a chip. Each chip input is passed through a NOT gate so that each input and its complement are available to each AND gate. The output of each AND gate is available to each OR gate, and the output of each OR gate is a chip output. By making the appropriate connections, arbitrary SOP expressions can be implemented.

Figure A-19a shows a PLA with three inputs, eight gates, and two outputs. Most larger PLAs contain several hundred gates, 15 to 25 inputs, and 5 to 15 outputs. The connections from the inputs to the AND gates, and from the AND gates to the OR gates, are not specified.

PLAs are manufactured in two different ways to allow easy programming (making of connections). In the first, every possible connection is made through a fuse at every intersection point. The undesired connections can then be later removed by blowing the fuses. This type of PLA is referred to as a *field-program-mable logic array*. Alternatively, the proper connections can be made during chip fabrication by using an appropriate mask supplied for a particular interconnection pattern. In either case, the PLA provides a flexible, inexpensive way of implementing digital logic functions.

Figure A-19b shows a design that realizes two boolean expressions.

Read-Only Memory (ROM)

Combinational circuits are often referred to as "memoryless" circuits, since their output depends only on their current input and no history of prior inputs is retained. However, there is one sort of memory that is implemented with combinational circuits, namely *read-only memory* (ROM).

Recall that a ROM is a memory unit that performs only the read operation. This implies that the binary information stored in a ROM is permanent and was created during the fabrication process. Thus a given input to the ROM (address lines) always produces the same output (data lines). Because the outputs are a function only of the present inputs, the ROM is in fact a combinational circuit.

A ROM can be implemented with a decoder and a set of OR gates. As an example, consider Table A-8. This can be viewed as a truth table with four inputs and four outputs. For each of the 16 possible input values, the corresponding set of values of the outputs is shown. It can also be viewed as defining the contents of a 64-bit ROM consisting of 16 words of 4 bits each. The four inputs specify an address, and the four outputs specify the contents of the location specified by the address. Figure A-20 shows how this memory could be implemented using a 4-to-16 decoder and four OR gates. As with the PLA, a regular organization is used, and the interconnections are made to reflect the desired result.

Adders

So far, we have seen how interconnected gates can be used to implement such functions as the routing of signals, decoding, and ROM. One essential area not

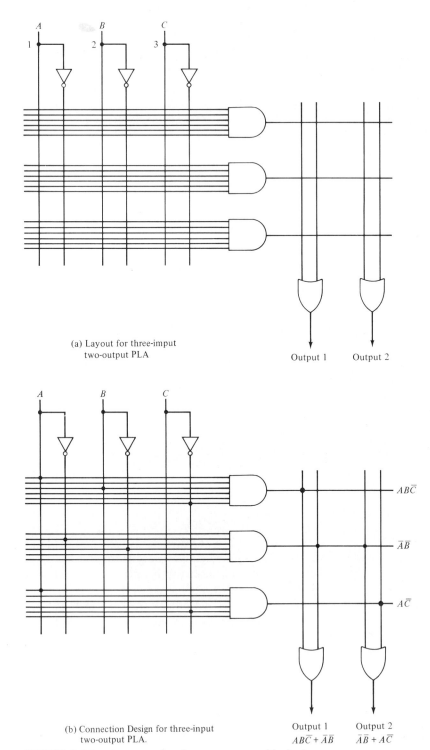

(a) Layout for three-imput
two-output PLA

Output 1   Output 2

$AB\overline{C}$

$\overline{A}\overline{B}$

$A\overline{C}$

(b) Connection Design for three-input
two-output PLA.

Output 1   Output 2
$AB\overline{C} + \overline{A}\overline{B}$ $\overline{A}\overline{B} + A\overline{C}$

FIGURE A-19.   An example of an programmable logic array

TABLE A-8   Truth Table for a ROM

Input				Output			
0	0	0	0	0	0	0	0
0	0	0	1	0	0	0	1
0	0	1	0	0	0	1	1
0	0	1	1	0	0	1	0
0	1	0	0	0	1	1	0
0	1	0	1	0	1	1	1
0	1	1	0	0	1	0	1
0	1	1	1	0	1	0	0
1	0	0	0	1	1	0	0
1	0	0	1	1	1	0	1
1	0	1	0	1	1	1	1
1	0	1	1	1	1	1	0
1	1	0	0	1	0	1	0
1	1	0	1	1	0	1	1
1	1	1	0	1	0	0	1
1	1	1	1	1	0	0	0

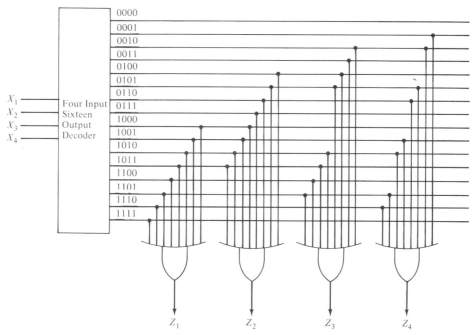

FIGURE A-20.   A 64-bit ROM

TABLE A-9   Binary Addition Truth Tables

(a) Single-Bit Addition				(b) Addition with Carry Input				
A	B	Sum	Carry	C_{in}	A	B	Sum	C_{out}
0	0	0	0	0	0	0	0	0
0	1	1	0	0	0	1	1	0
1	0	1	0	0	1	0	1	0
1	1	0	1	0	1	1	0	1
				1	0	0	1	0
				1	0	1	0	1
				1	1	0	0	1
				1	1	1	1	1

yet addressed is that of arithmetic. In this brief overview, we will content our-
selves with looking at the addition function.

Binary addition differs from boolean algebra in that the result includes a carry
term. Thus,

$$\begin{array}{cccc} 0 & 0 & 1 & 1 \\ +\ 0 & +\ 1 & +\ 0 & +\ 1 \\ \hline 0 & 1 & 1 & 11 \end{array}$$

However, addition can still be dealt with in boolean terms. In Table A-9a, we
show the logic for adding 2 input bits to produce a 1-bit sum and a carry bit. This
truth table could easily be implemented in digital logic. However, we are not
interested in performing addition on just a single pair of bits. Rather, we wish to
add two n-bit numbers. This can be done by putting together a set of adders so
that the carry from one adder is provided as input to the next. A 4-bit adder is
depicted in Figure A-21.

For a multiple-bit adder to work, each of the single-bit adders must have three
inputs, including the carry from the next-lower-order adder. The revised truth
table appears in Table A-9b. The two outputs can be expressed:

$Sum = \overline{A}\,\overline{B}C + \overline{A}B\overline{C} + ABC + A\overline{B}\,\overline{C}$

$Carry = AB + AC + BC$

Figure A-22 is an implementation using AND, OR, and NOT gates.

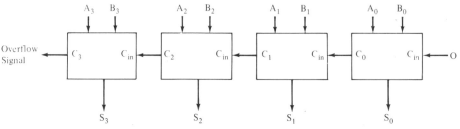

FIGURE A-21.   4-bit adder

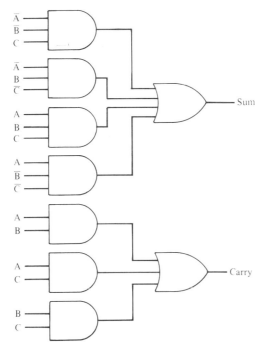

FIGURE A-22. Implementation of an adder

Thus we have the necessary logic to implement a multiple-bit adder such as shown in Figure A-23. Note that since the output from each adder depends on the carry from the previous adder, there is an increasing delay from the least significant to the most significant bit. Each single-bit adder experiences a certain amount of gate delay, and this gate delay accumulates. For larger adders, the accumulated delay can become unacceptably high.

If the carry values could be determined without having to ripple through all the previous stages, then each single-bit adder could function independently and delay would not accumulate. This can be achieved with an approach known as *carry lookahead*. Let us look again at the 4-bit adder to explain this approach.

We would like to come up with an expression that specifies the carry input to any stage of the adder without reference to previous carry values. We have

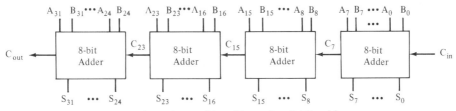

FIGURE A-23.   Construction of a 32-bit adder using 8-bit adders

$$C_0 = A_0 B_0 \tag{A-4}$$
$$C_1 = A_1 B_1 + (A_1 + B_1)C_0 \tag{A-5}$$

Substituting Equation A-4 into A-5,

$$C_1 = A_1 B_1 + A_1 A_0 B_0 + B_1 A_0 B_0$$

Following the same procedure, we get

$$C_2 = A_2 B_2 + A_2 A_1 B_1 + A_2 A_1 A_0 B_0 + A_2 B_1 A_0 B_0$$
$$+ B_2 A_1 B_1 + B_2 A_1 A_0 B_0 + B_2 B_1 A_0 B_0$$

This process can be repeated for arbitrarily long adders. Each carry term can be expressed in SOP form as a function only of the original inputs, with no dependence on the carries. Thus, only two levels of gate delay occur regardless of the length of the adder.

For long numbers, this approach becomes excessively complicated. Evaluating the expression for the most significant bit of an n-bit adder requires an OR gate with $n - 1$ inputs and n AND gates with from 2 to $n + 1$ inputs. Accordingly, full carry lookahead is typically done only 4 to 8 bits at a time. Figure A-23 shows how a 32-bit adder can be constructed out of four 8-bit adders. In this case, the carry must ripple through the four 8-bit adders, but this will be substantially quicker than a ripple through 32 1-bit adders.

A.4

SEQUENTIAL CIRCUITS

Combinational circuits implement the essential functions of a digital computer. However, except for the special case of ROM, they provide no memory or state information, elements also essential to the operation of a digital computer. For the latter purposes a more complex form of digital logic circuit is used: the sequential circuit. The current output of a sequential circuit depends not only on the current input, but also on the past history of inputs. Another and generally more useful way to view it is that the current output of a sequential circuit depends on the current input and the current state of that circuit.

In this section, we examine some simple but useful examples of sequential circuits. As will be seen, the sequential circuit makes use of combinational circuits.

Flip-Flops

The simplest form of sequential circuit is the flip-flop. There are a variety of flip-flops, all of which share two properties:

- The flip-flop is a bistable device. It exists in one of two states and, in the absence of input, remains in that state. Thus the flip-flop can function as a 1-bit memory.
- The flip-flop has two outputs, which are always the complements of each other. These are generally labeled Q and $\overline{Q}$.

The S–R Latch

Figure A-24 shows a common configuration known as the S-R flip-flop or *S-R latch*. The circuit has two inputs, S (Set) and R (Reset), and two outputs, Q and $\overline{Q}$, and consists of two NOR gates hooked together in a feedback arrangement.

First, let us show that the circuit is bistable. Assume that both S and R are 0 and that Q is 0. The inputs to the lower NOR gate are $Q = 0$ and $S = 0$. Thus the output $\overline{Q} = 1$ means that the inputs to the upper NOR gate are $\overline{Q} = 1$ and $R = 0$, which has the output $Q = 0$. Thus, the state of the circuit is internally consistent and remains stable as long as $S = R = 0$. A similar line of reasoning shows that the state $Q = 1$, $\overline{Q} = 0$ is also stable for $R = S = 0$.

Thus, this circuit can function as a 1-bit memory. We can view the output Q as the "value" of the bit. The inputs S and R serve to write the values 1 and 0, respectively, into memory. To see this, consider the state $Q = 0$, $\overline{Q} = 1$, $S = 0$, $R = 0$. Suppose that S changes to the value 1. Now the inputs to the lower NOR gate are $S = 1$, $Q = 0$. After some time delay Δt, the output of the lower NOR gate will be $\overline{Q} = 0$ (see Figure A-25). So, at this point in time, the inputs to the upper NOR gate become $R = 0$, $\overline{Q} = 0$. After another gate delay of Δt, the output Q becomes 1. This is again a stable state. The inputs to the lower gate are now $S = 1$, $Q = 1$, which maintain the output $Q = 0$. As long as $S = 1$ and $R = 0$, the outputs will remain $Q = 1$, $Q = 0$. Furthermore, if S returns to 0, the outputs will remain unchanged.

The R output performs the opposite function. When R goes to 1, it forces $Q = 0$, $Q = 1$ regardless of the previous state of Q and $\overline{Q}$. Again, a time delay of $2\Delta t$ occurs before stability is re-established (Figure A-25).

The S-R latch can be defined with a table similar to a truth table, called a *characteristic table*, which shows the next state or states of a sequential circuit as a

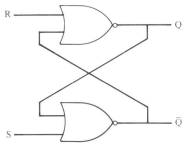

FIGURE A-24.   The S-R latch implemented with NOR gates

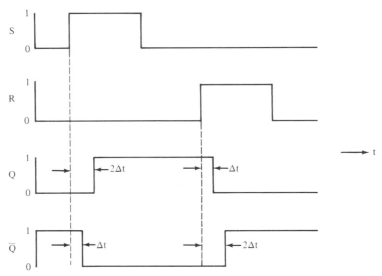

FIGURE A-25. NOR S-R latch timing diagram

function of current states and inputs. In the case of the S-R latch, the state can be defined by the value of Q. Table A-10a shows the resulting characteristic table. Observe that the inputs $S = 1$, $R = 1$ are not allowed, since these would produce an inconsistent output (both Q and $\overline{Q}$ equal 0). The table can be expressed more

TABLE A-10   The S–R Latch

(a) Characteristic Table

Current Inputs	Current State	Next State
SR	Q_n	Q_{n+1}
00	0	0
00	1	1
01	0	0
01	1	0
10	0	1
10	1	1
11	0	—
11	1	—

(b) Simplified Characteristic Table

S	R	Q_{n+1}
0	0	Q_n
0	1	0
1	0	1
1	1	—

(c) Response to Series of Inputs

t	0	1	2	3	4	5	6	7	8	9
S	1	0	0	0	0	0	0	0	1	0
R	0	0	0	1	0	0	1	0	0	0
Q_{n+1}	1	1	1	0	0	0	0	0	1	1

compactly, as in Table A-10b. An illustration of the behavior of the S-R latch is shown in Table A-10c.

Clocked S–R Flip-Flop

The output of the S-R latch changes, after a brief time delay, in response to a change in the input. This is referred to as *asynchronous operation*. More typically, events in the digital computer are synchronized to a clock pulse, so that changes occur only when a clock pulse occurs. Figure A-26 shows this arrangement. This device is referred to as a *clocked S-R flip-flop*. Note that the R and S inputs are passed to the NOR gates only during the clock pulse.

D Flip-Flop

One problem with S-R flip-flop is that the condition $R = 1$, $S = 1$ must be avoided. One way to do this is to allow just a single input. The D flip-flop accomplishes this. Figure A-27 shows a gate implementation and the character-

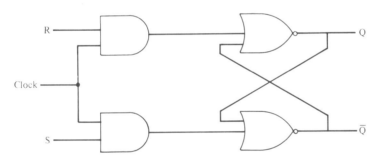

FIGURE A-26. Clocked S-R flip-flop

D	Q_{n+1}
0	0
1	1

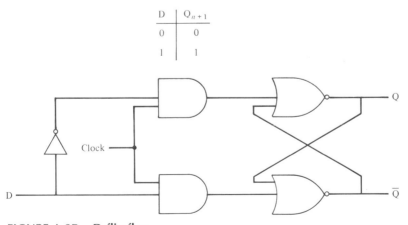

FIGURE A-27. D flip-flop

istic table of the D flip-flop. By using an inverter, the nonclock inputs to the two AND gates are guaranteed to be the opposite of each other.

The D flip-flop is sometimes referred to as the data flip-flop because it is, in effect, storage for one bit of data. The output of the D flip-flop is always equal to the most recent value applied to the input. Hence, it remembers and produces the last input. It is also referred to as the delay flip-flop, because it delays a 0 or 1 applied to its input for a single clock pulse.

J-K Flip-Flop

Another useful flip-flop is the J-K flip-flop. Like the S-R flip-flop, it has two inputs. However, in this case all possible combinations of input values are valid. Figure A-28 shows a gate implementation of the J-K flip-flop, and Figure A-29 shows its characteristic table (along with those for the S-R and D flip-flops). Note that the first three combinations are the same as for the S-R flip-flop. With no input, the output is stable. The J input alone performs a set function, causing the output to be 1; the K input alone performs a reset function, causing the output to be 0. When both J and K are 1, the function performed is referred to as the *toggle* function: the output is reversed. Thus, if Q is 1 and 1 is applied to J and K, then Q becomes 0. The reader should verify that the implementation of Figure A-28 produces this characteristic function.

Registers

As an example of the use of flip-flops, let us first examine one of the essential elements of the CPU: the register. As we know, a register is a digital circuit used within the CPU to store one or more bits of data. Two basic types of registers are commonly used: parallel registers and shift registers.

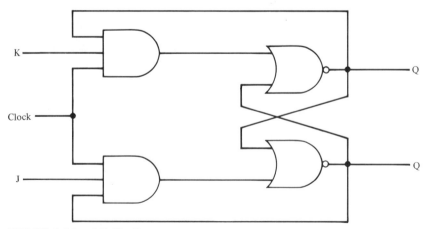

FIGURE A-28.   J-K flip-flop

Name	Graphic Symbol	Characteristic Table		

S-R

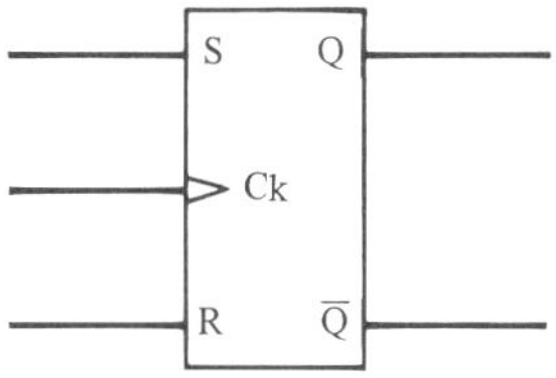

S	R	Q_{n+1}
0	0	Q_n
0	1	0
1	0	1
1	1	—

J-K

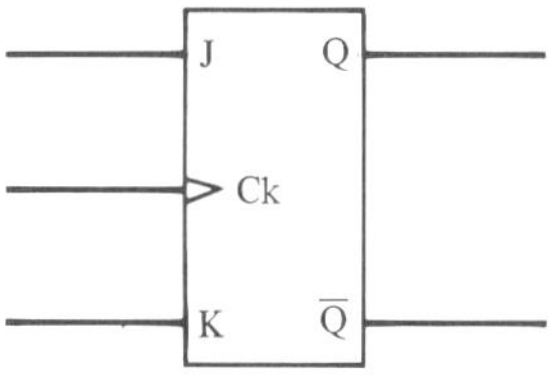

J	K	Q_{n+1}
0	0	Q_n
0	1	0
1	0	1
1	1	$\overline{Q_n}$

D

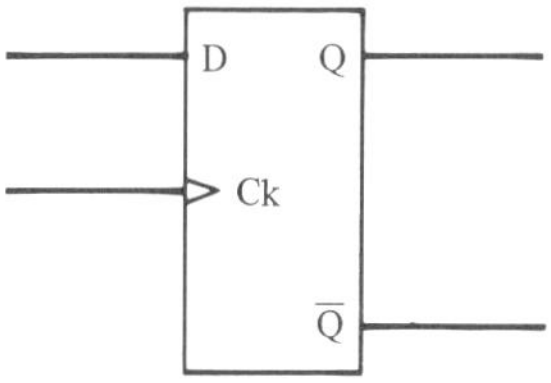

D	Q_{n+1}
0	0
1	1

FIGURE A-29. Basic flip-flops

Parallel Registers

A parallel register consists of a set of 1-bit memories that can be read or written simultaneously. It is used to store data. The registers that we have discussed throughout this book are parallel registers.

The 8-bit register of Figure A-30 illustrates the operation of a parallel register. S-R latches are used. A control signal, labeled *input data strobe*, controls writing into the register from signal lines, D11 through D18. These lines might be the output of multiplexers, so that data from a variety of sources can be loaded into the register. Output is controlled in a similar fashion. As an extra feature, a reset line is available that allows the register to be easily set to 0. Note that this could not be accomplished as easily with a register constructed from D flip-flops.

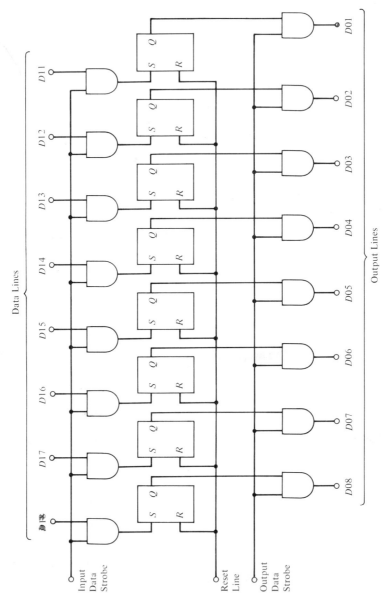

FIGURE A-30.   8-bit parallel register

Shift Register

A shift register accepts and/or transfers information serially. Consider, for example, Figure A-31, which shows a 5-bit shift register constructed from clocked S-R flip-flops. Data are input only to the leftmost flip-flop. With each clock pulse, data are shifted to the right one position, and the rightmost bit is transferred out.

Shift registers can be used to interface to serial I/O devices. In addition, they can be used within the ALU to perform logical shift and rotate functions. In this latter capacity, they need to be equipped with parallel read/write circuitry as well as serial.

Counters

Another useful category of sequential circuit is the counter. A counter is a register whose value is easily incremented by 1 modulo the capacity of the register. Thus, a register made up of n flip-flops can count up to $2^n - 1$. When the counter is incremented beyond its maximum value, it is set to 0. An example of a counter in the CPU is the program counter.

Counters can be designated as asynchronous or synchronous, depending on the way in which they operate. Asynchronous counters are relatively slow since the output of one flip-flop triggers a change in the status of the next flip-flop. In a synchronous counter, all of the flip-flops change state at the same time. Because the latter type is much faster, it is the kind used in CPUs. However, it is useful to begin the discussion with a description of an asynchronous counter.

Ripple Counter

An asynchronous counter is also referred to as a ripple counter, since the change that occurs in order to increment the counter starts at one end and "ripples" through to the other end. Figure A-32 shows an implementation of a 4-bit counter using J-K flip-flops, together with a timing diagram that illustrates its behavior. The timing diagram is idealized in that it does not show the propagation delay that occurs as the signals move down the series of flip-flops. The output of the left-most flip-flop (Q_0) is the least significant bit. The design could clearly be extended to an arbitrary number of bits by cascading more flip-flops.

In the illustrated implementation, the counter is incremented with each clock pulse. The J and K inputs to each flip-flop are held at a constant one. This means

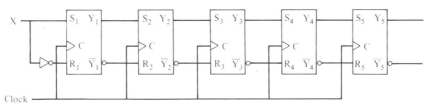

FIGURE A-31.   5-bit shift register

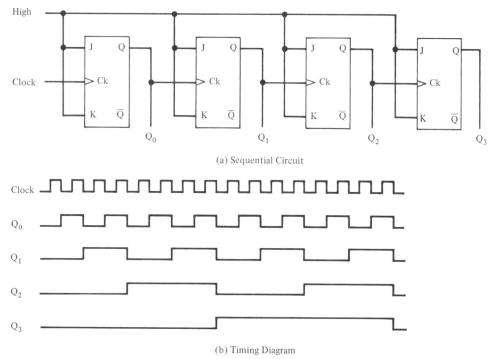

(a) Sequential Circuit

(b) Timing Diagram

FIGURE A-32.   Ripple counter

that, when there is a clock pulse, the output at Q will be inverted (1 to 0; 0 to 1). Note that the change in state is shown as occurring with the falling edge of the clock pulse; this is known as an edge-triggered flip-flop. Using flip-flops that respond to the transition in a clock pulse rather than the pulse itself provides better timing control in complex circuits. If one looks at patterns of output for this counter, it can be seen that it cycles through 0000, 0001, . . . , 1110, 1111, 0000, and so on.

Synchronous Counters

The ripple counter has the disadvantage of the delay involved in changing value, which is proportional to the length of the counter. To overcome this disadvantage, CPUs make use of synchronous counters, in which all of the flip-flops of the counter change at the same time. In this subsection, we present a design for a 3-bit synchronous counter. In doing so, we illustrate some basic concepts in the design of a synchronous circuit.

For a 3-bit counter, three flip-flops will be needed. Let us use J-K flip-flops. Label the uncomplemented output of the three flip-flops A, B, C respectively, with C representing the least significant bit. The first step is to construct a truth table that relates the J-K inputs and outputs, to allow us to design the overall circuit. Such a truth table is shown in Figure A-33a. The first three columns show the possible combinations of outputs A, B, and C. They are listed in the order that they will appear as the counter is incremented. Each row lists the current value of A, B, C and the inputs to the three flip-flops that will be required to reach the next value of A, B, C.

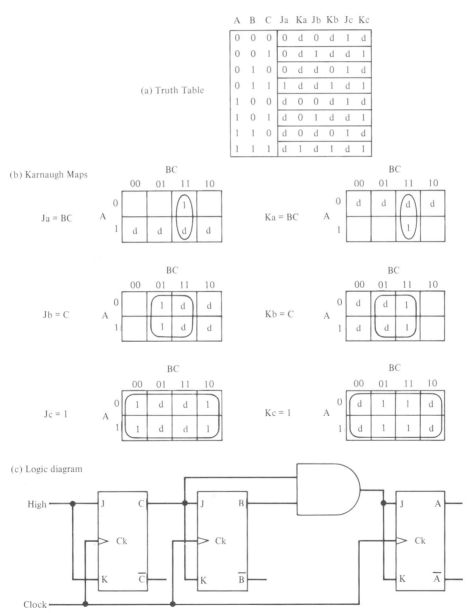

FIGURE A-33. Design of a synchronous counter

To understand the way in which the truth table of Figure A-33a is constructed, it may be helpful to recast the characteristic table for the J-K flip-flop. Recall that this table was presented as follows:

J	K	Q_{n+1}
0	0	Q_n
0	1	0
1	0	$\overline{Q}x_{n+1}$

In this form, the table shows the effect that the J and K inputs have on the output. Now consider the following organization of the same information:

Q_n	J	K	Q_{n+1}
0	0	d	0
0	1	d	1
1	d	1	0
1	d	0	1

In this form, the table provides the value of the next output when the inputs and the present output are known. This is exactly the information needed to design the counter or, indeed, any sequential circuit. In this form, the table is referred to as an *excitation table*.

Let us return to Figure A-33a. Consider the first row. We want the value of A to remain 0, the value of B to remain 0, and the value of C to go from 0 to 1 with the next application of a clock pulse. The excitation table shows that to maintain an output of 0, we must have inputs of $J = 0$ and don't care for K. To effect a transition from 0 to 1, the inputs must be $J = 1$ and $K = d$. These values are shown in the first row of the table. By similar reasoning, the remainder of the table can be filled in.

Having constructed the truth table of Figure A-33a, we see that the table shows the required values of all of the J and K inputs as functions of the current value of A, B, and C. With the aid of Karnaugh maps we can develop boolean expressions for these six functions. This is shown in part b of the figure. For example, the Karnaugh map for the variable Ja (the J input to the flip-flop that produces the A output) yields the expression Ja = BC. When all six expressions are derived, it is a straightforward matter to design the actual circuit, as shown in part c of the figure.

A.5

RECOMMENDED READING

The literature in this area is vast, and the following recommendations are just samples of what is available. [FLOY90] and [REIS91] are both easy-to-follow yet thorough accounts that cover the material of this appendix. More rigorous treatments that can be highly recommended are [MANO91] and [WAKE90]. Another good text, with a somewhat different emphasis than most texts, is [UNGE89].

A.6

PROBLEMS

A.1 Construct a truth table for the following boolean expressions:
   (a) $ABC + \overline{AB}\,\overline{C}$ (b) $ABC + AB\overline{C} + \overline{A}\,\overline{B}\,\overline{C}$
   (c) $A(B\overline{C} + \overline{B}C)$ (d) $(A + B)(A + C)(\overline{A} + \overline{B})$

A.2 Simplify the following expressions according to the commutative law:
   (a) $A \cdot \overline{B} + \overline{B} \cdot A + C \cdot D \cdot E + \overline{C} \cdot D \cdot E + E \cdot \overline{C} \cdot D$
   (b) $A \cdot B + A \cdot C + B \cdot A$
   (c) $(L \cdot M \cdot N)(A \cdot B)(C \cdot D \cdot E)(M \cdot N \cdot L)$
   (d) $F \cdot (K + R) + S \cdot V + W \cdot \overline{X} + V \cdot S + \overline{X} \cdot W + (R + K) \cdot F$

A.3 Apply deMorgan's theorem to the following equations:
   (a) $F = \overline{V + A + L}$
   (b) $F = \overline{A} + \overline{B} + \overline{C} + \overline{D}$

A.4 Simplify the following expressions:
   (a) $A = S \cdot T + V \cdot W + R \cdot S \cdot T$
   (b) $A = T \cdot U \cdot V + X \cdot Y + Y$
   (c) $A = F \cdot (E + F + G)$
   (d) $A = (P \cdot Q + R + S \cdot T)T \cdot S$
   (e) $A = \overline{\overline{D} \cdot \overline{D} \cdot E}$
   (f) $A = Y \cdot (W + X + \overline{Y} + \overline{Z}) \cdot Z$
   (g) $A = (B \cdot E + C + F) \cdot C$

A.5 Construct the operation XOR from the basic boolean operations AND, OR, and NOT.

A.6 Given the following boolean expression:

$$F = \overline{A}\overline{B}\overline{C} + \overline{A}BC + A\overline{B}C$$

   (a) Develop an equivalent expression using only NAND operations, and draw the logic diagram.
   (b) Develop an equivalent expression using only NOR operations, and draw the logic diagram.

A.7 Given a NOR gate and NOT gates, draw a logic diagram that will perform the 3-input AND function.

A.8 Write the boolean expression for a 4-input NAND gate.

A.9 A combinational circuit is used to control a 7-segment display of decimal digits, as shown in Figure A-34. The circuit has four inputs, which provide the 4-bit code used in packed decimal representation ($0_{10} = 0000$, . . . , $9_{10} = 1001$). The seven outputs define which segments will be activated to display a given decimal digit. Note that some combinations of inputs and outputs are not needed.
   (a) Develop a truth table for this circuit.
   (b) Express the truth table in SOP form.
   (c) Express the truth table in POS form.
   (d) Provide a simplified expression.

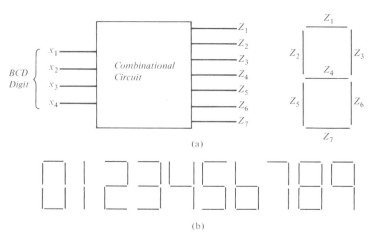

(a)

(b)

FIGURE A-34.   Seven-segment LED display example

A.10 Design an 8-to-1 multiplexer.

A.11 Add an additional line to Figure A-15 so that it functions as a demultiplexer.

A.12 The Gray code is a binary code for integers. It differs from the ordinary binary representation in that there is just a single bit change between the representations of any two numbers. This is useful for applications such as counters or analog-to-digital converters where a sequence of numbers is generated. Because only one bit changes at a time, there is never any ambiguity due to slight timing differences. The first eight elements of the code are

Binary Code	Gray Code
000	000
001	001
010	011
011	010
100	110
101	111
110	101
111	100

Design a circuit that converts from binary to Gray code.

A.13 Design a 5 × 32 decoder using four 3 × 8 decoders (with enable inputs) and one 2 × 4 decoder.

A.14 Derive a PLA and a ROM implementation for the following set of combinational functions:

$$Z_1 = X_1X_2X_3\overline{X_4} + X_1X_2\overline{X_3}\overline{X_4} + X_1\overline{X_2}X_3X_4 + \overline{X_1}X_2X_3X_4$$
$$+ \overline{X_1}\overline{X_2}X_3X_4 + \overline{X_1}X_2\overline{X_3}X_4 + \overline{X_1}\overline{X_2}\overline{X_3}\overline{X_4}$$

$$Z_2 = X_1X_2X_3X_4 + X_1X_2X_3\overline{X_4} + X_1\overline{X_2}X_3\overline{X_4} + \overline{X_1}X_2X_3X_4$$
$$\qquad + \overline{X_1}\overline{X_2}X_3X_4$$
$$Z_3 = X_1X_2\overline{X_3}X_4 + X_1\overline{X_2}X_3X_4 + X_1\overline{X_2}X_3\overline{X_4} + X_1\overline{X_2}X_3X_4$$
$$\qquad + \overline{X_1}\overline{X_2}X_3\overline{X_4} + \overline{X_1}\overline{X_2}\overline{X_3}\overline{X_4}$$

A.15 Implement the full adder of Figure A-22 with just five gates.
(Hint: Some of the gates are XOR gates.)

A.16 Consider Figure A-22. Assume that each gate produces a delay of 10 ns.
Thus the sum output is valid after 30 ns and the carry output after 0 ns.
What is the total add time for a 32-bit adder:
(a) Implemented without carry lookahead, as in Figure A-21?
(b) Implemented with carry lookahead and using 8-bit adders, as in Figure A-23?

A.17 Draw a realization of a D flip-flop using only NAND gates.

References

ABAD83 ABADIR, M., AND REGHBATI, H. "Functional Testing of Semiconductor Random Access Memories." *Computing Surveys*, September, 1983.

ACOS86 ACOSTA, R.; KJELSTRUP, J.; AND TORNG, H. "An Instruction Issuing Approach to Enhancing Performance in Multiple Functional Unit Processors." *IEEE Transactions on Computers*, September 1986.

AGAR89a AGARWAL, A. *Analysis of Cache Performance for Operating Systems and Multiprogramming*. Boston: Kluwer Academic Publishers, 1989.

AGAR89b AGARWAL, A.; HOROWITZ, M.; AND HENNESSY, J. "An Analytical Cache Model." *ACM Transactions on Computer Systems*, May 1989.

AGER87 AGERWALA, T., AND COCKE, J. *High Performance Reduced Instruction Set Processors*. Technical Report RC12434 (#55845). Yorktown, NY: IBM Thomas J. Watson Research Center, January 1987.

AGRA76 AGRAWALA, A., AND RAUSCHER, T. *Foundations of Microprogramming: Architecture, Software, and Applications*. New York: Academic Press, 1976.

ALLI88 ALLISON, A. "Where There's RISC, There's Opportunity." *Mini-Micro Systems*, January 1988.

ALPE88 ALPERT, D., AND FLYNN, M. "Performance Trade-offs for Microprocessor Cache Memories." *IEEE Micro*, August 1988.

ALSU90 ALSUP, M. "The Motorola's 88000 Family Architecture." *IEEE Micro*, June 1990.

ALTN79 ALTNETHER, J. *Error Detecting and Correcting Codes*. Intel Application Note AP-46, 1979. Reprinted in [INTE85a].

AMDA79 AMDAHL, G. "The Early Chapters of the PCM Story." *Datamation*, February, 1979.

ANDE67 ANDERSON, D.; SPARACIO, F.; AND TOMASULO, F. "The IBM System/360 Model 91: Machine Philosophy and Instruction Handling." *IBM Journal of Research and Development*, January, 1967.

ANDR80 ANDREWS, M. *Principles of Firmware Engineering in Microprogram Control*. Silver Spring, MD: Computer Science Press, 1980.

ANDR90 ANDREWS, W. "Futurebus+ Spec Completed—Almost." *Computer Design*, February 1, 1990.

ANDR91 ANDREWS, W. "Enhancing the Performance of Standard Buses." *Computer Design,* September 1991.

ANSI90 AMERICAN NATIONAL STANDARDS INSTITUTE. *American National Standard Dictionary for Information Systems.* ANSI X3.172-1990, 1990.

ARDE80 ARDEN, B. *What Can Be Automated?* Cambridge, MA: The MIT Press, 1980.

AUER79 Auerbach Publishers, Inc. "Basic Architectures for System Control Mechanisms." *Computer Technology Reports: Mainframe Computers,* Pennsauken, NJ, 1979.

BAKE90 BAKER, T. "Headroom and Legroom in the 80960 Architecture." *Proceedings, COMPCON Spring '90,* March 1990.

BANE82 BANERJI, D., AND RAYMOND, J. *Elements of Microprogramming.* Englewood Cliffs, NJ: Prentice-Hall, 1982.

BARR68 BARRON, D. *Recursive Techniques in Programming.* New York: American Elsevier, 1968.

BART85 BARTEE, T. *Digital Computer Fundamentals.* New York: McGraw-Hill, 1985.

BASH81 BASHE, C.; BUCHOLTZ, W.; HAWKINS, G.; INGRAM, J.; AND ROCHESTER, N. "The Architecture of IBM's Early Computers." *IBM Journal of Research and Development,* September, 1981.

BASH91 BASHTEEN, A.; LUI, I.; AND MULLAN, J. "A Superpipeline Approach to the MIPS Architecture." *Proceedings, COMPCON Spring '91,* February 1991.

BELL70 BELL, C.; CADY, R.; McFARLAND, H.; DELAGI, B.; O'LOUGHLIN, J.; AND NOONAN, R. "A New Architecture for Minicomputers—The DEC PDP-11." *Proceedings, Spring Joint Computer Conference,* 1970.

BELL71A BELL, C., AND NEWELL, A. *Computer Structures: Readings and Examples.* New York: McGraw-Hill, 1971.

BELL71B BELL, C., AND NEWELL, A. "The IBM 1401." in [BELL71a].

BELL78A BELL, C.; MUDGE, J.; AND McNAMARA, J. *Computer Engineering: A DEC View of Hardware Systems Design.* Bedford, MA: Digital Press, 1978.

BELL78B BELL, C.; NEWELL, A.; AND SIEWIOREK, D. "Structural Levels of the PDP-8." in [BELL78a].

BELL78C BELL, C.; KOTOK, A.; HASTINGS, T.; AND HILL, R. "The Evolution of the DEC System-10." *Communications of the ACM,* January, 1978.

BHAN79 BHANDARKAR, D., AND ROTHMAN, S. "The VAX-11, DEC's 32-Bit Version of the PDP-11." *Datamation,* February, 1979.

BIC88 BIC, L., AND SHAW, A. *The Logical Design of Operating Systems.* Englewood Cliffs, NJ: Prentice-Hall, 1988.

BOND83 BOND, R. "XA: The View from White Plains." *Datamation,* May, 1983.

BOOT51 BOOTH, A. "A Signed Binary Multiplication Technique." *Quarterly Journal of Mechanical and Applied Mathematics,* vol. 4, pt. 2, 1951.

BRAD91A BRADLEE, D.; EGGERS, S.; AND HENRY, R. "The Effect on RISC Performance of Register Set Size and Structure Versus Code Generation Strategy." *Proceedings, 18th Annual International Symposium on Computer Architecture,* May 1991.

BRAD91B   BRADLEE, D.; EGGERS, S.; AND HENRY, R. "Integrating Register Allocation and Instruction Scheduling for RISCs." *Proceedings, Fourth International Conference on Architectural Support for Programming Languages and Operating Systems*, April 1991.

BREY91   BREY, B. *The Intel Microprocessors—8086/8088, 80186, 80286, 80386, and 80486: Architecture, Programming, and Interfacing.* New York: Merrill/Macmillan, 1991.

BUCH86   BUCHHOLZ, W. "The IBM System/370 Vector Architecture." *IBM Systems Journal*, No. 1, 1986.

BUDD87   BUDDINE, L., AND YOUNG, E. *The Brady Guide to CD-ROM.* New York: Prentice-Hall Press, 1987.

BURG75   BURGE, W. *Recursive Programming Techniques.* Reading, MA: Addison-Wesley, 1975.

BURK46   BURKS, A.; GOLDSTINE, H.; AND VON NEUMANN, J. *Preliminary Discussion of the Logical Design of an Electronic Computer Instrument.* Report prepared for U.S. Army Ordnance Dept., 1946, reprinted in [BELL71a].

BUZE75   BUZEN, J. "I/O Subsystem Architecture." *Proceedings of the IEEE*, June, 1975.

CHAI82   CHAITIN, G. "Register Allocation and Spilling via Graph Coloring." *Proceedings, SIGPLAN Symposium on Compiler Construction*, June 1982.

CHEN84   CHEN, C., AND HSIAO, M. "Error-Correcting Codes for Semiconductor Memory Applications: A State of the Art Review." *IBM Journal of Research and Development*, March, 1984.

CHOW86   CHOW, F.; HIMMELSTEIN, M.; KILLIAN, E.; AND WEBER, L. "Engineering a RISC Compiler System." *Proceedings, COMPCON Spring '86*, March 1986.

CHOW87   CHOW, F.; CORRELL, S.; HIMMELSTEIN, M.; KILLIAN, E.; AND WEBER, L. "How Many Addressing Modes Are Enough?" *Proceedings, Second International Conference on Architectural Support for Programming Languages and Operating Systems*, October 1987.

CHOW90   CHOW, F., AND HENNESSY, J. "The Priority-Based Coloring Approach to Register Allocation." *ACM Transactions on Programming Languages*, October 1990.

CLAR80   CLARK, W. "From Electron Mobility to Logical Structure: A View of Integrated Circuits." *Computing Surveys*, September, 1980.

CLAR82   CLARK, D., AND LEVY, H. "Measurement and Analysis of Instruction Use in the VAX-11/780." *Proceedings, Ninth Annual Symposium on Computer Architecture*, April, 1982.

CLAR83   CLARK, D. "Cache Performance in the VAX-11/780." *ACM Transactions on Computer Systems*, February, 1983.

CLAR85   CLARK, D., AND EMER, J. "Performance of the VAX-11/780 Translation Buffer: Simulation and Measurement." *ACM Transactions on Computer Systems*, February 1985.

CLIN81   CLINE, B. *Microprogramming Concepts and Techniques.* New York: Petrocelli, 1981.

CODY84   Cody, W., et al. "A Proposed Radix- and Word-Length-Independent Standard for Floating-Point Arithmetic." *IEEE Micro,* August, 1984.

COLW85a   Colwell, R.; Hitchcock, C.; Jensen, E.; Brinkley-Sprunt, H.; and Kollar, C. "Computers, Complexity, and Controversy." *Computer,* September, 1985.

COLW85b   Colwell, R.; Hitchcock, D.; Jensen, E.; and Sprunt, H. "More Controversy About 'Computers, Complexity, and Controversy.'" *Computer,* December 1985.

CONN79   Connors, W.; Florkowski, J.; and Patton, S. "The IBM 3033: An Inside Look." *Datamation,* May, 1979.

CONW77   Conway, J. "Approach to Unified Bus Architecture Sidestepping Inherent Drawbacks." *Computer Design,* January, 1977.

COOK82   Cook, R., and Dande, N. "An Experiment to Improve Operand Addressing." *Proceedings, Symposium on Architecture Support for Programming Languages and Operating Systems,* March, 1982.

COON80   Coonen, J. "An Implementation Guide to a Proposed Standard for Floating-Point Arithmetic." *Computer,* January, 1980. (Errata in *Computer,* March, 1981.)

CORM83   Cormier, R.; Dugan, R.; and Guyette, R. "System/370 Extended Architecture: The Channel Subsystem." *IBM Journal of Research and Development,* May, 1983.

COUT86   Coutant, D.; Hammond, C.; and Kelley, J. "Compilers for the New Generation of Hewlett-Packard Computers." *Proceedings, COMPCON Spring '86,* March 1986.

CRAG79   Cragon, H. "An Evaluation of Code Space Requirements and Performance of Various Architectures." *Computer Architecture News,* February, 1979.

CRAW90   Crawford, J. "The i486 CPU: Executing Instructions in One Clock Cycle." *IEEE Micro,* February 1990.

DAVI87   Davidson, J., and Vaughan, R. "The Effect of Instruction Set Complexity on Program Size and Memory Performance." *Proceedings, Second International Conference on Architectural Support for Programming Languages and Operating Systems,* October 1987.

DAWS86   Dawson, W., and Dobinson, R. "A Framework for Computer Design." *IEEE Spectrum,* October, 1986.

DAWS87   Dawson, W., and Dobinson, R. "Buses and Bus Standards." *Computer Standards and Interfaces,* June 1987.

DEC78a   Digital Equipment Corporation. *Translation Buffer, Cache, and SBI Control Technical Description.* 1978.

DEC78b   Digital Equipment Corporation. *LSI-11 WCS User's Guide.* 1978.

DEC82   Digital Equipment Corporation. *VAX Technical Summary.* 1982.

DEC83   Digital Equipment Corporation. *PDP-11 Architecture Handbook.* 1983.

DEC86   Digital Equipment Corporation. *VAX Hardware Handbook; Volume 1—1986.* 1986.

DEIT90   DEITEL, H. *An Introduction to Operating Systems.* Reading, MA: Addison-Wesley, 1990.

DENN68   DENNING, P. "The Working Set Model for Program Behavior." *Communications of the ACM*, May, 1968.

DENN84   DENNING, P., AND BROWN, R. "Operating Systems." *Scientific American*, September, 1984.

DERO85   DEROSA, J.; GLACKEMEYER, R.; AND KNIGHT, T. "Design and Implementation of the VAX 8600 Pipeline." *Computer*, May, 1985.

DEST87   DESROCHERS, G. *Principles of Parallel and Multiprocessing.* New York: McGraw-Hill, 1987.

DEWA90   DEWAR, R., AND SMOSNA, M. *"Microprocessors: A Programmer's View."* New York: McGraw-Hill, 1990.

DIJK63   DIJKSTRA, E. "Making an ALGOL Translator for the X1." in *Annual Review of Automatic Programming, Volume 4*, Pergamon, 1963.

DORA82   DORAN, R. "The Amdahl 470V/8 and the IBM 3033: A Comparison of Processor Designs." *Computer*, April, 1982.

DUBB78   DUBBEY, J. *The Mathematical Work of Charles Babbage.* Cambridge, England: Cambridge University Press, 1978.

DUBE91   DUBEY, P., AND FLYNN, M. "Branch Strategies: Modeling and Optimization." *IEEE Transactions on Computers*, October 1991.

DUBO82   DUBOIS, M., AND BRIGGS, F. "Effects of Cache Coherency in Multiprocessors." *IEEE Transactions on Computers*, November, 1982.

DUGA83   DUGAN, R. "System/370 Extended Architecture: A Program View of the Channel Subsystem." *Proceedings, Tenth Annual International Symposium on Computer Architecture*, June, 1983.

ECKE90   ECKERT, R. "Communication Between Computers and Peripheral Devices—An Analogy." *ACM SIGSCE Bulletin*, September 1990.

EDEN83   EDEN, R.; LIVINGSTON, A.; AND WELCH, B. "Integrated Circuits: The Case for Gallium Arsenide." *IEEE Spectrum*, December 1983.

ELAS84   EL-ASFOURI, S.; JOHNSON, O.; AND KING, W. *Computer Organization and Programming: VAX-11.* Reading, MA: Addison-Wesley, 1984.

ELAY79   EL-AYAT, K. "The Intel 8089: An Integrated I/O Processor." *Computer*, June, 1979.

ELAY85   EL-AYAT, K., AND AGARWAL, R. "The Intel 80386—Architecture and Implementation." *IEEE Micro*, December 1985.

ENSL77   ENSLOW, P. "Multiprocessor Organization—A Survey." *ACM Computing Surveys*, March, 1977.

EVAN81   EVANS, C. *The Making of the Micro: A History of the Computer.* New York: Van Nostrand Reinhold, 1981.

FINK88   FINKEL, R. *An Operating System's Vade Mecum.* Englewood Cliffs, NJ: Prentice-Hall, 1988.

FITZ81   FITZPATRICK, D., ET AL. "A RISCy Approach to VLSI." *VLSI Design*, 4th quarter, 1981. Reprinted in *Computer Architecture News*, March, 1982.

FLOY90   FLOYD, T. *Digital Fundamentals.* New York: Merrill/Macmillan, 1990.

FLYN71 FLYNN, M., AND ROSIN, R. "Microprogramming: An Introduction and a Viewpoint." *IEEE Transactions on Computers,* July, 1971. Also in [GALE75].

FLYN85 FLYNN, M.; JOHNSON, J.; AND WAKEFIELD, S. "On Instruction Sets and Their Formats." *IEEE Transactions on Computers,* March, 1985.

FLYN87 FLYNN, M.; MITCHELL, C.; AND MULDER, J. "And Now a Case for More Complex Instruction Sets." *Computer,* September 1987.

FOSS85A FOSSUM, T.; McELROY, J.; AND ENGLISH, B. "New VAX Squeezes Mainframe Power into Mini Package." *Computer Design,* March, 1985.

FOSS85B FOSSUM, T.; GRUNDMANN, W.; AND BLAHA, V. "Floating-Point Processor for the VAX 8600." *Proceedings, COMPCON Spring '85,* 1985.

FOSS85C FOSSUM, T.; McELROY, J.; AND ENGLISH, W. "An Overview of the VAX 8600 System." *Digital Technical Journal,* August 1985.

FOST67 FOSTER, J. *List Processing.* New York: American Elsevier, 1967.

FOX87 FOX, G., AND MESSINA, G. "Advanced Computer Architectures." *Scientific American,* October 1987.

FRAI83 FRAILEY, D. "Word Length of a Computer Architecture: Definitions and Applications." *Computer Architecture News,* June, 1983.

FREE88 FREESE, R. "Optical Disks Become Erasable." *IEEE Spectrum,* February, 1988.

FUJI84 FUJITANI, L. "Laser Optical Disk: The Coming Revolution in On-Line Storage." *Communications of the ACM,* June 1984.

FURH87 FURHT, B., AND MILUTINOVIC, V. "A Survey of Microprocessor Architectures for Memory Management." *Computer,* March 1987.

GALE75 GALEY, J., AND KLEIR, R. *Microprogramming: A Tutorial on the Queen Mary.* Silver Spring, MD: IEEE Computer Society, 1975.

GEHR88 GEHRINGER, E.; ABULLARADE, J.; AND GULYN, M. "A Survey of Commercial Parallel Processors." *Computer Architecture News,* September 1988.

GIBS88 GIBSON, S. "Hardware Roundup: Large and Medium-Scale Systems." *Computerworld,* September 19, 1988.

GIFF87 GIFFORD, D., AND SPECTOR, A. "Case Study: IBM's System/360-370 Architecture." *Communications of the ACM,* April 1987.

GIMA87 GIMARC, C., AND MILUTINOVIC, V. "A Survey of RISC Processors and Computers of the Mid-1980s." *Computer,* September 1987.

GLAS91 GLASS, B. "The MIPS R4000." *Byte,* December 1991.

GOLD72 GOLDSTINE, H. *The Computer from Pascal to von Neumann.* Princeton: Princeton University Press, 1972.

GOOD83 GOODMAN, J. "Using Cache Memory to Reduce Processor-Memory Traffic." *Proceedings, Tenth Annual International Symposium on Computer Architecture,* June, 1983.

GOOR89 GOOR, A. *Computer Architecture and Design.* Reading, MA: Addison-Wesley, 1989.

GOSL80 GOSLING, J. *Design of Arithmetic Units for Digital Computers.* London: Macmillan Press, 1980.

GOSS89 GOSS, R. "Motorola's 88000: Integration, Performance and Applications." *Proceedings, COMPCOM Spring '89,* March 1989.

GUPT83 GUPTA, A., AND TOONG, H. "Microprocessors—The First Twelve Years." *Proceedings of the IEEE*, November, 1983.

GUST84 GUSTAVSON, D. "Computer Buses—A Tutorial." *IEEE Micro*, August, 1984.

GUTE88 GUTERL, F. "Compact Disc." *IEEE Spectrum*, November 1988.

HAAV71 HAAVIND, R. "The Many Faces of Microprogramming." *Computer Decisions*, September, 1971. Also in [GALE75].

HABE85 HABER, L. "Multiprocessor Technology Means More Muscle, Less Fat." *Mini-Micro Systems*, June, 1985.

HALL91 HALL, C., AND O'BRIEN, K. "Performance Characteristics of Architectural Features of the IBM RISC System/6000. *Proceedings, Fourth International Conference on Architectural Support for Programming Languages and Operating Systems*, April 1991.

HAYE88 HAYES, J. *Computer Architecture and Organization, Second Edition.* New York: McGraw-Hill, 1988.

HEAL83 HEALEY, M. "Junking the Mainframe." *Datamation*, August, 1983.

HEAT84 HEATH, J. "Re-evaluation of RISC I." *Computer Architecture News*, March, 1984.

HENN82 HENNESSY, J., ET AL. "Hardware/Software Tradeoffs for Increased Performance." *Proceedings, Symposium on Architectural Support for Programming Languages and Operating Systems*, March, 1982.

HENN84 HENNESSY, J. "VLSI Processor Architecture." *IEEE Transactions on Computers*, December, 1984.

HENN90 HENNESSY, J., AND PATTERSON, D. *Computer Architecture: A Quantitative Approach.* San Mateo, CA: Morgan Kaufmann, 1990.

HENN91 HENNESSY, J., AND JOUPPI, N. "Computer Technology and Architecture: An Evolving Interaction." *Computer*, September 1991.

HEYW83 HEYWOOD, S. "The 8086—An Architecture for the Future." *Byte*, June, 1983.

HIGB83 HIGBIE, L. "A Vector Processing Tutorial." *Datamation*, August, 1983.

HIGB90 HIGBIE, L. "Quick and Easy Cache Performance Analysis." *Computer Architecture News*, June 1990.

HIGM67 HIGMAN, B. *A Comparative Study of Programming Languages.* New York: American Elsevier, 1967.

HILL64 HILL, R. "Stored Logic Programming and Applications." *Datamation*, February, 1964.

HILL89 HILL, M. "Evaluating Associativity in CPU Caches." *IEEE Transactions on Computers*, December 1989.

HITC85 HITCHCOCK, C., AND BRINKLEY, H. "Analyzing Multiple Register Sets." *The 12th Annual International Symposium on Computer Architecture*, June 17–19, 1985.

HOPK87 HOPKINS, M. "A Perspective on the 801/Reduced Instruction Set Computer." *IBM Systems Journal*, Vol. 26, No. 1, 1987.

HUCK83 HUCK, T. *Comparative Analysis of Computer Architectures.* Stanford University Technical Report No. 83-243, May, 1983.

HUGU91   HUGUET, M., AND LANG, T. "Architectural Support for Reduced Register Saving/Restoring in Single-Window Register Files." *ACM Transactions on Computer Systems*, February 1991.

HWAN85   HWANG, K. "Multiprocessor Supercomputers for Scientific/Engineering Applications." *Computer*, June, 1985.

IBM83A   IBM Corp. *IBM System/370: Principles of Operation*. GA22-7000-9, May, 1983.

IBM83B   IBM Corp. *IBM System/370 Extended Architecture: Principles of Operation*. SA22-7085-0, May, 1983.

IBM90A   IBM Corp. Special Issue on the RS/6000. *IBM Journal of Research and Development*, January 1990.

IBM90B   IBM Corp. *IBM RISC System/6000 Technology*. SA23-2619, 1990.

IEEE84   Institute of Electrical and Electronics Engineers. *IEEE Standard Graphic Symbols for Logic Functions*. ANSI/IEEE Std 91-1984, 1984.

IEEE85   Institute of Electrical and Electronics Engineers. *IEEE Standard for Binary Floating-Point Arithmetic*. ANSI/IEEE Std 754-1985, 1985.

INTE81   Intel Corp. "8085AH/8085AH-2/8085AH-1 8-Bit HMOS Microprocessor." 1981.

INTE84   Intel Corp. "8087 Numeric Data Coprocessor." Intel Data Sheet 205835, October, 1984. Reprinted in [INTE85b].

INTE85A   Intel Corp. *Memory Components Handbook*, Santa Clara, CA, 1985.

INTE85B   Intel Corp. *Microsystem Components Handbook*, Santa Clara, CA, 1985.

INTE85C   Intel Corporation. *Multibus II Bus Architecture Specification Handbook*. 1985.

INTE86   Intel Corporation. *80386 Programmer's Reference Manual*. 1986.

INTE87   Intel Corporation. "Cache Subsystems." in *80386 Hardware Reference Manual*, 1987.

INTE88   Intel Corporation. *Microprocessor and Peripheral Handbook*. 1988.

INTE90   Intel Corporation. *i486 Microprocessor Data Book*. 1990.

JEND83   JENDRO, J. "Extending the Megabus." *Mini-Micro Systems*, September, 1983.

JOHN71   JOHNSON, A. "The Microdiagnostics for the IBM System/360 Model 30." *IEEE Transactions on Computers*, July, 1971. Also in [GALE75].

JOHN84   JOHNSON, J., AND KASSEL, S. *The Multibus Design Guidebook*. New York: McGraw-Hill, 1984.

JOHN91   JOHNSON, M. *Superscalar Microprocessor Design*. Englewood Cliffs, NJ: Prentice-Hall, 1991.

JONE91   JONES, S. "A Futurebus Interface from Off-the-Shelf Parts." *IEEE Micro*, February 1991.

JOUP88   JOUPPI, N. "Superscalar versus Superpipelined Machines." *Computer Architecture News*, June 1988.

JOUP89A   JOUPPI, N., AND WALL, D. "Available Instruction-Level Parallelism for Superscalar and Superpipelined Machines." *Proceedings, Third International Conference on Architectural Support for Programming Languages and Operating Systems*, April 1989.

JOUP89b JOUPPI, N. "The Nonuniform Distribution of Instruction-Level and Machine Parallelism and Its Effect on Performance." *IEEE Transactions on Computers,* December 1989.

KAEL91 KAELI, D., AND EMMA, P. "Branch History Table Prediction of Moving Target Branches Due to Subroutine Returns." *Proceedings, 18th Annual International Symposium on Computer Architecture,* May 1991.

KANE92 KANE, G., AND HEINRICH, J. *MIPS RISC Architecture.* Englewood Cliffs, NJ: Prentice-Hall, 1992.

KARP87 KARP, A. "Programming for Parallelism." *Computer,* 1987.

KATE83 KATEVENIS, M. *Reduced Instruction Set Computer Architectures for VLSI.* PhD dissertation, Computer Science Department, University of California at Berkeley, October, 1983. Reprinted by MIT Press, Cambridge, MA, 1985.

KENA84 KENAH, L., AND BATE, S. *VAX/VMS Internals and Data Structures.* Bedford, MA: Digital Press, 1984.

KHAM82 KHAMBATA, A. *Microprocessors/Microcomputers: Architecture, Software, and Systems.* New York: Wiley, 1982.

KING88 KING, W. "Special Section on Microprogramming." *IEEE Transactions on Software Engineering,* May 1988.

KNUT71 KNUTH, D. "An Empirical Study of FORTRAN Programs." *Software Practice and Experience,* vol. 1, 1971.

KNUT81 KNUTH, D. *The Art of Computer Programming, Volume 2: Seminumerical Algorithms, Second Edition.* Reading, MA: Addison-Wesley, 1981.

KOES78 KOESTLER, A. *Janus.* New York: Random House, 1978.

KOP81 KOP, H. *Hard Disk Controller Design Using the Intel 8089.* Intel Application Note AP-122, 1981. Reprinted in [INTE84].

KOZD80 KOZDROWICKI, E., AND THEIS, D. "Second Generation of Vector Supercomputers." *Computer,* November, 1980.

KRAF81 KRAFF, G., AND TOY, W. *Microprogrammed Control and Reliable Design of Small Computers.* Englewood Cliffs, NJ: Prentice-Hall, 1981.

KRUT88 KRUTZ, R. *Interfacing Techniques in Digital Design with Emphasis on Microprocessors.* New York, Wiley, 1988.

KRYD86 KRYDER, M., ED. "Special Section on Magnetic Information Storage Retrieval." *Proceedings of the IEEE,* November 1986.

KRYD87 KRYDER, M. "Data-Storage Technologies for Advanced Computing." *Scientific American,* October 1987.

KUCK72 KUCK, D.; MURAOKA, Y.; AND CHEN, S. "On the Number of Operations Simultaneously Executable in Fortran-like Programs and Their Resulting Speedup." *IEEE Transactions on Computers,* December 1972.

KUGA91 KUGA, M.; MURAKAMI, K.; AND TOMITA, S. "DSNS (Dynamically-hazard resolved, Statically-code-scheduled, Nonuniform Superscalar): Yet Another Superscalar Processor Architecture." *Computer Architecture News,* June 1991.

KUHN81 KUHN, R., AND PADUA, D. *Tutorial on Parallel Processing.* Washington, DC: IEEE Computer Society Press, 1981.

KULI81 KULISCH, U., AND MIRANKER, W. *Computer Arithmetic in Theory and Practice.* New York: Academic Press, 1981.

LAHT90 LAHTI, W., AND McCARRON, D. "Store Data in a Flash." *Byte,* November 1990.

LARS82 LARSON, R.; McENTIRE, P.; AND O'REILLY, J. *Tutorial: Distributed Control.* Washington, DC: IEEE Computer Society Press, 1982.

LEBA84A LEBAN, J., AND ARNOLD, J. *IBM I/O Architecture and Virtual Storage Concepts: System/370-Mode and 370/XA-Mode Processors.* New York: Wiley, 1984.

LEBA84B LEBAN, J., AND ARNOLD, J. *IBM CPU and Storage Architecture: System/370-Mode and 370/XA-Mode Processors.* New York: Wiley, 1984.

LEE84 LEE, J., AND SMITH, A. "Branch Prediction Strategies and Branch Target Buffer Design." *Computer,* January, 1984.

LEE91 LEE, R.; KWOK, A.; AND BRIGGS, F. "The Floating Point Performance of a Superscalar SPARC Processor." *Proceedings, Fourth International Conference on Architectural Support for Programming Languages and Operating Systems,* April 1991.

LEVI76 LEVINE, L., AND MEYERS, W. "Semiconductor Memory Reliability with Error Detecting and Correcting Codes." *Computer,* October, 1976.

LEVI82 LEVINE, R. "Supercomputers." *Scientific American,* January, 1982.

LEVY78 LEVY, J. "Buses, the Skeleton of Computer Structures." in [BELL78A].

LEVY89 LEVY, H., AND ECKHOUSE, R. *Computer Programming and Architecture: The VAX-11.* Bedford, MA: Digital Press, 1989.

LILJ88 LILJA, D. "Reducing the Branch Penalty in Pipelined Processors." *Computer,* July 1988.

LUHN84 LUHN, R. "The Ups and Downs of Bubble Memory." *Computerworld,* December 3, 1984.

LUND77 LUNDE, A. "Empirical Evaluation of Some Features of Instruction Set Processor Architectures." *Communications of the ACM,* March, 1977.

MACG84 MACGREGOR, D.; MOTHERSOLE, D.; AND MOYER, B. "The Motorola MC68020." *IEEE Micro,* August 1984.

MAJU83 MAJUMDER, D., AND DAS, J. *Digital Computers' Memory Technology.* New York: Wiley, 1983.

MALL75 MALLACH, E. "Emulation Architecture." *Computer,* August, 1975.

MALL79 MALLACH, E. "The Evolution of an Architecture." *Datamation,* April, 1979.

MALL82 MALLACH, E. "Computer Architecture." *Mini-Micro Systems,* December, 1982.

MALL83 MALLACH, E., AND SONDAK, N. *Advances in Microprogramming.* Dedham, MA: Artech House, 1983.

MANO88 MANO, M. *Computer Engineering Hardware Design.* Englewood Cliffs, NJ: Prentice-Hall, 1988.

MANO91 MANO, M. *Digital Design.* Englewood Cliffs, NJ: Prentice-Hall, 1991.

MAYB84 MAYBERRY, W., AND EFLAND, G. "Cache Boosts Multiprocessor Performance." *Computer Design,* November, 1984.

MCEL85 McEliece, R. "The Reliability of Computer Memories." *Scientific American,* January, 1985.

MCFA86 McFarling, S., and Hennessy, J. "Reducing the Cost of Branches." *Proceedings, 13th Annual Symposium on Computer Architecture,* June 1986.

MCGE89 McGeady, S. "A Programmer's View of the 80960 Architecture." *Proceedings, COMPCON Spring '89,* March 1989.

MCGE90 McGeady, S. "The i960CA Superscalar Implementation of the 80960 Architecture." *Proceedings, COMPCON Spring '90,* March 1990.

MCGE91 McGeady, S., et al. "Performance Enhancements in the Superscalar i960MM Embedded Microprocessor." *Proceedings, COMPCON Spring '91,* February 1991.

MEIK86 Meiklejohn, W. "Magnetooptics: A Thermomagnetic Recording Technology." *Proceedings of the IEEE,* November 1986.

MEIN87 Meindl, J. "Chips for Advanced Computing." *Scientific American,* October 1987.

MELE89 Melear, C. "The Design of the 88000 RISC Family." *IEEE Micro,* April 1989.

MEND91 Mendelsohn, A. "Will Monolithic or Multichip Processors Win the Performance Race?" *Computer Design,* May 1, 1991.

MILE87 Milenkovic, M. *Operating Systems: Concepts and Design.* New York: McGraw-Hill, 1987.

MILU86 Milutinovic, V. "GaAs Microprocessor Technology." *Computer,* October 1986.

MILU89 Milutinovic, V. *Microprogramming and Firmware Engineering.* Los Alamitos, CA: IEEE Computer Society Press, 1989.

MILU91 Milutinovic, V.; Fura, D.; and Helbig, W. "Pipeline Design Trade-offs in a 32-bit Gallium Arsenide Microprocessor." *IEEE Transactions on Computers,* November 1991.

MOKH84 Mokhoff, N. "Magnetic Bubble Memories Making a Comeback." *Computer Design,* November, 1984.

MOOR87 Moore, B.; Padegs, A.; Smith, R.; and Buchholz, W. "Concepts of the System/370 Vector Architecture." *Proceedings, Fourteenth Annual International Symposium on Computer Architecture,* June 1987.

MORE84 Moreau, R. *The Computer Comes of Age.* Cambridge, MA: MIT Press, 1984.

MORS78 Morse, S.; Pohlman, W.; and Ravenel, B. "The Intel 8086 Microprocessor: A 16-bit Evolution of the 8080." *Computer,* June, 1978.

MORS87 Morse, S.; Isaacson, E.; and Albert, D. *The 80386/387 Architecture,* New York: Wiley, 1987.

MYER78 Myers, G. "The Evaluation of Expressions in a Storage-to-Storage Architecture." *Computer Architecture News,* June, 1978.

MYER88 Myers, G., and Budde, D. *The 80960 Microprocessor Architecture.* New York: Wiley, 1988.

NATU87 Natusch, P.; Senerchia, D.; and Yu, E. "The Memory System in the VAX 8800 Family." *Digital Technical Journal,* February 1987.

NBS79 National Bureau of Standards. *I/O Channel Interface.* FIPS PUB 60-1, August 27, 1979.

OBER88 OBERMEIER, K. "Side by Side." *Byte,* November 1988.

OEHL91 OEHLER, R., AND BLASGEN, M. "IBM RISC System/6000: Architecture and Performance." *IEEE Micro,* June 1991.

PADE81 PADEGS, A. "System/360 and Beyond." *IBM Journal of Research and Development,* September, 1981.

PADE88 PADEGS, A.; MOORE, B.; SMITH, R.; AND BUCHHOLZ, W. "The IBM System/370 Vector Architecture: Design Considerations." *IEEE Transactions on Communications,* May 1988.

PARK89 PARKER, A., AND HAMBLEN, J. *An Introduction to Microprogramming with Exercises Designed for the Texas Instruments SN74ACT8800 Software Development Board.* Dallas, TX: Texas Instruments, 1989.

PASH89 PASHLEY, R., AND LAI, S. "Flash Memories: The Best of Two Worlds." *IEEE Spectrum,* December 1989.

PATT82A PATTERSON, D., AND SEQUIN, C. "A VLSI RISC." *Computer,* September, 1982.

PATT82B PATTERSON, D., AND PIEPHO, R. "Assessing RISCs in High-Level Language Support." *IEEE Micro,* November, 1982.

PATT84 PATTERSON, D. "RISC Watch." *Computer Architecture News,* March 1984.

PATT85A PATTERSON, D. "Reduced Instruction Set Computers." *Communications of the ACM.* January, 1985.

PATT85B PATTERSON, D., AND HENNESSY, J. "Response to 'Computers, Complexity, and Controversy.'" *Computer,* November 1985.

PAYN80 PAYNE, M., AND BHANDARKAR, D. "VAX Floating Point: A Solid Foundation for Numerical Computation." *Computer Architecture News,* June, 1980.

PEUT79 PEUTO, B. "Architecture of a New Microprocessor." *Computer,* February, 1979.

PHIL85 PHILLIPS, D. "The Z80000 Microprocessor." *IEEE Micro,* December 1985.

PIER84 PIERCE, R. "Diskless Computers Emerge with Proper Mix of Firmware, Processor, and Bubble Memory." *Electronic Design,* October 13, 1984.

PINK89 PINKERT, J., AND WEAR, L. *Operating Systems: Concepts, Policies, and Mechanisms.* Englewood Cliffs, NJ: Prentice-Hall, 1989.

POHL81 POHL, I., AND SHAW, A. *The Nature of Computation: An Introduction to Computer Science.* Rockville, MD: Computer Science Press, 1981.

POHM83 POHM, A., AND AGRAWAL, O. *High-Speed Memory Systems.* Reston, VA: Reston Publishing Co., 1983.

POHM84 POHM, A. "High-Speed Memory Systems." *Computer,* October, 1984.

POPE91 POPESCU, V., ET AL. "The Metaflow Architecture." *IEEE Micro,* June 1991.

POWE83 POWELL, D. "The Everlasting Mainframe." *Computer World,* June 27, 1983.

PRAS81 PRASAD, N. *Architecture and Implementation of Large Scale IBM Computer Systems.* Wellesley, MA: QED Information Sciences, Inc., 1981.

PRZY88 PRZYBYLSKI, S.; HOROWITZ, M.; AND HENNESSY, J. "Performance Trade-offs in Cache Design." *Proceedings, Fifteenth Annual International Symposium on Computer Architecture,* June 1988.

PRZY90 PRZYBYLSKI, S. "The Performance Impact of Block Size and Fetch Strategies." *Proceedings, 17th Annual International Symposium on Computer Architecture,* May 1990.

RADI83 RADIN, G. "The 801 Minicomputer." *IBM Journal of Research and Development,* May, 1983.

RAGA83 RAGAN-KELLEY, R., AND CLARK, R. "Applying RISC Theory to a Large Computer." *Computer Design,* November, 1983.

RAMA77 RAMAMOORTHY, C. "Pipeline Architecture." *Computing Surveys,* March, 1977.

RAUS80 RAUSCHER, T., AND ADAMS, P. "Microprogramming: A Tutorial and Survey of Recent Developments." *IEEE Transactions on Computers,* January, 1980.

REIS91 REIS, R. *Digital Electronics Through Project Analysis.* New York: Merrill/Macmillan, 1991.

RIGA84 RIGANATI, J., AND SCHNECK, P. "Supercomputing." *Computer,* October, 1984.

RUSS78 RUSSELL, R. "The CRAY-1 Computer System." *Communications of the ACM,* January, 1978.

RYAN88A RYAN, A. "Hardware Roundup: PCs, Workstations and Small Systems." *Computerworld,* October 3, 1988.

RYAN88B RYAN, D. "Intel's 80960: An Architecture Optimized for Embedded Control." *IEEE Micro,* June 1988.

SALI76 SALISBURY, A. *Microprogrammable Computer Architectures.* New York: Elsevier, 1976.

SARR84 SARRIZIN, D., AND MALEK, M. "Fault-Tolerant Semiconductor Memories." *Computer,* August, 1984.

SATY80 SATYANARAYANAN, M. "Commercial Multiprocessing Systems." *Computer,* May, 1980.

SATY81 SATYANARAYANAN, M., AND BHANDARKAR, D. "Design Trade-Offs in VAX-11 Translation Buffer Organization." *Computer,* December, 1981.

SCHL89 SCHLEICHER, D., AND TAYLOR, R. "Systems Overview of the Application System/400." *IBM Systems Journal,* No. 3, 1989.

SEBE76 SEBERN, M. "A Minicomputer-compatible Microcomputer System: The DEC LSI-11." *Proceedings of the IEEE,* June, 1976.

SEGE91 SEGEE, B., AND FIELD, J. *Microprogramming and Computer Architecture.* New York: Wiley, 1991.

SERL86 SERLIN, O. "MIPS, Dhrystones, and Other Tales." *Datamation,* June 1, 1986.

SHAN38 SHANNON, C. "Symbolic Analysis of Relay and Switching Circuits." *AIEE Transactions,* vol. 57, 1938.

SHER84 Sherburne, R. *Processor Design Tradeoffs in VLSI*. PhD thesis, Report No. UCB/CSD 84/173, University of California at Berkeley, April, 1984.

SHUR84 Shurkin, J. *Engines of the Mind: A History of the Computer*. New York: Norton, 1984.

SIER90 Sierra, H. *An Introduction to Direct Access Storage Devices*. Boston, MA: Academic Press, 1990.

SIEW82a Siewiorek, D.; Bell, C.; and Newell, A. *Computer Structures: Principles and Examples*. New York: McGraw-Hill, 1982.

SIEW82b Siewiorek, D. "Multiple-Processor Systems." in [SIEW82a].

SILB91 Silberschatz, A.; Peterson, J.; and Galvin, P. *Operating System Concepts*. Reading, MA: Addison-Wesley, 1991.

SIMO69 Simon, H. *The Sciences of the Artificial*. Cambridge, MA: MIT Press, 1969.

SIMP87 Simpson, R., and Hester, P. "The IBM RT PC ROMP Processor and Memory Management Unit." *IBM Systems Journal*, Vol. 26, No. 4, 1987.

SING86 Singh, Y.; King, G.; and Anderson, J. "IBM 3090 Performance: A Balanced System Approach." *IBM Systems Journal*, No. 1, 1986.

SLAT89 Slater, M., and Wharton, J. "Revenge of the CISCs." *Byte,* November 1989.

SMIT82 Smith, A. "Cache Memories." *ACM Computing Surveys*, September, 1982.

SMIT87a Smith, A. "Line (Block) Size Choice for CPU Cache Memories." *IEEE Transactions on Communications*, September 1987.

SMIT87b Smith, A. "Cache Memory Design: An Evolving Art." *IEEE Spectrum*, December 1987.

SMIT89 Smith, M.; Johnson, M.; and Horowitz, M. "Limits on Multiple Instruction Issue." *Proceedings, Third International Conference on Architectural Support for Programming Languages and Operating Systems,* April 1989.

SOHI90 Sohi, G. "Instruction Issue Logic for High-Performance Interruptable, Multiple Functional Unit, Pipelined Computers." *IEEE Transactions on Computers,* March 1990.

SPAN81 Spaniol, O. *Computer Arithmetic*. New York: Wiley, 1981.

STAL90 Stallings, W. *Local Networks: An Introduction, Third Edition*. New York: Macmillan, 1990.

STAL91a Stallings, W. *Data and Computer Communications, Third Edition*. New York: Macmillan, 1991.

STAL91b Stallings, W. *Reduced Instruction Set Computers, Third Edition*. Washington, DC: IEEE Computer Society Press, 1991.

STAL92 Stallings, W. *Operating Systems*. New York: Macmillan, 1992.

STAM79 Stamm, D.; Kopec, S.; and McCormick, B. "Free the MC's CPU from I/O Hassles with a Special I/O Processor." *Electronic Design*, March 29, 1979.

STEP91 Stephens, C., et al. "Instruction Level Profiling and Evaluation of the IBM RS/6000. *Proceedings, 18th Annual International Symposium on Computer Architecture*, May 1991.

STEV64 STEVENS, W. "The Structure of System/360, Part II: System Implementation." *IBM Systems Journal*, Vol. 3, No. 2, 1964. Reprinted in [BELL71A] and [SIEW82A].

STON80 STONE, H., EDITOR. *Introduction to Computer Architecture*. Chicago: SRA, 1980.

STON90 STONE, H. *High-Performance Computer Architecture*. Reading, MA: Addison-Wesley, 1990.

STRE78A STRECKER, W. "Cache Memories for PDP-11 Family Computers." in [BELL78A].

STRE78B STRECKER, W. "VAX-11/780: A Virtual Address Extension to the DEC PDP-11 Family." *Proceedings, National Computer Conference*, 1978.

STRE83 STRECKER, W. "Transient Behavior of Cache Memories." *ACM Transactions on Computer Systems*, November, 1983.

STRI79 STRITTER, E., AND GUNTER, T. "A Microprocessor Architecture for a Changing World: The Motorola 68000." *Computer*, February, 1979.

SWAR90A SWARTZLANDER, E., EDITOR. *Computer Arithmetic, Volumes I and II*. Los Alamitos, CA: IEEE Computer Society Press, 1990.

SWAR90B SWARTZLANDER, E., EDITOR. Special Issue on Computer Arithmetic. *IEEE Transactions on Computers*, August 1990.

TABA87 TABAK, D. *RISC Architecture*. New York: Wiley, 1987.

TABA91 TABAK, D. *Advanced Microprocessors*. New York: McGraw-Hill, 1991.

TAMI83 TAMIR, Y., AND SEQUIN, C. "Strategies for Managing the Register File in RISC." *IEEE Transactions on Computers*, November, 1983.

TANE78 TANENBAUM, A. "Implications of Structured Programming for Machine Architecture." *Communications of the ACM*, March, 1978.

TANE84 TANENBAUM, A. *Structured Computer Organization*. Englewood Cliffs, NJ: Prentice-Hall, 1984.

TANE87 TANENBAUM, A. *Operating System Design and Implementation*. Englewood Cliffs, NJ: Prentice-Hall, 1987.

TEJA85 TEJA, E. *The Designer's Guide to Disk Drives*. Reston, VA: Reston Publishing, 1985.

THUR79 THURBER, K. *Tutorial: Distributed Processor Communication Architecture*. Washington, DC: IEEE Computer Society Press, 1979.

THUR80 THURBER, K. *Tutorial: A Pragmatic View of Distributed Processing*. Washington, DC: IEEE Computer Society Press, 1980.

TI90 Texas Instruments Inc. *SN74ACT880 Family Data Manual*. SCSS006C, 1990.

TJAD70 TJADEN, G., AND FLYNN, M. "Detection and Parallel Execution of Independent Instructions." *IEEE Transactions on Computers*, October 1970.

TOON81 TOONG, H., AND GUPTA, A. "An Architectural Comparison of Contemporary 16-Bit Microprocessors." *IEEE Micro*, May, 1981.

TRIE82 TRIEBEL, W., AND CHU, A. *Handbook of Semiconductor and Bubble Memories*. Englewood Cliffs, NJ: Prentice-Hall, 1982.

TROI85 TROIANI, M.; CHING, S.; QUAYNOR, N.; BLOEM, J.; AND OSORIO, F. "The VAX 8600 I Box, A Pipelined Implementation of the VAX Architecture." *Digital Technical Journal*, August 1985.

TUCK67 TUCKER, S. "Microprogram Control for System/360." *IBM Systems Journal*, No. 4, 1967. Also in [MALL83].

TUCK87 TUCKER, S. "The IBM 3090 System Design with Emphasis on the Vector Facility." *Proceedings, COMPCON Spring '87*, February 1987.

TURN86 TURNER, R. *Operating Systems: Design and Implementation.* New York: Macmillan, 1986.

UNGE89 UNGER, S. *The Essence of Logic Circuits.* Englewood Cliffs, NJ: Prentice-Hall, 1989.

VERI87 VERITY, J., AND LEWIS, G. "Computers: The New Look." *Business Week*, November 30, 1987.

VERN88 VERNON, M., AND MANBER, U. "Distributed Round-Robin and First-Come-First-Serve Protocols and Their Application to Multiprocessor Bus Arbitration." *Proceedings, Fifteenth Annual International Symposium on Computer Architecture*, June 1988.

VOEL88 VOELKER, J. "The PDP-8." *IEEE Spectrum*, November 1988.

VONN45 VON NEUMANN, J. *First Draft of a Report on the EDVAC.* Moore School, University of Pennsylvania, 1945.

VRAN80 VRANESIC, Z., AND THURBER, K. "Teaching Computer Structures." *Computer*, June, 1980.

WAKE77 WAKERLY, J. "Microprocessor Input/Output Architecture." *Computer*, February, 1977.

WAKE90 WAKERLY, J. *Digital Design Principles and Practices.* Englewood Cliffs, NJ: Prentice-Hall, 1990.

WALL85 WALLICH, P. "Toward Simpler, Faster Computers." *IEEE Spectrum*, August, 1985.

WALL91 WALL, D. "Limits of Instruction-Level Parallelism." *Proceedings, Fourth International Conference on Architectural Support for Programming Languages and Operating Systems*, April 1991.

WARD90 WARD, S., AND HALSTEAD, R. *Computation Structures.* Cambridge, MA: MIT Press, 1990.

WATE86 WATERS, F., ED. *IBM RT Personal Computer Technology*, IBM Corp. SA23-1057, 1986.

WAYN92 WAYNER, P. "Processor Pipelines." *Byte*, January 1992.

WEBE67 WEBER, H. "A Microprogrammed Implementation of EULER on IBM System/360 Model 30." *Communications of the ACM*, September, 1967.

WEIN75 WEINBERG, G. *An Introduction to General Systems Thinking.* New York: Wiley, 1975.

WEIS84 WEISS, S., AND SMITH, J. "Instruction Issue Logic in Pipelined Supercomputers." *IEEE Transactions on Computers*, November 1984.

WEIS87 WEISS, R. "RISC Processors: The New Wave in Computer Systems." *Computer Design*, May 15, 1987.

WEIZ81 WEIZER, N. "A History of Operating Systems." *Datamation*, January, 1981.

WEIZ91 WEIZER, N., ET AL. *The Arthur D. Little Forecast on Information Technology and Productivity.* New York: Wiley, 1991.

WIEC82   Wiecek, L. "A Case Study of VAX-11 Instruction Set Usage for Compiler Execution." *Proceedings, Symposium on Architectural Support for Programming Languages and Operating Systems,* March, 1982.

WILK51   Wilkes, M. "The Best Way to Design an Automatic Calculating Machine." *Proceedings, Manchester University Computer Inaugural Conference,* July, 1951.

WILK53   Wilkes, M., and Stringer, J. "Microprogramming and the Design of the Control Circuits in an Electronic Digital Computer." *Proceedings of the Cambridge Philosophical Society,* April, 1953. Also in [SIEW82a].

WILL84   Williams, T. "Semiconductor Memories: Density and Diversity." *Computer Design,* August, 1984.

WILL90   Williams, F., and Steven, G. "Address and Data Register Separation on the M68000 Family." *Computer Architecture News,* June 1990.

WILS84   Wilson, K. "Science, Industry, and the New Japanese Challenge." *Proceedings of the IEEE,* January, 1984.

WILS90   Wilson, R. "RISC Chips Get Trimmed to Satisfy Embedded Applications." *Computer Design,* May 1, 1990.

WIND85   Windsor, W. "IEEE Floating-Point Chips Implement DSP Architectures." *Computer Design,* January, 1985.

WONG80   Wong, C. "Minimizing Expected Head Movement in One-Dimensional and Two-Dimensional Mass Storage Systems." *Computing Surveys,* June, 1980.

WULF82   Wulforst, H. *Breakthrough to the Computer Age.* New York: Charles Scribner's Sons, 1982.

YEN85   Yen, W.; Yen, D.; and Fu, K. "Data Coherence in a Multicache System." *IEEE Transactions on Computers,* January, 1985.

YOSH91   Yoshida, N.; Goto, E.; and Ichikawa, S. "Pseudorandom Rounding for Truncated Multipliers." *IEEE Transactions on Computers,* September 1991.

ZECH88   Zech, R. "Systems, Applications, and Implications of Optical Storage." *Proceedings, COMPCON Spring '88,* March 1988.

ZORP85   Zorpette, G. "The Beauty of 32 Bits." *IEEE Spectrum,* September 1985.

Glossary

Some of the terms in this glossary are from the *American National Dictionary for Information Systems* [ANSI90]. These are indicated in the glossary by an asterisk.

Absolute Address* An address in a computer language that identifies a storage location or a device without the use of any intermediate reference.

Accumulator The name of the CPU register in a single-address instruction format. The accumulator, or AC, is implicitly one of the two operands for the instruction.

Address Bus That portion of a system bus used for the transfer of an address. Typically, the address identifies a main memory location or an I/O device.

Address Space The range of addresses (memory, I/O) that can be referenced.

Arithmetic And Logic Unit (ALU)* A part of a computer that performs arithmetic operations, logic operations, and related operations.

ASCII American Standard Code for Information Interchange. ASCII is a 7-bit code used to represent numeric, alphabetic, and special printable characters. It also includes codes for *control characters*, which are not printed or displayed but specify some control function.

Assembly Language* A computer-oriented language whose instructions are usually in one-to-one correspondence with computer instructions and that may provide facilities such as the use of macroinstructions. Synonymous with *computer-dependent language*.

Associative Memory* A memory whose storage locations are identified by their contents, or by a part of their contents, rather than by their names or positions.

Asynchronous Timing A technique in which the occurrence of one event on a bus follows and depends on the occurrence of a previous event.

Autoindexing A form of indexed addressing in which the index register is automatically incremented or decremented with each memory reference.

Base (*ANS) In the numeration system commonly used in scientific papers, the number that is raised to the power denoted by the exponent and then multiplied by the mantissa to determine the real number represented (e.g., the number 6.25 in the expression $2.7 \times 6.25^{1.5} = 42.1875$).

Base Address*   A numeric value that is used as a reference in the calculation of addresses in the execution of a computer program.

Binary Operator*   An operator that represents an operation on two and only two operands.

Bit*   In the pure binary numeration system, either of the digits 0 and 1.

Block Multiplexer Channel   A multiplexer channel that interleaves blocks of data. See also *byte multiplexer channel*. Contrast with *selector channel*.

Bubble Memory   A solid-state magnetic memory device. Binary 1s and 0s are represented by the presence or absence of tiny magnetic domains, called *bubbles*.

Buffer*   Storage used to compensate for a difference in rate of flow of data, or time of occurrence of events, when transferring data from one device to another.

Bus   A shared communications path consisting of one or a collection of lines. In some computer systems, CPU, memory, and I/O components are connected by a common bus. Since the lines are shared by all components, only one component at a time can successfully transmit.

Byte   Eight bits. Also referred to as an *octet*.

Byte Multiplexer Channel*   A multiplexer channel that interleaves bytes of data. See also *block multiplexer channel*. Contrast with *selector channel*.

Cache Memory*   A special buffer storage, smaller and faster than main storage, that is used to hold a copy of instructions and data in main storage that are likely to be needed next by the processor, and that have been obtained automatically from main storage.

CD-ROM   Compact Disk Read-Only Memory. A nonerasable disk used for storing computer data. The standard system uses 12-cm disks and can hold more thn 550 Mbytes.

Central Processing Unit (CPU)   That portion of a computer that fetches and executes instructions. It consists of an Arithmetic and Logic Unit (ALU), a control unit, and registers. Often simply referred to as a *processor*.

Combinational Circuit*   A logic device whose output values, at any given instant, depend only upon the input values at that time. A combinational circuit is a special case of a sequential circuit that does not have a storage capability. Synonymous with *combinatorial circuit*.

Compact Disk (CD)   A nonerasable disk that stores digitized audio information. The standard system uses 12-cm disks and can record more than 60 minutes of uninterrupted playing time.

Computer Instruction*   An instruction that can be recognized by the processing unit of the computer for which it is designed. Synonymous with *machine instruction*.

Computer Instruction Set*   A complete set of the operators of the instructions of a computer together with a description of the types of meanings that can be attributed to their operands. Synonymous with *machine instruction set*.

Condition Code   A code that reflects the result of a previous operation (e.g., arithmetic). A CPU may include one or more condition codes, which may be stored separately within the CPU or as part of a larger control register. Also known as a *flag*.

Conditional Jump*   A jump that takes place only when the instruction that specifies it is executed and specified conditions are satisfied. Contrast with *unconditional jump*.

Control Bus   That portion of a system bus used for the transfer of control signals.

Control Registers   CPU registers employed to control CPU operation. Most of these registers are not user visible.

Control Storage   A portion of storage that contains microcode.

Control Unit   That part of the CPU that controls CPU operations, including ALU operations, the movement of data within the CPU, and the exchange of data and control signals across external interfaces (e.g., the system bus).

Daisy Chain*   A method of device interconnection for determining interrupt priority by connecting the interrupt sources serially.

Data Bus   That portion of a system bus used for the transfer of data.

Data Communication   Data transfer between devices. The term generally excludes I/O.

Decoder*   A device that has a number of input lines of which any number may carry signals and a number of output lines of which not more than one may carry a signal, there being a one-to-one correspondence between the outputs and the combinations of input signals.

Demand Paging*   The transfer of a page from auxiliary storage to real storage at the moment of need.

Direct Access*   The capability to obtain data from a storage device or to enter data into a storage device in a sequence independent of their relative position, by means of addresses that indicate the physical location of the data.

Direct Address*   An address that designates the storage location of an item of data to be treated as operand. Synonymous with *one-level address*.

Direct Memory Access (DMA)   A form of I/O in which a special module, called a *DMA module*, controls the exchange of data between main memory and an I/O module. The CPU sends a request for the transfer of a block of data to the DMA module and is interrupted only after the entire block has been transferred.

Disabled Interrupt   A condition, usually created by the CPU, during which the CPU will ignore interrupt request signals of a specified class.

Diskette*   A flexible magnetic disk enclosed in a protective container. Synonymous with *flexible disk*.

Disk Pack*   An assembly of magnetic disks that can be removed as a whole from a disk drive, together with a container from which the assembly must be separated when operating.

Dynamic RAM   A RAM whose cells are implemented using capacitors. A dynamic RAM will gradually lose its data unless it is periodically refreshed.

Emulation* The imitation of all or part of one system by another, primarily by hardware, so that the imitating system accepts the same data, executes the same programs, and achieves the same results as the imitated system.

Enabled Interrupt A condition, usually created by the CPU, during which the CPU will respond to interrupt request signals of a specified class.

Erasable Optical Disk A disk that uses optical technology but that can be easily erased and rewritten. Both 3.25-inch and 5.25-inch disks are in use. A typical capacity is 650 Mbytes.

Error-Correcting Code* A code in which each character or signal conforms to specific rules of construction so that deviations from these rules indicate the presence of an error and in which some or all of the detected errors can be corrected automatically.

Error-Detecting Code* A code in which each character or signal conforms to specific rules of construction so that deviations from these rules indicate the presence of an error.

Execute Cycle That portion of the instruction cycle during which the CPU performs the operation specified by the instruction op code.

Fetch Cycle That portion of the instruction cycle during which the CPU fetches from memory the instruction to be executed.

Firmware* Microcode stored in read-only memory.

Fixed-Point Representation System* A radix numeration system in which the radix point is implicitly fixed in the series of digit places by some convention upon which agreement has been reached.

Flip-Flop* A circuit or device containing active elements, capable of assuming either one of two stable states at a given time. Synonymous with *bistable circuit, toggle*.

Floating-Point Representation System* A numeration system in which a real number is represented by a pair of distinct numerals, the real number being the product of the fixed-point part, one of the numerals, and a value obtained by raising the implicit floating-point base to a power denoted by the exponent in the floating-point representation, indicated by the second numeral.

G Prefix meaning *billion*.

Gate An electronic circuit that produces an output signal that is a simple boolean operation on its input signals.

General-Purpose Register* A register, usually explicitly addressable, within a set of registers, that can be used for different purposes, for example, as an accumulator, as an index register, or as a special handler of data.

Global Variable A variable defined in one portion of a computer program and used in at least one other portion of that computer program.

Immediate Address* The contents of an address part that contains the value of an operand rather than an address. Synonymous with *zero-level address*.

Indexed Address* An address that is modified by the content of an index register prior to or during the execution of a computer instruction.

Indexing A technique of address modification by means of index registers.

Index Register* A register whose contents can be used to modify an operand address during the execution of computer instructions; it can also be used as a counter. An index register may be used to control the execution of a loop, to control the use of an array, as a switch, for table lookup, or as a pointer.

Indirect Address* An address of a storage location that contains an address.

Indirect Cycle That portion of the instruction cycle during which the CPU performs a memory access to convert an indirect address into a direct address.

Input-Output (I/O) Pertaining to either input or output, or both. Refers to the movement of data between a computer and a directly attached peripheral.

Instruction Address Register* A special purpose register used to hold the address of the next instruction to be executed.

Instruction Cycle The processing performed by a CPU to execute a single instruction.

Instruction Format The layout of a computer instruction as a sequence of bits. The format divides the instruction into fields, corresponding to the constituent elements of the instruction (e.g., op code, operands).

Instruction Register* A register that is used to hold an instruction for interpretation.

Integrated Circuit (IC) A tiny piece of solid material, such as silicon, upon which is etched or imprinted a collection of electronic components and their interconnections.

Interrupt* A suspension of a process, such as the execution of a computer program, caused by an event external to that process, and performed in such a way that the process can be resumed. Synonymous with *interruption.*

Interrupt Cycle That portion of the instruction cycle during which the CPU checks for interrupts. If an enabled interrupt is pending, the CPU saves the current program state and resumes processing at an interrupt handler routine.

Interupt-Driven I/O A form of I/O. The CPU issues an I/O command, continues to execute subsequent instructions, and is interrupted by the I/O module when the latter has completed its work.

I/O Channel A relatively complex I/O module that relieves the CPU of the details of I/O operations. An I/O channel will execute a sequence of I/O commands from main memory without the need for CPU involvement.

I/O Controller A relatively simple I/O module that requires detailed control from the CPU or an I/O channel. Synonymous with *device controller.*

I/O Module One of the major component types of a computer. It is responsible for the control of one or more external devices (peripherals) and for the exchange of data between those devices and main memory and/or CPU registers.

I/O Processor An I/O module with its own processor, capable of executing its own specialized I/O instructions or, in some cases, general-purpose machine instructions.

Isolated I/O   A method of addressing I/O modules and external devices. The I/O address space is treated separately from main memory address space. Specific I/O machine instructions must be used. Compare *memory-mapped* I/O.

K   Prefix meaning $2^{10} = 1,024$. Thus 2Kb = 2,048 bits.

Local Variable   A variable that is defined and used only in one specified portion of a computer program.

M   Prefix meaning $2^{20} = 1,048,576$. Thus 2Mb = 2 X 2^{20} bits.

Magnetic Disk*   A flat circular plate with a magnetizable surface layer, on one or both sides of which data can be stored.

Magnetic Tape*   A tape with a magnetizable surface layer on which data can be stored by magnetic recording.

Main Memory*   Program-addressable storage from which instructions and other data can be loaded directly into registers for subsequent execution or processing.

Memory Address Register (MAR)*   A register, in a processing unit, that contains the address of the storage location being accessed.

Memory Buffer Register (MBR)   A register that contains data read from memory or data to be written to memory.

Memory Cycle Time   The inverse of the rate at which memory can be accessed. It is the minimum time between the response to one access request (read or write) and the response to the next access request.

Memory-Mapped I/O   A method of addressing I/O modules and external devices. A single address space is used for both main memory and I/O addresses, and the same machine instructions are used both for memory read/write and for I/O.

Microcomputer*   A computer system whose processing unit is a microprocessor. A basic microcomputer includes a microprocessor, storage, and an input/output facility, which may or may not be on one chip.

Microinstruction*   An instruction that controls data flow and sequencing in a processor at a more fundamental level than machine instructions. Individual machine instructions and perhaps other functions may be implemented by microprograms.

Micro-Operation   An elementary CPU operation, performed during one clock pulse.

Microprocessor*   A processor whose elements have been miniaturized into one or a few integrated circuits.

Microprogram*   A sequence of microinstructions that are in special storage where they can be dynamically accessed to perform various functions.

Microprogrammed CPU   A CPU whose control unit is implemented using microprogramming.

Microprogramming Language   An instruction set used to specify microprograms.

Multiplexer   A combinational circuit that connects multiple inputs to a single output. At any time, only one of the inputs is selected to be passed to the output.

Multiplexer Channel   A channel designed to operate with a number of I/O devices simultaneously. Several I/O devices can transfer records at the same time by interleaving items of data. See also *byte multiplexer channel, block multiplexer channel*.

Multiprogramming*   A mode of operation that provides for the interleaved execution of two or more computer programs by a single processor.

Nonvolatile Memory   Memory whose contents are stable and do not require a constant power source.

Nucleus   That portion of an operating system that contains its basic and most frequently used functions. Often, the nucleus remains resident in main memory.

One's-complement Representation   Used to represent binary integers. A positive integer is represented as in sign-magnitude. A negative integer is represented by reversing each bit in the representation of a positive integer of the same magnitude.

Op Code   Abbreviated form for *operation code*.

Operand*   An entity on which an operation is performed.

Operating System*   Software that controls the execution of programs; and that provides services such as resource allocation, scheduling, input/output control, and data management.

Operation Code*   A code used to represent the operations of a computer. Usually abbreviated to op code.

Orthogonality   A principle by which two variables or dimensions are independent of one another. In the context of an instruction set, the term is generally used to indicate that other elements of an instruction (address mode, number of operands, length of operand) are independent of (not determined by) op code.

Page*   In a virtual storage system, a fixed-length block that has a virtual address and that is transferred as a unit between real storage and auxiliary storage.

Page Fault   Occurs when the page containing a referenced word is not in main memory. This causes an interrupt and requires the operating system to bring in the needed page.

Page Frame*   An area of main storage used to hold a page.

Parity Bit*   A binary digit appended to a group of binary digits to make the sum of all the digits either always odd (odd parity) or always even (even parity).

Peripheral Equipment (IBM)   In a computer system, with respect to a particular processing unit, any equipment that provides the processing unit with outside communication. Synonymous with *peripheral device*.

Process   A program in execution. A process is controlled and scheduled by the operating system.

Process Control Block   The manifestation of a process in an operating system. It is a data structure containing information about the characteristics and state of the process.

Processor*   In a computer, a functional unit that interprets and executes instructions. A processor consists of at least an instruction control unit and an arithmetic unit.

Processor Cycle Time   The time required for the shortest well-defined CPU micro-operation. It is the basic unit of time for measuring all CPU actions. Synonymous with *machine cycle time*.

Program Counter   Instruction address register.

Programmable Logic Array (PLA)*   An array of gates whose interconnections can be programmed to perform a specific logical function.

Programmable Read-Only Memory (PROM)   Semiconductor memory whose contents may be set only once. The writing process is performed electrically and may be performed by the user at a time later than original chip fabrication.

Programmed I/O   A form of I/O in which the CPU issues an I/O command to an I/O module and must then wait for the operation to be complete before proceeding.

Program Status Word (PSW)   An area in storage used to indicate the order in which instructions are executed, and to hold and indicate the status of the computer system. Synonymous with *processor status word*.

Random-Access Memory (RAM)   Memory in which each addressable location has a unique addressing mechanism. The time to access a given location is independent of the sequence of prior access.

Read-Only Memory (ROM)   Semiconductor memory whose contents cannot be altered, except by destroying the storage unit. Nonerasable memory.

Registers   High-speed memory internal to the CPU. Some registers are user visible, that is, available to the programmer via the machine instruction set. Other registers are used only by the CPU, for control purposes.

Scalar*   A quantity characterized by a single value.

Secondary Memory   Memory located outside the computer system itself, including disk and tape.

Selector Channel   An I/O channel designed to operate with only one I/O device at a time. Once the I/O device is selected, a complete record is transferred one byte at a time. Contrast with *block multiplexer channel, multiplexer channel*.

Semiconductor   A solid crystalline substance, such as silicon or germanium, whose electrical conductivity is intermediate between insulators and good conductors. Used to fabricate transistors and solid-state components.

Sequential Circuit   A digital logic circuit whose output depends on the current input plus the state of the circuit. Sequential circuits thus possess the attribute of memory.

Sign-Magnitude Representation   Used to represent binary integers. In an N-bit word the leftmost bit is the sign (0 = positive, 1 = negative) and the remaining $N - 1$ bits comprise the magnitude of the number.

Solid-State Component*   A component whose operation depends on the control of electric or magnetic phenomena in solids (e.g., transistor crystal diode, ferrite core).

Stack*   A list that is constructed and maintained so that the next item to be retrieved is the most recently stored item in the list, last-in-first-out (LIFO).

Static RAM   A RAM whose cells are implemented using flip-flops. A static RAM will hold its data as long as power is supplied to it; no periodic refresh is required.

Superpipelined Processor   A processor design in which the instruction pipeline consists of many very small stages, so that more than one pipeline stage can be executed during one clock cycle and so that a large number of instructions may be in the pipeline at the same time.

Superscalar Processor   A processor design which includes multiple-instruction pipelines, so that more than one instruction can be executing in the same pipeline stage simultaneously.

Synchronous Timing   A technique in which the occurrence of events on a bus is determined by a clock. The clock defines equal-width time slots, and events begin only at the beginning of a time slot.

System Bus   A bus used to interconnect major computer components (CPU, memory, I/O).

Truth Table*   A table that describes a logic function by listing all possible combinations of input values and indicating, for each combination, the output value.

Two's-Complement Representation   Used to represent binary integers. A positive integer is represented as in sign-magnitude. A negative number is represented by adding one to the 1's-complement representation of the same number.

Unary Operator*   An operator that represents an operation on one and only one operand.

Unconditional Jump*   A jump that takes place whenever the instruction that specified it is executed.

Uniprocessing   Sequential execution of instructions by a processing unit or independent use of a processing unit in a multiprocessing system.

User-Visible Registers   CPU registers that may be referenced by the programmer. The instruction set format allows one or more registers to be specified as operands or addresses of operands.

Vector* A quantity usually characterized by an ordered set of scalars.

Virtual Storage* The storage space that may be regarded as addressable main storage by the user of a computer system in which virtual addresses are mapped into real addresses. The size of virtual storage is limited by the addressing scheme of the computer system and by the amount of auxiliary storage available, and not by the actual number of main storage locations.

Volatile Memory A memory in which a constant electrical power source is required to maintain the contents of memory. If the power is switched off, the stored information is lost.

WORM Write-Once Read-Many. A disk that is more easily written than CD-ROM, making single-copy disks commercially feasible. As with CD-ROM, after the write operation is performed, the disk is read-only. The most popular size is 5.25-in, which can hold from 200 to 800 Mbytes of data.

Index

College Division
Macmillan Publishing Company
Front & Brown Streets
Riverside, NJ 08075

ORDER FORM

Ship To:
(Please print or type)

Name _____

Co. _____

Address _____

_____

City _____ St _____ Zip _____

Bill To:
(If different from shipping address)

Name _____

Co. _____

Address _____

_____

City _____ St _____ Zip _____

Mail your order to the above address or call 800-548-9939 (in New Jersey call 609-461-6500 or Fax 609-461-9265

Shipping Method **(select one)**
_____ UPS ground
_____ 2nd Day Air
_____ Book Rate

Payment Method **(select one)**	
_____ Check	_____ Visa
_____ Bill Me	_____ MasterCard
_____	
Authorized Signature	
_____ _____	
Card Number	Exp Date

(continued)

TEAR OUT THIS PAGE TO ORDER OTHER TITLES BY WILLIAM STALLINGS:

SEQ.	QTY.	ISBN NO.	TITLE	PRICE	TOTAL
1	_____	002-415495-4	Computer Organization & Architecture 3/e	$69.00	_____
2	_____	002-415454-7	Data and Computer Communications 3/e	$69.00	_____
3	_____	002-415465-2	Local and Metropolitan Area Networks 4/e	$60.00	_____
4	_____	002-415431-8	Business Data Communications	$49.00	_____
5	_____	002-415475-X	ISDN and Broadband ISDN 2/e	$55.00	_____
6	_____	002-415481-4	Operating Systems	$56.00	_____

Handbooks of Computer Communications Standards

7	_____	002-415521-7	Volume 1, The Open Systems Interconnection (OSI) Model and OSI-Related Standards, 2/e	$47.00	_____
8	_____	002-415522-5	Volume 2, Local Area Network Standards, 2/e	$47.00	_____
9	_____	002-415523-3	Volume 3, The TCP/IP Protocol Suite, 2/e	$47.00	_____

GRAND TOTAL _____

A small shipping charge will be added. Prices subject to change without prior notification.

PSR-PSL 350-3500   FC# 1355

ACRONYMS

ALU	Arithmetic and Logic Unit
ASCII	American Standard Code for Information Interchange
ANSI	American National Standards Institute
BCD	Binary-Coded Decimal
CD	Compact Disk
CD-ROM	Compact Disk–Read Only Memory
CPU	Central Processing Unit
CISC	Complex Instruction Set Computer
DMA	Direct Memory Access
DEC	Digital Equipment Corporation
EPROM	Erasable Programmable Read-Only Memory
EEPROM	Electrically Erasable Programmable Read-Only Memory
HLL	High-Level Language
I/O	Input/Output
IAR	Instruction Address Register
IR	Instruction Register
IC	Integrated Circuit
IEEE	Institute of Electrical and Electronics Engineers
IBM	International Business Machines Corporation